Eastern Africa Series

LOST
NATIONALISM

Eastern Africa Series

Women's Land Rights & Privatization in Eastern Africa
BIRGIT ENGLERT & ELIZABETH DALEY (EDS)

War & the Politics of Identity in Ethiopia
KJETIL TRONVOLL

Moving People in Ethiopia
ALULA PANKHURST & FRANÇOIS PIGUET (EDS)

Living Terraces in Ethiopia
ELIZABETH E. WATSON

Eritrea
GAIM KIBREAB

Borders & Borderlands as Resources in the Horn of Africa
DEREJE FEYISSA & MARKUS VIRGIL HOEHNE (EDS)

After the Comprehensive Peace Agreement in Sudan
ELKE GRAWERT (ED.)

Land, Governance, Conflict & the Nuba of Sudan
GUMA KUNDA KOMEY

Ethiopia
JOHN MARKAKIS

Resurrecting Cannibals
HEIKE BEHREND

Pastoralism & Politics in Northern Kenya & Southern Ethiopia
GŨNTHER SCHLEE & ABDULLAHI A. SHONGOLO

Islam & Ethnicity in Northern Kenya & Southern Ethiopia
GŨNTHER SCHLEE with ABDULLAHI A. SHONGOLO

Foundations of an African Civilisation
DAVID W. PHILLIPSON

Regional Integration, Identity & Citizenship in the Greater Horn of Africa
KIDANE MENGISTEAB & REDIE BEREKETEAB (EDS)

Dealing with Government in South Sudan
CHERRY LEONARDI

The Quest for Socialist Utopia
BAHRU ZEWDE

Disrupting Territories
JÖRG GERTEL, RICHARD ROTTENBURG & SANDRA CALKINS (EDS)

The African Garrison State
KJETIL TRONVOLL & DANIEL R. MEKONNEN

The State of Post-conflict Reconstruction
NASEEM BADIEY

Gender, Home & Identity
KATARZYNA GRABSKA

Remaking Mutirikwi
JOOST FONTEIN

Lost Nationalism
ELENA VEZZADINI

The Oromo & the Christian Kingdom of Ethiopia
MOHAMMED HASSEN

Darfur
CHRIS VAUGHAN

The Eritrean National Service
GAIM KIBREAB

Ploughing New Ground
GETNET BEKELE

Hawks & Doves in Sudan's Armed Conflict
SUAD M. E. MUSA

Ethiopian Warriorhood
TSEHAI BERHANE-SELASSIE

Land, Migration & Belonging
JOSEPH MUJERE

Land Tenure Security *
SVEIN EGE (ED.)

Tanzanian Development *
DAVID POTTS (ED.)

* *forthcoming*

Lost Nationalism

Revolution, Memory and Anti-colonial Resistance in Sudan

ELENA VEZZADINI
CNRS, Institut des Mondes Africains, Paris

JAMES CURREY

James Currey
is an imprint of Boydell & Brewer Ltd
PO Box 9, Woodbridge, Suffolk IP12 3DF (GB)
www. jamescurrey.com

and of

Boydell & Brewer Inc.
668 Mt Hope Avenue, Rochester, NY 14620-2731 (US)
www.boydellandbrewer.com

First published in hardback 2015
First published in paperback 2019

British Library Cataloguing in Publication Data
A catalogue record for this book is available from the British Library

ISBN 978-1-84701-115-2 (James Currey cloth)
ISBN 978-1-84701-209-8 (James Currey paperback)

Typeset in 10 on 12 pt Cordale with Gill Bold display
by Kate Kirkwood Publishing Services

To Anna Maria and Paolo
And to my Sudanese brothers and sisters

Contents

List of Illustrations ix
Acknowledgements x
Note on Transliteration xiii
List of Abbreviations xiii

Prologue 1
Introduction: Nationalism and Memory 5

PART ONE 17
THE NATIONALIST MOVEMENT IN SUDAN 1919-1923
Transnational Perspectives

1 Rethinking Nationalism in Colonial Sudan 19

2 The Spring of the Colonial Nations 38

PART TWO 65
THE REVOLUTION OF 1924
Organization of the Movement and its Spread to the Provinces

3 The 1924 Revolution 67

4 The White Flag League: The Structure of the Nationalist Movement 96

5 1924 in Port Sudan and El Obeid 122

PART THREE 147
IDEOLOGY AND STRATEGIES

6 'The Word is for the Nation Alone': Telegrams, Petitions and Political Writings 149

7 A Community of Protesters: Symbols, Songs and Emotions 164

PART FOUR 177
THE 1924 PROTESTERS
Reconsidering Social Bonds after the First World War

Prologue 178

8 The Sociology of Colonial Education and the 1924 Insurgents 182

9 A Military Elite: The Army in the 1924 Revolution 206

10 'I Was Very Famous in *Sūq al-'Arabī*': Nationalism and Sudanese Workers 234

11 The Colonial Gaze, History and the Archive 255

Epilogue: Memory and the Racialization of the 1924 Revolution 273

Appendix 1: Telegrams of the White Flag League and Other Protesters 278
Appendix 2: Sources on Members of Political Associations in 1924 288
Bibliography 294
Index 313

List of Illustrations

Maps

1 Centres in which White Flag League activities were reported 107
2 Transfers of Sayyid Shahāta 227

Figures

1 Exterior view of the old house of the family of 'Alī 'Abd al-Laṭīf in Khartoum, 2015 6
2 Table of contents reproduced from the two volumes of Thomas Frost, *Secret Societies of European Revolution, 1776–1876* 64
3 Four of the founders of the White Flag League, 15 May 1924 68
4 The parade of the cadets of the Military School, 8 August 1924 81
5 List of White Flag Members, 1924 99
6 The cadets of the Military School, 1912 xiv and 207

Tables

1 Professional distribution of political activists in Khartoum 111
2 Profession of the political activists in Port Sudan 128
3 Profession of protesters in El Obeid 138
4 Profession of all the people suspected in El Obeid 138
5 Merchants' origin 142
6 Addressees of telegrams 151
7 Difference of the texts according to four locations 154
8 Number of students in Elementary Vernacular Schools, Primary Schools, and Gordon College, 1906-1916 189
9 List showing number of boys in each class in Sudan government primary schools in January of each year from 1906 onwards 192
10 Number of boys leaving primary schools, 1917-1925 193
11 Origin of pupils in some EVS for 1913 196
12 Origin of pupils in primary schools in 1913 197
13 Nationality of students of Gordon College Upper School 198
14 The grading system 201
15 Geographical distribution of texts, including telegrams 278
16 Occupation and origin of individuals arrested for participating in the disturbances of June and July in Khartoum 292

Acknowledgements

This book has been my companion for so many years, and in so many countries and research environments, that it is no easy task to condense all the people that have contributed to it in such a short space.

When I arrived in Khartoum for the first time in 2004, two years after beginning my PhD, I still had only a very abstract idea about what I really wanted to do. Then I fell ill with the disease the late Professor Collins used to call 'Sudanitis': your heart starts beating faster, and you feel insanely happy just looking at ostensibly meaningless objects such as a teaspoon entangled in mint leaves, or a local bus, or the ochre shade of the streets, regardless of the extreme heat, the traffic, and the solemn glances of people overloaded with their difficult daily lives – it is no wonder that one of the first words I heard in Sudan was *mushkila* (problem).

I have only been able to come so far in my study of 1924 thanks to the fact that I have had the opportunity to hammer out the subject with Sudanese 'informants' ranging from intimate friends to acquaintances and passers-by. A list of interviews is given, but does not cover the number of discussions woven into this work. My first debt is to the personnel of the National Record Office in Khartoum, to its former director 'Alī Karrār, but even more to the staff with whom I shared my mornings, teas, and conversations: 'Awwād, Khaldā, Ḥanafī, Nyamāt and Fātiḥ, and their respective families. Others I met briefly during my five trips also facilitated my work, such as Muḥammad Azraq. Second, I wish to thank Dr Fadwā 'Abd al-Raḥman 'Alī Ṭaha, who welcomed me to Sudan and introduced me to Yāsmīna Hāshim Khalīfa, who has become like a sister to me. I am indebted to her family, with whom I lived for months in Omdurman. I wish to thank my closest friends: Aḥmad 'Abd al-Wāḥid and Naṣr al-Dīn Kafī and his family: the latter had me travel to Angola (Omdurman), Jebel Awlia, and Kadugli, showing me new shades of ochre. 'Abd al-Qādir Atwa's selfless generosity has been unconditional throughout the years, especially considering his two jobs and fourteen-hour work day. Durriyya and Mu'awiyya Aḥmad Badrī never grew tired of being pestered with questions. As for the many colleagues and friends I should thank, I would like to make special mention of anthropologists Munzūl 'Assāl and 'Abd al-Ghaffār Muḥammad Aḥmad; Professor al-Mu'taṣim of al-Nilayn university; Aḥmad Ibrāhīm Diyāb, who was so generous with sharing his knowledge of 1924; 'Abdallāh Bashīr; and finally the staff of the Afro-Asian Institute. I shall not forget the people of the 'Abd al-Karīm Mīrghanī Centre, an intellectual beacon in Omdurman. In Sudan I also met Yoshiko Kurita, to whom I owe an enormous intellectual debt. Many other people made my stay in Khartoum memorable; this book is truly dedicated to them.

This work has been carried out thanks to a series of generous grants: first, the PhD scholarship and fieldwork grant I received from the University of Bergen; since 2011, I have held a fellowship from the Norwegian Research Council, allowing me to have very fine working conditions. Before 2012, I completed two periods of fieldwork with the support of the Nordic Africa Institute of Uppsala and the Centre d'Études et de Documentation Économiques, Juridiques et Sociales of Khartoum. On the subject of philanthropy, I am especially indebted to late Maḥmūd Ṣāliḥ, whose generosity has affected a generation of Sudan scholars. I also spent about four months in Cairo, and would like to thank my dear teacher Āmal.

Both the Centre for Middle Eastern and Islamic Studies and the AHKR (Institute of Archaeology, History, Religion and Cultural Studies) of the University of Bergen provided institutional support. My dear friends Anwar 'Abd al-Majīd, Anders Bjørkelo, Anne Bang, Leif Manger, Knut Vikør, Sean O'Fahey, Alexandros Tsakos, and Henriette Hafsas, and many other academic and non-academic staff at the SMI and Uniglobal have been essential for their intellectual and logistical help. Most of all, it has been wonderful to be a part of one of the most important intellectual hubs of Sudan Studies. It has meant, among other things, that many colleagues and PhD students were working, or had worked, on Sudan; that there was a distinct imbalance in the Centre's library in favour of rare prints on Sudan; and finally that I could listen to countless presentations given by Sudan specialists, such as the late Bob Collins, Aḥmad Abū Shūk, Enrico Ille, Øystein Rolandsen, Cherry Leonardi, Bob Kramer, Mohanad Hāshim, and many others, all of whom nourished my thought.

The second intellectual tradition that is woven into this work is French social history. The École des Hautes Études en Sciences Sociales reciprocated this affinity with a one-year fellowship, and I am thankful to Francis Zimmerman for this opportunity. I am also grateful to EHESS historians of the 'new social history school' and 'micro-history' such as Simona Cerutti, Jacques Revel, and Giovanni Levi.

This work is born out of exchanges with a number of members of the IMAF (Institut des Mondes Africains, Paris 1-EHESS): Henri Medard, Roger Botte, Pierre Guidi, Silvia Bruzzi, Ophelie Rillon, Camille Lefebvre, Séverine Awenengo, Rémi Dewière, Marie-Laure Derat, Anne Hugon, Claire Bosc-Tiessé, Eric Jolly, Catarina Madeira-Santos, Pascale Barthélémy, Christine Douxami, Françoise Blum, and Jean Schmitz; and the heads of the centres for which I worked, Jean-Paul Colleyn, Fabienne Samson, Pierre Boilley and Bernard Heyberger, who truly welcomed me; but also Vincent Bonnecase, David Ambrosetti, and Céline Thiriot of LAM Bordeaux; Barbara Casciarri of Paris VIII; Ismael Moya of the LESC Paris X-Nanterre who so often pulled me up; and last but not least, Iris Seri-Hersch of Aix-Marseille University.

Other Sudan scholars have also been important inspirations for this work, and I wish especially to thank Heather Sharkey. I am also grateful to Jay Spaulding for reading and commenting on my PhD thesis, Douglas H. Johnson, the late Richard Gray and his wife Gabriella, Gerard Prunier, and Noah Salomon; and in Durham, Justin Willis and Jane Hogan.

Finally, I need to mention the place where this all started – Bologna – and Irma Taddia, who on one fateful day in 2000 asked me which African country I wished to study. Together with her, I am grateful to the late Cesare Rossi, Anna Laura Cola and Gianna Pomata for the different yet decisive impacts they have had on my work.

A number of people who are dear to me have made this work possible, putting up with the unreasonable schedule imposed by this all-consuming task. In particular, I wish to thank those who have had to endure the most: Gildas, Anders, Marianna, Ana Belen, Souad, Lorenzo, Alexander and Silvia. Simon Dix has worked hard to make sense of my linguistic confusion, and so did Rola Shabayek and Āmal for Arabic.

Last, but by no means least, this work is dedicated to my family in Bologna: Anna Maria, Paolo, Chiara, and Stefano, and my nephews Diego and Beatrice. They have been my bedrock in every sense of the word, and it is to them that I owe the hard work, stubbornness and consuming love that I have put into this book.

Note on Transliteration

Arabic names will generally be transliterated according to the JMES standard, with some degree of adaptation to Sudanese Arabic where it diverges substantially from Modern Standard Arabic. Arabic names of authors quoted for their publications in English will be spelled as the authors spell their own name in English. Names of places are spelled according to their most common English usage. Finally, in the footnotes, I have been faithful to the sources, and I have spelled Arabic names in the way in which they were transliterated in British colonial documents, in spite of their inconsistency. Thus, the attempt to be as faithful as possible to the sources has won over consistency.

List of Uncommon Abbreviations

DI	Director of Intelligence
DC	District Commissioner
Civsec	Civil Secretary
IAAS	Institute of Afro-Asian Studies, University of Khartoum
NA	The National Archive, Kew, London
NRO	National Record Office, Khartoum
SA	Sudan Agent
SAD	Sudan Archives, Durham University, UK

The cadets of the Military School, 1912 (see pp.206-9)

Prologue

In 1919, millions of Egyptian men and women took to the streets to protest against Great Britain's refusal to lift the protectorate that had been imposed on Egypt at the beginning of World War I. On its close, Sa'd Zaghlūl, a seasoned politician who had previously been aligned with the moderate party, gathered a few of his associates for a meeting with the British High Commissioner, General Wingate. The group expressed their wish to form a delegation – a *wafd* – that would travel to London and then on to the Paris Peace Conference to plead the Egyptian 'case' for an end to the protectorate. Their request was rejected, and Sa'd Zaghlūl was exiled to Malta. Egyptians reacted by taking to the streets.

The events in Egypt had immediate reverberations in Sudan. Sudan, which had been an Anglo-Egyptian Condominium since 1899, was theoretically a colony of two States. In practice, the British had had the upper hand from the beginning, but Egypt retained an important influence, not least due to the fact that the Sudan did not have its own armed forces, and relied on the Egyptian Army. Furthermore, thousands of Egyptians were serving as employees at all levels of the Sudan government. For as long as Egypt had been an informal colony and later a protectorate of Great Britain, however, the problem of Egyptian 'infection', as the British put it, had somehow been kept in check. Everything changed with the outbreak of the Egyptian Revolution.

In July 1919, to offset any effect Egyptian unrest might have on Sudan's status as a *de facto* British dominion, British administrators decided to take steps to demonstrate that the Sudanese had no desire to stand beside the Egyptians. They organized a delegation of ten notables, who included Sudan's highest religious leaders, to meet King George V in London to congratulate him on Great Britain's victory in the War. They praised British colonization, and thanked the King for all Britain's efforts in 'assist[ing] in [Sudan's] material and moral advancement.'[1] Their mission was vigorously condemned in the Egyptian press, however, likewise in Sudan: they began to be attacked as traitors or puppets of the British. In 1920, in an attempt to counter this image, the three religious leaders – 'Alī al-Mīrghanī, the

1 Address of the Sudan Delegation, annex to Lee Stack to the High Commissioner for Egypt, 28.6.1919, FO 141/582/3, The National Archives, London.

head of the Sufi *tarīqa* Khatmiyya, 'Abd al-Raḥman al-Mahdī, the son and spiritual heir of the *mahdī* Muḥammad Aḥmad, and Sharīf Yūsif al-Hindī, the leader of the *tarīqa* al-Hindiyya – decided to sponsor *Ḥaḍārat al-Sūdān*, or simply *al-Ḥaḍāra* (in Arabic *The Civilization of Sudan*), the first Sudanese journal in the country's history.

In Egypt, meanwhile, continuing unrest, demonstrations, and violence prompted the establishment in 1920 of a special commission led by the Secretary of State for the Colonies, Lord Milner. It determined that the time was ripe to accede to certain of Egypt's national aspirations. As the unrest persisted, in 1922 Great Britain unilaterally granted a form of independence to Egypt that was limited by four 'Reserved Points': the security of imperial communications, the protection of foreign minorities, the defence of Egypt, and finally, the status of Sudan.[2] Zaghlūl and his Wafd party strongly opposed these conditions, and as Egypt requested the renegotiation of the Condominium Agreement, the issue of Sudan became a major concern. No Sudanese were invited to take part in any of the various stages of the negotiations. After yet another period in exile, Zaghlūl was allowed to return to Egypt in 1923, a new constitution was approved by Parliament, and in January 1924, Zaghlūl was finally elected as Prime Minister of Egypt, and the Wafd obtained the overwhelming majority of the seats in Parliament.

The turmoil in Egypt and the negotiations on the status of Sudan had direct consequences on political life within Sudan. The debate on the country's status prompted the polarization of Sudanese politics around two main factions. The first supported the slogan 'Sudan for the Sudanese' (*sūdān lil-sūdāniyyn*), and believed that Sudan should become independent from Egypt. However because it was still unprepared for full independence, Sudan would need British tutelage for some years to come. The second faction, whose slogan was 'Unity of the Nile Valley', or *waḥda wadī al-nīl*, claimed that Sudan should unite with Egypt to fulfil the 'perfect unity of the Nile Valley', and cast off the British yoke. This proposal was endorsed by the best-known secret society of this period, the Society of the Sudan Union (*Jam'iyyat al-Ittiḥad al-Sūdān*), which had been founded at some point during 1920 by 'Ubayd al-Ḥājj al-Amīn, the poet Tawfīq Ṣāliḥ Jibrīl, Sulaymān Kisha, and others.

In 1922, *Mulazim Awal* (First Lieutenant) 'Alī 'Abd al-Laṭīf attempted to publish an anti-colonial text in *al-Ḥaḍāra* in which he demanded complete independence for Sudan from both Egypt and Great Britain. He was arrested and imprisoned for a year between 1922 and 1923. By 1924, however, he had changed his political line and aligned himself with the pro-Egyptian faction. He joined forces with two former members of the Society of the Sudan Union, 'Ubayd al-Ḥājj al-'Amīn and Ṣāliḥ 'Abd al-Qādir, who had become dissatisfied with the Society's policies. Together with two employees of the Department of Post and Telegraphs, Ḥassan Sharīf and Ḥassan Ṣāliḥ al-Maṭbājī, they formed the *Jam'iyyat al-Liwā' al-Abyaḍ*, or White Flag League, sometime between 1923 and 1924, although

[2] Albert P. Blaustein, Jay J. A. Sigler, and Benjamin R. Beede eds, *Independence Documents of the World* (Dobbs Ferry, N.Y.: Oceana Publications, 1977), pp. 204-205.

the official founding date of the society was 15 May 1924, the day on which they sent the first in a long series of protest telegrams.

The White Flag League's objective was to demonstrate openly and peacefully that the Sudanese nation supported the 'Unity of the Nile Valley' and wanted independence from Britain. Initially, their main activity was to collect letters and petitions of support to be sent to Egypt and to be used by politicians in the negotiations. Its second task was the organization of a large-scale campaign of telegrams and petitions to be addressed to the Sudanese government and the Egyptian authorities, giving expression to the will of Sudanese people. Between June and July, however, the White Flag broadened the scope of its activities, and decided to stage a series of political protests. This phase began on 14 June with the organization of a two-man delegation to Cairo: Muḥammad al-Mahdī, an employee of the Irrigation Department, and Egyptian Army officer Zayn al-'Ābdīn 'Abd al-Tām. The delegation, which was allegedly carrying petitions in support of Egypt, was intercepted on a train between Khartoum and Wadi Halfa. On 19 June, the first large demonstration took place at the funeral of the Mamur of Omdurman, ignited by a political speech, after which protests followed one after the other. Even when the government declared demonstrations illegal after 23 June and the League stopped organizing such events, people who were either members or supporters of the movement continued to demonstrate. Furthermore, the movement began to spread beyond Khartoum.

In June and July, the movement mobilized provincial networks of disaffected officers and officials, who were encouraged to form local branches of the White Flag League. Branches were set up in Port Sudan, Wad Medani, Shendi, El Obeid, and so on. In this way, the main provincial urban centres, as well as more remote areas in the south, north, and west, became involved in the movement.

At the beginning of July, the British began a crackdown against the White Flag League. On 4 July, they arrested 'Alī 'Abd al-Laṭīf, the chosen leader of the movement. By the beginning of August, all its founders and most important members had been imprisoned, and a few others had been exiled to remote places. The arrests only provoked an intensification of protests. Ṣāliḥ Abd al-Qādir had been transferred to Port Sudan at the end of June, only to organize a new branch of the League. A series of demonstrations of increasing gravity shook that city from 27 July to the middle of August. When Ṣāliḥ 'Abd al-Qādir was arrested and put on a train to Khartoum, people in Atbara, a stop between Port Sudan and Khartoum, decided to organize a demonstration. The protesters, mostly Egyptian men from the Railways Battalion and Sudanese artisans, continued their action for hours, and the situation became increasingly riotous, until some men were accidentally shot by the police, and four died. On 9 August, while these events took place in Atbara, all 51 cadets of the Khartoum Military College decided to leave their barracks and form a demonstration. The following week, what was perhaps the largest demonstration of 1924 was held in the capital, and thousands people were involved. Abortive attempts at demonstrations were simultaneously organized in several smaller centres, such as Wad Medani, Shendi, and El Obeid.

In September, as the Anglo-Egyptian negotiations got under way, a tense calm reigned. Hundreds of activists had been arrested and were awaiting trial in inhumane conditions in Kober, the main prison of Khartoum North. In the meantime, disturbances occurred in Wau and Malakal in Southern Sudan led by Sudanese and Egyptian officers, although these were swiftly quelled. The Anglo-Egyptian negotiations rapidly broke down, and by October were concluded without any satisfactory agreement. The atmosphere in Sudan remained overwrought, future developments unclear, and the situation at an impasse.

On 19 November, the Governor General of Sudan, Sir Lee Stack, was assassinated in Cairo by Egyptian political extremists. In retaliation, the British High Commissioner in Cairo, Viscount Allenby, launched his famous ultimatum, in which – among other things – he demanded the immediate withdrawal of the Egyptian Army from Sudan. When Zaghlūl refused, evacuation orders were immediately carried out. In Khartoum, the army's Egyptian battalions began to gather near the train station. On 27 November, the 11th Sudanese battalion of the Egyptian Army attempted to join them, led by six Sudanese officers: Sayyid Faraḥ, 'Abd al-Faḍīl al-Māẓ, Ḥassan Faḍl al-Mūlā, 'Alī al-Bannā, Sulaymān Muḥammad and Thābit 'Abd al-Raḥīm. They were stopped by British troops led by Acting Governor General Huddleston. When they refused to take orders from anybody but an Egyptian authority, Huddleston ordered his troops to open fire. A desperate two-day confrontation ensued, in which the mutinous officers and soldiers put up exceptional resistance. The mutiny was quashed. Sayyid Faraḥ managed to escape to Egypt and 'Abd al-Faḍīl al-Māẓ was killed in action. The other four of the six leading officers were condemned to death. Three of them, Thābit 'Abd al-Raḥīm, Ḥassan Faḍl al-Mūlā, and Sulaymān Muḥammad, were executed on 5 December 1924, and one, 'Alī al-Bannā, was pardoned at the last minute.

This book is my attempt to strip away the outer layers of this episode, and to disentangle its complexities and anomalies in relation to the master narrative of modern Sudanese history.

1

Introduction: Nationalism and Memory

'The house of the leader 'Alī 'Abd al-Laṭīf, a local restaurant. The most evident manifestation of the neglect of the heritage and the symbols of nationalism.'[1] This was the title of a newspaper article published in 2009 by *Ajrās al-Ḥurriyya*, the organ of the then principal Northern Sudanese opposition party, the SPLM-North (Sudan People Liberation Movement, North Branch). The article appeared two years before the government closed down the newspaper. The reference was to the home of the man who is known as the leader of the 1924 Revolution. The photograph of 'Alī 'Abd al-Laṭīf's home that accompanied the article is a visual corroboration of its title; it shows a rather dilapidated one-storey house, indistinguishable from any of the other homes that surround *sūq al-'arabī*, one of the central and most overcrowded areas of Khartoum. The article went on to blame the government for this neglect and suggested that the house be restored and 'turned into a sacred museum that contains the belongings of the 1924 movements and the White Flag League dispersed between individuals', concluding that 'this much is the simplest thing we can offer them, as they fought at a time when the struggle was very tough.'

Other sites in Khartoum bear witness to unheeded pleas that 1924 be remembered. For example, a neglected obelisk in *shari'a al-Jāma'a* is a memorial to the death of 'Abd al-Faḍīl al-Māẓ, one of the protagonists of the last mutiny in November 1924. The monument is plastered with all kinds of advertising; a passer-by would scarcely notice it. The obelisk bears witness to the fact that the state itself had participated at some point in the effort to commemorate 1924. In the 1970s, the similar conjunction of events that brought Ja'far Numayrī to power also encouraged a significant effort to retrieve memories of that crucial year. The result was an impressive number of publications sponsored by the Afro-Asian Institute of the University of Khartoum, including *Al Riwāyāt al-Shafawiyya li-Thuwwār 1924*, consisting of two volumes of typescripts of dozens of interviews with protagonists of 1924; a volume on the trials of the members of the White Flag League and other supporters; and a comprehensive bibliography of the primary and secondary sources on the

[1] *Ajrās al-Ḥurriyya*, 3.11.2009, issue 540, p. 1.

Fig 1 Exterior view of the old house of the family of ʿAlī ʿAbd al-Laṭīf in Khartoum. In 2009 part of the house was a restaurant; by 2014–15 it had changed into a travel agency and construction work was underway to renovate part of the house (Photograph © Elena Vezzadini, January 2015)

events.[2] The 'heroes of 1924' were given a medal for their patriotism at a state ceremony, and were also granted a lifetime pension. However, in the 1980s the government turned towards political Islam, and 1924 once again slipped from State memory.

Today, the families of the 1924 insurgents that I met bitterly regret that the State and Sudanese society have forgotten their 'Revolution'. The grandson of 'Alī 'Abd al-Laṭīf told me this story: in 2005, a few months after the peace agreement that brought thirty years of civil war between the North and the South to an end, one of the party's advertisements reproduced an image of Garang, the beloved former leader of the SPLM, standing side by side with 'Alī 'Abd al-Laṭīf to mark the ideological continuity between the two movements. However, most people had no idea who' Alī 'Abd al-Laṭīf was, mistaking him for Garang's son.[3]

This is why in some respects, the revolution has been lost twice: first in 1924, when it was violently quelled; and then historically, because it never really achieved the status of a stable element of the national narrative. This fluctuation between the duty to remember and the drive to forget is one of the many paradoxes of the 1924 Revolution, but it is also what makes it one of the densest and richest subjects for historical investigation, and one of the most crucial episodes in the modern history of Sudan.

The revolution was bloodily crushed and highly discredited by the British administration and the urban elites. Typical of this derogatory attitude were the British descriptions of insurgents as 'rabbles of nobodies' and 'ill-balanced' puppets in the hands of malicious Egyptian politicians, but the deeper cause was the alleged origin and status of the insurgents. A Sudanese contributor to the journal *Ḥaḍārat al-Sūdān* in June 1924, at the beginning of the demonstrations, scornfully commented that 'low is the nation if it can be led by 'Alī 'Abd al-Laṭīf', while another proclaimed that 'the country is insulted when its smallest and humblest men, without status in its society, pretend to come forward and express the country's opinion.'[4] In fact, 'Alī's father was originally from the Nuba Mountains, was captured as a slave during Turco-Egyptian rule, enrolled in the Mahdi's army, left it to join the Anglo-Egyptian forces before and during the 'reconquest', and finally became a (free) farmer in the Northern Province. 'Alī's mother was originally from the Dinka, in Southern Sudan. Several officers of the Egyptian Army[5] who participated to political activities were also descendants of slave families. Thus, the revolution was

2 *Al-Riwāyāt al-Shafawiyya li-Thuwwār 1924* (Al-Khurṭūm: Ma'had al-Dirāsāt al-Ifrīqīya wa al-Āsīwīya, 1974). *Index for Primary and Secondary Sources on the 1924 Revolution in the Sudan* (Khartoum: Institute of African and Asian Studies, University of Khartoum, 1973). Saeed Mohammed Ahmed El Mahdi, (ed.), *The White Flag Trials* (Khartoum: Institute of African and Asian Studies and the Dept. of Private Law, University of Khartoum, 1974). 'Abd al-Karīm Al-Sayyid, *al-Liwā' al-Abyaḍ, Thawrat 1924: mudhakkirāt wa-mushāhadāt sajīn* (Al-Khurṭūm: Jāmi'at Al-Khurṭūm, Kullīyat al-Ādāb, Shu'bat Abḥāth al-Sūdān, 1970).

3 Mentioned in several conversations between the author and the grandsons of 'Alī 'Abd al-Laṭīf in their house in Omdurman, 2005-2014.

4 Both quoted in Jafaar Bakheit, 'British Administration and Sudanese Nationalism 1919-1939' (PhD Thesis, University of Cambridge, 1965), p. 88.

led by elements of society seen as illegitimate. The most telling example is a statement from Muḥammad Ṣāliḥ Shinqīṭī, a prominent politician and speaker of the Legislative assembly, reported in 1946: '[Judge M.S.] Shangetti boasted that the Sudanese had come from Arabia. He spoke very contemptuously of Abdel Latif (now in an insane asylum). He said his mother was a Negress, his father was unknown, and that he, Latif, had at one time collected old tins from barracks.'[5]

The drive to forget 1924 appears to reflect the subaltern position attached to people such as 'Alī 'Abd al-Laṭīf labelled 'sūdānī' (in local Arabic), or 'detribalized negroids' (in British sources) – Northern Sudanese of southern and/or slave descent.[6] Southern Sudanese intellectuals claim that the drive to forget 1924 is associated with the racist attitudes held by Northern Sudanese 'Arabs' towards Southern Sudanese 'Africans'.[7] Hence, the memory of 1924 lies at the very heart of the traumas that have marked the postcolonial history of the country: the politics of representation that in the North define any southern genealogy as a sign of social inferiority; the failure of the Northern Sudanese to acknowledge the demands of the Southerners; the identity struggle between a north that sees itself as a part of the Arab world and an 'African' south, and consequently the explosion of one of the most murderous civil wars on the African continent (1962-1972; 1983-2005; with the Darfur crisis exploding in 2003).

Memories of the events of 1924 are full of contradictions and paradoxes, mostly because, as this volume argues, the revolution was definitely not an issue of only 'detribalized negroids'. They were a minority in a movement that included a rainbow social spectrum, comprised of officers and officials, wage-workers, artisans, and traders, as well the sons and relatives of those notables who attacked it.[8] Yet the remarkable social diversity of the 1924 revolution has not survived in the nation's collective memory.

This leads to the reason why 1924 is a peculiar historical subject. In their fight to rescue their revolution from oblivion, those who were participants and their descendants (both from notable backgrounds and descendants of *sūdānī*), have made countless efforts to demonstrate that it was a

5 Douglas H. Johnson (ed.), *Sudan. Part I 1942-1950, British Documents on the End of Empire* (Series B, Volume 5, London: The Stationery Office, 1998), p. 235.

6 In classical Arabic, the word 'sūdānī' is masculine and singular; however, in local colloquial Arabic it is used in a plural sense, as in the expression 'nās sūdānī', the *sūdānī* people. E-mail conversation with Prof. Gerasimos Makris on 13 November 2013. I am very grateful to Prof. Makris for this clarification.

7 Francis M. Deng, 'Green Is the Color of the Master. The Legacy of Slavery and the Crisis of National Identity in Modern Sudan.' Paper presented at 'From Chattel Bondage to State Servitude: Slavery in the 20th Century', 6th International Conference of Gilder Lehrman Center for the Study of Slavery, Resistance, and Abolition, 2004. Francis M. Deng, *War of Visions: Conflict of Identities in the Sudan* (Brookings Institution Press, 1995), pp. 101-111. Amir H. Idris, *Identity, Citizenship, and Violence in Two Sudans: Reimagining a Common Future* (Basingstoke: Palgrave Macmillan, 2013), pp. 70-71.

8 I have discussed the 'memory problem' related to 1924 in: 'Spies, Secrets, and a Story Waiting to Be (re)told: Memories of the 1924 Revolution and the Racialization of Sudanese History', *Northeast African Studies* (2013), vol. 13, n. 2, pp. 53–92.

significant event and to accumulate evidence to prove it.[9] This is precisely what makes the 1924 Revolution perhaps the best documented episode of the history of the Anglo-Egyptian Condominium, with thousands of documents produced by a worried colonial government while the events were taking place, and with numerous recollections and memoirs, either published in books and newspaper articles, or written down on pieces of scrap paper by key participants anguished by the fear that their testimonies might be lost, often common people whose memories have not 'made it' into the historiography. The sources of the Revolution of 1924 are of exceptional value for a social historian, because they include traces of the lives of 'common' people, whose whereabouts are usually not only beyond the range of vision of the state, but also outside the canons of classical Sudanese high culture and historiography.

This wealth of sources, which has been collected through interviews and archival research, is what has prompted this book. It is also what has made it long, and difficult to write, as each time I believed the last word had been said, I would discover new pieces of the story, and I think I probably always will. Indeed, the research material is so rich that it has not been possible to include it all in one book, and this story has only just begun to be told.

This study has a circularity in structure: it opens with a reflection on the place of 1924 in Sudanese historiography, and returns to that topic in the last chapter – more accurately to the making of 'the story of the story' – when and how 1924 began to be perceived as a minor event led by unrepresentative individuals. Even if the book is not about memories, memory is what has prompted it. The contradiction between the homogeneous and linear way in which the revolution is described in historiography, compared with the heterogeneity, multiplicity, and dissonances of its memories has compelled me to keep digging.

1924 IN HISTORIOGRAPHY: A NON-EVENT

In order to trace the genealogy of this work, an analysis of the way historiography has depicted the revolution of 1924 is needed. There are a number of excellent, specialized works on 1924, such as those by Jafaar Bakheit, Hasan Abdin, Aḥmad Ibrāhīm Diyāb, or Yoshiko Kurita.[10] The last-mentioned author in particular has produced a ground-breaking work

[9] The clearest evidence is found in the *Index for Primary and Secondary Sources on the 1924 Revolution in the Sudan*, a long list of primary sources up to 1973.

[10] Bakheit, 'British Administration and Sudanese Nationalism 1919-1939'. Hasan Abdin, *Early Sudanese Nationalism, 1919-1925* (Khartoum: Institute of African & Asian Studies, University of Khartoum, 1985). Aḥmad Ibrāhīm Diyāb, *Thawrat 1924 : dirāsa wa-waqā'i'* (Khartoum, 1977). Aḥmad Ibrāhīm Diyāb, *al-'Alāqāt al-miṣrīya al-sūdāniyya: 1919-1924* (al-Qāhira: al-Hai'a al-Miṣrīya al-'Āmma lil-Kitāb, 1985). Yoshiko Kurita, 'The Concept of Nationalism in the White Flag League Movement' in *The Nationalist Movement in the Sudan.* Ed. Mahasin Abdel Gadir Hag Al-Safi (Khartoum: Institute of African and Asian Studies, University of Khartoum, 1989), pp. 14-63.

on 'Alī 'Abd al-Laṭīf that has proved essential to my research.[11] However, these works have not shaken the foundations of the paradigm that has shaped the historiography of 1924. Outside this specialized group, the most well-established volumes on modern Sudanese history have exhibited a remarkable narrative consistency. In spite of different interpretations, the conclusions have always been the same: that 1924 was a minor event with serious consequences, as it accelerated the move towards Indirect Rule in Sudan and the formalization of the administrative separation between North and South Sudan. Thus 1924 is seen as laying the foundation of the postcolonial civil war.

If we take one of the classics, Holt and Daly's *A History of the Sudan*, a somewhat out-of-date but often reprinted volume which is also the first essential reading for anyone who is interested in Sudanese history – the verdict is clear. After briefly narrating the events of 1924, the authors conclude: 'The White Flag League and its shadowy counterparts had a very limited appeal, and were composed mainly of minor officials and ex-officers.'[12] In another classic on the modern history of Sudan, *Islam, Nationalism and Communism in a Traditional Society*, the author Gabriel Warburg reaches a similar conclusion: '...the leaders of the White Flag League had little support outside the small and politically immature intelligentsia and the handful of Sudanese Army Officers who founded it.'[13] Finally, in *Empire on the Nile*, the most important and extensive work on colonial Sudan to date, Martin Daly writes:

> ...the Sudan Government was justified in arguing that the supporters of the White Flag League and parallel groups were a tiny, unrepresentative minority. The demonstrations were never very large, and contemporary reports agree that the vast majority even of the urban population had nothing to do with them ... significantly, there was unequivocal support for the British from the traditional religious and tribal leaders.[14]

Small, minor, and unsupported by local forces, 1924 suffered from one final flaw: inauthenticity. The general view of 1924 offered by many works see it as the result of the struggle between Great Britain and Egypt, in which Sudan acted as a sort of proxy in a spiralling rivalry that was exacerbated after the First World War. I had these assertions firmly in my mind during my research, and was very surprised to see them debunked sometimes by the very sources used in these works. In other words, 1924 is a blind spot of modern Sudanese history not as a consequence of the unavailability of sources, but because of the reluctance of historians to fully acknowledge it as a meaningful historical event.

[11] Yoshiko Kurita, *'Alī 'Abd Al-Laṭīf Wa-Thawrat 1924: Baḥth Fī Maṣādir Al-Thawra Al-Sūdāniyya* (al-Qāhira: Markaz al-Dirāsāt al-Sūdāniyya, 1997).

[12] P. M. Holt and M. W. Daly, *A History of the Sudan: From the Coming of Islam to the Present Day* (Harlow, England; New York: Longman, 2000), p. 113.

[13] Gabriel R. Warburg, *Islam, nationalism and communism in a traditional society: the case of Sudan* (London: F. Cass, 1978), p. 94.

[14] Martin Daly, *Empire on the Nile: The Anglo-Egyptian Sudan, 1898-1934* (Cambridge: Cambridge University Press, 2000), p. 295.

Historians from Sudan have not questioned the general tenets of the paradigm that describes 1924 as a failed event. There is a difference here, however: Sudanese nationalist historians usually do not consider the 1924 Revolution as provoked from the outside. It may still be described as a small and badly-organized event, but at least it was 'purely Sudanese'. One of the most important historians of nationalism, Mohamed Omer Beshir, describes 1924 as a foundational event on the march towards independence – 'Sudan's first major revolt after the Mahdiya defeat' – and he dedicates an entire chapter of his *Revolution and Nationalism in Sudan* to this theme. Nonetheless, he, too, concludes that 'the main cause for failure ... was the absence of mass support. Indeed, support came only from the few urban centres and the small group of intelligentsia.'[15]

Paradoxically, Beshir offers one of the most positive views of the event. Many Sudanese historians tend to lose any semblance of neutrality, neglect historical accuracy, and blame the 1924 activists for having prevented a smoother and more rapid progress towards independence (see most notably the collected volumes of Maḥāsin 'Abd al-Qādir Ḥājj al-Ṣāfī).[16] Such hostility towards an event that occurred almost ninety years ago demonstrates that it is anything but in the past.

The most significant common denominator in the literature of the 1924 Revolution is the perception of it as a non-event, lacking substance. It is as if something should have happened, but did not, and so something was lost; hence the sense of bitter disappointment. The teleology of failure becomes the organizing principle of the narratives; in other words, the main question that seems to inform historical works is: 'why did 1924 not work out?' It is true that all research is positional, and so 1924 is seen in the light of the later nationalist movements that developed from the late 1930s on, and which eventually led the country to independence. In that, the 1924 Revolution in Sudan is by no means a unique case. One only need mention the historiography of the East African Association of Harry Thuku, also described as a 'failure' in the nationalist historiography of Kenya, or the uprising of John Chilembwe in Malawi, besides others, dubbed as 'protonationalisms', in itself an evidence of the shortcomings of nationalist studies in the African context.[17] As in those cases, evaluations of the 1924 nationalist movement rise out of its positional relationship with later versions, as an 'immature' form of what would later become 'ripe.' Positioning of this kind deprives 1924 of its autonomy as a historical event. We end up knowing much more about what the movement was *not*, than what it was all about: the movement did *not* include the masses,

[15] Mohamed Omar Beshir, *Revolution and Nationalism in the Sudan* (New York: Barnes & Noble Books, 1974), p. 90.

[16] Maḥāsin 'Abd al-Qādir Ḥājj al-Ṣāfī, *Al-Ḥaraka al-Waṭaniyya Fī al-Sūdān: Thawra 1924* (al-Khurṭūm: Ma'had al-Dirāsāt al-Ifriqiya wa al-Asiyawiya, Jāmi'a al-Khurṭūm, 1992).

[17] Keith Kyle, 'Gandhi, Harry Thuku and Early Kenya Nationalism', *Transition* (1966), vol. 27, pp. 16-22; J. M. Lonsdale, 'Some Origins of Nationalism in East Africa', *Journal of African History* (1968), vol. 9, n. 1, pp. 119-146. George Shepperson, 'The Place of John Chilembwe in Malawi Historiography', *The Early History of Malawi*, B. Pachai ed. (London: Longman, 1972), pp. 405-28.

was *not* widespread, *not* representative, *not* well-organized, and finally *not* even endogenous. This is why in mainstream historiography, 1924 is a *non-event*.

ON REVOLUTIONS

Perhaps the best case in point on 1924 as a *non-event* is the issue of whether historians can or cannot properly call it a 'revolution'. Since I began this study, I have been asked on countless occasions to state, from my standpoint as 'expert' of Sudanese history, whether 1924 was a 'true' revolution or not, because this is one of the most heated debates surrounding the event, both in formal and informal settings such as internet forums. One example of the academic debate is an article by 'Abd al-Wahhāb Aḥmad 'Abd al-Raḥīm, in which he seeks to demonstrate that 1924 was definitely not a revolution.[18] After spending considerable time offering definitions of what revolutions are ('the occurrence of essential sudden radical and inclusive changes to the better in some countries through violence or using legitimate power'),[19] and then defining *coups d'état*, uprisings, insurrections, events, and movements, he arrives at the conclusion that 1924 can at best be defined as a movement (*ḥaraka*). His position is that a certain event can only be called a revolution if 'x' factors are present. If we have a situation of 'x – a', then it is an uprising; if we have 'x – a – b', it is an insurrection; and if we have 'x – a – b – c', it is a movement. This argument is challanged on two fronts here and in the following section: first, by looking briefly at the social science debate on revolutions, and second by reflecting on whether this equation can possibly be so simple.

Among the many theories of revolutions, two definitions have long been considered the most authoritative. The first is Huntington's, who describes revolutions as 'a rapid, fundamental, and violent domestic change in the dominant values and myths of a society, in its political institutions',[20] and the second is that of Theda Skocpol, according to whom 'social revolutions are rapid, basic transformations of a society's state and class structures; and they are accompanied, and in part carried through, by class-based revolts from below.'[21] But if this is the criterion by which revolutions are scaled, there have been very few 'real' revolutions; and indeed, according to one scholar, 'many upheavals are labelled revolutions, but few actually qualify for them.'[22] For instance, various encyclopaedias of political sciences in their entries on 'revolution' do not include the American Revolution, the

[18] 'Abd al-Wahāb Aḥmad al-Raḥīm, 'Naḥwa ta'rīf jadīd "lithawra" 1924', *Al-Ḥaraka al-Waṭaniyya Fī al-Sūdān: Thawra 1924*, pp. 11-84.
[19] Ibid., p. 11.
[20] Samuel P. Huntington, *Political Order in Changing Societies* (New Haven: Yale University Press, 1968), p. 264.
[21] Theda Skocpol, *States and Social Revolutions: A Comparative Analysis of France, Russia, and China* (Cambridge; New York: Cambridge University Press, 1979), p. 4.
[22] J. Leith, 'Revolutions, History of' *International Encyclopedia of the Social & Behavioral Sciences*, Neil J. Smelser and Paul B. Baltes eds, (Oxford: Pergamon, 2001), p. 13303.

Glorious British Revolution, or any of the various European struggles for independence such as the Italian Risorgimento.[23] Yet in the USA, Italy, or the UK, in collective memory today they are considered to be so, and millions of people would feel robbed of their past if they were told that those events were not after all, 'real' revolutions. This leads to the old '*querelle*' between the analytical and emic approaches. It must be recognized that a 'revolution' is both an object of sociological enquiry that can be analytically apprehended, and a way in which a community experiences its past. These two aspects overlap and cannot be definitely disjointed.

Clear evidence of that is found in the Eurocentrism of Huntington's and Skocpol's definitions. There is an evident affinity between today's sociological category of revolution and the concept that emerged from the specific historical context of 18th-century France. Some authors consider that revolutions were originally a European phenomenon, inseparable from the spread of democracy and modernity.[24] How does this definition fit with other political experiences beyond Europe? The difficulty with translating the concept of revolution to other contexts is evident if we look at the question from a linguistic point of view. In Arabic, the word '*thawra*' translates the concepts of both revolution and revolt. Thus, we have the 'great Iraqi revolt', *al-thawra al-'irāqiyya al-kubrā*, the great Syrian revolt, *al-thawra al-sūriyya al-kubrā*, the Urabi revolt, *al-thawra al-'urābiyya*, and the Egyptian Revolution of 1919, *thawra 1919*. Whether the word *thawra* is translated as 'revolution' or 'revolt' depend more on political considerations than it does on the thoroughness of social processes.

But even considering 'revolution' as an analytical sociological category, classical structuralist and state-centred theories such as Skocpol's have been increasingly challenged from a wide array of different positions. While structuralist theories stress that revolutions are the outcome of a more or less determined set of conditions ('revolutions are not made, they come'),[25] since the 1990s the so-called 'fourth-generation' theories of revolution have brought 'agents' back into the picture.[26] They have pointed to the importance of understanding the motives of different actors for participating in protests, including chronically understudied groups such as women, workers, and peasants; they have also insisted on the importance of studying 'revolutionary cultures' and the ideological and cultural factors that prompt these events; and finally they have stressed that revolutions are multi-causal phenomena, the complexity of which

23 Social scientists have drawn up lists of revolutionary events, which, according to the literature, range from eighteen to one hundred and fifty: Jack A. Goldstone, 'Toward a Fourth Generation of Revolutionary Theory,' p. 142. Jeff Goodwin, and Adam Isaiah Green. 'Revolutions', *Encyclopedia of Violence, Peace, and Conflict*, Lester K. Kurtz ed. (Academic Press, 2008), p. 1871.

24 See, for example, Charles Tilly, Richard Tilly, and Louise Tilly, *The Rebellious Century, 1830-1930* (Cambridge, Ma: Harvard University Press, 1975).

25 Skocpol, *States and Social Revolutions*, p. 17.

26 Rod Aya, 'The Third Man; Or, Agency in History; Or, Rationality in Revolution', *History and Theory* (2001) vol. 40, n. 4, pp. 143–52. Eric Selbin, *Revolution in the Real World: Bringing Agency Back in* (New York: Routledge, 1997).

defies any attempt at prediction.[27] This in turn has had an impact on the definition of revolution as an analytical category, and shifted the focus of interest.

Definitions of revolutions become authoritative because they set the rules for inclusion or exclusion (what is and what is not a revolution) by suggesting the conditions that generate them. Thus, Skocpol's definition was believed to be the best (and still is, many think) because the causes of revolutions she identifies, notably class struggles, the 'health' of the state, and international conjuncture, were thought to be the most convincing. But since the time scholars began to acknowledge the multiplicity of the factors that cause revolutions, definitions have become progressively looser. This has also led to a shift in interest from revolutions as a sociological object *per se* and from compilations of taxonomies of revolutions to something quite different. What now occupies a central position in research is the analysis of the many agents and means, both tangible and intangible, that go to make up social and political protest; this explains the ever-increasing interest in the sociology of social movements, a branch of social science that has inspired parts of this book.

In the end, if there is one common denominator in all these interpretations of what revolutions are, it may be this: revolutions are social movements of protest that cross social hierarchies and involve both popular and elite groups, and which produce forms of radical change. In this purposely loose sense, 1924 was a true revolution, as this work will argue.

POWER IN HISTORY

From the point of view of a historian who deals with archives, the argument that if a certain number of conditions are present we can define an event as a revolution is also flawed for another reason. It presupposes that knowledge of all these conditions is somewhere there in the archives, simply waiting to be recovered, and that once it has been retrieved, the historian merely has to draw the resulting conclusions. As a consequence, the better the sources are, the more accurate the writing of history can be. But 1924 demonstrates exactly the opposite: the wealth and density of sources is not matched by scholarship that takes the event seriously. The problem with this argument, therefore, is that it omits politics and power from the equation.

Trouillot's reflections on power and narration offer powerful tools towards the understanding of how history, memory and power are intertwined.[28] According to the Haitian historian, there is an irreducible

[27] John Foran and Jeff Goodwin, 'Revolutionary Outcomes in Iran and Nicaragua: Coalition Fragmentation, War, and the Limits of Social Transformation', *Theory and Society* (1993), vol. 22, n. 2, pp. 209–47. Mustafa Emirbayer and Jeff Goodwin, 'Symbols, Positions, Objects: Toward a New Theory of Revolutions and Collective Action', *History and Theory* (1996), vol. 35, n. 3, pp. 358–74.

[28] Michel-Rolph Trouillot, *Silencing the Past: Power and the Production of History*

distinction between history as a series of facts and history as a narrative, but there is also an irreducible overlapping between the two which is inherent in the very word 'history': that is, something that is both narrated and located in the past: 'history reveals itself only through the production of specific narratives'; every piece of written history 'renews a claim to truth' as the most authoritative version of a certain past; however, every narrative is subject to a certain set of conditions for its production, which are inherently political: 'power is constitutive of the story'.[29] Thus, every historical narrative is strewn with silences. In an oft-quoted evocative passage, Trouillot makes this point:

> Silences enter the process of historical production at four crucial moments: the moment of fact creation (the making of sources); the moment of fact assembly (the making of archives); the moment of fact retrieval (the making of narratives); and the moment of retrospective significance (the making of history in the final instance) ... any historical narrative is a particular bundle of silences ...[30]

This analysis is clearly echoed in the making of 1924 into an historical object. The extent to which the transformation of events into sources is political is the subject of the last chapter of this book; similarly, that is where I discuss the way in which archival information is selected, processed, and brought together to write history. In the case of 1924, only a limited amount of information has been selected from among the vast array of sources and versions available in the national archives or as published autobiographies, and this selection has then been reiterated from one work to the next.

One case in point is the idea that the White Flag League consisted of only a 120 people, a figure that is systematically cited in the secondary literature.[31] In reality, the colonial archives (and personal ones, too) yield various lists of members, to the point where I have been able to build a database of activists that includes slightly more than 900 names, all collected from the colonial files (and if we also include a list kept by a descendant of a Sudanese officer, the number rises to about 1,100 names). In spite of all their limitations, produced as they were from judicial and intelligence records, these lists have been fundamental to this work, not only to obtain a complex overview of the structure of the national movement and its regional differences, but also, more simply, to grasp fragments of stories of people who were otherwise invisible to the colonial state.

Similarly, in contrast to the idea that the movement had a limited impact, both the colonial documents and insurgents' testimony bear witness to the extent to which the League spread to even small villages, the organization of demonstrations on a daily basis, and the participation of thousands of people in some of them. The movement is described in secondary literature as lacking ideological cohesiveness, and yet the

(*contd*) (Boston, Mass.: Beacon Press, 1995).

29 Ibid., pp. 25, 6, 28.

30 Ibid., pp. 26-27.

31 See for instance: Beshir, *Revolution and Nationalism*, p. 75. Daly, *Empire on the Nile*, p. 293.

archives have kept dozens of telegrams that reveal that the activists had a very precise idea of what it was they wanted.

The reason for this selective forgetfulness may be found in the difficulty with overcoming a colonial paradigm of historical interpretation, and in the intensely political reading of this event.

Plan of the book

This book's first concern lies with the protagonists of 1924 and their backgrounds, life-stories, beliefs, values, and motives; but it will also focus on the resources, both tangible and intangible, that were mobilized by the nationalist movement to attract supporters and turn the Sudanese into protesters. For this, the book is heavily indebted to the theories of social movements that explore how ideological, emotional, and cultural resources are employed to frame a political movement and to convince people that it is worth fighting for the nation. Otherwise, it would be hard to understand why people like Zayn al-ʿĀbdīn ʿAbd al-Tām, a well-off army officer with excellent relations with his British superiors, or ʿUbayd al-Ḥājj al-Amīn, a young graduate with a brilliant future, decided to join the movement. These two had far more to lose than they had to gain from a struggle against a government of whose constantly looming violence they had had direct experience; and yet, they joined it.

Following a research agenda that seeks to overcome the view of 1924 as a non-event, I have tried to find room for what 1924 *was* for its actors, to the extent the sources have allowed me to see it and to the degree that I have been able to interpret them. It was a revolt framed by the nationalist wind that was blowing across many parts of the colonial world after the First World War, and so the movement's political demands were justified as the will of the Sudanese nation (Chapters 1 and 2). It was led by a political society, the White Flag League, which had a fairly complex organization and whose aim was to convince the largest possible number of people to join the national struggle (Chapters 3 and 4). However, it was also characterized by a considerable diversity in structure and coordination according to location, a point evident in the study of two cases, that of Port Sudan and El Obeid (Chapter 5). Its spread is reflected in the ideology of the movement, which outlined an extremely subtle and loose idea of national unity (Chapters 6 and 7). A close-knit network of classmates and colleagues, mostly army officers and civilian government employees, formed its leadership. This group was socially rather diverse, however, and in many aspects was not very distant from skilled urban workers, who formed another crucial component of the national movement (Chapters 8 to 10). Finally, Chapter 11 returns to the question of memory, with an analysis of the first layer of silence that set the tone for the historical interpretation of 1924. The Epilogue shall delve more into this issue.

Part One

The Nationalist Movement in Sudan 1919–1923

Transnational Perspectives

I

Rethinking Nationalism in Colonial Sudan

After the First World War, a wave of political unrest swept through the colonial world. It was of such force that the historical period rightfully deserves to be called the 'spring of the colonial nations' as an analogy with the wave of nationalist agitations that crossed Europe in 1848, and which similarly ended with severe blows to the nationalist cause. After the Great War, as far as the Middle East and North Africa were concerned, this wave included, besides Sudan, the Egyptian Revolution of 1919, the Great Iraqi Revolt of 1920, the Great Syrian Revolt between 1925 and 1927, and last but not least, the wars from 1919 to 1923 that led to the creation of the independent Republic of Turkey. Besides these kinds of agitation, which sought direct confrontation with colonial forces, milder forms of resistance also developed in the Mediterranean area. Various political movements were created or restructured during this period that sought increased political rights for national citizens, and in some cases independence. Examples of this may be found in Tunisia, with the reorganization of the Young Tunisians into the Dustour party by 'Abd al-'Azīz Tha'ālbī and others in 1921, or in Algeria, with the 'Mouvement pour l'Egalité et la Reforme', which was founded in 1919 by Khālid Bin El-Hāshimī (also known as the 'Emir Khalid'); this would later lead to the foundation of the most important Algerian nationalist party, the 'Étoile Nord-Africaine'.[1]

Revolts and protests were by no means confined to the shores of the Mediterranean or the Middle East, however. In 1921, after a wave of mass demonstrations and violence, Gandhi launched the *Ahimsaa*, the non-violence movement, in India; one year later the Irish Free State became independent after a war of liberation that had begun in 1919. In 1922, millions of Koreans participated in peaceful demonstrations to protest against Japanese occupation in the name of Woodrow Wilson's principle of self-determination.[2] In 1920, in Accra, the National Congress of British West Africa was formed to discuss reforms in the Gold Coast, while in

[1] For references on these movements and on the following ones, see the Bibliography.

[2] Erez Manela, *The Wilsonian Moment: Self-Determination and the International Origins of Anticolonial Nationalism* (Oxford; New York: Oxford University Press, 2007).

Kenya in 1921, the Young Kikuyu association (soon to be renamed the East African Association) was founded by Harry Thuku in order to ask for more political rights for Kenyan people. In South-West Africa, a wave of anti-colonial protests took place as a reaction to the nomination of South Africa as a mandatory power.[3] Surely, a global wave of political unrest of this magnitude, taking place more or less simultaneously within ten years of the end of the First World War, cannot be a coincidence.

Obviously these political movements developed out of entirely diverse political conjunctures. What is more, the extent to which the masses were involved differed greatly, as the movements varied between elite organizations with little contact with popular elements, such as in Ghana, to mass movements that included millions of protesters, as was the case in Egypt. And yet, in spite of their differences, there is no doubt that these movements shared an isomorphic transnational language: they claimed that the inhabitants of the colonies were national citizens with a right to self-determination; they should be masters of their own destiny, both political and economic; and they knew best how to make their country 'civilized' enough to be independent. To quote James McDougall, a historian of Algeria, 'the right of nations to self-determination was the principal gain of the war.'[4] For David Killingray, the West African Conference expressed 'the demands for greater African participation in the colonial administration and greater influence over the economy'.[5]

Sudanese nationalism was fully a part of this global moment. However, its transnational dimensions not only go undetected, but nationalism is also narrowly reduced to a derivative discourse coming either from Egypt or from Great Britain.[6] For example, for one historian, William Hanes,

> ...it might well be argued (polemically no doubt) that Sudanese nationalism itself was largely a creation of the [Sudan] Political Service as a part of its struggle against any Anglo-Egyptian agreement that would jeopardize its agenda in the Sudan.[7]

This approach is even more present in studies of Sudanese nationalism after the First World War. As no political faction asked for the full independence of Sudan, the political movement of the 1920s is often dubbed as 'proto-nationalism'.

3 For and overview, see Jonathan Derrick, *Africa's 'Agitators': Militant Anti-Colonialism in Africa and the West, 1918-1939* (New York: Columbia University Press, 2008).

4 James McDougall, *History and the Culture of Nationalism in Algeria* (Cambridge: Cambridge University Press, 2006), p. 44.

5 David Killingray, 'Repercussions of World War I in the Gold Coast', *The Journal of African History* (1978), vol. 19, n. 1, p. 57.

6 For an example of the Egyptian interpretation of 1924, see Mohammed Nuri El-Amin, 'Britain, the 1924 Sudanese Uprising, and the Impact of Egypt on the Sudan', *The International Journal of African Historical Studies* (1986), vol. 19, n. 2, pp. 235-260; for Britain, see Martin Daly, *Empire on the Nile*.

7 William T. Hanes, *Imperial Diplomacy in the Era of Decolonization: The Sudan and Anglo-Egyptian Relations, 1945-1956* (Westport, Conn.: Greenwood Press, 1995), p.10.

This chapter and the following argue that there has been a real problem in historiography in seeing African nationalisms as a popular political force, and this problem is even more acute in the case of the nationalism after the Great War. The discussion covers two chapters because for the purposes of shedding light on nationalism in Sudan as a connected history, it is necessary to tie together ostensibly unrelated elements. These range from a discussion on 'origin' and nationalism to the history of the Sudanese press, and from the international spread of protest techniques to the circulation of radical ideas. It is hoped these strands will end up making sense as a single whole, and corroborate the argument that any analysis that takes insufficient account of the global interconnectedness of political ideas, people, and resistance strategies among colonized countries (and radical parties) is highly reductive.

POST-WAR NATIONALISM AS A DERIVATIVE DISCOURSE?

Broadly speaking, nationalism as a political force able to move the masses is an overlooked topic in African studies. A number of factors have contributed to this neglect, from the way in which colonial historians have portrayed nationalism to the prominence of ethnic conflicts in the continent. Nationalism is often described as a political force not 'originally African': first embraced and diffused by local elites of colonial intermediaries, who because of their colonial education had been estranged from their own society, nationalism never 'made it' to the masses. Moreover, particularly in the case of sub-Saharan Africa, nationalism is more often than not seen as a failed ideology, one that has been and is unable to resolve ethnic conflicts and religious fractures.

The failure to take seriously the nationalisms of the African continent goes hand in hand with the inadequacy of the current theories to seize it; in other words, nationalism in Africa is somehow theoretically impossible. The dominant theories of nationalism, often labelled as 'modernist' theories, consider nationalism as the ideology of choice of the 'modern' world, and they connect its birth with the industrial revolution, the shift from absolute monarchies to a centralized bureaucratic states, and the spread of mass literacy. Because it is closely associated to modernity, in those areas that are deemed 'not modern enough', nationalism is often seen as a weak political force. One example is how perhaps the most popular book of the last thirty years in nationalism studies, Benedict Anderson's *Imagined Communities,* describes African nationalisms. After considering nationalism as the outcome of a series of epochal changes in a ('Westernizing') world increasingly marked by religious, political, and cultural pluralism, Anderson maintains that nationalism in Africa was a part of the colonial imperial legacy, and that this ambiguity marked its development from the start: 'in the 'nation-building' policies of the new states, one sees both a genuine, popular nationalist enthusiasm and a systematic, even Machiavellian, instilling of nationalist ideology through the mass media'[8]. An interpretation such as this cannot but recall the way colonial rulers described the various African nationalist movements as being composed of malicious political entrepreneurs who 'mimicked' exogenous ideas from the West for their own interests and benefit.

The interpretation of African nationalism as a 'mimicry' of a European concept has been disputed by a generation of nationalist historians, usually based in the former colonies, who have insisted that nationalism was a genuine ideology born as a *reaction* to European imperialism.[9] To use the specific terminology of theories on nationalism, one might say that the disagreement concerns exogenous versus endogenous models of nationalism, and imitative versus reactive versions.

To overcome such dichotomy, one has to return to Anderson, because in other parts of his *Imagined Communities* he sets forth a type of interpretation (which he does not follow through consistently) that is crucial for the present work. Anderson hints at the fact that, far from being a European exclusivity, nationalism was instead a global phenomenon, which expanded in 'modular', isomorphic forms, capable of adjusting to entirely dissimilar contexts, yet retaining a similar language.[10] And indeed in the case of Sudanese nationalism of the 1920s, it makes little sense to distinguish the endogenous from the exogenous, the reactive versus the imitative models. It was intrinsically both: it made sense locally, but at the same time it had clear modular characteristics that lent it affinity with many anti-colonial nationalist movements elsewhere in the colonial world. To focus only on the Anglo-Egyptian-Sudanese triangle would limit our vision to an unacceptable degree, because political developments in Sudan after the Great War were a reflection and a consequence not only of the Anglo-Egyptian dispute, but also of the 'spring of the colonial nations' that was sweeping through many parts of the world. For that reason, what is needed is a connected history of Sudanese nationalism that applies the following oft-quoted passage from Sanjay Subrahmanyam to the letter:

> [I]deas and mental constructs, too, flowed across political boundaries in that world, and – even if they found specific local expression – enable us to see that what we are dealing with are not separate and comparable, but connected histories.[11]

[8] Benedict Anderson, *Imagined Communities: Reflections on the Origin and Spread of Nationalism* (London; New York: Verso, 1991), pp. 113-114.

[9] Terence Ranger, 'The 'New Historiography' in Dar Es Salaam: An Answer', *African Affairs* (1971), vol. 70, n. 278, pp. 50-61; Terence Ranger, 'Nationalist Historiography, Patriotic History and the History of the Nation: The Struggle Over the Past in Zimbabwe', *Journal of Southern African Studies* (2004), vol. 30, n. 2, pp. 215-234. More generally, this is considered to be the line of the well-known UNESCO History of Africa: *General History of Africa* (London; Berkeley: Heinemann Educational Books, 1981).

[10] Anderson, *Imagined Communities*, p. 113.

[11] Sanjay Subrahmanyam, 'Connected Histories: Notes Towards a Reconfiguration of Early Modern Eurasia' (1997), *Modern Asian Studies*. vol. 31, n. 3, p. 747.

NATIONALISM AS AN IDEOLOGICAL RESOURCE

If generally the topic of grass-root dimensions of nationalist movements is overlooked in African Studies, even more neglected is the wave of nationalist movements that developed in Africa after the First World War. If at all mentioned, these movements are systematically dubbed as 'proto-nationalisms', as 'early' or 'pioneer' movements, or as 'nationalisms' in inverted commas. Such denominations underline that they are generally perceived as faltering, precarious, precocious, and usually failed attempts, especially if compared with their later more 'successful' versions.[12]

There are various factors that explain the genealogy of such a perception. First of all, as they were (or are considered as) ineffective, they simply attract less attention than later nationalist movements. Second, their timing does not fit with how the period after the First World War is generally understood. There is a widespread tendency to see this stage as the apogee of imperialism, to the point where it has been called a time of 'predatory imperialism'[13], because not only Africa but also most of the world fell victim of the appetite of a bunch of imperial powers. The third factor is again connected to how nationalism is theorized. Another mainstay of modernist theories is that nationalism is the result of social, political and economic 'earthquakes' (industrialization, the French revolution, and so on). Applied to the African context, this leads to the assumption that nationalism 'proper' developed as a consequence of the tremendous changes in the social, politic and economic orders that affected very many aspects of people's lives after the Second World War: demographic explosion, urbanization, economic restructuring, an unprecedented development of state services, political turmoil, and rapid changes from colonies, to independent republics, and ultimately to one-party regimes.[14] Thus, in the same way that in Europe nationalism coincided with the socio-economic dislocations occurred with the advent of the Modern Age, so in Africa the spread of nationalism occurred in connection with the socio-economic and political disruptions of decolonization.

This model fits the period after the First World War much less well, however. The First World War brought dramatic transformations to the Middle East, but much less so to Africa. Yet, even places relatively untouched by the global war such as Sudan or Tunisia experienced the advent or rise of nationalist movements. Thus, just as nationalism as a political force must not be tied to a European brand of 'modernity', so it should also be free from being associated with dramatic local dislocations.

[12] See for instance the telling title, *Early Sudanese Nationalism, 1919-1925,* by one of the historians of 1924, Hasan Abdin.

[13] Barbara Bush, *Imperialism, Race and Resistance: Africa and Britain, 1919-1945* (London, New York: Routledge, 2002), p. 20, and generally her discussion in pp. 20-46.

[14] Frederick Cooper, *Decolonization and African Society: The Labor Question in French and British Africa* (Cambridge [England]; New York: Cambridge University Press, 1996).

This issue has been brought to light in recent studies on social movements: one example of an integration of this social theory into history is the work of historian Juan Cole on the so-called ʻUrābī Revolution of 1881-1882 in Egypt. This revolt toppled the rule of the Khedive Tawfīq, and *de facto* marked the beginning of the British occupation of Egypt.[15] Cole, influenced by the strand of the sociology of social movements that focuses on resource mobilization, maintains that this uprising, which had a distinctly nationalist character, was possible because of a complex series of interrelated factors that cannot all be described as political or economic strains.[16] While conceding that the worsening of the political condition of Egypt, most notably its *de facto* loss of sovereignty after 1876, was one of the causes of the revolution, he also demonstrates that the revolution took place because a set of new resources, in form of ideas, technologies and organizational strategies, became available to the nationalists.

The point is crucial to the study of the 1924 Revolution and of the nationalist movement that triggered it. In Sudan the reverberations from the Great War were more subtle and more widespread than they are usually believed to have been, and cannot be described in terms of social dislocation. As in many other parts of the colonial world, post-war nationalism in Sudan was a result of the new opportunities that opened up to political activists as a consequence of the historical conjuncture that came about after the Great War, in which nationalism became a powerful resource of political mobilization, and gave people who were dissatisfied with colonial and semi-colonial situations a particularly powerful toolkit of ideas, strategies, and structures for political action. Among anti-colonial activists, this conjuncture shaped a sense of belonging to a 'community of the oppressed', which provided a common language that was at the same time supranational and fully grounded into local colonial situations. Last but not least, the emergence of nationalism as an ideology implied a change in the power relations between the colonizers and the colonized. Nationalism represented a radical departure for Sudanese, because it permitted them to imagine colonialism not only as having a time limit, but also as being dialectically determined by the national will of the Sudanese. Nationalism in the 1920s was much more than a product of British or Egyptian influences in Sudan: it was an unobtrusive revolution.

FOR A NATIONALISM WITHOUT ORIGINS

The last methodological point to be introduced here is a critique of nationalism as something linear and progressive, having a point of origin which somehow set the modalities in which it would deploy later. The

[15] Juan R. Cole, *Colonialism and Revolution in the Middle East Social and Cultural Origins of Egypt's 'Urabi Movement* (Princeton, N.J.: Princeton University Press, 1993).

[16] Della Porta and Diani, *Social Movements.* For Africa, Stephen Ellis and Ineke I. V. Kessel eds. *Movers and Shakers: Social Movements in Africa* (Leiden; Boston: Brill, 2009).

mythology of the 'origins' of nationalism, and the intellectual search for them, is very powerful in both the scholarship on Middle East and Africa, and also in Sudan Studies. As seen above, some scholars believe that the 'origins' of nationalism are exogenous to Sudan, so that the 1924 activists were pawns in the hands of foreign powers. In a similar vein, other historians consider that the 'true origins' of Sudanese nationalism do not lie in the White Flag League, but in its predecessor, the Society of the Sudan Union, which is commonly credited for its less radical outlook and more prominent social composition.[17]

In an important note on the theoretical advancement of studies on Arab nationalism, James Gelvin, a historian of colonial Syria, has drawn attention to the anguished search for the origins of nationalism.[18] The search for origins is a quest for an archetypical nationalism, inherently related to all its subsequent historical manifestations, just as a seed is related to a plant. This assumption is founded on the supposition that it exists in one single, discrete place where everything began, and that by knowing this one place one would understand all that happened later once and for all. But as Gelvin notes, in this way we are attributing a characteristic of essentialism to this origin; we can all agree that nations are social constructs, yet they remain essentially set by the way in which they were born. This is the reasoning that leads some scholars to consider that the White Flag League was not the 'true origin' of Sudanese nationalism but the product of an external import: it was too radically different from later versions of nationalism to represent an archetypical model.

And yet, the works of Gelvin and those of a wave of new historians of the Middle East from the 1990s has led to a profound reconceptualization of Arab nationalism, which represents a very important contribution to the study of nationalism in general, and in particular in the non-Western world. These historians unravel the complex configuration of the Ottoman Middle East from the end of the 19th century to the 1920s.[19] The study of the political debates in places such as Ottoman Mesopotamia or Greater Syria demonstrates that allegiances to a supposed concept of 'Arabness' were far more volatile and unstable than had been described in earlier works on Arab nationalism; second, that only a series of unpredictable historical contingencies led to the affirmation of this specific form of nationalism; and finally, that the way Arab nationalism was originally formulated bore little resemblance to later types of nationalism, such as

[17] Martin Daly, *British Administration and the Northern Sudan*, p. 131. Holt and Daly, *A History of the Sudan*, pp. 113-114.

[18] James L. Gelvin, 'Arab Nationalism Meets Social Theory' in 'Questions and Pensées: "Arab Nationalism": Has a New Framework Emerged?', AAVV, *International Journal of Middle East Studies* (2009), 41, n. 1, pp. 10-21.

[19] Israel Gershoni and James Jankowski, *Egypt, Islam, and the Arabs the Search for Egyptian Nationhood, 1900-1930.* (New York: Oxford University Press, 1986). James P. Jankowski and Israel Gershoni, *Rethinking Nationalism in the Arab Middle East* (New York: Columbia University Press, 1997). Arthur Goldschmidt, Amy J. Johnson, and Barak A. Salmoni, *Re-envisioning Egypt 1919-1952* (Cairo; New York: American University in Cairo Press, 2005).

pan-Arabism or the Arab nationalism of the Ba'ath party in Syria after the 1950s.[20]

Perhaps the clearest example of this is Egyptian nationalism. According to James Jankowski and others, national debates on Egyptian nationalism from the end of the nineteenth century until the eve of the Great War revolved around the opposition between the moderates and the radicals. The moderates were represented by the Umma Party – the party to which Sa'd Zaghlūl himself adhered before the war – whose ideology was 'Egypt for the Egyptians' that is, that Egypt must gradually reach full autonomy, but under British guidance; the radicals instead supported the Watanist (in Arabic, Nationalist) Party of Muṣṭafā Kāmil.[21] Although the Watanist Party was the most radical in the spectrum of Egyptian politics, it did not ask for Egyptian independence, just as Sudanese radical party after the Great War. For Kāmil, Egypt was an integral part of the Ottoman Empire. Moreover, neither the Umma nor the Watanist party in Egypt would have ever contemplated the idea of joining forces with the Arabs, or worse, that Egyptians were even Arabs. At the time, this term described the nomadic inhabitants of places such as Greater Syria and the Arabic Peninsula, who were considered by Egyptians to be unsophisticated and uncivilized Bedouins at best, and – especially during and after the Great War – at worst, as traitors sold to the British and enemies who wished to destroy the Ottoman Empire. And so, in 1920, Egyptians would have never defined themselves as Arabs – which may seem to be a contradiction of the pan-Arab ideology that was extensively employed by Jamāl 'Abd al-Nāṣir from the 1950s on.

The second point that the theoretical shift on Arab nationalism has brought to light is that the beginnings of nationalism can hardly be seen as situated in just one place, one social group, or political movement. Despite the fact that various movements adopted a nationalist ideology, the political scene was systematically characterized by heterogeneity and divided loyalties. Not only did political entrepreneurs from dissimilar social and ideological backgrounds have quite disparate projects for the nation and its future, they also conceived it in radically different ways, including through the symbols that brought these projects together.[22] Similarly, there were wide differences of opinion on the means for achieving political objectives, ranging from moderation and gradualism to the most uncompromising of attitudes.

Nevertheless, in spite of the diversity of these projects, we must not fail to take account of the isomorphism of contentious politics across different countries, such as Sudan for the Sudanese, Egypt for the Egyptians, an

[20] James L. Gelvin, *Divided Loyalties: Nationalism and Mass Politics in Syria at the Close of Empire* (Berkeley: University of California Press, 1998).

[21] James P. Jankowski, 'Egypt and Early Arab Nationalism, 1908-1922', in Rashid Khalidi, *The Origins of Arab Nationalism* (New York: Columbia University Press, 1991), pp. 243-270.

[22] See, for instance, the link between Pharaonism and nationalism in Egypt: Donald M. Reid, *Whose Pharaohs?: Archaeology, Museums, and Egyptian National Identity from Napoleon to World War I.* (Berkeley: University of California Press, 2002).

independent Morocco but under French 'guidance', or further, Greater Syria with the Ottomans, Egypt with the Caliphate, Sudan with the Egyptians, and so on.

The final point emphasized by this new scholarship is the volatility of the political scene. In Greater Syria, unstable allegiances might push nationalist entrepreneurs to be staunch supporters of Ottomanism at the outset, and then within a very short period of time turn them into passionate Arab nationalists.[23] Similar patterns can be traced in Sudan and Egypt: we have seen that before the Great War, Zaghlūl was a member of the moderate and pro-British Umma party; but after the war, his Wafd became one of the most radical parties of the political spectrum, to the point where it attracted people who had previously supported the Watanist party of his old enemy Muṣṭafā Kāmil. Similarly, in Sudan, in 1922 'Alī 'Abd al-Laṭīf sought to publish a document, known as 'The Claim of the Nation' in which he asked for the full independence for Sudan from Egypt and Great Britain. However, in 1924, as a leader of the White Flag League, he claimed the unity between Sudan and Egypt.

The new historians of Arab nationalism have stressed that these political entrepreneurs must not be seen as 'false moderates' who 'deep down' were radicals, or 'false radicals' who maliciously hid their moderate views; for example, Zaghlūl is sometimes accused of having been an opportunist, embracing a radical ideology only for his own political gains. Instead, these historians remind us that the politicians acted within – and reacted to – a setting that was evolving at a dramatically fast pace, and that by consequence had to adapt and respond swiftly to the new context. This interpretative framework is directly relevant to how the White Flag League and the Revolution of 1924 will be analysed here: above all, the 1924 Revolution is a story of complex and shifting alliances among disparate social groups; of swift changes in leadership and direction within the national movement; and of several uprisings rolled into one revolution. This study proposes that all these complexities, far from being signs of the immaturity or fatuity of the movement, are common to any broad social movement and evidence of its wide scope.

INTERPRETING THE CONNECTIONS AND CONTRADICTIONS BETWEEN NATIONALISM AND STATUS

Narratives

As previously mentioned, the 'moderate' Sudan Union is considered to have been more similar to the movement that led the country to independence than the 'radical' White Flag League, and as such the Sudan Union is treated as the real 'origin' of Sudanese nationalism. The Sudan Union included an impressive number of soon-to-be-famous Sudanese and intellectual voices of the time, such as Khalīl Faraḥ, one of the most popular Sudanese musicians and songwriters; 'Abdallāh Khalīl, Prime

[23] Gelvin, 'Arab Nationalism Meets Social Theory', p. 12.

Minister from 1956 to 1958; 'Arafāt Muḥammad 'Abdallāh, who was in the 1930s the editor-in-chief of the nationalist journal *al-Fajr* (The Dawn); Khalfallāh Khalīl, later to become the first Minister of Defence; or finally Muḥammad Ṣāliḥ Shinqīṭī, whom we have already met (see page 8).[24] It is quite easy, therefore, to establish a correlation between political models and the status and origin of political activists.[25] As mentioned previously, the leader of the White Flag League, ex-army officer 'Alī 'Abd al-Laṭīf, was a so-called *sūdānī*, as were several members of the White Flag League; today people in Sudan would say that he was 'an African'. Moreover, 'Alī 'Abd al-Laṭīf was no moderate. He was among the very few Sudanese to be arrested for nationalist anti-colonial sedition during the period between 1919 and 1924, for having attempted to publish in a pro-government journal a call for the independence of Sudan.[26] For these reasons, historians usually assume that 'Alī was not a member of the Sudan Union as much on the grounds of his 'low' background as his 'radical' standing, because the Sudan Union is believed to have included only Sudanese from the 'best' Northern Sudanese families, and only 'Arabs'.

The paradigm associating 'African-ness', low status and radical politics can be seen as the convergence of two different sets of narratives. The first consists of the official reports written by senior Sudan officials such as Governor General Lee Stack (1916-1924) and members of the Intelligence Department. According to these reports, the political spectrum was neatly divided into pro-British and pro-Egyptian factions. The pro-British faction was, in turn, composed of two elements: the first of these was made up of older Sudanese notables, such as the principal merchants of Khartoum, senior Sudanese officials, leaders of 'tribal' confederations who lived in Khartoum, and all three religious leaders of the country, *sayyid* 'Abd al-Raḥman al-Mahdī, *sayyid* 'Alī al-Mīrghanī and *sayyid* Yūsuf al-Hindī. The first two in particular were consulted frequently and extensively on matters that were considered to be politically sensitive. It should also be noted that even though the name of 'Alī al-Mīrghanī would be associated with the pro-Egyptian political faction in the 1930s, in the 1920s he was an outspoken advocate for the complete independence of Sudan from Egypt.[27] The second element of the pro-British faction included elite

[24] Their biography can be found, for instance, in Richard L. Hill, *A Biographical Dictionary of the Sudan* (London: Frank Cass, 1967) and Maḥjūb Muḥammad Bāshirī, *Rūwād al-Fikr al-Sūdānī* (Bayrūt: Dār al-Jīl, 1991). On the development of nationalism in Sudan in the period from 1918 to 1924, see the fundamental work by the late Sudanese historian Bakheit, 'British Administration and Sudanese Nationalism 1919-1939'; Diyāb, *al-'Alāqāt al-miṣrīya al-Sūdāniyya*, pp. 56-64; Beshir, *Revolution and Nationalism in the Sudan*; Mahasin Abdel Gadir Hag Al-Safi ed., *The Nationalist Movement in the Sudan* (Khartoum: Institute of African and Asian Studies, University of Khartoum, 1989); Muḥammad Sayyid al-Qaddāl, *Tārīkh Al-Sūdān Al-Ḥadīth: 1820-1955* (al-Khurṭūm: Markaz 'Abd-al-Karīm Mīrghanī, 2002).

[25] Bakheit, 'British Administration and Sudanese Nationalism'. Yoshiko Kurita, 'The Role of 'Negroid but Detribalized' People in Modern Sudanese History', *Nilo-Ethiopian Studies* (2003), no. 8-9, pp. 1-11.

[26] Kurita, *'Alī 'Abd al-Laṭīf wa-Thawrat 1924.*

[27] 'The Governor General saw Sayed Ali a few days ago and had a long confidential

Sudanese youth with 'national aspirations'. One report described them as 'the party of the more senior native officers and senior graduates ... most of the young Province Kadis, District Kadis, Schoolmasters, Officers of Arab origin and well to do merchants nearly everywhere, (with a small minority) belongs to this party.'[28] These descriptions associate 'Arabness' with political moderation and prestigious careers.

On the other hand, British sources describe the pro-Egyptian faction in a quite different way. Its members were considered to be 'inexperienced' Sudanese born after the end of the Turco-Egyptian era, the new generation. The contrast with the pro-British faction was not simply a matter of age, however. These sources point definitely at a difference in terms of background and careers between the pro-British and the pro-Egyptian parties, as a report filed at the beginning of 1924 affirmed:

> This party may be said to be composed of the majority of the employees in the lowest two grades of discharged and discontented officers and employees, etc. *They are exerting great efforts to get sons of good families into their association*, such as Ahmed Mudasir Ibrahim and Imam Doleib (both of whom have been disowned by their families), but without success. This party will undoubtedly grow in the future and will be the 'noisy' party.[29]

One point should not be missed, however, from the above quotation: first, at this stage, the government did not make any explicit connection between the non-Arab background of the activists and their pro-Egyptian political orientation; instead, from this quote, it is clear that this party included people of diverse origins, because officers were often *sūdānī*.

The second set of narratives that feeds the historiography of the period is built from testimonies by former members of the Sudan Union, either from their own memories, as in the case of the famous poet Tawfīq Ṣāliḥ Jibrīl, or journalist Sulaymān Kisha, or as a part of the secondary literature by historians who collected their accounts, such as Ḥassan Najīla or Gafaar Bakheit.[30] These sources describe the pro-Egyptian Sudan Union as composed of people from well-established Northern Sudanese families, educated at Gordon College – at that time the only institution of secondary education – and mostly working as civil servants. In sources

(*contd*) talk with him on the present situation..... The Governor General told him that... he hoped it would be found possible for an announcement to be made defining the status of the Sudan and giving it a separate Government which would enable the Sudanese to develop on their own lines under the guidance of the British Government. Sayed Ali's pleasure and satisfaction at the possibility were only too evident.' GG Office to Keown Boyd, 8.4.1920, FO 141/810/1, NA.

28 C. A. Willis, 'The Political Situation', Intel. Dept., Khartoum, 16.6.1924, FO 141/806/1, NA.

29 Ibidem. My italics. See also: Report received from ADI, Intel. Dept., Khartoum, 14.3.1919, FO 407/154, NA.

30 Bakheit, 'British Administration and Sudanese Nationalism 1919-1939'; Muḥammad 'Uthmān Yāsīn ed., *Al-Shā'ir Tawfīq Ṣāliḥ Jibrīl: Dhikrayāt Wa-aḥādīth* (Bayrūt: Dār al-Thaqāfa, 1971), Sulaymān Kisha, *Sūq al-Dhikryāt* (al-Khurṭūm: sharika al-ṭab'a wal-nasha, 1963), Sulaymān Kisha, *Al-Liwā' al-Abyaḍ* (al-Khurṭūm, 1969). The work of Ḥassan Najīla, *Malāmiḥ Min al-Mujtama' al-Sūdānī* (Bayrut: Dār Maktabat al-Ḥayāh, 1964), is one of the most important sources on the intellectual history and high culture of these times.

such as memoirs and biographies, direct reference to an alleged Arab background of Sudan Union members is usually omitted, but it is implicit that its members considered themselves to be the elite of Sudan.[31] As such, historians have described them as part of the Arab establishment that since these times has dominated Sudan's political life.[32]

It is quite baffling that in the surviving colonial records, references to the Sudan Union are conspicuous for their absence.[33] And yet, accounts left by former Sudan Union members such as Mudaththir al-Būshī or Ṣāliḥ 'Abd al-Qādir leave little doubt that the government was monitoring the activities of many members.[34] Yet, not only it decided to take no action, but also any trace of their activities was left off the records. Therefore, one may wonder whether the Intelligence Department glossed over their political involvement, not only in order to give as little visibility as possible to the pro-Egyptian movement, but also to cover the fact that people from well-established families, the elite of the Gordon College, was turning anti-colonial.

This short overview is quite emblematic of the historiographical problems connected to the nationalism of the 1920s. On the one hand, the existing historiographical narratives strongly shape the impression that the situation at the time was quite clear, politically: moderate against radicals, high status against low status, and 'Arabs' against 'Africans'; on the other hand, the various versions available differ quite substantially: in the version of the British intelligence, the political divide was set between a pro-British upper-class against a pro-Egyptian miscellaneous group of 'low' junior employees; in the versions of Sudan Union members, the divide was between a pro-Egyptian upper-class of (Arab) moderates and another pro-Egyptian group that was more radical, lower-class and certainly included fewer famous names. A part of these contradictions are connected to the memory problem related with 1924; and a part are related to the fact that that such divisions so clearly correspond to the multiple dichotomies by which scholars are used to seeing Sudan. It takes a great deal of patience to see the many cracks in these narratives.

Cracks and secrets

The first element that emerges from cross-checking the various sources is that it is not possible to associate moderates with people from notable families, and radicals with Sudanese of lower status. A case in point is 'Alī 'Abd al-Laṭīf himself. If he is usually considered not to be a member of the

[31] I have dealt with this question in Vezzadini, 'Spies, Secrets, and a Story Waiting to Be (re)told'.

[32] Bakheit, 'British Administration and Sudanese Nationalism 1919-1939'; Daly, *British Administration and the Northern Sudan*.

[33] One of the few existing documents, which dates from January 1923, described the Sudan Union as a secret society formed in Egypt to fight for the independence of Sudan that had founded a parallel organization based in Khartoum. Director S.S. [sic], Cairo, to the Chancery, the Residency, 16.1.1923, FO 141/806/1, NA.

[34] Mudaththir al-Būshī states that he was not arrested because the British were afraid to make the situation worse: *Al-Riwāyāt*, p. 106. Similarly, Ṣāliḥ 'Abd al-Qādir was known to the Intelligence Dept. since 1922: 20.7.1924. FO 141/806/1, NA. 'Notes on the signatories of the Telegram to Governor General, 15.5.1924'.

Sudan Union, the existing narratives relate different stories. Sulaymān Kisha, a member of the Sudan Union, states that 'Alī did not belong to it, while 'Abd al-Karīm al-Sayyid, who was a White Flag League member, claims that he was. As for colonial documents, a rare fragment, apparently written by a member of the Sudan Union and discovered by the Intelligence Department after 'Alī's arrest in 1922, stated:

> I impart my views or rather the views of the members of the Sudan Union Society, to my beloved countrymen, trusting that any failure on my part in describing the atrocities fully will be overlooked. It is clear to all who can see what has befallen a member of this Society Mulazim Awal Ali Eff Abdel Latif... who wished to express our views by means of publishing an article in a newspaper and was oppressively tried.[35]

Another case in point is drawn from a later event that took place just a few days before the beginning of the demonstrations. On June 10, a meeting took place at *sayyid* 'Abd al-Raḥman al-Mahdī's house in Omdurman, usually known as *ijtimā' al-'abbāsiyya* [the meeting of al-Abbasiyya, the neighbourhood where he lived], which was meant to represent the pro-British political faction. It was attended by the most important notables of Khartoum and by young graduates from notable families. During the gathering, the participants drafted a 'Declaration' in which they stated 'the general principle upon which the whole Sudan has agreed, namely, the choice of England to be the guardian of the Sudan and to bring up the country until they become a self-governing nation.' Indeed, the declaration contained no ambiguity as to the allegiance of its signatories to Britain, and it concluded:

> The party assembled today in the house of Sayed Abdel Rahman el-Mahdi at Omdurman comprises personages of Sudanese nationality who are enlightened and competent to form an opinion. ... They request that the English Government remain as their guardian until they reach the age of majority, the age when they are able to stand alone on their feet, they further charge the Government in London to represent the Sudan in the forthcoming negotiations, on this basis.[36]

Later, one activist humorously commented that 'when the meeting was finished the English went out safe and happy that all their wishes were fulfilled,' and that on the following day, Ḥusayn Sharīf published an article in *al-Ḥaḍāra* declaring that the Sudanese had decided to rid themselves of the Egyptians.[37]

And yet, there were incongruences. The declaration was followed by a list of signatures, and at least five of the thirteen signatories would soon reveal themselves to be members or supporters of the White Flag League: these included 'Abdallāh Khalīl, future prime minister and well known League member;[38] Ṭaha Ṣāliḥ, also member of the White Flag and signatory

35 F. C. C. Balfour, ADI to the Private, Civil, Legal Secretaries, SA, General Manager SGR&AG, and all Governors and DC Omdurman, Khartoum 9.7.1922, Darfur 3/2/16, National Record Office, Khartoum [NRO].

36 Declaration, Omdurman, 10.6.1924, Encl. 2 in No. 101, Allenby to MacDonald, 13.6.1924, FO 407/199, NA.

37 Al-Sayyid, *Al-Liwā' al-Abyaḍ*, p. 11.

38 Gov. Khartoum Prov. to Civsec, Khartoum 12.10.1924, Palace 4/9/56, NRO.

of an anti-British protest;[39] and 'Ibrahim Israil [sic],'[40] who would later be reported as a member of the League with his brother Muḥammad al-Makkī Ibrāhīm, and brother-in-law of one of the founders, Ṣāliḥ 'Abd al-Qādir. Secondly, the signatures of 'older' pro-British notables included the names of individuals whose sons would be involved in the events of 1924: people such as shaykh Bābikr al-Ḥājj al-Shafī, father of a Military College cadet who demonstrated in August 1924, and shaykh Aḥmad al-Imām Dūlayb, father of one of the earliest members of the White Flag League, al-Imām Dūlayb Khalīl.[41] One of the notables who signed the above declaration, 'Alī al-Mārdī, was even brought to trial as a League member.[42]

The picture that emerges from these accounts may seem to be confusing, and to bring chaos to an orderly situation rather than lead anywhere. Was 'Alī in the Sudan Union or not? Were the people on the Intelligence Department's list pro-British or pro-Egyptian? The catalogue of contradictory elements goes on and on: to give just one more example, in September 1924, the editor of the pro-British journal *Ḥaḍārat al-Sūdān*, Ḥusayn Sharīf, attempted to send to *The Times* a long and virulent anti-British article in which he accused the Sudan Government of thinking only of its 'imperialistic and exploiting aims'.[43]

These elements do not make particular sense as long as Sudanese political life continues to be viewed as orderly organized around two visible poles. Rather, the political situation was highly volatile, not only because it evolved very rapidly in relation to events in Egypt, but also because activists were continually testing whether levels of repression could be renegotiated, and if so, how. Furthermore, the configuration of politics in Sudan is hard to comprehend if one fails to take account of one essential factor: secrecy. At that time, political work needed secrecy if it was to survive. This fundamental element structured political associations such as the Sudan Union and the White Flag League. The need for secrecy explains some of the contradictions we have alluded to above: pro-Egyptian activists concealed their political opinion to a point where they were misidentified as outspoken pro-British activists. Because the Sudan Union was structured as a secret society, all its members did not necessarily know each other, even if they wanted to believe they did. But the main point is that the organization of Sudanese activists in the

39 'Translation of attached telegram from Taha Saleh to the Governor General through the Director of Education', Khartoum 30.7.1924, Palace 4/10/50, NRO. List of members of the White Flag League, undated and unsigned. In pencil: 'Usual distribution asking to inform us which of these men are Govt. employees and to which department they belong,' Palace 4/10/50, NRO.

40 This name signalled the fact that they belonged to a Jewish Sudanese family that had converted to Islam. See Robert Kramer, 'The Death of Bassiouni: A Case of Complex Identity in the Sudan,' forthcoming, *Canadian Journal of African Studies.*

41 C. A. Willis, 'The League of the White Flag,' Khartoum 20.7.1924, FO 141/810/3, NA.

42 *The White Flag Trials*. During his evidence he denied any connection with the White Flag.

43 'Copy of the article Hussein Sherif intended to send to The Times', from Ass. Private Sec. to Civsec, Khartoum, 13.9.1924, Palace 4/9/44, NRO.

period 1919 to 1924 was far more fragmentary than it is believed to be in historiography.

Local accounts and colonial sources all make passing references to the presence of numerous secret societies in Sudan after the War, in addition to the Sudan Union. For instance, the Ewart Report of 1925 commented in a few lines that before 1924, politics had been characterized by a number of 'nebulous,' loosely organized and, for Ewart, ultimately insignificant political organizations.[44] Ḥassan Najīla also refers briefly to the existence of many 'patriotic' societies besides the Sudan Union.[45] Most sources treat this question very summarily, however, with the result that historians tend to make reference to this configuration almost as a minor feature, an accidental detail that might easily be omitted.

The light shed on Sudan Union has obscured all that happened beyond and outside it. And yet, the presence of multiple secret societies and the complexity of the situation was a major feature of the political culture of that time. In turn this political culture had a direct impact on the information that the Intelligence Department managed to gather, and hence on what we as historians are able to learn about this period.

ARABS, SUDANESE, EGYPTIANS, AND OTHER LABELS

Labels such as 'Arab', 'Black, 'Muwallad' and Egyptian will be used frequently in this book, because they were a part of the language of colonial and Sudanese sources. This final section reflects on their meanings, and more generally on all the 'nationality' labels that were used to define activists, such as the words 'Berberine', 'Shaigi' or 'Denka'. This is all the more important because these labels are also used in historiography, not only to define people, but also to connote specific brands of nationalism. Thus, it is often noted that the nationalism of 1924 was a form of (proto)-Sudanese nationalism, unlike the 'Arab' nationalism that would develop in the 1930s and 1940s. It is commonly believed that later nationalists strongly resisted defining themselves as 'Sudanese', because the word still carried a meaning that was associated with slavery.

This paradigm does not necessarily work for the 1920s, however. First of all, in colonial sources, the overarching categories of 'Arab' or 'Black'/'Sudanese' were only rarely used to define individuals. The word 'Sudanese' was applied to a person of southern background only when it was impossible to establish his or her 'tribe' of origin with precision. More frequently, people were attributed a specific ethnic origin. Second, some of the ethnic labels that were used bore witness to the complexity of the question of origins and belonging in Sudan, as in 'Moorish muwallad', or

44 Ewart Report on Political Agitation in the Sudan, Khartoum, 21.4.1925, FO 407/201, NA, p. 157. Henceforth: 'Ewart Report'.

45 Najīla, however, does not mention either the names or the number of such societies. Najīla, *Malāmiḥ Min al-Mujtama' al-Sūdānī*, p. 165.

'Jaalin-Sudanese', or 'Turk-Sudanese'.[46] They also reflected the history of migration and intermarriage of the Sudanese people and the way in which history impacted the demographic composition of the country, such as the Ottoman-Egyptian invasion and the slave trade. Yet, as many stories in this book will illustrate, the ethnic labels applied to insurgents can at best be seen as fragments of this complex history, and never as categorical identity markers. Even colonial sources barely mention the ethnic make-up of the protesters: in two-thirds of cases, the activists' descriptions do not include their ethnic background at all.

Yet colonial sources did employ the labels 'Black', 'Arab' and 'Egyptian', especially in longer reports that attempted to draw a broad portrait of the political situation in Sudan. This terminology was also frequently employed in the government administration, for example in statistics and in descriptions of the army. What was the meaning of these labels as they were used in these contexts?

Egyptians and Muwalladīn...

In 1924, the British believed that 'Egyptian' people were responsible for the country's political unrest, and they often identified Egyptians as participants in the events. However, in the Sudan of the 1920s, it was no easy matter to establish whether a person was or was not Egyptian. This label was attached to people who may have had an entirely different relationship with Sudan: some would have spent only a few years of their lives there, while others were born in that country and were as much Sudanese as they were Egyptian. Some of the Egyptians who chose to work in Sudan did so for family reasons, because a part of their family came from there, as was the case with the Egyptian president Muḥammad Najīb, whose mother was Sudanese. Second, there were those Sudanese whose families stretched across the two countries. In particular, in northern provinces such as Halfa and Dongola, population movement between Egypt and Sudan was continuous, and annually, during the agricultural off-season, Sudanese labourers left to work in Egypt, only to return for the harvest. This movement was so conspicuous that every year, British officers expressed the fear that these provinces would become completely depopulated.

Besides this geographical contiguity and the political and economic connections, there are obvious historical explanations for the blurred nature of the identity frontier between Egypt and Sudan. In the 19th century, political consolidation of dominant indigenous families in Northern Sudan had been carried out by a close alliance with the Ottoman-Egyptian establishment, and was achieved, among other things, through a policy of intermarriage.[47] Even today, there is a popular adage in North

46 Muwallad-Moorish: Aḥmad Idrīs 'Abū Ghālib: Baily, Assistant Gov. Khartoum to Civsec 29.6.1924, Palace 4/10/49. Jaalin-Sudanese: Farajallāh Muḥammad, Intelligence Notes, 21.10.1924, Khartoum, Palace 4/9/47. Turk-Sudanese was attributed to a certain 'Attia Shafie', in List of persons tried for Offences of a political nature from June 1st to May 31st 1925, Kordofan 1/14/68, all in NRO.

47 Richard L. Hill, *Egypt in the Sudan, 1820-1881* (London: Oxford University

Sudan that every Sudanese has at least one relative in Egypt. This was particularly true of the old 'Effendi' class, that is old elite families whose members had served as clerical staff under the Ottoman-Egyptian government – and who had married Sudanese women.

Nothing reveals the blurred nature of the borders between Egyptians and Sudanese better than the category of *Muwallad* (plural *Muwalladīn*) which is extremely important in colonial sources on 1924, as it was attributed to a large number of political activists. The term indicated first of all people born of an intermarriage between an Egyptian father and a Sudanese mother. In practice, however, everyone who had fair skin and a vague link with Egypt could be conveniently defined by that term. This was the case, for instance, with White Flag founder, Ṣāliḥ 'Abd al-Qādir.[48] He was the son of a Sudanese from Shendi and Metemma on his father's side, while the family of his mother, Fāṭima Ibrāhīm ibn Mushlī (one of the first midwives in Sudan), came from a family originally from Anatolia or Iraq. Thus, even though Ṣāliḥ's Ottoman descent was from his mother's side and dated back to his grandparents, he was still consistently looked upon as a *Muwallad*. Another telling example is that of Ḥassan Ṣāliḥ, one of the League founders. According to his personal file, '[he] is a muwallad, but registers himself as a Sudanese', and the file adds that the mother was Egyptian (which meant that the father was Sudanese).[49] These two cases show that attribution of the label 'Muwallad' overrode rules of patrilineality, personal definitions and affiliation with broader identities such as national citizenship, and marked the activists as still being partially foreign by blood, at least in the eyes of those who were describing them. This element of foreignness was seen as responsible for their nationalist leanings. The Muwalladīn are one of the most visible groups of 1924, but it is extremely problematic to assess whether the White Flag League was indeed most popular among them, or whether every activist was a 'Muwallad' on the ground of his pro-Egyptian orientation.

'Sudanese' and 'Arabs'

In colonial sources, few terms are so confusing as the labels 'Sudanese' and 'Arab'. First of all, the term 'Sudanese' was used to indicate both the inhabitants of Sudan and those people who were of southern, Nuba or slave extraction. In the latter meaning the word was interchangeable with another fuzzy term – 'black' – and was translated by the Arabic word '*sūdānī*'. Sometimes, this double meaning was embedded in the same

(*contd*) Press, 1959); Heather J. Sharkey, 'The Egyptian Colonial Presence in the Anglo-Egyptian Sudan, 1898-1932', *White Nile, Black Blood: War, Leadership, and Ethnicity from Khartoum to Kampala,* Jay Spaulding and Stephanie Beswick eds. (Lawrenceville NJ: Red Sea Press, 2000), pp. 273-314.

48 Author interview with one of his sons, Sa'd Ṣāliḥ 'Abd al-Qādir at his home, Khartoum North, 26.1.2005. See also the testimony of 'Izz al-Dīn Ḥusayn Rasīq (IAAS n. 1575), in which he mentions that the mother of Ṣāliḥ was very brave. See also 'Awāṭif 'Umar 'Abdallāh, *Ṣāliḥ 'Abd Al-Qādir: Ḥayātuhu Wa Shi 'ruhu* (Bayirūt) (Dār al-Jīl, 1991), pp. 44-46.

49 Notes on signatories to a telegram of protest to his Excellency the Governor General, Khartoum, 10.6.1924, FO 141/806/1, NA.

sentence, as in this telling example from Governor General Lee Stack, when describing 'Sudanese' battalions: 'the Sudanese looked upon the Sudanese battalions as 'Abid' [slaves].'[50] Moreover, there was no systematic use of the term 'Sudanese' to indicate a specific origin: for example, there are numerous documents entitled 'List of Sudanese officers', or 'List of Sudanese officers and officials', where the people included came from all Sudan, and certainly did include also people from the North.[51] Finally, it is to be noted that even when the term 'Sudanese' hinted at a slave past, it remained adamantly indeterminate. It was applied, first, to people with a family background in Sudan's peripheral areas, such as Southern Sudan and the Nuba Mountains, who did not necessarily have a direct connection to slavery except for the fact that in the 19th century these areas were slave reservoirs; second, to people who had a slave descent dating of one, two or more generations before; and third, it was applied both to people who were still enslaved, and to manumitted and runaway slaves.[52]

Unlike the term 'Sudanese', 'Arab' is surprisingly rarely employed in the sources of 1924, both colonial and local. It is mostly used in the context of the army, but once again in a remarkably ill-defined way. For example, a British veteran of the Camel Corps explained that one of the Arab units was composed of recruits who were 'Shaigi from Omdurman', and thus Arabic-speaking Northern Sudanese town-dwellers; and that another battalion was made up of Baqqāra, one of the largest Arabic-speaking nomadic pastoral groups of Kordofan.[53] Therefore, the term 'Arab' defined groups with very different, if not actually contrary, ways of life. These people had historically been in opposed to each other, including during the time of the Mahdiyya.

This terminology corresponded to a British racial grid that translated the varied nature of Sudan's populations heuristically. Such inconsistencies simultaneously indicated the blurred nature of this categorization and its *ad hoc* use, almost on a case-by-case basis. Yet in spite of the ambiguity, the 'Arab' and 'Black' categories did work as a general principle for organizing the army, the school, the workplace. It had a direct impact on the recruitment of soldiers and officers, clerks and judges, schoolteachers and district administrators, as the section on the background of the protesters, later in this book, will illustrate.

[50] Memorandum, Enclosures in no. 167, Major General Sir L. Stack to Mr MacDonald, 18.8.1924, FO 407/199, NA.

[51] For example, the 36 officers who signed a petition against the arrest of Zayn al-'Ābdīn 'Abd al-Tām were all described as 'Sudanese', even if the list included people such as Muḥammad Jabr al-Dār, from a prominent Northern Sudanese family. List of Sudanese officers and officials who are signatory of telegram of 28.6, Palace 4/10/49, NRO.

[52] Elena Vezzadini, 'Making the Sudanese: Slavery Policies and Hegemony Construction in Early Colonial Sudan', *Sudan's Wars and Peace Agreements*, Jay Spaulding, Stephanie Beswick, Caroline Fluher Lobban, and Richard Lobban eds. (Newcastle: Cambridge Scholars Publishing, 2010), pp. 71-101.

[53] G. A. V. Keays, 'A Note on the History of the Camel Corps', *Sudan Notes and Records,* (1939), vol. 22, p. 106.

The final issue to be discussed here is what the White Flag League did with the labels 'Sudanese' and 'Arab'. In one famous episode (which is recounted by Kurita, drawing from Ḥassan Najīla), when Sulaymān Kisha dedicated a book of poems to the 'Noble Arab People' (*Sha'b 'Arabī karīm*), 'Alī 'Abd al-Laṭīf protested that it should have been dedicated to the 'Noble Sudanese People' (*Sha'b Sūdānī karīm*).[54] This episode shows that there was resistance among certain groups to associating nationalism with a term connected to slavery, a feeling that became widespread among the nationalists from the 1940s.[55] However, it does not appear from the available sources that the League was waging a war against an 'Arab' brand of nationalism. First, various local sources, including the *Trials of the White Flag*, recount that when asked about their ethnic belonging, 1924 activists made a point of stating that they were Sudanese. However, it appears that they were opposing the British desire to catalogue people into 'tribes' – which the activists interpreted as a scheme to weaken national unity – rather than combating any alleged identification as Arabs. Finally, the texts written by the White Flag League during 1924 never use any terminology other than 'Sudanese nation' and 'Sudanese people'. The term 'Arab' is used only twice in all the texts I have collected. If a sense of belonging to the Arab world was widespread in some nationalist circles it did not become dominant in 1924: at this time anti-colonial nationalists were committed to the Unity of the Nile Valley and the liberation of Sudan and the Sudanese people with the help of the Egyptians, who, as we have seen, certainly in the 1920s did not define themselves as Arabs.

54 Yoshiko Kurita, 'The concept of nationalism in the White Flag League movement'.

55 Heather J. Sharkey, *Living with Colonialism: Nationalism and Culture in the Anglo-Egyptian Sudan* (Berkeley and Los Angeles: University of California Press, 2003) Chapter 2.

2

The Spring of the Colonial Nations

Colonial documents describing Sudanese nationalism between 1918 and 1923 treated it as an existing force that had to be confronted by the authorities: British discussions revolved on *how* – and not *if* – nationalist feelings existed, and above all on how they could be controlled. As early as 1918, a report observed laconically:

> The Nationalist movement ... is ... at present limited to the areas from Khartoum northwards. This is partly due to the considerable connection between merchants of Omdurman and the towns of the north with people in Egypt.[1]

In 1919, a document tellingly entitled 'Note on the Growth of National Aspirations in the Sudan' also noted the presence of a pro-British nationalist faction:

> Three of the principal religious leaders ... have asked to be allowed to institute among their followers a kind of propaganda which will endeavour to foster loyalty and co-operation with the British Imperial idea, with the ultimate object of cultivating a spirit of national unity among the Soudanese.[2]

The latter document also makes it clear that as far as the British were concerned, nationalism was an idea that was being nurtured by the elites. What went ostensibly unremarked was that these elites had adopted the language of nationalism as an integral part of their political arguments, whether they were pro- or anti-British. In an article published in *Ḥaḍārat al-Sūdān* in 1924, the editor Ḥusayn Sharīf wrote: 'Nations are not herds of goats to be shared to graze, they are human groups that by principle should govern themselves.'[3]

The point that must not be missed is that if even a heavily censored and state-monitored newspaper such as *Ḥaḍārat al-Sūdān* could include a piece – one of the many – in which its author stated that the Sudanese people must choose their own rule, it meant that this kind of statement fell within the limits of what had become politically acceptable for a colonial government. The deployment of this language by the Sudanese was the most important novelty of the time.

[1] Willis, undated, Enclosure in Major Lee Stack to Sir R. Wingate, Khartoum, 22.12.1918, FO 407/18, NA.

[2] 'Note on the Growth of National Aspirations in the Sudan', Major-General Lee Stack, Khartoum, 23.2.1919, FO 407/184, NA.

[3] Najīla, *Malāmiḥ Min al-Mujtama' al-Sūdānī*, p. 22.

Already before the Great War, the Sudanese had been exposed to anticolonial nationalism through the Egyptian press smuggled into Sudan and by Egyptian militants working there.[4] But it is only after the War that the Sudanese began to produce their own political pieces. The major difference of this period, thus, consisted neither in the circulation of anticolonial nationalist ideas, nor in the Sudanese political struggle against colonialism, as numerous upheavals had taken place long before 1919.[5] Instead, what was new and surprising was the ease and speed with which Sudanese intellectuals began to speak the language of nationalism, suddenly and effortlessly, as if they had always talked that way.

How did this happen? First, the nationalist ideology represented a formidable tool of political struggle for anticolonial activists, as it allowed them to crack the justifications upon which colonization was based. This is evident from the political texts written during that time. Second, activists became increasingly exposed to this ideological repertoire because of a set of new resources, such as the press, the post and telegraph, and more frequent interactions with other 'radicals'. Third, this exposure allowed them to learn a set of techniques of political struggle, such as demonstrations and petitions, which in turn contributed to spread this new ideology and ignite mass reactions. They also learnt ways to organize themselves, and the most important case in point from the perspective of this work is the formation of secret societies. Post-war nationalism – in Sudan, as elsewhere – was the outcome not so much of the direct impact of the war on the colonies, but rather of the new opportunities, strategies and tools that become available to political activists after the Great War.

'PATRIOTISM BY POST'

Between 1919 and 1923, a good part of the political battle was fought by means of texts in the form of letters, circulars, pamphlets, and journal articles. Only in a few cases were there public acts of protest, such as that of 15 May 1919, when an unknown number of men from the Railways Battalion paraded in Atbara, cheering for Egypt, or on 30 May 1919 when in Omdurman, a retired officer, Muḥammad 'Amīn Hudayb, 'stepped into the pulpit immediately after the sermon and read a seditious speech, calling upon Sudan to join with the Egyptians to eject the British.'[6] But such events were exceptional, and took place mostly during the time of the Egyptian Revolution.

4 Examples are in Gabriel Warburg, 'The Sudan, Egypt and Britain, 1899-1916', *Middle Eastern Studies* (1970): 6, n. 2, p. 169.

5 For an overview on the armed revolts against Anglo-Egyptian rule during this first phase of colonization, see Alexander S. Cudsi, 'Sudanese Resistance to British Rule, 1900-1920' (PhD Thesis, University of Khartoum, 1969). However this work should be treated with some caution, as in his catalogue of primary resistance he includes some highly debatable examples.

6 Sudan Monthly Intelligence Report [SMIR], No. 298, May 1919, WO 33/997, NA.

What where the arenas of political debate and the themes handled? The first textual arena was *Ḥaḍārat al-Sūdān*. Founded in 1918, the journal really began to become a serious publication under the editorship of Ḥusayn Sharīf in 1919. The editor was indeed a strange figure: according to the historian Martin Daly, his father, Muḥammad Sharīf, was the second *khalīfa* of the Mahdi, and was executed by the British in 1899.[7] Ḥusayn himself was arrested for having written a 'seditious circular' in 1915, of which no trace remains. It was sufficiently serious for him to be exiled to Southern Sudan and then to Dongola, and he was only allowed to return to Khartoum in 1917. Despite all this, in 1919, Ḥusayn Sharīf represented for the British the best kind of enlightened moderate, something that clearly demonstrates the intricate background of some of Britain's most trusted allies.

What is known about the political position of Ḥusayn Sharīf is usually taken from a series of four articles that he wrote in 1920. He argued at length as to why the Condominium had to be ended, why the Sudanese had to choose one of the two partners in dominion, and why the preferred – if not the only – choice was Great Britain. Ḥusayn maintained that while Egypt and Sudan shared the same religion and language, the former had also committed gross abuses over the course of history. Just as Egypt had striven to be independent from the Ottoman Empire, so it was natural that Sudan should fight for her own independence. However, Ḥusayn argued, the time was not ripe for complete freedom. In his third article, he explained why:

> Let us look at which situation is applicable in our case that can lead to our independence. Firstly, for the time being we are not qualified enough to govern ourselves. Secondly, although our brothers the Egyptians are among the leading Eastern nations yearning for freedom and independence, yet they did not attain the stage of mastering the government ... if the evidence, experiences or events can help us to believe that our neighbours can keep our *sacred national trust* we wouldn't have preferred or chosen other than them, but as it is not the case it will be an act of folly to deceive ourselves, to risk our identity and to throw our future in a bottomless pit. Now it is only the British gate that is left for us, no one can deny that they are the best to navigate and rule a nation as much as the human capacity allows for an invader and a colonizing nation.[8]

Thus, for Ḥusayn Sharīf, guardianship by Great Britain was necessary because Sudan was not sufficiently far along the path of 'civilization',

[7] Daly, *British Administration and the Northern Sudan*, p. 110. Hill, *A Biographical Dictionary of the Sudan*, p. 273; conversation between the author and Zayn al-'Ābdīn Ḥusayn Sharīf, nephew of Ḥusayn, in his house in Khartoum, 29.4.2006. There is also a volume, of which probably only a few copies were published, which collects the essays of Sharīf written between 1919 and 1920: *Bākūra al-wa'ī bil-thāt. Silsilat maqālat katabahā al-marḥūm. Al-sayyid Ḥusayn Sharīf al-sanatayn 1919-1920* (out of print, undated; publisher unspecified). I am grateful to Zayn al-'Ābdīn Ḥusayn Sharīf for having shown me this volume and for making a copy for me, especially because I was not able to locate the originals of *al-Ḥaḍāra* in any of the archives I consulted.

[8] Najīla, *Malāmiḥ Min al-Mujtama' al-Sūdānī*, p. 23-24 (my italics). Sharkey, *Living with Colonialism: Nationalism and Culture in the Anglo-Egyptian Sudan*.

and because Britain had much more experience than Egypt in governing other countries. It should be noted also that the themes of civilization and progress occupied a considerable amount of space in the journal. The various contributors wrote pieces discussing all sorts of issues relating to how to achieve a 'civilized' state: the spread of literacy, improvements in educational standards in secondary education, social assistance for the poor and orphans, the importance of overcoming the country's 'backward' customs, and finally, education for women.[9]

As the censored *Ḥaḍārat al-Sūdān* offered no space for the anti-British opposition, anti-colonial activists had two main channels of expression: clandestine propaganda and Egyptian newspapers. Writing clandestine texts was one of the main activities of societies such as the Sudan Union, to the extent that the historian Gafaar Bakheit identifies the period after the war as one of 'patriotism by post'.[10] According to one witness, their frequency dramatically increased during these years: 'not a single day passes without the civilians receiving circulars about the colonial intrigues and despotism.'[11] Clandestine literature came in different types: it included letters to leading Sudanese notables, circulars posted or scattered across the main urban centres of northern Sudan, and anti-British pamphlets.[12] They were sent by post or delivered by hand to their designated recipient, which meant that he had to make contact with a government official if he wished to reveal that he had received a text, and it is quite probable that many did not.[13]

In this chapter, only the surviving texts written between 1919 and 1923 are considered, because the telegrams composed by White Flag League members deserve a discussion on their own, as the most important source for grasping the ideology of the movement. For the period before 1924, about 20 nationalist anticolonial texts have survived. This material is problematic, however, because not only have the originals been lost, but we also only know of them from sketchy summaries compiled by the Intelligence Department. In one case, for instance, a summary was condensed from a two-page text into a couple of lines.[14] These scanty

9 *Bākūra al-wa'ī bil-thāt*; Bakheit, 'British Administration and Sudanese Nationalism'; Heather J. Sharkey, 'A Century in Print: Arabic Journalism and Nationalism in Sudan, 1899-1999', *International Journal of Middle East Studies* (1999), vol. 31, n. 4, pp. 534-535; Mahjoub Al-Malik Babiker, *Press and Politics in the Sudan* (Khartoum: University of Khartoum, 1985); Mahgoub Mohammed Salih, 'The Sudanese Press', *Sudan Notes and Records* (1965), n. 46, pp. 4-5.

10 Bakheit, 'British Administration and Sudanese Nationalism', p. 67.

11 Najīla, *Malāmiḥ Min al-Mujtama' al-Sūdānī*, p. 165.

12 Anticolonial pamphlets had already been circulated during the war, but both their content and their senders are unknown. Many are mentioned in SMIR 331, February 1922, WO 33/997, NA.

13 Apparently, the Intelligence Department disposed of some. Daly recounts that at some point, the Director of Intelligence gave the order to destroy all files concerning Egyptian propaganda in Sudan: Daly, *British Administration and the Northern Sudan*, pp. 113-114.

14 Compare, for instance, the circular entitled 'A call to the Natives of Sudan' reported by the Intelligence Department on 1.11.1919 in FO 141/806/1, NA, and its summary in SMIR 331, February 1922, WO 33/997, NA. The summary compacted

descriptions hardly ever mention the conditions under which the texts were distributed, the extent to which they were spread, or offer information about their authors.

While bearing these important limitations in mind, it is possible to gather some general elements as to their production and the topics they touched on. First, the texts were anonymous, and were signed using pseudonyms such as 'the Society to Promote the Deliverance of the Country', 'the Society to Defend Faith in the Sudan', the 'Committee of Urgent Affairs', the 'Society to Promote the Safety of the Country', and finally the 'White Hand and Black Hand'.[15] The person allegedly responsible for this last circular was expelled to Egypt; but on 25 December 1919, another circular was sent to the Director of Intelligence, signed once more by the 'Society of the Black Hand.'

Some of these names hark back to names used in Egypt for similar purposes. For instance, 'The Urgent Committee' signed three pamphlets in Sudan and dozens in Egypt during the same period.[16] From the content of some of these texts, it is possible to infer that a number of them, but certainly not all, came from Egypt. In one case, the officer noted at the side of the text that the handwriting was that 'commonly taught in Government schools.'[17] Sharkey recounts that former Sudan Union members 'printed its circulars locally, using a type of rudimentary hand-press (*baluza*) that government employees readily found in their offices in Khartoum.'[18]

Circulars and texts were often written following some politically significant event – such as the notables' journey to London in 1919, the publication of the four articles in *al-Ḥaḍāra*, the visits by Egyptian High Commissioner Lord Allenby to Sudan in 1921 and 1922 – and during special celebrations, such as the King's Day.[19] The example below is a colonial comment on a series of circulars that were distributed in response to the three articles by Ḥusayn Sharīf:

> A set of three pamphlets has been distributed over the country, apparently as propaganda directed against the articles published in the native paper Hedaret El Sudan. They advise the natives to beware of British machinations, warn them that the British will deprive them of their land to enrich a British syndicate, that

(*contd*) in one single paragraph a two pages long, detailed anti-British pamphlet.

15 Appendix to SMIR no. 331, February 1922, WO 33/997, NA.

16 'A Call to the Natives of Sudan' by The Urgent Committee, marked as 'Translation of printed pamphlet (in Arabic),' Intel. Dept., War Office, Cairo, 1.11.1919, FO 141/806/1, NA, 'High Treason to the Country' by 'A free Sudanese, Urgent Committee' 18.7.1919, FO 141/582/3, NA. As to Egypt, a number of petitions signed by 'The Urgent Committee' and also sent in 1919 are included in the following file: FO 141/807, NA.

17 SMIR no. 330, January 1922 and July 1922, WO 33/997, NA. SMIR 351, October 1923, WO 33/999, NA.

18 Sharkey, *Living with Colonialism*, p. 105; but see also pp. 103 to 107. On the importance of Egyptian press see also Diyāb, *al-ʿAlāqāt al-miṣrīya al-sūdāniyya*, p.49.

19 For Allenby: SMIR 331, SMIR February 1922 and SMIR 334, May 1922; for the King's day: SMIR 330, January 1922, all in WO 33/997, NA; for the notables' journey, 'A Call to the Natives of Sudan' by 'The Urgent Committee', Intel. Dept., War Office, Cairo, 1.11.1919, FO 141/806/1, NA.

> the British are trying to evangelise them, and the proper refuge of the Sudanese is with the Egyptians, their co-religionists, who have always been their best friends.[20]

This summary identifies some of the favourite topics of this literature: British 'machinations'; unity with Egypt; and the call for all Muslims to unite. However, these subjects were not equally frequent. By far the most recurrent was an attack on British colonization, the main theme in at least eight circulars.[21] In May 1921, for example, a pamphlet signed by 'the Society to Promote the Deliverance of the Country' condemned the Gezira and Jebel Awlia irrigation schemes, and alerted the Sudanese to its 'development under British auspices or with British capital'.[22] In October 1923, a circular drafted in Sudan and addressed 'to the free Sudanese ... [and] ... specially directed against the Gezira Scheme' was disseminated in the streets of Khartoum, Omdurman, and Khartoum North.'[23] The use of words such as 'British capital' and the accusation that the British were 'exploiting' Sudan is noteworthy, and cannot help but make us think of the impact of Leninist anti-imperialist ideas in the colonial world. The second most frequently-recurring topic was the incitement to unite with Egypt in order to fight the British. In its pamphlet of October 1919, the 'Committee of Urgent Affairs' 'urged the Sudanese to rise and demand their independence simultaneously with the Egyptian movement'; in January 1921, another pamphlet incited a 'revolt against the British Government in Egypt and the Sudan.'[24] Finally, on the subject of religion, several pamphlets argued that British colonization would lead to the advance of Christianity. For instance, in the famous circular signed by 'An Honest Adviser', written by a Sudan Union member and reported at length by the historian Ḥassan Najīla, the author complained:

> As to religious freedom I don't need to state how retarded and oppressing it is, that our schools in Omdurman, Khartoum and other parts force our sons to study the Bible and the southern civilians to become Christians. There are six churches in Khartoum and one mosque that has remained incomplete for 20 years.[25]

It is worth noting that the texts did not plead for the fusion of Egypt and Sudan. The two countries were to struggle together against a common enemy, but not become one. Moreover, none of these texts referred to a common Arab identity, in line with what we observed earlier in relation to Egypt. To conclude, both pro- and anti-British texts seem to share a common set of ideas: Sudan was a nation endowed with certain rights, the Sudanese were citizens – that is, individuals able to make choices on their own, and not subjects – and finally Sudan was a country striving

20 SMIR 316, November 1920, WO 33/997, NA.
21 Three sent in 1919, one in 1920, two in 1921 and two in 1922. They may all be found in the following files: WO 33/997; WO 33/999; FO 141/806/1; FO 141/582/3, all in NA; Darfur 3/12/16; Intel 1/21/111, NRO.
22 SMIR 322, May 1921, WO 33/997, NA.
23 SMIR 351, October 1923, WO 33/999, NA.
24 Both reported in the Appendix to SMIR 331, February 1922, WO 33/997, NA.
25 Najīla, *Malāmiḥ Min al-Mujtama' al-Sūdānī*, p. 26.

to attain material and moral progress. However, in the absence of more information, it is impossible to assess to what extent these publications were circulated.

DECODING NATIONALISM: INTERNATIONAL RELATIONS 'FROM BELOW' AFTER THE GREAT WAR

Sanjay Subrahmayam makes the case that it is not only people, technologies, and goods that flow, but also ideas and 'mental constructs': '[we must consider] the permeability of what are often assumed to be closed "cultural zones", *and the existence of vocabularies that cut across local religious traditions.*'[26] This section develops the idea through an analysis of two crucial terms in the 'vocabulary of nationalism': self-determination, and what may be termed 'the rights of the civilized nations'. Obviously, many more ideas were in circulation transnationally after the Great War. For instance, surprisingly similar discourses were promulgated about the importance of women as a civilizing element, as pillars of nation-building, and 'mothers' in the development of their male companions in different countries. These themes stand out in the pages of *Ḥaḍārat al-Sūdān* in 1920, *The Liberation of Women* by Qasim Amin in 1899, and in Rabindranath Tagore's novels set in Bengal between 1900 and 1915.[27]

However, from this complex and intertwined set of discourses, the principle of self-determination and the idea of civilization permeated to an outstanding degree Sudanese political literature.

a) Self-determination, petitions and delegations

The Great War marked a complete reconceptualization of international relations, not only 'from above', as the heads of the victorious powers met in the various peace conferences, seeking to redesign the world, but also 'from below', because the outcome of the war transformed the way in which political activists framed their relations with the colonial powers. Well before the Great War, however, anti-colonial nationalism was already an important political force in countries such as India or Egypt. Nevertheless, a number of factors made the situation after the Great War highly propitious for anticolonial activists.

The most obvious of these is the war itself and its geopolitical consequences, notably the dismantlement of three of the largest Empires in the world – the Austro-Hungarian, the Ottoman and Russian Empires – the Russian Revolution, and the emergence of many new nations. Second, anticolonial criticism after the war came from entirely new places, notably the United States. As the historian Erez Manela remarks, the peculiarity of Woodrow Wilson's 14 Points was that they were not uttered by an anticolonial campaigner, but by the President of a country that had only

[26] Subrahmanyam, 'Connected Histories', p. 748, my italics.

[27] Indrani Mitra, ''I Will Make Bimala One With My Country': Gender and Nationalism in Tagore's The Home and the World', *MFS Modern Fiction Studies* (1995), 41, no. 2, pp. 243–64.

just risen to the status of hegemonic member of the 'family of the civilized nations' – a term that indicated the world's dominant countries, which also included colonial powers such as Great Britain, France, Portugal, and Italy.[28] When anticolonial activists asked for self-determination after the Great War, they could make the point that they were merely demanding what was by now an established principle of international relations. In a telling anecdote, Manela describes an episode that took place in Cairo in 1918:

> Muhammad Husayn Haykal, a prominent Egyptian journalist and intellectual, wrote of an encounter he had with a friend on the streets of Cairo on a summer day in 1918. The texts of President Wilson's addresses had appeared in Egyptian newspapers over the previous month... "That is it, Sir!" exclaimed the friend. "We have the right to self-determination and therefore the English will leave Egypt." Why did he think that Wilson's promises would be implemented? Haykal tells us he asked the friend. Could they not be yet more empty words from the mouth of a politician? "No!!" came the reply. "The United States is the one who won the war. She is not an imperialist country. She truly wants that there will not be another war. Therefore, she will enforce right to self-determination and enforce the withdrawal."[29]

There is also scattered evidence of the impact of Wilson on Sudanese nationalism. In *Ḥaḍārat al-Sūdān*, Ḥusayn Sharīf commented how the Great War and Woodrow Wilson's policies had been the spark for nationalist agitation in Egypt: '[After the war] the principles of Wilson spread among the population, the Egyptians began their movement of the complete independence of Egypt and Sudan.'[30]

In an interview taken in the 1970s, one of the leading activists of the White Flag League in Wad Medani, Mudaththir al-Būshī, also recollected Wilson's principles:

> There were things produced by the end of the war, as the general freedom and the 14 points of [W]Nilson (sic). It paved the way for people towards self-determination ..., and also the movement in Egypt was growing faster and we started to think why the Sudan should have no share in self-determination?[31]

The very possibility of seeking independence within the legal framework of the League of Nations was a third significant catalyst for political activity in the colonial world after the Great War. Even after Wilson had left the scene, the understanding that the relationship between colonizers and colonized had changed persisted. The League of Nations superseded Wilson in the popular imagination; it reinforced the sense that a new international order was in place, incarnated by a supranational entity charged with the task to safeguard international justice.[32] The perception of its presence was a dynamo for nationalist activities,

[28] Manela, *The Wilsonian Moment*, pp. 3-53.
[29] Ibid. p. 63.
[30] *Bākūra al-waʿī bil-thāt*, p. 38.
[31] *Al-Riwāyāt*, p. 64.
[32] Michael D. Callahan, *Mandates and Empire. The League of Nations and Africa* (Brighton: Sussex Academic Press, 1999). Michael D. Callahan, *A Sacred Trust: The League of Nations and Africa, 1929-1946* (Brighton; Portland OR: Sussex Academic Press, 2004).

because it shaped the belief that the anticolonial struggle was no longer an unequal confrontation between the powerful and the powerless; there was a supranational institution out there that would hear people's demands and assess their legitimacy. The League of Nations contributed to this image with the provision of a mechanism for filing complaints by petition. Although it hardly ever worked to safeguard 'indigenous' rights, what mattered was the perception that such a mechanism existed.

All this had a decisive influence on the shaping of the practices of political protest, exemplified in the impact made by petitions.[33] Although this form of political protest was by no means a post-war novelty, signing petitions became one of the most recurrent means of expressing a certain political opinion after the war.[34] Their function was to let citizens speak up about what they wanted for their nation, and to legitimize the claims of certain political movements to represent the will of the people.[35] Petitions were sent to the League of Nations, to the relevant colonial authority, and to heads of government. For example, in the period between 1919 and 1924, Sudanese notables addressed anti-Egyptian petitions to the Sudan Government; in Egypt, during the years from 1919 to 1924, hundreds of petitions were sent to the Egyptian heads of government; in Syria after the Great War, sending petitions was a common way for various constituencies to declare their political positions.[36] In South West Africa, Rehoboth Basters put in place a broad petitioning campaign to the League of Nations, and similarly many petitions were filed by Africans in Togo and Cameroun.[37]

Just as with petitions, and often in pair, the forming of 'delegations' became another popular way to express dissent. It is no coincidence that Zaghlūl's party was named Wafd, in Arabic 'the delegation'. Their function was the same: a delegation 'spoke up' for the nation at international venues such as the Paris Peace Conferences or before the League of Nations. That some delegations had been admitted at the peace conferences and the countries that they represented had subsequently succeeded to be granted independence had such an impact on the political imagination of the time

[33] Tilman Dedering, 'Petitioning Geneva: Transnational Aspects of Protest and Resistance in South West Africa/Namibia After the First World War', *Journal of Southern African Studies* (2009), vol. 35, n. 4, pp. 785-801. The system of petitions was not new in the Middle East: John Chalcraft, 'Engaging the State: Peasants and Petitions in Egypt on the Eve of Colonial Rule', *International Journal of Middle East Studies* (2005), vol. 37, n. 3, pp. 303-325; James E. Baldwin, 'Petitioning the Sultan in Ottoman Egypt', *Bulletin of the School of Oriental and African Studies, University of London* (2012), vol. 75, n. 3, pp. 499-524.

[34] Manela, *The Wilsonian Moment*; other examples may be found in Kenneth J. Perkins, *A History of Modern Tunisia* (New York: Cambridge University Press, 2004), pp. 73-89; Callahan, *Mandates and Empire*, pp. 43–52.

[35] Dederin, 'Petitioning Geneva'.

[36] Gelvin, *Divided Loyalties*, pp. 225-283; Keith D. Watenpaugh, *Being Modern in the Middle East: Revolution, Nationalism, Colonialism, and the Arab Middle Class* (Princeton, N.J.: Princeton University Press, 2006), p. 181.

[37] Tilman Dedering, 'Petitioning Geneva'; Paul Hibbeln, 'Supervising Imperialism: Petitions to the League of Nations Permanent Mandates Commission, 1920-1939', *Proceedings of the Ohio Academy of History* (2001).

that 'delegations' became one of the modular forms of nationalist protests virtually everywhere. There are many examples of that: in 1924, a small delegation of two Sudanese attempted to travel to Egypt to meet Egyptian politicians, and to present a bagful of petitions signed by Sudanese citizens. In Paris, as Manela recounts, a host of disparate delegations representing 'oppressed nations' asked to be heard at the Peace Conference. These included Sinn Fein leaders, Catalan nationalists, and committees from countries such as Albania, Armenia, Syria, Lebanon, and Ukraine.[38] When political leaders could not attend in person, they would at least send petitions, as in the famous case of the Algerian-Tunisian petition seeking full independence for the two countries.[39]

b) Civilization

The second concept that carried a central meaning in international politics after the Great War was that of 'civilization'. The term is so thick, polysemous, and intimately connected to the justifications of colonization that it requires some clarification.

As discussed above, even a superficial glance at Sudanese political literature after the Great War reveals the centrality of the question of civilization in the various political debates: it was no coincidence that the first and only Sudanese journal in the early 1920s was called *Ḥaḍārat al-Sūdān*, or 'Sudanese Civilization'. For the moderate party, civilization was to be attained under the auspices of British colonization, as Britain was the best and most capable power to make Sudan develop; while the pro-Egyptian faction considered that the 'civilizing process' could well be carried through with the help of Egypt, for it could never be achieved unless Sudan were free from British colonization. Above all, both factions agreed that Sudan was not 'civilized enough' to be fully independent.

Why was the theme of civilization so essential to the debate? It was certainly connected to legacy of the reformist ideas that had been in circulation in the Ottoman Empire and Egypt since the end of the 19th century, associated with figures such as Muḥammad 'Abduh or Jamāl al-Dīn al-Afghānī, who believed that religious and social decadence had prompted the decline and the colonization of the Muslim world.[40] Yet, in the legalist framework that inspired much of contentious politics after the Great War, one might also see the insistence on civilization from another point of view. Once again there are echoes of Subrahmanyam's idea that 'by moving laterally' and searching for connections, new configurations of sense may sometimes emerge.[41]

This 'moving laterally' consists in observing that from the end of the

38 Manela, *The Wilsonian Moment*, p. 60.

39 McDougall, *History and the Culture of Nationalism in Algeria*, pp. 43-39.

40 Nissim Rejwan, *Arabs Face the Modern World: Religious, Cultural, and Political Responses to the West* (Gainesville FL: University Press of Florida, 1998). Jamal Mohammed Ahmed, *The Intellectual Origins of Egyptian Nationalism* (London; New York: Oxford University Press, 1960).

41 Sanjay Subrahmanyam, *Explorations in Connected History* (New Delhi: Oxford University Press, 2005), p. 11.

nineteenth century, 'civilization' – or rather, 'the standard of civilization' – emerged as a powerful legal concept that regulated the capital aspects of international relations. According to Gong, the 'standard of civilization' came to be a keyword in the language of international politics from the moment in which contacts between Europe and the rest of the world became more intensive as a consequence of territorial conquest. By 1905, the standard of civilization was an 'explicit legal principle and an integral part of the doctrines of international law prevailing at the time'.[42]

According to international law, the 'standard of civilization' meant that in order for a state to be considered as civilized, four essential conditions had to be satisfied: first, the ability of a state to guarantee basic rights to foreign nationals; second, the presence of an organized bureaucracy 'with some efficiency in running the state machinery, and with some capacity to organize self-defence'; third, the adherence of a state to international law and diplomacy; and fourth, the existence of a properly functioning domestic system of justice.[43] If these conditions were satisfied, the state gained entry to the 'family of nations', a term applied to nations that enjoyed full rights in international relations. Initially, the family of nations included only European countries, but, firmly grounded on the idea that any nation may sooner or later 'progress' and reach such a standard as to enable her to become part of the 'family', any state that succeeded in complying with the standard could become a member. Indeed, first the United States and later Japan came to join this 'family'. The standard was crucial because it fixed the dividing line between colonisable and non-colonisable countries. In other word, an 'uncivilized' country was also a colonisable one. Thus it was that at the beginning of the 20th century, Japan was no longer colonisable.

After the First World War, the 'standard of civilization' became a crucial argument in the redefinition of the colonial world. It became a means of determining whether a territory that claimed the right to self-determination was ready to become independent. This is obvious, for example, from the very formulation of the system of mandates as defined by the League of Nation. The famous Article 22 of the Covenant declares that:

> [F]or people yet not able to stand by themselves under the strenuous conditions of the modern world, there should be applied the principle that the well-being and development of such people form a *sacred trust of civilisation* the tutelage of such peoples should be entrusted to advanced nations...[44]

Thus, in the colonial world of the 1920s the term 'civilization' embraced one essential concern: how to achieve a form of progress that might justify a country's demand for independence. Indeed, the petitions sent

[42] Gerrit W. Gong, *The Standard of 'civilization' in International Society* (Oxford: Clarendon Press, 1984), p. 14. For an expression of the application of standards of civilization to Native Administration in Sudan see D. K. Cooke, 'Native Administration in Practice: Historical Outline', in J.A. de C. Hamilton (ed.), *The Anglo-Egyptian Sudan from Within*, (London, 1935)

[43] Gong, *The Standard of Civilization*, pp. 14-15.

[44] As cited in Callahan, *Mandates and Empire*, p. 198 (My italics).

to the League of Nations and to the peace conferences often used the argument that a certain 'nation' was 'civilized enough' to stand on its own feet. For example, according to Manela, at the Paris Peace Conference, Zaghlūl maintained that if the 'uncivilized' and 'barbarous' Arabs of the Hijaz had been granted the privilege of participating in the conference, it was unthinkable that the Egyptians might be refused a hearing, as their civilization was far more ancient and sophisticated than that of the Hijazi. He also relates that at the Paris Conference the various delegations from oppressed nations laid 'their people's long histories of civilization' before the participants.[45]

To sum up, the issue of civilization came to have a central role in the political discourse of the post-war years. Because the question of civilization came to be so intimately associated with the colonial situation, the degree of civilization of a certain nation became a heated subject of discussion in political debates in Sudan as elsewhere. As will be discussed later, in 1924 it was essential for the White Flag League to insist that they were a legal movement. Sudanese intellectuals wanted to demonstrate that their countrymen were 'civilized enough' to choose their own destiny and govern themselves.

A TIME-SPACE COMPRESSION OF POLITICAL INTELLIGENCE

Nationalist ideas did not circulate in thin air: they were carried by people, on paper, and by wire. They crossed oceans and continents, spreading unevenly yet ubiquitously. In Sudan in 1919-1923, anticolonial pamphlets were sent by post, printed and posted in the streets, and smuggled by merchants, officers, and officials. Two aspects of this circulation had a direct effect on the form of political mobilization in Sudan in the 1920s: the first is the type of technology that was used to spread discontent, and the second is the connection between the press and politics.[46] This determined another crucial setting that characterized the Sudanese situation after the Great War: namely, the time-space compression of political intelligence. This will provide us with a partial explanation of why nationalism 'infected' so fast not only large and central cities, but also peripheral medium- to small-sized provincial cities and villages in Sudan.

a) Politics across the Wire

The time-space compression of political intelligence was not a novelty in the period after the Great War; the globalization of political news had begun far earlier, and was the result of the combination of disparate factors, such as the interdependent development of the press, the telegraph, and

45 Manela, *The Wilsonian Moment*, p. 60.

46 This term was first developed by the geographer David Harvey, *The Condition of Postmodernity: An Enquiry into the Origins of Cultural Change,* (Oxford [England]; Cambridge, Mass., USA: Blackwell, 1990); see also B. A. S. Warf, *The Spatial Turn: Interdisciplinary Perspectives* (London; New York: Routledge, 2009).

international news agencies, and later the symbiosis between press and politics.

In the 18th century, international news was a scarce resource, which explains why the telegraph technology developed after the 1830s met with immediate success.[47] The telegraph made it possible to make extremely fast connections between the centres and peripheries of Empires and states, and to keep governments informed about sensitive political news on foreign countries. The entire world – and not only Europe – began to be covered by telegraph poles; for example, Istanbul was connected to Baghdad in 1861, and Britain to India in 1865, one year before Europe was successfully connected to the United States, in 1866.[48] The technology also facilitated the military advance of Empires.[49]

With the worldwide spread of the telegraph, the distribution of international news became increasingly efficient and well-organized. News agencies such as Reuters or Havas became specialists at gathering, circulating and spreading international news to be sold to national newspapers and to governments. It was not only from the Rest to the West that the news circulated; Reuters established an agency in Cairo as early as 1866, and systematically fed the extremely vibrant Egyptian press from that time on.[50] News agencies also came to have privileged relations with colonial governments, which enjoyed priority access to politically sensitive news.[51] In Anglo-Egyptian Sudan, for example, provincial governors were to receive regular news from Reuters together with news from the provinces, so that 'those in charge of the administration of the country may be fully alive to the local and general situation.'[52]

During the Great War, the wire permitted the worldwide dissemination of much more than just military news and political ideas. One example of this is provided by Manela, who describes how the rapid spread of the 14 Points of Wilson after 1917 was aggressively promoted by the Committee on Public Information, which had been created by associates of Wilson.[53] In Sudan, the information that news agencies such as Reuters provided directly to the government played an especially significant role in radical

[47] Menahem Blondheim, *News over the Wires: The Telegraph and the Flow of Public Information in America, 1844-1897* (Cambridge, Mass.: Harvard University Press, 1994), pp. 12–27.

[48] Daniel R. Headrick, *The Tools of Empire: Technology and European Imperialism in the Nineteenth Century* (New York: Oxford University Press, 1981), pp. 157–59; Soli Shahvar, 'Tribes and Telegraphs in Lower Iraq: The Muntafiq and the Baghdad-Basrah Telegraph Line of 1863-65', *Middle Eastern Studies* (2003), n. 39, vol. 11, pp. 89-116.

[49] Headrick, *The Tools of Empire,* and Daniel R. Headrick, *The Tentacles of Progress: Technology Transfer in the Age of Imperialism, 1850-1940* (New York: Oxford University Press, 1988).

[50] Ami Ayalon, *The Press in the Arab Middle East: A History* (New York: Oxford University Press, 1995), p. 19.

[51] Donald Read, *The Power of News: The History of the Reuters* (Oxford, New York: Oxford University Press, 1999).

[52] ADI, Khartoum to Governors, All Provinces, 24.10.1914, Intel 2/48/407, NRO.

[53] Manela, *The Wilsonian Moment*, pp. 48-53.

politics in the 1920s. As the government depended on local telegraph operators, and as postmasters were also in charge of the telegraph in their local post offices, there was a small group of Sudanese who were fluent in English and always fully updated on the most important international events. 'Alī Malāsī, a Post and Telegraph employee and White Flag League member in Port Sudan, painted a vivid picture of the impact of Reuters:

> Reuters was produced three times a day. We were the employees of the post. We used to take a copy of this and read it and summarize it, and know things like 'the Germans did that' and 'this happened to the Allies'.[54]

It is also no coincidence that in 1924 four out of five founders of the White Flag League worked, or had worked, in the Post and Telegraph Department. There were also other types of wire that carried political information: for instance, some of the telephone operators who worked in the Palace in Khartoum, where the Governor General resided, were White Flag League members, and reported what they heard to the League.[55] The British were so alarmed when they discovered this that Sudanese would be banned from the job and replaced by female Syrians until the 1930s.[56]

b) Press and politics

In countries like India, Egypt, and Syria, the press had been becoming increasingly political starting from the beginning of the nineteenth century. In Egypt, at the end of that century, all the most famous newspapers, such as *al-Ahrām*, *al-Muqaṭṭam*, and *al-Mu'ayyad*, had clear political orientations.[57] *Al-Liwā'*, the organ of the radical Watanist Party, and *al-Jarīda*, the newspaper of the moderate *Ḥizb al-Umma*, were directly connected to political parties. What is most crucial is that their arguments were fed by international news. In other words, these newspapers did more than report news from the Empire: they translated – and in some cases moulded – it into a political language. They offered a reading of what was happening in the world that was extremely, and consistently, political. For instance, Eldon Gorst, High Commissioner of Egypt between 1907 and 1911, complained bitterly: 'Many of the articles

54 *Al-Riwāyāt*, p. 302. The League's leaders used to speak English among themselves if they did not wish to be understood. See 'Alī Aḥmad Ṣāliḥ, 'Confession,' pp. 9–11, 28.7.1924, FO 141/805/2, NA.

55 Sharkey, *Living with Colonialism*, pp. 105-106. One example is Aḥmad Mudaththir Ibrāhīm, who was a telephone operator at the Palace, in Notes on the signatories of the telegram of 3.6.1924, FO 141/806/1, NA.

56 'As far as I remember it was for political reasons that after the 1924 trouble it was decided to employ non-Sudanese in the telephone exchange' and again: 'This work should be taken away from females of foreign extraction and given back as heretofore to males of the country, 4th year primary boys.' In 'View of certain responsible educated native officials on matters arising from or pertaining to the present situation of Government 10.1.1931', by Williams, Civsec 1/58/165, NRO.

57 For an overview on its history before the First World War, see Abbas Kelidar, 'The Political Press in Egypt, 1882-1914.' In *Contemporary Egypt Through Egyptian Eyes: Essays in Honour of Professor P. J. Vatikiotis,* Charles Tripp ed. (London; New York: Routledge, 1993).

published in these newspapers are calculated to arouse the passion of the mass of people who are far too ignorant to appreciate the absurdities and falsehood of the diatribes which are out daily in the villages.'[58]

In Sudan, too, the press became steadily more political in the period between 1915 and 1924, but always under the watchful eye of the Sudan Government.[59] The first journal to be founded was the bilingual *al-Sūdān*, or *The Sudan Times,* which appeared in 1903 and belonged to the government. The paper was fed by Reuter cables and Government provincial news, but also by its partner in Cairo, the pro-British *al-Muqaṭṭam*. The second paper, which was privately owned, was *al-Rā'id al-Sūdān*. It was founded in 1911, and published by two Greek merchants who owned their own printing press (the Victoria Press, where worked some anti-British activists such as 'Alī Aḥmad Ṣāliḥ). Unlike *The Sudan Times, Al-Rā'id* was a literary-cum-political journal. In 1917, its Syrian editor, Muṣṭafa Qalīlat, was dismissed and exiled for writing an article critical of British rule. He was replaced by Ḥusayn Sharīf, who began his editorial career there, and remained there until the journal was closed down in 1918.

Ḥaḍārat al-Sūdān never made any effort to conceal its political purpose. In July 1920, an article explicated the paper main aims:[60]

1 National reforms based on conciliation between the government and the people.
2 Awakening national feeling.
3 Advocating that loyalty and frankness are the best medium for creating an understanding between the government and the people.
4 Paying great attention to the question of education and the need to spread it.
5 Reviewing the economic situation and discussing the country's problems.

However, besides being closely censored, it also had other limitations. For instance, it did not include fresh news, either international or national, so that in order to be up-to-date on the current international situation, Sudanese people had to turn to the Egyptian press.

A number of 1924 activists recounted that they were avid readers of Egyptian, and sometimes British, newspapers. Such accounts are taken from the two-volume *Al-Riwāyāt al-Shafawiyya li-Thuwwār 1924* ('Oral Testimony by the Revolutionaries of 1924'), which is a capital source of the present work. For example, Aḥmad Ṣabrī Zāyd recalled:

> We were influenced by the Egyptian revolution of 1919, and we read a lot about that, and we learnt that Egypt and Sudan should be like a united body. We were

[58] Kelidar, 'The Political Press in Egypt, 1882-1914', p. 11.

[59] Martial Law was still enforced in 1924, it was noted in a report, and therefore a Press Law was deemed unnecessary: 'Report of Censorship in the Sudan from the outbreak of hostilities in August 1914,' Intel 1/20/106, NRO.

[60] Salih, 'The Sudanese Press', p. 4. The intimate connection between the journal and politics is best expressed by this famous sentence, which is attributed to Ḥusayn Sharīf: 'A nation without a journal is like a heart without a tongue.' Quoted in Sharkey, 'A Century in Print', p. 534.

> used to read Egyptian newspapers continuously, and Egyptian books also, because the mail ferry was not censored. We used to take ideas from what we read to be applied to the Sudanese society.[61]

According to Mudaththir al-Būshī, 'Alī 'Abd al-Laṭīf read a great deal of the Egyptian press,[62] and the Military College officers and cadets kept themselves busy reading.[63] The clerk 'Alī Malāsī also recalled:

> At that time we understood for the first time the idea of the nation, of a homeland, and there are those who fight for their countries. ... So the activities continued until the day of the ceasefire [of the Great War]. At that time I was agent in al-Nuhud, I was already mature in my full capabilities, reading Egyptian and British press.[64]

During the trials of the White Flag League, a witness for the prosecution mentioned that the League received Egyptian newspapers: 'All days they would collect to read the papers, 'El Ahram' 'Mokottam' [sic] 'El Siassa - 'El Nil' 'El Dataif' and others were brought [sic].' [65]

Crucially, the anti-British Egyptian press, which was often smuggled into Sudan, trained readers to read British colonial policy in a certain manner. Thus, the Gezira scheme was not simply an agricultural project, but a capitalist, imperialist scheme developed to steal resources from the Sudanese; the delay in building the Omdurman mosque was not due to lack of money and labour but because of the attempt by the British to Christianize Sudan, and so on. This is exactly what the protest texts discussed above show.

Just as Egyptian newspapers fed the Sudanese political imagination, however, the opposite was also true. Sudanese sent regularly pieces of news from Sudan that fed Egyptian radical press. Unfortunately, it is impossible for a historian to recognize who wrote what, as the texts written by Sudanese militants were heavily 'retouched', if not entirely rewritten, by Egyptian journalists. According to Najīla,

> Al-Ahrām was the favourite Egyptian newspaper for Sudanese. It had offered much space for the Sudanese pens that supported the Egyptian revolution and Sa'd Zaghlūl. However the intelligence failed to recognize that because the members of Sudanese Union Society were clever enough not leave a written evidence that can reveal their efforts.[66]

Still, these collaborations were indispensable for Sudanese anticolonial militants, not only because they were their only means of public expression, but also because they were the only possible way by which Sudan's case could attain international visibility. This point was emphasized by one

61 *Al-Riwāyāt*, p. 262.
62 Ibid. p. 87.
63 Ibid. p. 61.
64 Ibid. pp. 303-304.
65 *The White Flag Trials*, p. 66.
66 Najīla, *Malāmiḥ Min al-Mujtama' al-Sūdānī*, p. 65. On the other hand, examples of how the Egyptian press covered Sudanese events show that they were entirely transformed in some cases. See, for example, the press resumé on the life of 'Alī 'Abd al-Laṭīf in 1923, which portray him as a 'savage'. Egyptian Press Resumé, Al-Akhbar of 26.07.1924, in FO 141/810/3, NA.

activist, Mudaththir al-Būshī who explained that the White Flag League hoped to 'bring their case abroad' through the press.[67]

Finally, if the Egyptian press fed Sudanese politics, and the Sudanese nourished Egyptian writers, this relationship must be viewed on a broader scale, because Egypt, too, was a recipient of international news and ideas, and its own politics developed with constant reference to what was happening outside. Consequently, the Egyptian press was significant not only for its political content, but also because it offered Sudanese politicians a window on what was happening in the colonial world and elsewhere, feeding their imagination and repertoire with examples and cases which stretched well beyond Egypt and Great Britain.

One example of this kind of circulation and of the connections between Egyptian and international radical politics, was studied by the historian Noor-Aiman Khan. This sheds light on the reverberation of the international situation. First of all Indian and Egyptian radicals were connected through the press.[68] News from India were frequently reported in Egyptian newspapers, and vice versa. But more importantly, news that bounced back and forth from one country to the other could also have an important feedback effect. Khan reports the case of the political assassination of British officer, Curzon Wyllie, in 1909 by an Indian nationalist named Madan Lal Dhingra. While the Indian press had to censure the case, things were viewed from a quite different light in Egypt. *Al-Liwā'*, the journal linked to the radical Watanist Party, published an article in which the author praised the murderer for his sacrifice and martyrdom. The journalist was immediately arrested, but his imprisonment, like the event itself, became a *cause celebre* in Egypt prompting all the other major newspapers to write about it, and then compare the colonial situation in the two countries.[69]

Egyptian and Indian radicals met in European capitals, and connected with even wider circuits there. One country with particular significance in anticolonial struggles was Ireland. According to Silvestri, 'For [Bengali nationalists], the Irish experience provided a heroic model of anticolonial resistance, as well as what seemed to be a blueprint for national liberation.'[70] Other circuits involved European members of socialist and communist parties, and collaborations were once again made concrete through the

[67] *Al-Riwāyāt*, p. 118.

[68] Egypt was considered to be 'the capital of Arab journalism', and, according to Ayalon, '[by World War I] the leading newspapers, al-Ahram, al-Muqattam, and al-Mu'ayyad ..., combined with a score of others, reached an audience of perhaps 200,000 readers in Egypt, according to one assessment' (Ayalon, *The Press in the Arab Middle East*, p. 58). The history of the press in India dates back to the early 19th century. By the 1920s, India had developed an extremely articulate press apparatus, including hundreds of journals in various vernacular languages. Swaminath Natarajan, *A History of the Press in India* (Bombay; New York: Asia Pub. House, 1962).

[69] Khan, *Egyptian-Indian Nationalist Collaboration*, pp. 40-41.

[70] Michael Silvestri, '"The Sinn Fein of India": Irish Nationalism and the Policing of Revolutionary Terrorism in Bengal', *Journal of British Studies* (2000), vol. 39, n. 4, p. 455.

press. According to Khan, the *Egyptian Standard,* the English version of the radical Watanist newspaper *al-Liwā'* was edited by an Irishman who was associated with Sinn Fein, while a Russian dissident worked at the French version of the same paper. 'Both the Egyptian and Indian extremist journals also carried notes from *The Gaelic American* and the British socialist paper *Justice!*'[71] Radical politics was a truly transnational business, and such hubs of radicals remind of other nineteenth century situations, as one described by the historian Bayly, when in 1822, Indian reformers and Portuguese, Eurasian, and British radicals 'toasted the Carbonari at a dinner in Calcutta.'[72]

These circulations must be kept in mind when looking at Sudanese politics. Oral accounts and political texts include scattered references to the situation in places like India, the United States, and Scotland, and to people such as Gandhi. For example, during the trial of League members, an activist, Aḥmad Ṣabrī Zāyd recalled ironically: 'We wanted to have an advocate from Egypt, but they refused to give us any kind of advocate except from Britain. But we said, we want Gandhi from India.'[73] These accounts provide scattered evidence of an awareness on the part of Sudanese militants that they were sharing the same situation and the same struggle as a number of countries in the colonial world. One anecdote on an episode from the Revolution of 1924, the revolt by convicts at the Khartoum North prison that happened simultaneously than the November mutiny, illustrates this point perfectly. The narrator, Abāyzīd Aḥmad Ḥusayn al-Shallālī, who was one of the convicts, recalled:

> While we were occupying the prison a Scottish division was guarding us. I talked to them, telling them that the Scottish are colonized as we are; we have to ask for independence. You and Ireland, you are colonized by England, why don't you ask for independence? Their commander took his cap and threw it against the wall and dismissed his soldiers.[74]

What is interesting about this story, which is obviously difficult to verify, is that it expresses the activist's belief that the colonial situation made all oppressed peoples, no matter where, equal and in solidarity with each other. This means that the circulation of international news made the Sudanese increasingly conscious that so many people in the world were struggling for self-determination as they were.

SECRET SOCIETIES IN SUDAN, EGYPT, AND BEYOND

In the previous sections, it has been suggested that various forms of political protests in different countries presented isomorphic characteristics. The organization of secret societies is the final aspect of this international

[71] Khan, *Egyptian-Indian Nationalist Collaboration*, pp. 47-48.
[72] C. A. Bayly and Eugenio Biagini, *Giuseppe Mazzini and the Globalization of Democratic Nationalism, 1830-1920* (Oxford: Oxford University Press, 2008), p. 6.
[73] *Al-Riwāyāt*, p. 290.
[74] Ibid., p. 148.

configuration explored here, not only because of their centrality, but also because their structure in Sudan reveals striking similarities with the organization of similar associations elsewhere.

On political secret societies

First, some general considerations on the nature and structure of political secret societies are needed, as these enlighten the case of the secret societies formed in Sudan between 1919 and 1923 and of the White Flag League. In a study on the organizational structure of secret societies, the sociologist Bonnie Erickson outlined a number of characteristics that distinguished secret societies from other forms of organization.[75] First, she underlined the fact that risk is the most important factor that determines both the scope and the meaning of these associations: 'risk is so important a consideration that it sets similar processes in motion even for societies differing in time, place, goals, and so on.'[76] The configuration of risk – in the form of the nature of retaliations, the degree of repression, the resources that the 'enemies' have for disclosing the association, and so on – determines not only the need for a series of carefully-devised processes for keeping the movement underground, but also affects the organization of the movement itself, for instance as regards the number of members, their functions and relations to each other. Because of the impending possibility of being discovered and arrested, recruitment is very selective: 'Clearly recruitment is not likely to take place unless the two people first trust each other, unless they have a prior tie outside the secret society and that tie is reasonably strong one.'[77] The nature of these networks will have consequences for the organization of the society; for instance, the existence of different networks within a society may lead to the creation of distinct branches. Finally, by comparing six different secret societies, Erickson noted that the fissiparous pattern of secret societies was directly linked to the environment in which they operated. The greater the uncertainties and constraints, the more societies tended to split and multiply. The political organizations of the 1920s correspond to this model point by point.

In Sudan...

As seen, the sources refer in vague terms to a plurality of 'nebulous' secret societies in Sudan after the Great War. Oral accounts by former White Flag League members add other fragmentary details to these descriptions, and seem to confirm that the panorama of secret societies was more variegated than it is usually believed to have been.

First, however, the term 'secret society' must be nuanced. Some associations were primarily discussion groups that were secret because of the anticolonial direction of their debates. For example, White Flag activists 'Alī Malāsī recounts that during the Great War, he was stationed

[75] Bonnie H. Erickson, 'Secret Societies and Social Structure', *Social Forces* (1981), vol. 60, n. 1, pp. 188-210.
[76] Ibid., p. 189.
[77] Ibid., p. 195.

in El Nuhud, an administrative centre in Kordofan, where he attended a club where people met and discussed politics. He adds: 'We continued exchanging news, even if we did not still have a specific goal, the revolutionary activity was there.'[78] Discussion clubs were a starting point that could lead to the creation of secret associations. This was the way in which, for Sulaymān Kisha, the Sudan Union developed:

> The first [patriotic] calling took the form of a literary association in Omdurman. Its members shared patriotic friendship that was revived by the meeting of the Graduate Club and it turned into public home meeting in the night, and then it turned into secret association.[79]

Among all these associations, the structure of the Sudan Union is certainly the best-known. In order to be admitted, a candidate had to take a special oath and carry out a number of anticolonial activities. Sulaymān Kisha described the process in detail:

> A member is not accepted in the cell unless he passes three stages: in the first the candidate has to go through a test given to him by the eldest of the association for a period of few months. A person would help watching the new member, a member [tutor] whose mission is to assist in the examination period of the candidate. If the eldest and the tutor decide that the candidate is competent, the member that suggested him would offer him to be part of the association to serve Sudan in pacific secret ways. If the candidate agrees, he would be presented as well as his assistant to the cell and would have to swear the oath, then he would meet the rest of his brothers in the cell and they would ask him to do tangible actions that are illegal, such as giving out flyers or writing a book or writing a letter, and then he would pay the membership fee and would participate in all the meetings.[80]

The society worked through a system of cells, organized hierarchically. According to Kisha, these cells were composed of ten members (although others say five):

> The association has ten founding members, who represent the presidency of the association, its mind, the ones that keeps its secret; then each of them runs a cell of ten members and he would be the tenth and he would work with this cell and the founders would give them assignments to accomplish and then this person would act as a mediator between his group and the senior members. He would be in charge of telling the founders how the nine were doing and telling the nine what the founders wanted from them.[81]

A member was not supposed to know who belonged to other parallel, inferior or superior cells, and above all, a member who was not in the top leadership was not supposed to know all the members of the society. This is likely one of the reasons why, in their memoirs, different Sudan Union members never named the same people as members of the society, and there are many inconsistencies in these accounts about who was and was not included, including, as seen, 'Alī 'Abd al-Laṭīf.[82]

78 *Al-Riwāyāt*, pp. 302-304.
79 Kisha, *Sūq al-Dhikryāt*, p. 164, and Kisha, *Al-Liwā' al-Abyaḍ*, p. 6.
80 Kisha, *Sūq al-Dhikryāt*, 164.
81 Ibid., p. 164.
82 *Al-Riwāyāt*, p. 528: in his oral account, Aḥmad al-Ṭrīfī Zubayr Pasha relates that the society was founded by Tawfīq Ṣāliḥ Jibrīl. As to the members of the Sudan Union: For Bakheit, 'British Administration and Sudanese Nationalism', pp. 65-67, the members were: Khalfallāh Khalīd, al-'Amīn al-Madanī, Makkāwī Ya'qūb,

Finally, there were other secret societies in Sudan, and they apparently adopted a similar structure. For instance, 'Alī Malāsī identified another association in Khartoum called the Society of the Five Brothers[83]:

> ['Alī Malāsī]: at that time there were some active societies. Of course I don't want to mention them now because it is the responsibility of its members, isn't it?
> [Interviewer]: Do you mean the [Sudan] Union society?
> ['Alī Malāsī]: The [Sudan] Union and others like the Five Brothers' League, and others.[84]

Secret associations not only existed in the capital. Ḥassan Ismā'īl al-Muftī, a Sudanese officer in the Camel Corps, recounted that in Bara – an administrative and trading centre of Kordofan – a society composed mostly of traders and officers of the Camel Corps had already been founded during the Great War.[85] Similarly, there was an association in El Obeid, the main administrative centre of Kordofan, not far from Bara. The same officer Ḥassan Ismā'īl al-Muftī, who was transferred to El Obeid after Bara, recounts that the society organized 'secret activities and meetings':

> [Around 1919] a lot of people contacted me and we established a society in El Obeid to stir British hatred among the people [... and] to show the bad standing of the British. ...
> [Interviewer] Which topics did you discuss?
> [Ismā'īl] Provoking nationalism against Britain.
> [Interviewer] Did you have any other goals, like the Unity of the Nile Valley?
> [Ismā'īl] We did, we told them that Sudan must be connected to Egypt and form a unity.[86]

Not much else is remembered about these associations, with one partial exception. This is a secret society based in Wad Medani, usually known as the United Tribes Society, which is the name that was used by 'Alī 'Abd al-Laṭīf to sign 'The Claim of the Nation'. The historian Hasan Abdin echoes colonial views when he writes, 'it is doubtful whether [such an association] existed at all beyond a small number of Ali's associates in Medani.'[87] But while historical works have glossed over it, various oral accounts point out that it was an important reference for activists, including those from outside Wad Medani. For example, officer 'Alī Mūsā was asked:

> There were organizations between Egyptian and Sudanese [during the Darfur Campaign of 1916]?' 'Yes I was one of the members.' 'Was it restricted to Kordofan only?' 'No, it was in Kordofan and in Wad Medani and in Khartoum'. [88]

(contd) 'Abdallāh Khalīl, Muḥammad Ṣāliḥ Shinqīṭī, Bābikr Qabbānī, Khalīl Faraḥ and Muḥammad al-Umm 'Arabī. Instead, Bāshirī mentions: Bāshirī 'Abd al-Raḥman, Ḥussayn Malāsī, Muḥammad Aḥmād Salīm, Ṣāliḥ 'Abd al-Qādir, Muḥammad 'Anīd, Aḥmād Fawzī, Muḥammad 'Uthmān Ṭāhir, and Khalafallāh Khalīd (Bāshirī, *Rūwād al-Fikr al-Sūdānī*, pp. 186-188). Aḥmad al-Ṭrīfī Zubayr Pasha (*al-Riwāyāt*, p. 528) adds the *Shaykh* 'Umar Daf'a Allāh.

83 *Al-Riwāyāt*, p. 305.

84 Ibid., p. 305.

85 Ibid., p. 131; according to him, the society also included one officer and four merchants.

86 Ibid., pp. 131-132.

87 Quoted in Deng, *War of Visions*, p. 104.

88 'Alī Mūsā, tape-recorded interview kept in the archive of the Afro-Asian Institute, University of Khartoum (hereafter IAAS), n. 1163.

Officer Ḥassan Ismāʿīl al-Muftī mentioned that his society in Bara 'had no contact with Khartoum or Wad Medani', thereby hinting that Wad Medani was as important as Khartoum. The wife of ʿAlī ʿAbd al-Laṭīf, al-ʿĀzza Muḥammad ʿAbdallāh, mentioned that when she and ʿAlī moved to Wad Medani, they found the society already up and running, and that it was composed mostly of officers.[89] Wad Medani was the place where some of the most prominent officers of 1924 met, already during and after the Great War. Officer Ḥassan Ismāʿīl al-Muftī was transferred to Wad Medani in 1922, and in the 1970s he still remembered some of the soon-to-be protesters whom he met there, all officers: Ibrāhīm ʿAbd al-Raḥman, ʿAbd al-ʿAzīz ʿAbd al-Ḥay, Muḥammad Surūr Rustum and 'that one who was shot, Ḥassan Faḍl al-Mūlā, and others I don't recall the names of'.[90] But the Wad Medani society included also civilians, such as judge Mudaththir al-Būshī.[91] Thus, even though the details of this story are unknown, it can still be concluded that there was a secret society that was based in Wad Medani; that it already existed during the Great War; and that was mostly, but not exclusively, made up of army officers. This was no coincidence, because the city hosted a large headquarters of the Egyptian Army.

Finally, it should be noted that there are puzzling intersections between the Wad Medani society and the Khartoum-based Sudan Union. In 1925, the Assistant Governor of Khartoum, Robin E. Baily, wrote a report on 'The Origins and History of the White Flag League', in which he described the Sudan Union:

> About 1921 there are the first indications that some of the members of the "League of the Sudan Union" were working subversively. ... They seemed to have operated by cells of "fives." ...
>
> Typical of this movement was the Egyptian officer who was then Mamur of Medani, Yuzbashi [Captain] Mohammed Effendi Fatuh. He was a member of an important "five," consisting of himself and four Sudanese officers. Of these four, one was Ali Abd al-Latif, a Dinka officer of the 14th Battalion, then serving at Medani. One of the four is now dead [Ḥassan Faḍl al-Mūlā]. The other two were Yuzbashi Abdulla Khalil and Yuzbashi Mohammed Saleh Gibril.[92]

Here, Baily seems to be confusing the Sudan Union with the Wad Medani society, or, to be more precise, he has merged them into one single society. For Baily, the Sudan Union 'was composed of Egyptians and Sudanese, nearly all of whom were serving officers', but also included civilians, people like Ṣāliḥ ʿAbd al-Qādir, co-founder of the White Flag League and a member of the Sudan Union. To add complexity to this already confusing picture, during 1924 another Sudan Union Society – even if it is unknown if it was a continuation of the old Sudan Union, or an entirely new society – became

89 *Al-Riwāyāt*, p. 374.

90 Ibid., p. 133.

91 His relative Ḥassan Ismāʿīl al-Muftī recounts: '[in 1919] also with us there was al-Būshī. He used to provide the society with the circulars and all the requirements of secret work... We used to meet in the house of my brother ʿAbd al-Qādir Ismāʿīl al-Muftī. He is a farmer there in Medani. There were officers among us.' *Al-Riwāyāt*: 133.

92 Baily Report, 'The Origin and History of the White Flag League', Appendix 7 to the Ewart Report, Khartoum, 21.4.1925, FO 407/201, NA, pp. 177-185.

active. It was composed mostly but not exclusively of army officers, and in August 1924 began signing a number of anticolonial circulars. Given these elements, one may wonder if there existed a sort of larger 'Sudan Union', which included people in Khartoum and in Wad Medani. However, pending further evidence, this remains only a hypothesis; the most that can be confirmed is that the Sudan Union and the officers' society in Wad Medani were connected in some imprecise way. This is easy to understand: army officers stationed outside Khartoum took their leave in the capital, where their families resided. If they were politically active in Wad Medani, it is likely that they continued their political activities in Khartoum, either in a group that represented a branch of the Sudan Union, or in another independent society that somehow overlapped with it.

Finally, is also likely that other secret societies, such as that mentioned by 'Alī Malāsī in Khartoum, also developed from socio-professional networks, as he seems to suggest:

> Meanwhile there were young people who belonged to two divisions ... the Railways and the Post and Telegraph. They were the most active in politics and in house meetings, because of the absence of clubs.[93]

Furthermore, there was some degree of porosity among secret societies and open associations, and participation in one did not exclude membership of another. For instance, many of those young graduates, secretly pro-Egyptian, reported as taking part in the meeting of June 10 in the house of *sayyid* 'Abd al-Raḥman al-Mahdī were also members of the Graduate Club, an official association formed in 1918 where only pro-British opinions could be aired. Young graduates of that time were highly politicized, and discussed politics whenever and wherever they had occasion to. The modalities, times and spaces of political exchange were multiple, each offering a chance of political confrontation.

... and beyond

British officers believed that Sudanese secret societies were the result of Egyptian political 'infection'. Indeed, there is little doubt that Egyptians working in Sudan not only were busy with politics but had also their own political associations. In the sources, the activism of Egyptian officers and officials living in Sudan before 1924 is invisible, and oral sources from Sudanese activists are silent on the issue, perhaps to clear any doubt that they were acting independently from Egypt. What is also surprising, however, is that the Intelligence Department overlooked Egyptian anticolonial organizations in Sudan entirely, to judge from the complete absence of reports on this important issue. Fragmentary evidence from Egyptians does exist, however. The collection of oral testimonies from the 1970s includes that of one Egyptian officer, 'Alī Mūsā, who participated in the Darfur campaign of 1916. He reveals that there was a secret society in Kordofan made up of Sudanese and Egyptian officers, and adds that this association was not unique in Sudan.[94] Muḥammad Najīb, who

[93] *Al-Riwāyāt*, p. 304.
[94] Interview with 'Alī Mūsā, 28.5.1974, IAAS 1163.

later became President of Egypt just prior to Nāṣir (1953-54), and whose mother was Sudanese, worked as an officer in Sudan for most of his early career. Before the Great War, he was already busy spreading anti-British propaganda in Sudan, an activity that he resumed in the early 1920s:

> At the end of my leave [in Egypt], I made contact with our secret society again, and started to write leaflets addressed to Sudanese politicians and leaders, staying up late at night to distribute them, either by mail or by leaving the letters on doorsteps.[95]

Unfortunately, Najīb does not dwell on this topic. He merely claims that his secret society was distinct from, but in contact with, the White Flag League (or possibly the Sudan Union). Precisely how the collaboration between Sudanese and Egyptian societies up to 1924 worked is not clear, however. It probably varied from one situation to another, but what is very likely is that Sudanese activists learnt a great deal from their Egyptian colleagues working in Sudan about the techniques of underground politics. Rather than focus on what the Egyptians 'taught' the Sudanese, it is of more interest to examine secret societies as a modular form of contentious politics that circulated in various parts of the colonial world, was adopted in Egypt at some point, and from there came to Sudan.

The history of Egyptian political secret societies after the Great War is one of the better-known compared to the general lack of information about their history elsewhere.[96] Unlike in Sudan, secret societies in Egypt were responsible for high-profile political assassinations, which prompted the police to carry out thorough and usually successful investigations; hence the availability of intelligence and judicial records about them. The first of a long series of political assassinations was that of Prime Minister Buṭrus Ghālī in 1909, killed by Egyptian nationalist Ibrāhīm Nāṣṣīf al-Wardānī. After a series of police investigations, fully covered and closely followed by the Egyptian press, the police discovered that al-Wardānī was a member of the *Jam'iyyat al- Taḍāmun al-Akhawī*, or 'Society of Brotherly Solidarity'. Further enquiries brought its structure and composition to light. These disclosed that most of its members came from the Engineering School in Cairo; that it was organized through a system of secret cells, and used coded language for communication.[97]

The al-Wardānī affair led to the creation of a special bureau dealing with secret political associations. It discovered no less than twenty-six secret societies, some of which had been created after Buṭrus Ghālī's

95 Mohammed Negib, *Memorie di Mohammed Negib (1919-1973)* (Firenze: La Nuova Italia, 1976), p. 4. Original in Italian. There is another version of Najīb's memoirs: Mohammad Neguib, *Egypt's Destiny* (London: Gollancz, 1955), but the English version does not include this passage.

96 See in particular Jacob M. Landau, 'Prolegomena to a Study of Secret Societies in Modern Egypt', *Middle Eastern Studies* (1965), vol. 1, n. 2, pp. 135-186; Malak Badrawi, *Political Violence in Egypt, 1910-1924: Secret Societies, Plots and Assassinations* (Richmond: Curzon, 2000); Eliezer Tauber, 'Egyptian Secret Societies, 1911', *Middle Eastern Studies* (2006), vol. 42, n. 4, pp. 603-623; Eliezer Tauber, 'Secrecy in Early Arab Nationalist Organizations', *Middle Eastern Studies* (1997), n. 33, vol. 1, pp. 119-127.

97 Badrawi, *Political Violence in Egypt*, p. 66.

assassination in the wake of the popularity of al-Wardānī, while others had existed previously.[98] The bureau revealed that the number of secret societies was a direct consequence of their volatility: for instance, the *Jam'iyyat al-Taḍāmun al-Akhawī* not only changed both its name and bylaws several times in its four years of existence, but also continually reshuffled its membership. Some members left to form new societies, while others joined it by splitting away from older societies, as happened in the case of al-Wardānī himself. In line with what Erickson noted on secret societies, this volatility was a consequence of the constant looming threat of being discovered and dismantled, as eventually happened. Repression did not put an end to this kind of political organization, however, as secret societies continued to engineer political assassinations well into the 1920s.

There were many similarities between the structure of these associations and the Sudanese ones. This was even noted in the Ewart Report on the 1924 Revolution. Its author maintained:

> The ["Leagues"] were extremely nebulous to start with and, even late in 1924, were by no means rigid. To some extent the methods of all secret societies were copied. There is testimony that one prominent feature was the formation of group of "five" ... The "five" grouping system has been a prominent feature of Egyptian secret conspiracies, and has also, of course, its Islamic significance ... Further obscurities arose from the merging in one another of societies originally formed independently in different localities ... More important than the formation of "leagues" was the insidious spreading of discontent by the working of "cells," and the cumulative process by which each Sudanese convert became in turn a "cell" more dangerous than any Egyptian could be.[99]

The origin of the White Flag League, at least according to one version, fits well into this description. During the trial of its members in October 1924, the main witness for the prosecution, 'Alī Aḥmad Ṣāliḥ, explained that this society had existed earlier than 1924 under different names. It is telling, in the light of the transnational circulation of nationalism discussed before, that one of the names was the 'Young Sudanese'.[100] According to al-Ḥājj, the last name chosen, 'White Flag League', was selected when the older society was reformed. It corresponded not only to a new strategy, but also to the fact that new people joined, notably two former members of the Sudan Union, 'Ubayd al-Ḥājj al-Amīn and Ṣāliḥ 'Abd al-Qādir, who were dissatisfied with the Sudan Union's leadership.

Apart from this problematic witness, other accounts relate that people came and went in different political associations. For instance, 'Alī Malāsī, who, it is known, worked for the Post and Telegraph Department, first joined a political club in El Nuhud, in Kordofan. When he was transferred, he initially attended secret political meetings in Khartoum and was ultimately responsible for the creation of a branch of the League in Port Sudan.[101] Similarly, Mudaththir al-Būshī related that he oscillated between the political society of Khartoum and that of Wad Medani, as apparently

[98] Tauber, 'Egyptian Secret Societies', p. 604.
[99] Ewart Report, p. 157.
[100] *The White Flag Trials*, p. 54.
[101] *Al-Riwāyāt*, pp. 302-328.

'Alī 'Abd al-Laṭīf did also.[102] Another reason why people left was because some members turned to King's witness, as happened in the Sudan Union, and later in the White Flag League.

Even if there were many similarities between Sudanese organizations and Egyptian secret societies, it is important to note from the start that the latter were a transnational form of contentious politics that spread worldwide, at least from the 19th and early 20th centuries. Far from being specific to the Egyptian or Sudanese context, they blossomed in a number of countries characterized by political repression and colonization, such as Greater Syria, Iraq, China, and India.[103] In Greater Syria, for instance, secret societies polarized political opinion between supporters of an independent Syria, or of a Greater Syria as a part of the Ottoman Empire from 1870 on.[104] In mandate Iraq, membership of secret societies was very popular among the elite military youth.[105]

Although they have not been object of any systematic comparative study, one anecdote clearly shows the circulation of this type of militant organization. According to the Rowlatt Committee Report on unrest in India, published in 1918, during the arrest of Indian radicals in London, the authorities discovered a copy of Thomas Frost's *Secret Societies of European Revolution, 1776–1876*, published in London in 1876.[106] Apparently, this was an essential text for Indian and Egyptian nationalists in exile. The book appears as a user's manual on secret societies. Its 660 pages are entirely dedicated to the history and organization of 19th-century secret societies in Europe and Russia, and the Table of Contents includes the Carbonari, the United Irishmen, the Tugenbund, Young Italy, Young Poland, the Communists, and the Russian Nihilists, among others. It is possible that this work had been the inspiration for the organization of secret societies in Egypt and had reached Sudan indirectly in this way. Indeed, during the trials of the White Flag League, 'Alī Aḥmad Ṣāliḥ mentioned, in a rather confused statement, that he was given a book by

[102] For Mudaththir al-Būshī, see his testimony in *Al-Riwāyāt*, pp. 64-129.
[103] As to Syria, see the discussion of al-Fatat in Gelvin, *Divided Loyalties*, pp. 55-66 and Eli'ezer Tauber, *The Formation of Modern Syria and Iraq* (Ilford, Essex, England; Portland OR: Frank Cass, 1995), pp. 1-10. For Iraq, see Orit Bashkin, *The Other Iraq: Pluralism and Culture in Hashemite Iraq* (Stanford CA: Stanford University Press, 2009), pp. 142: 'Rashid al-Hashimi, the editor of the daily Al-Dijla, hailed the role that secret societies played in the formation of Arab nationalism.' These works do not give much information on the structure of the society, however, but focus on their composition and political programme. On China: David Ownby and Mary F. Somers Heidhues, *Secret Societies Reconsidered: Perspectives on the Social History of Modern South China and Southeast Asia* (Armonk NY: M.E. Sharpe, 1993). For India, sparse information in Bayly and Biagini, *Giuseppe Mazzini*, p. 280; Richard Sisson and Stanley A. Wolpert, *Congress and Indian Nationalism: The Pre-independence Phase* (Berkeley CA: University of California Press, 1988), pp. 81-85.
[104] Khalidi, *The Origins of Arab Nationalism*, p. 8.
[105] Reeva S. Simon, 'The Education of An Iraqi Ottoman Army Officer', *The Origins of Arab Nationalism*, Rashid Khalidi ed. (New York: Columbia University Press, 1991), pp. 151-166.
[106] Khan, *Egyptian-Indian Nationalist Collaboration*, p. 48.

CONTENTS

OF

THE FIRST VOLUME.

		PAGE
INTRODUCTION		1
CHAP.	I. THE ILLUMINATI	23
"	II. THE UNITED IRISHMEN	55
"	III. THE PHILADELPHIANS	142
"	IV. THE TUGENDBUND	181
"	V. THE CARBONARI	209
"	VI. THE ASSOCIATED PATRIOTS	266
"	VII. THE COMMUNEROS	281

CONTENTS

OF

THE SECOND VOLUME.

		PAGE
CHAP.	VIII. THE REFORMED CARBONARI	1
"	IX. THE HETAIRIA	45
"	X. THE UNITED SCLAVONIANS	95
"	XI. THE TEMPLARS	118
"	XII. YOUNG ITALY	141
"	XIII. THE FAMILIES	200
"	XIV. YOUNG GERMANY	236
"	XV. YOUNG POLAND	255
"	XVI. YOUNG SWITZERLAND	262
"	XVII. THE COMMUNISTS	268
"	XVIII. THE FENIANS	275
"	XIX. THE NIHILISTS	303
"	XX. THE OMLADINA	316

Fig 2 Table of contents reproduced from the two volumes of Thomas Frost, *Secret Societies of European Revolution, 1776–1876* (Tinsely Bros, 1876)

an Egyptian official called the 'History of Societies' [the rest is illegible].[107]

In conclusion, a few important questions remain unanswered: to what extent did these societies contribute to the popularization of anti-colonial nationalism? Were they exclusively an elite phenomenon? What contact did they have with illiterate Sudanese, without access to the press, but the overwhelming majority of the people? The available sources provide very limited evidence. However, popular nationalism and secret associations were not mutually exclusive, as is evident in the case of Egypt, Iraq, and Syria. Moreover, looking the question retrospectively, it is hard to conceive how an event such as the Revolution of 1924 could have taken place without the popular element being to some extent exposed to the international political situation. Seditious circulars were not only sent to notables, but were also scattered throughout urban centres, and posted on walls, the idea undoubtedly being that even without being able to read them, people would know what they stood for: that it was time for people to stand up and protest.

[107] *The White Flag Trials*, p. 48.

Part Two

The Revolution of 1924

Organization of the Movement and its Spread to the Provinces

3

The 1924 Revolution

The photograph overleaf which belongs to the family of Zayn al-'Ābdīn 'Abd al-Tām, one of the earliest members of the White Flag League, has become an icon of the 1924 national movement. It was taken on May 15, when the League sent its first protest telegram, a day that can be rightfully considered as setting the start of the 1924 Revolution.[1] It reproduces four of the five founding members: from left to right, 'Ubayd al-Ḥājj al-Amīn, Ṣāliḥ 'Abd al-Qādir, 'Alī 'Abd al-Laṭīf, and Ḥassan Sharīf, the one who gave this picture to Zayn.[2] It is also a vivid representation of the fact that the White Flag League was not a movement made up solely of 'Black' army officers, but of people who were from all over Sudan: the origins of 'Alī 'Abd al-Laṭīf were in southern Kordofan and south Sudan, those of 'Ubayd al-Ḥājj al-Amīn[3] were in the Nubian northern Sudan, Ṣāliḥ 'Abd al-Qādir's family came from Turkey and Metemma, and Ḥassan Sharīf and Ḥassan Ṣāliḥ had unknown origins of mixed Egyptian and Sudanese backgrounds.

In the background to the photograph, there is a white flag, the symbol that gave the name to the movement. It is barely discernible in this picture, but on the left of the flag there is another small green flag, the national emblem for Egypt at the time, and on the right there is a representation of the river Nile, from the delta to its source. At the bottom of the flag are the words *ilā al-amāmi*, in Arabic, meaning '[to go] forward', reflecting the idea that the main target of the League was to make the country 'progress'.

1 And indeed this is reflected in the caption, that reads: "This historic picture was taken on the day of the beginning of the public [open] struggle, 15 May 1924."

2 The fifth founding member, Ḥassan Ṣāliḥ, is missing (who, according to popular accounts, came too late to be included). There is another very interesting version of the same image in which each of the four men is wearing a Fez – an Egyptian hat.

3 Interview by the author with the late nephew of 'Ubayd al-Ḥājj al-Amīn, 'Abd al-Mājid Muḥammad, Omdurman, 17.1. 2005. For a background on one of the branches of his family tree, the Hāshimāb, see Rex Seán O'Fahey, *Arabic Literature of Africa. Vol. III: The Writings of the Muslim Peoples of Northeastern Africa* (Leiden: Brill, 2003), pp. 289–329.

Fig 3 Four of the founders of the White Flag League, 15 May 1924. From left to right: 'Ubayd al-Ḥājj al-Amīn, Ṣāliḥ 'Abd al-Qādir, 'Alī 'Abd al-Laṭīf, and Ḥassan Sharīf
(Reproduced by kind permission of Amīna Bilāl Riziq, the wife of Zayn al-'Ābdin 'Abd al-Tām)

Below the picture, Ḥassan Sharīf copied a poem he had written at some unknown date, which is quite eloquent about the way in which the protesters retrospectively perceived 1924:[4]

> Truly we are the first to have disobeyed the government
> The sword is hanging threatening over our head, and the law is really blind
> We do not care, even if the shadows of the dead around us are pitch dark
> The dumbfounded inhabitants are doing nothing
> Even if this destiny guides us with irony
> To the prison, to exile, to death
> The people let us down on the day of calamity
> Even if they don't agree with us, we do not blame them
> Those who were hidden in a state of weakness and in a state of accusation, they rejected us
> We are the pioneers and history knows us
> In our records there is no accusation
> What is in our records is different to that of those who sold their conscience to the greedy usurper

[4] I am grateful to Āmal Aḥmad and to 'Abd al-Qādir Atwa for their generous help in explaining the poem to me.

The atmosphere in May 1924 was of course entirely different. After his election, Zaghlūl organized the creation of a special 'Sudan Committee' in Parliament, presided over by Ḥamdī Bey Sayf al-Naṣr. The Sudan Committee launched a request through Egyptian newspapers for the collaboration of any Sudanese willing to provide information to the commission about the situation in Sudan, which would be used during the negotiations. This appeal had an immediate effect. At the end of May, dispatches from the Intelligence Department noted that 'some Sudanese officers on pension and *disponibilité* at Omdurman' were sending information to the Sudan Committee through the collaboration of Egyptian employees.[5]

Second, Egyptian newspapers began to spread the news that the Sudanese government was secretly collecting signatures in support of Britain to use during the negotiations, an allegation that was probably not unfounded.[6] There is a general consensus among former activists that this is what drove to the foundation of the League, and that the British were supported by the notables and by the newspaper *Ḥaḍārat al-Sūdān*.[7] Many narratives taken from people who did not know each other at the time state that when the Sudanese patriots heard about this, they began collecting their own petitions in support of Egypt. For example, in Port Sudan, Muḥammad 'Abd al-Mun'im Zāyd reported: 'From al-Ahrām newspaper we knew that the British were collecting loyalty petitions, and that the Sudanese did not want Egyptian rule. We were upset by reading this.'[8] In the account of Zayn al-'Ābdīn 'Abd al-Tām,

> The political field was filled with clouds and the secret political associations were meeting and reflected about what had appeared from the intentions of the colonizers: their (British) project to contact the chiefs of the tribes and clans to make them write petitions of trust, that they would sign, choosing the British to be the sole ruler of Sudan instead than the Condominium that was present at the time, that was Egypt and Britain.[9]

It would be misleading to suggest that this is the 'true' story of the origins of the White Flag League. For example, the British version is totally different from those above: according to official reports such as that of Ewart, which was based on the testimony of informants, the League was created after the visit in June of that year of Muḥammad Bey Ḥāfiẓ Ramaḍān, leader of the Watanist Party in Egypt, who had come supposedly

5 C.A. Willis, Intelligence Note, Khartoum 21.5.1924, FO 141/806/1, NA. '*En disponibilité*' here means on leave, but ready to be recalled when needed.

6 The Sudanese Government was formally opposed to any active steps to foster pro-British public opinion for fear of escalation; on the other hand, nobody knew precisely what the Intelligence Department was doing in these early months of 1924, not even senior British officials, as they were to realize much later. In August, the Intelligence Department was requested to clarify the steps taken in May. The reply was as follows: 'Owing to the absence of the Director of Intelligence, I cannot categorically state whether steps to stimulate expression of loyalty were taken or not.' Unsigned telegram, Khartoum, 9.8.1924, FO 141/810/3, NA.

7 *Al-Riwāyāt*, p. 106, but see also pp. 75 (by Mudaththir al-Būshī, Wad Medani), 265 (Aḥmad Ṣabrī Zāyd, Port Sudan), 305-306 ('Alī Malāsī, Port Sudan).

8 Ibid., p. 257.

9 Ibid., p. 329.

to make contacts with Sudanese nationalists.[10] However, whatever the exact circumstances leading to creation of the White Flag League, the most important point is that ordinary Sudanese people turned into protesters as a consequence of feeling that somebody was 'stealing their rights' of self-determination, and that neither the British nor the notables had the right to 'speak for the nation' (See Chapter 6).

Thus, there was no time to waste: something had to be done to counter the 'secret works' of the British. One activist recounts:

> It had not been two days from the day of the petition [he is referring to the *al-'abbāsiyya* meeting] that the house of 'Alī 'Abd al-Laṭīf became a place that the people would visit all the time, day and night, and his doors became wide open to everyone who cared about the issue and wanted to participate in what these liberals agreed about.[11]

These 'liberals' decided that they had to collect their own petitions, and to be truly representative of all the people, these petitions had to come from all over Sudan. Apparently, each of the League's member was responsible for a certain area. According to Amīna Bilāl Riziq, the wife of Zayn al-'Ābdīn 'Abd al-Tām, Zayn was responsible for the Nuba Mountains, where he worked as a sub-*mamur* from the beginning of 1924.[12] Government reports also described attempts to collect petitions in the Gezira, around Berber and in Kordofan.[13]

THE FIRST PHASE: THE DEMONSTRATIONS OF JUNE 1924

After collecting some of such petitions – even if how many and from where is subject to speculation – the next step was to send them to Egypt, most probably to the Sudan Commission and the press. Two League members were selected to form a delegation to do so.

The composition of the 'strange couple' of men charged with this task is so puzzling that it should be described at some length. The small delegation included Officer Zayn al-'Ābdīn 'Abd al-Tām, a friend of 'Alī 'Abd al-Laṭīf, of Dinka family background, and coming from a (slave)soldier family.[14] The second man was Muḥammad al-Mahdī, nephew of the *mahdī* Muḥammad Aḥmad and son of the *khalīfa* Abdallāhi, the successor to the

10 Baily Report, Appendix 7 to Ewart Report, p. 178.

11 Al-Sayyid, *Al-Liwā' Al-Abyaḍ*, p. 13.

12 *Al-Riwāyāt*, p. 574. Aḥmad Ṣabrī Zāyd, one of the White Flag members in Port Sudan, also confirmed this version, mentioning that he believed that another White Flag League member, 'Alī Malāsī, collected petitions among the Beja of Eastern Sudan. Ibid., p. 265. The *ma'mūr* was a government appointee positioned between the British District Commissioner and the Sudanese people. The plural of the name *ma'mūr* is *mūmāra*, but in British sources the term is never transliterated and the plural is consistently formed just by adding the English plural ending –s, thus: *mamurs*. I have followed both conventions here.

13 C.A. Willis, DI, Intelligence Note, Khartoum 21.5.1924, FO 141/806/1, NA.

14 Interview by the author with Amīna Bilāl Riziq, taken at her home in Khartoum, Spring 2005. The assumption that because he was an officer his father had been taken into slavery at some point is, however, the author's.

mahdī after his death in Omdurman in 1885. Thus he belonged to a family that was not only locally very powerful, but was one of the closest allies of the British at the time.[15] The two took the train northwards to Wadi Halfa on 14 June, but after some time the train was stopped and the two were ordered to go back to Khartoum. It is to be noted that they were neither arrested nor accused of sedition, but simply sent back on the ground of a telling irregularity, that Zayn had bought for Muḥammad a half-price ticket reserved for officers' 'servants' (a word often used as euphemism for slave), when in reality Muḥammad was a civilian government employee. This chapter proceeds with a narrative of the events, but the topic of this unlikely pair and the choice to pass Muḥammad al-Mahdī off as a servant/ slave is discussed further in the Prologue to Part 4 of this book.

The two men managed to destroy the documents that they were carrying and nothing was found on them. Muḥammad al-Mahdī was sent back to Khartoum, while Zayn remained in Wadi Halfa for unknown reasons. On 17 June, White Flag members and supporters gathered at the train station to meet Muḥammad al-Mahdī and to protest against what they called 'the boycott of the delegation', but the British authorities got wind of their intention and made Muḥammad leave the train one stop before, in Khartoum North.[16] About 200 people gathered at the main station, but as they could not find him, they dispersed peacefully.[17]

On 19 June, the first large demonstration of 1924 took place. The occasion was the funeral of the beloved Egyptian *mamur* of Omdurman, *Yuzbashi* (Captain) 'Abd al-Khāliq Ḥassan. According to British estimates, 20,000 people gathered for his funeral.[18] Various speeches were made, initially of a non-political nature, but the final speech came from a young religious student from the Omdurman Islamic School, al-Ḥājj al-Shaykh Wad 'Umar. He called on the crowd 'to work for the unity of Egypt and the Sudan, and the downfall of the English.'[19] People were dispersed by the police, and only Wad 'Umar was arrested. The season of demonstrations had begun.

Events accelerated considerably after this first demonstration. Local narratives are hardly accurate as to the timing and the factual details of the various demonstrations, so this account mostly relies on colonial documents. On Friday 20 June, 'a crowd of about 100 small tradesmen and Effendis' asked for the release of al-Shaykh Wad 'Umar, but were

[15] Indeed, the British believed that Muḥammad al-Mahdī had been chosen in order to represent in the delegation the Mahdi's and Khalifa's family. Intelligence Notes, DI, Khartoum, 11.7.1924, FO 141/806/1, NA.

[16] Telegram from El Tayeb Babikr, Sheik Omar Dafalla, Izzeidin Rashek, Mohammed El Amin Abu El Gasem, Mohammed Sirr El Khatim Sulayman, and Ali Abd El Latif to Egyptian newspapers (the Editors of *El Balagh*, *El Akhbar*, and *El Ahram*) and the President of the Chamber, Khartoum, 19.6.1924, FO 141/806/1, NA.

[17] SA to the First Secretary, The Residency, Ramleh, Cairo, 19.6.1924, FO 141/806/1, NA.

[18] *The White Flag Trials*, p. 16.

[19] Telegram from DI, Khartoum to SA, Cairo, 20.6.1924, FO 141/806/1, NA.

dispersed.[20] On the same day, shaykh Ḥassan al-Amīn al-Darīr, another religious man from a notable family, gave 'a most seditious speech' at the Khartoum mosque. [21]A large crowd gathered in support.

On 22 June, the authorities issued an ordinance prohibiting demonstrations in the capital. News about this ordinance did not spread quickly enough for the White Flag League members to stop the demonstration that was organized for the day after.[22] One of the core tenets of the League was to stay within a legal framework, so that the demonstration of 23 June was the last to take place under the aegis of the League. According to British estimates, the crowd consisted of five hundred people, 'unsavoury-looking riff-raff', some of whom began throwing stones at the police and at foreign shops.[23] Four people were arrested, including officer Zayn al-'Ābdīn 'Abd al-Tām. His wife related the events of this demonstration from her husband's account, (however, adding flavour to the narrative, as from what is known from the sources, no one died in this demonstration):

> It was really a successful demonstration; a man called 'Abd al-Qādir Aḥmad Sayyid was holding the flag of the league and Zayn was photographing the demonstration. They clashed with the police, people were injured and bones were broken and people died, and Zayn photographed all this. In the same evening the houses of all the members were surrounded and they were taken into prison, and Zayn was brought to the military prison because he was an officer, and the others were brought to Kober [the civil prison] ... Every mission assigned to him by the League, he successfully completed it without being suspected or found guilty of anything by the British. He was released from prison many times due to lack of evidence.[24]

Various people were arrested during these first demonstrations and were given quite varied sentences: for example, 'Abd al-Qādir Sayyid, one of the heads of the demonstration of June 23, was given six months, Wad 'Umar, who uttered a very anticolonial speech at the mosque, got 67 days; yet Zayn al-'Ābdīn 'Abd al-Tām was released immediately.[25]

After this last demonstration, the five founders of the White Flag League were separated, but again, not arrested. Between 23 and 25 June, Ṣāliḥ 'Abd al-Qādir was transferred from Khartoum to Port Sudan to work in the Post and Telegraph Department.[26] Ḥassan Sharīf was sent to Barakat, a small village near Wad Medani, and Ḥassan Ṣāliḥ was dispatched to Merowe,

[20] Chronicle of the events during the period of political excitement in Khartoum, FO 141/805/2, NA.
[21] Ibid.
[22] *The White Flag Trials*, p. 18-22.
[23] Report on the demonstration held in Khartoum on 26.6.1924, Palace 4/10/49, NRO.
[24] *Al-Riwāyāt*, p. 580.
[25] DI to More, SA, 3.7.1924, FO 141/806/1, NA; Chronicle of the events during the period of political excitement in Khartoum, FO 141/805/2, NA.
[26] This is not mentioned by the Intelligence Department, but is inferred from the telegrams sent by the White Flag League, as Ṣāliḥ 'Abd al-Qādir began sending telegrams from Port Sudan starting from 25 June. Telegram from Saleh Abdel Gadir, Ali Malassi, and Bashari Abdel Rahman to Governor General, 25.6.1924, Port Sudan, FO 141/810/3, NA.

another minor centre north of Khartoum.[27] 'Ubayd al-Ḥājj al-Amīn could not be transferred as he was no longer a government employee, having been dismissed at the beginning of 1924, and so he was simply given a warning. Other people known to be associated with the League were also warned and transferred: Muḥammad al-Mahdī, for instance, was forced to return to El Dueim.[28] The only one picked up immediately was 'Alī 'Abd al-Laṭīf, because he was considered too dangerous to remain free. Arrested on 4 July, he was tried on 7 July and sentenced to three years' imprisonment under Section 90 of the Sudan Penal Code.

In spite of the fact that the League stopped supporting demonstrations and that its leaders had been, ostensibly, 'neutralized', protests continued. On 25 June, a small demonstration was organized but was rapidly dispersed.[29] On 26 June, another took place, but with some significant differences from the previous ones: first, instead of the League's flag, the demonstrators used the Egyptian green flag, probably to signal that they did not represent the White Flag League. However, of the four people arrested, at least one, al-Tuhāmī Muḥammad 'Uthmān, was certainly a member of the League. Second, unlike the other demonstrations in which those who were arrested were predominantly educated Sudanese, the four men imprisoned belonged to the popular element: two carpenters, a tailor, and a pedlar bookseller.[30] One of the four, 'Abd al-Karīm al-Sayyid, would later write a long memoir of his participation in the 1924 Revolution, an important source for this book.[31]

Protest continued. On Friday 27 June, another political speech was made at the Khartoum mosque, this time by Aḥmad Idrīs Abū Ghallāb, a clerk at the Department of Health. He told the crowd: 'We must all work for one cause, and as the Copts speak our language, they should be with us.'[32] A small number of demonstrators gathered, and once again were dispersed.

At the beginning of July, senior officials from the Sudan Government looked at the events of the past fifteen days with concern, and yet with confidence. On 1 July, the Director of the Intelligence Department, C. A. Willis, wrote: 'My own belief is that the League of the White Flag is for the time being moribund.'[33] The demonstrations had begun suddenly and had escalated rapidly, but once the ordinance prohibiting them had been issued, the atmosphere had cooled down just as quickly. The authorities had flexed their muscles during the disturbances, but at the same time they had carefully avoided using too much force and making

[27] For Ḥassan Sharīf: Notes on the signatories of the telegram to the Governor General, 3.6.1924 In C. A. Willis, The League of the White Flag, Khartoum, 20.7.1924, FO 141/806, NA; for Ḥassan Ṣāliḥ: al-Sayyid, *Al Liwā' al-Abyaḍ*, p. 13.

[28] DI, Khartoum, 11.7.24, FO 141/806/1, NA.

[29] See Appendix no. 13 that is a table of the chronology of 1924 and the distribution of events in the various provinces. Undated, unsigned, Kordofan 1/13/62, NRO.

[30] Chronicle of the events during the period of political excitement in Khartoum. FO 141/805/2, NA. In this document he is defined as a shoemaker, but in actual fact he sold books. Statement of Fuad Ali, Khartoum, 7.9.1924, Palace 4/11/55, NRO.

[31] Al-Sayyid, *Al-Liwā' al-Abyaḍ*.

[32] Baily, Ass. Gov. Khartoum to Civsec, 29.6.1924, Palace 4/10/49, NRO.

[33] C.A. Willis to Private Secretary, Khartoum, 1.7.1924, FO 141/806/1, NA.

too great a fuss about the events taking place – just enough to scare people and convince some to turn King's witness, which had allowed them to track the leaders down and seemingly 'neutralize' them.[34] The police force had been strengthened and had received valuable help from a sort of irregular corps of 'Arabs' – here, read 'nomadic people' – from Western Sudan, particularly Baqqāra and Ta'āishī, and who were seen by the protesters as supporters (*anṣār*) of *sayyid* 'Abd al-Raḥman al-Mahdī.[35] It is probable that the popular disturbances that took place after 23 June did not worry the British authorities unduly because they were smaller and led by 'unimportant natives' who no longer had a leader.[36] However, the continuation of small, apparently insignificant events in Khartoum somewhat eroded the government's confidence.

DEVELOPMENTS FROM JULY 1924

After the arrest of 'Alī 'Abd al-Laṭīf, a new leadership committee was chosen. Headed by 'Ubayd al-Ḥājj al-Amīn, its vice-president was 'Arafāt Muḥammad 'Abdallāh, and its secretary 'Alī Mūsā Lāz; the latter became a witness for the prosecution during the trials of the League.[37] However, the League was becoming side-lined by events. On 6 July, two men – 'two tailors, both the worse for drink' – attempted to hold a demonstration, once more carrying a white flag, but failed to raise a following and were arrested. On 12 July, a 'miserable-looking berberine effendi from the Irrigation Department' gave a speech at the mosque, reading a passage from the Qur'ān and shouting the usual cry that had rallied people at the previous demonstrations: 'Long Live Fu'ād, King of Egypt and the Sudan.'[38] The Government undoubtedly considered that these two events were last-ditch efforts by a moribund League, but this was not the case. This 'miserable-looking' clerk was Muḥammad Sirr al-Khātim, a Gordon College-educated man who could count on a large network of supporters and powerful protectors. His trial at the end of July was accompanied by a wave of telegrams and protests. Some of his colleagues at the Irrigation Department in Khartoum and Jebel Awlia went on strike for several days. The notables of the capital also mobilized. In August Muḥammad Sirr al-Khātim was released (only to be arrested again in September), and after his release, the Grand Mufti of the Sudan went to congratulate the Legal Secretary, Sir Wasey Sterry.[39]

[34] People were wounded by blows from the flat sides of swords, and some hospitalised. See the Chronicle of the events during the period of political excitement in Khartoum, FO 141/805/2, NA.

[35] *Al-Riwāyāt*, p. 44, in the account by Muzammil 'Alī Dinār. Among the people who mentioned the attack of the *ansār* is al-'Āzza, the wife of 'Alī 'Abd al-Laṭīf, *Al-Riwāyāt*, p. 411.

[36] Telegram, (unsigned), Khartoum, to High Commissioner for Egypt, Cairo, 4.7.1924 (re: sequence of events), FO 141/806/1, NA.

[37] Al-Sayyid, *Al-Liwā' al-Abyaḍ*, p. 13. *The White Flag Trials*, pp. xxxix, 76-113.

[38] Daily Bulletin, Sunday July 6th, Palace 4/10/49, NRO.

[39] Mr. Sterry to Mr. Kerr, Khartoum, 14.8.1924, FO 407/199, NA.

This affair and the disturbance raised began to worry the government once more, while the eagerly awaited end to the disturbances did not come. On 22 July, another small demonstration was raised by 'Alī Ḥassan Dabba. Setting out once again from the Khartoum mosque, and 'waving a green flag', he strode towards the Egyptian Officers' Club: 'The members of the club greeted him with acclamations and many of them descended into the street and crowded around him cheering for the King of Egypt.'[40] A section of the crowd began throwing stones at the police. 'Alī Ḥassan Dabba was sentenced to no less than one year of imprisonment, ostensibly also on the grounds of his low 'morals'. Small events such as this continued to occur: on 1 August, a boy attempted to start a demonstration by shouting at the Omdurman mosque, without success. On the following day, 2 August, Muḥammad 'Abd al-'Āl Fawzī, a carpenter and stonecutter, appeared in Khartoum Market waving a green flag in an attempt to incite people to demonstrate, but he was immediately arrested.[41]

The Intelligence Department slowly realized that the 'neutralization' of the League's leaders had not been sufficient to prevent problems. More worrying for the Department was the fact that political agitation had spread outside Khartoum. First, in June and July, nationalists sent telegrams not only from Khartoum, but also from Port Sudan, Wad Medani, Hassahissa, Barakat, and Merowe. This was followed by a number of small incidents in the provinces.

Confronted with a situation that was apparently deteriorating, at the end of July the British authorities concluded that a new strategy was to be pursued. Baily, the Deputy Governor of Khartoum, made an emphatic summary of the situation in the middle of August:

> I hold the opinion that there is only one thing to do with people whose mentality is so constituted as is that of the people of this country, and that is – when individuals give trouble, to hit and hit and go on hitting.[42]

Indeed, a new wave of arrests, more extensive than the previous one, swept the nationalist movement. On 30 July, 'Ubayd al-Ḥājj al-Amīn, Mūsā Lāz, Ḥassan Midḥat – the new leaders of the White Flag League – and Muḥammad 'Abd al-Bakhīt, a discharged officer from the Egyptian Army, were arrested. At the same time the British authorities allegedly found the list of 120 members of the White Flag League to which historians refer so often (see Appendix 2). During the month of August, the two last original founders of the White Flag League, Ḥassan Sharīf and Ḥassan Ṣāliḥ, were also arrested.[43] Protesters continued to be imprisoned throughout August and September. While the authorities had previously been careful to arrest 'agitators' only when they had obvious legal

[40] Chronicle of the events during the period of political excitement in Khartoum. FO 141/805/2, NA.
[41] Ibid.
[42] Corbyn, Gov. Khartoum Prov., to DI, Khartoum, (wrongly dated 16 June 1924: the correct date is 16.8.1924) FO 141/805/2, NA.
[43] In Gov. Khartoum Prov. to Civsec, 4.10.1924, Palace 4/9/46, NRO.

grounds for doing so, as in the case of participation in a demonstration, they now began arresting anyone who was suspected of sedition.

CLIMAX: AUGUST 1924

The hard line adopted by British authorities brought the situation to a crisis point. August was one of the most intense months of 1924, with significant popular mobilizations in the provinces and the capital and the increasing visibility of the army. The peculiarity of the events of August is that they were the product of a series of chain reactions: agitation in Port Sudan sparked agitation in Atbara, which in turn led to things escalating in Khartoum. All this happened when the Intelligence Department was left leaderless: its director, Charles A. Willis, has begun the customary long summer leave at the beginning of August.

Port Sudan

Some of the most successful demonstrations of 1924 took place in Port Sudan, and for that reason they are the focus of Chapter 5; however a general outline of events is useful here. At the end of July, the Intelligence Department organized the transfer of three political prisoners from Khartoum to Port Sudan under police escort (their names are never mentioned either in Sudanese or in colonial sources). The Port Sudan authorities were not informed or did not receive the information in time, but the Port Sudan members of the White Flag League were alerted and on 27 July organized a demonstration at the railway station to meet the prisoners. About 1,000 people, described in British sources as consisting of 'every description of person, Blacks, Muwahid [Muwalladīn] servants and Egyptians, and men wearing gallabers[44] and Effendia', were waiting for them.[45] They followed the political prisoners in good order as far as the jail, where speeches were made. Apparently there was none of the confusion and stone-throwing that had marked the demonstrations in the capital.[46] But matters did not end there.

Believing that the man behind the demonstration was the former White Flag leader Ṣāliḥ 'Abd al-Qādir, who, as mentioned previously had been transferred to Port Sudan around 25 June, the authorities arrested him on 5 August. The following day, the clerks of the Customs and Post and Telegraph Office went on strike. On 7 August, the day of Ṣāliḥ 'Abd al-Qādir's departure by train to Khartoum to be prosecuted, another demonstration was organized. The colonial response to this event was

44 Sing. *jalābiyya*, pl. *jalālīb*, typical Sudanese male dress.

45 Proceedings of the court of inquiry held to inquire into recent events at Port Sudan as far as they affect the Army, from G. D. Yeatman, Kaimakam, OC Troops Port Sudan, to the CSO & AG, Egyptian Army, Khartoum, 19.8.1924, Palace 4/9/45, NRO.

46 Copies of correspondence re. demonstration at Port Sudan 27.7.1924 on occasion of the transfer of political prisoners from Khartoum to Port Sudan, Port Sudan, 30.7.1924, Palace 4/10/50, NRO.

tougher; some protesters were injured by the police. This triggered a chain reaction of demonstrations, and matters became so serious that the British authorities lost control of the city for days.

Summarizing the events in 1925, Ewart nonchalantly reported that the demonstrations 'were controlled without difficulty and the situation was restored to normal within ten days.'[47] Yet, the gravity of the situation can be well appreciated by the fact that ten whole days were needed to restore order. Furthermore, to impress the population and make clear that these demonstrations would not lead anywhere, it was deemed necessary to summon no less than a war cruiser, the HMS Weymouth, which was subsequently replaced by another war ship, the sloop Clematis. Finally, a battalion of the British Army, the Argyll and Southerland Highlanders, arrived to Port Sudan on 20 August.[48]

Atbara

Running along the railway tracks, the spark of protest moved from Port Sudan to the next important train stop, the city of Atbara, on the line connecting the capital to the port city.[49] The sources for this episode are also mostly drawn from colonial records. Few local accounts of the riots of Atbara have survived, probably because so many of its protagonists were Egyptians.[50] On the one hand, colonial records, including witnesses' testimonies, are particularly rich in detail, so that this short paragraph does not do justice to the complexity of this event. On the other hand, there is no record of how the political movement was organized there, how it was formed, and even to what extent the leaders of the uprising were in contact with the League.

The events began with the transit of Ṣāliḥ 'Abd al-Qādir to Atbara after his imprisonment in Port Sudan. Political activists there organized a demonstration to meet him at the train station on 9 August. About 500 civilians and 120 soldiers from the Railways Battalion[51] arrived at the station, 'carrying branches of trees, shouting cheers to Saad Pasha and for the King of Egypt', and this is how the riots began.[52]

Because of its crucial role in the events of Atbara, a brief background of the Railways Battalion is useful at this point. Before 1924, the Railways were still administered by the military authorities – the first railway line had been built to facilitate the military operations during the Sudan campaign that began in 1896. Most of its workers belonged to the so-called Railways Battalion. Its employees had the status of soldiers, but

47 Ewart Report, p. 163.
48 Ibid., p. 163; Chronology - Appendix no. 13, Kordofan 1/13/62, NRO.
49 Ahmad A. Sikainga, *City of Steel and Fire: A Social History of Atbara, Sudan's Railway Town, 1906-1984* (Portsmouth NH: Heinemann, 2002), p. 33.
50 There is only one witness in *Al-Riwāyāt* that deals with Atbara, Abāyazīd Aḥmad Ḥusayn al-Shallālī, but his testimony is quite confusing and above all it deals very little with the specific events at Atbara.
51 Witness for the prosecution no. 4, Bash Shawish Mohammed Shalabi, Railways Battalion, Palace 4/10/52, NRO.
52 Memorandum on events at Atbara from the 9th August 1924 onwards, Palace 4/10/52, NRO.

they were unarmed and untrained, so that they were rather wage-earners employed by the army. The second peculiarity of the Railways Battalion is that it was mostly composed of Egyptian 'soldiers', or men of Egyptian origin, and staffed with Egyptian officers. For this reason, the Sudan Government regarded it with great suspicion, and one of the government's imminent plans was to get rid of it. Besides this battalion, the whole city of Atbara, which was to a large extent a new colonial city, revolved around the railways, and its inhabitants were mostly employed by the Railways Department.

On 9 August, after cheering the prisoner Ṣāliḥ 'Abd al-Qādir, the demonstrators were dispersed; but during the rest of the day tensions mounted, in particular among the men of the battalion, and it was reported that two civilian artisans, a Sudanese and an Egyptian, went to their barracks in the evening to speak with them. Exact details of that conversation are not known, but at dawn on 10 August, the men of the Railways Battalion decided to take action. They left their barracks, went to their workshops, and in a Luddite-style action, they began smashing tools and machines. They moved on to the central market where they were joined by a crowd of civilians, then marched on to the offices of the Headquarters of the Traffic and Engineering Department where much further destruction of property occurred.[53]

On the following day, 11 August, early in the morning, the 'Arab' troops of the Mounted Rifles, despatched from Shendi, arrived. They met the demonstrators in the central market, separated the civilians from the soldiers of the Railways Battalion, and pushed them back to their barracks, where they were surrounded. The Arab troops kept the soldiers of the Railways under fire, but were continually provoked. The demonstrators threw bricks, shouted at them, and tried to tear down and escape through the fences around the barracks.[54] At this point, a British officer gave an order to fire one round into the air in the hope of scaring the protesters, but the order was misunderstood, and the men begun to fire directly into the crowd of strikers. Firing continued for over a minute. When it stopped, 19 people had been wounded, of whom four later died.[55]

On the following day, a large crowd attended the funerals of the four victims, chanting 'Long Live Sa'd.'[56] All the men of the Railways Battalion who were working outside Atbara went on strike and asked to join their comrades still being held in the barracks in Atbara. In the days that followed, the authorities quickly organized the evacuation of the entire

53 During the trials, the British authorities noted that the damage was more spectacular than it was substantial: for instance, the offices of British superiors were vandalized, but expensive machines incurred only superficial damage. A. C. Parker, Acting General Manager, Sudan Govt. Railways and Steamers to Acting GG, 24.8.1924, FO 141/805/2, NA.

54 First Witness, M. Fadil, Lewa, Atbara, 12.8.1924, Palace 4/10/52, NRO.

55 Atbara: Narrative of Events, Enclosure 3 in no. 154 Sterry to Allenby, Khartoum, 21.8.1924, FO 407/199, NA.

56 Telegram from Parker, Atbara to Hakiman Huddleston, Khartoum, 12.8.1924, Northern Prov. 1/20/191, NRO.

Railways Battalion to Egypt. This task was carried out in just ten days – and was completed on 28 August.

This event provoked a wave of protests in Egypt and Sudan. Dozens of telegrams were sent by Egyptians in Egypt to the Parliament, mostly from the provinces and rural areas, all protesting against the murder of unarmed men.[57] More telegrams were sent to Egypt and to the Sudan Government from within Sudan. The question was discussed at length in the Egyptian Parliament, while the Sudan Government let the Egyptian authorities know that it considered Egypt to be solely responsible for the incident.[58] However, '...both Lord Allenby and Sir Lee Stack expressed doubt as to the possibility of producing conclusive evidence of Egyptian Government complicity.'[59]

The Mutiny of the Military School Cadets

The demonstrations of the cadets of the Military School and those in Atbara happened at the same time as the deteriorating situation in Port Sudan. Whether these three events were coordinated, and if so how, will probably never be known.

Among all the events of August, the protest at the Military School seemed the most worrying in the eyes of the Sudan Government. The very term 'mutiny' attributed to it by the authorities (while the cadets themselves called it a demonstration, *maẓāhira*[60]), reinforced the official line that it was a grave attack on the establishment; and yet this event was entirely peaceful, and its purpose was no different from that of the June demonstrations: to express the will of the Sudanese in a visible and peaceful manner.

There were many reasons why the mutiny shocked the colonial establishment; some will be explored here, while others will become clearer after the discussion of the role of the army in the colonial state in Chapter 9. The first is that the Military School was a jewel in the crown of the Sudanese educational system. Its discipline and standards were universally praised, and episodes of insubordination were unknown. The British teachers and supervisors at the school were proud of their pupils who were the 'product' of four years of advanced military and educational training. As one report stressed, the Military School was 'considered by everybody the most reliable and highly disciplined unit in the Army'.[61] This is why the British instructors at the school reacted to the demonstration

[57] List of telegrams sent as a protest against the incidents in Sudan, originals in Arabic, undated and unsigned, 0075-049751 Cairo Records Office [CRO].

[58] With regard to the diplomatic consequences of the events in Atabara, see the file entitled 'Sudan. Evenements and Troubles', which is divided into three sections: CRO 0075-049754; CRO 0075-09755; and CRO 0075-049752.

[59] See for instance: Record of conference held in the room of the Secretary of State at the Foreign Office on 13 August at 11 a.m., Palace 4/9/44, NRO. On the subject of Zaghlūl's denial of any responsibility, see: Translation of letter dated Paris 29.8, received by Prime Minister from Zaghlul, Palace 4/9/44, NRO.

[60] For example in: *Al-Riwāyāt*, p. 178.

[61] Huddleston, Notes on a discussion with Colonel J. B. Wells, CMG, DSC, on 15.10.1924, Palace 4/9/47, NRO.

almost with incredulity. Perhaps the best quotation to illustrate this sense of shock and awe is by Acting Governor General and Kaimakam (Colonel) Huddleston:

> El Bimbashi Pease ... was in the closest possible touch with the cadets, with whom he was most popular .... This morning he visited all the cadets, both those in close arrest and those confined in the school. He reports that their manner, although not insubordinate, is defiant and entirely unrepentant and he admits that he has entirely lost touch with them, including those upon whom he looked as personal friends.
>
> The continuation of this defiant attitude, the secrecy with which the conspiracy was hatched, and the firm belief of the cadets that at least one Sudanese unit in Omdurman would have joined them, appears to be the result of the most skilful anti-British propaganda which has been successful to an unexpected extent. This incident must definitely put an end to the present system of providing native officers for Arab and Sudanese units.[62]

The details of this mutiny – or demonstration, depending on the point of view – are known not only from British sources, but also from a wealth of interviews with former cadets. The two volumes of oral testimonies of the Revolution of 1924, *Al-Riwāyāt al-Shafawiyya li-Thuwwār 1924*, include as many as eight interviews with cadets out of a total of 39. The dynamic of the events was roughly as follows: in July, cadet Idrīs 'Abd al-Ḥay, who was acting as a contact person between the League and the cadets, met the various senior cadets and discussed how to respond to the political situation. Former cadet Ibrāhīm Sayyid Uthmān described this early phase:

> Idrīs 'Abd al-Ḥay was closely connected to 'Alī 'Abd al-Laṭīf and after his arrest, which had a strong effect on us, he talked to the senior cadets. It was the time of holiday at the school; then the college opened again at the beginning of August 1924. Afterwards we had a meeting in the dormitory, and the chairman of the meeting was al-Shinnāwī, *shawish*, senior cadet. We were discussing during the meeting that we must show ourselves and we must do something similar to that of the Egyptian military college of 1919.[63]

The cadets held a final meeting all together on 7 August to discuss the details of the demonstration. Ibrāhīm Sayyid Uthmān continued his account:

> The demonstration was intended to be a peaceful one but we were armed in case of attack to defend ourselves, and we, all the 51, agreed about that. ...We had 60 bullets each and we were dressed in parade uniform, the one for celebration, with feathers on the top. [Somebody asked cadet 'Alī Ṭāhir] why you are putting the feathers,[64] you know that today is sports training-day, and not the day of parade. 'Alī answered him: you wait and you will soon see.[65]

In the early morning of 9 August, the cadets sent a message to the authorities announcing that they would be holding a demonstration. They began their march from the Military School holding up a green

[62] Demonstration by Cadets of Khartoum Military School, Encl. 2 in Sterry to Allenby, Khartoum, 21.8.1924, FO 407/199, NA.
[63] *Al-Riwāyāt*, pp. 178-179.
[64] Plumes were attached to headgear as part of the dress uniform.
[65] *Al-Riwāyāt*, pp. 178-179.

Fig 4 The parade of the cadets of the Military School, 8 August 1924
(Source: SAD.1/21/14 from the W.J.R. Andrews collection. Reproduced by permission of Durham University Library)

flag, and a picture of King Fu'ād carried by two cadets in the centre.[66] The flag seemed to represent a modified version of the Egyptian one, bearing Arabic writings that cannot be deciphered. According to young Nafīsa Surūr, a friend of Idrīs 'Abd al-Ḥay who had sewn the flag, it bore slogans in support of King Fu'ād and Sa'd Zaghlūl, but also for 'Alī 'Abd al-Laṭīf.[67]

The cadets marched to the barracks of the 4th Egyptian Battalion. According to senior cadet Muḥammad Faḍlallāh al-Shinnāwī, one of the heads of the demonstration, and who left a detailed account of the events:

> [they] joined the cadets in 'Arms Salutation' then the senior cadet shouted three times Long Live King Fu'ād, Sa'd Zaghlūl, 'Alī 'Abd al-Laṭīf and Long Live the Nile Valley, both the cadets and the force of the battalion repeated after him.[68]

Then they marched to the Khartoum railway station, where a crowd surrounded them, but the police made sure that civilians did not join in. They formed a cordon around the demonstrators, and 'as several tried to evade the civil constabulary they received minor injuries during the rush to get past the cordon.'[69] The cadets continued their march regardless, and reached the centre of Khartoum, near today's *sūq al-'arabī,* to go to the home of 'Alī 'Abd al-Laṭīf. There they met al-'Āzza, the wife of 'Alī, who also had a vivid account of this meeting, as she was probably the

66 The same flag was sent to El Obeid to be used in the demonstrations organized there. Notes on the activity of the White Flag Society at El Obeid, Gov. Kordofan Prov. to DI, El Obeid, 8.8.1924, Kordofan 1/14/68, NRO.

67 *Al-Riwāyāt*, pp. 230-233 and 467.

68 The quote is taken from there. For a British account of the same events – the sequence is the same – see: Demonstration by Cadets of Khartoum Military School, August 9, Encl. 2 in Mr. Kerr to Mr. MacDonald, 31.8.1924, FO 141/199, NA.

69 Chronicle of events during the period of Political excitement in Khartoum, FO 141/805/2, NA.

first Sudanese woman to have participated in a demonstration in the 20th century.[70]

> Al-'Āzza is at home. Someone knocks at the door, and asks 'is al-'Āzza inside?' and asks her to come out. Her mother was making 'zaghrur' (a sound of encouragement) for the cadets, she asks her, why you are making this sound, they are going to Kober [the prison of Khartoum North], and she answers, I want to make them brave. So al-'Āzza got dressed and joined them. [71]
>
> ... then I went out with them and I began shouting with them as if I were not a woman, my steps in the earth were not woman steps, and I was shouting with them.[72]

From there they moved on to the Government Palace. They began to be followed by the irregular police, who were usually sent in against demonstrators, but this time they were not overly concerned, as one of them made clear: 'the senior cadet commanded stop, load the guns; when we did that, they all ran away.[73] They crossed the bridge between Khartoum and Khartoum North, and marched to the barracks of the 3rd Egyptian Battalion.[74] From there, they went to Kober, the main prison for political detainees, to render homage to 'Alī 'Abd al-Laṭīf. Finally, the cadets marched towards the steamer that connected Khartoum North and Omdurman – there was no bridge at that time – with the intention of meeting another Sudanese battalion,[75] but the steamer had been summoned back to the Omdurman side, and the cadets had no choice but to return to the Military School, where they found all their ammunition gone. They had been marching for hours, under the severe heat of the August sun.

Back in their barracks, they were surrounded by British troops, and yet a sense of having accomplished something extraordinary remained vividly in their memory for decades after. This is not only clear from the many recollections and the language used to describe this event, both by cadets and by other activists, but also from accounts recorded in the immediate aftermath. For instance, one of the cadets wrote in a letter to a friend:

> A wonderful event took place on the 10th instant, all the cadets marched out and made a demonstration in order to show that we did not want the British to be our rulers, we carried our rifles and ammunition and went along shouting out in the streets, and intended to kill anyone who obstructed us... British troops arrived on the scene with the object of firing on us. We were ready to fight them but some Egyptian, Arab and Sudanese Officers calmed us down and prevented us firing unless the British first opened fire on us.[76]

[70] *Al-Riwāyāt*, pp. 387-92, Yoshiko Kurita, 'The Daughters of Omdurman: The Role of Women in the Sudanese Mahdist Movement and Its Significance for the Subsequent Historical Process', *JCAS Symposium Series* 2004.

[71] Al-'Āzza Muḥammad 'Abdallāh Rīḥān, tape-recorded interview with Aḥmad Ibrāhīm Diyāb, unknown date and unknown place.

[72] *Al-Riwāyāt*, pp. 397-388.

[73] Ibid., p. 182.

[74] The usual custom in writing the numerals of the Egyptian and Sudanese battalions was to use Arabic numerals for the Egyptians (e.g. 4th Egyptians) and roman numerals for the Sudanese (e.g. XIth Sudanese).

[75] Diary of Muḥammad Faḍlallāh al-Shinnāwī. I am grateful to his relative, Majdī Sumīt for showing me these documents.

[76] Translation of a letter written by cadet Ahmed Ali Rahma, Military School, Khartoum, intercepted by DC Bara, undated, Kordofan 1/12/54, NRO.

On the following day, some of the 'ringleaders' were arrested, and the other cadets were kept inside the school. Eventually, on 18 August, the rest of the cadets were transferred to a special gunboat on the Nile in an attempt to isolate them from the rest of the population pending their trial. There, they chanted and sang all day and night, and urged people to continue with demonstrations.[77]

The aftermath in Khartoum and the provinces

The events in Port Sudan and Atbara, and the demonstration of the cadets shook both the capital and the provinces. In Khartoum, the situation remained tense. On 12 August, the police persuaded workers at the docks not to hold a demonstration. On Friday 15 August, what was perhaps the largest demonstration in the capital of the whole 1924 took place.

Again, details of how it started and developed are known only from police records. At first, a small demonstration began in the morning after prayers in the great Omdurman mosque. The crowd that gathered was faced by the police, who 'had to use force before the crowd would disperse.'[78] But in the afternoon, a person carrying a green flag started another demonstration. The police tried to get hold of the man but he ran to the Egyptian Officers Club, where officers surrounded him and cheered; passers-by gathered, and when the police tried to disperse the crowd they were pelted with stones.[79] The flag-bearer was arrested, but then yet another crowd, 'estimated at between 2,000 and 3,000', formed at the central railway station; this demonstration, too, was suppressed by the police.[80] In Ewart's own words, 'large crowds of the rabble of the town collected at different times and in different places, without any preliminary organisation, but because the general atmosphere was one of insecurity and tension.'[81] Seventeen people were eventually arrested, of whom nine were boys. More detail is given on the socio-professional background of these protesters in the following chapter.

Other demonstrations were attempted again on 19 and 21 August, but each time the police intervened before people could gather. The situation was such that a British detachment of the Argyll and Sutherland Highlanders had to be dispatched to Khartoum on 22 August; previously, on 19 August, airplanes had constantly buzzed the city to deter the rioters. Increasingly, reports on the activities of the White Flag League in the provinces began to pile up on the desks of Intelligence Department employees.

In Shendi, a demonstration took place on 10 August on the occasion of the departure of the Arab Mounted Rifles who had played such a fatal role in Atbara. A second was held a few days later, on 14 August, by the

77 Gov. Khartoum Prov. to Private Secretary, the Palace, 18.8.1924, Palace 4/10/48, NRO.
78 SMIR No. 361 August 1924, WO 33/999, NA.
79 Ibid.
80 Ibid.
81 Ewart Report, p. 164.

same four people who had organized the first, all members of the White Flag League. There the League was led by Ṭayyib Bābikr, who left a rich account, to which it is impossible to do justice here.[82]

In Kordofan, dissenters did their best to organize protests, but they were far less successful than their colleagues in eastern Sudan. In El Obeid, during the first fifteen days of August, the authorities managed to dismantle the local branch of the White Flag (see Chapter 5). The two individuals identified as its leaders were removed from the city. A demonstration was planned for 13 August to protest against the departure of one leader, but the authorities were informed beforehand and there was a heavy police presence at the railway station. The situation remained tense, however, and eventually the authorities decided to substitute the Egyptian battalion stationed there with British troops. They also sought to impress people by making an aeroplane to fly over the city, even if admittedly with limited success, as it crashed on landing![83]

News of agitations in the provinces continued to pour in, none of which is described in oral witnesses, unfortunately: in Wadi Halfa on 15 August, an activist gave a political speech at the mosque and attempted a demonstration.[84] On 16 August, in Umm Ruwaba, a small assembly composed of 'goldsmiths, merchants and employees' met the train carrying a political prisoner, a certain Muḥammad 'Alī 'Abd al-Raḥīm 'al-Saig' who was apparently the leader of the League there.[85] This local branch was subsequently dismantled. There were similar events in Dongola, in the Northern Province. On the same day, 16 August, a small demonstration was organized at the railway station to meet a White Flag League political prisoner captured in Argo.[86]

More was to come. In Abu Deleiq, between Shendi and Khartoum, rumours spread of a local Shaykh who was inciting disaffection.[87] In Abu Hamed, quite close to Merowe, the existence of a large network of protesters was disclosed.[88] Another person was denounced for talking seditiously to the Bisharin in Nurayet, on the Red Sea.[89] There is no space in this volume for a discussion of all of these events; suffice to say that between the end of July and October, anticolonial activities were recorded

[82] There, the cheers varied somewhat, as people hailed the King of Egypt, but also 'Abd al-Raḥman al-Mahdī and 'Alī al-Mīrghanī. Chronology - Appendix n. 13 in Kordofan 1/13/62, NRO; SMIR No. 361 August 1924, WO 33/999, NA; Intelligence Note on Tayeb Babiker of Shendi, Khartoum, 18.8.1924, Palace 4/10/50, NRO. This is confirmed by Ṭayyib's own account in *al-Riwāyāt*, p. 343.

[83] Telegram (Unsigned) to High Commissioner for Egypt, Cairo, 4.9.1924, FO 141/805/2, NA.

[84] Chronology - Appendix n. 13 in Kordofan 1/13/62, NRO.

[85] El Bahieir to E. G. Sarsfield Hall, Gov. Kordofan, Umm Rwaba 18.8.1924, and McLaren to Gov. Kordofan, El Obeid, 18.8 Kordofan 1/12/55; see also Kordofan 1/12/57

[86] Chronology- Appendix no. 13 in Kordofan 1/13/62, NRO.

[87] DI, Information, Khartoum, 18.7.1924, Northern Prov. 1/20/192, NRO.

[88] T. A. Leach to DC Berber, Atbara 17.8.1924, Northern Prov. 1/21/207, NRO.

[89] Gov. Berber Prov. to DC Berber, El Damer 27.9.1924, Northern Prov., 1/21/215, NRO.

in the following centres (see Appendix 2): in Northern Sudan, in Argo, Kabushiya, Delgo, Damer, and Dongola; in Western Sudan, El Fasher, Bara, Dilling, Talodi, Umm Ruwaba, and Sharkayla, (a hamlet close to El Obeid); in the Blue Nile, in Singa, Kamlin, and Hassahissa (this was, incidentally, the place where Tawfīq Sāliḥ Jibrīl was working as a sub-*mamur*), as well as in Wad Medani; in the White Nile, El Dueim, Geteina, and Kosti; and in Southern Sudan, Wau, Renk, Shembe, Kodok, and Malakal. In the Bahr al-Ghazal, a fairly substantial network of anticolonial activists was discovered between September and October.

QUIET TIMES AND HEAVY DISCUSSION

'The Secret Police are scattered like locusts'

Compared with the previous months, September and October 1924 may have seemed oddly quiet. At this point, the attitude of the government was uncompromising: signing a protest telegram was enough to lead to imprisonment. For example, Aḥmad al-Ṭrīfī al-Zubayr Bāshā relates: '...me and my nephew sent a letter to the Khartoum commissioner condemning the interdiction of demonstrations. We were arrested and put to prison. That was on 10 October 1924.'[90] In the same month, the trials of the White Flag League members began,[91] while arrests continued and intensified in Khartoum and the provinces among civilians and a few officers.[92] In particular, imprisonments involved a number of people considered to be members of a mysterious 'Workmen's League'.[93] Suspected activists who had not been arrested were closely watched and house searches were frequent. One witness observed at the end of September: 'Conditions are bad: wholesale arrests of innocent people are being made. ... The total number of arrests up to now from all districts amounts to more than 250.'[94] Even though many were released after a short period, a climate of general fear reigned; in the telling words of one witness: 'the Secret Police are scattered like locusts.'[95] The gaol of Kober became overcrowded, and many accounts relate the dire conditions in which the political prisoners were held. Finally, the government established tight censorship of all mail. One letter intercepted at the end of September mentioned that it was pointless to print circulars in Cairo, 'because it is very difficult to pass them through Halfa'.[96]

This turning of the screw led activists to cease visible protest. The only

90 *Al-Riwāyāt*, p. 522.

91 *The White Flag Trials*, p. 2.

92 For a list of the arrests in Khartoum, see DI, Khartoum to SA, Cairo, 4.9.1924, FO 141/805/2, NA.

93 Report from Gov. Khartoum to DI, Khartoum 31.(8).1924 Palace 4/9/44; and DI to Private Secretary, Khartoum, 12.9.1924, Palace 4/10/48, both in NRO.

94 Censored Letters, Nashid to Negib Eff Ghubriel, 24.9.1924, Kordofan1/14/68, NRO.

95 Censored Letters, Mohammed Ratib to Yousuf Eff. Hussein, Cairo, 25.9.1924, Kordofan 1/14/68, NRO.

96 DI to SA, 23.9.1924, Palace 4/9/45, NRO.

attempt at mobilizing people again was an abortive demonstration in Khartoum on 21 September, which was repressed immediately. This event took place after a wave of imprisonments of artisans and wage-workers that had occurred just few days earlier, all members of the 'Workmen's League', and this last abortive demonstration was also dominated by labourers: the five people arrested were a cook, a washer-man, a fishmonger, a coffee stall keeper, and a boy employed in a coffee shop.[97]

On the other hand, the activists resorted to underground activities. Anonymous political texts began to circulate again, in a fashion similar to the period between 1919 and 1923. They were signed with the name of various societies – but never with that of the White Flag League – the most frequent of which was, tellingly, a 'Society of the Sudan Union'. These texts were to remind the Intelligence Department that the national movement was not dead.

The South

As things quietened down in Northern Sudan, the end of August marked the beginning of a new wave of disturbances in Southern Sudan. Contrary to agitations in the rest of the country, in the South events were initiated by army officers. No first-hand accounts have survived, except in colonial papers, so that the history of this period is inevitably sketchy.

The first disturbance took place at Wau and it is known as 'the flag incident'. At the end of August, the local British authority substituted an old Egyptian green flag with a red civilian flag, pending 'the supply of the new Egyptian green flag for use at the Mudiriya.'[98] In response, a group of officers sent a protest telegram to the Egyptian Ministry of War, complaining about the hauling down of the flag. Two Egyptian officers were held responsible for that, *Mulazim Awal* (First Lieutenant) Aḥmad Fawzī and *Mulazim Tani* (Second Lieutenant) Maḥmūd Ra'fat and were repatriated to Egypt.[99] This event led the authority to suspect that a local branch of the League existed in Wau; and indeed, with the help of a double agent, they managed to learn of its organization and intentions. The leader was an army officer, Farajallāh Muḥammad, who in June was mentioned in one report as the contact of the White Flag in El Fashir, where he was stationed before to be sent to Wau.[100] As elsewhere in Sudan, however, at this stage his objectives were somewhat limited: 'At the present time he says they are afraid to do anything openly as the recent arrests etc had frightened them, but they want to collect signatures from the Chiefs and people to a petition demanding that the Sudan should be given to Egypt.'[101] However, as it was impossible to provide evidence against Farajallāh and his associates, which included not only, once more, Zayn al-'Ābdīn 'Abd al-Tām, but also the

[97] Copy of telegram, DI, Khartoum, to SA, Cairo, Khartoum 23.9.1924, FO 141/805/2, NA.
[98] SMIR No. 361 August 1924, WO 33/999, NA.
[99] Assistant AG to Private Secretary, Military Secretary, Civil Secretary, etc, Headquarters Egyptian Army, Khartoum, 21.9.1924, FO 141/669/8, NA.
[100] Intelligence information, 28.6.1924, Palace 4/10/49, NRO.
[101] Telegram from Gov. Wau to Civsec, Khartoum, 9.10.1924, Palace 4/9/46, NRO.

soon-to-be famous Ḥassan Faḍl al-Mūlā, the usual method was adopted, and Farajallāh was warned and transferred to Malakal.[102]

Thus, agitation moved to Malakal. The events in this location were more serious and worrying than those of Wau, but due to a bottleneck in the flow of information, the government managed to keep them fairly low key, including accounts in official reports. On 22 September, some army people (names unknown) from the 13th Sudanese Battalion organized a parade in which they held a picture of King Fu'ād. In the days that followed, as retaliation to their arrest, there was an attempt to set fire to the British headquarters, and another demonstration on 25 September. It is at this point, upon receiving the news that the officers were trying to convince their men to revolt, the British authorities realized with great anxiety that all their COs and NCOs, both Sudanese and Egyptians, were disaffected. The men did not follow them, however: a large-scale mutiny was avoided, an event that could have been disastrous in a region where the colonial rule was still as indecisive as in Upper Nile. As a British officer complained, 'We have been through a beastly time and almost the worst was that we did not know whom to trust at first.'[103] Only after the arrival of a Royal Leicestershire Regiment on September 30 could the mutinous officers be arrested; they were sentenced to 18 months of prison and dismissal from the army.[104]

Moderates into radicals

Although the situation in the north remained quiet, the incidents of the previous months had a dramatic impact on the political arena, although adequate attention to this has never been paid to this phase in studies on 1924.

It is evident that the events of August brought about a change in the political sensibilities of the local Sudanese establishment. Senior Sudanese officers, religious notables such as the three *sadā'*, leading merchants, and so on, reconsidered their position – not so much as regards the White Flag League and its supporters, which they continued to regard as illegitimate political actors – but rather towards what they could and should ask of the Sudanese Government. There were several reasons: first, the political incidents of the past months placed the British more in need that ever before of the loyalty of their Sudanese allies. This gave the latter unusually wide bargaining powers. Second, the notables felt that they were being overtaken by events and that their political role was de facto downplayed by the 'vociferous party': the White Flag League had been in the spotlight for months. Although they had been regularly consulted by senior British officers informally, they had been unable to foresee the

[102] For CSO&AG, to OC District, Khartoum 27.9.1924, FO 141/669/8, NA

[103] KPC Struvé to MacMichael, Malakal, 27.9.1924, Palace 4/9/46, NRO.

[104] On Malakal, see: SMIR No. 362, September 1924, WO 33/999, NA. Telegram Gov. Upper Nile Prov. HH Latem (?) Bimb. of OC XII Sudanese, Malakal 30.12.1925, UNP 1/25/192; Telegram Knapp Bey to CSO&AG, Malakal 24.9.1924, Palace 4/9/45, Telegram Knapp Bey, Malakal, to CSO&AG, Khartoum, 8.10.1924, Palace 4/9/46, Knapp Bey to Civsec 24.9.1924, Palace 4/9/45, all in NRO.

current evolution of the situation, not to mention influence it. Now they felt that they had to play their hand.

There were various signs that made this change visible. The notables gathered several times in Khartoum and Omdurman to discuss the political situation. The Intelligence Department got wind of these meetings, but probably only after that they had taken place. The first event was a tea party organized by the Grand Mufti on 22 August, and a second was held at the home of a notable named 'Abd al-Ḥalīm al-Aṭbānī on 8 September. These were followed by two meetings, held by shaykh Abū Zāyd Sulaymān on 9 September, and by *sayyid* Aḥmad Suwar al-Dahab, the most important trader of the capital, about two weeks later.[105]

The Intelligence Department reported in depth on only the first of these meetings, because the Egyptian press had heard about it and published an article claiming that that *sayyid* 'Alī al-Mīrghanī had 'held a meeting in favour of Zaghlūl.'[106] Some of the individuals who participated in this meeting, as shaykh Abū al-Qāsim, the head of the board of the '*Ulamā*', or Aḥmad Suwar al-Dahab, were the same people who had attended the gathering on 10 June at the house of *sayyid* 'Abd al-Raḥman al-Mahdī in al-'Abbāsiyya. The document that was produced after this second event, however, was radically different from the 'Declaration' drafted at the first. The notables put forward the following demands:

> Firstly: that the sugar trade should be handed over to native merchants.
> Secondly: that taxes and rates should be reduced.
> Thirdly: that Martial Law should be suppressed.
> Fourthly: that a certain number of native members be elected to sit on the Governor-General's Council, and will be free to give their opinions.
> Fifthly: that the duties of the Municipal Council should be limited to a certain extent and that the current members should be relieved by more efficient men.
> Sixthly: that the Gezira Scheme should be modified.[107]

Sayyid 'Alī al-Mīrghanī eventually convinced the other notables by some sleight of hand to await submission of this document until the conclusion of the negotiations between Egypt and Britain. A step was taken, nonetheless. When informed of the meeting, Viscount Edmund Allenby, the High Commissioner to Egypt noted that it was almost incredible that 'natives of considerable standing in Omdurman should have been ready to discuss proposals of such a nature and to consider the possibility of withholding their support from the Government if those proposals were not favourably received.'[108] Legal Secretary Sterry also reported:

> If we get a satisfactory end of negotiations we shall have to meet in some way our subjects desire to jaw and give some facilities for it on the lines of Municipal Council. Sheikh Ismail El Azhari told MacMichael in a heart to heart talk that ... it would be a good thing to establish consultative bodies in the provinces....[109]

105 Chronology - Appendix no. 13 in Kordofan 1/13/62, NRO.
106 Copy of telegram, Skrine to More, 10.9.1924, Palace 4/9/44, NRO.
107 Copy of telegram, DI, Khartoum, to SA, Cairo, 2.9.1924, FO 141/805/1, NA.
108 The Residency, Ramleh, to J. R. MacDonald, 20.9.1924, Palace 4/9/46, NRO.
109 Extract from a letter from Mr. Sterry to Mr. More, Cairo, 21.9.1924, FO 141/669/8, NA.

The balance of power was shifting, and the government had to face the consequences. The idea that some form of political participation by the Sudanese had to be integrated into the current system of government was taking shape in the minds of senior officers. One report in September also observed that the notables were 'manoeuvring for tactical positions in view of possible *constitutional* developments'.[110]

The issue of creating consultative bodies was raised several times during the following months.[111] At the beginning of October, Governor General Lee Stack consulted Legal Secretary Sterry from London on the possibility of issuing the following proclamation: 'the Government takes this opportunity of announcing that in future leading natives throughout the Provinces will be enlisted to a greater extent in advisory and consultative capacities.'[112] In the event, this note was not published for fear that it might be interpreted by pro-Egyptian supporters as a sign of the government's weakness. However, a broad agreement emerged among senior British officials on the importance of implementing it. Stack also suggested to Sterry: '...if you think fit[,] prominent natives who have raised that question such as Hussein Sharif might be told privately that is our intention to deal with it.'[113]

The idea was that once Stack had returned to Khartoum after the end of negotiations with Zaghlūl, the government would have put itself to the task of drafting a policy on native councils. Huddleston, the Assistant Governor General noted:

> I share your opinion as to non-reference to policy of forming native Councils and importance of putting it into practice as soon as possible after your return. Comments from Governors are mostly in and are distinctly favourable. As ... the idea is popular it is important to lose no time in starting the scheme before extraneous pressure begins. It will be complete by the time you return.[114]

All these activities demonstrate the extent to which the political pressure placed on the government by the events of August was bearing fruit. But fate and the actions of Egyptian extremists decided otherwise: Stack was assassinated before he returned to Sudan.

THE FINAL OUTBREAK

Just as the beginning of the protests in Sudan corresponded to the coming to power of two new governments in Britain and in Egypt, so their end coincided with a steady weakening of the same governments. The eagerly awaited negotiations between Great Britain and Egypt on the Sudan

[110] Telegram Skrine to More, 10.9.1924, FO 141/805/2, NA, my italics.
[111] Extract from a letter from Mr. Sterry to Mr More, Cairo, 21.9.1924, FO 141/669/8, NA.
[112] Copy of telegram from Stack, London, to Sterry, Khartoum, 7.10.1924, Palace 4/10/46, NRO. Various letters were exchanged between Stack and other British authorities on this issue, all in Palace 4/10/46, NRO.
[113] Ibid.
[114] Copy of telegram, Huddleston, Hakiman, Khartoum, to Stack, London, 8.10.1924, Palace 4/10/46, NRO.

question which were scheduled to start in London on 25 September broke down within just a few days and Zaghlūl hurriedly left London 'due to the inclement weather', as was sarcastically noted.[115] At around the same time, the British press broke a scandal involving the Labour Party which contributed to the crisis in its Government, and eventually led to its fall in early November.

The line adopted by the Sudan Government to explain unrest in Sudan to London had been to attribute full responsibility for the events to Egypt. Governor-General Stack was at pains to convince MacDonald that the only solution to these political problems was to eliminate the Egyptian component from Sudan. If the Condominium could not be terminated, at least the symbols of Egyptian sovereignty in Sudan had to be outshone, and the first and most important step was to get rid of Egyptian officers and soldiers. He noted in a memorandum written few days before his assassination that 'practically all of the young Sudanese officers' had been converted into nationalists by their Egyptian colleagues, and that the situation of the army had to be 'cleared up'.[116] The Sudanese Government demanded that command of the Egyptian Army be split in two, creating one *sirdar* (Commander-in-Chief) for Egypt and another for Sudan. Were this condition not to be met, the government was prepared to withdraw the Egyptian Army from Sudan unilaterally.[117]

However, no matter how much the British establishment in Sudan wanted this withdrawal, it was downright impossible. The Egyptian Government's direct involvement in events in Sudan could not be proved; Egypt would have interpreted a withdrawal as a direct attack on its rights of sovereignty in Sudan, as stated in the Condominium Agreement of 1899. Stack therefore reported:

> Owing to [the] approaching dissolution of Parliament, Mr MacDonald felt unable to take the drastic measure of evacuating the Egyptian Army from the Sudan, *which would be tantamount to declaring war with Egypt.*[118]

Then, while on his way from London to Khartoum, stopping off for a few days in Cairo, on 19 November 1924 Governor General Stack was shot dead by a member of an Egyptian extremist organization.[119]

As is well known, his assassination finally gave the British authorities carte blanche for their demands. The High Commissioner to Egypt Allenby forwarded a seven-point 'ultimatum' to the Egyptian Government that

[115] Daly, *Empire on the Nile*, p. 152, quoting Schuster to More, 23.10.1924.
[116] Memorandum on the Position of the Sudan, 8.11.1924 FO 407/199, NA, 278-279.
[117] Detailed plans for the withdrawal of the Egyptian Army and the formation of a new army – the Sudan Defence Force – had been laid out months before the assassination of Stack, so that when the latter was killed, all was ready to evacuate the Egyptian battalions from Sudan. Memorandum, Enclosures in n. 167, Major General Sir L. Stack to Mr. MacDonald, 18.8.1924, FO 407/199, NA.
[118] Report of a telegram from Stack, London, to Hakiman, Khartoum, 8.10.1924, Palace 4/9/46, NRO, my italics.
[119] For details about the dynamic of the event, see Badrawi, *Political Violence in Egypt*, pp. 200-206.

the historian M. W. Daly defines as 'a catch all for every irritant to British interests in Egypt and the Sudan'.[120] It included, among other things, the immediate withdrawal of the Egyptian Army, an extension of the budget for the Gezira project from the current 300,000 feddans to an unlimited amount, payment of a large fine, and a public apology. Even though the Egyptian Government rejected the ultimatum, it still marked a complete political victory for Britain. Zaghlūl, the great enemy of the British, had to resign from his position as Prime Minister, never to return to power. He died a few years later, in 1927. The Sudan Government proceeded to eliminate the elements that symbolized Egyptian sovereignty over Sudan.

Upon Zaghlūl's rejection of the ultimatum, the plan to withdraw the Egyptian battalions from Sudan was carried out immediately. On 24 November, the 3rd and 4th Egyptian Battalions and the Egyptian Artillery stationed in Khartoum were surrounded by British troops while the evacuation plan began. According to the Sudan Monthly Intelligence Report for November, 'the IVth Battalion, after a great deal of difficulty, and not before they had been threatened with machine guns, consented to move' but the 3rd Battalion and the Artillery 'refused to leave unless they received orders to do so from the Egyptian Government.'[121] Egyptian troops began being evacuated from the provinces as well; tensions were running high everywhere, but it was only in Talodi, in the Nuba Mountains, that they led to a potentially serious crisis.

While the Egyptian troops were being evacuated, a number Sudanese officers stationed in Talodi requested that they be deported together with the Egyptians, and in consequence were arrested.[122] They escaped from prison, took possession of all the ammunition, and began a demonstration, weapons in hand, joined by Egyptian officers. The situation cooled down somewhat, but the town remained under the control of the mutineers.[123] The officers resumed their duties and 'took charge of the order and discipline' while still holding the town.[124] The situation was only resolved when the officers received news from Khartoum that the Egyptian Ministry of War had ordered the Egyptian officers to withdraw, and negotiations began between the British and the various Egyptian and Sudanese officers. Eventually, all the officers agreed to hand over the ammunition and leave the town.[125] Troops were despatched from Khartoum over the days that followed, to arrest the mutinous officers and ensure the completion of the evacuation.[126]

The second event that clearly signalled the high levels of tension caused by the withdrawal of the Egyptian Army was the rioting at the

120 M. W. Daly, *Empire on the Nile*, p. 155.

121 Diary of Events Affecting the Sudan subsequent to the Murder of Sir Lee Stack, 19th to 39th November 1924, Appendix 1 to SMIR No. 364, November 1924, WO 33/999, NA.

122 Telegram, CSO&AG Khartoum to Spinks, Cairo, 26.11.1924, Palace 4/11/54, NRO.

123 C. District, Talodi, to CSO&AG, Khartoum, 26.11.1924, Palace 4/11/54, NRO.

124 Ibid.

125 Report by the Director of Prisons, Khartoum, 6.12.1924, FO 141/494/3, NA.

126 The whole file Palace 4/11/54 is dedicated to this mutiny.

civilian prison of Khartoum North, Kober, where political prisoners were held, including White Flag League members and supporters, some cadets from the Military School, and other non-political prisoners. Conditions inside the prison had been poor for a long time, and the treatment of prisoners was harsh and humiliating, as painfully recalled in the memoirs of those who experienced it.[127] They were kept in chains, could walk very little, ate badly, and hardly slept; they were kept awake by the yelling of people afflicted by psychiatric problems who were kept in the same prison: needless to say this was not the heyday of psychiatric treatment in Sudan. Prisoners could not bathe and were covered in lice; to be washed, they were simply stripped naked and hosed down.

On 18 November, a number of prisoners began a hunger strike in protest against such conditions, and two days later, they demanded to have their chains removed. The intensity of their demonstrations escalated after the news broke of the death of Stack and the plans of withdrawal of the army. Finally, on the morning of 24 November, while the 4th Egyptian Battalion and the Artillery were refusing to be moved pending direct orders from Egypt, the cadets began the mutiny by breaking out of their cells. They released the other prisoners, armed themselves with sticks and iron bars, and took control of the prison interior. Their plan was to hold it until they could be rescued by the army, as they were confident that the whole Egyptian army would have revolted.[128] During the mutiny of the 11th Battalion, they were kept constantly informed of what was going on through the cadets, who signalled back and forth with the Egyptian Artillery, and also stole signals from British battalions.[129]

The prison mutiny died down without bloodshed. The government authorities acted carefully, avoiding violence, also because 'had a single shot been fired from the prison, the Egyptian Artillery and Infantry [also stationed in Khartoum North] would have become involved.'[130] The prisoners continued to send messages asking for help from the Egyptian battalions, but the latter did not take action, surrounded as they were by British troops and unwilling to start fire. One of the ex-cadets who took part in the prison mutiny, Muzammil 'Alī Dinār, commented on the behaviour of Egyptians thus:

> Yes, I had the feeling at that time that the Egyptians betrayed us, but I was not so deceived after all, because in any case the whole matter is our country and it is our concern more than their one.[131]

Finally, on 1 December, exhausted and starving, the prisoners surrendered.

[127] Many witnesses have described conditions in the prison. One of the most detailed accounts is by Muzammil 'Alī Dinār, *Al-Riwāyāt*, pp. 45 *et seq.*; see also Sayyid, *Al-Liwā' al-Abiaḍ*, in particular p. 58 onwards.
[128] 3rd Witness for Prosecution, Kapsun el Gak, Palace 4/1/51, NRO, and Précis of Events in Central Prison, FO 141/494/3, NA.
[129] *Al-Riwāyāt*, p. 53.
[130] Report by the Director of Prisons, Sudan Govt., on mutiny in the Central Prison, Khartoum North, Khartoum, 6.12.1924, FO 141/494/3, NA.
[131] *Al-Riwāyāt*, p. 53.

While the prison riot was going on, the most serious event of 1924 took place: the mutiny of the 11th Sudanese Battalion. It was not unexpected, at least for Sudanese activists:

> ...for a week before, since the Sirdar's death and proposed removal of Egyptian troops, the whole place was full of rumours of Sudanese units joining up with Egyptian troops. You couldn't pick a Sudanese officer who hasn't been approached by Egyptians and hear the plot discussed ad nauseam.[132]

On 27 November, the letter from the Defence Ministry in Cairo that Egyptian battalions were waiting in order to leave Khartoum finally arrived, and the evacuation began. The dynamics were similar to those in Talodi. Some Sudanese officers, stationed in Khartoum, manifested their intention to be evacuated with the Egyptian battalions.[133] Officer 'Abd al-Faḍīl al-Māẓ was the first to leave the Khartoum barracks, and moved from there with two platoons of his 11th Battalion, but instead of joining the Egyptian troops in Khartoum North, he moved westwards. They first went to the Military Prison, where they were joined by Sayyid Faraḥ, the officer in charge, and his soldiers – about 30 men. From the Military Prison, they moved further west towards the Musketry School, where the two officers were joined by four others, Thābit 'Abd al-Raḥīm, 'Ali al-Bannā, Ḥassan Faḍl al-Mūlā and Sulaymān Muḥammad.[134] They commandeered a stock of ammunition and weapons kept in the Arms Store at the school.

From there, the six officers and their men, amounting to no more than 200 individuals, moved eastwards towards the bridge between Khartoum and Khartoum North to join the Egyptian troops. On their way, they met a British officer, named Cowan. When asked what they intended to do, they replied, 'To join our brothers of the 3rd Battalion in Khartoum North.'[135] Cowan told them that he would only allow the officers to go to Khartoum North, but not the men. The officers refused, and continued their march. After some time, they were met by Huddleston, the Acting Governor General and *sirdar* of the army after the death of Stack, who confronted them with a British platoon, already in firing positions. Huddleston asked the mutineers if they were willing to take orders from him, but they refused, stating that they would only take orders from an Egyptian superior officer. At this point, Huddleston gave his men the order to open fire,[136] which was returned by the mutineers, 'but their shooting was inaccurate and high and [provoked] no casualties.'[137] The mutineers took

132 Statement of Ali Mohammed Effendi El Banna, taken down by Newbold, 4.12.1924, FO 141/494/3, NA.

133 Besides the various witnesses mentioned, a good summary of the events may be found in Charles W. Gwynn, *Imperial Policing* (London: Macmillan & Co, 1934), pp. 150-180.

134 C.A. Willis, the Mutiny of 27th and 28th November 1924, Khartoum, 22.12.1924, Northern Prov., 2/21/211, NRO, and also Statement by MT Hassan Fadl al Mula, Camel Corps, FO 141/494/3, NA.

135 The Mutiny of 27th and 28th November 1924, Appendix 2 to SMIR No. 364, November 1924, WO 33/999, NA.

136 Second Witness for Prosecution, at the summary Court Martial, El Lewa Huddleston Pasha, Khartoum, 3.12.1924 FO 141/494/3, NA.

137 The Mutiny of 27th and 28th November 1924, Appendix 2 to SMIR No. 364,

refuge in the Military Hospital of Khartoum and the shooting continued from 6 p.m. to 10 p.m. 'Abd al-Faḍīl al-Māẓ, who had been wounded, was killed in the hospital by a Syrian doctor, who in turn was murdered by one of al-Māẓ's men. Other men joined the mutineers during the late afternoon, but when further volunteers, such as officers and men from the Army Transport Company, tried to do the same, they were intercepted by the British and turned away.

After an overnight break, the Sudanese officers resumed fire at dawn. The British responded, but as their continuous fire was insufficient to repulse the officers, the artillery was brought up to the Military Hospital. A Howitzer demolished most of the hospital, and the British troops attempted to rush it, but the Sudanese who were still alive inside it continued firing fiercely. According to Huddleston, who led the offensive, 'it was only after four hours continuous slow shell fire, bombing, machine gun fire, and rifle fire that all fire ceased and house was occupied without further casualties.'[138] In the end, the casualties were as high on the British side as they were among the mutineers. Six British COs and NCOs were killed, as well as other ranks. The resistance put up by the mutineers was described by all as exceptional, and some of them, including the leaders of the mutiny, managed to leave the hospital alive in spite of the fact that the shelling had lasted for many hours.

On the following day, the mutinous officers Thābit 'Abd al-Raḥīm, 'Alī al-Bannā, Ḥassan Faḍl al-Mūlā and Sulaymān Muḥammad handed themselves over to the authorities; only one of them, Sayyid Faraḥ, ran away to Egypt. During the trial, the four officers all related similar stories. A few days before the mutiny, rumours had been spreading among Sudanese officers that the Egyptian Artillery and other Egyptian battalions were ready for a mutiny. One such rumour was that Rif'at Bey, an Egyptian senior artillery officer, had written a letter to 'Abd al-Faḍīl al-Māẓ, stating: 'I have issued [an] order to all Sudanese units of the Egyptian Army, and as soon as I hear a shot fired I will fire on the Fort, the Palace and the British Barracks.'[139]

No Egyptian troops moved, however. It is hard to understand why. Was it impossible militarily because the Egyptian troops were surrounded; did they lacked the right leadership, or was it a case of a lack of coordination and communication, or simply betrayals amongst the officers? In any event, the Sudanese mutineers were abandoned, and despite their exceptional resistance, they were annihilated. The four mutinous officers were condemned to death, and the sentence was carried out on 5 December.

(contd) November 1924, WO 33/999, NA. According to another witness, Fūmī Jāmā, there were few casualties because one of the men had managed to cut the electricity cables so that there was not enough light to shoot accurately. *Al-Riwāyāt*, p. 27

138 Telegram, Huddleston to Spinks, 28.11.1924, FO 141/494/3, NA

139 Statement by Mulazim Awal Suleiman Effendi Mohammed, Camel Corps, in Notes of information give to the DI, Sudan Govt., Khartoum, on 2nd of December 1924, FO 141/494/3. NA. See also the Proceeding of a Summary Court-Martial on Active Service held at Khartoum on December 3rd 1924, Sterry to Allenby, Khartoum, 7.12.1924, FO 141/9494/3, NA.

Only 'Alī al-Bannā was spared at the last minute, his sentence commuted to 15 years in prison.[140]

The death sentences not only marked the end of the 1924 revolution, but also that of an institution, the Egyptian Army. It had been central to the history of Sudan since the Anglo-Egyptian 're-conquest,' and of a whole system of government that had profoundly relied on this institution. As al-'Āzza put it, 'the battle of Al-Māẓ ... turned everything upside down and everything changed after it.'[141] Moreover, the execution of these young brilliant officers provoked a general shock. In his personal diary, Baily, Deputy Governor of Khartoum, himself admittedly in a state of nervous breakdown, recorded that the execution squad, made up of officers reputed for their excellence, was so distressed that the men repeatedly missed the target. After three rounds of fire, one of the three officers, Thābit 'Abd al-Raḥīm, was still alive and had to be shot with a handgun.[142]

[140] Extract from the Army Orders, Khartoum Headquarters, 7.12.1924, FO 141/494/3, NA.

[141] *Al-Riwāyāt*, p. 389.

[142] Baily's diary, 5 December 1924, 422/13/23, Sudan Archive, Durham University.

4

The White Flag League: The Structure of the National Movement

There are a number of enigmatic features about how events unfolded in 1924. First, it is quite bewildering to observe the rapidity with which the movement, started by a handful of people based in Khartoum, spread in Sudan, attaining a variety of social groups in both rural and urban locations. Second, the most serious events occurred after the leaders of White Flag League had been imprisoned. The various demonstrations from August onwards appear at first sight as 'spontaneous' ocurrences. However, not only were they organized beforehand, but also none of them was disconnected from the network of activists surrounding the White Flag League: looking carefully, one might observe that either members or close supporters of the League were always within reach if not at the very heart of riots and demonstrations.

These aspects go hand in hand with the fact that it is particularly difficult for a historian to grasp how this society functioned. Even if the White Flag League chose a strategy of visibility and above all accountability, it was still structured as a secret society. Once more, that shapes the nature of the sources. The overwhelming majority comes from judicial records fed by informants who were at times quite dubious. The Intelligence Department was aware of that, but they simply needed their accounts. As for local and oral sources, the members and supporters of the White Flag rarely discussed directly or in detail the organization of the League and its sister organizations. Not only did few people know exactly how it worked and who were its members, but also members of the League and of other secret societies swore an oath of secrecy to which many remained bound until death.

Because direct testimonies about the organization of the League are unavailable, the historian can only reconstruct them by being sensitive to small fragments, then by searching for other ways to approach this problem. One such is to uncover the structure of society from patterns of participation in protests. Of course, when a historical fact can only be revealed from the existence of a pattern, it is impossible to know whether it is merely due to chance or coincidence, and even whether it only exists in the mind of the historian who is searching for it. However, sometimes, as in this case, a pattern is all we have.

By following this approach, it is hoped to achieve a number of goals: first, to add nuance and deepen historical knowledge of how the White Flag League worked. It is almost undisputed in historiography that the League was a small, elite, unorganized movement: small because it allegedly included no more than just over a hundred members; elite, because it is believed that its members were mostly drawn from the 'Effendi', that is, educated Sudanese working as government officers and officials; finally, it was disorganized because it was easily dismantled only a month after the demonstrations began. In this chapter, I shall argue that this image is distorted by the very organization of the League, which actually had a very complex and multi-layered structure. This is why, from its early phase, the 1924 Revolution was an uprising of railway workers, dockworkers, small traders, and so on, as much as of the educated elites.

A study of the composition and structure of the League is important at another level. The organization of social movements also has an expressive value, which communicates a movement's ideological identity in a performative manner. For instance, the need for the Sudanese to unite was both vocally expressed during, and performed through, demonstrations. In these events Sudanese of different extractions all shared the same risk of being imprisoned for their ideas. To quote sociologists Jasper and Polletta, in a social movement 'strategic choices are not simply neutral decisions about what will be most effective... they are statements about identity.'[1] Thus, the organization of the League was an important means of expression of its ideology.

THE COMPOSITION AND ORGANIZATION OF THE WHITE FLAG LEAGUE

The White Flag League presents another enigma. All in all, about 920 names of protesters appear at least once in the colonial sources consulted. If to this we add those mentioned in local Sudanese lists, the total number exceeds 1,100. However, it is certain from the records, both oral and colonial, that the majority were not members of the White Flag League.[2] For example, of the many people interviewed in *Al-Riwāyāt*, only six declared themselves as members of the White Flag.[3] Taking into account

1 Francesca Polletta and James Jasper, 'Collective Identity and Social Movements', *Annual Review of Sociology*, vol. 27, p. 293.

2 It is very difficult to ascertain to what extent this figure represents the actual number of protesters. On the one hand, there were personal vendettas, and some of the people who appear in the colonial records were probably not actually involved in politics; on the other, even these hundreds of names still do not include certain political activists who are commonly associated with 1924, such as the beloved nationalist singer Khalīl Faraḥ or Mudaththir al-Būshī, who described himself as one of the main activists of Wad Medani. At least three people whose interviews are included in *Al-Riwāyāt* are never mentioned in colonial records: Mudaththir al-Būshī, Qasim al-Sayyid Khalafallāh and 'Alī Sayyid Aḥmad Rakhā.

3 Muḥammad 'Abd al-Mun'im Zāyd, Aḥmad Ṣabrī Zāyd, 'Alī Malāsī, Ṭayyib Bābikr, Zayn al-'Ābdīn 'Abd al-Tām, Aḥmad al-Ṭrīfī Zubayr Pasha.

all the various lists of White Flag members (see Appendix 2) found by the Intelligence Department, the total number of White Flag League members approaches 200. And yet, some of the most prominent political activists are not included in any of these records. Hence it is impossible to draw up a definitive list of members.

How, then, can a historian assess the composition of political protests in 1924? What was the difference between members and supporters of the League, and how to distinguish them? This section and the following will demonstrate that this problem is directly linked to how the movement worked and was organized. The League was able to spread the movement nationwide, by creating a very flexible structure capable of effectively disseminating radical anticolonial political ideas.

The Leaders of the White Flag

How did the League succeed in spreading so fast? How could only five people, imprisoned after two weeks from the beginning of their activities, ignite Sudan? The first element of the answer is found in the composition of the White Flag League.

Of the many lists of members that have survived in private or public archives, there is a short one that can be identified as authentic. Before ʻAlī ʻAbd al-Laṭīf was arrested, he burnt most of the documents in his possession. Others were destroyed later, whenever the family had to submit to house searches. The few texts that have survived did so because of the courage of al-ʻĀzza, his wife, who kept them on her person all the time, hidden in her clothes. One of these is an early list of members of the White Flag. It is undated and unsigned, but can be ascribed to the end of June, before the first wave of arrests. It names 20 individuals, and is divided into three parts: a first group of five, indicated as the *markazia 1* (the first committee), five more members of *markazia 2* (the second committee), and finally ten other names.

Cross-checking this list with the Intelligence Department's records (local oral and written accounts do not offer such detailed information on the socio-professional background of activists), a clear picture of these very early members of the movement emerges. Four out of the five members of the first committee, Ṣāliḥ ʻAbd al-Qādir, ʻUbayd al-Ḥājj al-Amīn, Ḥassan Sharīf, Ḥassan Ṣāliḥ, were civilian government employees. They all worked, or had worked, for the same Post and Telegraph Department. Only ʻAlī ʻAbd al-Laṭīf had been an officer in the Egyptian Army. They had all attended colonial schools in Khartoum or Omdurman. Ṣāliḥ ʻAbd al-Qādir and ʻAlī ʻAbd al-Laṭīf were between 30-35 years old, the other three between 25-30. They were relatively young, but it should not be forgotten that at this age they had already been employed for ten years or more (the starting age for work was usually 17 for educated people at that time: see Chapter 8). At least two of the men were already married with children. They were a fairly homogeneous group in terms of education and employment, in that they all worked for the colonial State. The only varying element of their social background was their family and geographical origins. As discussed earlier, ʻAlī's origins were with the

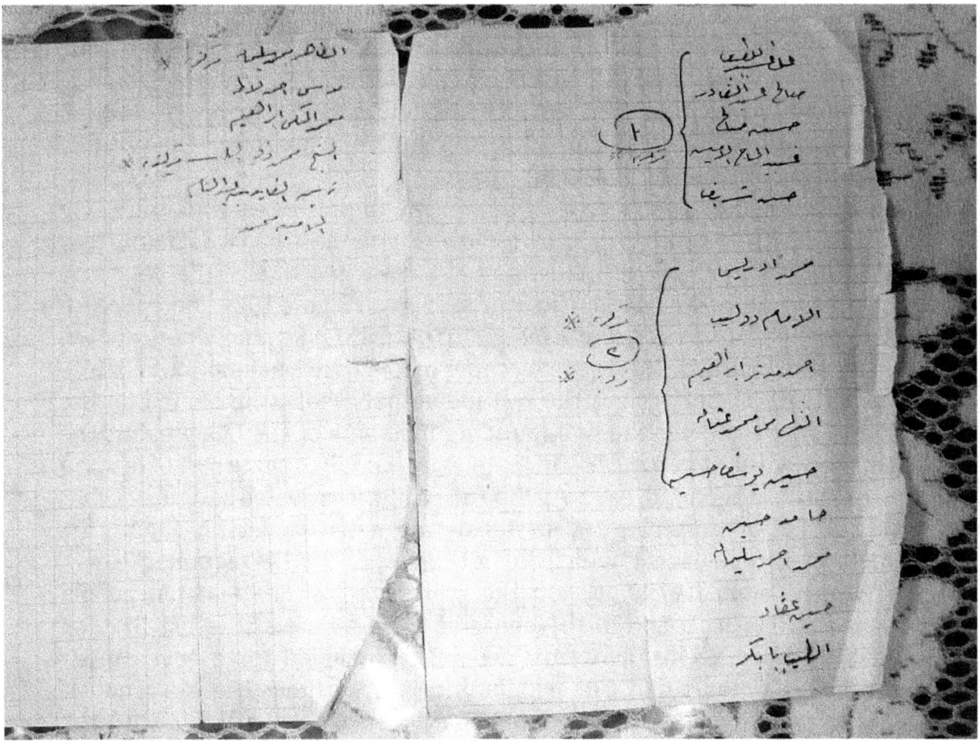

Fig 5 List of White Flag Members, 1924
(Photo taken by the author in the house of the family of 'Alī 'Abd al-Laṭīf in Thawra, Omdurman, on 30 February 2005, by permission of Durriyya 'Abdallāh Rīhān, grand-daughter of 'Alī 'Abd al-Laṭīf)

Dinka and Nuba; Ṣāliḥ 'Abd al-Qādir's father came from Metemma and his mother's family from Anatolia; 'Ubayd al-Ḥājj al-Amīn's family was based in Omdurman and had a Nubian background; and the two others were described as having a mixed Egyptian descent.

In contrast to the relative homogeneity of the first committee, the *markazia 2* was more diverse. The first of the five names on the list is Muḥammad Idrīs Bābikr. His personal record described him as being a Ja'ali, a graduate of Omdurman Primary School, and employed as a telephonist in the village of Singa, in the Blue Nile.[4] The second individual, al-Imām Dūlayb, was described as a 'social asset' for the League, as he came from a well-known religious family of Kordofan.[5] He was himself a religious man who had worked as a government employee, but in 1924 he had no post. Next, there was Aḥmad Mudaththir Ibrāhīm, a telephone operator at the Government Palace, who belonged to a famous family that was closely related to the Mahdī. In contrast, the fourth member, Al-Tuhāmī

[4] Notes on the Signatories. Enclosed in: Translation of a Telegram to His Excellency the Governor General, 3.6.1924. FO 141/810/3, NA.

[5] On this family, see Harold A. MacMichael, *A History of the Arabs in the Sudan* (London: F. Cass, 1967 [1922]), pp. 333-34, and O'Fahey, *Arabic Literature of Africa. Vol. III*, pp. 20-21.

Muḥammad 'Uthmān, was a carpenter, and according to the British a man 'of no standing or position'. He was described as a Shayqi or as a Ja'ali. The fifth member, Ḥusayn Yūsif Ḥusayn, was the owner of a small bakery and a contractor for the canteen of the 9th Sudanese Battalion. Other than being listed as the son of a discharged shaykh of a quarter of Omdurman, there are no further details on his origins.[6]

The relationship between the two central committees of the White Flag League is unclear. What is known, however, is that the two committees sent the first two protest telegrams, the first on 15 May (the very first telegram sent by the League) and the second on 3 June 1924. Moreover, on 18 June, the Cairo Police sent a telegram to the Intelligence Department in Khartoum, in which they gave warning of the five 'Leaders of the White Lewa [Flag] Society.' Now, the five individuals that were named by the Cairo Police were not the five founding members of the League, but the members of the *markazia 2*![7] This suggests that it had some sort of leading role. On the other hand, after 'Alī 'Abd al-Laṭīf was arrested and three other members of the *markazia 1* were transferred, a new leadership committee was formed to replace it, which did not correspond to the *markazia 2*.

A brief summary follows on the professions of the last ten people named in the list found in the house of 'Alī 'Abd al-Laṭīf (a list that, as seen, included all in all twenty people): it included three government employees (Muḥammad al-Makkī Ibrāhīm, Mūsā Aḥmad Lāz, Muḥammad Aḥmad Sulaymān), an officer (Zayn al-'Ābdīn 'Abd al-Tām), two students of religion (Muḥammad Ḍayfallāh and Muḥammad al-Amīn), a small landowner-cum-trader from Shendi (and leader of the White Flag there, Ṭayyib Bābikr), and a carpenter from the Gordon College workshops (Ḥāmid Ḥusayn). Two others (Ḥusayn 'Aqqād and Ṭāhir Muḥammad Sulaymān) never came to the attention of the Intelligence Department, so nothing is known about them.[8]

Thus, it can be observed that the League from the start was comprised of people of diverse status and professional backgrounds, with a slight majority of government employees, but with a strong popular element as well. This might suggest that the five founders deliberately sought to select people with diverse backgrounds. However, it is difficult to prove this point beyond any doubt on the basis of this document alone, because nothing is known of its history. The question must be approached from a different angle: the pattern of participation to protest.

6 Notes on the Signatories. Enclosed in: Translation of a Telegram to His Excellency the Governor General, 3.6.1924. FO 141/810/3, NA.

7 T. W. Russell, Commandant Cairo City Police, to Director General, European Parliament, Ministry of the Interior, Cairo, 18.6.1924, FO 141/806/1, NA.

8 For Muḥammad al-Makkī Ibrāhīm, Ḥāmid Ḥusayn and Mūsā Aḥmad Lāz, various references of which the longest in 'Alī Aḥmad Ṣāliḥ, 'Confession,' pp. 9–11, 28.7.1924, FO 141/805/2, NA; For Muḥammad Aḥmad Sulaymān: Corbyn to Private Secretary, Palace, 19.8.1924 Palace 4/10/48 (unless he is the person with the same name of the November mutiny); for Muḥammad Ḍayfallāh, Notes on the signatories of the telegram of 18.7.1924, FO 141/806/1, NA; Muḥammad Amīn: Ryed for SA to DI Cairo, 8.9.1924, FO 141/669/9, NA.

Members who demonstrated

In the period before it was dismantled, the White Flag League organized two main types of open protest: a campaign of petitions and a series of demonstrations. Colonial sources and judicial records allow us to reconstruct precisely who signed the telegrams of petition and who led the demonstrations: thus we can get a grasp of who did what, and why.

An analysis of the individuals arrested for making political speeches or leading demonstrations from June to September 1924 presents several interesting pieces of information (a detailed list is in Appendix 2, Table 16). This analysis takes into account all demonstrations, including those that were not organized under the aegis of the League, in order to emphasize their difference. First, none of the five founders and members of the *markazia 1* participated in any demonstration; and in fact none of them were arrested for such activity.[9] Secondly, from the moment when the League stopped supporting demonstrations, these events came to be more and more led by people from artisan, skilled worker and small merchant backgrounds; there were certainly fewer 'Effendi' – Sudanese civil servants – than in demonstrations organized by the League. Nevertheless, it is important to note that members of the *markazia 2* and some of the other people known to be League members took part in demonstrations *even after* the League had ceased supporting them. For example, al-Tuhāmī Muḥammad 'Uthmān was arrested following the demonstration of 26 June. It must be noted as well that the demonstrations that took place after 23 June can be hardly called 'spontaneous': for example, the Cadets' demonstration was prepared beforehand, and was influenced by people close to 'Alī 'Abd al-Laṭīf.[10] It should be mentioned that the people who participated in the demonstrations came mostly, but not exclusively, from Northern Sudanese groups. However, it is important to underline that this is more a reflection of the socio-professional division of roles within the national movement than evidence of the average origin of protesters, as analysed below.

Members who signed telegrams

The second strategy adopted by the White Flag League was its campaign of protest telegrams. For this chapter, the meaning and function of these telegrams is not under discussion, but only who wrote and signed them. A total of 53 signed telegrams have survived in archives in Khartoum, London, and Cairo. They were all sent between May and August 1924, mostly between June and July, after which the texts in the archives consist only of circulars and letters which were anonymous and only intended to be circulated inside Sudan.

Many telegrams were signed by the five founding members of the League. This means that the five did not go to demonstrations but were responsible for writing political texts. Five were sent by 'Alī 'Abd al-Laṭīf

9 Apparently, the only gathering at which 'Alī 'Abd al-Laṭīf was present was the first, when people assembled at the railway station to meet the 'delegation' that was intercepted in Wadi Halfa on June 17.

10 *Al-Riwāyāt*, pp. 44 and 178.

alone, and after he was imprisoned, five more were signed by 'Ubayd al-Ḥājj al-Amīn alone, as 'Vice-President of the League'.[11] After 'Ubayd, single-signature telegrams were signed by Ḥassan Sharīf (one)[12] and Ṣāliḥ 'Abd al-Qādir (two). Another such telegram was signed by 'Umar Bakhrībā, who described himself as the 'Vice-President of the White Flag in the Blue Nile'.[13] It therefore appears that single-signature telegrams were signed by people who had assumed the risk of acting as White Flag League 'spokesmen' in certain locations. Moreover, only White Flag League members could sign telegrams (but this did not apply to large petitions). According to Abd al-Karīm al-Sayyid, '...anyone who signed a telegram of protest was member of the league. Only members of the league signed such messages'.[14]

In total, more than 200 people signed at least one collective petition, and 40 signed at least one telegram either in small groups of signatories or alone. However, the same 13 people, all members of the White Flag League, signed more than the half of the texts. Their background was fairly similar. Nine of the 13 were employees of the Sudan Government in Port Sudan or Khartoum (in departments such as the Post and Telegraph Department and the Customs Department); one was a lawyer (Aḥmad 'Umar Bakhrībā, in Wad Medani); one an ex-officer ('Alī 'Abd al-Laṭīf); one a farmer-cum-trader (Ṭayyib Bābikr); and one from an unknown profession (a certain Aḥmad 'Alī, of Port Sudan[15]). As far as their origins and status were concerned, they mostly belonged to the Northern Sudanese urban middle class.

If we consider the larger number of about 200 signatories of petitions, however, a much greater variety of professions and origins is apparent. The signatories included ex-officers (two petition telegrams were signed by groups of between 17 and 38 ex-officers); skilled and unskilled workers (cooks, servants, or carpenters); merchants (from pedlars to well-established El Obeid traders); religious men; and employees in private firms, especially the multinational shipping company Gellatly & Hankey, which had its headquarters in Port Sudan.[16] In addition, there were

[11] Translation of a telegram from Obeid al-Haj al-Amin, Vice-President of the League, to the GG of Sudan and the DI, Khartoum, 5.7.1924, FO 141/806/1, NA.
[12] Not to be confused with Ḥusayn Sharīf, the editor of *Ḥaḍārat al-Sūdān*.
[13] Telegram from Ahmed Omar Bakhreiba, 'Vice-President of the White Flag in the Blue Nile', to the President of the Egyptian Parliament and the Honourable Members, Cairo, 21.6.1924, FO 141/806/1, NA (wrongly dated 11.6.1924). This telegram has an additional paragraph in a separate document, also in FO 141/806/1, NA.
[14] *White Flag Trials*, p. 63.
[15] It is possible that Aḥmad 'Alī is 'Alī Malāsī, because there is no trace in the archives of any other Aḥmad 'Alī in Port Sudan.
[16] The list of those who signed petitions can be found here: 1) List of the signatories of the telegram against the imprisonment of Sirr El Khatim, 27.7.1924, Palace 4/10/49, NRO. There are several versions of this telegram, with different signatories; 2) Signatory of telegram to HH The Prime Minister, the President of the Parliament, the Minister of War, the Chief of Ceremonies, the Press Syndicate, Cairo, signed by 53 people by name, 11.8.1924, Atbara, Northern Prov., 1/21/213, NRO; and 3) Translation of Arabic telegrams, the first copy signed by thirty-six and the second by thirty-eight discharged officers, to the President of the Parliament,

employees from all levels and types of occupation from railway battalion workers in Atbara to clerks in the Irrigation Department.[17]

As previously mentioned, the League's leading members sent the majority of the telegrams but were absent from the demonstrations. There were a number of reasons that explain this choice. First, the core 13 signatories were literate Sudanese who knew more than simply how to read and write; they were able to summarize a series of grievances into a strong political language. Second, until the end of July, it was much less dangerous to send a telegram than it was to lead a demonstration, at least in the sense that writing telegrams did not lead to immediate imprisonment. Indeed, the five leaders were not arrested on the ground of having written them. There was no law against sending protest telegrams, and before August the British probably considered that to arrest somebody because he had sent a telegram in support of Egypt was a politically dangerous step. Avoiding participating in a demonstration meant avoiding excessively rapid imprisonment, although they knew the time would come, sooner or later. The longer the leaders could avoid imprisonment, the more protests they could organize behind the scenes. A final factor is that several telegram signatories were members of the Post and Telegraph Department, and therefore had the necessary contacts to send telegrams undercover.[18] This shows that the role of a person in the League was related to his abilities, skills and connections, which in turn were connected to his professional background.

Indeed, the five members were not the only ones to keep away from demonstrations: members with specific abilities, for instance 'technical' skills, also remained behind the scenes. For example, 'Izz al-Dīn Ḥusayn Rāsiq was a postal agent between Khartoum and Wadi Halfa, and his role in the League was to bring anticolonial material from Egypt to Sudan. This is why he reported: 'I didn't participate in any demonstrations, because the League's policy is that the members of the League doing specific, important jobs like this should not be arrested.'[19] He certainly took no less risk than others, and in fact he was eventually arrested.[20] 'Izz al-Dīn's case was far from unique: many League members who held positions such as telephone operators – like Mudaththir Ibrāhīm, 'telefongi' at the Government Palace – or postmasters, telegraphers, and so on, and who played a vital role in

(contd) The Minister of War, and the Press Syndicate, Cairo, 24.6.1924, FO 141/806/1 and FO 141/810/3, NA, copy in Appendix K to the Willis Report, FO 141/810/3, NA and Telegram, the first copy signed by seventeen and the second by eighteen discharged officers to the Press Syndicate, President of Council of Ministers, Cairo, 24.6.1924, FO 141/806/1, FO 141/810/3, NA.

17 The telegram that best illustrates the differences among the signatories is one regarding the imprisonment of Muḥammad Sirr al-Khātim signed by 44 people and addressed to the GG, Khartoum, 27.7.1924, FO 141/806/1, NA; this telegram lists the professions of almost all the signatories.

18 *The White Flag Trials*, p. 45: 'Most telegrams were sent for free.'

19 'Izz al-Dīn Ḥusayn Rāsiq, IAAS 1575.

20 His name is among the list of people sentenced: White Flag League Conspiracy, results of trial, March April 1925, C. A. Willis, Intel. Dept., Khartoum 8.4.1925, Northern Prov. 1/21/207, NA.

helping circulate information among members, were kept safe. This, for instance, is how the activists found out about the arrival of a political prisoner in a certain city, or how they learnt about demonstrations that were taking place in some distant location. However, all members were involved in some sort of public activity: if it was not taking part in demonstration, it involved at least signing a telegram. For that reason, the White Flag League was not a typical secret society, because its members, at least the ones who swore an oath, never went completely underground.

As discussed for the demonstrations, not all the petitions were organized by the White Flag League. This is particularly the case for larger petitions, as with the forty or more signatures collected to protest against the arrest of Muḥammad Sirr al-Khātim in July. Who was responsible for organizing such a petition, if not League members? This brings us once again to the question of the structure and organization of the White Flag League, and more precisely the modalities of its expansion.

Working for the League, from the outside or the inside

The founding committee of the White Flag League attempted to include new people very early on. Crucially, this expansion was planned to be limited. For example, when Ṭayyib Bābikr, one of those on the list found at Laṭīf's home, 'opened' his own branch in Shendi, he agreed with his companions on 'the number of members and the oath to be sworn'.[21] Officer Ḥassan Ismā'īl al-Muftī also related that membership of the society was restricted in Wad Medani.[22]

In order to become a member of the White Flag League, a candidate had to swear an oath of allegiance.[23] The oath implied a willingness to dedicate oneself entirely to the League and a readiness to be arrested. It also opened to a new member the League's 'secrets'. Secrecy was an essential point as many activists attested to in their recollections, and the breaking of such oath was considered disgraceful and dishonourable. One of the cadets related: 'Of course they had secrets, those White Flag people. Some of them betrayed, and then [once in Kober] we tied them up inside the prison... and we gave them a good beating.'[24]

As being able to keep the League's secret was so essential, membership

[21] *Al-Riwāyāt*, p. 353.

[22] Ibid., p. 134.

[23] Many activists recount the oath (i.e. Ṭayyib Bābikr, *Al-Riwāyāt*, p. 337), but without giving details. An alleged oath is reported in colonial documents, but it is difficult to ascertain its reliability: 'the object of the Society is to spread the national ideal in the Sudan and to refuse to allow the Sudan to be separated from Egypt. If any member should commit a crime, all members are to assist him to escape the results of it and if they cannot help him otherwise, they should offer themselves for punishment with him. Every member is to carry out the rules of the Society on condition that nothing is done against the British Government.' DI, [Note on the] forthcoming Anglo-Egyptian negotiations on the Sudan, Khartoum, 25.6.1924, Palace 4/10/49, NRO.

[24] Mentioned by Muzammil 'Alī Dinār, *Al-Riwāyāt*, p. 55, and confirmed by Abdallāh Mabrūk, ibid., p. 494. See also Vezzadini, 'Secrets, spies, and a history to be (re) told'.

was not only restricted but a person had be totally committed before taking it up. The story of how ʻIzz al-Dīn Ḥusayn Rāsiq was recruited demonstrates this well:

> I was nominated in the Post and Telegraph Department, I found Ṣāliḥ ʻAbd al-Qādir already working there. We were close friends, colleagues and neighbours, and both of us were neighbours of ʻAlī ʻAbd al-Laṭīf. I used to meet and stay with them and they used to talk about the White Flag League. They told me that the goal of the League is the independence of the Sudan, and as I was their friend, they trusted me, they asked me to join, and I became a member.[25]

The members of the League did not trust a person fully or disclose their plans to him unless he had taken the oath, as is well illustrated by one particular episode. During his testimony to the Intelligence, ʻAlī Aḥmad Ṣāliḥ recounted that he had not sworn the oath of the League, and so ʻAlī ʻAbd al-Laṭīf and others spoke English in front of him if they needed to discuss League matters.[26]

However, it was not necessary to take the oath in order to be involved in the activities of the League; on the contrary, many people who had not taken it still participated in political activities and were arrested. This happened to ʻAlī Aḥmad Ṣāliḥ himself, for leading the demonstration of June 23. Another example is that of Wad Medani, where the political society included the civilian judge Mudaththir al-Būshī, who was not a League member. According to his relative Ḥassan Ismāʻīl al-Muftī '...shaykh Mudaththir was our centre [in Wad Medani]. He used to print the secret flyers for us, the ones that promoted hatred for the English and joining Egypt; he used to distribute them himself in the provinces'.[27]

What distinguished a member from a non-member? Why were some selected while others were kept on the outside? The pattern of participation in anti-colonial activities clarifies the situation: different people had different functions within the national movement, so that some stayed away from demonstrations to avoid imprisonment. Applying the same logic, some people served the White Flag League better by staying on the outside. When asked if he ever refused membership of the League to anyone, Ṭayyib Bābikr, answered:

> We refused the membership only to Aḥmad Effendi al-Shaykh, who wanted to join, but we preferred him to be outside the League, to support us. I wanted him not to be arrested, and to be safe. He was a brave and good man. Every time we were arrested he went to discuss our situation with Sulaymān ʻAysā.[28]

Similarly, according to Officer Muḥammad Ṣāliḥ al-Mak, who worked near El Obeid, '[we] did not tell anyone except those we already knew, like the *ʻumda*. We were careful that they were not arrested by the British.'[29]

25 ʻIzz al-Dīn Ḥusayn Rāsiq, IAAS, no. 1575.
26 Confession of Ali Ahmed Saleh, p. 10, 28.7.1924, FO 141/805/2, NA.
27 *Al-Riwāyāt*, pp. 133-134.
28 Ibid., p. 352.
29 Ibid., p. 563. Also, ʻAlī Aḥmad Ṣāliḥ mentioned in his confession that the mamur of Omdurman, ʻAlī al-Mardī, was secretly supporting the League (Ali Ahmed Saleh, Confession, 19.8.1924, p. 7, FO 141/805/2, NA), which the latter naturally denied during the trials.

This means that people with positions of responsibility or connections with the Government did not became members of the League because it was more important that they should remain free.

Last but not least, a third group of people was systematically absent from any visible activity of the White Flag League, whether for signing petitions or participating in demonstrations: these were officers and other army ranks, with few exceptions (such as in the case of Zayn al-ʿĀbdīn ʿAbd al-Tām). As Officer Aḥmad ʿAbd al-Farrāj put it in an interview, 'the soldiers are not allowed to know about politics, or to talk politics, and even the officers, because army laws forbid officers and soldiers from constituting or participating in political societies'.[30] Indeed, the case of ʿAlī ʿAbd al-Laṭīf, who was discharged from the army because of his text 'The Claim of the Nation', shows that political involvement meant the end of an army career. It is worth noting that the only army men 'visible' in politics, at least before late August, were discharged and pensioned officers, even if they limited themselves to signing petitions. At least four of such petitions have survived in the archives, and the famous list of 120 members of the White Flag League 'recovered' by the Intelligence Service included all but two of such signatories (a total of 34).[31]

The second reason why army personnel were not members of the League was that their undercover support was vital. Typically, officers would 'fail' to react to a political gathering immediately, or to report a political event to their superiors at once. This happened in Umm Ruwaba, for example, where an officer named Yūsif Sharīf 'failed' to inform his superior about the gathering at the station when Doctor Muḥammad ʿAbd al-Fatāḥ Sharīf, one of the leaders of the movement in El Obeid, passed through.[32] The League thus avoided involving people who were in a position to protect its political activities, or whose support was too important for them to be compromised by having their anti-colonial stance exposed.

This is perhaps the most important characteristic of people who embraced membership: by participating in the League, people accepted that their opposition to the government became visible. Even supporters such as Mudaththir Ibrāhīm or ʿIzz al-Dīn Ḥusayn Rāsiq, who were helping out behind the scenes through their jobs, signed at least one protest telegram. In one way or another, they all had to take responsibility for carrying out political protests and face the consequences.

In effect, the League members should be seen more as organizers of political actions, as agents with certain missions, rather than simply as men who shared a certain political ideal. Their first task was to organize

[30] *Al-Riwāyāt*, pp. 430-31. This is confirmed also by cadet Muzammil ʿAlī Dinār, who stated: 'We never met with the White Flag League, because in the military environment is banned to get involved in politics and such thing', ibid., p. 62.

[31] Cf. 'List of 120 Members of the WFL and the suggested leaders in the future', undated and unsigned, Northern Prov. 1/21/207, NRO and two petitions sent to Press Syndicate, Minister of War and President of Parliament, one in FO 141/806/1, and one in FO 141/810/3, NA. See also Appendix 2.

[32] DC Eastern Kordofan to Gov., Kordofan Prov., Um Ruaba, 24.8.1924, Kordofan 1/12/55, NRO.

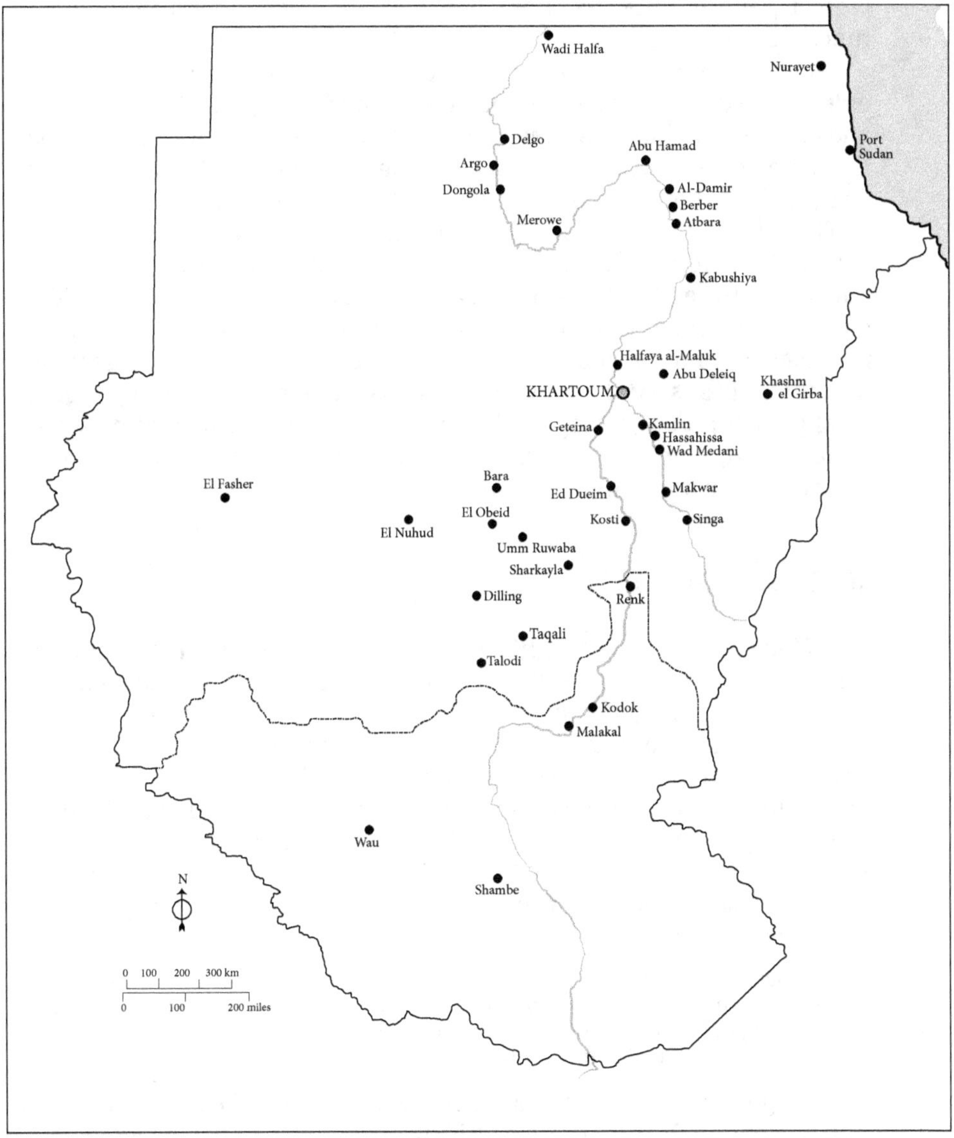

Map 1 Centres in which White Flag activities were reported

protests, and in order to attain this goal, they were assigned different functions according to how they could best 'serve' the League. By becoming a member, a candidate agreed to give up his personal safety and career in order to carry out acts of protest using all means appropriate to his position and profession. Thus, some members organized demonstrations, some led them, and others helped by disseminating information. Everyone had to do something, however, and agreed to be held accountable for his actions.

There was another task associated with being a full member of the League, however: to spread the anticolonial cause. This was the third most important strategy of the White Flag which represents another piece of the puzzle to explain both its geographical spread and the division between members and non-members. For the League, the objective of spreading unrest was best served not by its own expansion, but by igniting a spark among other groups, riding on the back of the frustrations that different social constituencies felt towards colonial rule, and of the expectations aroused by the international situation.

SPREADING DISCONTENT

The White Flag League sought to operate through a system of branches created in order to reach diverse socio-professional and geographical communities more effectively. This consisted in practice in sending 'agents' to make contact with various individuals or groups in different locations. If these targets were receptive to the League members' ideas, they were encouraged to set up a structure that would enable them to carry out protests on their own. They would initiate the formation of 'committees' to coordinate political activities, branches of the White Flag, or separate societies. One of the clearest accounts of this strategy is that of Ṭayyib Bābikr:

> I came and I met with the committee and I swore the oath of the League. I attended many meetings of the League and the members suggested that instead than working in Khartoum I continued my activities in Shendi to spread the League's principles there and to constitute a sub-committee.[33]

It is possible to distinguish two types of branches: geographical and occupational. It is a fairly artificial division, because geographical branches also included socio-professional divisions. This distinction is made primarily for the sake of convenience, to show two parallel patterns of diffusion of political agitation.

Occupation-based branches

The exact details of the operation are unknown, but what can be evinced from the sources is that members of the League were asked to approach people close to them and convince them to join protests against the British. For example, Aḥmad Mudaththir Ibrāhīm, whose father had been the Keeper of the Privy Seal of the Mahdī, was reported to have met with the

[33] *Al-Riwāyāt*, p. 337.

Head of the Board of Ulema and the Grand Mufti, probably in an attempt to exploit his family connections.[34] Similarly, Muḥammad al-Mahdī was reported to have contacted his uncle, *sayyid* 'Abd al-Raḥman al-Mahdī, to convince him to support the White Flag League.[35] Other affiliations could be mobilized: for example 'Nubians' were called on to protest against the arrest of Muḥammad Sirr al-Khātim. It was also reported that Muḥammad al-Mahdī claimed that 'if he only had money he could enrol 3,000 members in White Nile Province.'[36] In fact Aba Island, on the White Nile, was the headquarters of the *anṣār* and followers of the Mahdī.

In some cases, League members did not meet with much success, as in the case of their attempt to co-opt notables, but in others there is clear evidence that their strategy paid off. For instance, before he was imprisoned, 'Ubayd al-Ḥājj al-Amīn used to hold meetings among primary school boys and apparently prompted the creation of a committee of primary school students.[37] In September, the Intelligence Department obtained circulars written by two students, one of which warned the government that they would hold a demonstration on the day the school reopened, including '600 boys from the elementary and Kuttab school'.[38] The same two youths were also discovered to have smuggled Egyptian newspapers and other leaflets into school.[39]

Another organization linked to the League involved discharged officers. 'Abdallāh al-Nūr, a retired *yuzbashi* officer, was identified as a member of the White Flag League and also as the head of the 'Society for Dismissed Officers in Omdurman'.[40] He signed a collective petition with other discharged officers and a single-signatory telegram against the arrest of 'Alī 'Abd al-Laṭīf, presenting himself a spokesperson for the discharged officers.[41] As for merchants, there was apparently another committee

[34] Translation (of informant?), to DI, Khartoum, 14.8.1924, Palace 4/10/50, and Notes to Telegram of Protest, addressed to Parliament, Press Society and High commissioner, Cairo, 13.7.1924, Palace 4/10/49, both in NRO.

[35] C.A. Willis, Intelligence Notes, Khartoum, 11.7.1924, FO 141/806/1, NA.

[36] The full quote: 'A letter from Mohammed al-Mahdi Khalifa Abudallhi to the Acting President of the League in Khartoum... laments the lack of money, and says that, if he only had money he could enrol 3,000 members in White Nile Province', Corbyn to Skrine, Khartoum, 16.8.1924 (wrongly dated 16.6.1924), FO 141/805/2, NA.

[37] DC Omdurman to Gov., Khartoum, 9.9.1924, Palace 4/9/45, NRO.

[38] Translation of an anonymous letter, undated, addressed in English to the DI, Khartoum, and posted in Omdurman on the 11th of September, FO 1441/805/2, NA.

[39] The two students accused were: Muḥammad Amīr Bashīr and Kamāl Faltas. DC Omdurman to Gov. Khartoum, 9.9.1924, Palace 4/9/45, NRO.

[40] As a member of the League: censored letter no. 3, from Masri Aswad to the Editor of al-Mokattam, not dated but c. 24 October, Palace 4/9/47, NRO; Reported to have joined the society, in J. E. T. Phipps, Intelligence Report, Khartoum, 17.7.1924, FO 141/806/1, NA.

[41] Translation of a telegram, signed by Abdalla Nur on behalf of the Sudanese Officers to Prime Minister, President of the Parliament and Press Syndicate Cairo, Khartoum, 8.7.1924, FO 141/810/3, NA. Intelligence Information by informer no. 150, El Obeid, 9.9.1924, Kordofan 1/12/55, NRO.

composed of long-distance traders formed in El Obeid, with branches in Khartoum.[42] Another important committee in 1924 involved skilled and unskilled workers, artisans and petty traders: the British called it the 'Workmen's League'. As seen, several people were arrested in August and September for being members of this association. Generally, these committees varied very much in size, organization, and strategy, as well as in relation to the opportunities they had to perform political tasks and the personality and potential of their members.

A second point: not everything must be attributed to the agency of the League. It is possible that groups already in existence sought to connect with the League in order to coordinate their efforts. Thus, the League did not always have to create a committee or an association from scratch, but only to reactivate, revive, or simply catalyse the actions of an existing association, as was certainly the case in El Obeid and Wad Medani. It is crucial to bear in mind that the 1924 Revolution could not have taken place without the more or less loose political associations that existed before 1924.

Political agitators in Khartoum

There is no single answer to the question whether the League was successful in mobilizing different social groups. The degree of success of the League varied very much according to location, but a glance at the socio-professional backgrounds of the activists in Khartoum offers some perspectives on this issue.

The Intelligence Department documents that were accessed for this study name 302 political activists who are explicitly mentioned as being situated in Khartoum, Khartoum North and Omdurman.[43] Of these 302, 59 came to the attention of the Department as members of the White Flag League, 29 as members of the Sudan Union, a parallel political association, which is discussed below, and 11 as members of both the White Flag League and the Sudan Union.

Table 1 shows three categories as predominant in Khartoum: students, civil servants and officers. However, as this data is drawn from judicial records for the whole 1924, it expresses also the categories that, all in all, became the most visible to the Intelligence Department. For instance, the Table includes all the 51 cadets who demonstrated on August 9. Civilian employees of the Sudan Government were also easy to watch. The government kept records of each of its employees in special personnel files, so that a person's life and career could be easily tracked, contrary

[42] Information, Intel. Dept., Sudan Govt., Khartoum, 24.8.1924, Northern Prov. 1/21/215, NRO. Information, Khartoum District, Intel. Dept., 7.9.1924, and Report of DI, 10.8.1924, both in Palace 4/9/44, NRO.

[43] Thus, for instance, the 17 discharged officers who signed a telegram to Cairo have not been included in the table below (Telegram sent to the Press Syndicate and the President of the Court of Ministers, Cairo, 24.6.24 in FO 141/806/1, NA). Even though we might surmise that some ex-officers were living in Khartoum, this is not always true, as in the case of a certain 'Rizgalla Adam,' from another file, who was living or working in Port Sudan (List of 120 Members of the WFL and the suggested leaders in the future, Northern Prov. 1/21/207, NRO).

Table 1 Professional distribution of political activists in Khartoum

Profession	Number
Civilian employees (Government and private)*	67
Army officers†	66
Merchants	20
Wage workers / small traders	51
Students (GMC and Military school)	66
Shaykhs or Omdas	3
Religious men	5
Unemployed	2
Unknown	22
Total	302

*This category includes also one lawyer, as he had been educated in colonial schools but worked in a private practice.
† I have made no distinction between officers in service and discharged and retired officers.

Sources: Palace 4/9/44, Palace 4/10/46, Palace 4/10/47, Palace 4/10/48, Palace 4/10/49, Palace 4/11/55, Kordofan 1/13/62, Northern Prov. 1/21/207, Northern Prov. 1/21/215. NA: FO 141/806/1, FO 141/810/3, FO 141/805/2, FO 141/669/8

to the attention paid to other groups such as artisans or wage-workers. Finally, the high number of officers visible from the Table is due to the fact that at the end of August, the Intelligence Department obtained a long list of names of officers who were allegedly members of the Sudan Union.

Table 1 also shows that that one of the most important social components of protesters in Khartoum was that of skilled and unskilled workers and small traders. This rather loose category included all sorts of wage-based activities that required some kind of apprenticeship and expertise, such as bakers, carpenters, tailors, cooks, or butchers, but it also comprised professions requiring relatively lower skill, such as washers, waiters, and shopkeepers (including people defined as greengrocers, fishmongers, pedlars, or booksellers). Another sizeable category is that of 'merchants,' although there is little detail on the size of the person's business, and virtually no distinction is made between well-established merchants and pedlars.

As for the origins of these people, they are only mentioned for about half the activists (177), and once more they are very mixed. Of these 177, 34 were 'Egyptians' (including some born in Sudan), 28 were 'Muwalladīn', and 20 were 'Dinka'. The last is correlated to the fact that numerous Army officers had their family origins in Southern Sudan. The next category covered several Ja'aliyyin (12) and Mahas (7), two Nubian groups of northern Sudan; the remainder came from all over the country. Even if, as we have seen, the 'origin' classification had little heuristic validity, the table certainly highlights the heterogeneity of the protesters in the Three Towns.

Provincial Branches

As discussed, political agitation developed widely outside Khartoum. Numerous reports describe the works of 'agents' sent to locations among various ethnic groups, and apparently the League sought to have 'agents' in most Sudanese towns.[44] For example, Aḥmad 'Umar Bakhrībā, who was based in Wad Medani, was the White Flag League member responsible for the Gezira, and Ṣāliḥ 'Abd al-Qādir became responsible for Port Sudan after his transfer. In the White Flag trials, 'Alī Aḥmad Ṣāliḥ maintained that the Three Towns were divided into different sections, each assigned to a member of the League.[45]

If there truly was a geographical division of tasks of this kind in the League, the details have been lost. Information on this aspect of political agitation is only available from Intelligence Department records through informants, and cannot be verified; yet these records may offer some idea of the way in which the League sought to spread. For instance, a certain 'El Hasan Mohamed' appeared during a tribal conference (*majlis*) in Nurayath, in the Red Sea Province, 'and suggested that if they would give him a signed petition complaining of tribute [sic] and asking the Egyptian Government to take them over as the Ababda are, [sic] he would ride to Cairo with it.'[46] The Shaykh of the Habbaniyya, in Kordofan, also reported that he had been contacted about giving his allegiance to Egypt (and was accused of it, too).[47] A report from the Gezira detailed a number of such 'agents' working in various small villages. For example, it describes how 'Abu El Gasim El Fiki of Hillet Shirgeila, Rufa'a District, arrived recently from Khartoum and talked wildly at Hideiba market in the presence of Shaykh Abdulla Abu Sin and a large audience, relating how Zaghlul Pasha had turned the English out of Egypt, etc.' [48] In the same vein, an informant in Dongola related:

> [The] Egyptian question is the general talk. This is attributed to the police clerk Sami Eff. Nasir – irrigation engineer, and the new kadi with some of the merchants... The employees arriving [sic] from Khartoum with the rest of the Egyptians; last year it was Yuzb. Mohammed Eff. Saleh Gibril [head of the League in El Obeid], now it is Ahmed Eff. Hassan Midhat [member of the new committee of five] with others.[49]

In Dilling, in the Nuba Mountains, a certain 'Hassaballa el Hashi' was 'selected to fight the British Govt. among the Dar Gawad Arabs ... and spread propaganda among them'.[50] Discharged officers were also active in this geographical expansion: ex-officer Ḥassan Tayallāh was described as

[44] *The White Flag Trials*, p. 47.
[45] Confession of Ali Ahmed Saleh, 23.8.1924, p. 22. FO 141/805/2, NA.
[46] Gov. Berber Prov. to DC Berber, El Damer 27.9.1924, Northern Prov., 1/21/215, NRO.
[47] E. S. Fiddes for DC, Eastern Kordofan, to Gov., Khartoum Prov. El Obeid, Palace 4/9/44, NRO.
[48] Summary of Agent's report received from the Gezira, Acting DI to Gov., Damer (Circulated to all Governors), Khartoum 25.8.1924, Northern Prov. 1/12/215, NRO.
[49] Translation of a letter of information, Intel. Dept., 28.7.1924, Palace 4/10/49, NRO.
[50] Assistant DI to Gov. Kordofan, Dilling, 21.8.1924, Kordofan 1/12/56, NRO.

'[the] head of the Gema'ab of Zubeir Pasha at Hilfayat el Meluk, and has considerable influence with the followers of Zubeir Pasha, which influence he uses to assist the White Flag Society to foment sedition.'[51] Finally, in some cases, agents were chosen for their affinity with the groups that might be most sensitive to the League's political message, or because they had strong local ties. For example, Muḥammad Jabr al-Dār was chosen to be agent of the League in El Obeid because he was the son of a local notable.[52]

Although 'agents' and 'agitators' were sent all over Sudan, only in a few cases did they attempt to replicate the organization of the White Flag League in Khartoum. This is evident, for instance, from the structure and strategies adopted in places such as Port Sudan and Shendi. In the former, there was a first committee and a second, 'shadow', committee ready to replace the first when its members were arrested. The first was headed by Ṣāliḥ 'Abd al-Qādir, and also included 'Alī Malāsī, and Bāshirī 'Abd al-Raḥman, while the second included Ṭayyib 'Ābdīn, 'Ubayd Idrīs, and Muḥammad Hādiyā Manṣūr. The two committees signed telegrams separately. Here, too, the strategies were threefold: to send telegrams, to organize demonstrations, and to reach out to other groups. Nevertheless, even in a branch that was created by one of the League's founding members, the activists progressively detached themselves from the Khartoum guidelines. This is clear from the example of demonstrations: when the League in Khartoum decided to stop organising these events, the activists of Port Sudan continued to do so. At his trial, Muḥammad Hādiyā Manṣūr stated with regard to the demonstrations of Port Sudan: 'The demonstrations which were made at Port Sudan were not made by the consent of the League and the League was not satisfied with the demonstrators.'[53]

However, in many other cases, the agents of the League aimed not so much to create new branches or recruit new members as they did to provide logistical and material assistance for local activists. This is particularly evident in El Obeid and Wad Medani. In both these locations, there was a core group of officers and civilians who had been active in politics at least since the First World War, who were critics of colonialism, and who were accustomed – or at least exposed – to some form of underground protest. The arrival of agents from the League motivated these associations or individuals to become organized again and to increase the scale of their activities. It also prompted a sort of transfer of protest technologies. Thus, as the case of El Obeid will show later on, provincial associations also began asking their members to swear an oath (although it was not necessarily the same as the League's), to establish rules for the inclusion and exclusion of members, to create by-laws, and then to begin to plan how to organize demonstrations, send protest telegrams, collect petitions, and involve other groups and individuals.

[51] Information by informer no. 150, El Obeid, 9.9.1924, Kordofan 1/12/55, NRO.
[52] For Jabr al-Dār, see Letter sent to DI, El Obeid 28.7.1924, Kordofan 1/12/56, NRO. He was subsequently noted in many reports as a prominent member of the League in El Obeid.
[53] *The White Flag Trials*, p. 120.

To conclude, in 1924, the spread of political agitation functioned through an underground network of agents whose aim was to disseminate the movement. They sometimes created, and in other cases revived, a constellation of political associations based in the provinces, but also ended up working independently of the League. Moreover, judging from the differences among local branches in terms of structure and composition (clarified in the next chapter by exploring the cases of Port Sudan and El Obeid), it is doubtful whether the League members imposed any form of hierarchy below the Khartoum central committee, or sought to force compliance with its by-laws. This also explains the significant discrepancy between the limited number of White Flag members and the hundreds of 1924 activists: being a member of one of these associations did not necessarily mean being a member of the White Flag League, taking its oath, or obeying its by-laws.

Finally, this configuration also explains why, even after the disintegration of the League, demonstration and petitions continued. The success of the League was that of reviving or prompting the creation of dozens of different political groups, more or less connected to the League: this network survived the League's breakdown. One case in point, the association of army officers, is discussed below.

Army officers and the 'Society of the Sudan Union'

In September, the Intelligence Department began receiving information about a new association called the Society of the Sudan Union. The choice of name is somewhat baffling, considering that it is the same as that of the famous pre-1924 political association; it is impossible to know what link there might have been between the two, if indeed there was one. It is also puzzling that no oral account mentions this society. It should be noted nevertheless that in the private archive of the family of one of the cadets, there is a list of some 200 'members', most of whom were army officers. It is possible that he was referring to this society.[54]

From August onwards, numerous political texts were being signed under this name. The Intelligence Department reported in September that 'an Egyptian translator of the 9th Sudanese', in whose house they had found telegrams, circulars and 'seditious songs', was its leader.[55] At the end of September, a list revealing the names of 67 members of the Sudan Union was found by the Intelligence Department.[56] Of these, 62 were serving or former officers of the Egyptian Army, while the other five were civilian employees of the Sudan Government. There were no artisans, wage-workers or traders on the list.

[54] List of Muḥammad Faḍlallāh al- Shinnāwī, family documents of Majdī Sumīt.

[55] Telegram From Hakiman, Khartoum, to Stack, London, and More, Cairo, 22.9.1924, and List of member of the 'Sudan Union' who are said to have recently taken the oath, Intelligence, 21.9.1924, both in Palace 4/9/45, NRO. Telegram from DI, Khartoum, to SA, Cairo, 22.9.1924, FO 141/805/2, NA.

[56] Also, only 18 of the approximately 200 people mentioned on the list of cadet 'Abdallāh Mabrūk Khalīl correspond to individuals appearing on the Intelligence Department list of Sudan Union members.

Nonetheless, the society had certainly existed before August 1924. Aḥmad 'Umar Bakhrībā, the League's agent in Wad Medani, mentioned its existence already at the beginning of July:

> The Public opinion, the White Flag League, the Sudan Union Committee and all the other native parties affirm British administration which may be contrary to the contents of the decision given by the members of the Parliament of the two nations. Long live King Fuad and the Parliament of the two nations.[57]

One important element of the relationship between the two associations is disclosed in an article written in September 1924 by one of its members, 'Uthmān Muḥammad Hāshim, and addressed to the Egyptian newspaper *al-Muqaṭṭam*:

> The Society [of the Sudan Union] was founded by the best and most enlightened of the natives of the country and of the most famous families and by leaders of opinion in it. Previous to its organization individual members were seeking to oppose the colonization by various methods and they were assisted in this by reason of their position in administrative posts in touch with the masses of the people. This Society has done good work in preparing the nation and rendering it inflammable and ready to respond to the first spark of true patriotism (nationalism) [sic]. There were also circumstances that assisted this work.
>
> Now when the White Flag League began to work openly the United Sudan Society was (had been) [sic] working unseen and no difficulty was experienced in leading the nation to its patriotic campaign. When member of the White Flag League were arrested the United Sudan Society broke into revolt and by its circulars gave an open lead and call to the nation to be as one mass in its support.[58]

Indeed, his article suggests that the Sudan Union was a sort of shadow organization of the White Flag League. Something similar was suggested by the Intelligence Department:

> The 'White Flag League' was formed as an offshoot to the 'League of Sudan Union' ... When, owing to the imprisonment of most of its members, the activities of the White Flag League were brought almost to a standstill, the League of Sudan Union began a less open form of propaganda, by publishing and distributing circulars, Egyptians could secretly assist this movement.[59]

In December, the British authorities believed that the Society of the Sudan Union was behind the mutiny of the 11th Battalion.[60] Indeed, this view was supported by the above note about army officers. The latter supported the League underground, and at the same time officers had been highly politicized for years.

It is thus possible to imagine that the Sudan Union was the underground or shadow organization of officers of the Egyptian Army, created to support the League behind the scenes, but also to intervene in a worst-

57 Omar Bakhreiba, notice attached on walls in the suk, streets, provincial HQ and the Zabtiah, Medani, 6.7.1924, Palace 4/10/49.

58 Translated article, Othman Mohammed Hashim, Published in Mokhattam 31.8 Khartoum FO 141/805/2. However, to add to the complexity, the writer of this article was neither an officer nor one of the civilians named on the list of Sudan Union members found by the Intelligence Department; he was a civilian who was related to the family of the Grand Mufti.

59 Memorandum on Egyptian complicity in the Mutiny of 27th and 28th November 1924, FO 141/494/3, NA.

60 Ibid.

case scenario, such as Britain taking over in Sudan and getting rid of the Egyptians. After the events of August and the breakdown of negotiations between Egypt and Great Britain, the officers began to feel that the time had come to act and finally stepped in when it appeared that Sudan was to be separated from Egypt. This point is clear for instance from the account of officer 'Abd al-'Azīz 'Abd al-Ḥay.

> There was a rumour at the time that after the assassination of Lee Stack they [the British] wanted to rule Sudan by power. A British warning was issued that the Egyptian Army would be evacuated from Sudan. So we said, we the Sudanese officers, we ... decided that anything of this sort happened we had to defend our people in the country and take over the Gezira if necessary.[61]

What others officers did, instead, was to organize a mutiny against the evacuation of Egyptian troops.

EGYPTIANS

Was this a revolution in which Egyptians participated too? The question of their involvement is one of the thorniest subjects in the historiography of the event, as there is wide disagreement among historians on this issue. To some extent, this debate reflects a rift within the sources. On the one hand, oral accounts and written memoirs systematically leave aside the question of Egyptian involvement, as if not part of the revolution at all. On the other hand, the colonial sources provide countless reports that attempted to prove the link between the Watanist and the Wafd Party in Egypt, and the League (see Chapter 11).

It is impossible to determine once and for all from the sources available, what the relation was between the leadership of the League and Egyptian political parties. However, it is a question that has only relative importance, especially from the perspective of social history. Even if the leaders of the League had connections with Egyptian politicians, they did not make much difference. First, even if they existed, these connections were sporadic and certainly much below expectations. Financially, for instance, the League was in dire straits: it was funded locally and the members were clearly worried about saving money.[62] Moreover, the whole story of 1924 concerns the absence, rather than the presence, of Egyptian support. Finally, it was mostly Sudanese, and not Egyptians, who took to the streets, demonstrated, signed petitions, and went to prison. To believe that Sudanese protested because Egyptian politicians manipulated them into doing so reduces the people to the passive tools of politicians, and this position cannot be seriously sustained.

More interesting is the question of the individual participation of

61 *Al-Riwāyāt*, p. 228.

62 The second document that has survived in 'Alī 'Abd al-Laṭīf's family is a single page showing the meagre accounts of the League. The Ewart Report mentions that the League allocated a part of its finance to the support of the families of arrested members, but because of their financial difficulties they were unable to maintain such subsidies.

Egyptians in the events of 1924: one of the by-laws of the League forbade their membership.[63] Since the League was intended to express the will of the Sudanese nation, the presence of Egyptians would have weakened its demands. Nevertheless, from the records of 1924, the individual participation of some Egyptians is clear and cannot be dismissed. As previously discussed, each secret organization tended to have its own by-laws and it is obvious that some did not ban Egyptians. For example, in El Obeid, the local political association was led by a Sudanese officer and an Egyptian medical doctor.

However, it is impossible to make a general statement on the participation of 'Egyptians' in 1924 – a word I put in inverted commas to emphasize that this category was vague and confused. First of all, one has to be mindful that this label incorporated groups of people who were widely different, both in terms of the nature of their connection to Sudan, as seen in an earlier chapter, and of their socio-professional categories. These went from 'Effendi' to traders, pedlars, and unskilled wage-workers.

As a condition of the dual sovereignty of Egypt and Great Britain, and also because of the lack of educated native personnel at the beginning of the Anglo-Egyptian Condominium, thousands of Egyptians had been recruited by the colonial government to work as clerks, teachers, soldiers, officials, and officers up to the *mamur* grade. Egyptians occupied intermediary positions between their British superiors and their Sudanese subordinates. Egyptian officers and officials were despatched to every province and administrative centre, working shoulder to shoulder with Sudanese, yet always one grade higher in rank and status. In 1920, the colonial state employed 1,824 Egyptians, compared with 1,554 Sudanese.[64] A very different group of Egyptians in Sudan were the hundreds, sometimes thousands, of unskilled or semi-skilled workers. For example, there were the 'saidis,' a term that British sources used to refer to workers who originally came from Upper Egypt, and who were transported to Sudan to complete large infrastructure projects, notably, around 1924, the Jebel Awlia Dam, in preparation for the Gezira irrigation scheme. There were also the employees of the Railways Battalion: Egyptians who had the status of soldiers and spent up to ten years in Sudan. Another profession in which Egyptians were customarily engaged was trade, and here again, specifics are needed. Some Egyptians merchants had moved to Sudan recently to benefit from the thriving economic situation. As the import-export figures in Government Annual Reports show, this was especially true during the first phase of the Condominium, up to the 1920s, when Egypt was the second-largest importer of Sudanese products after Britain.[65] In contrast, other Egyptians came from families whose commercial and family links with Sudan were very old – at least as old as the Turco-Egyptian regime.

63 This is mentioned both in the secondary literature, such as Kurita, 'The Concept of Nationalism,' and in primary sources, such as in the *White Flag Trials*, p. 39.
64 Mohamed Omer Beshir, *Educational Development in the Sudan, 1898-1956* (Oxford: Clarendon Press, 1969), p. 198.
65 See Beshir, *Revolution and Nationalism*, p. 37.

It is therefore more useful to consider that their involvement was not so much a function of their origin – otherwise all Egyptians would have participated in 1924, which was not the case, of course – but of a series of complex factors that depended to a large extent on local configurations and also on the needs of the Sudanese national movement. A few examples will serve to make this clearer.

Perhaps one of the most famous Egyptians of 1924 was the lawyer al-Amīn Labīb al-Shahīd, who defended all the members of the White Flag League on trial, including ʻAlī ʻAbd al-Laṭīf. During the hearings in August of Muḥammad Sirr al-Khātim, the lawyer's closing statement became so famous that it forced the British to release the accused, after the direct intercession of some notables. In one letter, a British officer noted contemptuously:

> [al-Amīn Labīb al-Shahīd] made no attempt to deal with the defence in other than a political attitude. His first question to any witness was 'Do you see anything wrong in shouting Long Live Fuad King of Egypt and the Sudan, seeing that this is his proper title?[66]

A similar line of defence was taken also for other trials. According to a witness:

> Shahīd was living in the Sudan and licenced to practise as a lawyer. His defence was very strong in the court. He said to them that ʻAlī ʻAbd al-Laṭīf was right to constitute the League, and that the League was loyal to Egypt, and that ʻAlī ʻAbd al-Laṭīf was an Egyptian officer and the Governor Generalship of the Sudan is Egyptian and all the British who are employed are all Egyptian employees, and their League is not anything more than shouting 'Long Live the King of Egypt' and the same to Egyptian leaders, because his loyalty is to Egypt and this is a legitimate activity. He asked the main prosecutor, from where do you take your salary, he answered, from Egypt, and who is employing you in your job? Egypt.[67]

However, after the affair of Muḥammad Sirr al-Khātim, the British learnt their lesson: when the main trial of White Flag members was about to begin in September, al-Amīn Labīb al-Shahīd was taken to the railway station with a one-way ticket to Cairo, and the accused men were left without legal representation.

Al-Amīn Labīb al-Shahīd was educated in Egypt, and obtained a licence to practise law in Sudan, where he lived for several years. Unfortunately, not much is known about his background or the reasons behind his political involvement, but he played an important role in the White Flag not only as defence attorney but also as a sort of legal advisor to the League itself. For example, during the main League trials, ʻAlī ʻAbd al-Laṭīf related that it was agreed among the participants that after a demonstration, its leaders had to go to al-Shahīd to be instructed on how to respond to the police interrogations.

Other Egyptians with a background in law also helped al-Shahīd as much as they could, showing that his case was far from being unique,

66 (Unknown sender) to Skrine, El Damer, 30.9.1924, Northern Prov. 1/21/215, NRO.

67 *Al-Riwāyāt*, p. 525.

and that there were a number of Egyptians working in Sudan were deeply committed to the Sudanese cause.[68]

The profile of the Egyptian 'Effendi' supporter of the Sudanese national movement was that of a person who had typically been active in the Egyptian Revolution and held strong anti-colonial and nationalist ideas. As regards his version of nationalism, Sudan and Egypt were one and the same. This was the case, for instance, with Ḥāmid al-Qarḍāwī. He was an officer in the Camel Corps who had participated in the 1919 Egyptian Revolution. There, he had escaped the death penalty by a whisker. Once dispatched to El Obeid, he involved himself heart and soul in the nationalist movement. This is how he was described in an Intelligence Department report:

> He was hand in glove with Mohammed Eff Saleh Gibril [the officer leader of the League] and insisted on making a most offensive speech at the station on the day of the latter's departure from el Obeid. He also made a most offensive speech at a farewell dinner given to Mohammed Eff Saleh Gibril in the Officers Club.
>
> He continually talks most vehemently against the British to Officers and Officials and says for instance: "Why do you submit to the British holding all the good posts in this country when you yourselves are capable of filling them?"
>
> He has a large notebook in the left hand drawer of his office table in which he enters all items of information which are interesting from a political point of view. When he fills the notebook he sends it down to Egypt with some Egyptian travelling on leave. He is the focus of all anti-British propaganda in the Camel Corps.[69]

Thus, Egyptians active in anti-British protest placed their energies and know-how at the service of issues of radical politics. As Ḥāmid al-Qarḍāwī put it, 'My belief that Egypt and the Sudan are inseparable is as my belief that God is one', and continued: 'remember that history never mentioned that any army overcame a nation or that a nation did not obtain its independence when it claimed it,' and this is why for him, the end of British sovereignty in Sudan was just a matter of time.[70] The same officer reckoned that Egyptians had an extraordinary role to play in Sudan by helping the Sudanese, while at the same time being quite safe. Sudanese went to prison and risked their lives, but at worst, Egyptians were deported to Egypt, and were freed once they arrived there there: 'God, who has protected us during the Egyptian revolt when I was liable to death sentence, will protect us again during the revolt in the Sudan, in which our position is exceptional...' And yet, he continued, Egyptians were at best helping the Sudanese:

> All that is happening in the Sudan is being done with the free will of the natives and all that our enemies allege is false. They are those who kindled the fire of revolt in the Sudan and not us, and they are those who commenced to obtain expression of loyalty and lead the people to play with fire.[71]

68 Censored letter no. 32, Nashid, Gellatly Hankey & Co, to Negib Eff. Ghubrial, Aswan (recently deported), Khartoum, 24.9.1924, in Kordofan 1/14/68, NRO.

69 Intelligence Note, undated, unsigned, Kordofan 1/12/55, NRO.

70 Censored letter no. 34, Hamid, Officers & Officials Club, El Obeid to Abd El Aziz Eff. Abd El Fattah El Ansari, Tanta, Egypt, 21.9.1924, Kordofan 1/14/68, NRO.

71 Censored letter no. 38, Hamid, Officers & Officials Club, El Obeid to Mohammed Eff. Unsi (his father), Chief Clerk, Recruiting Dept., Alexandria, 23.9.1924, Kordofan 1/14/68, NRO.

The writer of another censored letter intercepted by the Intelligence Department, who was the son of an Egyptian army officer, and was born in Sudan and working for the Irrigation Department, expressed a similar opinion:

> With astonishment, I read in the last newspaper a conversation between the Daily Express's correspondent and Mr MacDonald, which it says [sic] that the Egyptian Government is responsible for the events in the Sudan and that men of the Egyptian Government have engineered them. Rot. Bosh. ... When the British suspect Egyptians of engineering the riots they forget, or try to forget, that they crushed Egyptian influence many years ago and that they have become the only rulers of the country. ... If we take it for granted that the Egyptians have instigated the riots in the Sudan against the British, is it conceivable that their small numbers can upset public opinion in this short time ... [?][72]

Indeed, the role of many Egyptian 'Effendi' should be seen as that of facilitation: they smuggled Egyptian newspapers and all kinds of 'subversive' literature – possibly even the book of secret societies that was mentioned by 'Alī Aḥmad Ṣāliḥ – into Sudan;[73] they helped send telegrams for free when they could; and when they uncovered British plans, they informed White Flag League members. It must be noted, however, that this assistance was offered on an individual basis: while there were indeed radical Egyptians who facilitated the work of the Sudanese, there were just as many who were apathetic about events in Sudan – as shown by the mutiny of November – while yet others clearly opposed the nationalist movement by turning king's evidence. In places such as El Obeid, Egyptian officers played a by no means minor role in breaking up the movement.[74]

Besides these Egyptian 'Effendi', the Egyptian working class also contributed, as in the famous example of the Railways Battalion men. Unfortunately, not much is known about these soldiers, except that they came from the working class, and that a sizeable minority of them had Coptic names.[75] The roots of their activism may be found in the politicization of wage-workers at the time of the 1919 Revolution. Wage-workers had been at the forefront of the Egyptian Revolution of 1919, and were the backbone of the Wafd Party.[76] In Atbara, the gulf between

[72] Censored letter no. 41, Mohammed Ali Mohammed, Malakal, to Ibrahim Bey Mohammed, Chief Engineer, Irrigation, Khartoum, 16.9.1924, Kordofan 1/14/68, NRO.

[73] *The White Flag Trials*, p. 48.

[74] Censored Letter no. 36, Hamid El Qardawi, Officers and Officials Club, El Obeid, 21.9.1924 to Dr Mohammed Eff. Sharif, Alexandria, (recently deported); Censored Letter no. 37, Hamid, Officers and Officials Club, El Obeid, 23.9.1924, to Mohammed Eff. Unsi (his father), Chief Clerk, Recruiting Dept. Alexandria, Kordofan 1/14/68, NRO.

[75] Signatories of telegram of 11.8.1924 to various personalities in Cairo protesting against the killing of Sudanese during the Atbara demonstrations. Intelligence Note 25.8.1924, Khartoum, from C. A. Willis to CSO & AG, EA Khartoum, Gov. Berber Prov., General Manager SGR & S, Atbara. In Northern Prov. 1/21/213, NRO. This petition was signed by 47 people.

[76] Joel Beinin and Zachary Lockman, *Workers on the Nile: Nationalism, Communism, Islam, and the Egyptian Working Class, 1882-1954* (Cairo: American University in Cairo Press, 1998), in particular Chapters IV and V. Unfortunately the background

wage-workers and their Egyptian superiors emerged clearly, as these officers, who were Egyptian, opposed the rebellion of their men and tried to contain it in different ways. This confirms other accounts of 1924: far from constituting a united front in support of the 1924 protesters, the reaction of Egyptians very much depended on individual political inclinations.

As will become evident in the next chapters, however, in the Sudanese national movement Egypt and the Egyptians were more crucial as symbols and metaphors of a successful liberation struggle than for anything they did in practice to facilitate the 1924 Revolution.

(contd) of these workers is completely unknown, and even Lockman's study makes no reference to wage-worker parties going to Sudan.

5

1924 in Port Sudan and El Obeid

In 1924 the national movement spread extensively through the provinces, reaching larger administrative centres and small hamlets, and arriving as far as Darfur and Upper Nile. The degree of success enjoyed by the League's 'agents' in turning the Sudanese into protesters was however very uneven. I have selected El Obeid and Port Sudan as cases in point of such unequal success, in part because of the sources available, but also because of their contrasting outcomes. Both were centres that hosted a vibrant group of activists, and yet, while the League in Port Sudan, succeeded in organizing a series of important demonstrations, nothing happened in El Obeid, despite the fact that the national movement there was older, larger, and more widespread. These two cases disclose the relationship between politics and economic change in Sudan, particularly in relation to domestic and international trade. Finally, they allow me to take a close-up shot of the modalities of participation of another group of protesters – the traders – whose presence in 1924 has so far been noted but never analysed.

These two case studies will show how failures are as important as 'success stories', if not actually more so. In 1924 the local conjunction of events, which was partly determined by structural elements and partly by unpredictable ones, determined the outcome of the protests. The leaders of the League in various locations did not make the same choices on how to attract supporters and organize the movement; they sought to adapt their strategies so that they would make sense locally and fit local needs. Conversely, the choices on the configuration of the national movement reveal a number of social, economic, and political elements that speak to the uneven integration of the provinces in international markets, their differing relations with the colonial state, and the multiple repercussions that this had at a local level.

PORT SUDAN

With the Three Towns and Atbara, Port Sudan became one of the most important sites of political agitation of 1924. Yet compared with other centres, the city was fairly new to political activism: at least, the existence of political associations was not recorded prior to that year. Before Ṣāliḥ 'Abd al-Qādir was transferred from Khartoum to Port Sudan at the end of June, the city appeared to be quiet. Several ex-Gordon College students who were associated with the Sudan Union worked there, but apparently they were not organized.[1] The day after his arrival, Ṣāliḥ 'Abd al-Qādir complained in a private letter that the people of the town were 'brutes' with no national feeling.[2] The following month would prove him wrong.

The narrative that follows is based on oral accounts combined with colonial sources. In the case of Port Sudan – in stark contrast to El Obeid – the historian can make use of a rich vein of oral material, such as the detailed interview of one of the leading figures in the protests, 'Alī Malāsī, and the accounts offered by the brothers Aḥmad Ṣabrī and 'Abd al-Mun'im Zāyd. On the other hand, the colonial sources to which I had access, from 2005 on, are mostly official in nature; confidential records are missing, their existence traceable only through the hints left by their deletion.[3] Even though the oral accounts and colonial sources diverge on a number of issues, and various aspects of how events developed are difficult to decipher, I shall attempt to draw the general lines along which proceedings unfolded.

Tense times in Port Sudan

Once he arrived in Port Sudan, and in spite of his disappointment with the situation there, White Flag League founding member Ṣāliḥ 'Abd al-Qādir did not despair, and set himself the task of organizing a branch of the League. He knew a number of Sudanese government clerks in Port Sudan, from his time at Gordon College and his activities with the Society of the Sudan Union there. Besides, he was a quite famous figure among radical educated Sudanese. The group that gathered around him was mostly composed of employees of the Railways, the Post and Telegraph, and the Customs Departments. Besides Ṣāliḥ himself and 'Alī Malāsī, the core members of the League included men such as Wahba Ibrāhīm, an 'Egyptian' working as a wireless operator for a private company; al-Ṭayyib 'Ābdīn, 'Ubayd Idrīs, Bāshirī 'Abd al-Raḥman, and Muḥammad Hādiyā, all employees of the Customs Department.[4] Their families came from different places in northern and central Sudan.

Ṣāliḥ 'Abd al-Qādir wasted no time: the first protest telegram sent from Port Sudan was dispatched around 25 June. During an initial phase, which lasted for most of July, the activists concentrated on sending protest

1 See also the witness of Aḥmad Ṣabrī Zāyid, *Al-Riwāyāt*, p. 266.

2 Kenneth J. Perkins, *Port Sudan : The Evolution of a Colonial City State, Culture, and Society in Arab North Africa* (Boulder CO: Westview Press, 1993), p. 177, note 75.

3 Perkins, in his chapter on Port Sudan in 1924, used sources which I could not find at the time of my visits to the archives in London and Khartoum from 2005 onwards. *Port Sudan*, 177-179.

4 For Wahba Ibrāhīm: Civsec, Newbold, to Private Secretary, 18.8.1924, Palace 4/10/50, NRO; on; al-Ṭayyib 'Ābdīn and 'Ubayd Idrīs: Intelligence Notes, Khartoum, 2.7.1924, Palace 4/10/49, NRO; for Bāshirī 'Abd al-Raḥman, Ryder for SA to DI, Cairo, 8.9.1924, Palace 4/9/44, NRO.

telegrams. Eventually, they decided to embrace a more provocative line of action in spite of the wave of arrests in Khartoum. The perfect occasion was provided by an error on the part of the Intelligence Department. The activists were informed by friends in Khartoum that three unnamed political prisoners were arriving in Port Sudan, probably to be sent back to Egypt by boat. In order for this information to remain as secret as possible, British officers in Khartoum did not inform their Port Sudan colleagues of the transfer. Thus, when the three men arrived at the railway station on 27 July, the nationalists were there but the police were not. It was too late to intervene, so the British let the demonstrators be. It should be noted that the proclamation against 'unlawful assembly' had not yet been issued in Port Sudan. The crowd was quite substantial and according to one witness there were about a thousand protesters; the demonstration, which was peaceful and orderly, was led by 'Egyptians', and was described as chiefly composed of people who were there by chance or out of curiosity.[5] They dispersed without incident, and no-one was arrested.

On 5 August, however, the authorities arrested Ṣāliḥ 'Abd al-Qādir, although he had not participated in the demonstration.[6] From this point on, the situation quickly deteriorated. Contradictory and vague colonial accounts suggest that the government in Port Sudan was particularly at a loss to understand what was going on. One reason is that Port Sudan was considered to be a 'safe' city, politically speaking, and this is probably why Ṣāliḥ 'Abd al-Qādir had been transferred there in the first place.[7] When the British authorities realized that this was not the case, they reacted somewhat randomly, without foresight. Eventually, they took the line of inaction, avoiding direct repression, in part because they were unsure whether they would be able to hold the city without armed reinforcements, especially in the middle of the climactic events of August, when it seemed that Sudan was on the brink of conflagration. Only after order had been restored in Atbara did the British send reinforcements and a warship to Port Sudan. Its presence in the harbour and the battalions patrolling the city were unequivocal signs of where power lay. The tactic had the merit of avoiding bloodshed.

[5] Copies of correspondence re demonstration at Port Sudan 27.7.24 on the occasion of the transfer of political prisoners from Khartoum to Port Sudan, Port Sudan 30.7.24, Palace 4/10/50. NRO. Proceedings of the court of inquiry held to inquire into recent events at Port Sudan as far as they affect the Army, From GD Yeatman, Kaimakam, OC Troops Port Sudan, the Chief staff officer and adjutant general, Egyptian army, Khartoum, 19.8.24, 1st Witness Yuzbashi Hussein Eff Mohammed, Prison Dept., Palace 4/9/45, NRO.

[6] Appendix to SMIR n. 361, August 1924, WO 33/999, NA, and Copies of correspondence re demonstration at Port Sudan 27.7.1924 on the occasion of the transfer of political prisoners from Khartoum to Port Sudan, Port Sudan 30.7.1924, Palace 4/10/50, NRO.

[7] Perkins reports: '...in a letter to the provincial governor on June 26, 1924, the commissioner insisted that "the happenings in Khartoum and Omdurman have had little interest for the people here, especially the townsfolk..."' Perkins, *Port Sudan*, p. 177.

To return to the events: the arrest of Ṣāliḥ only generated more trouble. The very next day, 6 August, some employees of the Customs Department left work early in protest.[8] On 7 August, the day on which Ṣāliḥ ʻAbd al-Qādir travelled by train to Khartoum to be tried there, a demonstration was organized at the railway station to cheer the prisoner.[9] This demonstration was similar to the first, but this time the police were decidedly more heavy-handed with the protesters. ʻAbd al-Munʻim Zāyd, for instance, related: 'The soldiers attacked us with batons. I went to the hospital. After I was discharged we demonstrated for the second time, all over the city; tradesmen and port workers went on strike in protest against us being beaten up.'[10] Some days later, the demonstrators sent a telegram claiming that the staff at the hospital had refused to treat the wounded people.[11]

On Friday, 8 August, ʻAlī Malāsī gave a speech at the Port Sudan mosque. It was an important event because spoke in Tu-Bedawi, the language of the Beja. The father of ʻAlī Malāsī had a Beja background, which is why ʻAlī knew the language. ʻAlī Malāsī described the speech in these words:

> I went up into the pulpit, and I made a speech in the Hadendowa[12] language for our brothers from the Hadendowa. I explained to them the intention of the British Government and that they are Christians, etc. and we are Muslims, and we must support the Egyptian negotiator because he is Muslim, that we had flesh and blood connection with him as such. Then I repeated the same in Arabic.[13]

From this moment onwards, Beja demonstrators were at the forefront of events, together with the members of the League and the men of the Port Sudan detachment of the Railways Battalion. Aḥmad Ṣabrī Zāyd version of the events is particularly telling:

> The people discovered that the demonstration was to start after the Friday prayer in the mosque by ʻAlī Malāsī. We prepared the Egyptian flag and two placards, one of King Fu'ād and the other Saʻd Zaghlūl. The Arabs (Hadendowa, Bisharin, Rashayda) had no idea who Fu'ād and Zaghlūl were; they had never heard of them. We told them who they were, and in front of the crowd we shouted out their names. It was our duty to carry the pictures and the flag, so after burning the British flag for the second time, we started to march away from the mosque, but the Hadendowa rushed after us, seized the flags and the pictures, protecting them with their shields and swords. The march continued; we were in the rear shouting and they repeated our slogans, holding up the pictures and the traditional

[8] It should be noted that ʻAlī Malāsī's employer asked that he be arrested, but for some reason this did not happen: Gov. of Red Sea to Civsec, Port Sudan, 7.8.1924, Palace 4710/48, NRO.

[9] Copies of correspondence re demonstration at Port Sudan 27.7.1924 on the occasion of the transfer of political prisoners from Khartoum to Port Sudan, Port Sudan, 30.7.1924, Palace 4/10/50, NRO.

[10] *Al-Riwāyāt*, p. 258, and SMIR No. 361, August 1924, WO 33/999, NA.

[11] Translation of attached telegram, Tayeb Abdin, Port Sudan, 8.8.1924, Palace 4/10/48, NRO.

[12] Like the colonial sources, the oral accounts also consistently call the Beja 'Hadendowa', even though the Hadendowa are but one of the many groups that make up the Beja. The majority of Beja workers in Port Sudan were not Hadendowa, but Amarar. B. A. Lewis, 'Deim El Arab and the Beja Stevedores of Port Sudan', *Sudan Notes and Records* (1962), vol. 43, pp. 16-49.

[13] *Al-Riwāyāt*, p. 309, and see also p. 257.

> weapons. The demonstration went around the city, no soldiers showed up that day, they remained in the barracks. It was a huge demonstration.[14]

Two days later, on 10 August, there was another large demonstration. By then, Railways Battalion soldiers in Atbara had clashed with the army and the cadets had just held their own demonstration in Khartoum. The demonstration on 10 August had been carefully organized. First, members of the League had been in contact with the Egyptian *mamur*, the head of the police, who had agreed to keep the police in their barracks. This officer was a supporter of the League, and he also wished to avoid bloodshed similar to that in Atbara, where the 'Arab' police had clashed with the Egyptian employees of the Railways Battalion. Also in Port Sudan, there was also a large detachment of that battalion, and as in Atbara the police force was made up of 'irregular Arabs.'[15] Another interpretation is that of 'Alī Malāsī who said that the police were not sent because 'they did not want to clash with them [the Hadendowa] because if they did the movement would be a real one.'[16] What is clear is that the city's police and army battalions remained in their barracks until reinforcements arrived a few days later.

What happened during the days between the 10th and 13th of August is rather difficult to fathom. On the one hand, British accounts maintain that control of the city was never completely lost, whereas oral accounts give a quite different impression. Another area of disagreement concerns the extent of the participation of Beja workers. According to three people interviewed, not only did the insurgents *de facto* manage to take over the city during this period, but also the collaboration of Beja and 'Arab' (here, nomadic Arabic speaking people) migrant workers was crucial. Alī Malāsī described what happened:

> I constituted a national guard to keep safe the government houses and the market to prevent looting. Then I came and I told the people what the situation was, that we were responsible for governing the city, the police were detained there, if they start to make trouble with us we would respond, but as long as they were inside, we were the owners of the town, so, what should we do? Then we divided the people present into ten groups: some in the market, some in the railways, some in the port, and in all places to keep watch on public buildings. Each of the Arabs was carrying a sword and a shield. I said to them, you stay put in front of these places ... during those four days and nights no British Governor was seen and the railways and the bank were working protected by the national guards led by myself.[17]

The protesters could not hold the city for long, however. 'Alī Malāsī said that he contacted the White Flag League in Khartoum to ask them what to do, and received the reply that it would be too dangerous to put up any more resistance, and that what they had done was enough.[18] It is clear that the movement in Khartoum did not wish to be responsible for more deaths than had already occurred, after the events of Atbara. On 13

14 Ibid., p. 267.

15 Secret Report on the conditions of Port Sudan, 19.9.1924, Palace 4/9/46, and Acting Sirdar to Acting GG, Khartoum, 9.10.1924, Palace 4/10/49, both in NRO.

16 *Al-Riwāyāt*, p. 310.

17 Ibid., p. 311.

18 Ibid., pp. 311- 313.

August, reinforcements of British and Egyptian troops arrived, but only the Egyptian soldiers were sent out to confront the mutineers, to avoid bloodshed.[19] What exactly happened is not known, but it is likely that the protesters were convinced to retreat. On 16 August, the men of the Railways Battalions left the quays and moved to their barracks. As for the Beja stevedores, the *nāẓir* (here: head) of the Amarar was sent to speak to his people to calm them down.[20] 'Alī Malāsī was arrested some time after, on 17 August. The authorities continued to feel insecure, however. On 20 August, when the captain of the cruiser H.M.S. Weymouth (which had been sent to 'impress' the inhabitants) was asked for his opinion on the situation in the city, he replied that he felt the outcome was still uncertain: 'The "Fuzzies" [the familiar British name for the Beja]... are not Arabs and are generally well-behaved, but again the prospect of free looting would have undoubtedly appealed to them.'[21]

For the rest of the month, as in Khartoum and Atbara, a number of small protests continued to occur followed by arrests: there were occasional strikes, attempts at demonstrations, and a flurry of telegrams. As late as 30 August, the authorities reported renewed attempts 'to incite disaffection among the local Arabs living in the *deims* and the Yemeni labourers on the East side of Port Sudan by intrigue'.[22] But as was the case everywhere else, the situation had reached a point of stability amidst the tension. The Railways Battalion would also be evacuated from Port Sudan towards the end of the month.

The trials of the mutineers took place in September, without the help of al-Amīn Labīb Shahīd, who was working for the defence of the White Flag in Khartoum. The heaviest punishment was meted out to 'Alī Malāsī, who was given a six-year prison sentence. According to Perkins, 'in the still highly charged atmosphere of the city, persistent, if unverified, rumours of Egyptian agents propagandizing among the nomads and the occasional appearance of pamphlets they deemed inflammatory aggravated their concerns.'[23] Yet nothing concrete happened, and in Port Sudan, as elsewhere, the mixture of bitterness and fear experienced after the quelling of the previous mutiny brought the episodes of 1924 to an uneasy close.

Composition and strategies of the White Flag League in Port Sudan

One of the characteristics of the White Flag in Port Sudan was that the core members of the movement were socially very homogeneous. The Intelligence Department recorded a total of 45 people as political activists. Of these, only 25 were eventually charged with taking part in some form

[19] Perkins, *Port Sudan*, p. 160. Interestingly, official reports are quite confusing as to which troops arrived and when exactly. See SMIR No. 361, August 1924, WO 33/999, NA.

[20] Appendix to SMIR No. 361, August 1924, WO 33/999, NA.

[21] Captain H.M.S. 'Weymouth' to the Secretary of Admiralty, Aden, 20.8.1924, Palace 4/9/47, NRO.

[22] Acting Civ. sec. to Private Secretary, Khartoum, 30.8.1924, Palace 4/10/48, NRO.

[23] Perkins, *Port Sudan*, p. 161.

of protest, such as signing petitions, or demonstrating; the other 20 were either named in lists of members or under suspicion more because they were Egyptians than for any other reason. If we look at the 40 suspects out of 45, of whom we know the professions, we see that the majority (28) were civilian educated Sudanese, mostly government employees:

Table 2 Profession of the political activists in Port Sudan[24]

Government employees	
Railways	6
Post and Telegraph	8
Customs	4
Public Works Department	1
Education (teacher)	1
Unspecified	4
Sub-Total	*24*
Clerks in private companies	4
Total educated civilians	*28*
Officers of the Egyptian Army (including ex-officers)	9
Traders	1
Workmen (both were tailors)	2
Grand total	*40*

Of the 25 people whose origins are known, there were 13 Egyptians – among whom there were five officers, all merely suspects, and seven others who were defined as *Muwalladīn*. Here too should be noted the usual official tendency to label everybody as such (to the point that 'Alī Malāsī himself, who as seen had a Beja background, was so designated by the authorities). The remainder came from various regions in Northern Sudan. [25] It is noteworthy that no Beja is 'seen' in colonial records as a participant in the agitations. On the one hand, the British dealt with the Beja dockworkers through their *nāẓir*, clearly on the premise that it would be more efficient to use clan structures than the penal code. But the absence of Beja workers is also to be interpreted in the light of the inability of the British authorities to treat these individuals as real political agents, and not as mere pawns in the hands of the nationalists.

The success of the protests in Port Sudan, therefore, was mostly due to the 'avalanche-effect' strategy: a first peaceful demonstration in which the government was taken by surprise, followed by other demonstrations that were repressed more aggressively, then by arrests, then by several larger demonstrations, and again by renewed repression. All this happened in a climate of increased tension, exacerbated by political speeches at the

[24] Sources: Palace 4/9/44; Palace 4/9/45, Palace 4/9/46, Palace 4/9/47; Palace 4/10/48; Palace 4/10/49, Palace 4/10/50; Northern Province 1/21/207, all in NRO; and FO 141/810/3; FO 141/805/2; FO 141/806/1, in NA.

[25] DI to Gov., Erkowit, 1.7.1924, FO 141/806/1, NA.

mosque, pamphlets, and breathtaking news from the rest of the country. The tipping point was 'Alī Malāsī's speech in Tu-Bedawi: he literally and metaphorically 'translated' local dissatisfaction into a nationalist discourse.

There was, however, a clear social gap between the members of the League and the Beja stevedores who participated in demonstrations. The first were educated northern Sudanese, posted to Port Sudan following a government job; the second were wage workers who barely spoke Arabic, and who did not mix with northern Sudanese. One cannot fail to notice a hint of surprise in the oral accounts at the unexpected success of the League among the Beja. Their response – the eagerness of the Beja in their traditional dress to hold the flag of Egypt and the portrait of King Fu'ād – is depicted as somewhere between comic and epic. Somehow this attracted the attention of the activists so much that not only all of the three oral accounts report the same episode but also the participation of other elements, such as the men of the Railways Battalion, goes unnoticed. This suggests a distance between the nationalists and the Beja stevedores, the implication being that even people as 'rough' as the Beja supported Egypt.

Why did the spark so quickly catch fire, and why did it take so little for the Beja stevedores to follow people with whom they had so little in common? Furthermore, why did they identify themselves with symbols of a government that they had fought only few decades before, when under Turco-Egyptian rule? The question certainly deserves more time, more space, and more research so only a few of the possible answers are discussed below.

Labour conflicts in Port Sudan

The first step is to change perspective from a close-up of the insurgents to a broader panorama of Port Sudan as a colonial city, a description that I shall complete in the next section, in which I will compare Port Sudan and El Obeid.[26] Both cities were engines of Sudanese commercial activity but in a different way, the former being the Sudan's newest city, and the latter an ancient centre of Sudanese trade.

The idea of constructing Port Sudan arose because the country's main commercial port, the old city of Sawakin, was totally inadequate for the volume of trade that was expected to develop. Port Sudan was also intended to reduce Sudan's dependence on Egyptian commercial routes by connecting the Red Sea to the Nile by railway. Port Sudan quickly became the gateway for the import and export trade, and the connection point between domestic and international markets, in particular Great Britain and other colonies of the British Empire, such as India. Port Sudan was the place through which many of the new goods that were symbols of the

[26] The work of Perkins is the best study so far on Port Sudan as a colonial city. Additional references are: Kenneth J. Perkins, '"The Best Laid Out Town on the Red Sea" The Creation of Port Sudan, 1904-09', *Middle Eastern Studies,* (1991), vol. 27, n. 2, pp. 283-302. J. Oliver, 'Port Sudan: Its Growth and Function', *Urbanization and Urban Life in the Sudan*, Valdo Pons ed. ([Hull, Humberside]: Dept. of Sociology and Social Anthropology of the University of Hull, 1980), pp. 297-321; Sudan Railways, *Port Sudan Harbour* (Quays: Port Manager's office, 1966).

British colonial rule passed, from tea to sugar and textiles. It was trade that impacted the planning rationale behind the whole city.

Built between 1905 and 1909, the city was a jewel of colonial urban planning, 'a showcase of European technology,'[27] and in the words of a British inspector it was 'the only place in actual touch with the rest of the world.'[28] As it was built from scratch, special attention was paid to questions of sanitation, and the city was endowed with modern infrastructures that were unique in Sudan. In 1909, the year of its official inauguration, the city already boasted 'twenty-one stone buildings, exclusive of offices, storehouses and residential quarters erected by Government.'[29] These services were necessary to satisfy the needs of a sizeable foreign population, and indeed were mostly addressed to them, because trade was run by European multinational shipping companies, and their employees had to have convenient accommodation.

As with other colonial centres that were built to serve international trade, as for example Port Said in Egypt, Port Sudan spatially incarnated colonial hierarchies in its architecture, with its sharp difference between the shiny European neighbourhoods, with their modern services such as water and light, and the *deims,* the working-class neighbourhoods, which lacked any kind of facilities, and where the quality of habitations was extremely poor.[30] While a significant part of the working population of the *deims* of Khartoum – also a working class area – resided there permanently, this was not the case with Port Sudan, where most of the workers continued to be seasonal or occasional migrants. For that reason one may imagine that the housing conditions were even worse than in Khartoum.

Until the First World War, a wide range of Sudanese converged on it, attracted by the possibility of employment and above all by the fact that the cost of labour in Port Sudan was the highest in the country. The *Handbook of the Anglo-Egyptian Sudan* of 1922 described the city as being composed of Sudanese (meaning inhabitants of Sudan), Arabs from the Red Sea (read, nomadic groups), Egyptians, Abyssinians, and Indians.[31] Other reports also noted the presence of West African 'Takruri' and of 'Berberine' (Nubian) migrant workers. The authorities looked at this mixing with limited sympathy, but workers for the port were badly needed.

Nonetheless, the most important labour force in Port Sudan was represented by two communities: that is, Beja, who were mostly from the Amarar group, and Yemenis. While a few Amarari were permanent settlers of Port Sudan, the majority were temporary workers, typically males working until they had enough money to return home. There were not enough Beja workers to satisfy all the needs of the port city, however, so work gangs from Yemen kept coming to Port Sudan.[32]

27 Perkins, *Port Sudan*, p. 54.
28 Ibid., p. 139.
29 *Annual Report of the Red Sea Prov. 1909*, pp. 775-776.
30 Perkins, *Port Sudan*, pp. 99-107.
31 *The Handbook of the Anglo-Egyptian Sudan 1922*, pp. 719-720.
32 Andrew Paul, *A History of the Beja Tribes of the Sudan* (Cambridge: Cambridge University Press, 1954). Janet C. M. Milne, 'The Impact of Labour Migration on

The Yemenis were considered to be far superior workers to the Beja. For instance, in 1912, an officer stated that: 'One Yemeni at 12 PT does more work and does it better than 2 Sudanese at 6 PT would.'[33] Yemenis were usually employed as porters, which was a lighter and easier job than being a stevedore, a task reserved for the Beja: 'stevedoring on the ships is all done by Sudanese who only get 8 pt but they are unsuitable for any other work.'[34] According to Perkins, being a stevedore was, 'one of the most difficult and undesirable [jobs] on the quays, entailed long and uncomfortable hours in the sweltering confines of the ships' holds,' with shifts that could be as long as eleven hours a day.[35]

After the First World War, the Yemenis had become essential to all the city's port activities, and at the same time, the number of Beja coming to Port Sudan to work became more significant. In the post-war years, unlike in the rest of the country, and contrary to all pre-war trends, Port Sudan was the only city in which the cost of labour did not rise. This is when tensions between the Beja and the Yemeni port workers became more serious.[36]

The Beja continued working as before: hard and low paid work, and long shifts. But something was different after the war. In times of famine and drought, going home was a complicated matter and the particular situation of the Beja workers in Port Sudan must be viewed in relation to the general situation of Beja pastoralists in the colonial state. In the years before the Great War, and in particular in 1913, a severe drought hit northern Sudan; official reports of the time downplayed it considerably, to the point where they barely mentioned it at all, but we know that it was serious because grain had to be imported from India, and because it remained in the collective memory and was described by Sudanese literary figures later on.[37] It is difficult to know how much it affected the Beja, as the rains in Sudan can be very uneven, but hints in the Annual Reports suggest that this region was not spared:

> The nomads are, on the whole, very prosperous. The generally heavy coastal rains of the last winter provided an abundance of grazing. This was particularly acceptable north of Port Sudan where there had been several years' continuous drought. The 'Kharif' rainfall has, however, been scanty and local, and the nomads have been compelled to wander far in search of grazing for their flocks.[38]

(contd) the Amarar in Port Sudan', *Sudan Notes and Records* (1974) vol. 55, pp. 70–87. B.A. Lewis, 'Deim El Arab and the Beja Stevedores of Port Sudan', *Sudan Notes and Records* (1962) vol. 43, pp. 16–49. G. E. R. Sandars, 'The Amarar', *Sudan Notes and Records* (1935), vol. 18, n. 2, pp. 195-220.

33 Miralai, Director Sudan Customs to Gov. Red Sea Prov., 12.3.1912, Intel 4/7/54, NRO.

34 Ibid.

35 Perkins, *Port Sudan,* p. 124; and Inspector Port Sudan to Gov. Red Sea, Port Sudan, 20.3.1912, Intelligence 4/7/54, NRO.

36 Perkins, *Port Sudan,* pp. 88, 123-36.

37 Najīla, *Malāmiḥ Min al-Mujtama' al-Sūdānī,* pp. 17-18; Kisha, *Sūq al-Dhikryāt,* pp. 66. Alexander De Waal, *Famine Crimes: Politics & the Disaster Relief Industry in Africa* (African Rights & the International African Institute, 1997), chapter 2.

38 *Annual Report of the Red Sea Prov., 1913,* p. 231.

This quote is fascinating from another angle: droughts were depicted as natural occurrences in relation to which the government had no responsibility to act. People were used to droughts and would know how to deal with them. In these descriptions, nomads were as much a part of nature as droughts were.

This and other reports reflect the extent to which the government disengaged from all those areas in which it had no direct economic interest. As a consequence of its very scarce resources, it needed to be careful as to where and to whom to allocate them. The Beja were hardly ever on the list of priorities. But by its lack of engagement, the British government was merely continuing a centuries-old process of interaction between the various riverain states and the Beja: a relationship of mistrust, conflicts and tension.[39]

In Port Sudan, where the Beja lived in shanty *deims*, underpaid, and assigned to the worst jobs, it was inevitable that relations with the government would become, if possible, worse. Given this underlying framework, the reaction of Beja workers to the anticolonial programme of nationalist agitators becomes easier to understand. It was nurtured not only by circumstantial injustices related to their working conditions and competition with Yemeni labourers, but also by broader issues relating to their 'invisibility' to an absentee state. For once, there was the hope that this could be overcome by participating in open, visible and roaring demonstrations.[40]

EL OBEID

The story of the nationalist movement in El Obeid is in many respects the antithesis of what happened in Port Sudan. This is due primarily to its entirely different setting, and to the city's very different relationship with the colonial state. If Port Sudan was a showcase for European urban technology, El Obeid was perpetually on the waiting list as regards construction of the 'most urgent' infrastructures. In 1908, a Report complained: 'the province [is] still much under-staffed in every-department.'[41] In 1912, the El Obeid hospital was still a temporary building made up of three *tukuls*, despite having 300 admissions each year and an annual average of approximately 3,000 outpatients.[42] Government buildings and the sanitation and water systems were poor, even if El Obeid was the seat of the provincial administration, the headquarters of

[39] On the relations between the state and the Beja, Leif O. Manger, 'Pastoralist-State Relationships among the Hadendowa Beja of Eastern Sudan', *Nomadic Peoples* (2001), vol. 5, n. 2, pp. 21–48.

[40] Barbara Casciarri, 'De l'altérité et de l'invisibilité des groupes pastoraux au Soudan. Repenser les études soudanaises en partant de leurs marges mobiles', *Canadian Journal of African Studies* (2015), vol. 49, n. 1.

[41] *Reports on the Finance, Administration, and Condition of the Sudan*, 1908, p. 483.

[42] *Reports on the Finance, Administration, and Condition of the Sudan*, 1912, vol. 1, p. 178.

the Camel Corps, and home to a shifting population between 11,500 and 40,000 inhabitants (variations were due to fluxes in herding, agriculture, and trade).[43] In 1921, the government was still pondering whether it was a good idea to build an 'expensive bank building' in El Obeid for the Bank of Egypt, which had opened ten years earlier.[44]

Other differences are linked to the structure of the national movement. In Kordofan, the League made extensive efforts to expand both to the entire province and beyond the initial group that had formed it. The situation appeared promising and ripe for protest. For example, White Flag member Muḥammad Jabr al-Dār estimated in August:

> There are a number of people who are in straightened circumstances in the Town owing to being turned out of the Animal Market etc. and to the fact that trade is stagnant at the moment. The most insidious propaganda is ceaselessly put about and if I arranged a demonstration thousands of people would join in and there might be a big row.[45]

Moreover, it should be remembered that political clubs and associations began to be formed during the First World War, so that political activism, particularly among officers, was not a novelty. In spite of this, however, the League failed to organize any significant open protests. In this section, I shall reconstruct the history of 1924 in El Obeid and explore some possible reasons for this immobility.

The types of sources available are the opposite of those available in Port Sudan. Oral accounts for Kordofan are scant: *Al-Riwāyāt* includes the testimony of only one activist, officer Muḥammad Ṣāliḥ al-Mak, who was not actually based in El Obeid in 1924, but in Bara (a city at about 60 km from the former).[46] Colonial sources, on the other hand, are exceptionally rich. The British authorities were particularly successful at infiltrating the movement without its members realizing it, and obtained almost daily accounts on its activities, projects, and members. Different informants told the authorities roughly similar versions of events, although they also contained improbable tales of murders and plots, *coups d'état*, and counter-spies. The significance of this gossip and rumour lies not in the accuracy of the details, but in the fact that when read against the grain they speak of power conflicts, personal rivalries, and complex interactions between the colonial power and its subjects in the town. It would not be feasible to undertake a thorough exploration of all the idiosyncrasies revealed by the sources here: the aim of this section is not to be exhaustive, but to reveal certain broad features of the nationalist movement in this location.

The wealth of sources is also related to the fact that the Kordofan branch of the White Flag was perhaps the most important in the entire country. The Intelligence Department recorded that as many as 100 people in El Obeid were either members or active supporters of the White Flag.

43 Ibid., p. 171

44 Percy Falcke Martin, *The Sudan in Evolution* (London, 1921), p. 486.

45 Notes on the activity of the White Flag Society at El Obeid, Gov. Kordofan Prov. to DI, El Obeid, 8.8.1924, Kordofan 1/14/68, NRO.

46 *Al-Riwāyāt*, pp. 563-583, District Commissioner, Northern Kordofan to Gov. Kordofan, Bara, 14.11.1924, Kordofan 1/12/57, NRO.

The League also established sub-provincial branches: three people were reported to be members in Bara, and as many as 24 in Umm Ruwaba; moreover, 'agents' of the movement were sent to Taqali (in the Nuba Mountains), El Nuhud, among the Baqqāra in the Feriks around El Obeid, the Habbāniyya in Shirgeila, the Dūlayb in Bara, and even further west. [47]

Thwarted demonstrations

The account of 1924 in El Obeid is more one of what did not happen, what was planned but failed, and of various thwarted attempts, rather than what actually occurred. As early as June, the Intelligence Department discovered that the White Flag League was planning to open branches in El Obeid, Shendi, Atbara, and El Fasher.[48] June passed without incident, however, as did most of July. On 25 July, Aḥmad Ismā'īl al-Dhākir (Zaki or Zakir in the British sources) made an 'inflammatory speech' at the El Obeid mosque, shouting 'God strengthen the Moslem and give victory to the King of Egypt and Sudan.'[49] Significantly, no demonstration followed, although 'the Imam ordered the Mosque ghaffir to arrest [Ahmed Zaki Ismail] but the worshippers rose to their feet', thereby protecting him from the police.[50] This man worked as a broker (*simsār,* pl. *samāsira*) at the cattle market in El Obeid, and the authorities explained his behaviour by that fact that he had been 'adversely affected by recent regulations re. brokers and wished to give effect to his feelings'.[51]

Much more information on the movement began to reach British intelligence from August onwards. First of all, the authorities managed to infiltrate it by contacting the father of the 'agent' appointed by the League in Khartoum to 'work' in Kordofan and support the local political movement. The latter was ex-officer Muḥammad Ḥāmid Jabr al-Dār who was a discharged Mulazim Tani.[52] Muḥammad came from a very prominent Kordofanese family, and his father put pressure on him to collaborate with the government.[53] This was a stroke of luck for the authorities, as

[47] For sources, see Appendix 2.

[48] DI to Gov. El Obeid, Khartoum, 26.6.1924, Kordofan 1/12/54 and a copy in Kordofan 1/14/68, NRO.

[49] SMIR No. 360, July 1924, WO 33/999, NA. See also Telegram from Gov., El Obeid to DI, 26.7.1924, Palace 4/10/49 and also Notes on the activity of the White Flag Society at El Obeid, Gov. Kordofan Prov. to DI, El Obeid, 8.8.1924, Kordofan 1/14/68, NRO.

[50] Gov. Kordofan to Mukhbarat Khartoum, 26.7.1924, Kordofan 1/12/56, NRO.

[51] Notes on the activity of the White Flag Society at El Obeid, Gov. Kordofan Prov. to DI, El Obeid, 8.8.1924, Kordofan 1/14/68, NRO.

[52] 'Most anxious not arrest him as he is invaluable.' Gov., Kordofan to Gov., Khartoum, 5.8.1924, Kordofan 1/12/57, NRO. In June, he was described as a discharged MT in a list of Sudanese officers and officials who were signatories to a telegram dated 28.6, Palace 4/10/49, NRO. There is a short biographical presentation of this individual on a sheet of handwritten notes, presumably from the Gov. of Kordofan, attached to a report, Gov. Kordofan to DI, 2.9.1924, FO 141/805/2, NA.

[53] See Assistant Gov., Kordofan Prov. to DI, El Obeid, 2.9.1924, FO 141/805/2, NA, and Notes on the activities of the White Flag Society in El Obeid, 8.8.1924, Kordofan 1/14/68, NRO. About this family, see Rex S. O'Fahey and Jay L. Spaulding.

Muḥammad Jabr al-Dār immediately joined the leadership of agitators and participated in all their meetings.

The central committee of the political movement was composed of Sudanese officers: besides ex-officer Jabr al-Dār, there were three officers from the Camel Corps who were all from Northern Sudan: *Yuzbashi* Muḥammad Ṣāliḥ Jibrīl, *Mulazim Awal* Aḥmad Idrīs, and *Mulazim Awal* Ṣāliḥ Raḥma.[54] But the real leaders of the movement were Muḥammad Ṣāliḥ Jibrīl and another individual connected to the fulcrum of El Obeid political life, the Officers' Club. Although the history of this club is not known, it appears to have been a well-consolidated institution in the town, and it was attended by both Sudanese and Egyptian officers. At some point in 1924, Muḥammad Ṣāliḥ Jibrīl and an Egyptian medical doctor, Muḥ ammad Sharīf, who also worked for the army, were elected as heads of the club. As a British official noted, 'As soon as [Muḥammad Ṣāliḥ Jibrīl] arrived here he joined the officers and officials club, and immediately set to work to do all in his power to change the club for a social club into a political club.'[55] Thus, the politicization of the club did not pass unnoticed. It was a public place, and the officers do not seem to have taken much care to remain low key.

Some peculiar features of the El Obeid movement can be gleaned from this description. First, unlike in other locations, army officers played a leading role. Moreover, they made themselves very visible, giving the British the pretext to remove them. This was especially the case with Muḥammad Ṣāliḥ Jibrīl. He was the brother of Sudan Union founder, poet and 'agitator' Tawfīq Ṣāliḥ Jibrīl, member of a well-known Kordofanese family of traders and scholars, and was married to the daughter of a prominent merchant from El Obeid.[56] The Assistant Governor of Kordofan described him thus:

> He is, as is well known, an extremely active member of the White Flag society. He is moreover a man of bad character and intensely anti-British... I trust that the Adjutant General will be able to transfer him without delay to some region where his political activities are unlikely to cause trouble.[57]

As a leader, Muḥammad Ṣāliḥ Jibrīl was quite a charismatic figure. According to his colleague Muḥammad Ṣāliḥ al-Mak, 'he was unable to control himself'[58] in the sense that he was unable to remain behind the scenes as he should have done as a White Flag League leader and an

(contd) 1972. 'Hāshim and the Musabba'āt.' *Bulletin of the School of Oriental and African Studies, University of London,* vol. 35, n.2, pp. 316-333.

54 This is confirmed both by Muḥammad Ṣāliḥ al-Mak (*al Riwāyāt*, p. 563) and in List of Members of White Flag Society at El Obeid, Kordofan 1/14/68, NRO.

55 Sarsfield Hall, Assistant Gov. Kordofan to Director Medical Dept., El Obeid 1.8.1924, Kordofan 1/12/47, NRO.

56 Extract form report of no. 34, Intel. Dept., not dated, Kordofan 1/12/57, NRO. See also Report from El Obeid by Assistant DI, Khartoum 20.3.1926, Kordofan 1/12/57, NRO.

57 Assistant Gov. Kordofan to Civsec, El Obeid 29.7.1924, see also the personal file of Muḥammad Ṣāliḥ Jibrīl, Kordofan 1/12/56, NRO.

58 *Al-Riwāyāt*, p. 564.

officer. Not only did he speak openly against the government, but he also used to accost people who were known supporters of the British and threaten them.[59] He was never scared of defying colonial rule: for instance, on the day of his transfer to Khartoum, he 'was ordered to go in a car to the station for fear of a demonstration, but he again refused and swore he would walk to the station and actually did so'.[60]

In his oral account, Muḥammad Ṣāliḥ al-Mak believed that the real reason behind the transfer of this officer was that he became involved in a row with an Egyptian *mamur* whom Muḥammad believed to be a spy: 'I think Muḥammad Ṣāliḥ Jibrīl said offensive words to him and said to him, this is the train of the King [of Egypt] and this is the country of the King.'[61] All this would seem to indicate that Muḥammad had not been to the League's 'school', in the sense that he acted very differently from the League's leaders in Khartoum. In El Obeid, therefore, a particular combination of events took place that proved decisive for hampering protests: on the one hand, the ability on the part of the government to infiltrate the movement, and on the other, an unusual self-assurance and boldness on the part of its leaders that did not pay off.

Because they were updated on every planned activity, the British were able to adopt an effective preventive line, and to thwart all attempts at demonstrations before they could take place. During the heated month of August, on the 7th, 'a demonstration was arranged to take place this day (demonstrators riff-raff, disgruntled simsars etc.) but police by this time had been armed with 'sunt' [hard wood] batons, and were held in readiness and no demonstration took place.'[62] Two more demonstrations were organized later, but again attempts to hold them were thwarted. The first was due to take place on the departure by train of Muḥammad Ṣāliḥ Jibrīl, on 13 August, when as many as 60 police officers were deployed around the station. Here the colonial sources and the oral account diverge. While for the former there was no demonstration, for Muḥammad Ṣāliḥ al-Mak, a small group of demonstrators definitely gathered and shouted for the independence of Egypt and Sudan.[63]

On 16 August, it was the turn of Muḥammad Sharīf to be deported to Egypt. This time, the authorities were even more careful: '...a police cordon was drawn round the Station yard and no Officers or Officials were admitted.'[64] It is also significant that the two leaders were not imprisoned, but were transferred, thereby avoiding the possibility that their arrest might spark protests. Ultimately, the only possible form of protest in this context was the distribution of anonymous, 'seditious' circulars, which

[59] For a full account, see (Gov. Kordofan Prov.) to Civsec, 13.9.1924, Kordofan 1/12/56, NRO.

[60] Letter from Iman Mohammed Osman, Veterinary Dept. to El Badry Mansour, El Obeid. News on 13th August 1924, Kordofan 1/14/68, NRO.

[61] *Al-Riwāyāt*, p. 564.

[62] Assistant Gov. Kordofan Prov. to DI, El Obeid, 2.9.1924, FO 141/805/2, NA.

[63] *Al-Riwāyāt*, p. 565.

[64] Assistant Gov. Kordofan Prov. to DI, El Obeid, 2.9.1924, FO 141/805/2, NA, and Chronicle of 1924, undated and unsigned, Kordofan 1/13/62, NRO.

took place fairly vigorously and was reported to the authorities constantly throughout the month of August. Here, however, there was little the government could do.

The political movement was unable to survive this series of disappointments; worse, its two leaders had failed to consolidate it sufficiently so that it could flourish after their departure. In the case of Port Sudan, we have seen that the arrest of Ṣāliḥ 'Abd al-Qādir did not bring the downfall of the movement, but actually set things in motion. In El Obeid, on the other hand, there was a power vacuum when the two leaders of the Officers' Club were transferred. The authorities reported that the League had 'died,' and that fifty-two people had resigned from it.[65] As another informant observed: '...we have no meetings as there is no head.'[66]

The strategy of frustrating the national movement by showing that it had no room for manoeuvre continued into the following month. Five people – two clerks, two unemployed men, and a *simsār* – were arrested in September and sentenced to three-years' imprisonment for sedition.[67] The local Egyptian battalion was recalled to Khartoum and replaced by a British battalion, which, in the words of an officer, 'provided tangible proof that the British Government meant what they said.'[68] The Officers Club split in September as the participants elected new and more moderate leaders.[69] Finally, the radical wing was further broken up when most of the Egyptian officers in El Obeid were expelled to Egypt during September and October.

The composition and organization of the League in El Obeid

In El Obeid alone, and in spite of a lack of demonstrations, the British registered as many as 100 people as suspected members or supporters of the League, more than double the number of Port Sudan. The information seized in El Obeid also incidentally cast light on the League's activities in Khartoum, which explains why so many documents on the League as a whole emanated from Kordofan.

We have seen that officers represented an important component of the political activists in El Obeid, and that in turn, civilian government

[65] Information, 10.8.1924, Meeting in the house of MA Ahmed Eff. Idris on 8.8.1924, Kordofan 1/14/68, NRO.

[66] Information, not signed, 17.8.1924, Kordofan 1/14/68, NRO.

[67] Telegram from DI, Khartoum, to SA, Cairo, 13.9.1924, FO 141/805/2, NA.

[68] DI to Gov., El Obeid, 12.9.1924, Kordofan 1/12/55, NRO.

[69] Censored letter no. 36, from Hamid El Qardawi, Officers and Officials Club, El Obeid, to Dr Mohammed Eff. Sherif, Alexandria (recently deported), 21.9.1924, Kordofan 1/14/68, NRO: 'I am sorry to tell you that, upon your departure, the wicked separated leaders of hesitation and who are the cause of our calamity and disease, have agreed to fight us. The Bimbashi Mustafa Fahmi and Hafez and others have made a covenant to exterminate the spirit of work, effort and vivacity which exist in the Club. It has been decided to elect Mustafa Fahmi and Basil Bulos as members of the Central Committee ... It has been decided at a hastily called meeting not to make any celebration without the permission of the Executive Committee and that all speeches should be submitted for confirmation. El Ansari and I have opposed but fruitlessly.'

employees had a much less prominent role. This was due to the fact that the Government was mostly present in El Obeid through the army (the town was a major army headquarters), and there were few civilian government employees because of the lack of public services and an elaborate government administration.

It would be a mistake to think that only officers became involved in politics, however: in fact, an analysis of the socio-professional background of the suspected activists reveals three main social components: officers and officials; merchants and middlemen; and skilled workers and artisans. In the two tables below, the first tabulates the 35 men who were directly involved in some sort of anti-government activity, of whom we know the professions of 28; the second table includes all the 91 individuals (out of 100) suspected in El Obeid whose profession we know, for instance people who had been named in lists of White Flag members.

Table 3 Profession of protesters in El Obeid[70]

Civilian employees (in private and public sectors)	4
Officers	12
Traders	6
Skilled and unskilled workers	2
Students	3
Headmen	1
Total	28

Table 4 Profession of all the people suspected in El Obeid

Civilian employees	23
Officers (including 2 ex-officers)	28
Traders	29
Merchants	(20)
Cattle brokers	(7)
Singer sewing machine salesmen	(2)
Skilled and unskilled workers	5
Students	3
Headmen	1
Others (an owner of a canteen and a policeman)	2

[70] Tables 3 and 4 have been constructed from the names of activists found in the following files: in NRO: Kordofan 1/12/54, Kordofan 1/12/55, Kordofan 1/12/56, Kordofan 1/12/57, Kordofan 1/12/58, Kordofan 1/13/59, Kordofan 1/13/61, Kordofan 1/14/65, Kordofan 1/14/68; Palace 4/9/44, Palace 4/9/45, Palace 4/9/46, Palace 4/9/47, Palace 4/10/48, Palace 4/10/49, Palace 4/10/50; in NA: FO 151/805/2.

Total	91

It should be observed that out of 100 suspects, the origins of only 36 are known. Apart from the fact that this is fairly similar to the situation elsewhere (it included Egyptians, *Muwalladīn*, northern Sudanese – above all Nubians – and some 'Black Sudanese'), it is not enough to give us a representative idea of their backgrounds.

These tables clearly highlight the greater heterogeneity in terms of socio-professional categories compared with the political activists of in Port Sudan. Indeed, various sources confirm this point. As Muḥammad Ṣāliḥ al-Mak put it:

> We started to spread the propaganda around and we used to receive funds form Khartoum by the intermediary of someone called Abū al-Ṭayyib... he was a trader.... The propaganda reached even the villages through the *'umād* [sg. *'umda*], for example, the Bidayriyya *'umda*, he was a young man, he was my friend.[71]

In a similar vein, an informant reported: 'We are just about to make arrangements for sending out "Mandubs" [agents] to all the tribes in the Province to stir them up and give them definite instructions as to what they are to do when they are given orders to rise.'[72] The same informant stated that each activist had to 'stir up' an allocated constituency, and that there existed a list specifying who had to do what.

It is fascinating to take a closer look at this list. As in Khartoum, also in El Obeid contacts with potential White Flag supporters were made according to socio-professional affiliations. For example, the Egyptian officer Ḥāmid al-Qarḍāwī had the 'duty to stir up CC [Civil Court] clerks and the members of the Club'. The trader 'Bayyid' Ibrāhīm had 'to work up the merchants'. This same list is of further interest because it also mentions the presence of skilled workers (a baker, a watchmaker, and a butcher), who apparently were not assigned to any specific duties, except for a certain 'Abdul Rabbo' who had to 'work up Muwalladin'.[73] Such list perhaps hints at one of the shortcomings of the political movement in El Obeid. Workers had clear grievances – some quite explicit anti-British talk was reported to the authorities[74] – and yet it seems that the movement did not think of mobilizing dissatisfied workers through their professional allegiances.

Instead, the movement sought to mobilize 'blood' connections. For example, it was reported that officer Ādam Adham refused to be section leader because 'it would be useless to him ... as he had no people of his tribe in El Obeid.'[75] It is also quite revealing that in order to hinder the spread of the League, the British authorities summoned all the heads of the main

71 *Al-Riwāyāt*, p. 563.

72 Notes on the activity of the White Flag Society at El Obeid, Gov. Kordofan Prov. to DI El Obeid, 8.8.1924, Kordofan 1/14/68, NRO.

73 List of Members of White Flag Society at El Obeid, undated, Kordofan 1/14/68, NRO.

74 See, for instance, the case of Khalīl Fahmī 'Saati', mentioned in Chapter 10.

75 Information given by El MA Abdul Rahim El Sheikh, 26.9.1924, Kordofan 1/14/68, NRO.

ethnic groups present in the city – Danaqla, Ja'alyyin, Ja'afra, Shayqi, Fellata, and so on – as well as the local heads responsible for the market and the various neighbourhoods, and informed them that 'in future they would be held responsible for loyal behaviour of the members of their tribes ... and be expected to hand over to the Government any person guilty of disloyal actions.'[76]

There is a final point to make on the number of people who turned Kings' witness. A review of the records reveals that the Intelligence Department could dispose of many informants, and they were quite diverse in terms of profession and status: there was a merchant, a supervisor of the vegetable market, and a guard, for example.[77] Similarly, there are many pages that bear witness to divisions and betrayals among the traders of El Obeid, heated rows among officers of the Camel Corps based on rifts that are difficult to decipher, and disputes among the heads of local communities. Taken together, these sources describe a highly divided society, marked by antagonism and conflicts; this in turn suggests that the national movement was not successful in creating solidarities across the social divides. In other words, the spark from the national movement did not ignite a process by which individuals and groups set aside their social, professional and ethnic differences through participation in a national movement.

One possible answer to the different situation of El Obeid compared to Khartoum or Port Sudan can be found in a perhaps unexpected factor: the level of salaries, which was in turn an indicator of the socio-economic situation in this town. Kordofan was one of the few regions in Sudan in which salaries remained low, before and after the First World War. Migrant workers – including pastoralists from Kordofan itself – who were looking to earn money for their various needs did not search for jobs in this region. For instance, Ta'aysha Baqqara from Kordofan were reported to go to Khartoum, but not to El Obeid, to search for salaried work (see Chapter 10). After the Great War, the province of Kordofan recorded a significant increase in production of cattle, sesame, sorghum, and above all gum arabic, which was historically the most important product from the region. In spite of this, wages in this province were among the lowest in the whole country. There are various reasons, principally associated with the type of agricultural products the region exported. First, extraction of gum arabic from trees combined very well with other types of agricultural production, without necessarily requiring an increase in the workforce.[78] A labour report from 1921 shows that cultivators in Kordofan were busy all year round: 'from June to January in growing dura [sorghum] and from January to June in the production of gum.'[79] There was no dead season

[76] They were summoned to a meeting in the Governor's office on the 17.8.24. Note (undated but around 17.8.24), Kordofan 1/14/68, NRO.
[77] See the whole file Kordofan 1/14/65, NRO.
[78] Stiansen, 'The Gum Arabic Trade in Kordofan in the mid-Nineteenth Century'. *Kordofan Invaded: Peripherial Incorporation and Social Transformation in Islamic Africa*, Endre Stiansen and Michael Kevane eds. (Leiden: Brill, 1998), pp. 60-85.
[79] Report of the Labour Committee 1921, p. 29, Intel 4/4/19, NRO.

when workers could leave to earn extra income except in the case of severe drought. Similarly, cattle herding was integrated with agricultural production and did not necessarily take time away from it.[80] Second, as seen, the infrastructure works carried out by the government in the region were very modest, especially compared with those of Khartoum and Port Sudan, or even along the Nile, where two large dams were constructed at Makwar on the Blue Nile and at Jabal Awlia on the White Nile, just south of Khartoum.

Further, the strength of patron-client relations may explain why the need for salaried work may not have been acute. In this province, British officers described how ancient slave communities were regularly tapped by their former owners to carry out agricultural work while they continued their pastoralist activities, as in the case of the Mandala, who were 'slaves' – or to be more precise, 'clients' – of the Baqqara.[81] An important report on slavery in Sudan written in the same years observed that this was the region where the issue of slavery had evolved the least, and where it was most difficult for slaves to leave their masters.[82] Thus, agricultural outputs could increase without any significant visible dislocation of the production structures – and hence the social structures – in existence. In other words, the labour force required for local needs was extracted through networks of clients. El Obeid's economic development consolidated, rather than weakened, established social structures.

To conclude, it could be suggested that in El Obeid the strength of the patron-client networks hampered the mechanisms that made the protests effective elsewhere. The activists sought to mobilize educated groups through their professional affiliations, but they used a different method with the population at large, attempting to recruit followers by contacting their reputed heads. This is exactly what the British also did when they sought to weaken the League by summoning all the 'leaders of the tribes'. When the movement contacted a leader, it created the opportunity for his rivals to denounce him to the government. The same phenomenon occurred among the trading community, that formed an important component of the national movement in El Obeid. The conspicuous number of traders who provided information to the government leads to the conclusion that, in so doing, they were attempting to side-line rivals by denouncing their actual or alleged adherence to the movement. Thus, in spite of the fact that Kordofan was overall a troublesome region (which is why there was a large army headquarters in El Obeid), the political potential offered by

[80] The literature is vast, but see: M.A.M. Salih, 'Agro-Pastoralists Response to Agricultural Policies: The Predicament of the Baggara, Western Sudan', *Adaptive Strategies in African Arid Lands,* Proceedings of the Scandinavian Institute of African Studies (1989), pp. 59–75. B. Casciarri, and Abdel Ghaffar Mohammed Ahmed, 'Pastoralists under Pressure in Present-Day Sudan: An Introduction', *Nomadic Peoples* (2009), vol. 13, n. 1, pp. 10–22.

[81] G. D. Lampen, 'The Baggara Tribes of Darfur,' *Sudan Notes and Records* (1933), vol. 16, n. 2, pp. 97–118; G. K. C. Hebbert, 'The Bandala of the Bahr El Ghazal', *Sudan Notes and Records* (1925), vol. 8, pp. 187–94.

[82] Willis Report on Slavery in the Sudan, quoted in Taj Hargey, 'The Suppression of Slavery in the Sudan, 1898-1939' (PhD Thesis, University of Oxford, 1981), p. 384.

such unrest was reduced by rivalries among individuals and networks of clients.

These considerations – in conjunction with the higher, yet carefully weighed, levels of repression – may explain why there was no outburst of protest. On closer inspection, it is evident that the two elements are intertwined: it was easier for the British to control a certain community if it was organized vertically and steered in some way by a 'tribal leader'. It was precisely this awareness that made the policy of Indirect Rule so attractive to the British in Sudan from the 1920s onwards.

NATIONALISM AND TRADE IN EL OBEID

The cases of El Obeid and Port Sudan cast light on the importance of domestic and international trade in bringing change to colonial Sudan, which on a larger scale reveals the political impact of economic transformations. El Obeid and Port Sudan were the two most important centres of Sudanese trade, yet local traders played a very uneven role both in economy and in politics. The final section of this chapter will take a closer look at this social component.

The first element of note is that most of the traders who supported the League were concentrated in two areas: colonial records include the names of 59 traders, 51 of whom were based in either Kordofan or Khartoum; while very few were based in the Red Sea province.

The reason for that is evident: Port Sudan was a city recently built to boost international trade; on the contrary, El Obeid was a fairly neglected centre in term of services and facilities, and yet, particularly before the

Table 5 Merchants' place of origin [83]

Origins of the merchants	Number
Atbara	1
Berber	1
Damer	1
Halfa	1
Medani	1
Port Sudan	1
Shendi	3
Umm Ruwaba	3
Sherkeila	6
El Obeid	20
Khartoum	21
Total	*59*

[83] Source: NRO: Palace 4/9/44, Palace 4/9/46, Palace 4/10/48, Palace 4/10/49, Palace 4/10/50, Kordofan 1/12/55, Kordofan 1/12/56, Kordofan 1/12/57, Kordofan 1/12/58, Kordofan 1/13/59, Kordofan 1/16/68, Northern Prov. 1/21/215; Northern

creation of the Gezira Irrigation Scheme with its cotton monoculture, El Obeid was one of the engines of the Sudanese economy. Its hinterland was the principal producer of gum arabic, which during this period represented about 39% of overall national exports (although major fluctuations were the norm).[84] Other agricultural products crucial to regional, national and international trade included cattle, sorghum, sesame, and groundnuts.[85]

The importance of El Obeid as a trading centre is recorded from at least the 18th century.[86] Under Turco-Egyptian rule, it was a prosperous base for large trading companies dealing in gum, ivory, and slaves. With the beginning of the Condominium, the goods changed but the commercial role of the city became more consolidated. In particular, the arrival of the railway line connecting El Obeid to Khartoum and Port Sudan in 1912 boosted the life of the city enormously, to the point where trade came to be siphoned off from other economic centres such as Kosti and El Dueim, on the White Nile, leading a number of traders to move to El Obeid. Similarly, other centres in Kordofan, in particular Bara and El Nuhud, prospered. To give an idea of the importance of these centres, suffice to say that in 1924, Port Sudan had about 15,000 inhabitants, but in that same year the population of El Nuhud – a smaller centre than El Obeid – had an estimated 7,000 to 12,000 inhabitants;[87] and as seen El Obeid population fluctuated between 11,500 and 40,000 people.

In 1920s Port Sudan, international companies, and not Sudanese ones, instead monopolized the trade. It is revealing that various members of the White Flag League were low-level clerks of the international shipping company Gellatly & Hankey. In El Obeid, on the other hand, trade was mostly carried out by a mixed group of Sudanese, often with close ties to Egypt, and by Egyptians with close ties to Sudanese. The trading community included newcomers and old merchants, and some individuals from Kordofan, but mostly from outside the province. In 1924, this diversity was reflected in the sample of merchants and market contractors of El Obeid whose nationality is known (10 out of 20): a 'Kenzi', a 'Berberi', a Danagla and two Jaali, two 'Copts' (one of which 'Egyptian'), an 'Egyptian of Aswan', a 'Furawi', a 'Muwallad', and a 'Syrian'.

It was the norm for Sudanese trading families to have extremely wide connections. Trade worked through these family connections, spreading

Prov. 1/19/133, Northern Prov. 1/20/192. NA: FO 141/805/1, FO 141/810/3.

84 Endre Stiansen, 'The Gum Arabic Trade in Kordofan in the Mid-Nineteenth Century', pp. 60-85.

85 See, for instance, the *Annual Report of the Kordofan Prov. 1913*, pp. 191-192, which describes an exceptionally abundant year for crops.

86 Taj-el-Anbia Ali El Dawi, 'The Residential Ecology of El Obeid', *Urbanization and Urban Life in the Sudan*, pp. 322-351 (in particular pages 325-327). Taj-el-Anbia Ali El-Dawi, 'Social Characteristics of Big Merchants and Businessmen in El Obeid', *Essays in Sudan Ethnography,* Ian Cunnison and Wendy James eds. (London: C. Hurst, 1972), pp. 201-216.

87 In 1906, Port Sudan had 2,275 inhabitants, in 1916 it had 6,300 and in 1926 16,674. Perkins, *Port Sudan*, p. 93.

all over the country, a pattern that scholars date from at least the 19th century.[88] Usually, the headquarters would be in Khartoum, but members of the extended family would settle in the most important commercial centres on the major the trade routes. This emerges clearly in the records of 1924. One document is worth quoting at some length: it is a report to the Intelligence Department, describing how traders' networks contributed to finance the national movement:

> The money is arriving from Egypt... in the name of one of the two named: Abdel Hamid El Mahdi, cattle merchants, Omdurman or El Sayed Id; and handed over to Habiballa Id, cattle merchant in Omdurman. This latter arrived in Omdurman coming from Egypt in April last. He is the uncle of El Sayed Id. Habiballa is said to be the person who undertakes the distribution of the money to the various places. In Berber Hussein Id – brother of Habiballa – is alleged to be responsible for that part of the country. He is supposed to be the medium of conveyance of documents which he receives from Omdurman, and is responsible for getting them from Berber to Shellal... Hussein Id has been to Egypt since 1921. He started a cattle trade in Berber, his native town, last July. He appointed a certain El Khidr Hamed, also a native of Berber, to represent him at El Obeid. Khidr Ahmed is now supposed to be the agent for Kordofan.[89]

This report reveals a dense network of traders who were either family members (an uncle and two brothers) or had other ties (such as being born in the same city, or the merchant and his agent). The family was scattered across Kordofan (El Obeid), Northern Sudan (Shellal, Berber), and Omdurman, and its members kept moving back and forth over these regions and between Egypt and Sudan. Doing business the Sudanese way did not simply mean exchanging goods, but also sharing a family.

The trading networks contributed to the spread of nationalism in 1924. For example, an informant reported about a merchant from El Obeid:

> This man has paid me another visit and informed me that if I want to send any letters to Egypt I can hand them to him and he will arrange to hand them to Loca Gulta [a Coptic merchant] who will forward them to Egypt.[90]

The records from 1924 also reveal that many of the Egyptian merchants of El Obeid had lived in Sudan their whole lives, and both their families and businesses were built on their dual allegiance to these two countries. For instance, one informant related:

> Sheikh Abd El Magid Gharib is a merchant and was delegated by the members of the club to make propaganda. He is an Egyptian who lives in the Sudan and knows the Sudan language and habits, and he was present during the Mahdia. The most of the people listens [sic] to his words, and he obtains all he wishes through the Egyptians.[91]

[88] Leif O. Manger, *Trade and Traders in the Sudan* ([Bergen]: Dept. of Social Anthropology, University of Bergen, 1984). Lidwien Kapteijns and J. Spaulding, 'Precolonial Trade Between States in the Eastern Sudan, ca 1700 - ca 1900', *African Economic History* (1982), vol. 11, pp. 29-62. Jane Ewald, *Soldiers, Traders, and Slaves: State Formation and Economic Transformation in the Greater Nile Valley, 1700-1885* (Madison: University of Wisconsin Press, 1990).

[89] Intelligence Information, Khartoum, 27.8.1924, Northern Prov. 1/21/215 (a copy is also in Kordofan 1/14/68), NRO.

[90] Information given by informant, 19.9.1924, Kordofan 1/12/55, NRO.

[91] Informant to the DI, Khartoum, El Obeid 20.7.1924, Kordofan 1/12/56, NRO.

It is evident that the distinction between being Sudanese and Egyptian made little sense for these people; the unity of the Nile Valley was much more than a matter of business or politics: it was a question of flesh and blood. Family connections between Egypt and Sudan had not only been inherited from the Turco-Egyptian rule; they also facilitated business during the Condominium, as Egypt had such a prominent place in Sudanese trade.

Things were changing rapidly, however. In 1921 and 1922, the market suffered a significant slump in prices, in what appears to have been the first crisis of overproduction in Sudan.[92] This coincided with a rise in taxes. After the war the British authorities introduced two very unpopular levies, the Traders' Tax and the Animal Tax, which directly affected the cattle trade, and thus trade with Egypt. The economic depression, followed by the new taxes, caused cattle merchants significant losses. For example, in 1921, cattle exports fell by one-third in a single year, and the sale of sheep and goats exactly halved compared with the period between 1911 and 1920.[93] As with the droughts in the Red Sea that were plaguing the Beja, the government saw these dramatic fluctuations in the markets as something people had to cope with on their own: interventions were outside the responsibility of a state. A government could facilitate trade by building infrastructures such as railways, dams, and irrigation ditches, but should not interfere with the invisible hand of international markets.

In addition to these difficulties, in these years there was much talk of the Gezira scheme and its impact on the Sudanese economy: indeed, studies on trade patterns have demonstrated that the Gezira Irrigation Scheme led to a drastic shift in the role of Egypt in the Sudanese economy.[94] Exports to Egypt in the period between 1925 and 1930 were half those of the period 1920-1925. Cotton produced in the Gezira and exported through Port Sudan became the most profitable item in the Sudanese economy, making it less attractive to cultivate other products. With the Gezira scheme, trade with Great Britain sidelined trade with Egypt. Although this change may not have been so obvious prior to 1924, Kordofanese traders were probably looking ahead, and were exposed via the Egyptian press to nationalist discourse about the 'imperialistic project', that is, the Gezira Irrigation Scheme.

Nevertheless, as noted, the trading community was far from united in its support of the nationalist movement compared with other socio-professional categories such as officers and officials. Traders had been one of the principal beneficiaries of the impressive economic growth the country had seen in the first 25 years of the Condominium; moreover, large merchants were well connected to and much respected by British

[92] Data on the crisis are available in the *Annual Report of the Sudan Govt., 1921*, pp. 249-254, and in the *Annual Report of the Sudan Govt., 1922*, p. 236.

[93] *Annual Report of the Sudan Govt., 1921*, pp. 249-254.

[94] R. H. B. Condie, 'Egypt's Trade with the Sudan', *Sudan Notes and Records* (1955), vol. 36, n. 1, pp. 57-63; D. E. Mills, 'A Failed Nationalist Endeavour: Egyptian-Sudanese Textile Trade', *British Journal of Middle Eastern Studies* (2004), vol. 3, n. 2, pp. 175-194.

government officials, who also sought their advice in difficult times. Their absence from protests was probably motivated by the idea that they would have had more to lose than to gain from open participation in the nationalist movement. Indeed, the leading merchants of Khartoum only began to show support for the nationalist movement in September and October, after the wave of revolts in August, when they realized that their bargaining power with the government had increased. Even though some might have been the victims of the post-war price slump and new taxes, it would be precisely because of their extremely flexible trading network that merchants would be able to bounce back from the crisis and adapt fast to the emergence of cotton as the monoculture of choice.

Part Three

Ideology and Strategies

6

'The Word is for the Nation Alone': Telegrams, Petitions and Political Writings

On 15 May 1924, 'Ubayd al-Ḥājj al-Amīn, Ḥassan Ṣāliḥ, Ḥassan Sharīf, Ṣāliḥ 'Abd al-Qādir sent the first of a long series of telegrams:[1]

> We beg to conveyance [sic] of this our protest to both the Egyptian and British Parliaments. Our dignity will not permit us to be bought and sold like animals who have no voice in their disposal. We protest with all our might that our people are not given the legal freedom to speak openly and demand that those who will be selected by the nation from her loyal sons should at least be made aware of the real decision on settlement of their future during the Negotiations. It is for no one but them, whatever the State may be, to settle the question of its future, because the word is for the Nation alone, and she is the owner of the right.[2]

This telegram inaugurated a protest strategy – the telegrams, petitions, and circulars campaign – that would become a hallmark of the 1924 Revolution. The campaign was intended to communicate the core values of the national movement to a wider public: the values for which the nationalists were ready, to use their own words, to 'sacrifice' themselves.

This chapter has been created from a repertoire of 85 texts composed of telegrams, petitions, and circulars sent in 1924. Some of the most significant are reported in Appendix 1. These texts are the only surviving documents written by political activists of 1924 while the events were actually taking place. In general, most of the existing Sudanese accounts were produced decades after the events. For this reason, they do not grasp the evolution of the movement's ideology in a comparable way as the political texts written during 1924 do.

With four exceptions, the texts are English translations of original Arabic documents that I was not able to locate in any of the archives I consulted. The quality of the translations varies a great deal, and is often poor, but only in a few cases does this hinder the comprehension of the document. Because of their nature as draft translations, a semantic analysis of these sources can only be approximate; the way in which I

1 Some of the material in this chapter has previously appeared in 'Nationalism by Telegrams: Political Writings and Anti-Colonial Resistance in Sudan, 1920-1924', *International Journal of African Historical Studies* (2013), vol. 48, n. 1, pp. 27–55.

2 The full references to all the telegrams quoted in this article are in Appendix 1, sorted according to date.

will approach them will therefore be to map the contents of the texts, analyse their circulation and readership, and finally trace their evolution and the way in which that sheds light on the history of the tense months of 1924.

POLITICAL WRITINGS IN 1924

During the course of 1924, the medium chosen by the nationalist movement to circulate its texts evolved significantly, reflecting changes in the political situation. During the first phase, from mid-May to mid-August, the texts consisted above all of telegrams: 51 of the 53 telegrams kept in the archives were sent between 15 May and 17 August, compared with three letters and six circulars sent during the same period. From 17 August until the last letter found in the archives (dated 28 November), the texts consist of eleven circulars, nine letters, three articles, and only two telegrams. We also need to consider that telegrams were far more visible than letters and circulars, which were disseminated secretly. For instance, al-ʻĀzza commented that one of the main activities of the League was to send secret circulars: 'they used to distribute their papers to El Obeid, Port Sudan, Atbara, Malakal, Talodi, and the Nuba Mountains.'[3] Thus, it is certain that some of this political material is now lost.

Telegrams as a Medium for Political Protest

There were a number of reasons why the 1924 protesters chose telegrams as a medium for expressing political discontent, of both a practical and symbolic nature.

First of all, telegrams were a relatively easy and safe way of expressing political protest, not least because no law explicitly prohibited them. Furthermore, while sending telegrams might have been extremely expensive for ordinary people, the fact that so many activists worked in the Post and Telegraph Department meant that the League could send most of them for free.[4] Moreover, they could count on Egyptians. In 1913, 311 of the 397 indoor employees of the Post and Telegraph Department in Sudan (thus not including travelling postmasters and messengers, who represented a sizeable number and who were mostly Sudanese) were Egyptians, and it is likely that this number was not so different in 1924.[5]

The majority of the telegrams had multiple recipients who belonged to two broad categories according to whether the messages were sent to Egypt or Britain. As shown in the table below, 25 of the 46 telegrams with known addressees were sent to Egyptian institutions or politicians, such as Saʻd Zaghlūl, the Parliament, the various Ministries, or to associations such as the Women's Society of Alexandria. In addition, 16 were addressed to the Egyptian Press Syndicate.

3 *Al-Riwāyāt*, p. 379.
4 *The White Flag Trials*, p. 45.
5 *Post and Telegraph Dept. Report, 1913*, p. 381.

Table 6 Addressees of telegrams[6]

Number of telegrams for which the addressees are known	46
Telegrams sent to Egypt	25
Egyptian political institutions	24
Egyptian press	16
Telegrams sent to the British	18
Telegrams sent to the British in Sudan	14
Telegrams sent to the British in Egypt	2
Telegrams sent to the British in Britain	2
Others	4

The second largest group of addressees were British individuals or institutions: first, the British government in Sudan, and mostly the Governor General and the Director of the Intelligence Department. One was sent to the Prime Minister, Ramsay MacDonald, and another to two British newspapers, *The Times* and *The Daily Herald*. Finally, two were sent to the British High Commissioner in Cairo. It is noteworthy that only two telegrams were specifically addressed to Sudanese individuals, demonstrating that telegrams were mainly used to reach an international public.[7] Finally, it should be borne in mind that the cost of telegrams increased with the distance covered, so that while it might not have been particularly difficult to send telegrams through compliant Egyptian officials in Egypt and Sudan, sending telegrams to Britain was probably more complicated, and certainly more expensive.

The fact that the addressees mostly consisted of Egyptian and British politicians and the press supports historian Keith Watenpaugh's view on the petition-telegrams that were being sent in Syria at about the same time: this kind of communication was particularly effective in bypassing spatial and social hierarchies.[8] In the case of Sudan, there was little or no possibility that Sudanese commoners could communicate with the British authorities even if they wished to do so. None of the signatories of the telegrams, most of whom were low-grade clerks, would ever have been allowed to meet the Governor General to discuss their grievances. Similarly, it was very difficult for common Sudanese to travel to Egypt and meet ministers and politicians there. The June delegation is a case in point.[9]

6 Sources: NA: FO 141/810/3, FO 141/806/1, FO 141/805/2; WO 33/999. NRO: Palace 4/9/44, Palace 4/9/46, Palace 4/9/49, Palace 4/10/50, Kordofan 1/12/53, Kordofan 1/14/65, Northern Province 1/21/213, Northern Province 1/20/191. CRO: 0075-049751

7 Ali Abdel Latif to Yuzbashi Mohammed Eff. Saleh Gibril, El Obeid, Ahmed Omar Bakhreiba, Wad Medani, 1.7.1924, FO 141/801/2, NA; Ali Abdel Latif to the leader of the Sudanese, Cairo, 1.7.1924, FO 141/806/1, NA.

8 Watenpaugh, *Being Modern in the Middle East*, p. 103.

9 Various intelligence reports mention a branch of the White Flag League that was formed in Cairo at some point in late 1924, which included individuals such as 'Arafāt Muḥammad 'Abdallāh, a former leader of the League in Khartoum. But the reports also bear witness to the League's problems with its survival in Cairo. See,

The choice of addressee casts light on the close ties – and feedback effect – between telegrams, international diplomacy, the masses and the press. First, these telegrams were meant to assist Egypt in negotiating with Great Britain. Second, by addressing telegrams to the Egyptian press, the nationalists aimed to reach the Egyptian masses. By publishing the telegrams, the press would contribute towards mobilizing Egyptian public opinion in favour of the Sudanese cause, and in turn, this would put pressure on Egyptian politicians to continue working on the Sudan question. Moreover, by sending telegrams to the Egyptian press, Sudanese activists counted on reaching a Sudanese public as well, since Egyptian newspapers were circulated and read in Sudan, as seen.

Finally, there was yet another layer of meaning in the use of telegrams. As Nickles remarks in his work on the impact of the telegraph on international diplomacy, 'because of such characteristics as expensiveness, rapidity, and association with scientific progress' telegrams also expressed the modernity of their senders.[10] Nickles' work focuses on Europe, but his observation carries even greater weight in the colonial context. By using the same medium of communication favoured by international diplomacy at the time, the nationalists were making a statement that they were 'modern enough', or to use the language of the time 'civilized enough' to participate in the arena of international politics, from which the Sudanese had been systematically excluded. It was a part of a broader strategy to assert that Sudan was on the path of becoming 'civilized enough' to be free from the British colonial government. Indeed, the form of the telegrams echoed the ideas expressed in them, as we shall see.

However, telegrams had significant shortcomings as a means of expressing dissent. The first and most important of these was that information was bottlenecked. The problem obviously lay with the recipients: if they were not willing to disseminate the contents of the telegrams, then it was as if they had never been sent. A second and related problem was that in order to have a real political impact, telegrams had to circulate beyond the person to whom they had been sent. In his study of political telegrams in late 19th century China, Zhou observed that their impact 'severely diminished if they [were not] widely publicized to focus public attention on them'.[11] As far as is known, however, telegrams were often stuck somewhere along the wire, ignored by their recipients or by journalists, or else censored by the British authorities.

From Telegrams to Circulars

As seen, the flow of telegrams began to dry up from August. The period between the beginning of July and the beginning of August was marked by a wave of arrests, which resulted in the imprisonment of all the

(*contd*) for instance, Extract from SA's Intelligence Summary, 8.11.1924, Palace 4/9/47, NRO, in which the League is described as being in a difficult financial situation.

10 David P. Nickles, *Under the Wire: How the Telegraph Changed Diplomacy* (Cambridge MA: Harvard University Press, 2003), p. 188.

11 Yongming Zhou, *Historicizing Online Politics: Telegraphy, the Internet, and Political Participation in China* (Stanford CA: Stanford University Press, 2006), p. 68.

leaders of the League. The subsequent period between the end of July and the middle of August was characterized by a severe wave of unrest (in Atbara, Port Sudan, Khartoum, and elsewhere). As a consequence, tighter controls were imposed on all mail correspondence to and from Egypt. Signing a telegram was enough to lead to arrest, and telegrams almost ceased to be sent, to be replaced by circulars and hand-delivered letters.

The most crucial difference compared with telegrams is that circulars were to be spread and 'consumed' inside Sudan. Available texts from this period consist of eleven circulars, nine letters, and three articles sent between August 17 and November 28.[12] Letters were usually sent or given to specific people, while circulars (often also called 'notices') were displayed in markets or mosques. Most of the texts from the collection under review are addressed to Sudanese (the addressees are known for 13 of the 23 texts). Examples include 'A call to the Sudanese generally and to the natives of Kordofan', 'the Sheiks', and *sayyid* 'Abd al-Raḥman al-Mahdī.

The origin of the circulars and letters varies slightly compared with the telegrams. The overwhelming majority of the latter were sent from Port Sudan (14) and Khartoum (12), with some from Atbara (5). Telegrams were also sent from smaller towns such as Abu Hamid, Wad Medani, Shendi, Hassahissa, Barakat, Merowe, and Wadi Halfa, which bears witness to the geographical extent of the movement (see Appendix 1). Circulars and letters, on the other hand, were overwhelmingly found in the Three Towns; a tiny minority of the circulars that have survived in archives were found in El Obeid, Wad Medani, Atbara, Port Sudan, Bara and al-Nuhud.

A final crucial difference between telegrams and circulars lies in their accountability: telegrams were mostly signed by the name of real individuals (42 out of 53), while circulars were anonymous or signed by the name of associations. The 'Sudan Union Society' was the name most frequently used in circulars. This society began signing texts on August 18 and endorsed 11 in total.[13] Other names used in the circulars were the Society of Sudan Progress, the Society for the National Defence, and the Society of the Crescent, or 'El Helal'. However, it is difficult to link these to specific activists or sections. Sudanese nationalists had returned to the one of the forms of protest used before 1924: the writing of anonymous texts.

[12] These articles are listed because they were included in the bulk of White Flag texts. Either the Intelligence Department found the originals of the articles or knew they came from League members. These are: 'Article by Othman Mohammed Hashim, member of the White Flag League, published in Muqattam 31.8.1924', FO 141/805/2, NA; Tayeb Babiker, 'What is there in the Sudan', published in El Akhbar, Cairo, 3.9.1924, FO 141/805/3, NA and 'Circular', 31.8.1924, included in the same sheet as the article by 'Uthmān Muḥammad Hāshim. They are English translations.

[13] These were five circulars, five letters, and one article.

Table 7 Differences in the form of texts according to four locations[14]

	Khartoum/Omdurman	Port Sudan	Medani	El Obeid*
Telegrams	12	14	1	0
Circulars	9	1	2	2
Letters	7	0	0	1
Articles	1	0	0	0
Total	29	15	3	3

The shift from signed telegrams to anonymous circulars marks an important change in the strategy of the nationalist movement. On the one hand, as seen, signing a telegram led directly to imprisonment after August. The openness of the period between June and July was no longer an option; if the national movement were to continue to exist, it had to act undercover. However, this change may also signify that the nationalists were losing heart about the effectiveness of the telegrams campaign, as if they had understood that it was hopeless to count on it to advance the national cause. They could have continued to send telegrams anonymously, but they did not. In any case, there is an unmistakeable link between the dismantling of the White Flag League and the move from telegram to anonymous circulars as a form of political protest.

MAKING A NATION IN THE PRESENT

Forms of political protests such as demonstrations were staged not only as a display of Sudanese public opinion, but also to 'move' the Sudanese and to force them into action. The telegrams, and later the circulars written in 1924 expressed similar concepts but with one substantial difference: while political protests in Sudan aimed at turning Sudanese into protesters, these texts reflected an image of the Sudanese as if this process had already been achieved – as if the Sudanese already constituted a body of citizens joined together in a united struggle. They also depicted the Sudanese as part of one nation. The telegrams told the story of an ongoing drama from which the Sudanese nation would eventually emerge free.

In their highly emotional vocabulary, these texts follow a narrative sequence reminiscent of the Hegelian dialectic of thesis, antithesis, and synthesis. They expressed a way of imagining the relationship of the Sudanese with colonialism as a form of struggle, which, once victorious, would lead to a liberation that was more than merely political. The three phases of the dialectic were as follows:

(a) British colonial rule oppressed and limited Sudanese freedom;

[14] One circular was found both in El Obeid and in Omdurman: 'A Call to the Sudanese Generally and to the Natives of Kordofan, Invocation of God, signed by Head of the Society of El Helal, Omdurman/El Obeid', 17.8.1924, FO 141/805/2, NA.

(b) The Sudanese had to engage in a battle to free themselves from the colonial yoke;
(c) The battle would lead to true liberation and the birth of the nation. The struggle against colonialism was not only a means of achieving more rights, but was also a rite of passage through which the nation manifested its coming into being.

Usually, the texts would address only one of the three dialectical movements: some focused on denouncing British injustice, others on the need to struggle to achieve freedom. There were also certain variations according to the media of choice and the period, although these lay more in the form in which a dialectic was expressed than in its structure. The telegrams written at the beginning of the 1924 Revolution were brief and focused on accusing the British rulers of something that had just happened, such as the arrest of an activist. Later, they would become longer and more dramatic, and similarly, circulars and letters even darker and more low-spirited. In the following two sections, this 'dialectic of oppression' is illustrated through some examples, and for the sake of convenience these are divided according to which dialectic moment was predominant in the texts. The second and third moments, those of struggle and liberation, are combined, because they are customarily joined together in the texts, often within the same sentence.

British Colonial Rule as a Rule of Oppression

The topic of the injustice of colonial rule is perhaps the most pervasive theme of the political texts written in 1924. It was generally expressed by this narrative structure: 'they' have committed a crime, and 'we' must redress the situation by protesting and demonstrating. Let us examine three examples, all taken from telegrams sent to Egypt in June and July:

> 24.6.1924: Whilst the officer Zein el Abdin was taking a picture of the demonstration he was arrested and imprisoned. We protest against this and against the imprisonment of four employees, and the beating of those who were shouting "Long live the King of Egypt and the Sudan" by [sic] swords.
>
> 30.6.1924: The peaceable demonstrators have been tried and sentenced to six months for shouting long live the King—It is an insult and it would please us [sic], and we the people of the Sudan shall wait to see how and when the noble Egyptian nation would come forward to wash it.
>
> 8.7.1924: The imprisoned liberals are being beaten and treated with cruelty which makes humanity tremble, in order to cause them to relinquish their principle and pretend that their acts were due to the abetment of the Egyptians. We have protested against this to the British Parliament.

Further examples are: the British did not ask for the opinion of the Sudanese in the negotiations (15.5); they boycotted the delegation of Zayn al-'Ābdīn 'Abd al-Tām and Muḥammad al-Mahdī to Cairo (19.6); they arrested demonstrators (24.6, 25.6, 28.6, 30.6, 5.7, etc.); and they carried out unlawful searches of activists' homes (5.7). Other telegrams complained about 'the severity used in dealing with our brethren the sons of the country' (27.6), or protested that '[t]here are animal reservations [sic] societies but none that ask about Sudanese' (7.8). Other texts maintained that by responding to patriotic initiatives with violence and illiberalism, the British had revealed the real nature of colonialism, broken their pledge to undertake reforms, and denied precisely those principles they were supposed to represent: 'British Government agents ... announce to all that they are alleys [sic] to justice, but in fact this is contrary' (7.8); British colonialism was painted as a tyranny (27.6).

In contrast, the nationalists depicted themselves as the positive 'alter ego' of the colonial rulers. Demonstrations by nationalists were 'peaceful', they were 'strong washouts [sic] but ... in good order' (28.6)· The nationalists were 'liberals,' and their actions 'legal,' 'lawful,' non-violent, and harmless (such as shouting and taking pictures). It was manifestly absurd, the telegrams maintained, to arrest somebody merely for shouting or taking a pictures of a demonstration in the street. The question of the legality of protests is so central that even in the very last letter of the series, sent on 28 November, exactly when the mutiny of the 11th Sudanese Battalion of the Egyptian Army was taking place in Khartoum, the author was still pleading for the organization of peaceful demonstrations (28.11).

At times, albeit less frequently, another pair of contrasts stood in opposition to one another. This was the conflict between the 'covert Empire' and the 'open' actions of the White Flag League.[15] The activists demonstrated, shouted, took photographs, signed telegrams, and in short sought visibility, while British rule was covert: it employed 'secret courts', stole signatures from unsuspecting natives, and used secret methods to divide the country (5.7).

Thus, the telegrams played on the contrast between the 'innocuous' and peaceful initiatives of the nationalists and the 'acts of terror' and 'persecutions' of the colonizers (5.7). The empowerment expressed by this contrast must not be overlooked. The nationalists maintained not only that the British were far from being the champions of civilization they claimed to be, but also that they were actually much worse than any Sudanese, which may alert the reader to the 'instructions' on how to join the White Flag League mentioned in the next chapter. Sudanese nationalists, with their passion for progress – as embodied by the slogan 'forward' (*ilā al-amāmi*) drawn on the flag of the White Flag League – considered themselves to be the real liberal elements in the country: 'Long live the progressive young men', stated one telegram (11.8).

In this way, the activists were contesting the image that had been imposed upon them by the colonial situation: the idea that the Sudanese were not 'mature' enough to decide for themselves. These texts also made a number of claims: they strongly emphasized the legitimacy of the nationalist movement; they painted the national struggle in intensely ethical terms; and finally, they referred to a system of values and justice that was conceived as being shared by the whole of humanity, independent of their origin and situation. Justice was thus presupposed

[15] This point is raised in Kurita: 'The Concept of Nationalism in the White Flag League Movement'. The term 'Covert Empire' is taken from Priya Satia, *Spies in Arabia: The Great War and the Cultural Foundations of Britain's Covert Empire in the Middle East* (New York: Oxford University Press, 2008).

to be a supranational and universal entity, enabling even a colonial power to be put on trial. According to this system of justice, the power that the British exerted over Sudan was rendered illegitimate by the 'crimes' Britain committed; the British 'sacred trusteeship' of Sudan was thus defused by the very principle justifying this trusteeship: the 'welfare' of colonial citizens.

The Struggle and Awakening of the Nation

Because British colonization was a rule of oppression, the Sudanese had the moral obligation to fight it. The struggle itself, independent of the outcome, was already a form of liberation. It represented a chance for every individual to become a patriot, a martyr for the country, and as such a national citizen (11.8). Colonization was depicted as a condition that limited not only a person's freedom but more importantly his humanity. It should be noted that this was a gender-biased discourse: only one telegram refers explicitly to the 'men and women of the future' (27.8). Perhaps the role of Sudanese women in the national movement was one of the topics on which the national movement of 1924 preferred to remain silent.

A common trope in these texts is the relationship between national struggle and redeemed humanity. A person under a foreign yoke is something less than a human being; he is an animal who lacks will, or a slave who lacks freedom, or a thing that cannot move; such metaphors are frequent in the texts: 'Are you mere bodies to be guided like a flock of sheep, or are you slaves to be trodden on, or are you articles of merchandise to be sold in the open markets?'(17.8). Passivity also stemmed from a lack of awareness: people had become accustomed to the colonial situation, as if they were asleep. A circular thus exhorted: 'Wake up from your slumber and fear not their forces ...' (19.8), and another:

> It is ... the biggest shame that a nation should come from overseas to strip you of your property and to enslave you, your children and your women and that you should be unaware of all this. You should be aware that the time for you to rise up has arrived. You should not be lazy; the hour when you should be awake has arrived... (13.9)

This state of unconsciousness was irreconcilable with the dignity of nationhood. The nation required people to be 'awake' from the state of sleep induced by colonialism and to be 'aware' of what the British were doing to Sudan. Once awake, the national community would have had no choice but to fight for its rights. The telegrams reminded their readers that this might mean 'extreme sacrifice'.

Sacrifice is another pervasive topic of these texts and it became even more present after the first wave of arrests from July onwards. The nationalists depicted themselves as the sacrificed generation who had given themselves to the national struggle. For instance, one telegram hailed 'Ali Bey Abdel Latif', as 'the sacrificed man'; a telegram praised 'the flower of young men ... sentenced to three years imprisonment by the tyrannical power' (8-24.7). Just as the nationalists had sacrificed themselves, they called on the people to do the same. A letter warned that 'no nation obtained her freedom without any sacrifice' (19.8); and the same idea was expressed in these two circulars:

> 8.7.1924, [excerpt]: steadily and bravely, young and old men without caring to the dark of prisons and heaviness of fetters, and every hardness that you met us with it will increase our hate on you and our despair from you and double our love to our country and our King Fuad I, the king of the Nile Valley.

> 10.8.1924, [excerpt]: Perseverance in the way of attaining your rights by exposing your lives and wealth and by so doing you would be showing the world that you are a prosperous nation. ... They desire to torture you and enslave you, and you desire to die in the way of your independence. ...

The nationalists portrayed themselves as perfect examples of the dedication, heroism and sacrifice required to 'make' the nation.

This insistence on sacrifice is worth further reflection. From what has been seen up to this point, there is something visibly missing from the nationalist discourse of the League compared with other versions of nationalism, in particular those rooted in the idea that nations expressed an 'ethnos', one people. Although Sudan is emphatically described as a nation in these texts, what remained rather vague was what really made it one. In particular, the theme of the Sudanese as Arabs and the topic of ancestry is conspicuous by its absence. Of course, this is also related to the nature of these political texts: the existence of a Sudanese nation was the precondition for the nationalists' demands, and it was neither necessary nor appropriate to dwell on what constituted nationhood in the telegrams. However, what is missing from any of the records of 1924, including later oral accounts, is any reflection on the 'roots' of the Sudanese nation. On the contrary, one of the telegrams incited the Sudanese to overcome any form of difference related to the origins of a person: 'Pay no attention to your races or religions, do not be traitors, do not be spies, but be united like brothers' (17.8). Even when describing the ties between Egypt and Sudan, the elements that were consistently highlighted were common language and religion, but not ancestry.

One might imagine that for the 1924 activists, perhaps because they themselves were a highly heterogeneous group, the origins of Sudan were not to be located in the past but in the present. Indeed, from these texts, the most evident element that unified the Sudanese was a sort of anti-colonial humanism: the idea that every human being, and every nation, deserved to be free, but that this freedom required a struggle in order for it to be forged. What made Sudan a nation was its ongoing titanic struggle against the colonial power. The nation was to be born from this battle, which was depicted in epic and intensely emotional terms; this is evident not only in the telegrams, but also in the elegies, poems, ballads, tunes and so on that spurred the Sudanese to fight. (See the following chapter).

If building a nation also entails creating a mythology, the 1924 nationalists were Sudan's myth-makers; these parables did not dwell on a mythological past, however, but referred to an epic present.

The International Community

This final section returns to the question of universal justice that concerned so many of the texts of 1924. There was an imagined public for whom the nationalists of 1924 wrote their texts and in particular the telegrams, and this was the international community of European powers, whose task was to protect and guarantee the principles of universal justice. Even though the name of the League of Nations may never have been explicitly evoked, it is probably something that the activists had in mind when they referred to the international community.

The imagined community seemed to incarnate the activists' core values. In the texts, the 'civilized nations' of Europe were portrayed as being shocked and horrified by the injustices of the British colonizers. For example, after the arrest of 'Alī 'Abd al-Laṭīf, one telegram warned the British that they would be 'held responsible before the European Governments' for his arrest (8.7). Another stated 'Let the advanced European nations bear witness of their treatment of humanity in the 20th Century' (5.7). The texts established a parallel between the lawfulness and morality of the Sudanese nationalists and the lawfulness and morality of the international community as compared with the immoral and unlawful actions of 'uncivilized' Britain. They portrayed the Sudanese activists as being a part of the modern world of high politics, sharing the same political language and belonging to the same international political and moral system that espoused the concept of the right to national self-determination.

This makes it easier to understand why the nationalist movement was so strict regarding questions of lawfulness and peacefulness. They felt that anything they did that was against the law would weaken their cause. For example, 'Umar Bakhrībā wrote in a telegram: 'You know that the matter is a peaceful one and does not require the raising of a stick or a whip, but requires management, reminding and calling attention of parliament in Europe and Egypt by legal means and proper arguments' (5.7). This theme was so important that it ran through every form of protest in 1924: even during the mutiny of November, the Sudanese officers only fired as a response to British fire, which metaphorically expressed the idea that violence was only a response to British brutality. There was a firm belief that by adhering to a legal framework, Sudanese rights would sooner or later be recognized; in turn, this was linked to the new international framework as it appeared in the 1920s: the 'oppressed' nations could now count on the institutions of supranational justice to defend their rights.

India inevitably comes to mind with regard to the movement's insistence on peacefulness, and once again through the medium of the Egyptian press, some Sudanese activists would certainly have read about Gandhi's non-violence campaign of 1921. Indeed, as one telegram bears witness, India was a presence in the imagination of the activists: 'The writers of this circular are the members of the White Flag League and the senders of the two deputations, the one that left a few weeks ago and the other that is known to the Almighty God[,] to Europe and

India'.[16] As discussed earlier, later accounts hint at an awareness that the Sudanese shared the same situation as many other countries across the colonial world. This shows that the 1924 activists not only looked to Great Britain and Europe; they were also aware that Sudan belonged to a sort of 'community of the oppressed nations' within a common imperial space inhabited by colonized nations seeking to break the yoke.[17]

CHOOSING EGYPT

The theme of the unity between Egypt and Sudan was another of the major topics of the 1924 texts: the two countries shared the same struggle and needed to join forces. Moreover, Sudan was a part of the Nile Valley, and as such its unity with Egypt was a 'natural' one from all points of view. The argument of the unity between Egypt and Sudan was based on two principal criteria: the cultural ties between the two countries and Egypt's responsibility for Sudan within the framework of their common struggle.

The issue of 'cultural ties' was articulated in various ways. In the first place, Egyptians and Sudanese were brothers, and their ties were therefore indestructible: 'The strong ties that bind us with our brethren the Egyptians are not dissolvable' (27.6), affirms one telegram; '[We] declare openly that we hate the unjust British government and want our brethren the Egyptians' (11.8). Second, Sudan and Egypt had a relatively long shared history which had begun with the Khedivate of Muḥammad 'Alī: 'the throne of the Kingdom ... legally founded in the Sudan for the last 100 years' (21.6). Then there was religion: as Aḥmad 'Umar Bakhrībā writes in a circular: 'You are an inseparable portion of Egypt united to it by "There is no God but God, Mohammed is the prophet of God"' (5.7). In many other cases, religion was referred to only in the most general terms.

What is puzzling, however, is that the theme of the common ties between the two countries is not pressed very far at all. Sudan is always portrayed as being distinct from Egypt as a nation. As we have seen, Egyptians are brothers, but are not exactly like the Sudanese. Nowhere is the idea expressed that the people of the two countries had the same ancestry.

As discussed previously, accusations of non-autochthonism have long marked the debate on 1924 and several historians consider the nationalism of this period to be a corollary of Egyptian nationalism. Far from shedding light on the debate, the texts analysed here are conspicuous for their lack

[16] General Circular, signed by the Vice-President and Members of the White Flag League, 6.9.1924, FO 141/805/2, NA.

[17] The expression 'community of the oppressed nations' is taken from Lenin's attack on imperialism in 1916: 'Mankind can proceed to the inevitable fusion of nations only through a transitional period of complete freedom of all oppressed nations', as in Terry D. Martin, *The Affirmative Action Empire: Nations and Nationalism in the Soviet Union, 1923-1939* (London: Cornell University Press, 2001), p. 5.

of precision with regard to the question of what unity between Egypt and Sudan meant. From one viewpoint, this lack of clarity reflects the complex and at times painful historical relations between the two countries, dating back to the 19th-century colonization of Sudan. The real ability of the League was to articulate the discourse on Egypt in a very finely-tuned manner, so that even people who had little sympathy with it could still support the White Flag League.

The first element of this strategy was to focus on the question of self-determination. In other words, Egyptian claims regarding Sudan were justified because they were legal, and they were legal above all because it was what the Sudanese people wanted. The telegrams insisted that as a national community, the Sudanese were entitled to certain sovereign rights, one of which was to choose Egypt, which the Sudanese had independently and consciously decided would be the most suitable partner for Sudan. An example is the affirmation that 'the aspiration of every Sudanese [and] the wish of the whole nation [is] the non-division of the Nile Valley' (5.8):

> The Nation has the right of choice to declare in lawful ways for deciding their fate and no one else than her sincere sons have the right to demand her designs.... We protest against the arrest of our brother Mulazmin Zein el Abdin Abdel Tam, Mohammed eff. Ibrahim Ismail, and their fellows, assuring you that they express the wish of the Sudanese Nation and her feelings towards her famous King Fuad I, the King of the Nile Valley (25.6).

Thus the end of Egyptian sovereignty in Sudan, or the elimination of Egyptian symbols, were to be fought against at all costs because they meant an infringement of Sudanese rights.

The second element of this strategy was connected to the argument raised in many telegrams, that because Egypt and Sudan were to be united, Egypt had a moral responsibility for the latter. The subtlety of this reasoning was that it pushed Egypt into a moral impasse. The telegrams called on Egypt to help and support Sudan because the Sudanese had entrusted Egypt with the responsibility of liberating them, 'because the whole Egyptian nation is responsible before History for any calamity that befalls the servants of the Egyptian Crown wherever they are found' (19.6). Egypt was charged by the nationalists to act and speak 'on behalf of' the Sudanese during the negotiations. The texts also communicated a sense of urgency, as the critical situation in Sudan required immediate reaction on the part of the Egyptians. As discussed previously, many telegrams contained powerful denunciations of British 'atrocities'; the latter were also deployed in order to push the Egyptian government to react, as in the following: 'We persistently demand the interference of the Government in the matter, with all the bravery and friendliness at her disposal, in order to put a stop to all kinds of persecution' (19.6). Others communicated an even greater sense of urgency for Egyptian intervention: 'The British officials are ... spreading the spirit of enmity against Egyptians with all the power they possess.... We beg for mercy' (4.7).

Sudanese nationalists may have sensed that the Sudan question was losing momentum under Zaghlūl. Hence, for example, one telegram declared: '...we the people of the Sudan shall wait to see how and when the noble Egyptian nation would come forward to wash [British crimes]' (30.6). At the beginning of September, Ṭayyib Bābikr wrote: 'We would however ask our Government [Egypt] to change her policy in regard to such actions. She has already been silent for a long time and it is time she said her last word to the English and defends us' (30.9). By entrusting Egypt to speak for the Sudanese nation, and by declaring that the Sudanese wanted Egyptian rule, Sudanese nationalists were trying to push Egypt to a firm commitment on the Sudanese question.

This is significant in the light of a reconceptualization of nationalism in the 1920s. The Egyptians did not manipulate the Sudanese intelligentsia to take action, as the British claimed. The reverse was true, or at least that is what the 1924 activists tried to do. In its battle against the British, Egypt had already achieved many victories, and the Sudan question was becoming burdensome. For that reason, the Sudanese reworked and dramatized accounts of the local situation to induce Egyptian intervention, trapped Egypt into a moral bind, to make it feel compelled to act, and insisted on Egypt's political responsibility, so that 'complete independence [may] come for Egypt and the Sudan' (8-21.7).

Was this 'love for Egypt' just a matter of convenience, a mere strategy to gain complete independence? This is a reductive view. 'Love for Egypt' was not necessarily heartfelt, or sincere, but it was nevertheless a *choice*, and as such it was an act in the struggle against imperialism, a form of resistance against a colonization that refused to acknowledge Sudanese political aspirations.

The ambiguity of the Sudanese nationalists' relations with Egypt was fully reflected in the telegrams. There were many nuances in the opacity of the concept of 'unity' of the Nile Valley. For instance, nowhere was it explained exactly how this unity should work, nor did the nationalists ever bother to clarify how two different nations could live within the same state. The vagueness of these expressions allowed space for different political positions: that of the nationalists who disliked Egypt but were anti-British, and that of the people who genuinely believed that Sudan was better off with Egypt. Thus the movement embraced activists such as Muzammil 'Alī Dinār, one of the sons of the Sultan 'Alī Dinār, or Muḥammad al-Mahdī, son of the Khalīfa 'Abdallāhi, both of whom came from families who had bitterly fought the Egyptians in the 19th century. This is well expressed by Muzammil himself:

> At that time everything was going towards the Unity of the Nile Valley, but this unity was like a ladder for us, because if we did not unite with the Egyptians we could never throw the English out of our land.[18]

Although Muzammil depicted unity with Egypt in functional terms, he was also stating that for many Sudanese at the time, the only possible solution to the national struggle was to combine with Egypt. The League sought to ride this feeling by compelling Egypt to join battle.

[18] *Al-Riwāyāt*, p. 62.

CONCLUSION

This chapter has focused on the 'seditious' telegrams, circulars and letters of this period as a form of political protest, and the way in which their form and content reverberated through each other. During an initial phase, the White Flag League organized a telegram campaign addressed to the Egyptian press, but more importantly to the higher echelons of Egyptian and British politicians to whom it exposed the injustice of British colonization. By denouncing the British for a 'cruelty that makes humanity tremble' (8.7) to an idealized international community of 'civilized nations', the nationalists were also making the point that there was no difference between colonizers and colonized, and that the colonial rulers were as accountable as any other power for what they did. They also stated that according to the principles of international justice, with which even Britain had to comply, the Sudanese had suffered enough under British colonization and wished to be free to choose Egypt.

These telegrams were also addressed to the press because the nationalists hoped that the situation of Sudan would be exposed internationally. Seeking such support as a medium of political protest symbolized their hope of a new era of global connectedness.

Then, quite suddenly, the telegrams were discontinued. Once again, internal circulars and letters began to gain momentum in their place, as they had in the period before 1924. The content of these texts did not differ substantially from that of the telegrams; they continued to refer to the need for Sudanese to make sacrifices in the struggle for the Unity of the Nile Valley. The change marked a new phase in the events of 1924, however, as if the nationalists had finally come to recognize the apathy of the international community towards Sudanese demands, or perhaps the importance of concentrating on enlisting the support of people inside Sudan rather than outside it.

The argument of this chapter has proposed that the nationalist language of the White Flag League was not free from ambiguities and contradictions. However, these served the purpose of making certain issues sufficiently imprecise for every constituency to be able to agree to them. What is more important is that the argument used to justify unity between Sudan and Egypt was first and foremost that the Sudanese wanted it; that this desire and the people's decision to support it was sovereign. In the words of the movement's leaders, 'Our dignity will not permit us to be bought and sold like animals who have no voice in their disposal' (15.5).

7

A Community of Protesters: Symbols, Songs and Emotions

'They were young and they wanted to work,
and their feeling for demanding their rights was great.'[1]

The 1924 Revolution, like any other, such as the 1919 Egyptian or the French Revolution of 1789, consisted of a number of separate uprisings rolled into one. In Sudan, each social group had different reasons and grievances behind their decision to participate, all of which were fused together in the slogans of the 1924 Revolution, such as 'Long live King Fu'ād, King of Egypt and the Sudan'. But what made such different social constituencies willing to participate, sometimes at great personal risk?

This chapter considers the question of participation in the national movement from a particular perspective: the emotions it raised.[2] This stems directly from the first hand narratives of activists. Indeed, many of them recounted that they participated in 1924 because, as Ṭayyib Bābikr put it, '...we wanted only to demonstrate our feelings for our nation'. These feelings were a mixture of shock and outrage after the arrests of League members, which led to a moral obligation to act.[3] Activists narrate that they experienced shock, fear, and anxiety, on witnessing British repression, followed by a sense of solidarity, pride and empowerment from their participation in demonstrations. As it is evident from the available sources, the members and supporters of the White Flag League deliberately strove to arouse passionate reactions among common people.

The discussion of emotions should also be connected to symbols. They have the power of summoning emotions and creating bonds between individuals. Thus, the symbolic apparatus of protest plays a central role in social movements, and this is particularly pertinent in the case of nationalist programmes, which always include a plethora of symbols presented as embodying the essence of the nation.

1 *Al-Riwāyāt*, p. 309.

2 This chapter is indebted to the sociology of social movements that highlights the centrality of the emotions in collective action, as in James M. Jasper, 'The Emotions of Protest: Affective and Reactive Emotions in and Around Social Movements', *Sociological Forum* (1998), vol. 13, n. 3, pp. 397-424; also Jeff Goodwin, James M. Jasper, and Francesca Polletta, *Passionate Politics: Emotions and Social Movements* (Chicago: University of Chicago Press, 2001).

3 *Al-Riwāyāt*, p. 345.

The literature on the role of symbols in making an imagined, 'emotional community' of national citizens is extensive. Suffice to say that analysis of symbolic events and items in nationalism owes much to the seminal work of Emile Durkheim, *The Elementary Forms of Religious Life,* and his discussion of 'totemism,' which is of particular relevance to 1924. For Durkheim, '[b]y expressing the social unit tangibly, [a symbolic object] makes the unit itself more tangible to all ... [T]he emblem is not only a convenient method of clarifying the awareness the society has on [sic] itself: it serves to create – and is a constitutive element of – that awareness.'[4] This is why certain objects, actions, speeches become so much more than their tangible form: a flag is not a piece of cloth, but a carefully crafted symbol standing for the core values of a nation, a group, a movement; a demonstration is much more than a march of people. As Gelvin observed, these forms of protest, which he defines as a 'secular ceremony', 'not only contain symbols, but the ceremony itself, in its entirety, acts as a symbol.'[5]

SOLIDARITY, PRIDE AND EMPOWERMENT

The practices of political struggle devised by the League can be seen as performances staged to arouse a complex of emotions in both those who participated and in the public viewing them. The first set of emotions associated with participation in political activities is solidarity, pride, and empowerment. To evoke this response was one of the explicit objectives of the League. For example, a document found by the Intelligence Department details the instructions that a new member received on joining the League. It is impossible to know whether the information is reliable, but even if the instructions were merely the product of rumours about the League, they are significant because they bear witness to popular perceptions of what the League wished to provoke in the Sudanese:[6]

a) Every [Sudanese] should realize that he is as important as any Englishman on earth, and wherever he meets an Englishman, he should by his behaviour show him that he is such.
b) The Englishmen have made donkeys of the Sudanese up till now and have ridden on their backs. If the Sudanese are brave and know their rights they will ride on the back of the Englishmen.
c) Whenever a member of the League meets people or sits with them he should abuse the British, talk of their oppression and speak good of the Egyptians, our Mohammedan brethren.
d) Do not believe that the Government is very strong. Right is on our side and through it we are much stronger.
e) Take part in any demonstration that you find taking place and do not be afraid. Shout as much as you can and especially your motto should be 'No God but God, Mohammed is the prophet of God.'
f) Our instructions now are to behave very peacefully and to obey the Police in whatever they tell us. But circumstances may change and we may receive other

4 Emile Durkheim, *The Elementary Forms of Religious Life* (Translated by Karen E. Fields. New York: Free Press, 1995 [1912]), p. 231.
5 James L. Gelvin, 'Demonstrating Communities in Post-Ottoman Syria', *The Journal of Interdisciplinary History* (1994), vol. 25, n. 1, p. 30.
6 DI, Summary of news, Khartoum 25.6.1924, Palace 4/10/49, NRO.

instructions. If these instructions are received then everybody should be ready to risk his life. It is better for most of us or all to die and our sons [to] live free ....

g) The Egyptian Government will shortly come to the Sudan and we will get rid of the British.

The bylaws of the League sought to address one of the main problems of the colonial situation: how Sudanese grew accustomed to be ruled by – and to submit to – a foreign power. Ṭayyib Bābikr elucidated this point in a sarcastic anecdote:

> When the British passed by, everyone had to stand. When one was lying down, he should stand up or when one was riding, he should dismount, even if it was a camel. Once there was an Englishman, [an Inspector] riding a camel, together with an officer. Then the man fell off; when the soldier saw it, he fell off too. He did this on purpose. Then the Inspector asked him, why did you fall off? He answered, what made you fall made me fall too. The British were much feared by the Sudanese. You must take off your shoes if you want to see an Inspector; even if you were a Judge, a *'umda*, a *nāẓir*, you had to enter barefooted.[7]

It is this problem that the League sought to address by organizing demonstrations.

Demonstrations

The 1924 Revolution marked the beginning of this form of political protest in the Sudan, but the Sudanese had to wait until the Second World War before they would be able to participate in large demonstrations again.[8] The League made these events a hallmark of the movement from the start, in line with political protests in several other colonial settings, as discussed in Chapters One and Two. The protesters, who constantly kept in mind what had happened in Egypt in 1919, considered protests to be a fundamental stepping-stone that would eventually lead to the liberation of their country from colonization.

As symbols, demonstrations were staged performances standing for the unity of the will of the community, or, to put it in the words of Gelvin, as ceremonies of the masses that simultaneously celebrated 'individuals in society both as they [were] and as they ought to be'.[9] In her work on the choreography of protest, Susan L. Foster compares the different ways in which bodies are staged during political protests, reflecting the target and framing those who staged them as '[a] physicality that ... deciphers the social and then choreographs an imagined alternative', or as bodies displaying 'a physical relationship... to the oppression they suffered'.[10] In other words, there is a connection between the nature of political demands and the way in which bodies are displayed during political protests. The sources on these events are, however, very sparing in details of how exactly demonstrations were performed, with the exception of the demonstration by the Military School cadets. The following, for instance, is a short description of the series

7 *Al-Riwāyāt*, p. 350.

8 After 1924, the most important manifestations of popular mobilization were in Atbara in the 1940s, such as the important strike that took place in July 1947. See Sikainga, *City of Steel and Fire*, pp. 103-111.

9 Gelvin, 'Demonstrating Communities', p. 30.

10 Susan Leigh Foster, 'Choreographies of Protest', *Theatre Journal* (2003), vol. 55, n. 3, pp. 411, 412.

of June demonstrations related by Amīna Bilāl Riziq, as she heard it from her husband, Zayn al-'Ābdīn 'Abd al-Tām:

> At [the] funeral [of the *mamur* of Omdurman] there was a huge procession and speeches were made beside his grave, and a demonstration was led by 'Umar al-Ḥājj Shaykh, one of the heroes, May God bless him. He was arrested and a group of White Flag League was arrested as well. On the 24th of June another demonstration took place in support of the first one. It was a really successful demonstration; a man called 'Abd al-Qādir Aḥmad Sayyid was holding the flag of the League and Zayn al-'Ābdīn 'Abd al-Tām was photographing the demonstration.[11]

However brief, this narrative is sufficient to illustrate the broad lines of a choreography dense with meaning. The demonstrators were always equipped with flags – until June 23, it was a League flag, and it then became the green flag of Egypt. They also carried pictures of Sa'd Zaghlūl and King Fu'ād. Both flags and images were usually positioned at the front and in the centre of the march. People shouted slogans such as 'Long Live King Fuad, King of Egypt and the Sudan,'[12] cheered for the life of Zaghlūl, and after 'Alī 'Abd al-Laṭīf had been arrested, they also cheered him as a *za'īm,* a leader, as Kurita notes.[13]

The starting point for any march was also carefully chosen. One of the preferred locations was the railway station – another emblematic site for the 1924 revolutionaries, echoing the circulation of ideas and people that were a hallmark of that time. During that period, activists used to go to the train station to get the latest news of demonstrations.[14] However, most frequently, the people began marching from a mosque, sometimes after the sermon following Friday prayers, or any day of the week using the mosque as a rallying point. By choosing this site, protesters associated the nationalist message with the moral world of religion, as if it was a sacred duty to fight for the country.

Indeed, demonstrations were to forge participants into a community by giving them the experience of fighting together in a dangerous but extraordinary venture. People shared the feeling that they were struggling for a cause that was intensely moral, while they were also at considerable personal risk. Even if, with the exception of Atbara and the final mutiny in November, there were no fatalities, people were beaten with sticks and swords, sometimes quite badly, as in Khartoum on 23 June and in Port Sudan on 10 August. Risk, moral commitment, and the sense of making history: all of these contributed towards the creation of bonds among protesters.

Finally, demonstrations were intended to be dramatic events, both for

[11] *Al-Riwāyāt*, pp. 579-80.

[12] The four ringleaders were: 'Hamed Hussein, a muwallad from the Gordon College Workshop, Ali Ahmed Saleh, a Mahassi, clerk in the Victoria Bookstore, Hamad Ibrahim Ismail, a Muwallad, clerk in the Tanzimat Office, Khartoum Mudiria. Abdel Salem Sid Ahmed, a Dinka of no occupation', Chronicle of events during the period of Political excitement in Khartoum, FO 141/805/2, NA.

[13] Kurita, 'The Concept of Nationalism'.

[14] Ṭayyib Bābikr: 'At that time I usually went to the station to see if there any news from the League in Khartoum', *Al-Riwāyāt*, p. 338.

their participants and for spectators. The very number of people taking part communicated a visually powerful message. With the exception of the first large demonstration of 19 June, the others staged in June were composed of a few hundred people – at least according to British estimates. The demonstrations of August, on the other hand, both in Khartoum and in the provinces, brought larger numbers together. In Port Sudan, the demonstration on 27 July was made up of approximately 1,000 people, a sizeable number for a city of about 15,000. At the demonstration in Atbara, the British authorities counted 500 civilians and 120 soldiers; the city was much smaller than Port Sudan.[15] However, the largest, held in Khartoum on the afternoon of 15 August, brought out between 2,000 and 3,000 protesters.[16]

At this point, it should be noted that demonstrations were gender-specific. Demonstrations in Sudan, unlike those in Egypt in 1919, included overwhelmingly male Sudanese, with the famous exception of al-'Āzza, who followed the cadets' demonstration for a short time before she was persuaded by an officer to go home. While it is likely that a few women at least witnessed the first great demonstration that took place in June, following the *mamur's* funeral, there is no concrete evidence. As far as is known, the participants in all the other demonstrations were men. The participation of women in politics was seen to be dangerous, ostensibly out of a fear for women's safety, or because it was deemed premature, or downright inappropriate. Whatever the case, some women did participate, but in the 'dis-comfort' of their homes, for instance by sewing flags or concealing documents for their revolutionary, absent husbands, brothers, and friends. This reflects the general absence of women from public spaces as well as politics, a characteristic of Khartoum society at that moment of history.

The cadets' demonstration is perhaps the best example of the carefully crafted symbolism of these events. In their march, the cadets came to a halt several times. They went to the house of 'Alī 'Abd al-Laṭīf and later to Kober, his prison, to honour him as the leader of the revolution; they went to the train station, which was very crowded at that hour, to ensure that the news of the demonstration would be spread by people leaving the city, and also to gather more civilians from the area – although the police were stopping people from joining in by then. They moved on to several colonial buildings, such as the Governor's General Palace, to express their opposition to colonization. Finally, they marched on several Egyptian battalions stationed in Khartoum North to show their loyalty to Egypt.[17] At

[15] For the number of demonstrators: see the fourth witness for prosecution for Atbara trial, Mohammed Shalabi, 19.8, Palace 4/10/52, NRO. For estimates of the population of Atbara, see Sikainga, *City of Steel and Fire,* p. 33. In 1914, the inhabitants of the railway cantonment in the city numbered 1,975, mostly Egyptians, but there are no statistics for residents in the rest of the city.

[16] Gov. Khartoum Prov. to Private Secretary, the Palace, Khartoum, 18.8.1924, Palace 4/10/48, NRO.

[17] In *Al-Riwāyāt,* see in particular the eye-witness accounts of Muzammil 'Alī (*contd*) Dinār, Ibrāhīm Sayyid Uthmān, and Abdallāh Mabrūk.

every point they were met with cheering from onlookers. All 51 students of the military school made a point of participating as one group in the march. During their demonstration, '...the senior cadets ordered that none show his grade', to affirm that there was no difference between them.[18]

The symbolism of equality and unity of this episode reverberates in many other stories of 1924 demonstrations. First, Sudanese from different social groups participated in these events. For example al-'Āzza, the wife of 'Alī 'Abd al-Laṭīf, in her account of the demonstration of August 15 in Khartoum, mentions: '[my mother and I] went to the market, and it was completely something new, because the butcher was shouting and the greengrocer was shouting.'[19] In demonstrations people sought to display themselves as equals and as equally engaged in the national struggle.

Indeed, the peaceful and legal demonstrations by relatively young male Sudanese challenged the image of Sudanese as minor subjects, passive and unable to act rationally, typical of the colonial situation. In contrast, the demonstrations presented Sudanese as active, responsible citizens, aware of their political rights, ready to stand up for them within the limits of what was legally acceptable, and taking control of their lives. In the eyes of the colonial power, there was something unmistakeably dangerous and subversive in this mass of bodies; the perception of their potential threat is clear from the derogatory language used to describe the event. For example, the Governor of Khartoum dismissed the demonstrators as 'a rabble of nobodies, led by shady characters and followed by naughty little boys'.[20]

The 'work' of demonstrations in creating horizontal communities must also be connected to the success of this form of protest among artisans and wage-workers. By taking an early lead in the demonstrations, this class of workers was asserting that they were as entitled as anybody else to participate. It was a moment in history in which only notable families were given a voice in politics. Instead, common Sudanese had very limited access to State institutions, in particular if they had to negotiate their rights. Demonstrations offered those consistently left out of the political realm a powerful means to become visible.

MORAL OUTRAGE AND SHOCK

The White Flag League as a political association was, as discussed, short-lived. On May 15, the founders of the League sent their first protest telegram, and just six weeks later, 'Alī 'Abd al-Laṭīf was arrested. The imprisonment of the other four founding members followed soon after, but it was not until some time later that events began to unfold. This

18 *Al-Riwāyāt*, p. 180.

19 *Al-Riwāyāt*, pp. 385–86. Al-'Āzza states that this was before the demonstration of the Cadets, which was held on August 8, but I believe it to be likely that she is referring to the large demonstration of August 15.

20 Baily Report, Appendix 7 to Ewart Report, p. 184.

delay has long been interpreted as the result of immature leadership: the founders of the League were unable to evade imprisonment, and so when the revolution reached its climax, it lacked leadership.

This interpretation does not, however, take into consideration the possibility that the arrests might have been a calculated risk that formed a part of the League's strategy, to 'wake up' the Sudanese. James Jasper, a leading sociologist of 'emotions in movements', writes: 'activists work hard to create moral outrage and anger and to provide a target against which these can be vented.' He also makes the point that moral affront and feelings of injustice are different from grievances such as forms of deprivation that may induce people to take part in a protest. In fact, moral shock 'helps a person think about her basic values and how the world diverges from them in some important ways.'[21] People are physically, morally, and psychologically affected by moral shock, which may prompt them to expose themselves to risks that they would have never have contemplated otherwise.

Indeed, provoking arrests that could be denounced by the nationalists as illegal was an important strategy for many branches of the League and other connected associations. This is clear, for instance, in many testimonies such as that of 'Alī Malāsī: '...we worked like that: we demonstrated and after the British beat us and arrested us, we sent protest telegrams.'[22] In other words, the sequence was the following: some 'crime' would be committed by the British (the stopping of the delegation of Zayn al-'Ābdīn 'Abd al-Tām, the arrest of 'Alī 'Abd al-Laṭīf, and so on), this crime would be denounced by the some of the League members by telegram, and a demonstration would be organized in protest. In consequence, more people would be arrested, and this would lead to yet more demonstrations. In all this, as seen, the main leaders of the League kept a low profile, and were absent from any demonstration, and this is why it was particularly easy to denounce their imprisonment as 'unjust' and to portray them as 'martyrs for the nation'. Thus, there was a real feedback effect between imprisonments, telegrams and demonstrations in various places (Atbara, Shendi, Khartoum, Port Sudan and so on). These were three acts in a scenario that was deliberately staged in order to push the Sudanese into such a state of anger, shock, and fear that it would be impossible not to react.

From the available sources, it emerges clearly that the League members were fully aware that they ran the risk of imprisonment at any time, and were prepared for it.[23] First, it was quite logical because political activists could be easily identified, even without the help of spies, from their personal signature in telegrams. Second, the possibility of imprisonment shaped the structure of the League. In Khartoum, Port Sudan and Shendi there existed two central committees of Leaguers, and the second looked as one of substitution. In his account, 'Izz al-Dīn Ḥusayn Rāsiq mentioned that many talks given by League members focused on the organization of

21 Jasper, 'Emotions of Protest', p. 409.
22 *Al-Riwāyāt*, p. 308.
23 *The White Flag Trials*, p. 47.

replacement committees and 'the means of making the League survive': 'for example, if the first cell was arrested the second should do so and so, if the second cell was arrested this should do so and so.'[24] Third, from the outset, the League created a fund to assist the families of imprisoned members, and a part of the money paid for subscription to the League was applied to this cause.[25]

In this respect, the strategy of provoking arrests to mobilize people was extremely successful. Several accounts of 1924 insist that the actors had no choice but to demonstrate because they felt morally compelled to do so by the great injustice that had befallen their country. For example, Cadet Muzammil 'Alī Dinār relates:

> [Muzammil] We decided to demonstrate because when we came back [to the Military School at the beginning of the school year] we found the whole city demonstrating already, the demonstration of our brothers the people of 'Alī 'Abd al-Laṭīf.
> [Interviewer] How did you take the decision? Did you have a meeting?
> [Muzammil] ... In fact Idrīs 'Abd al-Ḥay came to us and said, groups are spreading and talking about so and so, and he said we'd better discuss this and decide... After the discussion we concluded that talking is not enough, we have to take the oath to keep this secret and demonstrate.[26]

For all these reasons, we should not seek the rationale behind the arrests in their direct consequences, but rather in their expressive capacity and symbolic meaning. People were not simply getting arrested: they were 'sacrificing' themselves for the nation. By letting themselves be arrested, the League's members wanted also to make it clear who was the villain of the piece, and to make people recognize that British colonization was an illegal and violent force. It is for that reason that some of the League leaders sought to discontinue demonstrations after June 23. It was very important for them that their protests should remain lawful, so to make clear to spectators of demonstrations that the British were in the wrong.

One final point to be made here is that the protests organized by the League also set an example and a model of how fear, outrage, and anger at colonial rule could be channelled and expressed politically. After the arrests of the League leaders, people continued to march and to send out petitions, thereby employing the same repertoire that had first been used by the League. The models were there - writing circulars, signing petitions, organizing demonstrations- people had seen how they worked, and now they were ready to make use of them. When the League was dismembered, the stage was set for new individuals and associations to take over. This 'learning process' of political activism is expressed very clearly by Mūsā

24 'Izz al-Dīn Ḥusayn Rāsiq, IAAS 1575.

25 One example was the family of al-Tuhāmī Muḥammad: 'one day Abdullahi Rihan the tailor, came to the prisoners and received the money they contributed for the household of El Tuhami', from Statement of Fuad Ali, Khartoum 7.9.24, Palace 4/11/55, NRO. Also, in the oath of the Sudan Union as it is quoted in Intelligence Dept. files, one of the conditions was that 'assistance should be given to the family of any member of the Society in any town he may be found in time of difficulty.' Intelligence Notes, Khartoum, 3.10.1924, Palace 4/9/46, NRO.

26 *Al-Riwāyāt*, p. 44.

'Antar, the owner of a coffee shop in the Khartoum central market, who first saw the demonstration by the cadets of the Military School, and then organized one on his own, turning from being a supporter into being a demonstration leader:

> I was staying in the house of Ḥassan Sālim, we were talking about the domination of the British, then 'Alī Hādiyā and Muḥammad Hādiyā were imprisoned (they were my friends in the market). Before that, when Idrīs 'Abd al-Ḥay and his colleagues the cadets demonstrated, I asked the people in the market to close their places, the coffee houses, the bars (bottles sellers) and shops, and we received the cadets who saluted us, we shouted with them for the life of Sa'd Zaghlūl, for Egypt and those kind of slogans.
>
> As to my own demonstration, it happened after when I saw my colleagues 'Alī and Muḥammad Hādiyā put in prison. I collected my people in the coffee house, the workers and everyone in this place and I asked them to go and shout in the street that there is a demonstration. After that I took my bike, and went to *Sūq al-'Arabī*, and I told the people there that a demonstration would take place. When I returned there were around 50 people. When we arrived beside the barracks, around 2000 joined. Ḥusayn 'Alī and me, and a man called Hamriti, were shouting and the whole people were shouting. A waiter, called 'Abbās, and 'Abd al-Raḥīm, a fish seller, until now they had not reached my coffee house. I shouted until my voice was hoarse. I could not speak any more, then we passed by the coffee house of Ḥassan Sa'd, we saluted him long live Ḥassan Sa'd the president of the coffee house owners, long live Egypt and Sudan, out with the British.[27]

When demonstrations stopped working because of heightened levels of repression, the time became ripe for the November mutiny. Some examples of the high levels of tension and fear, and the bitterness of feelings against the colonial rulers that could no longer be channelled in open protest are vividly presented in the following excerpts from letters censored by the Intelligence Department:

> Abd El Majid Abd El Hadi, 25.9.1924: Zaghlul Pasha is expected in London today. May God strengthen him against the colonisers – Amen. Five Egyptians have been arrested and interned in the Civil Prison, Khartoum North. One of them is employed in the Army and other four in the Sudan Government. House searching is done in [sic] wholesale. I am ready for them to search my house at any time and shall find nothing but the photograph of Saad Pasha and the members of the Wafd. The curse of God may be upon the usurpers.
>
> Mohd Ratib 25.9.1924: I have ... found most of my friends in every Province either interned or under trial as has been the case after the incidents of 1919. ... May God have mercy on his people.[28]

The mutiny was thus also a response to a situation that was generally nerve-wracking not only politically but above all emotionally. At this point, the only solution was for Sudanese and Egyptian troops to unite against colonial rule. Even al-'Āzza, the wife of 'Alī 'Abd al-Laṭīf, heard about this: 'At the end of the demonstrations, they had the so-called Article 18 which meant firing, the war, it was agreed between them.'[29]

Through its strategies of protest, the League offered people strong emotional reasons for joining in the national struggle: to 'feel love' for

[27] *Al-Riwāyāt*, pp. 452-53.
[28] All in Kordofan 1/14/60, NRO.
[29] *Al-Riwāyāt*, p. 377.

their nation, solidarity with each other, and empowerment in relation to their position as colonial subjects, but also to 'feel hatred,' contempt, rage and outrage for what the colonial rule was doing to Sudan, and not only to its 'patriots', but also to any Sudanese, by making them accustomed to the colonial situation.

SYMBOLS OF COMMUNITY

Egypt as a symbol

As noted earlier, the direct intervention by Egyptians in the events of 1924 was at least as important as the use of Egypt as a symbol of liberation. According to Kurita, Egyptian protesters represented 'role models' for the Sudanese rebels, and the Egyptian revolution of 1919 was a powerful metaphor for what they wished for Sudan.[30] Both because it represented a 'success story', and because the independence of Egypt possibly had direct implications for Sudan, the Egyptian Revolution came to assume a particularly emotional meaning. Kurita has argued that 1924 saw an escalation in the intensity of 'feelings' towards Egypt.[31]

Unity was also built on the emotional premise that Sudan and Egypt were 'brothers' fighting an unequal battle against an enemy that was much more powerful than they were, and for this reason they had to unite to stand against colonization. Thus, Aḥmad Ṣabrī Zāyd recounted: 'We were influenced by the Egyptian Revolution of 1919, and we read a lot about that, and we learnt that Egypt and Sudan should be like a united body.'[32] Even clearer is the testimony of 'Alī Malāsī on the relations between the two countries:

> The demonstrations continued in 1919 and the Sudan contributed to it. Of course our capabilities were limited, but we followed the Egyptian activities because our destiny was connected with theirs. ... We were sticking to the agreement of the Egyptian delegation, as they were demanding we should demand as well because their demands apply to the whole of Nile Valley.[33]

In their patriotic fervour, Sudanese continually compared themselves with the Egyptians who had sacrificed their lives in 1919. Events in Egypt became metaphors of what could happen in Sudan and protests were organized in memory of events that happened in Cairo. For example, the cadets' demonstration was inspired by that of the Military School of Cairo in 1919, during which a number of cadets were killed. According to Ibrāhīm Sayyid 'Uthmān, the cadets decided that 'we must show ourselves and we must do something similar to that of the Egyptian military college of 1919.'[34]

30 Kurita, '*Alī 'Abd Al-Laṭīf wa Thawrat 1924*'.
31 Kurita, 'The Concept of Nationalism', p. 35.
32 *Al-Riwāyāt*, p. 262.
33 Ibid., p. 304.
34 Ibid., p. 178.

The perception that any of the symbols of Egyptian sovereignty in Sudan were being disregarded or insulted, or that the British were creating problems between Egyptians and Sudanese, was read as an attempt to divide the Nile Valley, and often became a catalyst for protest. Three examples will show this point. First, as seen, the lowering of the Egyptian flag at the military headquarters sparkled a wave of protests in Wau.[35] Second, situations in which Egyptians employees were evidently favoured by the Sudan Government over Sudanese were interpreted as ways to undermine the Unity of the Nile Valley. For instance, the cadets complained of the 'unfair appointment of commissions' that favoured cadets from the Cairo Military School. However, instead of nurturing resentment towards their Egyptian colleagues, they considered such appointments as means used by the British who wanted to create tensions between Egyptian and Sudanese officers.[36] Third, the real issue behind the evacuation of the Egyptian Army was much more than its simple physical removal. The evacuation was not meant to affect the careers of Sudanese officers, at least according to the plans laid down by Stack.[37] However, the Egyptian Army was the most important symbol of Egyptian sovereignty, and for the nationalist officers such an action was equated to the British taking over Sudan, and the beginning of an era of 'enslavement'.

Songs and poetry

One of the most fascinating aspects of the 1924 Revolution is the literary output it prompted. It is not the purpose of this work to discuss this point exhaustively, both because it a such large a topic that it deserves a study of its own and because it has already been discussed by a number of Sudanese historians. The period after the First World War represented a turning point in the history of Sudanese literature, and was marked by a literary renaissance linked to Sudan's political development.[38] As this chapter deals with emotions and symbols, however, it is relevant to consider some of the nationalist poems that were recited or sung during the events of 1924 and also voiced the emotions evoked by the struggle with Egypt against colonialism.

The work by Ḥassan Najīla, *Malāmiḥ min al-mujtama' al-sūdānī*, or *'Features of the Sudanese Society'*, is perhaps the best history of nationalist literature after the Great War. He describes the literary debates and the way in which different political opinions were reflected in poetic compositions. He also describes the special place enjoyed by music and songs

[35] Acting Sirdar to Acting GG, 9.10.1924, Palace 4/9/46, NRO.

[36] Appendix to SMIR No. 362, September 1924, WO 33/999, NA. Account of events connected with pro-Egyptian propaganda in various parts of the Sudan during August 1924. Appendix to SMIR No. 361, WO 33/999

[37] Memorandum (Sudan Defence Force), Enclosure to no. 67, Major-General Sir L. Stack to Mr MacDonald, London, 18.8.1924, FO 409/199, NA.

[38] For full references, see Sharkey, *Living with Colonialism*; 'Colonialism, Character Building and the Culture of Nationalism in Sudan'; 'Arabic Literature and Nationalist Imagination in Kordofan'; 'Arab Identity and Ideology in Sudan,' in addition to the bibliography of sources in Arabic here.

during these years. Graduates and members of the Sudan Union used to gather at *Dār Fawzi*, the home of Fawz, a Sudanese female singer whose beauty charmed the educated youth of the time. As she sang, she was accompanied by the music of Khalīl Faraḥ, himself a musician and singer, who is still today considered the most important Sudanese nationalist musician. During these evenings, Sudan Union members shared their concerns about their clandestine activities, drank alcohol, discussed politics, composed and recited anti-colonial poems, and sang with Fawz and Khalīl. Tellingly, in Najīla's work the chapters dedicated to *Dār Fawzi* are entitled 'Between Seriousness and Amusement' (*bayna al-jidd wa al-lahū*).[39]

Khalīl Faraḥ was a poet and musician of Nubian origin. He was not from a notable family, but managed to attend primary school and became an employee of the Post and Telegraph Department.[40] He was also a member of the Sudan Union. His political activity shaped his style and his themes. The language of his poems, which were written to be sung, was a blend of classical Arabic and Sudanese dialect. Their powerful political message was expressed through metaphors.[41] For example, one of his most famous songs, which was composed in 1927, and thus after the event discussed here, is entitled *'azza fi-hawāk* (which can be translated as 'I love you, Azza') remains one of the most beloved of Sudanese patriotic songs, standing for a passionate and consuming love for Sudan.

Another of the famous singers of the time was 'Ubayd 'Abd al-Nūr, a primary school teacher at Gordon College, a member of the White Flag League, a playwright, and a composer, who wrote another very famous song from 1924 entitled 'The Girl with the Braided Hair' (*yā umm ḍafāyr*).[42] Some of his songs were quite explicit attacks to colonization. Bakheit cites one of them, of which I shall quote only the first and last paragraphs:

> O youth rising at dawn, bid farewell to your families
> And join in the struggle. Stiffen your sinews and die in
> Peace. The beautiful women will come and weep for
> You. O young women cry 'Long live the nation'
> ...
> You are dear and precious; they made you cheap.
> You are beautiful and virgin, and they deflowered you.
> But you are for us and we take the oath
> We shall walk through fire and walk on thorns to rescue you[43]

[39] Six chapters of Najīla's book are dedicated to *Dār Fawzi*, pp. 148-195.

[40] His most important collection of poems is Khalīl Faraḥ, *Diwan Khalīl Faraḥ* (al-Khurṭūm: Dār Jāmi'at al-Khurṭūm lil-Nashr, 1977).

[41] Sharkey, *Living with Colonialism*, p.105. Besides Najīila, an analysis of his poetry appears in Thorraya Soghayroon 'Sudanese Literature in English Translation: An Analytical Study of the Translation with a Historical Introduction to the Literature' (PhD, University of Westminster, 2010), pp. 68-69.

[42] Sogayroon, 'Sudanese literature', pp. 66. He is also discussed in Heather Sharkey, 'Colonialism, Character-Building and the Culture of Nationalism in the Sudan, 1898-1956', in particular p. 10 *International Journal of the History of Sport* (1998), vol. 15, n. 1, pp. 1-26.

[43] Bakheit, 'British Administration and Sudanese Nationalism', p. 79.

The Intelligence Department also discovered many other such songs, such as one entitled 'The National Tune'.[44] It is significant, however, that neither Khalīl Faraḥ nor 'Ubayd 'Abd al-Nūr were ever discovered to have been their authors, and were barely known to the Intelligence Department in 1924. This casts some light not only on the ubiquity of nationalist songs, but also on the fact that they belonged to a layer of Sudanese culture to which British officers did not have access.

Patriotic songs were not sung in any public setting, such as during demonstrations, but only in exceptional or private occurrences. For example, while the cadets were awaiting trial, they were put on gunboats on the Nile for more than a month, and during this time they were heard singing patriotic songs.[45] It was reported on 16 September that officers of the Egyptian Club sang back to them.[46] Otherwise, precisely how the songs circulated is not known, and the era of mass media was yet to arrive on the scene. A national radio network was not created until the Second World War, and the recording industry was in its infancy, the first recording studio having opened in Omdurman in 1921.[47] Nevertheless, patriotic songs certainly circulated in private settings, in close and protected houses such as that of Fawz.

The patriotic tunes sang in 1924, composed in colloquial Sudanese Arabic, expressed dramatic emotions of love, death, generosity, pride, and sacrifice. Songs, recited poems, literary compositions, and so on greatly contributed, during these tense times to 'move' the audience, adding a further layer of emotion to the already volatile and galvanized atmosphere of the times.

44 Appendix I to the Ewart Report.
45 Corbyn to Private Secretary, Khartoum, 18.9.1924, Palace 4/10/48. Corbyn informed the Private Secretary that the cadets had been moved to the civil prison because they were shouting. Previous correspondence between the two shows that they had been shouting for several days.
46 Telegram, unsigned, Khartoum to Mr Kerr, Cairo, 17.9.1924, FO 141/805/2, NA.
47 Ahmad A. Sikainga, 'A Short History of Sudanese Popular Music', *The Sudan Handbook*, John Ryle, Justin Willis, Suliman Baldo, and Jok Madut Jok eds. (Oxford: James Currey, 2011), p. 149. For a comparison with Egypt and a discussion of the role of 'media-capitalism', and in particular patriotic songs in mobilizing the Egyptian urban masses, see Ziad Fahmy, *Ordinary Egyptians: Creating the Modern Nation Through Popular Culture* (Stanford, California: Stanford University Press, 2011).

Part Four

The 1924 Protesters

Reconsidering Social Bonds after the First World War

Prologue

One of the most puzzling aspects of 1924 is that divisions based on social origins, ethnicity, status, profession, and education did not work or seem as they are imagined today. As anticipated earlier, the most remarkable example of this is the story of the 'delegation' formed of officer Zayn al-'Ābdīn 'Abd al-Tām and Muḥammad al-Mahdī. On 19 June 1924, the Sudan Agent in Cairo reported 'the following news' that he had just received from Khartoum:

> Mulazim Awal Zein El Abdin Abd El Tam left for Egypt on the train which was conveying the returning Saidi labourers on June 14th and took with him Mohammed El Mahdi (a son of the Khalifa and grand-son of the Mahdi), who is at present a translator in the White Nile Province. This man was travelling as his servant. On their arrival to Wadi Halfa both were detained on the ground of misuse of Government warrant, and Mohammed El Mahdi returned to Khartoum on the mail arriving there on the evening of June 17th.
>
> Mulazim Awal Zein El Abdin telegraphed to Ali Abd El Latif (recently released after serving a sentence of one year's imprisonment for sedition) and a demonstration was arranged to take place at Khartoum Railway Station. Mohammed El Mahdi, however, had been removed from the train at Khartoum North, so that there was no subject for the projected demonstration at Khartoum.[1]

That concise and carefully worded report could hardly be expected to raise any suspicions about the oddity of the situation. As seen in an earlier chapter, Zayn al-'Ābdīn 'Abd al-Tām was an officer in the Egyptian Army with Dinka family origins. The Dinka had been one of the main targets of the nineteenth-century slave trade. His companion, Muḥammad al-Mahdī, was a son of the Khalīfa 'Abdallāhi, a grandson of the Mahdī himself, and a relative of *sayyid* 'Abd al-Raḥman al-Mahdī, whose political influence both locally and with the British was on the rise. Muḥammad thus belonged to one of the holiest and most reputed northern Sudanese families; yet, Zayn, the son of a slave-soldier, had bought Muḥammad al-Mahdī a special half-price train ticket reserved for servants/ slaves of officers using the privileges associated with his rank, with the intention of saving money for the League's limited finances. How did a grandson of the Mahdī agree to play the role of the slave of somebody

[1] SA to the First Secretary, Cairo, 19.6.1924, FO 141/806/1, NA.

who had 'real' slave ancestry? Conversely, how did a person like Zayn agree to collaborate with a direct descendant of those who had caused his ancestors so much suffering?

In 1924, this story was not unique. It was rumoured that 'Alī' 'Abd al-Laṭīf's father was a slave belonging to a family in al-Khandaq, a small centre not far from Dongola, in the Northern Province. It was alleged that the owners of 'Alī's father were the family of the mother of 'Ubayd al-Ḥājj al-Amīn (another of the League's founders), and this is how the two met for the first time, 'Alī as a son of a family slave, and 'Ubayd as a freeborn child.[2] Even though this story has been disproved, there was clearly a difference in background status between these two men, who were also close friends.

Inside the League, the members were well aware of 'Alī 'Abd al-Laṭīf's background. The Port Sudan activist 'Alī Malāsī provides a fascinating account of the way 'Alī was chosen as a leader of the League:

> After the meeting of the notables [of 10 June] and its decision to support the British Government, 'Alī 'Abd al-Laṭīf held a meeting in his house. Graduates and officers were present. [He said] 'Now *sayyid* 'Abd al-Raḥman has already held his own meeting and he announced his opinion; but we don't think that [they] represent us, because we also have an opinion. We want to fight the government, which was the principle of the League, to fight the government openly. And now we want a president for this league.'
>
> The meeting continued until very late, discussing who would be the president. The meeting was on the brink of failure.
>
> Then 'Alī 'Abd al-Laṭīf said to them, 'It's 2 o'clock now, what do you think if I become the president? And [even] if I do not honour you among the notables, sons of the tribes (because Abū Diqn and Abū Qash were sons of notables), I accept the burden of responsibility, being the president of the White Flag League.' Everybody said '*mabrūk*' [congratulations].[3]

The retrospective account of 'Abd al-Karīm al-Sayyid was even more explicit in emphasising the political meaning of 'Alī's background:

> The choice of 'Alī 'Abd al-Laṭīf had another political dimension: at the time, the English were working on separating the peoples of northern Sudan and southern Sudan and since 'Alī 'Abd al-Laṭīf was from the Dinka, the choice fell on him. In presenting his memorandum he made a gesture of defiance* at colonization to show that there are men in Sudan who do not recognize the political division and they are enemies of the colonization wherever it comes from.[4]

It is clear from these stories is that 'Alī's ancestry was no secret for anybody. However, for him as well as for his fellow members, this mattered less than the strength of his patriotism and political commitment.

Kurita and other historians have argued that the inclusive ideology and composition of the White Flag League resulted from the background of *sūdānī* people such as 'Alī 'Abd al-Laṭīf, whose ancestors had been

2 See for instance: Muḥammad Ibrāhīm Ḥatīkābī: "'Ubayd min qabīla al-maḥas wa 'Alī 'Abd al-Laṭīf khandaqāwī wa laysa min al-dīnkā' ['Ubayd from al-mahasī tribe and 'Ali 'Abd al-Laṭīf from Khadaq and not from Dinka,] *Al-Rāy al-'ām*, 17.5.2002. In *'Alī 'Abd al-Laṭīf* Kurita has demonstrated that this version of 'Alī's origin does not coincide with factual evidences.

3 *Al-Riwāyāt*, pp. 306-307.

4 Al-Sayyid, *al-Liwā' al-Abyaḍ*, p. 10. *Lit. 'slapped the face' of colonization.

captives from the South or the Nuba Mountains. It is also because of that background – they argue – that the League leaders enjoined its members to consider themselves first and foremost as Sudanese. Finally, because people such as ʻAlī came from marginalized and non-Arab groups, the *sūdānī* were able to build an idea of nation that took account of the diversity of the Sudanese people. Kurita notes that in 1924 ʻAlī was known by the protesters as *al-zaʻīm*, the leader, which was the same title used for Zaghlūl in Egypt.[5]

However, although ʻAlī's slave ancestry may have played a role in shaping the League's inclusive ideology and structure, this element is not in itself sufficient to explain why people from notable backgrounds also abided by this vision and, moreover, came to choose a person such as ʻAlī as leader of the national movement. It is not enough to suggest that people because of their patriotism, 'forgot' the issues of ʻAlī's origins. It is a contradiction to state that people became patriots because ʻAlī's origins allowed him to build bridges among various groups, and yet their patriotism made them ignore the issue of his origins.

It should be noted, on the other hand, that some historians consider that it is because of such origins that the 1924 Revolution failed. For instance, it is often maintained that some Sudan Union members, such as Sulaymān Kisha, refused to join the League because ʻAlī was a *sūdānī*. However, had this attitude been predominant in that moment of Sudanese history, the 1924 Revolution would have never occurred. Indeed, unlikely couples such as Zayn and Muḥammad, and ʻAlī ʻAbd al-Laṭīf and ʻUbayd al-Ḥājj al-Amīn were more the rule than the exception in 1924. In this part, I shall argue that these kinds of relationship were not the consequence of an exceptional state of affairs provoked by the impending revolution, in which people 'forgot' about status in the name of a common struggle. On the contrary, they were the outcome of a complex social, economic, and political conjuncture that had begun with the British 'reconquest', as a result of which people labelled as *sūdānī* managed to achieve a central role in the colonial state *together with*, rather than in opposition to, the Northern Sudanese elites. Couples such as that of Zayn and Muḥammad, are surprising only if we believe that social relations are static, and that throughout the 19th and 20th centuries, the Northern Sudanese had adopted a clear, unwavering derogatory attitude towards 'African' people – as today people from southern Sudan, the Nuba Mountains and some parts of Darfur are defined. This would mean extracting social relations from history, and considering them unaffected by change.

The chapters that follow address the question of social hierarchies from a structural point of view, suggesting that they came to be affected by the colonial situation in very unexpected ways, through state institutions, economic change, educational possibilities, and new patterns of employment. This is of particular note in three groups of people who were to play leading roles in 1924: civilian government employees, army officers, and wage-workers employed in all sorts of jobs, mostly related

5 Kurita, *ʻAlī ʻAbd al-Laṭīf*, p. 74.

to the burgeoning urban economy. The 1924 Revolution was not an 'anomaly' in Sudanese history, but was fully grounded in the conditions of the time. And only after the revolution, and as a backlash to it, there would be a significant change in the Northern Sudanese society, with the intensification of the racialization of various state institutions, as well as of the political and cultural life of Northern Sudan

8

The Sociology of Colonial Education and the 1924 Insurgents

> 'When I arrived at Kober prison, I met 'Ubayd al-Ḥājj al-Amīn. We had the opportunity to be in one cell to continue our laughs. After being in one class in college, now we were in one cell in prison.'[1]

In 1924, the White Flag League managed to connect to various social constituencies through its structure. However, three groups stood out as being the most significant: civilian employees of the Sudan government; army officers; and skilled and unskilled workers, small traders, and artisans. In an earlier chapter reference was made to Erickson's idea that one of the prerequisites for the formation of secret societies is mutual trust among prospective members. Thus, recruitment usually works through relatively tight and previously established networks: friends, neighbours, or colleagues. How these bonds were formed is explored in this and subsequent chapters. Here, I study the structure of colonial schools and the career paths of educated Sudanese: the way in which education shaped their lives as a whole, from the types of employment open to them after school; the city to which they were sent to work; the type of people they met and the networks developed. This chapter is closely connected to the one that follows, which focuses on the officers of the Egyptian Army, because civilians and officers followed the same curriculum until the end of primary school.

Education policy and its social and political consequences in the period starting from 1925 has been studied extensively, but the era in which people like 'Alī 'Abd al-Laṭīf and 'Ubayd al-Ḥājj al-Amīn attended school – between 1905 and 1925 – has received far less attention. It is crucial to the events of 1924, however, in the light of the fact that colonial sources describe White Flag League members as 'low' government clerks, in contrast to their 'smarter' (Arab) superiors supposedly loyal to the government. However, there is scattered evidence here and there in the records of 1924 that the picture was more complex than that, such as a remark made by a colonial officer that 'Blacks' had risen to 'unnaturally' high positions through education.[2] This comment, inadvertently dropped

1 *Al-Riwāyāt*, p. 280.

2 J. M. Ewart, Report on Political Agitation in the Sudan, Khartoum, 21.4.1925, FO 407/201, NA, p. 171.

into a long report aiming at proving the worthlessness of political agitation, calls for further study on the sociology of education in Sudan, that is, on the composition of the student population before 1924.

Considering the extensive literature on education in Sudan, limitations are necessary.[3] How the school curriculum influenced Sudanese self-perceptions; whether it was a form of cultural imperialism; or a vehicle for enlightened ideas, is beyond the remit of this study.[4] The focus is on the structure and management of education, on how it worked, on the way people were selected, and on what they did after the end of their school career, because the focus is first of all on their *entanglements*. Being able to perceive this structure means being more aware of the numerous contacts and connections that made 1924 possible.

First, some personal stories of activists are examined, to illustrate the ways in which education and politics intertwined. The quotation at the head of this chapter, the words of a member of the White Flag League on his lifelong friendship with 'Ubayd al-Ḥājj al-Amīn, sets the tone for this narrative.

CLASSMATES AND COMRADES

Among the many accounts by members of the Sudan Union and the White Flag League collected in *Al-Riwāyāt al-Shafawiyya li-Thuwwār 1924* only a few dwell on memories of their lives, networks, and careers before 1924, so many years before these interviews were taken in the 1970s. In 2005, the families of activists I met knew even less about this period of their fathers' or relatives' lives. Still, some of the accounts in *Al-Riwāyāt* are fairly detailed, as in the case of the brothers Aḥmad Ṣabrī Zāyd and Muḥammad 'Abd al-Mun'im Zāyd, who were members of the White Flag League in Port Sudan.

Aḥmad and Muḥammad were known by the Intelligence Department as ringleaders of the demonstration of 27 July 1924 in Port Sudan. The brothers also took part in the prison riot at the end of November.[5] Their family background and ethnicity are not mentioned in their personal files and their names do not figure in the *tabaqāt*.[6] Aḥmad only specified that they were born in Argo, near Dongola, more or less half way between Khartoum and the border with Egypt, which is suggestive of Nubian

3 Beshir, *Educational Development in the Sudan*, Sharkey, *Living with Colonialism*.

4 This question was at the centre of the debate of some of the early postcolonial thinkers, such as Fanon or Ngugi Wa Thiongo. For some positions on the debate, see: J. A. Mangan, *The Imperial Curriculum: Racial Images and Education in the British Colonial Experience* (London; New York: Routledge, 1993).

5 For the participants in the demonstration: Copies of correspondence re. Demonstration at Port Sudan 27.7.1924 on the occasion of the transfer of political prisoner from Khartoum to Port Sudan, Port Sudan 30.7.1924, Palace 4/10/50, NRO. For the prison riots, *The White Flag Trials*, pp. iv-v.

6 The tabaqāt, biographical dictionaries, consulted were: Bāshirī, *Rūwād Al-fikr Al-Sūdānī* and 'Awn al-Sharīf Qāsim, *Mawsū'at al-Qabā'il wa-al-Ansāb Fī al-Sūdān Wa-ashhar Asmā' al-'Ālam wa-al-Amākin,* 6 vols. (Khartoum: Maktabat Āfiruqrāf, 1996).

origin. Muḥammad ʻAbd al-Munʻim was born in 1901, and was probably slightly older than Aḥmad.[7] At some point, and for unknown reasons, they moved from Argo to Khartoum and were enrolled at the Gordon College Primary School. It should be noted that the Gordon College, besides being a secondary school (called at that time the Upper School), included also a primary and an elementary school (in vernacular Arabic, *kuttāb*).

The brothers were already involved in politics while they were at school. As narrated in his interview, Aḥmad had 'secret work' with a certain Tawfīq Aḥmad Bakrī, who in turn put him in contact with ʻUbayd al-Ḥājj al-Amīn. Aḥmad's 'secret work' consisted of writing and posting seditious circulars written by Sudan Union members. Tawfīq Aḥmad Bakrī, ʻUbayd al-Ḥājj al-Amīn, and Muḥyī al-Dīn Abū Sayf 'were the dynamo of the circulars at the college'.[8]

The brothers belonged to one of many groups of politicized young men who had attended Gordon College Primary School. Several political activists who gave accounts of their lives in *Al-Riwāyāt* had studied there: Sayyid Shahāta, an officer of the Egyptian Army of Egyptian origins who was suspected of seditious behaviour in 1924, attended the Gordon College *kuttāb* between 1902 and 1906 and then joined Gordon College Primary School (or Khartoum Primary School), while ʻAbd al-ʻAzīz ʻAbd al-Ḥay, another officer who was involved in the officers' mutiny to some degree, was admitted to Omdurman Primary School around 1911 after attending elementary school in Wad Medani, and moved to Gordon College Primary School in his fourth year. Cadets Muzammil ʻAlī Dinār, Maḥmūd Khamīs Aḥmad, and Ibrāhīm Sayyid ʻUthmān all also attended the Khartoum Primary School at one time or another.[9] Three others, telegraph operator (and later railway employee) Abāyazīd Aḥmad Ḥusayn al-Shallālī, who was sentenced to one year's imprisonment for his participation in the Atbara riots; Aḥmad al-Ṭrīfī Zubayr Bāshā, who was probably a member of the White Flag, and who worked for a private company at the Makwar Dam; and last but not least, Ṣāliḥ ʻAbd al-Qādir, the oldest of the five founders, all attended Gordon College Primary School.[10]

7 *Al-Riwāyāt*, p. 262.

8 Ibid., and Notes on the signatory of the telegram dated 15.5.1924 (Saleh Abdel Gadir, Ali Abdel Latif, Hassan Sharif, Hassan Saleh, Obeid El Haj El Amin to Governor General, Khartoum), undated, unsigned, FO 141/806/1, NA.

9 For Sayyid Shahāta: *Al-Riwāyāt*, p. 160. For ʻAbd al-ʻAzīz ʻAbd al-Ḥay: Ibid., p. 224. Maḥmūd Khamīs Aḥmad attended the Khartoum *kuttāb* from 1910 and then entered the primary school in 1914; in 1916, he joined the army and studied at the battalion school. He became a soldier in 1920, and was selected for the Military School in 1924. *Al-Riwāyāt*, p. 356. Muzammil ʻAlī Dinār attended it between 1920 and 1922: *Al-Riwāyāt*, pp. 42-43. Ibrāhīm Sayyid ʻUthmān did so at some date between 1906 and 1917, as he entered the Military College in 1922, *Al-Riwāyāt*, p. 173.

10 For Abāyazīd Aḥmad Ḥusayn al-Shallālī: Gov. Berber to DI, El Damer 5.10.1924, Northern Prov. 1/21/215 and *Al-Riwāyāt*, p. 141, NRO. For Aḥmad al-Ṭrīfī Zubayr Bāshā, *Al-Riwāyāt*, p. 521. For Ṣāliḥ ʻAbd al-Qādir: Notes on the signatory of the telegram dated 15.5.1924, undated, unsigned, FO 141/806/1, NA, he is listed as a Gordon College student, without clarifying whether he was at the primary

Many, if not most of the people interviewed in *Al-Riwāyāt* had wanted to continue to the Gordon College Upper School. For example, Ṣāliḥ 'Abd al-Qādir wished to attend the Teachers' Branch of the college, but he was not allowed to do so. After completing primary school, he was appointed to the Post and Telegraph Department as a travelling postmaster between Khartoum and Wadi Halfa.[11] This was also the case of the brothers Zāyd. Muḥammad 'Abd al-Mun'im Zāyd remarked bitterly, 'the British did not allow students to continue to secondary education, and appointed us to simple jobs in the Sudan administration'. His brother also complained that, because of his limited education, he was hired in 'low government employment.'[12] Only a small number of activists was allowed to continue to the Gordon College Upper School, for example, 'Ubayd al-Ḥājj al-Amīn (although he left after the second year) and Mudaththir al-Būshī.[13]

One should not jump to the conclusion that the White Flag League was composed only of students from this school. The educational backgrounds of only a small number of the political activists is known and since Gordon College was still a prestigious institution in the 1970s (having become the most famous university of the country), those who had attended it were more likely to mention it than students of other institutions. [14] Activists often called it 'Gordon College' without specifying that it was actually the primary school.

The narratives in *Al-Riwāyāt* cast light on how political engagement began at school and continued at work. Once in Atbara, Aḥmad Ṣabrī Zāyd met 'Ubayd al-Ḥājj al-Amīn in the Railways Department, as well as two other former classmates, and probably also two Sudan Union members who were working there, Ṭayyib al-Mīrghanī and Ibrāhīm 'Abd al-Hādī.[15] In an Intelligence Note, Willis mentions that the four graduates were all sent to Atbara in 1920, and were all discharged by 1922.[16] Indeed, Aḥmad Ṣabrī Zāyd complained in his interview that his period at the Railways was a difficult one, because 'they' knew that he belonged to a political group, so 'they started making trouble with us and assigning us missions

(contd) or secondary school. His son Sa'd Ṣāliḥ 'Abd al-Qādir said that his father had completed the fourth year of primary school. Author interview with Sa'd Ṣāliḥ 'Abd al-Qādir at his home, tape recorded, Khartoum 26.1.2005.

11 Notes on the signatory of the telegram 15.5.1924, undated, unsigned, FO 141/806/1, NA.

12 *Al-Riwāyāt*, p. 257 and p. 262.

13 Coming from a prestigious family of *'ulamā* of Wad Medani, Mudaththir attended both elementary and primary school there, but obtained a place at the Upper School, more precisely in the prestigious *qāḍi* branch – that is, the branch that trained judges for the *sharī'a* courts – around 1918. *Al-Riwāyāt*, p. 64.

14 Only in a few cases do we know the educational career of the activists who studied outside Khartoum: for example, 'Izz al-Dīn Ḥusayn Rāsiq had studied in Berber, and 'Alī Malāsī in Sawakin. 'Izz al-Dīn Ḥusayn Rāsiq IAAS 1575; for 'Alī Malāsī, *Al-Riwāyāt*, p. 302.

15 For Ibrāhīm 'Abd al-Hādī, see 'List of 120 Members of the White Flag League and suggested leaders in the future', Northern Prov. 1/21/207; for Ṭayyib al-Mīrghanī, see 'List of political agitators', unsigned, undated, Kordofan 1/13/61, both in NRO.

16 Notes on the signatory of the telegram dated 15.5.1924, undated, unsigned, FO 141/806/1, NA.

in distant places.'[17] After being discharged, they probably returned to their respective homes in El Dueim, El Obeid and Omdurman. At least two quickly found work again: 'Ubayd al-Ḥājj al-Amīn in the Post and Telegraph Department,[18] while Aḥmad Ṣabrī Zāyd moved to Port Sudan, to work for the multinational shipping company Gellatly & Hankey. In Port Sudan, Aḥmad Ṣabrī Zāyd found a new cell of protesters which included his brother Muḥammad 'Abd al-Mun'im, now working for the Port Sudan office of the Railways Department, and Alī Malāsī, in the Post and Telegraph. He had completed the Sawakin Primary School in 1913. In common with other activists he had wanted to continue to the Gordon College Upper School, but he was not admitted, and after being hired by the Post and Telegraph, he was sent to work in Kordofan, and then back to the Red Sea.[19] These stories show that educated government employees were frequently transferred from one city to another, and from one administrative post to another. There were many ways, therefore, in which educated people could get to know each other and create bonds: they may have attended the same school, worked for the same department, or moved to the same city during one of their many transfers.

EDUCATION, ORIGIN AND STATUS BETWEEN 1900 AND 1925

During the entire period under review, the British authorities considered education to be a privilege for a few carefully chosen individuals. This was clearly a reflection of the broader policy of the British Empire in Africa, which was to keep educational infrastructures as restricted as possible, and to leave education in the hands of Christian missionaries wherever appropriate.[20] But in post-Mahdist Sudan, the British thought it inadvisable to open Christian missionary schools in the North, because it would have offended local religious sentiment. Therefore, in the North, with few exceptions, the schools were public and run by the colonial state, while in the South the educational system was left to the missionaries.[21]

From the outset, senior British officials agreed in principle that education should favour the natural 'leaders' of Sudan. In practice, however, things went quite differently, especially at the beginning: many of these 'leaders' were not particularly eager to send their sons to colonial schools, while other groups pushed to obtain a formal education. In addition, the colonial

[17] *Al-Riwāyāt*, p. 264.

[18] Notes on the signatory of the telegram dated 15.5.1924, undated, unsigned, FO 141/806/1, NA. See also Bāshirī, *Rūwād al-Fikr al-Sūdānī*, p. 203.

[19] *Al-Riwāyāt*, p. 302.

[20] Aaron Windel, 'British Colonial Education in Africa: Policy and Practice in the Era of Trusteeship', *HIC3 History Compass* (2009), vol. 7, n. 1, pp. 1-21.

[21] A number of private schools existed in Northern Sudan, such as the Greek school or the Comboniani Missionary School (which would become the prestigious Comboni College in the 1940s), but in the period covered here, they were always a second choice compared to Gordon College. For the Church Missionary Society, see Heather J. Sharkey, 'Christians Among Muslims: The Church Missionary Society in the Northern Sudan', *The Journal of African History* (2002), vol. 43, n. 1, pp. 51-75.

authorities did not all share the same opinion about who precisely these 'leaders' were. Variations in the practical application of this general principle led to substantial differences in the types of pupils recruited.

At the time of Governor General Reginald Wingate, the Director of Education, James Currie, believed in the importance of providing elementary instruction for a wider stratum of the Sudanese population than future government employees. For instance, he created a few girls' elementary schools that offered a limited form of education for females, alongside the Rufa'a school, founded by Bābikr Badrī, and the various missionary schools for girls.[22] On the other hand, secondary education under Currie was extremely restricted and limited to a very small number of Sudanese. This situation was reversed with the Governor Generalship of Lee Stack.

The period after the Great War presented a turning point in the educational policies of the Sudanese Government, connected to wider changes in native policies. In the early 1920s, a new generation of administrators replaced the old guard of senior British Officers that had surrounded Wingate, who had left in 1916. Mainly composed of civilians, the new administration was influenced by the growing popularity of Indirect Rule elsewhere in the British Empire, and believed that native policies should be based on the co-optation of local authorities, and on decentralization. Stack was caught between the two eras, however. He was convinced that devolution to traditional authorities could and should coexist with a gradual empowerment of educated Sudanese. These two groups might be made to cohere through a careful screening of school pupils, who would be selected from the same social strata as notables. This native policy, which is known as the Dual Policy, inevitably had a crucial impact on the entire structure of education. In practice, it led to the restriction of access to elementary and primary schools, and an expansion of secondary education. Another, less expensive form of basic education began to be subsidized, in the shape of Quranic schools known as *khalwa*.

During the period in question, the school system was organized over four levels. After a 'preparatory' year in a religious *khalwa*, which was not compulsory, at around the age of seven a pupil would enter elementary school – EVS (Elementary Vernacular School) in colonial jargon – for a period of three to four years.[23] If allowed to continue, at about age twelve a student would begin primary education, which lasted for four years, or attend one of the Vocational Workshops, where he would learn a craft such as stonecutting or iron working. At about sixteen, a pupil could start secondary education at Gordon College, which also lasted four years, or be admitted to the Military School. It should be noted that the ages of pupils beginning the various school levels was very flexible, both because they might repeat the same year several times and because they could be admitted even if they were older.

[22] For girls' schools, see Summary of number of pupils attending elementary vernacular schools, state-aided khalwas, girls' schools and instructional workshops from 1904-1926, Palace 4/1/3, NRO.

[23] *Regulation and Syllabus of Studies for Elementary Vernacular Schools under the Sudan Government*, Education Dept., 1929, Dept. Reports 6/5/60, NRO.

During the mid-1920s, there were frequent debates on the need to reform the school system. The changes in education, in particular with Indirect Rule, exposed the differences between the old guard of government officials of the Wingate era and the new. In 1934, Currie, the former Director of Education, wrote two articles in which he expressed his dismay, and denounced the educational policy of Indirect Rule.[24] After his retirement, Currie remained involved in a number of high-profile educational institutions such as the Imperial College of Science and Technology, London, and was an influential figure in the English educational system. His complaints could not be ignored. The Civil Secretary MacMichael (1926-1933) and other government officials did their best to defend their line, providing figures on the school system before and after the Dual Policy and Indirect Rule.

Another heated discussion that took place in the 1920s concerned the fees students had to pay to attend primary and secondary schools (elementary education was free, as the costs were borne by a local education tax).[25] For some British officers, this eliminated the very people for whom the education system had been created: the sons of headmen and notables whose assets were intangible or could not be converted into money. This sparked even broader criticism of the system as a whole: for instance, in 1923 the Governor of the White Nile Province bemoaned the fact that elementary education benefited only 'townees'. The text is worth quoting, as it demonstrates what colonial officials of the time understood the goals of the educational system to be:

> Our chief aim should be to educate our future Sheikhs and Omdas. Should we fail to do so, and we are failing to a large extent at present, we render impossible any future scheme of decentralisation which I consider should be the ultimate aim of our administration. Instead of coordinating our efforts towards this very desirable end we are flooding our towns with more or less educated youths who can only be a source of danger and trouble in the future.[26]

These debates, which are of great interest but beyond the scope of this discussion, provide enlightening snippets of information about the educational background of educated 1924 protesters, who on average had attended school for some years between 1905 and 1924.

Education and the labour market

In the period covered for this study (and well beyond it) access to public education was conspicuous in its scarcity. Not only was it extremely restricted at an elementary level, but the chances of continuing an education were ridiculously low. In comparison to the overall student population (100%), in 1906 Gordon College Upper School pupils represented 3.5% of all

[24] James Currie, 'The Educational Experiment in the Anglo-Egyptian Sudan, 1900-33. Part I', *African Affairs, Journal of the Royal African Society* (1934), vol. 33, n. 133, pp. 361-371. James Currie, 'The Educational Experiment in the Anglo-Egyptian Sudan, 1900-33. Part II', *African Affairs, Journal of the Royal African Society* (1935), vol. 34, n.134, pp. 41-59.

[25] A large file including some of these debates may be found in Civsec 1/59/171, NRO.

[26] Memorandum on Education Policy, submitted by Gov. White Nile Prov., to be discussed at the GG Council, el Dueim, 4.1.1923, Civsec 17/6/34, NRO.

Table 8 Number of students in Elementary Vernacular Schools, Primary Schools, and Gordon College, 1906–1916

Year	Number of boys in EVS	Number of boys in Khalwa	Total 4 years Primary School	Total 4 years Gordon College
1906	935	0	792	29
1907	1280	0	934	38
1908	1781	0	887	49
1909	2123	0	799	49
1910	2504	0	952	49
1911	2782	0	939	67
1912	3223	0	895	60
1913	3674	0	947	60
1914	4220	0	987	67
1915	4377	0	1019	70
1916	5025	0	985	70
1917	5366	0	1018	74
1918	5881	189	1060	86
1919	6451	188	1089	114
1920	7311	183	1133	134
1921	8367	254	1191	180
1922	8456	424	1220	191
1923	8043	889	1161	207
1924	8318	2700	1147	212
1925	7852	5444	1101	235
1926	8342	9503	1153	303

Source: Summary of number of pupils attending EVS, state aided khalwas, girls' schools and instructional workshops from 1904-1926, Palace 4/1/3, NRO.

primary school students and 3% of all elementary school pupils; in 1910, the figure was 5% and 2% respectively, and in 1915 it was 7% and 1.5%. Thus, out of 100 pupils who attended elementary school, an average of just over one would reach secondary school level – a thoroughly inadequate provision. These figures explain the centrality of the topic of education among nationalist circles: it was the most obvious evidence of the failings of British colonization.

A more detailed look at the table on the growth of the student population in Sudan between 1906 and 1926 reveals a number of interesting details. Overall, it shows a soaring disproportion in access between elementary and primary education during the two decades in question, and also between elementary and secondary education. The number of pupils attending the *kuttāb* continued to grow, but the number of places in primary schools did not. In 1926, the number of admissions to primary schools was only slightly higher than it was in 1907! Securing a place at a primary school was so difficult that according to the historian Beshir, no student was admitted without the specific approval of the Governor General.[27]

Nonetheless, a comparison of the decades 1906-1915 and 1916-1926 reveals a number of differences. The chance of continuing from elementary to primary school was higher during the former decade, which was also the period when the first nationalists attended the *kuttāb*: people like ʿAlī ʿAbd al-Laṭīf or Ṣāliḥ ʿAbd al-Qādir, who were born around 1890-1895.[28] For instance, in 1905, a total of 783 students attended elementary schools: this means that the output of fourth-year students from the all the elementary schools in Sudan, which must have included roughly 150 to 200 students, was lower than the number of students recruited in the first year of primary school in 1906 (361 pupils).[29] In other words, theoretically, all the students who finished elementary school could continue with primary education. Ten years later, in 1915, less than one pupil out of four made it into primary school, and ten years later, in 1925, the number had fallen as low as 3 out of 20 pupils, around 15%.

As for Gordon College Upper School, while admission was always extremely difficult, the decades from 1906 to 1915 and 1916 to 1926 are not completely alike. The enrolment patterns are the opposite of those between primary school and *kuttāb*: before the war, it was easier to gain admission to primary school after the *kuttāb*, but it was more difficult for primary school students to continue on to Gordon College Upper School: for example, in 1917, only 27 out of 187 pupils who left primary school made it to the next level, while in 1925 the number was 91 out of 289, a little less than one out of three. The educational pyramid was also very uneven with regard to geographical distribution and numbers of schools. In 1913, there were only 6 primary schools in the Northern Province and in the Gezira, compared to 49 elementary schools; they were located in Omdurman, Khartoum, Berber, Halfa, Sawakin, and Wad Medani.[30] About ten years later, in 1925, there were only four more – Rufaʿa, Atbara, El Obeid, and El Dueim – compared with 91 elementary schools.[31] Primary schools were thus concentrated in riverain Sudan.

[27] Beshir, *Educational Development in the Sudan*, p. 40, quoting the Sudan Govt. Gazette No. 8, November 1902.

[28] For Ṣāliḥ ʿAbd al-Qādir, interview by the author with Saʿd Ṣāliḥ ʿAbd al-Qādir in his home, tape recorded, Khartoum 26.1.2005. For ʿAlī ʿAbd al-Laṭīf, see Kurita, *ʿAlī ʿAbd al-Laṭīf wa-Thawrat 1924*.

[29] Compare the Summary of Number of Pupils Attending Elementary Vernacular Schools, state-aided khalwas, girls' schools and instructional workshops from 1904-1926, and the List showing number of boys in each class in Sudan Govt. Primary Schools in January of each year from 1906 onwards, both in Palace 4/1/3, NRO.

[30] *Annual Report of the Education Dept. 1913*, pp. 247-48.

[31] Number of boys attending Sudan Govt. primary schools, January 1925, and

Finally, there is one figure in the Education Department statistics that is especially remarkable, and its very presence shows that it must have represented a real problem for early educators. This is the exceptionally high attrition rate: that is, the number of pupils who dropped out of schools. This is significant for our purposes to put in context the educational background of the 1924 activists, and it is worth reflecting for a moment on the statistics for this period. At the end of 1909, only 61 out of 361 pupils from the class of 1906 had reached the fourth year of primary school, and in 1915, only 86 of the 370 students from the class of 1912 had done so; this means that in 1909, 83%, and in 1915, 77% of pupils left primary school without completing it.[32] Things improved significantly after the end of the Great War, and in 1926, 203 of the 317 pupils who had started primary school in 1923 were still there. The figures for the levels above and below primary school are scarce, and yet the few existing show a similarly high attrition rate. As for Gordon College Upper School, we know that in 1928, of the 150 students in the first two years, 60 dropped out at the end of the second year.[33]

Considering that most of the 1924 protesters who had graduated studied in the period between 1905 and 1920, we can conclude that they belonged to a generation in which most students would not complete primary school, and yet, as Table 10 shows, would still easily be able to find employment in the public or private sectors. To look at it from another angle, the overwhelming majority of the Sudanese clerical staff in the period between 1900 and 1920 had not finished primary school.

There were many reasons behind the high rate of students withdrawing from primary schools, but the most important factor was that the labour market for clerks was so in need of individuals with some degree of literacy that employers were willing to take whoever they could. Even students who had only attended one or two years could still find good employment. The table on the careers of students following primary school confirms this (Table 10); between 1917 and 1925, the rate of unemployment for people who had attended primary schools, including those who had dropped out, was almost zero, to the point that more students died each year than were unemployed. The trend of drop-outs was certainly reinforced by the fact that many Sudanese families struggled economically to keep their sons at school because of the school fees, and by other factors such as a suspicion of colonial education, as many colonial officers reported.[34]

(contd) Summary of Number of Pupils Attending Elementary Vernacular Schools, state-aided khalwas, girls' schools and instructional workshops from 1904-1926, both in Palace 4/1/3, NRO.

32 It should be remembered that until 1910, completing four years of primary school was not a pre-requisite for admission to the Upper School; however, as we have seen, the number of admissions in this period was so small that it cannot be a justification for so many withdrawals. Currie, *Report, dated 8th September, 1911, on the Gordon Memorial College at Khartoum, for the Year 1910*, p. 12.

33 Note after conversation with Mr Udal about the possibility of enlarging the Gordon College to produce more full secondary course boys. Matthew, Khartoum 3.2.1928, Civsec1 17/2/6, NRO.

34 Beshir, *Educational Development in the Sudan*; Daly, *Empire on the Nile*, Chapter 6.

Table 9 List showing number of boys in each class in Sudan government primary schools (PS) in January of each year from 1906 onwards[35]

Class	1st	Drop-outs	2nd	Drop-outs	3rd	Drop-outs	4th	Total drop-outs over 4-year period	Total drop-outs per year	Total PS pupils per year	Variation in number of pupils per year
1906	361	-	252	-	121	-	58	-	-	792	-
1907	449	-94	267	-97	155	-58	63	-	-249	934	142
1908	342	-147	302	-89	178	-90	65	-	-326	887	-47
1909	305	-87	255	-124	178	-117	61	-300	-328	799	-88
1910	353	0	305	-42	213	-97	81	-368	-139	952	153
1911	326	-94	259	-115	190	-149	64	-278	-358	839	-113
1912	370	-63	263	-63	196	-124	66	-239	-250	895	56
1913	377	-91	279	-46	217	-122	74	-279	-259	947	52
1914	371	-53	324	-73	206	-131	86	-240	-257	987	40
1915	369	-41	330	-90	234	-120	86	-284	-251	1019	32
1916	323	-92	277	-65	265	-124	110	-267	-281	975	-44
1917	333	-26	297	-28	249	-126	139	-232	-180	1018	43
1918	326	3	336	-55	242	-93	156	-213	-145	1060	42
1919	335	-35	291	-37	299	-78	164	-159	-150	1089	29
1920	356	-31	304	-9	282	-108	191	-142	-148	1133	44
1921	366	-39	317	-22	282	-56	226	-100	-117	1191	58
1922	345	-14	352	-11	306	-65	217	-118	-90	1220	29
1923	317	-36	309	-54	298	-69	237	-119	-159	1161	-59
1924	350	-47	270	-29	280	-49	249	-117	-125	1149	-12
1925	337	-44	306	-42	228	-50	230	-115	-136	1101	-48
1926	347	-33	304	-7	299	-25	203	-114	-65	1153	52

The table on the employment of primary school pupils deserves a closer look. It shows that during the period under consideration, the government was their first employer, absorbing between a quarter and one-half of school leavers. This trend was even more evident at the Upper School level: in 1919, out of 20 Gordon College Upper School students, the government hired 19 and only one went into 'non-government employment'; in 1921 none did; and in 1924, 48 went into the public sector and only three into other occupations.[36]

[35] Source: Palace 4/1/3, NRO.
[36] Statistic of boys employed from Gordon College Upper School and Sudan govt. school (primary) since 1919, Palace 4/1/3, NRO.

Table 10 Number of boys leaving primary schools, 1917-1925[37]

Year	G C Upper school	Employed in government	Joined private schools	Left Sudan	Gordon College Workshop	Died	Employed in agriculture	Employed as merchants	In private employment	Joined military school	Enlisted in army	Different trades	Doing nothing	Total
1917	27	42	7	24	4	1	13	39	7	10	3	10	--	187
1918	35	80	4	32	2	3	14	35	32	11	2	8	1	259
1919	43	76	--	34	3	2	6	32	13	16	4	7	3	239
1920	59	57	3	38	7	1	5	33	6	5	6	3	1	224
1921	71	85	5	48	--	3	13	29	14	5	1	--	4	278
1922	55	102	8	46	6	2	8	31	3	5	2	2	1	271
1923	83	91	11	38	5	1	17	26	16	5	4	25	--	322
1924	90	106	19	29	--	3	22	24	14	--	--	32	1	340
1925	91	115	11	20	--	1	11	15	4	--	--	19	1	289

37 Source: Palace 4/1/3, NRO. There are elements of inconsistency between Tables 9 and 10, but they have been reported as they appear in the sources.

Tables 9 and 10 demonstrate that in the 1910s and early 1920s, the term 'graduate' or 'educated' Sudanese largely indicated primary school students. It is of interest now to look further at the career opportunities they enjoyed. After government, the main employer was the trading sector, although the percentage decreased with the passing of the years (as in 1925, when only 15 out of 289 pupils were employed as merchants). A fairly high percentage left Sudan. Those who travelled abroad were Egyptians and 'Other' foreigners, mostly because Sudanese were barred from studying in Egypt. As for the Vocational Workshops, the number of primary school students choosing that route was much smaller than the actual number of pupils who attended them. To secure a place at these workshops, it was only necessary to have completed the *kuttāb*, and thus it was rather unusual for young graduates to choose this path.[38] Finally, a steady but small percentage of students joined the Military School or the army straight out of primary school.

To sum up, these statistics reveal several features of education prior to the Great War. First, the overall educational infrastructure remained extremely limited throughout the whole period and did not improve with the passing of time. In addition, the educational pyramid was structured in such a way that it had an extremely wide base and an extremely narrow top: very few made it from elementary to primary school, and fewer still from primary school to Gordon College.

Second, the overwhelming majority of educated Sudanese who worked as clerks for the government or in private firms had only been reading in primary schools for a few years, or at best had attended a few years of Upper School. This trend continued to be visible after the Great War: in 1919, only one out of four government employees had an Upper School background. In the same year, of the 76 primary school students employed by the government, only 47 had completed the fourth year, and as late as 1924, of the 106 primary school student recruited by the government, only 33 had completed primary school.[39] Things were changing fast, however: by 1922, half of those entering government employment came from the Upper School, as it became increasingly difficult to obtain a classified government position (see below) without an Upper School diploma.[40]

The 1924 activists were disparagingly called a 'half-baked intelligentsia', which referred to the limited amount of time they had spent at school. However, an intelligentsia of this kind was actually representative of average students trained in the colonial educational system.

Family background, nationality, and 'race'

As seen, schools were indisputably exclusive institutions, and open to very few Sudanese. There were a number of criteria for the selection of such a

[38] Details of instruction in instructional workshops, Intel 4/3/15, NRO.

[39] Cf. Statistics of boys employed from Gordon College Upper School and Sudan govt. school (primary) since 1919 and Number of boys who left primary schools from 1917-25, in Palace 4/1/3, NRO.

[40] Statistics of boys employed from Gordon College Upper School and Sudan govt. school (primary) since 1919, Palace 4/1/3, NRO.

limited amount of pupils: aptitude and interest in education; the type of connection between the family and the government; the origins and status of the family; and finally its ability to pay the school fees, which were waived in the case of exceptional students, usually from notable families. The government had a clear priority which it had stated from the outset. Its aim was to target 'future Sheikhs and Omdas... the very class whom Kitchener desired to benefit'.[41] Yet there is a legitimate suspicion that, at least in the period between 1900 and 1925, before the turn to Indirect Rule, the situation was quite different from the policy stated above.

According to Beshir, until the 1920s, the system benefited three main groups of people. First were the Egyptians, at least until 1924. Because they represented around 40% of government officials, the number of Egyptian pupils educated at colonial schools was fairly high (see Tables 11 and 12).[42] With the exception of the Military School, all educational institutions were open to this group, which is probably something Egyptian officials had negotiated as a condition for staying in Sudan; moreover, as we have seen, it was also a result of the interconnections between Egyptian and Sudanese families. Second, there were the urban and rural notables who were not as interested in education, and certainly did not have enough cash to pay the school fees. However, as the government had a political interest in educating the offspring of precisely this group, it tried to encourage them in different ways, such as waiving fees, but with limited success. The third group with an interest in education were the Sudanese who worked for the British government. This varied group included people who did not enjoy the same degree of influence. At the very beginning of the Condominium, before the first Sudanese had completed their training in colonial school, the first – and only – natives to secure senior positions in government were educated urban notables, some of whom had already served as clerks in the Mahdiyya or Turkiyya governments: families such as the al-Azharī, the Hāshimāb, or the Abū Sinn. They valued formal education and the power it yielded, and were interested in educating their sons. Second were Sudanese who did not necessarily come from well-known families, but had some connection with the government. This was the case with some families of merchants, who could pay school fees and had the necessary links with senior British officials. Another important sub-group included the higher ranks of the Egyptian Army, discussed in more detail in the following chapter. Suffice to to mention here that their important role in the Sudan Government up to the 1920s is confirmed by the presence in the statistics of the Education Department of Sudanese labelled as 'Blacks' up to the level of Gordon College Upper School.

This general description drawn from existing scholarship on education provides little detail, however, which is often where the most intriguing information may lie. Detailed statistics on the pupils' parentage are almost

41 The first quote is from Memorandum on Education Policy, submitted by Gov. White Nile Prov. to be discussed at the GG Council, el Dueim, 4.1.1923, Civsec 17/6/34, NRO. The second is from [MacMichael] to Simpson, Ministry of Education, Cairo, 16.11.1933, Palace 4/1/4, NRO.

42 Beshir, *Educational Development in the Sudan*, p. 198.

Table 11 Origin of pupils in some EVS for 1913[43]

Kuttabs	Arabs	Blacks	Berberine	Mixed	Egyptians	Miscellaneous	Total
Berber	17	0	0	34	1	1	53
Shendi	21	9	0	28	10	-	68
Kassala	30	12	0	13	7	2	64
Gedarif	60	15	0	33	0	0	108
Sennar	26	40	0	4	4	1	75
Wad al-Abbas	33	10	0	0	0	0	43
El-Obeid	74	9	0	0	9	5	97
Bara	54	0	0	0	0	0	54
Khartoum	52	65	24	46	54	1	242
Omdurman	51	22	3	43	17	4	140
Wad Medani	27	12	0	31	9	1	80
Port Sudan	15	8	4	5	16	11	59
Tokar	61	40	0	39	0	0	141
Total	**521**	**242**	**31**	**276**	**127**	**25**	**1224**
Grand total in Sudan	2738	547	395	1039	426	81	5226

completely lacking for all levels of education for the period before 1925. Some information as to their background can, however, be deduced from another category relating to the 'nationality' of pupils attending. Unfortunately, these figures are not available for every year, especially for elementary schools.

Note that the 'nationality' category does not indicate a geographical or ethnic background but is a tentative reading of Sudanese society and notions of intimacy and foreignness. As seen, the label 'Arabs' was used to indicate Northern Sudanese; the term 'Blacks' represented people who were considered to be racially 'negroids', people with origins from the South or the West. The term 'Mixed' referred mostly to the *Muwalladīn*. 'Berberine' was the name given during this period to inhabitants of Upper Nubia, who at that time were believed to be racially distinct from Arabs.[44] Lastly were the foreigners, the closest being the Egyptians followed by the others – 'Miscellaneous' – in the main, Christians from Greater Syria.

These statistics are remarkable because they serve a dual purpose: they demonstrate the racial scrutiny of the colonial government and the system applied to describe Sudanese people. The regional variations in the origins of pupils suggest that enrolment reflected more an emphasis on the part

[43] Source: *Annual Report of the Education Dept. 1913*: 247-8. Not all elementary schools are reported in this list; this is why I have made the distinction between a total and a grand total.

[44] See Harold A. Macmichael, *A History of the Arabs in the Sudan* (Cambridge: Cambridge University Press, 1922), Vol. 1, Chapter 1, pp. 3-34.

of certain groups in literacy than in government provisos on which groups to favour. And the most interesting element is the very sizeable number of people defined as 'Blacks'. This is exactly what the Governor of the White Nile complained about in 1923 in the quote reported earlier, affirming that the 'right' people were not getting into schools.[45]

It is worth noting that the *kuttāb* of Khartoum, attended by several of the *Al-Riwāyāt* interviewees such as Sayyid Faraḥ or Maḥmūd Khamīs Aḥmad, was the one where pupils defined as 'Blacks' represented the most significant student group.[46] This reflects the fact that many serving officers lived in special housing in the centre of Khartoum, and that the *deims* south of Khartoum were also places where 'Blacks' lived.[47] Besides this group, however, the Khartoum elementary school was extremely heterogeneous, almost evenly divided among pupils defined as 'Egyptians,' 'Arabs,' 'Mixed', and 'Berberine'. Similarly, the high number of pupils defined as 'blacks' in towns such as Tokar and Sinnar was connected to the presence of the *radīf*, veteran soldiers who were relocated by the Government in special settlements (see next chapter).

The diversity of the student population was not unique to Khartoum *kuttāb*: in Port Sudan, 'Egyptians' outnumbered 'Arabs' and 'Blacks' outnumbered 'Berberines'. Even schools in which there were few 'Blacks' such as in Wad Medani, the student population was fairly varied, including a high proportion of 'Mixed' and 'Egyptians'. The only exception to this trend are the two schools in Kordofan, El Obeid and Bara, reflecting what was discussed earlier, that the region offered the fewest avenues to social mobility.[48]

In primary schools, however, there were notable variations, as illustrated in the following table for the same year.

Table 12 Origin of the pupils in primary schools in 1913[49]

	Arabs	Blacks	Berberine	Mixed	Egyptians	Miscellaneous	Total
Khartoum	91	26	3	38	110	4	272
Omdurman	102	33	57	126	18	6	342
Halfa	0	2	56	3	29	1	91
Sawakin	27	7	0	42	9	20	105
Wad Medani	34	7	0	28	16	1	86
Berber	29	1	4	44	11	4	93
Total	283	76	120	281	193	36	989

45 Education Dept, Budgeting for education service. Memorandum on Education Policy, submitted by Gov. White Nile Prov. To be discussed in GG Council, El Dueim, 4.1.1923; and Director of Education to Civsec, Khartoum 22.1.1923, both Civsec 17/6/34, NRO.

46 *Al-Riwāyāt*, pp. 1 and 356.

47 Sikainga, *Slaves into Workers*, Chapters 3 and 6.

48 See Chapter 5.

49 Source: *Annual Report of the Education Dept. 1913*, pp. 247-8.

Table 13 Nationality of students of Gordon College Upper School[50]

	Arab	Blacks	Mixed	Berberine	Egyptians	Miscellane-ous	Total
1913	41	2	30	4	17	3	97
1914	42	2	28	4	19	4	99
1925	155	10	60	11	1	3	240
1926	203	13	66	18	-	3	303

While the diversity of the pupils is still remarkable, there are some differences. In primary school, the proportion of people defined as 'Blacks' was more stable: 3% to 10% of the student population, with a peak in Khartoum and Omdurman. The 'Arab' population was equally stable at some 30% in every school with the exception of Halfa, where there was a preponderance of Nubians. In this respect, the difference between this table and that of the *kuttāb* school dated the same year may suggest that there were racial considerations at work as to how to select the pupils of primary schools. On the other hand, pupils defined as Egyptians and 'Mixed' continued to be numerous in certain places until the 1920s: in 1915, they constituted the 20% of the student population, while in 1925, the percentage was roughly 7%.[51] The 'Mixed' category is unclear. On the one hand, as discussed previously, family connections with either Egypt or the Ottoman Empire were widespread, while on the other, it is doubtful whether this category indicated people with Egyptian descent in all cases. These statistics were compiled from provincial government reports and thus the meaning of the word may have varied according to different locations.

Finally, Table 13 provides figures of the origins of pupils at Gordon College Upper School. Gordon College reflected the tendency seen in primary schools, with some enlargement of it. On the one hand, there was an increasing preference for people defined as 'Arabs', who had replaced the Egyptians over time. In 1933, the Education Department showed that the percentage of 'Arabs' at Gordon College had skyrocketed from 42% in 1914 to 73% in 1933 to the detriment of 'Egyptians'.[52] On the other hand, the number of 'Blacks' (2-4%), 'Berberine' (4-6%), and 'Mixed' (20-25%) remained remarkably stable throughout the decade.

Two branches of the Upper School in particular were intensely screened, and were open only to Sudanese of impeccable 'pedigree,' as the British used to call the claim of notable families to high Arab ancestry. These were the 'Kadi' (judge, *qāḍi* in Arabic) and teachers' sections. These occupations were seen as requiring social standing, and so 'Blacks', for instance, would not be admitted because it was believed that they would

50 Source: Statistics showing nationality of the GMC boys, 1914 & 1925 to 1933, Palace 4/1/4, NRO; and *Annual Report of the Education Dept.* 1913, p. 247.

51 Number of boys attending Sudan Govt. primary schools, January 1925, Palace 4/1/3, NRO.

52 [MacMichael] to Simpson, Ministry of Education, Cairo, 16.11.1933, Palace 4/1/4, NRO.

not command sufficient respect. The social homogeneity of these sections was highlighted throughout all the reports: for instance, in 1901 Currie praised the law students, who were all members of 'good Arab families.'[53] In 1907, the Annual Report boasted that in the teacher training colleges in Omdurman, Khartoum, Sawakin and Rufa'a, '174 sons and relatives of the most influential or religious families of the Sudan, between the ages of 17 and 24, are now undergoing a five-year course of instruction.'[54]

In conclusion, it is evident that admission to the Upper School was a privilege reserved to a fortunate few on the basis of the prominence of a family and its connection to the colonial administration. This is undoubtedly the main reason why people such as 'Ubayd al-Ḥājj al-Amīn or Mudaththir al Būshī went to the Upper School, while 'Alī Malāsī or the brothers Zāyd were not accepted.

However, the statistics given above reveal as well that family background was a criteria of enrolment applied unevenly throughout the educational pyramid. The most diverse student population existed at the base of the pyramid. The more selective the institution, the more difficult the admission and the more careful the screening to pick the 'right' people according to their status, but also according to some kind of unwritten racial quota, although this latter factor was unofficial and low-key.

These privileges went unnoticed in 1924. The nationalists reproached the government about the limited access to education, but not that it was favouring certain families and groups over others. From the 1970s interviews, it is evident that educated protesters who were forbidden to continue to Upper School understood the reason to be that the British did not want to educate Sudanese in general, and in particular potential political enemies, and not that the protesters' background was not famous enough. For instance Muḥammad 'Abd al-Mun'im Zāyd complained: 'the British did not allow students to continue to secondary education.'[55] It is also important to underline that the way in which the British applied their own racial grid probably made little sense locally, which is why it was hard for Sudanese nationalists to detect. For instance, the label 'Arab' could be attributed to wealthy notables and obscure former government employees indiscriminately.

WORKING LIFE

It is impossible to describe all the government jobs that educated people might have found following their schooling, which were as varied as translators and postmasters, accountants and tax collectors, veterinary assistants and teachers, judges and inspectors. There are, however, some general features common to most of the Sudanese who found jobs as

53 *Annual Report of the Sudan Govt. 1901*, p. 66.

54 *Annual Report of the Sudan Govt. 1901*, p. 133. These 173 were not all pupils of Gordon College Upper School however, which in that year counted 38 all in all, at least according to Education Dept. Figures.

55 *Al-Riwāyāt*, p. 257.

civil servants. These highlight certain characteristics of this group that, in turn explain some of the patterns of the spread of the 1924 political protest. The civil service was not the destiny of all graduates; there was, however, some switching between the private and public sectors, even if educated Sudanese always preferred to work as civil servants. Students employed in government posts could find jobs in private firms, and vice versa. For example, once he had been discharged in Atbara, Aḥmad Ṣabrī Zāyd readily found employment with Gellatly & Hankey in Port Sudan, and 'Alī Aḥmad Ṣāliḥ was in and out of government jobs and even served in the army for a period.[56] It must be mentioned here that this moment of history, Sudanese women were barred from civil servant positions as from private clerical works. Thus, the following section only concerns male Sudanese.

The typical positions that educated Sudanese were able to find immediately after school were somewhat mundane, at the base of a hierarchy to the top of which Sudanese were forbidden to climb. This question merits a digression on the professional grading of Sudan Government employees. Until the early 1930s, these men were divided into classified, unclassified, and ungraded personnel. In the early 1920s, a new category was introduced, the 'SPG' (meaning Special Primary Grade), which was the starting grade for people with only a primary school education, probably because of the higher number of people graduated from Upper School competing for jobs. Unclassified and ungraded personnel included those with 'very poor educational qualifications', without specifying what this meant (probably only elementary school).[57] A list of pay grades in the Sudan Government identifies unclassified personnel as those with professions such as driver, 'greaser', 'sanitaryman', 'cattleboy', 'guard', 'messenger', and so on.[58]

The classified personnel were divided into eight hierarchical grades.[59] Until 1935, the same scale applied to the British, Egyptian and Sudanese.[60] The highest four grades were open only to British; Grade V was the starting grade for the British and the highest grade a Sudanese could attain; Grades IV to VII were also open to Egyptians; finally, Grades V to VIII were open to Sudanese (with some degree of flexibility depending on departments). The assignment of subordinate positions to Sudanese was justified on the grounds of both poor education and of 'character'. For example, in 1929, Hubert Huddleston, a veteran of

[56] Appendix J in CA Willis, The League of the White Flag, FO 141/810/3, NA; Confession of Ali Ahmed Saleh, p. 5, 12.8.1924, FO 141/805/2, NA; *Al-Riwāyāt*, p. 264.

[57] Matthew to Huddleston. Subject: the grading system 17.4.1929, Civsec 20/1/4. NRO.

[58] Samples of pay, list of officials transferred to WTR laboratories, Civsec 2 39/8/7, NRO.

[59] The system was described in detail during a debate among British officers in 1929 about how to amend it, but it had existed for a while, and in any case it worked in 1924.

[60] Finance Circular letter no. 54 (1934), Revision of the grading system, Civsec 10/2/5, NRO.

Table 14 The grading system [61]

Grades	Pay per annum, in Egyptian pounds (LE)	Nationality
Classified staff		
Grade I to III		British
Grade IV		British, Egyptian
Grade V	396-252 (*figures for 1924*)	British Egyptian Sudanese
Grade VI	276-192	Egyptian Sudanese
Grade VII	180 -96	Egyptian Sudanese
Grade VIII	108-72	Sudanese
continued	72-54	Sudanese
SPG	48-	Sudanese
Unclassified officials	*(figures for 1922)*	
Electrician:	72	Sudanese
Apprentice:	48-36	
Storeman	42	
Kholi	42	
Car driver	42	
Greaser:	30-25	
Sanitaryman	26.4	
Cattlemen	25-21	
Cattleboy	18-12	
Farrah	25	
Waterman	21-25	
Messenger	21	
Attendant	18	

the Sudan Government, expressed his reluctance to replace his foreign personnel with educated Sudanese:

> ...the lack of continuity of effort and an inclination to avoid responsibility on the part of Sudanese employees are two reasons that preclude the possibility of a general replacement taking place in the next ten years...[62]

[61] Source: Matthew to Huddleston. Subject: the grading system 17.4.1929, Civsec 20/1/4. NRO, Samples of pay, list of officials transferred to WTR laboratories in 1922, Civsec 2 39/8/7, NRO. NB: From 1898 to 1945, the exchange rate was 1 GBP= LE (Egyptian Pound) 0.975.

[62] Huddleston Kaid El Amm to Secretary for Education and Health, Sudan Govt., Khartoum, 14.12.1929, Civsec1 17/2/6, NRO.

Grade VIII was 'the initial grade for clerks and accountants', with Grade VII the initial level for judges, teachers, and engineers, that is, people from Gordon College Upper School.[63] The difference in terms of pay, but also in the nature of the jobs, between the lowest grades and unclassified personnel was not substantial; on the other hand, the difference of pay (as shown in Table 14), as well as the levels of responsibility and prestige among the grades were considerable. As an example of Grade VIII jobs, we can take Muzammil 'Alī Dinār, who after various vicissitudes obtained a position as 'Technical Assistant, Plant Breeding Section'.[64] Other openings were for postmasters, telephonists, and bookkeepers.

However, not only did unclassified personnel not enjoy the same benefits in gratuities, leave, and above all, pensions as classified staff, but also the nature of the jobs performed was such that *de facto* the dividing line between the low grades and the unclassified personnel was thin. In theory, advancement through the grades was defined by length of service: it took 12 years to move from Grade VIII to Grade V. In practice, it worked quite differently. Grade V was the so-called *Bash-Katib* grade (Ottoman for 'chief secretary'), and since it was the highest grade a Sudanese could obtain, it was usually assigned on the basis of birth, trustworthiness and capabilities. In 1929, Grade V was defined as 'the aim of most natives ... a Grade that carries definite position and responsibility ... Grade V to the native is Super Grade.'[65] The grade immediately below, Grade VI, was the first level at which a certain amount of responsibility and independent duties were given to an employee. In Grade VI, a person had to prove himself: '...it is taken as a general rule that a man is not promoted to Grade VI until he has promoted himself fit to be considered as a potential Bash Katib.'[66] For that reason, only a very few Sudanese breached the barrier from Grade VII to Grade VI.

As was the case with schools, the grading system was pyramidal. In 1920, in the whole of Sudan, there were only 20 Sudanese in the 'super grade', Grade V, compared to 150 Egyptians, 76 Syrians, and 245 British.[67] Likewise, a 1924 table on the establishment of Khartoum province lists four employees in Grade V, 10 in Grade VI (most Egyptians were in these two grades), 26 in Grade VII and 27 in Grade VIII (generally a majority of Sudanese), compared to 607 'unclassified staff'. This administration also included seven 'officers.'[68] Finally, in 1932 in all Sudan, there were 1,278 employees in Grade VIII; 789 in Grade VII, and 271 in Grade VI.[69] The data is interesting at the light of the fact that White Flag Leaguers were disparagingly termed 'low' government employees, as they belonged

63 Ibid.

64 Personal file of Muzammil Ali Dinar, Intel 2/10/71, NRO.

65 Matthew to Huddleston. Subject: the grading system 17.4.1929 Civsec 20/1/4, NRO.

66 Ibid.

67 The figure is provided for grades IV and V, but it is likely that they were mostly in Grade V. Table: Nationality Analysis, Sudan Govt., 1920, Civsec 1/58/167, NRO

68 Source of the Table: Particulars of Establishment 1924-1932, Civsec 50/14/61; Provinces, Analysis of Staff, 1933, Civsec 20/2/6, NRO.

69 Establishment, 1932, Civsec 10/2/5, NRO.

to Grades VIII and VII.[70] However the overwhelming majority of graded government employees were found in these two levels.

Another characteristic of the civil servants in this period is that, unless totally incompetent, they were never fired. When a person had an unsatisfactory record with a department, was found to be 'inefficient' or culpable of some offence, the practice was to transfer him. This was the case in the early 1920s when people started to commit professional errors as forms of political insubordination, or when they were discovered to have political orientations. Thus, when 'Ubayd al-Ḥājj al-Amīn caused trouble in Atbara in 1920, he was discharged and then rapidly re-employed in Khartoum in the Post and Telegraph Department. Ḥusayn Mukhtār Maḥmūd, a schoolmaster in Kosti, who was caught sending an article to the Egyptian press in October 1924, was transferred to work in Bara, where his father lived.[71] The authorities in Atbara noted that Iskander Sa'd, an accountant in the Railways Department, a member of the White Flag League, and a signatory of a telegram was '[a] graded but unpensionable employee, one of the signatories of a seditious telegram; it was discussed if dismiss him but finally it was decided to give him another possibility.'[72] A final example is that of 'Alī Aḥmad Ṣāliḥ, accused in 1922 of falsifying court receipts and imprisoned. He was already released in 1923 and back at work, surprisingly, as an assistant tax collector![73] Similar treatment applied to League's founders Ṣāliḥ 'Abd al-Qādir and Ḥassan Sharīf.

As seen above, there was an exceedingly high attrition rate in primary schools. This was caused by the fact that the labour market was exceedingly hungry for educated Sudanese. The scarcity of individuals with the kind of skills offered by colonial schools meant that the government could not afford to dismiss them. In 1929, when asked what he thought about an expansion of the Upper School and whether his department needed more personnel, the Director of the Public Works Department replied: 'At the present time, the output of the College is not sufficient to meet demands. Certainly as far as Engineering students are concerned, and probably as regards others, it is always the fact that something is better than nothing where there is shortage supply.'[74] In 1927, a government official reported laconically: 'Only 53 boys were available for Government employment this year, although 129 were required.'[75]

70 C. A. Willis, The Political Situation, Khartoum 16.6.1924, FO 141/806/1, NA; Telegram from DI to Gov., El Obeid, 21.6.1924, Kordofan 1/12/54, NRO.
71 ADC Northern Kordofan to Gov. Kordofan, Bara, 3.12.1924, Kordofan 1/13/60, NRO.
72 Havercroft to DI, Atbara, 13.10.24, Palace 4/9/47, NRO.
73 Appendix J in C.A. Willis, The League of the White Flag, FO 141/810/3, NA.
74 Director of Works, Sudan Govt. to Civsec Khartoum, 29.11.29, Civsec1 17/2/6, NRO. The head of the Legal Dept. also complained: 'This department has been treated badly as regards Engineering graduates in the last few years. The Registrar-General of Lands states that the last engineering graduate to join the Land Registry did so in 1921, since when in spite of repeated application nobody with engineering qualifications has been given to him with the exception of one student who failed in the final examination in 1923 and joined the department in 1924.'
75 Gordon Memorial College, reports and accounts to 31st December 1927, Dept.

The final but not least important point to highlight about the careers of these educated Sudanese is their mobility both in terms of occupation and of geographical location. This feature is illustrated more by personal accounts of 1924 activists than by statistics. The likelihood that educated people would begin their working lives far from home was very great: the Zāyd brothers, originally from Argo, were sent to Port Sudan and Atbara; Aḥmad al-Ṭrīfī Zubayr Bāshā, born and brought up in Omdurman, secured his first job in Makwar, on the Blue Nile. Also colonial personal files of 'agitators' confirm this point: Bayūmī 'Sayah', a known member of the White Flag League, was born in Khartoum; in 1924 he was employed in the Stores and Ordnances Department there; in 1934 he worked in Shendi as a civilian armourer for the Army; and in 1940 he was still in Shendi but employed in an agricultural scheme.[76] Although at times this mobility was due to political activities, it was not always the case. The personal file of a civilian *mamur*, born about the same time as some of the 1924 League leaders but who did not participate in the protests, states: 'Ali Hamid. Born 1.10.05. ... Appointed as clerk game preservation 20.1.24, ungraded, constant rise in pay and grade (to Grade VII). Service: Game preservation, Khartoum, Red Sea, Darfur, 1924-31.'[77] Thus, over a period of seven years, this individual had switched departments four times and had crossed Sudan from east to west.

CONCLUSION

Civilian educated Sudanese during the first half of colonial rule in the Sudan presented a number of characteristics. First, receiving an education was a difficult endeavour achieved through an extremely selective process. Pupils were selected according to a number of factors that included family background, merits, ability to pay school fees, and the 'race' by which they were classified. In spite of the government's determination to include in school only the 'best' Sudanese, the sons of the most important families of the country, the system also allowed Sudanese from non-notable backgrounds to access education. In a period when literacy was rare this opened doors to economic and professional stability and to upward social mobility. Their training gave educated people automatic entry to the labour market, and guaranteed them employment.

In spite of this, opportunities opened up by formal education were limited. Civil servants usually started in subordinate positions and had few chances to progress. Civil servants started generally in very subordinate positions, and concretely with few opportunities to progress. However, those who had studied at government schools before 1924 were still in the early phase of their careers. Various 1924 activists complained of their low education and uninteresting jobs, but they could still hope for a better future.

(contd) Reports 20/1/1, NRO.

76 Personal File of Bayoumi Sayah, Shendi, Northern Prov. 1/19/128, NRO.

77 Civsec Dept., Mamurs and sub-mamurs, recruitment, 1934, Civsec1 50/1/4, NRO.

As young men, they moved from their parents' home to school, and from school to their first job, often located far from their home towns. This first employment was followed by numerous other posts, often in different cities. School, literacy, and jobs exposed educated Sudanese to politics: many had mixed with politicized Egyptians at school, as they would later in their workplace, and where they met other activists in their progress from one job to the next.

Finally, in spite of being routinely depicted by the colonial rulers as low clerks in menial positions, this description should not lead to an underestimation both of their importance within the colonial state, and their self-perception as the progressive elements of Sudanese society. Much of their dissatisfaction came exactly from the gap between their self-perceptions and the tasks that they were called to perform.

Indeed, colonial institutions contributed towards the creation of a group of educated Sudanese who fell in some respects between two worlds, and made of them an unaccomplished elite, or at least an ambiguous one. On the one hand, education set these people apart from the rest of the society, opening to them the exclusive club of those who had access to 'modern' instruction and to government jobs. On the other, the type of tasks that most educated Sudanese were asked to carry out, their salaries, and the levels of responsibility granted to them in this period were hardly rewarding, and barely distinguishable from those of skilled wage-workers. Because most of civil servants had only a primary school education, and because this institution was quite more open than the Upper School, the background of educated Sudanese was so varied that the connection between education and prominent status was, at this point, rather invisible. Most pupils were able to enter a school because their families were associated with the government in one way or another, but this did not imply necessarily that they belonged to a notable family. The stories of educated activists of 1924 show that it was not only the son of the Grand Mufti who, by his connections to the government, obtained a place at school for his sons, but also the Beja policeman of Sawakin father of 'Alī Malāsī, or the Dinka artisan working for the Public Works Department, who was the father of one of the first demonstrators of 1924, clerk 'Abd al-Qādir Aḥmad Sayyid.

9

A Military Elite: The Army in the 1924 Revolution

FROM A PHOTOGRAPH OF THE STUDENTS OF THE MILITARY COLLEGE, 1912

A photograph of the students at the Military College in the possession of the family of the late officer Zayn al-'Ābdīn 'Abd al-Tām[1] provides us with the names of most the students who were at the college in 1912. The picture has been compared with colonial records and with the interviews of some 1924 activists, and it reveals the extent of disaffection within the socio-professional category. Visible in the picture are the names of 35 out of the 40 cadets (the four in the front row were commissioned officers). At least 14 of 35 were involved in the 1924 revolution, albeit to different degrees. Besides Zayn al-'Ābdīn 'Abd al-Tām, the photograph includes 'Alī 'Abd al-Laṭīf,[2] Sulaymān Muḥammad – one of the officers executed for the November Mutiny[3] – and Sayyid Shahāta[4] who is discussed later in this chapter. Other officers pictured who participated in the mutiny are 'Abd al-Wahhāb Bīhārī,[5] who belonged to a political society in Bara around 1919, and who was suspected of being the leader of the White Flag League in Umm Rwaba, Kordofan, in 1924; and 'Abd al-Raḥman 'Abd al-Rāḍī,[6] who in 1924 was *mamur* in Tumbura, Bahr al-Ghazal, where he was accused of spreading disaffection. 'Abd al-Raḥman 'Abd al-Rāḍī was also married to a sister of Thābit 'Abd al-Raḥīm, one of the three young officers executed for having led the November mutiny.[7]

1 Left, 3rd row up. (See p. xiv for enlarged view.)
2 First on the left, 2nd row up.
3 Ninth from the left, second row up.
4 Seventh from the left, third row up.
5 Standing alone in the top row.
6 13th from left, 4th row up.
7 Intelligence Dept. to General Staff, Khartoum, 10.12.1924 Palace 4/11/55, NRO. For 'Abd al-Wahhāb Bīhārī: *Al-Riwāyāt*, p. 131; District Commissioner Eastern Kordofan to Gov. Kordofan, 24.8.1924, Korodfan 1/12/55, NRO. For 'Abd al-Raḥman 'Abd al-Rāḍī: his membership is recorded in oral accounts: namely, Muḥammad Faḍlallāh al- Shinnāwī's list, and he is mentioned in the 'Confession of Ali Ahmed

Fig 6 The cadets of the Military School, 1912 (Reproduced courtesy of Amīna Bilāl Riziq)

Each of these cadets is as a thread that leads to more insurgents. Several of Zayn al-ʿĀbdīn ʿAbd al-Tām's relatives and friends were involved in the events of 1924. *Yuzbashi* Bilāl Riziq, the father of Amīna, who would later become Zayn al-ʿĀbdīn's second wife, attempted to inspire more Sudanese units to rise up during the November Mutiny. His brother-in-law, Adam Adham, *Yuzbashi* of the Camel Corps, came to the attention of the Intelligence Department as a staunch member of the political movement in El Obeid. It was claimed that '[He] has been filling up the soldiers with anti-British ideas ... He is a thoroughly bad influence in the Camel Corps.'[8] His son was the founder of the 'Black Block', a political association created in the 1940s to defend the interests of 'black Sudanese' in which several descendants of 1924 officers participated.[9]

Two other figures with political connections among officers are Zayn al-ʿĀbdīn Ṣāliḥ and Ḥassan al-Zayn who were accused in 1924 of forming a League in Darfur called the 'Black Block' (not to be confused with the 'Black Block' of the 1940s mentioned above) with *Mulazim Tani* Muḥammad Surūr Rustum and others.[10] Ḥassan al-Zayn had previously

(contd) Saleh,' pp. 5 and 8, 12.8.1924, FO 141/805/2, NA.

8 A detailed description of the deeds of this officer in El Obeid in Assistant DI, Intelligence Notes, Report: Credibility factor 'A', Intelligence Dept., Khartoum, 9.10.1924, Kordofan 1/13/59, NRO.

9 Sikainga, *Slaves into Workers*, pp. 168-172. Kurita, 'The Role of 'Negroid but Detribalized' People in Modern Sudanese History'.

10 In order of mention, 1st from the left, 2nd row up, and 8th from the left, the 4th row up.

belonged to the secret society in Wad Medani, at least according to officer Ḥassan Ismāʿīl al-Muftī,[11] with a number of soon-to-be mutinous officers such as ʿAlī ʿAbd al-Laṭīf, ʿAbd al-ʿAzīz ʿAbd al-Ḥay, and Ḥassan Faḍl al-Mūlā.[12]

Muḥammad ʿAbd al-Bakhīt and Ḥassan Sharaf, who also appear in the photograph[13] were both discharged from the army (for reasons unknown). Their names reappear in 1924 among the signatories of various petitions organized by discharged officers. Several other names in these petitions open up another web of connections; suffice to mention that one of the signatories, ʿAbdallāh al-Nūr, honorary *Yuzbashi*, was reputed to be the 'Head of the Society for Dismissed Officers' in Omdurman. He was a veteran elite officer, who among other things had been appointed as *sub-mamur* in Bahr al-Ghazal. He spoke French, Italian, and some English and was an 'uncle' of Ḥassan Faḍl al-Mūlā.[14] Another of al-Mūlā's 'uncles' was *Yuzbashi* Kabsūn al-Jak,[15] a member of the same society of dismissed officers. One of al-Jak's sons, Khalīl Khabsūn, was a 'teacher in the American Mission.'[16] The civilian Khalīl, contrary to all the officers seen so far (except for Zayn al-ʿĀbdīn ʿAbd al-Tām and ʿAlī ʿAbd al-Laṭīf), was a member of the White Flag. He participated in a demonstration of the League in June, and was arrested. Other officers involved in 1924 who stand in the photograph include Ḥusayn Rīḥān, son of ʿAbdallāh Rīḥān, in whose house ʿAlī ʿAbd al-Laṭīf grew up; Fatḥallāh Nadā; Muḥammad ʿAbdallāh, and finally Gharīb Aḥmad.[17] They were all mentioned in lists of political agitators, but their exact involvement in 1924 is not known.

11 He is also in the photograph, although his name does not appear (as part of the picture is missing). According to his account he graduated in 1914.
12 Telegram from DI to Gov., El Fasher, 18.12.1924, Palace 4/9/47, NRO; see also *Al-Riwāyāt*, p. 588. In this account, however, he denies any involvement with the League. *Al-Riwāyāt*, p. 133. However, Ismāʿīl does not mention ʿAlī ʿAbd al-Laṭīf, probably because by the time he arrived in Medani, ʿAlī had already left.
13 First from the left, 5th row from the bottom, and 4th from the left in the 3rd row, respectively.
14 Intelligence Information by informer no. 150, Kordofan 1/12/55, NRO. Diary of MT Hassan Eff. Fadl El Mula, Palace 4/9/47, NRO.
15 On these two 'uncles', see Diary of MT Hassan Eff. Fadl El Mula, Palace 4/9/47, NRO. Khalīl is also mentioned at several points in the Confession of Ali Ahmed Saleh, FO 141/805/2, NA. Chronicle of the events during the period of political excitement in Khartoum, FO 141/805/2, and List of members of the 'Sudan Union' who are said to have recently taken the oath, Intelligence, 21.9.24, Palace 4/9/45, NRO.
16 List of signatories of telegram sent to the Press Syndicate and the President of the Court of Ministers, Cairo, 24.6.1924 in FO 141/806/1, NA.
17 For Ḥusayn Rīḥān: Confession of Ali Ahmed Saleh, p. 10, 19.8.1924, FO 141/805/2, NA. His political participation is confirmed from oral accounts: list of Muḥammad Faḍlallāh al-Shinnāwī. For Fatḥallah Nadā: List of members of the 'Sudan Union' who are said to have recently taken the oath, Intelligence Note, 21.9.1924, Palace 4/9/45, NRO. For Muḥammad ʿAbdallāh, this name is so common that one cannot be certain, but an ʿAbdallāh Muḥammad, MA of the XII Sudanese, is mentioned in the 'List of members of the 'Sudan Union' who are said to have recently taken the oath,' Intelligence, 21.9.24, Palace 4/9/45, NRO. For Gharīb Aḥmad: List of political agitators, undated, unsigned, Kordofan 1/13/61, NRO.

This photograph is one of the many pieces of evidence that prove the extent of disaffection among army officers and how nationalist ideas penetrated this socio-professional category. It also hints at an issue discussed in previous chapters: in many cases this disaffection arose well before 1924. The officers' memoirs tell of their involvement in political societies in centres such as El Obeid, Bara or Wad Medani both during and just after World War I. The aim of this chapter is to elucidate the configurations that led to this extensive involvement, first by analysing the historical connections between army officers and Egypt, then by investigating the specific situation experienced by them from the time of the establishment of the Condominium, and finally by reviewing the changes that took place after the war.

ARMY OFFICERS BETWEEN EGYPT AND BRITAIN

At the end of 1924, in their cogitations about the November mutiny, British officials concluded that the motives of the mutiny rested in the impossible situation in which Sudanese officers had been placed, trapped between divided loyalties. Sudanese soldiers served under British officers, led by a British *sirdar,* but the army was an Egyptian institution in which officers swore an oath of allegiance to the Egyptian Crown. It was not a sudden discovery that this situation was rife with problems; discussions on how to reform the army had been under way for some time. However, the November mutiny represented the concrete realization of the British authorities' worst-case scenario. The extent and the strength of the bonds between Egypt and Sudanese officers had not been fully appreciated by British administrators.

The ties between the army – its officers in particular – and Egypt ran deep. The personal stories of 1924 revolutionaries highlight this fact; for example, Sayyid Shahāta, one of the officers in the photograph, talked about his life in *Al-Riwāyāt*. He was born in Wadi Halfa in 1894 (at that time the city belonged to Egypt), and began his schooling there. He did not describe his family background in much detail; however, his name and place of birth are revealing.[18] His family name, Shahāta, in Sudan is considered to be typically Egyptian. We know also from his account that his father was an officer in the Turco-Egyptian army, so it can be deduced that on the outbreak of the Anglo-Egyptian 'reconquest' of Sudan (as the Anglo-Egyptian invasion of 1895-1898 is usually called) Sayyid's father joined up and headed to Omdurman, leaving his family behind in what was at that time Egypt. Several other 'black' officers of 1924 had classic Egyptian or Ottoman names: the former in the case of Muḥammad Faḍlallāh al-Shinnāwī, and the latter in the case of 'Abd al-Wahhāb Bīhārī.

Of course, the link with Egypt was not only a matter of family names; on the contrary, it was a living memory and remains so today. In the 1980s, Janet Ewald, a historian of the Taqali Sultanate, in the Nuba Mountains, recorded that there were still people who remembered their forefathers'

[18] See his interview in *Al-Riwāyāt*, pp. 160-172.

participation in the 19th-century Egyptian Army and took great pride in their link with that country.[19] The descendants of officers to this day express the same attachment. The family of Cadet Muḥammad Faḍlallāh al-Shinnāwī, for instance, was proud to recount that one of their forefathers was sent to Mexico with the Sudanese battalion to fight for Napoleon III between 1863 and 1867. In 2004, when asked about the relations between the officers and Egypt, the late Thābit 'Abd al-Raḥīm (named after his uncle, one of the officers killed for the November mutiny) told me:[20]

> Muḥammad 'Alī took people from the south by force to work as soldiers, because they are brave. This is the first relation; then, what happened after is that they learnt in Egypt, received there their training, some of them were even taken to Mexico. This is the reason why my tribe [the Dinka] supports Egypt. ... Every Dinka who was Muslim knew about [this religion] via Egypt. They took them to Egypt, and they taught them things, about religion and Islam and they gave them Egyptian names, like Fu'ād, Badrī, Thābit. ... Even weddings happened between Dinka and Egyptians.... If it were not for Egypt, we would not have been here.

So many officers from 1924 had old family links with the army; suffice to recall that the father of 'Alī 'Abd al-Laṭīf was an enslaved Nuba who was later requisitioned by the Mahdist army before deserting and joining the Anglo-Egyptian camp. The fathers of Cadets Idrīs 'Abd al-Ḥay, Sayyid Uthmān and 'Abdallāh Mabrūk were all in the Anglo-Egyptian army that took part in the invasion of Sudan, and possibly served in the Khedival army.[21] Maḥmūd Khamīs Aḥmad, an NCO who had been admitted to the Military School in 1924, just before it was closed down, recalled that '[my father] was working in the Egyptian reserve police, which afterwards turned into a battalion'. He participated in many military battles at the time of Khedive Pasha' and later 'joined the military administration' during the Condominium.[22]

These memories provide evidence of the continuity between pre-colonial and colonial times in the army, and require a summary of the history and role of the Egyptian army from Turco-Egyptian rule to 1924.

The Turco-Egyptian Jihādiyya

It is a well-known fact that one of the aims of the Turco-Egyptian invasion of Sudan that began in 1820 was to constitute *al-niẓām al-jadīd* (the new order), a modern army based on the Napoleonic model but composed of Sudanese slaves that would enable the *khedive* Muḥammad 'Alī of Egypt to conquer nothing less than the entire Ottoman Empire. The failed invasion of Syria forced the Khedive to reconsider his ambitions. His attempts to bring Sudanese slaves into Egypt as recruits were catastrophic and led him to introduce a system of mass conscription, at least in Egypt. Within Sudan, however, his project was partially successful: the Turco-Egyptian government launched waves of raids in areas such Southern Kordofan and

[19] Ewald, *Soldiers, Traders, and Slaves*.

[20] Interview by the author with Thābit Ḥamza 'Abd al-Raḥīm, taken at his home in Omdurman, 30.12.2004. He was the son of Thābit's brother.

[21] For Idrīs 'Abd al-Ḥay, *Al-Riwāyāt*, p. 224; for Sayyid Uthmān, p. 173; for 'Abdallāh Mabrūk, p. 492.

[22] Ibid., p. 356.

the Blue Nile, enabling it to create a slave army that came to be known as the *Jihādiyya.* [23] This contributed towards a chain of events in motion that made the slave trade, together with the ivory trade, one of the most lucrative businesses in Sudan from the mid-19th century. It expanded the trading frontier to the Bahr al-Ghazal, Southern White and Blue Nile, and Southern Darfur. Although the government was no longer the main protagonist in the slave trade after 1850, slave soldiers continued to pour into the army, as much as non-soldier slaves went to work in Northern Sudanese homes and lands.

The fate of slave-soldiers was substantially different from that of slaves in domestic work or agriculture, however. The *Jihādiyya* quickly earned a reputation for excellence. Comparisons between Sudanese and Egyptian soldiers were always being made, with the former always being preferred to the latter, who were deemed to be inept, inane, and unreliable. According to the historian Dunn, the Sudanese were praised as 'the best fighters' and 'warriors by instinct'.[24] They were chosen for special missions, as was the case with the battalion mentioned above that was selected to be sent to Mexico between 1863 and 1867, or to the Crimean War of 1853-1855.[25] Compared with the general situation enslaved Sudanese found themselves in, therefore, slave-soldiers enjoyed a 'higher' destiny: they were 'slaves of fortune', as the historian Lamothe calls them.[26]

Slave-soldiers were enlisted for life, and in this sense they were slaves of the State, although they were regularly manumitted, so that they were as free as a soldier could be. They received a regular wage – at least when the government was able to pay it – training, and weapons. Although the majority were trained in Sudan, a lucky few were sent to the Military College in Cairo, which gave them positions of distinction. It was also common practice to assign administrative responsibilities to high-ranking soldiers and officers. Dunn notes that Sudanese soldiers acted 'both as

23 On this subject, see: Douglas H. Johnson, 'Sudanese Military Slavery from the Eighteenth to the Twentieth Century', in *Slavery and Other Forms of Unfree Labour*, L. Archer ed. (London: Routledge, 1988), pp. 142-156; Douglas H. Johnson, 'The Structure of a Legacy: Military Slavery in Northeast Africa', *Ethnohistory* (1989), vol. 36, no. 1, pp. 72-88; Ahmad A. Sikainga, 'Military Slavery and the Emergence of a Southern Sudanese Diaspora in the Northern Sudan, 1884-1956', *White Nile, Black Blood: War, Leadership, and Ethnicity From Khartoum to Kampala*, Stephanie Beswick and Jay Spaulding eds (Lawrenceville, NJ: Red Sea Press, 2000), pp. 23-37. Recent works on the *nizām al-jadīd*: Khalid Fahmy, *All the Pasha's Men: Mehmed Ali, His Army and the Making of Modern Egypt* (Cambridge: Cambridge University Press, 1998); and John P. Dunn, *Khedive Ismail's Army* (London; New York: Routledge, 2005).

24 Dunn, *Khedive Ismail's Army*, p. 34.

25 For Mexico, the most important work is Richard L. Hill and Peter C Hogg, *A Black Corps d'Élite. An Egyptian Sudanese Conscript Battalion with the French Army in Mexico, 1863-1867, and Its Survivors in Subsequent African History* (East Lansing: Michigan State University Press, 1995); for the Crimean war, Ronald M. Lamothe, *Slaves of Fortune: Sudanese Soldiers and the River War, 1896-1898* (Woodbridge, Suffolk; Rochester NY: James Currey; Boydell & Brewer Inc.), p. 19, and Hill, *Biographical Dictionary*, p. 27.

26 Lamothe, *Slaves of Fortune*, pp. 122-134.

soldiers in wars of conquest, and as a paramilitary force to maintain law and order, collect taxes, and assist in public works projects', very much as would occur later during the Condominium.[27] One of the best-known examples of this is Adham Pasha al-'Ārifī, who was originally from Taqali was trained at the Cairo Military School, and became acting Governor General of the Sudan for few months in 1872.[28]

Under the Mahdist rule, the Turco-Egyptian *Jihādiyya* was absorbed into the Mahdist army and the slaves of private owners were requisitioned to swell the ranks. We know, for instance, that one of the most famous Mahdist generals, Ḥamadān Abū 'Anja, came from this background.[29] When the Mahdist army took control of Sudan, some battalions of the Turco-Egyptian *Jihādiyya* withdrew towards Egypt, settling around Wadi Halfa, a region that was never annexed by the Mahdiyya, and in Upper Egypt to the north. They represented a fighting force that knew Sudan very well from a military point of view, and was ready to be incorporated anew into the Anglo-Egyptian forces that were advancing from Egypt. Similarly, when the Mahdist state began to collapse under the pressure of the Anglo-Egyptian offensive, slave-soldiers from the Mahdist army deserted for the opposite camp, carrying strategic information with them.

Incidentally, the role of slave-soldiers in the Anglo-Egyptian invasion of Sudan clarifies the geographical variations in the Education Department in relation to those who were defined as 'Blacks'. During the Mahdiyya, slave soldiers were concentrated in Omdurman, and were so numerous that some witnesses estimated that between a half or three-quarters of the population of Omdurman were of slave background.[30] As all the troops converged on the Three Towns during the Anglo-Egyptian advance, the capital ended up with the largest population of Sudanese soldiers and officers in Sudan. At the beginning of Condominium, the standing army had to be reduced, the government disbanding several battalions. Former soldiers became reservists – *radīf* – and resettled in special villages called *malakiyyāt*, which were mostly located along the Blue and White Nile and other militarily strategic locations such as the Nuba Mountains and the Red Sea.[31] For this reason, the largest number of 'Blacks' attending schools were, first, in Khartoum, where serving officers of the Egyptian Army had

[27] Dunn, *Khedive Ismail's Army*, p. 34.

[28] For al-'Ārifī, Hill, *Biographical Dictionary*, p. 27. See also the story of *Yuzbashi* 'Abdallāh 'Adlān: G. R. F. Bredin, 'The Life Story of Yuzbashi 'Abdullah Adlan', *Sudan Notes and Records* (1961), vol. 42, pp. 37–52. Hill and Hogg, *A Black Corps d'Élite*, pp. 154-155; Lamothe, *Slaves of Fortune*, pp. 21-23;

[29] For the Mahdist *Jihādiyya*, see Sikainga, *Slaves into Workers*, and Sikainga, 'Military Slavery and the Emergence of a Southern Sudanese Diaspora in the Northern Sudan, 1884-1956'. On Abū 'Anja, see Hill, *A Biographical Dictionary*, p. 147. He had previously belonged to the slave army of Sudan's most important slave trader, Zubayr Pasha. Zakī Ṭamal, Ḥamadān's successor after Ḥamadān died in the war with Abyssinia, was another slave soldier from the same group, the Mandala (Hill, *A Biographical Dictionary*, p. 389).

[30] Robert S. Kramer, *Holy City on the Nile: Omdurman during the Mahdiyya, 1885-1898* (Princeton: Markus Wiener Publishers, 2010), p. 52.

[31] Sikainga, *Slaves into Workers*, pp. 63-65.

their homes, then in Omdurman, where retired officers lived, and finally in those provinces in which *malakiyyāt* were located, such as the Blue and White Nile.

The Anglo-Egyptian 'reconquest' and the British 'martial race'

According to Lamothe, it was during the Anglo-Egyptian campaign that bonds of comradeship and solidarity were forged between British officers and their Sudanese subordinates. He argues that the men of the Sudanese army were the unacknowledged champions of the Anglo-Egyptian invasion, and it is to their credit that the campaign was so swift and casualties in the Anglo-Egyptian camp so limited (unlike the fate of the Mahdists, who suffered a bloodbath). On the British side, there was sincere appreciation for both the military abilities and the loyalty and character of many subordinate officers. The Sudanese soldier was described as 'the ideal fighting man' and 'full of the military instinct'.[32] For instance, in the foreword to a book on Sudan and the military, written by Officer Alexander Pott, Wingate recalled the Darfur campaign in 1916:

> I gave [Pott] two of the best companies, one of which was Mabruk Fiki (you will remember him, I am sure, as one of the best type of Sudanese officer). The combination of Pott and Mabruk could not have been improved upon.... On that Darfur expedition I always felt extremely proud and lucky to have with me such a backbone as Pott, Almaz Mursi, Said Mohammed, Mabruk Fiki and Abdel Hai Idris.[33]

However, one must not overlook that fact that the relationship between these colonial governments and their slave or 'black' armies was one of power, and fraught with ambiguities. For instance, Wingate expressed a very different opinion of the 'black' soldiers in other contexts. As he put it in 1901: '...these blacks are little better than savages & childish to a degree – rifles in the hands of such men must always be fraught with a certain amount of risk...'[34] Similar ambiguities were frequent in British descriptions of what became their 'martial race'.

In many colonial settings in both Asia and in Africa, certain individuals labelled as belonging to specific 'tribes' or 'races' were considered to be more disposed to display martial virtues than others because of their physical characteristics and their 'natural inclination' towards nerve and courage. This process of labeling often represented one stage in the creation of the very group that was being identified in this way. This was the case, for instance, with the 'Nilotic' troops in Uganda, the 'Yoruba' in British West Africa, the 'Kamba' or the 'Nubi' in Kenya, and the 'Gurkhas' in India.[35] People labelled as 'martial races' were more often than not taken

32 Lamothe, *Slaves of Fortune*, p. 127.

33 Alexander J. Pott, *People of the Book* (Edinburgh and London: W. Blackwood & Sons, 1932), pp. xvi-xvii.

34 Wingate to Cromer, 21.02.01, SAD 271/2/4. I am grateful to Douglas Johnson for indicating this source.

35 H. Streets, *Martial Races: The Military, Race and Masculinity in British Imperial Culture, 1857-1914* (Manchester University Press, 2004). P. Barua, 'Inventing Race: The British and India's Martial Races', *Historian* (1995), vol. 58, no. 1, pp. 107-116. Risto Marjomaa, 'The Martial Spirit: Yao Soldiers in British Service in Nyasaland

either from former supplies of slaves or from groups that for one reason or another were kinds of 'internal others' in a certain establishment. The perception of their martial predispositions went hand in hand with the stereotyping of what made them different from the population in which they served: this dynamic has been extensively studied with regard to slave armies in the Ottoman Empire or the Maghreb.[36] One advantage of these distinctions was that governments maintained a certain degree of separation between the armies and the rest, but they were also at the origins of the contradictory descriptions that typically characterized 'martial races' in different societies and empires. 'Martial races' were essential to maintaining imperial rule, yet were perceived at the same time as being different or 'abnormal' compared with the majority of the people.

In the Sudan of the 19th and early 20th century, the various governments heavily relied on military power. Because the army was at the very heart of rule, and because colonial administrators worked so closely with the military, these governments fostered the dread that the army might be disloyal and attempt to take over. Although Sudanese battalions had a track record of excellence, they were also perceived as a threat that might explode at any time. Indeed, episodes of insubordination occurred quite regularly. When the Sudanese battalion was sent to Mexico, a revolt of all the Sudanese troops broke out in Kassala (Adham Pasha al-ʿĀrifī was the officer who managed to handle the mutiny). Because the Khalīfa suspected that the soldiers of the *Jihādiyya*, which was partly composed of former conscripts from the Egyptian Army, were not entirely loyal, he formed his own special corps, known as the *Mulazmīn*, largely made up of people from his own group, the Baqqara. In 1900, a number of Sudanese battalions of the Egyptian army mutinied in Omdurman, apparently on rumours that they were to be disbanded, and as a result of 'infection' by Egyptian officers. It was precisely to avoid any possibility of contamination from nationalist ideas that the Military School was created in Khartoum in 1905. Rumours of disaffection resurfaced periodically: for instance, during a tour of inspection in Wau in 1911, a British officer complained about the state of discipline in one of the companies stationed there, 'being commanded by an officer ... who is a politician.'[37]

Nevertheless, in spite of the mistrust and criticism of the Egyptian army as an institution and of its soldiers and officers routinely voiced by the British authorities, the army was central to the functioning of the colonial state.

(contd) (Malawi), 1895-1939', *The Journal of African History* (2003), vol. 44, no. 3, pp. 413-432. Timothy H. Parsons, "Wakamba Warriors Are Soldiers of the Queen': The Evolution of the Kamba As a Martial Race, 1890-1970', *Ethnohistory* (1999), vol. 46, no. 4, pp. 671-701. Douglas H. Johnson, 'Tribe or Nationality? The Sudanese Diaspora and the Kenyan Nubis', *Journal of Eastern African Studies* (2009), vol. 3, no. 1, pp. 112-131.

[36] Toru Miura and John J. E. Philips, *Slave Elites in the Middle East and Africa: A Comparative Study* (London; New York: Kegan Paul International, 2000).

[37] J. J. Asser, 'Report on tour of Bahr el-Ghazal, Tewfikia and Malakal, 08.09.1911, SAD 301/3/29-30. I am grateful to Douglas Johnson for this source.

THE EGYPTIAN ARMY, 1900-1924

The end of a 'long comradeship-in-arms'

Although the politicization of officers in the Egyptian Army began very early on during the Condominium, and in spite of the fact that some British observers occasionally raised the issue, the senior British authorities did not focus on this problem until 1924, at least according to the available sources. Even during that year, the importance of the officers' participation in the national movement is not reflected in their low-key presence in colonial records. One striking case is the mutiny of November 27. The six officers who were held responsible had not made much of an impression on the Intelligence Department before the mutiny, and in at least two cases – Sayyid Faraḥ and 'Abd al-Faḍīl al-Māẓ – there are no previous records at all.[38] There are undoubtedly many reasons for this. First, as the officers were administered by the military authorities, it is possible that army records may have been held separately, not the national archives, and therefore were inaccessible to me.[39] Second, as mentioned earlier, the involvement of these officers was a well-kept secret. Third, allowing insubordination to spread among the officers may have been a calculated risk on the part of a British government that was searching for a pretext to do away with the Egyptian Army and completely restructure the military force.[40]

Nevertheless, there can be no doubt that the government's line towards its officers was quite different from that adopted towards White Flag League members. When a list of 78 officers, all members of the 'Sudan Union,' was given to the authorities in September, the consequences were minor compared to the crackdown on the White Flag League in July. This lack of response equals the leniency shown towards officers who were suspected of insubordination. For example, as late as August (thus at a time when most of the League leaders were already in prison), when it became impossible to turn a blind eye to the 'subversive' activities of Officer Muḥammad Ṣāliḥ Jibrīl in El Obeid, he was simply transferred to Khartoum and given a warning to abstain from politics (which he ignored). Oral accounts confirm this pattern, as the story of officer 'Abd al-'Azīz 'Abd al-Ḥay, a close friend of 'Alī 'Abd al-Laṭīf, shows:

> [In 1924] I came back to Wad Medani in the 14th battalion in which I was working, and ... it happened that the commandant called me to his office and told me: 'Abd al-'Azīz, there is a report against you, issued by the head of the secret service in Khartoum, where he says that you are a member of the White Flag League and that you are a member in the Sudan Union association and this is related to 'Alī

[38] Ḥassan Faḍl al-Mūlā was noticed in connection with the incidents in Wau (CSO Adjutant General to OC District, Khartoum 27.9.1924, FO 141/669/8, NA). Thābit 'Abd al-Raḥīm's name was mentioned once by 'Alī Aḥmad Ṣāliḥ (Confession of Ali Ahmed Saleh, p. 8, 19.8.1924, FO 141/805/2, NA); 'Abd al-Faḍīl al-Māẓ's name is in the List of members of the 'Sudan Union' who are said to have recently taken the oath, Intelligence Note, 21.9.1924, Palace 4/9/45, NRO.

[39] This can be evinced from the introduction to *The White Flag Trials*, for instance.

[40] Memorandum, Enclosures in no. 167, Major General Sir L. Stack to Mr MacDonald, 18.8.1924, FO 407/199, NA.

> 'Abd al-Laṭīf. He is giving out words to watch on you, and you are being watched, but you are a good officer in our battalion and your work is good, and we cannot restrain your liberty, but we wish that you would not go to Wad Medani very often.' So I said, 'I cannot stop going to Wad Medani, I used to go every day after work ... to see my friend, the deceased Ḥassan Faḍl al-Mūlā.'[41]

'Abd al-'Azīz 'Abd al-Ḥay continued to visit Wad Medani but he was not arrested. It was only in December – and therefore after the mutiny – that *Al-Riwāyāt* and the records of the Intelligence Department provide evidence that officers began to be discharged or suspended. For example, Sayyid Shahāta states:

> I was granted leave and I found that the Egyptians were being evacuated. I went to the station in Omdurman to see.... They cancelled my leave and ordered me to return to Medani, and there was a kind of secret investigation. ... After finishing with the Egyptians they turned their attention to us, and they claimed that Sayyid Shahāta and Ibrāhīm 'Abd al-Raḥman were disloyal to the government ... so they dismissed us from the service.[42]

Even if downplaying the participation of the army was deliberate, it is impossible to ignore the emotional effect on British officers of the breakdown of trust between them and their Sudanese subordinates. In Chapter 3, the shock felt by the administration following the cadets' demonstration was discussed; a further example of this may be found in the Sudanese memoirs of Sir Charles Gwynn, who was serving in the Egyptian Army in 1924.

> No one who ever served with the Egyptian Army can think without the deepest regret of an episode which marked the termination of a long comradeship-in-arms maintained through fierce fighting and many hardships: a comradeship which rescued a great territory from chaos and misery and, under a purely military Government, gave it a fresh start towards prosperity. ... the Egyptian Army was a force of which the British Army was justly proud, and of which many British officers had affectionate memories. Competition to serve in it was always keen, and, specially [sic] in the Sudanese battalion, the relations between British officers and the men were of the happiest.[43]

The low awareness in the military authorities of the politicization of their cadets and officers had its origins in the structure of the colonial government during this phase of colonization, when the army was the most important institution of the colonial state, at least until the end of World War I.

The period up to the war is described in Sudanese historiography as the time of the 'soldier-administrators', because British military men made up the majority of the establishment within the government. [44] For example, Governor General Wingate, Inspector-General Slatin Pasha (his right-hand man), and other early members of the Sudan Political Service, such as Jackson, Pipps, and Savile, had fought the Mahdist troops during the joint Anglo-Egyptian invasion of 1895-1898. They considered Mahdism to be a dangerous evil that had thrown Sudan into chaos, and suspected former

[41] *Al-Riwāyāt*, p. 227.
[42] Ibid., p. 166; see also the testimony of 'Abd al-'Azīz 'Abd al-Ḥay, Ibid, p. 224.
[43] Gwynn, *Imperial Policing*, p. 150.
[44] See Daly, *Empire on the Nile*, p. 106.

Mahdist followers of plotting to take over the country. As a consequence, they were convinced that the country had to be ruled by a strong military presence because at this stage of the occupation military knowledge and authority were the most indispensable skills.[45] In turn, civil servants, especially those in senior positions, resented being subordinated to the military, but there was little they could do about it. With the onset of World War I, as British officers gradually retired or left the country, the new cadre of civilian administrators took further steps to withdraw military elements from civil duties. However, this transformation was still in process during the Stack administration.

The term 'soldiers-administrators' accurately defines the role of the army in this first phase of colonization, not only because the country had not yet been 'pacified' – a word that hinted at the violent suppression of anticolonial resistance – but also because the army was involved in the overall running of the colonial state. The careers of the 1924 officers make this clear.

A phase of this nature was by no means peculiar to Sudan. According to Killingray, the period between 1885 and 1914 was characterized by the prolonged presence of a military or paramilitary administrations in various parts of Africa. Colonial rule rested on the principle of 'a minimum of force' applied by a numerically small police and army whose 'disciplined fire-power, machine guns and artillery usually ensured victory over numerically larger African opponents'.[46] This is echoed in a comment by Wingate in the Annual Report of 1908:

> [A]s time has progressed, the areas to be brought within the sphere of settled administrative government have enlarged, with the result that further demands have to be made upon the troops at the disposal of the Government, to supply the *necessary small modicum of material force* without which, in a primitive country, it is impossible to establish any form of peaceful administration.[47]

Practical application of this 'modicum of material force' was provided by the number of patrols, listed monthly in the Sudan Intelligence Reports, that were sent to the various border and non-border areas of Sudan, from South Kordofan to Eastern Sudan, and from Darfur (which became a part of Sudan in 1916) to the Upper Nile. For example, the 1911 Annual Report listed as many as cight patrols.[48]

These patrols had to be successful. The assistance of veteran Sudanese officers, with their profound knowledge of the country, was indispensable, even more so as the older generation of British military who had fought the

45 Only the Education and Legal Departments had civil servants at senior and junior levels, and the first civilian Provincial Governor was appointed in 1909, and then only after considerable discussion. Daly, *Empire on the Nile*, p. 90.

46 Anthony Clayton and David Killingray, eds, *Khaki and Blue: Military and Police in British Colonial Africa* (Athens, Ohio: Ohio University Center for International Studies, 1989), p. 422.

47 *GG Annual Report, 1908*, p. 206. (Author's italics)

48 *Annual Report of the Sudan Govt. 1911*, p. 150. For instance, the SMIR of January 1915 mentions a slavery patrol to the Dinder river, a patrol against the Lokoia in Mongalla province, and another the following month to the Upper Nile; FO 371/2349, NA.

Mahdi began to be replaced by younger men. They may have had limited knowledge of the country, but displayed the same eagerness to advance their military careers speedily. According to Justin Willis, the frequency and number of patrols was a consequence of the military administration itself being led by the ambitions of officers with few scruples about using their terms of service to obtain rapid career advancement. This situation was therefore a cause, not a consequence of what should be called low-intensity warfare rather than 'pacification', a situation that persisted even after the end of World War I.[49] Such ambitions could only be realized by victorious campaigns, which in turn required the knowledge, experience, and support of Sudanese veterans. This is what made British officers both close to and dependent on their 'black' soldiers and officers. For the historian Lamothe, they were the secret behind so many victories. This dependence contributed to the generation of highly ambiguous sentiments as well as contradictory narratives that were usually expressed in racial terms. For the British soldier-administrators, the racial background of 'Black' army men determined both their exceptional military abilities and their untrustworthiness, just as their courage and strength witnessed their inherent savagery. Simply stated, however, a military government could not do without its army.

RECRUITING SUDANESE

The composition of the army

During the Condominium, the army maintained a distinctively Ottoman-Egyptian character as an institution, even though it employed fewer Egyptians than other branches of the administration. While its overall structure did not change until the creation of the Sudan Defence Force in 1925, its composition evolved in relation to the strategic and pragmatic needs of the State.

During the early period, most of the army recruits were manumitted or runaway slaves. The army administration, however, routinely complained that they could not find all the new recruits they needed[50] – about five

[49] Justin Willis, 'Violence, Authority, and the State in the Nuba Mountains of Condominium Sudan', *The Historical Journal* (2003), vol. 46, n. 1, pp. 89-114.

[50] This is referred to in several works, in both the primary and secondary literature. For primary sources, see for example: Notes on the recruits for Sudanese units of the Egyptian army, Khartoum General Office, 27.5.1946, Palace 4/8/41, NRO: 'From the advance to Dongola in 1896 to the death of the Khalifa at Um Debeikerat in 1899 every young able bodied black who was taken prisoner was forcibly enlisted in a Sudanese unit. From 1899 to 1917 there was practically no enlistment in Sudanese units with the exception of a few reprieved murderers etc.; the Sudanese looked upon the Sudanese battalions as "Abid" and absolutely refused to enlist in them. In 1917, recruitment was opened up to Nubas and a very large number enlisted and a correspondingly large number of old soldiers were retired.' In 1924, Lee stack affirmed: 'The army is not a popular profession in the Sudan. For many years recruiting was almost at a standstill.'

hundred a year.[51] Colonial rulers, like historians today, believed that this was because the army was closely associated with slavery, but other considerations must also be taken into account. The *Handbook of the Egyptian Army* makes clear that the salary was no better than that for other unskilled jobs, and may have been lower. Joining the army was no small undertaking. Enlistment for soldiers who were recruited lasted for life before 1903, and thereafter for ten years, with the possibility of renewal for further ten-year periods. Those who had been recruited prior to 1903 could only be discharged 'on producing a voluntary substitute.'[52] Compared with the pattern of salaried work in Sudan in this period, when wage workers were mostly seasonal labourers who returned to their land and families during the agricultural season and moved from one employer to the next if they believed they were not being paid enough,[53] enlistment in the army entailed much worse conditions.

Recruitment changed as a consequence of the patrols, however, and began to reproduce a pattern reminiscent of the Turco-Egyptian slave raids. According to a British officer, Sir Angus Gillan, who was Deputy Governor in Kordofan after World War I:

> The Sudanese Battalions (that is the 9th to the 16th Sudanese) were recruited nominally voluntarily. There was a certain amount of – I wouldn't say pressgang work – but, for instance, after a patrol a good many prisoners were persuaded to go into the Sudanese Battalions for the good of their souls, and in the interests of civilisation. [54]

The account given by Fūmī Jāmā (also called Fūmī Ajmā) in *Al-Riwāyāt* is illuminating in this respect.[55] In 1924, he was an *onbashi*, a corporal, and thus an Non-Commissioned Officer (NCO). He became involved in the November Mutiny almost by accident because he was stationed with the 13th Battalion in Bahr al-Ghazal in 1924, but had been recalled in Khartoum for training. There he was caught in action during the mutiny and joined the insurgents.

Fūmī became a soldier in 1918 when he was seized during a patrol launched in the Nyima Hills to quash an uprising by Sultan Ajabna the previous year.[56] The patrols in the Nyima Hills during 1917 and 1918 used the same brutal methods of slave raids: villages were burnt, cattle seized, crops destroyed, access to water barred and heavy artillery brought in.

51 *Handbook of the Egyptian Army [HEA]* 1912, p. 55.

52 *HEA* 1912, p. 55.

53 This was also observed by Governor General Stack in his memorandum on the future Sudan Defence Force: Memorandum, Enclosure in no. 167, Major General Sir L. Stack to Mr MacDonald, 18.8.1924, FO 407/199, NA: 239. He also compares the high rate of pay of officers to the inadequate pay of the rank and file.

54 Douglas H. Johnson, interview with Sir Angus Gillan, K.B.E., C.M.G., Order of the Nile, 9 May 1979, 'The Role of British Forces in Africa - The Sudan Defence Force', Oxford Development Records Project, Rhodes House.

55 *Al-Riwāyāt*, pp. 23-39.

56 Ahmed Uthman Muhammad Ibrahim, *The Dilemma of British Rule in the Nuba Mountains, 1898-1947*, ([Khartoum]; London: Graduate College, University of Khartoum, 1985), Willis, 'Violence, Authority, and the State in the Nuba Mountains of Condominium Sudan'.

Fūmī Jāmā recalled that the British surrounded the hills and obliged the people to capitulate by shooting everybody who approached the river to drink.[57] As a result of this campaign, 4,000 people were captured and all their animals seized. The majority were released quickly but forced to move from their hills to the plains. 500 men and children were abducted by the army, sent to Khartoum, and divided among various battalions.[58] Fūmī Jāmā was one of that number, and began his military career as a child soldier at the age of about ten or eleven. [59] Separated from his family, and alone in Khartoum, he accepted his fate. He started to earn a small salary and develop new bonds in his battalion and in Khartoum. When asked if he had taken part in any political activity before 1924 or knew any of the leaders of the mutiny, he denied any such links and said that he participated in the mutiny because 'we are all Sudanese'.[60]

Although battalions tended to be organized according to the origins of their soldiers – such as the 11th Battalion, predominantly Nuba – only two categories, 'Arabs' and 'Sudanese' are found in colonial sources. [61] Thus the army was divided between Sudanese battalions, Egyptians battalions, and the Arab Corps. Each required a certain number of officers. There, racial considerations once again played a role. It was suggested that 'Arab soldiers would be likely to do better under men fitted by race, age and experience to be their leaders than under young officers of the regular army with no experience of Arabs.'[62] This preference for assigning 'Arab' officers to the Arab Corps and vice-versa was never strictly applied.

The size, composition, and number of the battalions varied, but in 1919 the army consisted of approximately 14,000 men, including six Sudanese (from the 9th to the 14th) and two Egyptian battalions.[63] In addition, there were a number of territorial battalions, one of the first being the Equatorial Battalion which was created in 1911 and later became known as the Equatorial Corps. In the Nuba Mountains there was the Nuba Territorial Company, formed in 1914. There were also various 'Arab' units in the north, such as the Eastern Arab Corps and the Western Arab Corps;[64] finally, there

57 *Al-Riwāyāt*, pp. 35-36.

58 Muhammad Ibrahim, *The Dilemma of British Rule in the Nuba Mountains*, pp. 19-22; Daly, *Empire on the Nile*, pp. 132-133.

59 *Al-Riwāyāt*, p. 35.

60 Ibid., p. 34.

61 Kamal O. Salih, 'British Colonial Military Recruitment Policy in the Southern Kordofan Region of Sudan, 1900-1945', *Middle Eastern Studies* (2005) vol. 41, n. 2, pp. 169-192.

62 G. A. V. Keays, 'A Note on the History of the Camel Corps', *Sudan Notes and Records* (1939), vol. 22, p. 105.

63 *Annual Report of the Sudan Govt. 1914-19*, p. 410. The 14th was disbanded early in the 20th century and reformed around 1910. The 15th and 17th Sudanese were originally raised as Egyptian battalions towards the end of the 'Reconquest' but were transformed into Sudanese battalions. They were then disbanded in 1921. A full description of the army in 1923 may be found in Composition of troops, 1923, WO 32/5588, NA.

64 Sikainga, 'Military Slavery, p. 27; *HEA* 1912, pp. 1-8. In 1912, the Arab Battalion consisted of one Camel Company and eight Infantry Companies, with a total of 1,176 'other ranks' (*HEA*, p. 23).

was the Camel Corps, formed in 1883, and reorganized as a permanent Sudanese unit in Kordofan from 1901. This last was originally made up of one 'Sudanese' and two 'Arab' units. Between 1909 and 1919, this changed to one 'Sudanese' and four 'Arab,' units. One such was stationed in Wad Medani but disbanded in 1924 because of its 'disaffection'.[65]

This overview also reveals that the government gradually began to prefer territorial battalions. Locally raised units were meant to know the region better, but also, at the turn of the 1920s, when Indirect Rule ideas were becoming increasingly popular among British administrators, it was considered to be in the best interests of the soldiers that they remain close to their 'homes'. The number of recruits into the territorial Arab Corps rose sharply: in 1923, there were seven companies in the Western Arab Corps, and seven in the Eastern Arab Corps, double the number of 1912.[66] Later, with the creation of the Sudan Defence Force in 1925, the army was composed of territorial battalions alone.

In the early 1920s, this change was under way. Not only were officers continually being transferred, but battalions, corps, and units also seem to have had a quite remarkable degree of flexibility and mobility. Battalions were often divided up into smaller units that were dispatched at some distance from the headquarters to form patrols or perform tasks that were semi-policing duties in character. During this period of history, the army infiltrated Sudanese provinces to a greater extent than the civil administration, as revealed in details by the lives of 1924 officers. It was marked by a tendency to swallow up institutions and skills that were unquestionably part of the civil administration in metropolitan areas.

The military elite: the officers of the Egyptian Army

Another important change introduced by the Condominium dealt with recruitment. Previously, soldiers had been promoted to be officers on the basis of seniority 'for good service, and not infrequently for gallantry in the field', but they were 'very often illiterate and unfitted educationally to carry on the office work of a company'.[67] In the Military School, young Sudanese graduated as officers, which meant that they were younger and had more experience behind school desks than they did in the field. The Military School made the country army's elite. Even more exclusive than Gordon College, the school recruited only between seven and ten pupils each year.[68]

[65] The first two 'Arab' units were composed of Baqqara and riverain groups; another 'Arab' company was raised in 1904. The fourth and fifth companies were raised 'from Shaigi Arabs in Omdurman' in 1906 and 1907, while the fifth was raised for the war in the Sinai Peninsula and was only annexed to the Camel Corps in 1908. The 2nd Company was transferred to the Western Arab Corps in 1919, and the 3rd Company to the Sudan Horse in 1907. The 5th Company was disbanded in 1925. Keays, 'A Note on the History of the Camel Corps', p. 106. In 1923, the Camel Corps was still made up of five companies. Composition of troops 1923, WO 32/5588, NA.

[66] Composition of the Troops in the Sudan, 1923, WO 32/5588, NA.

[67] *HEA* 1912, p. 44.

[68] Initially, the Military School was to include 30 cadets all in all: this number

The students in the photograph at the beginning of the chapter were between fifteen and twenty years of age, although they look much older in their uniforms. Most of them had been selected directly from primary school, while a smaller number had been handpicked from among the most promising and best educated NCOs. This is due to the practice that if a pupil left school to enrol in the army, he would have the opportunity to continue his studies at the barracks schools, reserved for soldiers.[69] Figures from the 1911 Annual Report, the year in which some of the students of the photograph in this chapter began Military School, show that the majority of the cadets had only completed the second or third year of primary school.[70] At the same time, it was compulsory for cadets to obtain a fourth-year primary school certificate, and if they had not finished school, they had to continue classes at Gordon College with other non-army students. Thus, the cadets were studying at Gordon College Primary School at the same time as some other political activists, such as the Zāyd brothers, and it is likely that they were involved in political debates at school. Sometimes, Upper School students might be selected to enter the Military School, although this was probably rare, as in the experience of Ismā'īl al-Muftī:

> I entered the Gordon College department of teachers and judges .... We used to play football against the Military School students. The Military School commander found that I am good at playing football and told me that the best is that I join the Military School and become an officer. I accepted and entered the Military School, which was a disgrace for our family, and a bad omen, because they were all Shaykhs.[71]

If some of the activists were barred from Upper School, others could obtain a secondary education only as cadets of the Military School. Ibrāhīm Sayyid Uthmān was admitted to the Military School in 1922, but 'unwillingly, because I wanted to continue my studies, but my two elders brothers were officers';[72] Muzammil 'Alī Dinār wanted to be a judge, but he could not, still he did not regret the change of direction:

> Mr Udal told me to go to the Military School. He said, your grades are good you can study whatever you want but the Governor General says you go to the Military School to be an officer. Then they will take you to the Western Corps. At that time I was interested in this, because when I was studying in the college I was thinking about taking revenge for my father .[73]

In spite of the potential danger of integrating the sons of old enemies, the British authorities appears surprisingly confident about the power of the school to instil discipline.

Although the cadets discussed above would have preferred to be civilians, various reports emphasize the fact that the Military School was an extremely popular institution, and the number of places was utterly

[(contd)] was increased to 40 in 1909. In 1924 there were 51 cadets.

69 *GG Annual Report 1911*, p. 112.

70 Ibid.

71 *Al-Riwāyāt*, p. 130.

72 Ibid., p. 173.

73 Ibid., pp. 42-43.

inadequate to satisfy demand.[74] The British were proud of the institution, and routinely expressed this confidence in the Annual Reports. For example, Wingate wrote in 1908:

> The results obtained by the school continue to be most satisfactory, the reports I receive regarding the young officers who have been gazetted to units from this establishment being universally excellent.[75]

Rules for the selection of candidates are set out in the *Handbook of the Egyptian Army*, where it is noted that recruits were 'chosen from the best families in the Sudan and from the sons of old officers and soldiers.'[76] Similarly, Wingate affirmed:

> [A] more than sufficient supply of the most suitable candidates is always forthcoming from the Gordon College and Government schools for vacancies in the Military school, which is happily thus enabled to obtain its cadets from among those who, not only possess qualifications of an excellent educational standard, but who are also sprung from some of the best families to be found in the Sudan.[77]

This reveals that there were two rationales at work in the choice of the Military School cadets. First, by choosing the sons of former officers and veterans, the British felt that their 'natural disposition' for war connected to their 'race' would be channelled and regulated through a consistent study curriculum. The school would further enhance these natural qualities and turn the recruits into even more redoubtable 'fighting material'.[78] Of course, they were not just any veterans. The privilege of entry to the Military School was bestowed upon the sons of the best and most trusted Sudanese army officers. For instance, in the foreword to Pott's book quoted above, Wingate mentioned the names of a number officers, one of whom was 'Abdel Hai Idris.' He was (most certainly) the father of the brothers 'Abd al-'Azīz and Idrīs 'Abd al-Ḥay, who were both admitted to the Military School, and were both 1924 revolutionaries.

The second type of pupils belonged to 'the best families to be found in Sudan'. Indeed, several of the 1924 officers were actually from well-established northern Sudanese families, as we have seen on more than one occasion. Examples of these students are MT 'Abdallāh Khalīl, a future President of Sudan; Yuzb. Aḥmad Ḥilmī Abū Sinn, a notable from the Shukriyya group;[79] or MA Ḥassan Ismā'īl al-Muftī, a nephew of Ismā'īl al-Azharī, Grand Mufti of Sudan between 1924 and 1932. The logic behind the selection of pupils from notable families is similar to that of the Upper School: education was used as a form of reward to be bestowed on government allies as a privilege in order to bolster alliances. This was even

[74] For instance, its popularity was noted in Currie, *Report, dated 8th September, 1911, on the Gordon Memorial College at Khartoum, for the Year 1910*, p. 13.

[75] *GG Annual Report 1908*, p. 210.

[76] *HEA* 1912, p. 70.

[77] *GG Annual Report 1908*, p. 209.

[78] Bennet Burleigh, *Sirdar and Khalifa; Or the Re-Conquest of the Soudan* (London: Chapman & Hall, 1898), p. 212; quoted in Lamothe, *Slaves of Fortune*, p. 131.

[79] On this individual, see Hill, *A Biographical Dictionary*, p. 32; as to his participation in 1924, nothing was proved, but he was suspected in several instances, such as the November mutiny: Intelligence Dept. to General Staff, Khartoum 10.12.1924 Palace 4/11/55, NRO.

more important during the time of the 'soldier administrators.' Because officialdom represented a prestigious form of elite activity, the notables of Sudan could not be left out.

Thus, while the Egyptian Army and officialdom is usually associated with 'Black' officers – that is, descendants of enslaved Sudanese – in reality, the composition of the elite of arms was much more varied. The 'origins' of the pupils who took part in the demonstration of August 8 is a fascinating case in point, and it also suggests that the times were changing. We know that in 1908, only three cadets were defined as 'Arab Sudanese',[80] and also the majority of the cadets represented in the 1912 photograph would have been categorized as 'Blacks'. Instead, in 1924, of the 44 cadets out the 51 whose origins are known, nine were defined as Dinka, four as Nuba, and one was from the province of Mongalla.[81] The rest of the cadets came from all corners of Sudan. Many were from the West: six were defined as 'Burnawi' (one from Kalakla), and thus originally from Chad, and three were Fur from Darfur. One was defined as Ta'aisha (a famous group because many of the Mahdi's soldiers came from it), and one as Ḥassaniyya; both thus came from nomadic groups from Kordofan. There were cadets from central Sudan: two from the 'Abbadi, three from the Jawama'a (a branch of the Ja'aliyyin), three Ja'aliyyin (one from Rufa'a) and two from the Shayqiyya, all fairly well-settled groups from central Sudan. From Eastern Sudan, one cadet came from the pastoral nomadic Hadendowa and two others from the 'Ababda. Lastly, there was one who was described as a relative of the *'umda* – the chief – of the city of Bara, and five were *Muwalladīn*.

The list reveals that although the cadets' origins were extremely diverse, they came predominantly from 'troublesome' groups that the government struggled to control. Yet, the application of ethnic labels also merits reflection. They were applied to these young cadets – just as they were to other Sudanese – in an attempt to decode ties that actually operated in complicated ways and translate them into simple, intelligible forms. Take, for instance, one of the leaders of the Cadets' Mutiny, Muḥammad Faḍlallāh al-Shinnāwī. He is defined as a Burnawi, having Nigerian origins, and yet he had an Egyptian family name (his father had fought in Mexico), was born in Fashoda in the Upper Nile and raised in Khartoum. Furthermore, his account reveals no visible association with the West African community.[82] In the case of the brothers Idrīs and 'Abd

[80] Beshir, *Educational Development in the Sudan*, p. 43.

[81] The origins of the 34 who were arrested is in White Flag League Conspiracy Trial, 1924, List of sentences, Northern Prov. 1/21/207, NRO. With regard to the other ten who were not convicted: for Muḥammad al-Ṭāhir Isḥāq: DI to Gov. Kordofan, 6.11.1924, Kordofan 1/12/54; Yaḥyā Aḥmad 'Umar: Gov. Khartoum Prov. to CSO & AG Egyptian Army, Khartoum 18.10.1924, Palace 4/9/47; for Aḥmad 'Abd al-Raḥman al-Nūr, Bābikr Sharīf, Muḥammad Ṣāliḥ Aḥmad, and 'Abd al-Mūlā Māhir: List of Military Cadets who took part in demonstration in August 1924, who were released under guarantee, 16 in all, n.d., n.s., Kordofan 1/11/45; Muḥammad 'Awād al-Nimr: Bimbashi General Staff, Egyptian Headquarters to DI, Khartoum, 18.10.1924, Palace 4/9/47; Muḥammad Abū Zāyd, 'Uthmān 'Abd al-'Aẓīm Khalifa, and Muḥammad 'Uthmān Bakhīt: Gov. Khartoum Prov. to CSO & AG, Egyptian Army, Khartoum, 18.10.1924, Palace 4/9/47. All these files are in NRO.

[82] From his own written account, documents in private possession of the family

al-'Azīz 'Abd al-Ḥay, they are labelled in colonial records as Dinka,[83] but they were born in Omdurman, grew up in Wad Medani, returned to Khartoum to study at the Military School and were later despatched all over Sudan.[84] There are a great number of similar accounts, which is why in a final report on the 1924 Revolution in 1925, Ewart would call such men 'detribalized negroids,' because their ties to their place of origin were weak or non-existent.

They were not the only ones in this category. Other cadets came from families whose ethnic label had no single, certain meaning. The fact that Cadet 'Alī Ṭāhir was labelled as Hadendowa does not clarify if he had just moved to the School from Eastern Sudan or his family had lived in Khartoum for one or two generations; if he had claimed that he was a Hadendowa despite the fact that his parents were of a different origin or that he was given this label because his main relationships were with Hadendowa. What is certain is that his family had personal links with the British establishment because this was a strict condition for entry into the Military School. It was of course easier for people who lived close to the establishment to fulfil it than those from more rural areas.

This does not mean that people's 'origin' was an unimportant distinction: it affected the lives of officers in numerous ways; it did so for any Sudanese. As Kurita relates, 'Alī 'Abd al-Laṭīf grew up in the home of Officer 'Abdallāh Rīḥān. The latter managed to get 'Alī into the Military School because he had connections with the British Army. 'Alī's mother and 'Abdallāh Rīḥān had a Dinka family background, at least partially: 'Alī's grandmother was also a Dinka, while his grandfather was from Dongola. Yet this was enough for 'Abdallāh to perceive 'Alī's mother as being related to him ('Alī called 'Abdallāh as his 'uncle'), and to open his house to her and her son. Not only was it irrelevant that the Dinka connection came from the mother's side, contrary to the habit of ascribing group membership to the patrilineal line, but also the 'Nuba' part of 'Alī's background was irrelevant and invisible in this context, to the point that until Kurita's account surfaced, it was widely believed that he was a Dinka. The description of 'Alī as Dinka corresponded very little with the 'tribes' that the British were beginning to conceptualize as the proper organization for a well-ordered Sudanese society.

LIVES AS OFFICERS OF THE EGYPTIAN ARMY

After completing Military School, the young officers of the Egyptian Army began to live in a style that set them apart from the majority of the population of Sudan in many ways. This is best illustrated through the accounts of several 1924 officers.

(contd) of Muḥammad Faḍlallāh al-Shinnāwī. See also: Mutiny of the military cadets, undated, unsigned, Palace 4/9/47, and A/Controller Public Security intelligence to Gov. Kordofan Prov., Khartoum 7.9.29, Kordofan 1/13/60, both in NRO.

83 White Flag League Conspiracy Trial, 1924, List of sentences, Northern Prov. 1/21/207, NRO.

84 See 'Abd al-'Azīz 'Abd al-Ḥay's narrative in *Al-Riwāyāt*, pp. 224-257.

Sayyid Shahāta's account is particularly detailed (see Map 2). After his graduation in 1914, Sayyid was sent to work in Wau, the first of the many places to which he would be posted:

> I was appointed to the 12th battalion in Wau. I was responsible for the shooting and firing section and for the new recruits ... Then I was selected for training. While there, I got the news of my appointment in the signalling corps; I found Egyptian officers in this branch of the army. They were Egyptian and Sudanese officers, among them 'Alī 'Abd al-Laṭīf. But I knew him earlier; we were members of the White Flag League and we were in the signalling corps as friends. I ended my period and returned to my battalion, I was very sick with black fever, so they had to transfer me to Khartoum where I joined the 13th Sudanese battalion and remained with it. I was despatched to Rahad to guard the airport ... In 1917 I was transferred again to Equatoria, to Tumbura, where I served for two years, then in Raja in 1919 in Bahr al-Ghazal, I was there for one year, then ... I was transferred to the 14th Battalion in Wad Medani. Then I joined the musketeer unit, my colleagues were Ḥassan Faḍl al-Mūlā and 'Alī al-Bannā. I left them in the musketeer unit and moved to the 14th Sudanese battalion ... I worked in Kurmuk, in 1922; then I returned to Wad Medani.[85]

Sayyid Shahāta was transferred seven times in ten years, not including transfers due to training, sickness, or leave.

Such mobility was one of the main features of the officers' profession, as many stories from the 1924 protesters confirm. For example, al-'Āzza, the wife of 'Alī 'Abd al-Laṭīf, complained that after they married '... we did not have a honeymoon, we travelled everywhere... I rode camels, donkeys and horses ... there was no rest.'[86] Her account shows that 'Alī was sent to a number of places, including Talodi in the Nuba Mountains, Dar Masalit in Darfur, and Wad Medani.[87] Similarly, officer 'Abd al-'Azīz 'Abd al-Ḥay was sent to Wau in Bahr al-Ghazal for three months after he graduated in 1919, then sent back to Khartoum to attend a special signalling course. Subsequently he was stationed in Omdurman, participated in another training course in Khartoum, and was posted in Wad Medani at the end of 1923.[88] Officer Ismā'īl al-Muftī also moved around a great deal, mostly within Kordofan. He graduated in 1913, joined the Camel Corps in 1916 in El Obeid, took part in the Darfur campaign from al-Nuhud in the same year, thence to Bara, where he stayed for a period that for him was 'a long time': three years. In 1919 he was transferred to El Obeid, thereafter to Wad Medani, where he joined the officers' association. In 1924, he went to Khartoum, only to be sent to Equatoria in 1925.[89]

There were compensations for these continuous transfers, and numerous benefits. First of all, officers were among the best-paid government employees. Second, their profession allowed them to reach positions of responsibility that were barred to civilians, at least until World War I. After graduation, cadets were immediately given the rank of *Mulazim*

85 *Al-Riwāyāt*, pp. 160-163.

86 Al-'Āzza Muḥammad 'Abdallāh Rīḥān, tape-recorded interview with Aḥmad Ibrāhīm Diyāb, unknown date and unknown place.

87 *Al-Riwāyāt*, pp. 44-52.

88 Ibid., pp. 224-228.

89 Ibid., p. 131.

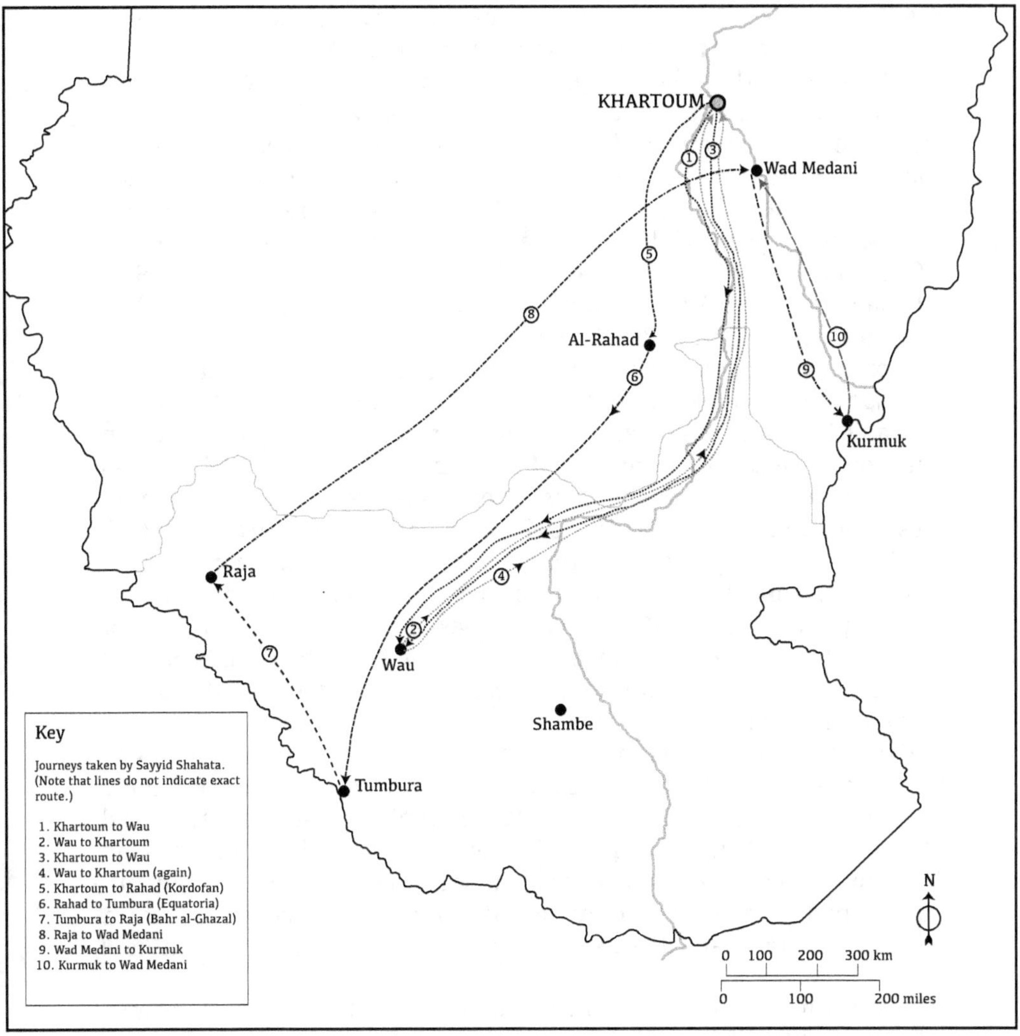

Map 2 Transfers of Sayyid Shahāta

Tani[90] (MT; Second Lieutenant), the lowest commissioned officer rank. The school marked the distinction between non-commissioned officers (NCOs) who worked their ways through the ranks and commissioned officers (COs), so that a subordinate to a *Mulazim Tani* was usually older and more experienced than a commissioned officer. There was a substantial difference in terms of pay, responsibilities, and status between the two categories. For example, in 1912, a newly graduated officer earned GB£ 98.10s. a year, while after years in the army, the highest ranked NCOs earned only GB£ 49.[91] It is also important to observe that in 1912, a freshly graduated *Mulazim Tani* earned more than a Grade VIII civilian government employee after World War I.

Promotion depended on seniority, the ability to pass special exams corresponding to rank, and recommendations from superiors. The ranks available to Sudanese officers were limited, however; during the period in question these usually went from MT to *Yuzbashi*, while the higher ranks were open to British and Egyptians.[92] Nonetheless, the *Yuzbashi* rank was prestigious and well paid, and in 1912 meant a starting salary of GB£ 147.[93] Another important point to observe is that it does not seem that promotion to *Yuzbashi* worked in the same way as that to *Bash Katib* among civilians. Various protagonists of 1924, from families of veteran 'Black' officers or from Northern Sudan were appointed as *Yuzbashi*. In the records of 1924 activists, there were 47 officers of Yuzbashi rank; eight were defined as Egyptian and the remainder Sudanese.

Other privileges reserved to officers included government housing in the very centre of Khartoum, near today's *Sūq al-'Arabī*, where we know 'Alī 'Abd al-Laṭīf, Zayn al-'Ābdīn 'Abd al-Tam, and 'Abd al-'Azīz 'Abd al-Ḥay lived.[94] Being an officer also involved gratuities and warrants (as in the case of Zayn, who was able to take the train with his 'servant' Muḥammad al-Mahdī and only pay half price for al-Mahdī's ticket); a pension for life after retirement; annual leave of one to two months;[95]

[90] In Arabic it should be *Mulāzim Thāni,* but the ranks of the Egyptian Army were taken from the old Ottoman-Egyptian ranks, and in Ottoman Turkish the rank was spelt as Mulazim Tani.

[91] *HEA* 1912, pp. 72-73 and 92-93. The original amounts are in Egyptian Pounds, respectively 96 and 48. From 1898 to 1945, the exchange rate was 1 GBP= 0.975 EGP.

[92] These were Sagh, or Adjutant-Major; Bimbashi, or Major; Kaimakam – Colonel; Miralai – Brigadier-General. The positions of Ferik – General of Division – and Sirdar – Commander-in-Chief of the Army, were always held by British. The ranks were in Ottoman Turkish. Before 1898, long-serving officers might reach Saghkoklaghasi (Adjutant Major). In the first two decades of the 20th Century, a few were given the rank of Bimbashi, and even Kaimakan, immediately before retirement so that they could draw the pension due to a higher rank. A number of such cases are recorded in the IX Sudanese Regimental Historical Record, SAD 110/11/1-89. I am grateful to Douglas Johnson for this information.

[93] *HEA* 1912, pp. 72-73.

[94] For 'Abd al-'Azīz, *Al-Riwāyāt*, p. 235; for Zayn, interview by the author with Amīna Bilāl Riziq in her home in Khartoum, Spring 2005.

[95] See the series of Army Orders of the Sudan Govt., published monthly. In the Mahmud Salih Collection, University of Bergen.

special arrangements for leisure time, such as dedicated officers' clubs;[96] and finally, continuing education for officers, who were periodically called on to take refresher courses and further training.

As we have seen, a theoretical rule existed according to which Sudanese officers who were defined as 'Black Sudanese' were to be sent to Southern Sudan, while those defined as Arabs would be sent to the north. In practice, racial considerations were superseded by pragmatism. One of the places to which Sayyid Shahāta was despatched was Al-Rahad, in Kordofan, between Umm Ruwaba and El Obeid. Officer Thābit 'Abd al-Raḥīm, who was labelled a 'Dinkawi', was a cavalry officer stationed in Shendi, in the Northern Province. In contrast, Officer 'Alī al-Bannā was sent to Malakal in Bahr al-Ghazal at one stage during 1924. All the officers of 1924 whose stories are found in *Al-Riwāyāt* had spent a more or less lengthy period in Wad Medani. Officers were sent wherever their abilities were needed, based on the training and skills.

Another important aspect of an officer's career was the variety of functions he covered. Officers commanded units that were dispatched all over the country, and carried out all sorts of tasks that lay somewhere between civilian and military jurisdictions. The units guarded airports, ensured the safety of commercial roads, or patrolled frontiers; officers were in charge of supervising the construction of colonial buildings in urban centres and dams and irrigation works in rural areas. For example, among the 1924 officers, 'Abdallāh Khalīl, who was a *Yuzbashi* at the time, worked for the Irrigation Department, as did officer 'Alī al-Bannā (the same whose death sentence was commuted at the very last minute).[97] Muḥammad Sayyid Uthmān worked for Sudan Transports between Kordofan and Darfur,[98] and Aḥmad Tawfīq for the Veterinary Department.[99]

These examples show that officers were frequently given tasks that were more administrative than military. In 1912, about a quarter of all the officers in the Egyptian Army were employed in civilian duties.[100] Army officers represented 10% of the establishment of Khartoum province in 1924; it is significant that in 1927, the province did not include a single officer in its list of administrative personnel.[101]

The porosity between the military and civil administrations also worked the other way around. Every month, the Army Ordnances published lists

[96] Mentioned for instance in the interview of 'Abd al-'Azīz 'Abd al-Ḥay, *Al-Riwāyāt*, p. 225. There was also a cadets' club, which was mentioned by Muzammil 'Alī Dinār, ibid., p. 45.

[97] For 'Abdallāh Khalīl, this is mentioned in several places, such as Gov. Wau to Civsec Khartoum, received 9.10.1924, FO 141/669/8, NA, and 'Information received on the 11th instant, Intelligence Dept., Khartoum. 13.8.1924, Palace 4/10/50, NRO. For 'Alī al-Bannā: Knapp Bey Malakal to CSO & AG Khartoum, 24.9.1924, FO 141/669/8, NA.

[98] Confession of Ali Ahmed Saleh, p. 15, FO 141/805/2, NA.

[99] Sanduk Talodi to Sanduk El Obeid, 4.12.1924, Kordofan 1/11/45, NRO.

[100] Appendix 4: Appointments under the Sudan Govt. held by officers of the Egyptian Army, *HEA* 1912, pp. 131-32 and 21.

[101] Particulars of establishment, Khartoum Prov., 1924-1932, Civsec 50/14/61, NRO.

of civilians who had been transferred to various departments administered by the army, such as the Medical Corps, the Department Staff and the battalions. Similarly, an officer usually served in a civilian function for a short period of time.

Nonetheless, the types of administrative tasks that were assigned to officers were quite different from those given to civilians, which also explains why the Military School was such a popular institution. In his history of the Camel Corps, British officer Keays noted:

> Soon after the conversion of the Egyptian units to Sudanese difficulties were experienced regarding the shortage of junior officers who looked upon service in the unit as a stepping stone to appointment to the political administration to which they were constantly being seconded.[102]

Keays also mentioned that the army's recruiting system produced officers who were 'junior leaders,' 'sheikhs [who] have grown up in the Corps itself.'[103]

Certainly, the meaning of the term 'political administration' was very broad, but the clearest case in point is the appointment of officers as sub-*mamurs*. A *mamur* was the first subaltern below the British Inspector (later called the District Commissioner) and the sub-*mamur* was his personal subordinate. Typically, the *mamur* would be Egyptian and the sub-*mamur* Sudanese (or also Egyptian), but in smaller administrative centres, there was usually only a (Sudanese) sub-*mamur*.

The latter position covered everything relating to the maintenance of colonial order and disciplining those who breached it.[104] Sharkey gives us an extensive idea of the breadth of its functions:

> They collected taxes ... , supervised police business, maintained public security, surveyed and registered lands, directed upkeep of government buildings, and helped semiliterate or literate 'sanitary barbers' (the *hakims*, or medical assistants) to register birth, death, and smallpox vaccinations. They supervised public health measures, such as anti-malarial mosquito control.[105]

It was quite common for officers to be given a *mamur* post; it was not necessary to have reached a high rank to hold it. Yet it was a position of responsibility. Its political importance can also be grasped from this comment by Lee Stack on how to recruit them, even though it was expressed in the context of the opening of the school for civilian *mamur*, a new Upper School branch, in 1918:

> The selection of these men does not depend merely on their educational or 'literary' qualifications, but due weight is given to their belonging to families of good repute

[102] Keays, 'A Note on the History of the Camel Corps', p. 105.

[103] Ibid., p. 106. More specifically, he was referring to NCOs who had been commissioned thanks to their experience and gallantry. At the same time, this argument could be applied to all officers.

[104] As Sharkey points out (in *Living with Colonialism*, p. 112), the word *mamur* comes from the Arabic verb 'to order' ('amr).

[105] Sharkey, *Living with Colonialism*, p. 112. See also *The Sub-Māmūr's Handbook. Lectures on the Penal, Criminal Procedure and Civil Codes, and Notes on Accounts, Agriculture, Forestry, Sanitation, &c.* Printed by McCorquodale & Co. Ltd, 1926.

> and showing the qualities of character necessary for a Government servant who has to exercise authority and accept a certain amount of responsibility[106]

In line with the general turn towards a civil administration, the government sought to replace military with civilian *mamurs,* but this transformation had not been achieved 1924. According to Stack, there were 138 sub-*mamurs* in that year, of whom 102 were Sudanese: 76 were civilians and 26 officers.[107] In his time, officers were chosen as sub-*mamurs* mostly to be despatched to 'difficult' areas. For example, Zayn al-'Ābdīn 'Abd al-Tam was a sub-mamur in Shiban, in the Nuba Mountains, Ḥassan Muḥammad Zayn in Zalingei, in Darfur, and 'Alī 'Abd al Laṭīf in Shambe, in the Bahr al-Ghazal.[108] They were all kept in post for a brief period, about one or two years. Colonial records indicate that at least 18 Sudanese *mamurs* and sub-*mamurs* were suspected of involvement in the events of 1924.

CONCLUSION: SUDANESE OFFICERS AND THE SPREAD OF POLITICAL PROTEST

Sudanese army officers formed an unusual elite. They were constantly transferred from one administrative centre to another, and from one post to another, meeting and working with other officers. Ties could rapidly be established because they had received the same education and had sometimes known each other since childhood. They might have been neighbours, or acquainted through relatives. The overriding factor was that they belonged to an institution marked by a formidable *esprit de corps*.

As with civilian employees, the multiple ties connecting groups of officers promoted a variety of intimacy and mutual trust that favoured underground politics. Incidentally, it should be noted that many of the secret societies formed across the Middle East during the same period were officers' societies. Political ideas travelled with the officers, and spread from one location to the other in the course of their constant transfers. Finally, at least for some periods of their career, officers were likely to work in close contact with civilian government employees, and most of them had spent one or two years at the Gordon College Primary School, which explains why they were able to establish ties with civil officials relatively easily.

[106] Lee Stack, Memorandum on the Future Status of the Sudan, 25.5.1924, 323, FO 407/198, NA. See also *Annual Report of the Sudan Govt., 1921*, p. 240.

[107] Lee Stack, Memorandum on the Future Status of the Sudan, 25.5.1924, p. 325, FO 407/198, NA. The figures are slightly different in Civsec Office, Khartoum, 7.9.1924, Palace 4/9/44, NRO, in which there were 45 Egyptians and 12 Sudanese mamurs, and 21 Egyptians and 114 Sudanese sub-mamurs.

[108] For Zayn: *Al-Riwāyāt*, p. 575. C.A. Willis, Notes on Persons arrested in connection with recent demonstrations in Khartoum, 23.6.1924, FO 141/810/3, NA. For 'Alī 'Abd al-Laṭīf, *Al-Riwāyāt*, p. 373. For Ḥassan Muḥammad Zayn, Telegram from DI to Gov., El Fasher, 18.12.1924, Palace 4/9/47, NRO.

At the same time, their profession set them apart from the rest of the society. First of all, their uniform shaped their lives entirely. There was no other institution in the colonial state that determined the training and work of individuals in such an all-encompassing way. There were personal files on each and every officer, carefully updated every year. Soldiers and officers were taught not only how to fight, but also how to carry themselves, how to talk, and how to walk. Army Ordnances reveal that every time an officer moved from one city to another, even during vacations and holidays, he had to submit a special application and wait until permission was granted. It is no coincidence that the way in which officers showed their insubordination, in Sudan as in Egypt and elsewhere, was not by participating in demonstrations but by refusing to salute a superior or to dismount when meeting a British officer, or by disobeying any other a minor order, however insignificant.[109]

The central position they enjoyed within the colonial state also generated a form of segregation between the army – in particular officers – and ordinary people that was expressed in spatial terms. During their period of service, officers and men lived in special barracks separated from the rest of the population, and tended to socialize among themselves. Their relationships with the population at large were mediated by their uniforms. An extract from the Annual Report of 1911 best expresses the function of these guardians of law and order. Although it refers to patrols, it is easy to see that it could apply to the army as a whole:

> The object aimed at in sending out all these patrols has been to uphold the prestige of the Government, and to prove to the natives that the Soudanese authorities are as determined to punish rebellion and disorder as to protect form aggression those who obey their orders and exert their influence for the maintenance of public tranquillity.[110]

This sheds light one of the most puzzling omissions in the tales of 1924 officers collected in *Al-Riwāyāt*. They recounted their frequent transfers, the forms of their political engagement, and their connections among each other, but the connections with the population among which they lived and with their subordinates, soldiers such as Fūmī Jāmā, are invisible. The officers were often asked to discuss this point with their interviewers because the latter were keen to know whether or not the military was associated with the civilians of the White Flag. The accounts all stated that there were contacts with Gordon College graduates, mostly through intermediaries who were relatives of the officers: for instance we know that in Wad Medani, the civilians were associated with the military through Mudaththir al-Būshī, a relative of officer Ismā'īl al-Muftī (the two of them were interviewed together). The officers were obviously more at ease with educated civilians, with whom they worked and whom they had met at school, than they were with their subalterns or the people they worked with or managed.

[109] This happened to 'Alī 'Abd al-Laṭīf (Kurita, *'Alī 'Abd al-Laṭīf*, p. 82), and several oral accounts confirm it.

[110] *Annual Report of the Sudan Govt., 1911*, p. 150.

Their role as guardians of colonial law and ultimately as agents of imperial domination limited their political contacts with the population at large, as the narratives of 1924 make clear. In peripheral places such as Wau or Talodi, in South Sudan and the Nuba Mountains, where the government chiefly operated through violence and coercion, officers who mutinied failed to 'ignite' the local population, despite the number of grievances and the degree of hostility against the colonial government in these areas. In central Sudan and in the capital the presence of the army was much less connected to the violence of the colonial state, but in the peripheries, patrols were sent year after year to 'pacify' the local population, so the latter saw the army mostly as enemies.

Nevertheless, Sudanese officers were the most important, and sometimes the only representative of the colonial state, in particular up to World War 1.[111] Even where they worked under an Egyptian or British officer, they were often the ones who established the link between their superiors and the people they governed. Those who gave interviews in the 1970s were keenly aware that their liminal status between the state and its subjects conferred on them a role that was unique and exceptional among the inhabitants of Sudan, without at the same time fully accounting for its ambiguity. This special status also explains why the actions that were organized by officers, such as the cadets' demonstration, arose such deep emotions on the population at large. The future bearers of colonial authority, the symbols of the coercive power of the colonial state, were rebelling against the very same government that bestowed them power. The demonstration by the cadets made it appear as though the very foundations of colonial rule were beginning to crumble. And it is no coincidence that the quelling of the November mutiny and the execution of the officers responsible for it marked the exact end of the 1924 Revolution.

[111] This discussion as much as that of the previous chapter owe much to Benjamin N. Lawrance, Emily L. Osborn, and Richard R. L. Roberts eds. *Intermediaries, Interpreters, and Clerks: African Employees in the Making of Colonial Africa* (Madison WI: University of Wisconsin Press, 2006).

10

'I Was Very Famous in *Sūq al-'Arabī*': Nationalism and Sudanese Workers

The British authorities attached no importance to the political participation of skilled and unskilled workers in the Revolution of 1924. They believed that 'ignorant' men in 'low' positions had no political opinions. In their view, the workers who participated in demonstrations did so because they were paid either by the White Flag League or by the Egyptians. British observers did not spare their contempt for those demonstrators who were not 'Effendi': 'A crowd of riff-raff collected as if by magic', 'large crowd of the rabble of the town', 'rabbles of nobodies led by shady characters and followed by naughty little boys', 'loafers':[1] these are just a few examples of the terms used to describe the crowd; yet their frequency bears witness to the fact that that the masses were always present, ominous, undisciplined, and unfamiliar.

Historiographical approaches to the politicization of labour in colonial Africa and the Middle East tend to perceive political activism, in particular within the framework of an anticolonial nationalist movement, as being directly connected to the further integration of a colonized territory into the world economy.[2] A capitalist economy would bring about the workers' progressive disengagement from patron-client relationships and would lead to a consequent strengthening of horizontal links. Socio-economic changes among peasants who had become workers also determined a shift in their political sociability. This is the thesis presented by Joel Beinin and Zachary Lockman in their analysis of the participation of the Egyptian working class in political movements up to the time of Nāṣir. The authors

[1] Chronicle of the events during the period of political excitement in Khartoum, FO 141/805/2, NA. Ewart Report, p. 164.

[2] Frederick Cooper, *Decolonization and African Society: The Labor Question in French and British Africa* (Cambridge & New York: Cambridge University Press, 1996), Beinin and Lockman, *Workers on the Nile,* p. 17. Z. Lockman, 'Imagining the working class: Culture, nationalism, and class formation in Egypt, 1899-1914', *Poetics Today* (1994), vol. 15, n. 2, pp. 157-190. James L. Gelvin, 'The Social Origins of Popular Nationalism in Syria: Evidence for a New Framework', *International Journal of Middle East Studies* (1994), vol. 26, n. 4, pp. 645-661.

identified a common historical pattern in the rise of the working classes in a number of countries in the colonial world:

> In these countries foreign capital and the requirements of the colonial power bring an urban working class into existence... the fact that economic and social grievances are directed against a foreign-run state apparatus as well as a foreign-dominated economy creates link between indigenous workers and the emerging nationalist political movement.[3]

This chapter explores the relevance of the paradigm to Sudan; the features of the political mobilization of workers during the 1924 Revolution; the make-up of the labour force, and its reasons for joining the national movement.

First, the category of wage-workers as discussed in this chapter is quite different from that described by Beinin and Lockman, who deal primarily with salaried workers in industrial jobs, employed by the State, chiefly in the Railways Department. In Sudan principally in Atbara and Port Sudan, railway wage-workers were also at the forefront of events in 1924, and would remain at the heart of political life in Sudan for many years to come.[4] However, this type of transport worker constituted a small part of the demonstrators. On the other hand, colonial descriptions such as 'rabbles of nobodies' do not reveal much about the composition of the crowds. The judicial records of those seized by the police indicate that they were made up of small shopkeepers, artisans, and unskilled workers, with significant variations according to location: in Khartoum, they were semi-skilled workers and small artisans-cum-traders: shoemakers, ivory-turners, cooks, tailors, servants, bakers, butchers, carpenters, coffee shop owners, book makers, and pedlars. In Atbara, the majority were workers and craftsmen from the railway workshops. In Port Sudan, the demonstrators were dockers and artisans of the *sūq*. In El Obeid, the White Flag League recruited people working in the cattle market, such as *samāsira* cattle brokers, besides craftsmen such as watchmakers and tailors. For this reason, it is difficult to categorize people: it is very unlikely that Sudanese workers would have seen themselves as a group, not because class consciousness had yet to develop, but rather because the conditions for recognizing themselves as a category were not yet present.[5] Further, the group was in the first place characterized by its very lack of homogeneity: the situation of a worker who received a fixed monthly salary could hardly be compared with that of a small artisan plying his trade in a stall. On this premise, the term 'workers' is used in this chapter as a heuristic category more associated with 'plebeian' than with 'proletariat', not in the sense that Sudanese workers lacked class consciousness in 1924 as opposed to 'proletarian' Sudanese later on, but rather because this latter category is mostly linked to the idea of a class tied to a form of industrial capitalism

3 Beinin and Lockman, *Workers on the Nile*, p. 17.

4 Sikainga, *City of Steel and Fire*.

5 Luc Boltanski, *Les Cadres : La Formation D'un Groupe Social* (Paris: Éditions de Minuit, 1990), Simona Cerutti, 'Histoire Pragmatique, Ou de La Rencontre Entre Histoire Sociale et Histoire Culturelle', *Tracés. Revue de Sciences Humaines* (2008), vol. 15, pp. 147–68.

that owned nothing but its labour. The term 'plebeian' covers a multiplicity of occupations, from craftsmen to unskilled workers, that includes both new and old types of livelihood.[6]

The broad category of Sudanese 'worker' is limited only by two conditions and one tendency: first, the people so designated usually had not attended primary school, and thus were not 'Effendi', although some may have attended the Sudan Government Instructional Workshop where they would have learnt elements of literacy; second, they usually received pay for their labour and services in cash; and third, workers tended to settle in urban centres. The fact that they did not have primary education points up another aspect that may be obvious but worth mentioning: the government considered it unnecessary (and also uneconomical) to educate this group. As the funds for education were limited, they were certainly not the group to be prioritized.

The approach taken in this chapter is of necessity quite different from that of the two previous chapters on the 'making' of educated civilians and officers. The category of Sudanese workers was much broader and more diversified. Career development, working conditions, and family backgrounds varied considerably according to the type of work and the setting. Finally, overall, research material on Sudanese workers is exceedingly fragmentary. Not only – as discussed previously – was it much easier for the Intelligence Department to track down officers and civilian employees of the government, but first-hand accounts are also very rare. Most workers were illiterate, not having attended school; even the few who may have kept diaries probably had difficulty in publishing them; and finally, the interviewers who compiled *Al-Riwāyāt* probably found it harder to comprehend the working-class element than the professional. For instance, *Al-Riwāyāt* includes only one interview with an artisan/ small trader, Mūsā 'Antar, who led the demonstration of September 21.[7] However, some memoirs have survived, such as the excellent account of 'Abd al-Karīm al-Sayyid, who in colonial sources was described as a carpenter.[8]

The scarcity of sources, coupled with the heterogeneity of workers 'category' explains why this chapter moves away from a microscopic analysis, which would mostly expose how little it is known about them, to a macroscopic review of the labour question in Sudan, that can still provide for useful answers as to workers' participation in 1924.

6 E. P. Thompson, 'Patrician Society, Plebeian Culture', *Journal of Social History* (1974), vol. 7, n. 4, pp. 382–405. For an example of use in African history, see: Jonathon Glassman, *Feasts and Riot: Revelry, Rebellion, and Popular Consciousness on the Swahili Coast, 1856-1888* (Portsmouth NH: Heinemann, 1995).

7 Mūsā Aḥmad 'Antar, *Al-Riwāyāt*, pp. 452-265.

8 Al-Sayyid, *Al-Liwā' al-Abyaḍ.* On his profession: Chronicle of the events during the period of political excitement in Khartoum. FO 141/805/2, NA. Here his name is misspelt as Abdel Gadir El Sayed (confusing him with another protester), but in other documents his correct names are given. Unfortunately, he makes no reference to his own profession, or to the organization of the League and his relations with other members.

WORKERS IN 1924

Far from being mere observers or passive supporters, workers were at the forefront of events in Khartoum, Atbara, and Port Sudan. They were among the first and most central members of the League, they headed and later organized demonstrations, and many went to gaol for their activism. Of the 31 people imprisoned for taking part in demonstrations and political speeches, as many as 15 were Sudanese workers (see Appendix 2). One man, for instance, 'Abd al-Raḥman Ḥassan, a 'Muwallad' fishmonger, who demonstrated at the end of September with Mūsā Aḥmad 'Antar and others, was sentenced to four months in prison; another, Muṣṭafā Yūsif, an ivory turner, probably originally from Aswan, was sentenced to two months for his participation in the demonstration of August 15. Others were found guilty on minor charges: Bashīr Na'īm, a Ja'ali butcher, who was at the demonstration of June 27 was given two months for throwing stones.[9] Workers also signed petitions, such as those sent after the arrest of Irrigation Department employee Muḥammad Sirr al-Khātim. These are of particular interest: 37 people signed one on 27 July, and a second, endorsed by 85 'Berberine', was sent at the beginning of August.[10] The Intelligence Department managed to trace the professions of the signatories; the records are particularly revealing. The petitions were signed mostly by artisans and wage-workers, including seven cooks, five servants, three small-scale merchants, one motor driver, and the owner of a coffee house. As one Intelligence Report noted, many wage-workers in occupations such as house servants and shopkeepers – but also artisans – belonged to the same broad group described by the British as 'Berberine', that is Nubians: 'Sirr el Khatm is said to be of a Berberin [sic] origin from Halfa, and all the servants of the British troops and others in Khartoum are of the same origin. Should Sirr el Khatm be convicted and sentenced, it is alleged that these latter people may try and do harm to the British.' [11]

The extent to which this participation was organized is unclear. Intelligence Department records mention a branch of the White Flag League called the Workmen's League. 'Alī Aḥmad Ṣāliḥ, the main British informant, was considered to be the leader of this association, and as such he is sometimes seen as a sort of proto-communist. In Bakhcit's words, he

[9] For 'Abd al-Raḥman Ḥassan: Gov. Khartoum Prov. to Private Secretary, Khartoum, 22.9.1924, Palace 4/10/48, NRO. For Muṣṭafā Yūsif: Corbyn to Private Secretary, Palace (Khartoum), 19.8.1924, Palace 4/10/48, NRO. For Bashīr Na'īm: SA to First Secretary, Residency, Ramleh, 13.7.1924, FO 141/806/1 NA; Baily, Gov. Khartoum Prov. to Civsec, 29.6.1924, Palace 4/10/49, NRO; Chronicle of the events during the period of political excitement in Khartoum, FO 141/805/2, NA.

[10] List of the signatories of the telegram against the imprisonment of Sirr El Khatim; Translation of attached telegram, Khartoum, 27.7.1924, Palace 4/10/49 and Petition by 85 signatories to Hakimam, Port Sudan, 4.8.1924, Palace 4/10/50, NRO. On the strike by the Irrigation Dept: Daily Bulletin, Gov. Khartoum Prov., 13 50 15.7.1924, Palace 4/10/50, NRO.

[11] Latest information regarding the movement of the White Flag League, Intel. Dept., Khartoum, 29.7.1924, FO 141/810/3, NA.

was a 'would-be trade union organizer'.[12] Another record describes him as being 'fond of Lenin'.[13] There was a rumour –still current – that he betrayed the League because the movement was not radical enough;[14] however, this does not match the colonial records, as the historian Nuri al-Amin has noted.[15] Although 'Alī Aḥmad Ṣāliḥ described himself as the leader of the Workmen's League, he never said much about the organization,[16] and yet, while he named others as members of the association, he added:

> If Ali Abdel Latif were not in prison, [the League] would by now have included the donkey-boys, the barbers, the tailors, the youth employed by shops, and everyone of the kind, and all these organisations would have been at the League's disposal for demonstration or anything. In proof of this some tailors are among those already arrested in the demonstration.[17]

For him, implicitly at least, the connection between the urban workers and 'Alī was that the latter was known to have worked as a donkey boy during his childhood; thus, even though he may have been an officer, his real background was in working-class Khartoum. Perhaps he was also implying that many workers had the same slave background as 'Alī, but that does not explain how then 'Alī Aḥmad Ṣāliḥ would have been appointed as the leader of the Workmen's League, as all the records about him indicate that he was of northern Sudanese origins.

The reliability of 'Alī Aḥmad Ṣāliḥ's statement may be in doubt, but there are good reasons for believing that the association existed. First, the League proceeded in analogy of the Egyptian revolution of 1919; and in Egypt, organized protests by wage-workers were an extremely important element of the uprising. Beinin and Lockman mention that by the end of 1919 'there were an estimated twenty-one unions functioning in Cairo, seventeen in Alexandria, and others in the Suez Canal cities, the Delta towns and elsewhere.'[18] The unions initiated waves of protests such as the Cairo tram strike of August 1919, which drew 15,000 workers. The parallel between the Wafd/unions and the White Flag League/Workmen's League was also drew comment from the Egyptian press: the journal *al-Muqaṭṭam* published an article on August 31 by 'Abd al-Raḥman Bey Fahmī, President of the 'General Union of the Labour Syndicate' in Egypt. He stated that

[12] Bakheit, 'British Administration and Sudanese Nationalism', p. 75, and Jaafar Muhammad Bakheit, *Communist Activities in the Middle East between 1919-1927, with Special Reference to Egypt and the Sudan* (Khartoum: Sudan Research Unit, Faculty of Arts, University of Khartoum, 1975), pp. 10-13.

[13] Maḥjūb 'Umar Bāshirī, *Ma'ālim al-Ḥaraka al-Waṭaniyya Fī al-Sūdān* (al-Khurṭūm: al-Maktaba al-Thaqāfiyya, 1996), p. 187.

[14] Mu'āwyyia Badrī, e-mail conversation, 22.10.2013.

[15] Mohammed Nuri El-Amin, 'A Leftist Labour Movement in the Sudan in the Early 1920s: Fact or Fiction?' *Middle Eastern Studies* (1984), vol. 20, n. 3, pp. 370-378. This article is a rebuttal of Bakheit's theory about the presence of communism in Sudan as early as the 1920s, but also includes a detailed analysis of the testimony of 'Alī Aḥmad Ṣāliḥ.

[16] For instance, in the *White Flag Trials*, p. 54: 'In White Flag League I represented the Labour party.'

[17] Confession, Ali Ahmed Saleh, p. 26, 24.08.1924, FO 141805/2, NA.

[18] Beinin and Lockman, *Workers on the Nile*, p. 119.

a Workers' League existed in Khartoum, and that it was 'a branch of the White Flag League, which was intended in due course to place at the disposal of the White Flag League all the local artisans and labourers and native craftsmen and traders, organized in Syndicates or Soviets of their own.'[19] Whatever the truth of this, the British authorities immediately became anxious. After the riots in Atbara, the demonstrations in Port Sudan, and those of the cadets and all the rest, a workers' movement would have been the last straw. Baily, the Deputy Governor of Khartoum, wrote in dismay at the end of August:

> The political movement under the White Flag League for the Unity of the Nile Valley under Egypt having failed, we are now threatened with a Syndicalist Labour movement on the worst Egyptian lines, attempting to unify the Nile Valley under cover of and by means of Labour Syndicates controlled from Cairo.[20]

On September 11, four people were arrested and accused of being the leaders of this branch.[21] They were 'Osta' [head artisan] Aḥmad, who was charged under Section 96 of the Sudan Penal Code on 'exciting disaffection'; tailor 'Abdallāh Rīḥān, who was charged with being the 'head of the Tailors syndicate'; Maḥmūd 'Guma', a grocer; and Mūsā Mirsāl, a workman at the *al-Ḥaḍāra* printing press.[22] Ten days later, on 21 September, a demonstration was attempted by coffee-shop owner Mūsā 'Antar and other workers.

Although these four were accused of being the heads of the Workmen's League, the existing fragmentary records suggest that the workers' organization was rather tentative and never evolved into anything elaborate. It seems the Workmen's League was the result of an attempt by some workers to get more organized, although there is no direct evidence. However, if this league was not particularly effective in the organization of workers' participation in protests, why and how were these actors mobilized?

First, networks existed between educated Sudanese and workers beyond their socio-professional differences and the different groups mingled to a large extent. Second, there was a sense of dissatisfaction among workers that the White Flag League managed to catalyse. They were so successful that when the League disbanded, the workers began acting *motu proprio*, demonstrating on their own account.

MEETING UP: COFFEE HOUSES AND MARKETS

Considering the paucity of the available sources, it is no easy task to discover exactly how nationalist ideas spread among workers, but more is known about where it took place. There were at least two locations where

19 Report from Gov., Khartoum, to DI, Khartoum, 31.8.1924, Palace 4/9/44, NRO.

20 Ibid.

21 Assistant DI to Private Secretary, Khartoum, 12.9.1924, Palace 4/10/48, NRO, re. the arrest of three people connected to the Workmen's branch.

22 Telegram, DI, Khartoum, to SA, Cairo, 13.9.1924, and another telegram, same senders, same date and place, about Aḥmad Sayyid, both in FO 141/805/2, NA.

government servants and workers met up and discussed politics: coffee houses and the market.

The relationship between coffee houses and radical politics has been noted elsewhere in the Middle East. In his study of Turkish coffee houses, Ozturk points out:

> ...coffeehouses had been male public spaces that enable the transgression of power configurations. They bridged social division by bringing together men of all social levels and lifestyles, offering ordinary people the opportunity to experience a way of life, outside the bazaar and the mosque, in a place whose boundaries had not been defined by one's duties to the family and God. And this social interaction encouraged discussion and subversive criticism of those in power.[23]

It is possible that this was the situation also in the colonial Sudan of the 1920s. The sources describe one particular coffee house in Khartoum, *Qahwat al-Halwānī* [Halwan's Café], owned by a certain Ḥusayn 'Abdūn. The café had been known to be 'political' since 1922. In 1924, after the arrest of Muḥammad Sirr al-Khātim, his colleagues, who were officers and employees of the Irrigation Department, were reported to meet there to discuss what to do in order to protest. When the authorities tried to find out more about the regulars at the café, they obtained a list of 28 names of people who were known to be the most loyal clients. The list also mentioned their professions, which included eight cooks, seven servants, a motor driver, a washer, and a merchant. Of the 28, therefore, 19 could be defined as small traders or salaried workers. But the list also included eight educated Sudanese who were employees of either Government Departments (the Civil Secretary's Office, the Financial Department, Irrigation, and *kuttāb* teachers) or private firms (Gellatly & Hankey and the Anglo-Egyptian Bank). The list shows that this café was a place where all levels of society met or mingled.[24]

The fluidity of social interactions in coffee houses is also indirectly confirmed in the interview of Mūsā Aḥmad 'Antar. Not much is known about this person except that he was himself the owner of a coffee house in the heart of Khartoum, in *sūq al-'arabī*. He recounted to his interviewers that he decided to demonstrate because his 'brothers' had been arrested. The 'brothers' he was referring to were (real brothers) 'Alī and Muḥammad Hādiyā.[25] Both had been educated in colonial schools and were government employees, the former in the Railways and Steamers Department in Khartoum, and the latter in the Customs Department in Port Sudan.[26] As

[23] Serdar Öztürk, 'The Struggle over Turkish Village Coffeehouses (1923–45)', *Middle Eastern Studies* (2008), vol. 44, n. 3, p. 435. See also Brian W Beeley, 'The Turkish Village Coffeehouse as a Social Institution', *Geographical Review* (1970), vol. 60, n. 4, pp. 475-493.

[24] 'List of gatherers in the coffee place of Hussein Abdun', Intelligence Information, Khartoum, 6.8.1924, Palace 4/10/50, NRO. Translation of information, Intel. Dept., 28.7.1924, Palace 4/10/49, NRO. 'Alī Aḥmad Ṣāliḥ mentioned that when 'Alī 'Abd al-Laṭīf knew that he would be arrested, he went to this café to write a telegram asking for the help of an Egyptian lawyer. In Confession, 20.8.1924, p. 9, FO 141/805/2, NA.

[25] *Al-Riwāyāt*, p. 452.

[26] Both names are in list of people arrested for the 1924 events, Northern Prov.,

Mūsā was apparently uneducated, it is likely that the brothers met him in his coffee house. One possible scenario is that he was approached by the brothers because he was known for his outspoken antipathy towards the British.

Finally, some activists' professions illustrate the proximity and fluidity of professional categories. Take 'Alī Aḥmad Ṣāliḥ, a man apparently illiterate. He worked first for the Survey Department, served as a soldier, returned to government job, and finally worked in a private printing press.[27] He was a polyvalent figure who does not fit any of the categories seen above, occupying a position somewhere between 'Effendi' and artisan.[28]

Generally, most anticolonial political meetings were held in private homes, where decisions were taken and tasks assigned. For example, Mūsā recounts that he attended meetings such as these, was given leaflets to distribute in the markets, and that he was 'very famous in *sūq al-'arabī*' for this reason.[29] House meetings were secret, however, and were quite highly charged, especially after the movement passed to open action. People could be discovered and arrested. They took place at night and a witness recounts that on one occasion members had to climb the wall at the back of the house in darkness to avoid being discovered.[30] Coffee houses, on the other hand, were places where politically-minded people shared their leisure time, where politics could only be discussed *sotto voce*, in the form of conversations that lay somewhere 'between seriousness and amusement', as Ḥassan Najīla put it. People did share information there, but the atmosphere was different from that of the nocturnal meetings.

Coffee houses should not be confused with places such as the 'home of Fawz', which was a private guest room. Here, people not only recited poems, sang music, and talked about politics, but also drank alcohol, usually forbidden in coffee houses.[31] Such guest rooms were similar to coffee houses in that they were the location of transgression, but not where strangers from different social groups would get to know each other.

Of course, cafés were not the only places of interaction between the small elite of educated Sudanese and the rest of the population. There were several others, such as the market. Aḥmad Mudaththir al-Būshī recounted in his interview: '...when I passed through the market I used to sit in front of the shops and talk about the new ideas. People were used to talk about such things; we were very enthusiastic.'[32] Similarly, an Intelligence Department report underlines that workers in the market were also active in the circulation of political ideas, as in this example taken from El Obeid,

(contd) 1/21/207, NRO. For 'Alī, see List of Govt. Officials arrested (in relation to their suspension of pay) Gov. Khartoum Prov., to Civsec, Khartoum, 4.10.1924, Palace 4/9/46, NRO.

27 See his full curriculum vitae in Appendix H dated 23.6.24, in C.A. Willis, 'The League of the White Flag', Khartoum, 20.7.1924, FO 141.810.3, NA.

28 See also his series of statements in FO 141/805/2 and in *The White Flag Trials*.

29 *Al-Riwāyāt*, p. 457.

30 Al-Sayyid, *Al-Liwā' al-Abyaḍ*, p. 20-21, where 'Abd al-Karīm recounts in detail the material and psychological complications of these nocturnal meetings.

31 Najīla, *Malāmiḥ Min al-Mujtama' al-Sūdānī*, p. 150.

32 *Al-Riwāyāt*, p. 74.

about a certain Khalīl Fahmī 'Saati'[33] – a watch repairer, as his name indicates:

> [he] is a member of the club and talks against the govt. and abuses the British. Whoever goes to him to repair a watch, he gives him a seat and talks politics. Every day he meets the travelling postmaster and asks him about demonstrations in Khartoum, then next day he published [sic] that demonstrations took place in Medani, Sennar.[34]

Socially, the gap between wage-workers and 'Effendi' was not so wide. The difference between the best paid clerical jobs and the worst paid unskilled jobs was a hair's breadth. We have seen that the majority of educated Sudanese had at best only completed primary school, and were assigned tasks for the most part subordinate and technical. A qualified artisan could earn almost double the pay of a man educated at primary school and at the beginning of his career. In 1924, in the Special Primary Grade – the starting grade of those who had not completed primary school – the salary was 48 LE per annum. In contrast, for certain skilled workers, such as electricians, the figure for 1922 was 72 LE.[35] To understand this discrepancy, some background on labour practices in the main urban centres of Northern Sudan up to the 1920s is required.

THE LABOUR QUESTION IN SUDAN UP TO 1924

There is a familiar paradigm in the historiography of colonial Sudan that associates wage labour with slaves and ex-slaves. Whether 'free' or 'hired-out' workers, slaves progressively obtained their freedom by seizing opportunities that opened up with the development of the economy and Sudan's integration with international markets. The most important study is Sikainga's *Slaves into Workers*, a remarkable account of the transformation of slave labour into a wage-earning force. However, this reading of the process of emancipation has had the effect of tying the question of slavery to the labour issue, identifying workers with people from a slave background.[36] Although Sikainga's fine study casts light on the composite nature of the labour force, his work has been interpreted as a confirmation of this paradigm. Furthermore, the association between labour and slavery becomes all the easier to make because of a widespread perception that 'manual' labour in Sudan means 'slave' labour, and that

33 Probably *al-sā'atī*, an Arabic construction that can be translated as 'of the watch'.
34 Extract from report of no. 34, Intel. Dept., undated, Kordofan 1/12/47, NRO.
35 Assistant Director of Education to DI, Khartoum, 10.12.1924, Intel 1/11/50, NRO. It is worth remembering here that, according to a sample of pay dated March 1922, an electrician earned 72 LE per annum, and an apprentice electrician between 48 and 36 LE. A 'sanitaryman' earned about half what an SPG did (26.4), and a 'car driver' 42 LE, Civsec2 39/8/7, NRO. See Table 14, p. 201.
36 This is a very common assumption. For instance, in the work by Daly, *Empire on the Nile*, the paragraph entitled 'Labour 1899-1919' covers only the question of slave labour and emancipation (pp. 231-239).

'Arabs' have a 'cultural' distaste for such work.[37] From another perspective, because workers were people of slave background, they were thus a marginal and marginalized group in society.

The problems with this approach are manifold. First, being of slave descent did not automatically imply socio-economic marginalization. Second, this approach equates wage-workers and urban poor; and third, it takes for granted that slaves and ex-slaves were the major component of the emerging Sudanese working class. Of course, the situation was more complicated.

Labour problems

Among the various colonial debates on how the economic development of Sudan should be steered, one issue stood out: the scarcity of wage-workers and the high cost of labour.

In the 1920s, it had been a sore point for years, as discussed in the economic section of the Annual Reports of the Sudan Government since the beginning of the Condominium. This should come as no surprise, given the overall economic development of Sudan. Its economy relied entirely on the export of agricultural, animal, and natural products: cattle, gum arabic, sorghum, and cotton (although this last was not as important as it would become after implementation of the Gezira agricultural scheme, mid-1920s onwards). The expansion in exports between the time of the establishment of the Condominium and the Great War was dramatic. As Wingate solemnly noted in 1910, 'the Sudan may seem to stand at the threshold of a new era.'[38] In the period 1906-1913 alone, the total amount of exports multiplied five times, from 197,950 LE to 1,007,494 LE.[39] According to British estimates, land under cultivation expanded from 529,239 acres in 1904 to 2,303,000 in 1913. Although the figures may be somewhat inflated, there was a significant increase in agricultural production.

Land was plentiful in Sudan; that was not a problem. The real issue was labour. In the same period in which exports multiplied by five, the population of Sudan increased only by three, from two to six million, although such demographic data must be viewed with caution.[40] Moreover, during this period, there were no substantial improvements in agricultural technology, so that to produce more, one had to hire more hands. Slave labour was also scarce, as witnessed by the fact that it was more profitable for owners to 'hire out' their slaves than to use them on their own land.[41]

[37] One of the first articles to expound this hypothesis was P. F. M McLoughlin, 'Economic Development and the Heritage of Slavery in the Sudan Republic', *Africa* (1962), vol. 32, n. 4, pp. 355-391. This discussion has been routinely debated by authors studying wage labour in both rural and urban areas. For the debate, see also: Jay O'Brien, 'Agricultural Labour Force and Development in the Sudan' (PhD dissertation, University of Connecticut, 1980).

[38] *Sudan Govt. Annual Report 1910*, p. 65.

[39] *Sudan Govt. Annual Reports*, 1906 to 1913.

[40] In 1905, the population estimate was 1,853,000 (*Sudan Govt. Annual Reports 1905*:195); in 1924, it had risen to 6,000,000: Intel. Dept., Annual Report 1924, WO 33/999, NA.

[41] Sikainga, *Slaves into Workers*; Taj Hargey, 'Festina Lente: Slavery Policy and

Agriculture was not the only sector in need of labour: so was the State. Schools, hospitals, residences for British officials, and the *markaz*, or municipal building, had to be reconstructed. Khartoum itself had been razed to the ground by the Mahdi's troops. Commercial infrastructure – the railway system, the city of Port Sudan, and later the dams for the Gezira irrigation scheme had to be developed. Thus the two decades between 1900 and 1920 were a period during which the State was in dire need of manpower.

The combination of the needs of both private and public employers led to a labour crisis, in which the salaries of wage-workers continued to rise. The 1904 Annual Report had already foreseen these problems; the Annual Report of 1905 confirmed that 'the rates of wage have risen everywhere and the demand ... is greater than the supply.'[42] The increase provoked a chorus of complaints, not only because it was a serious obstacle to 'sound' economic development, but also because wages were deemed 'unnaturally' high. In 1908, during the peak season, a man could earn an average of between 90 and 100 pt. a month (100 pt.= 1LE), while in colonial documents his expenses were described to be as low as 10 to 15 pt. a month.[43] Salaries in rural areas were even higher during peak seasons than they were in urban centres: one report from 1909 observed that despite the 600-1000 men applying for a job at the Central Labour Bureau,

> There is, however, considerable difficulty in inducing any of them to accept 3½ piastres a day ... Meanwhile, 60 miles south, native cultivators are offering, unsuccessfully, anything from 5-10 pt. to attract labourers for a few days' work on their crops which will otherwise be ruined.[44]

Wages were highest where competition for labourers between private landowners and the state was the sharpest. Importing foreign labourers had always been thought of as a last resort, however, one which should not be encouraged over the long term. This is why, for instance, the government made occasional use of labour gangs from Egypt during construction of the Nile dams, with the intention that they would return home immediately after. Before the Great War, the Red Sea Province set an all-time record for wage levels, because Port Sudan could not function without workers, and in a situation of scarcity labour costs soared.[45] Wages could be as high as 12 pt. a day during the agricultural season, compared to the average for the rest of the country of 3-5 pt. a day.[46] In other words, if an unskilled man worked in Port Sudan every day, he would earn something like 43.2 LE a year – half of what an officer in the Egyptian Army who had graduated from the Military School earned in a

(contd) Practice in the Anglo-Egyptian Sudan', *Slavery & Abolition* (1998), vol. 19, n. 2, pp. 250–72.

42 *Sudan Govt. Annual Report, 1904*, p. 116 and *Sudan Govt. Annual Report, 1905*, p. 195.

43 Draft for the GG Annual Report for 1908, Labour, Intel 4/4/29, NRO.

44 Report on the Labour Bureau, 1909, Intel 4/3/15, NRO.

45 See the whole file: Intel 4/7/54, Wages of labour at Port Sudan, NRO.

46 Report of the Labour Bureau, 1911, Rates of Wages, Intel 4/3/15, NRO.

year. In reality, this never happened because workers rarely stayed in the city all the year round.

For the colonial administrators, the critical situation was due not to a lack of workers, but to the fact that 'the sources of supply have not yet been fully opened up.'[47] To be more precise, for the British the real cause of the situation was a reluctance on the part of hired-out and freed slaves to carry out their roles as workers. The government responded to this in 1905 by creating an institution known as the Central Labour Bureau (CLB) to work as a platform for connecting supply in the labour market with demand. Its strategy was to force 'Sudanese servants' into work. This generalized category included both slaves and ex-slaves, as the term 'slave' was banned in official documents because this status had been legally abolished since the beginning of the Condominium.[48] The rationale was that, once freed, ex-slaves, accustomed to being forced to work by their masters, would not know what to do with their freedom and would have spent their time being idle. Masterless 'Sudanese servants' were to be registered by the CLB and kept in readiness, to be sent off wherever there was a need for labourers. If a 'registered Sudanese' refused to work, he could be arrested as a vagrant.[49]

This scheme turned out very differently from how it had been conceived, however, and worked to only a very limited extent. Registration was launched and ended up including several thousand 'Sudanese', but apparently it only helped, rather than forced, ex-slaves to work. Registered Sudanese moved quite freely from one employer to the other, enjoyed good earnings, and used the CLB as a *de facto* employment agency. By 1921, the authorities had completely lost track of these 'Soudanese' but concluded that they had settled down and augmented Sudan's 'artisan' class. The text is worth quoting for its vagueness:

> The old registration scheme shows about 7000 registered labourers. We have no means of knowing where they are but they are presumably somewhere and they are for most part of the artisan class and it is at any rate some sort of a figure as a basis for the number of artisan labour available in the country.[50]

The composite nature of the labour force

When the CLB registration scheme was launched, many government officials were highly perplexed. In 1913, the Governor of the Red Sea asked why it was only applicable to 'registered Sudanese' if its objective was to stabilize the work force and turn 'vagabonds' into workers, offering the comment that 'most of the vagabonds and idle persons in this province' were 'Danaqla, Shaigi, and the like'. He asked for a clearer definition of the word 'Sudanese workers', and suggested that the scheme be extended to 'Arabs.' The Director of the Intelligence responded hurriedly that the word 'Sudanese' 'simply' meant 'Blacks', apparently seriously thinking that in Sudan – literally the 'land of the Blacks' – this would clarify the

47 *Sudan Govt. Annual Report, 1905*, p. 196.

48 Memorandum on the agricultural labour condition in the Anglo-Egyptian Sudan, 1910, Intel 4/4/29, NRO.

49 Hargey, 'The Suppression of Slavery in the Sudan', pp. 227-248.

50 CA Willis to Huddleston, 31.1.1921, Intel 4/1/7, NRO.

matter. He also opined that 'any forced registration of Arabs would be unfavourable and at the same time hard to put into operation.'[51] Colonial discussions such as this were frequent – colonial officers were desperate to find solutions to labour problems – and at least they have the merit of casting light on the complex question of labour and capturing a process that saw an increasing number of actors becoming wage-workers.

During the years between 1910 and 1913, when labour problems were at their height, the labour reports attempted to track down the main sources of labour to be tapped. Three were mentioned on a regular basis: Sudanese, Western African immigrants – the so-called Fellata – and Arabs. Each of these groups was described by certain characteristics that were considered 'natural' for their 'race' and 'culture':

> The Arabs: a migratory population, most of them owners of and connected with land, who visit the towns for short periods to earn some money and return to their villages, a percentage of them, mostly belonging to the Baggara tribes form the West, are now regular labourers and remain in the towns. ...
>
> The Sudanese ... form a more sedentary population, moving about occasionally in search of work, most of them are ex-slaves, adapt themselves readily to urban existence, and show no strong inclination to return to their own districts. They are the unskilled 'work-men' of the Sudan, and excellent manual labourers when the wish of the moment or the rare pressure of necessity induces them to labour. The women works as well as the men, and are employed on light earth-shifting, water carrying, etc., but at slightly lower wages.
>
> The Fellata ... They are a thrifty hard-working people, willing to work for small wages, though not expert agriculturalists or capable of heavy manual labour, they are willing to learn and are said to be excellent cotton pickers, especially the women.[52]

Several other reports confirm the multiple sources of labour. The Governor of the White Nile reported that the labourers hired for public works in his province, a total of 641 men, were two-thirds 'Sudanese', most of whom were slaves hired out by their masters, and one-third 'riverain Arabs'.[53] In other areas, the percentage was reversed; for instance, in the private estates of Khartoum Province, 70% of labourers were 'riverine Arabs'.[54] British officers noted that Hadendowa pastoralists from Eastern Sudan 'proved so satisfactory that they will be used for work on the Shendi-Khartoum section of the [railway] line.'[55] Hadendowa workers in Port Sudan were well known for their skills in bridge construction. The 1908 Annual Report noted the migration of people from the Rashayda and 'Abadba – two pastoralist groups from along the Red Sea Hills – to Berber Province to work on agricultural schemes, and remarked on the migration of Ta'aysha from south-eastern Darfur to the White Nile: 'These Taaisha are almost alone among the Arabs of this province in the enterprise they

[51] Assistant Gov. Red Sea Prov., to Assistant DI, 13.7.1913, Intel 4/1/6, NRO. And Assistant DI to Assistant Gov. Red Sea Prov., 10.8.1913, Intel 4/1/6, NRO.

[52] Memorandum on the agricultural labour in the Sudan, undated, unsigned, but from previous correspondence datable to 1910, Intel 4/4/29, NRO.

[53] Gov. White Nile Prov. to Assistant DI, Dueim, 16.11.1911, Intel 4/3/15, NRO.

[54] Report of the Labour Bureau 1911, Riverain estate labour supply, Intel 4/3/15, NRO.

[55] *Sudan Govt. Annual Report, 1908*, p. 103.

show in going to Khartoum where they work until they have earned enough money to purchase a few cattle... Their example is also followed by the Homr, another Baggara tribe.'[56] Thus, even though these types of worker hardly constituted a stable labour force, and their availability was rather unpredictable, they were sufficiently significant to merit a yearly mention in the labour reports of the time.

This plurality is well reflected in the records of the 1924 Revolution. Reports by the Intelligence Department do not reveal a clear association among wage-workers, small artisans and former slaves; if there was one, it cannot be evinced from the activists' personal files. In Khartoum, for instance, of the 51 people 'seen' by the Intelligence Department who might be defined as 'workers and small artisans', only the origins of 21 people are known. These include three Egyptians, seven 'Muwalladīn,' five Ja'aliyyin, a Furawi, a 'Harbabi', an 'Elegi' (probably from near Merowe), two defined as 'Black Sudanese,' and one 'Berberine.'[57]

Records depicting the labour situation in urban centres again confirm the multiple origins of workers – in particular in Khartoum and Port Sudan, but also Kassala and Gedarif, Tokar, Wad Medani, and Atbara – the most important centres for skilled and semi-skilled labourers and artisans. These centres were the preferred destinations for migrants in search of work. Precise figures on urban migration are unavailable, with only a few exceptions. For instance, in the Khartoum Province Report in 1913, of the 4,439 new inhabitants of Omdurman in a single year, only 1,369, or about 30%, were attributed to births.[58] Although it is difficult to ascertain the margin of error in the birth rate and the population census, the impact made by immigration is clear.[59] Centres such as Khartoum and Port Sudan were magnets for migrant wage labour. This is witnessed by the names of working class neighbourhoods. In both Khartoum and Port Sudan, some of the *deims* were named according to both the ethnic groups that had originally inhabited them, such as *Deim Banda* or *Deim Berti Niala*, and the occupations of those who settled in them: for example, both cities had a neighbourhood called *Deim Telegraf*.[60] However, migrant workers hardly satisfied the demand for labour. As late as 1921, the Labour Bureau remarked that the numbers of all categories of workers, including the most expensive, skilled artisans, were insufficient for all needs: 'Considerably

56 *Sudan Govt. Annual Report, 1908*: on Berber, p. 472; on White Nile, p. 672.

57 Sources: Palace 4/9/44, Palace 4/10/46, Palace 4/10/47, Palace 4/10/48, Palace 4/10/49, Palace 4/11/55, Kordofan 1/13/62, Northern Prov. 1/21/207, Northern Prov. 1/21/215. NA: FO 141/806/1, FO 141/810/3, FO 141/805/2, FO 141/669/8.

58 *Khartoum Province Annual Report, 1913*, pp. 126 and 156-157.

59 Sikainga, *Slaves into Workers*, pp. 76-81. See also Saad Ed Din Fawzi, *The Labour Movement in the Sudan, 1946-1955* (London, New York: Oxford University Press, 1957).

60 Sikainga, *Slaves into Workers*, p. 80. It does not seem, however, that there was a correspondence between a person's origins and the place where he or she lived. For example, the *osta* Aḥmad Sayyid of whom I wrote above, and who had grown up in Cairo, apparently lived in *deims al-nuba,* even though his forefathers were apparently Dinka. Confession of Ali Ahmed Saleh, p. 25, 24.08.1924, FO 141805/2, NA.

more labour would be employed in the Khartoum District if it were available, but there are no signs of its being forthcoming to any extent.'[61]

The final misconception is that 'Sudanese' only took jobs that 'Arabs' refused to do. This was perhaps the situation in Khartoum in 1930. According to Sikainga, the most degrading jobs, such as sewage work, were taken by Nuba.[62] This had not always been the case, however, as the 1912 Report of the Sanitary Commission of Khartoum noted with regard to precisely the same jobs:

> Most of the old Sudanese ex-soldier labourers are dead, or are no longer fit for work, and have to be replaced by young Arabs. ... The work is very hard, but wages are good, and these Arabs ... have overcome their aversion to the unclean nature of the work, as they can save up, in about a year's time, sufficient to allow them to return to their homes as wealthy men.[63]

This extract is also interesting because it highlights why people became workers: during this period, occasional salaried work offered the possibility of more rapid upward mobility to which workers would not have had access had they remained in their villages. By taking on these jobs, a young man could earn money fast enough to return home, marry and settle down, but they also instilled a habit among the early workers of going off to search for work every time a financial difficulty, like a failed harvest or drought, had to be overcome.

Strikes and negotiations

The scarcity of labour made the first wage labourers a relatively privileged group. During the first 25 years of colonial rule, workers had relatively strong negotiating powers, and they made good use of them. There must have been many ways in which labourers struggled for better working conditions, but two reactions held the attention of the British authorities: the volatility of the labour force and strikes.

According to the various labour reports, salaried workers mostly chose their employers based on the salary and working conditions offered. What is more, they had no hesitation in leaving from one day to the next if their demands were not met, and as a result, salaries continued to increase. This was a particularly successful strategy during harvest time, when a threat to down tools left an employer with little choice but to offer a raise in pay. As an example, just one among many, a British official complained bitterly in 1921 of his problems with the 2,285 Sudanese labourers allocated by the Central Labour Bureau to work for a private employer. Of these 2,285 men, only 241 accepted the pay scale proposed by the employer, which was 6 pt. per day; another 691 were paid at a higher rate because they were skilled workers; and 'the remaining 1,352 labourers refused absolutely to work at this rate', and left.[64]

[61] Report of the Labour Committee 1921, p. 22-25, Intel 4/4/19, NRO.

[62] Sikainga, *Slaves into Workers*, pp. 124-125.

[63] 'Annual Report of the chief sanitary inspector for the year ending 30th September 1923', p. 31, in *Report on the Health and Sanitation of Khartoum, Khartoum-North and Omdurman*, Dept. Reports 9/4/33, NRO.

[64] (Letter from) Y. Cantonis to M. Pizzigalli, 13.9.1921, Intel 4/2/9, NRO.

When workers did not succeed in negotiating better conditions, they were ready to strike. Labourers did so from very early on in the Condominium period, and often. Colonial sources mostly describe the strikes that involved government-sponsored enterprises, but from their frequency and the fearlessness of the workers when it came to abandoning even closely-monitored colonial operations, one might well assume that the practice was widespread. Sikainga reports that as early as 1903, the men working for the Forest Department went on strike, as did the workers on the Fadlab agricultural estate in 1909.[65] In the same year, 40 workers on the Kamlin estate came out for an increase in pay or shorter working hours.[66] They were all dismissed, but this did not prevent other labourers working on construction of the engine house at the Kamlin farm to go on strike again. In 1910, labourers sent by the Central Labour Bureau from Khartoum to the Tayiba experimental farm, a government-run agricultural estate, went on strike because they were given dirty grain for food. The following year, the Tayiba workers walked out again, but this time the authorities lost their patience and sent the Camel Corps to persuade them to return to work.[67] There were also strikes as a show of solidarity with fellow-workers who had not been treated fairly; for instance, in Kamlin in 1909, the entire workforce downed tools in solidarity with a colleague who had been dismissed for repeated absence.[68]

Even in Port Sudan, the city with the highest wage levels, strikes took place on several occasions. In his work on colonial Port Sudan, Kenneth Perkins narrates in detail the history of labour negotiations in 1912, when Beja workers struck in protest against the use of Yemeni labourers. In retaliation, the Inspector of Port Sudan first dismissed 30 men, and then tried to imprison four others for vagrancy. This tactic failed, and shortly thereafter there was another strike at the docks. Eventually, the authorities had to accept the demands of the workers for increased wages to keep the harbour functioning.[69]

To conclude, the significant participation of workers in nationalist protests can be read at the light of their relatively prosperous situation in this period of colonial history, when labour was plentiful and salaries quite high. Workers were confident of finding employment, and were able to change their employer if they found a better offer. At least some of them had land and a community to which they could return if things turned out badly, and were therefore relatively confident that participation in protests would neither lead to the end of their working life nor a stop in their careers, contrary to the case of officers and civil servants.

65 Sikainga, *Slaves into Workers*, p. 90.

66 Extract form the Blue Nile Prov. diary for the month of May 1909, Intel 4/3/15, NRO.

67 Sikainga, *Slaves into Workers*, pp. 90-91.

68 Extract from the Blue Nile Prov. Diary for the month of May 1909, Intel 4/3/15, NRO.

69 Kenneth J. Perkins, *Port Sudan: The Evolution of a Colonial City State, Culture, and Society in Arab North Africa* (Boulder: Westview Press, 1993), pp. 70-1.

ON WORKERS AND NATIONALISM

At the start of this chapter, the question of why the 'masses' came to participate in White Flag League demonstrations was raised. True, it should be said that if the word 'masses' signifies the participation of hundreds of thousands of people – which is difficult to imagine in a country with low urbanization levels, where the largest urban conglomeration, the Three Towns, counted 40,000 inhabitants, and where women were not politically mobilized – then indeed 1924 did not draw the masses. According to British estimates, the largest demonstrations brought out perhaps 2–3,000 participants. But this insurgency was also an uprising of the unskilled worker, the *sūq* merchant, or the artisan, and as such the 1924 revolution was a revolution of the masses. Even though the participation of the common people was overlooked – and if recorded, usually denigrated – they were there at each demonstration. Eventually, when most of the 'Effendi' had been sent to prison and the League had stopped to support demonstrations, they continued to demonstrate alone. Indeed, the common people represented the majority of the protesters of 1924, and actually made the revolution happen. There is no better description of 1924 as a popular revolution than that of al-'Āzza, the wife of 'Alī 'Abd al-Laṭīf:

> Next morning a big demonstration occurred.... [A] woman, one of our neighbours, went to the market and told me that the whole market was upside down and all the market was in demonstration.... My mother and I wanted to go and see what was happening, so we went to the market, and it was completely something new, because the butcher was shouting and the greengrocer was shouting. We followed them until they reached the headquarters of the District Commissioner. They used to spray hot water on the demonstrators from hose pipes. People started to run, and I was asking—what is going on, what is there? One of them, whose name was Bābikr, said to me, what do you want to understand, the revolution is coming out of your house and you still want to understand.[70]

Far from being a weak and marginalized category, labourers were in this period of history more able to control their conditions of work than they would be later. Because the labour force did not to satisfy Sudan's need at this time, and because most of the workers were migrants who were ready to move to meet the best offer, they had fairly wide room to manoeuvre in negotiating adequate working conditions. The situation allowed a part of this group to accumulate capital and reinvest it, and to realize a certain upward social mobility, both for themselves and for their descendants.

Two stories show different aspects of this situation. The first is that of *osta* Aḥmad Sayyid. The judicial records note that he was a Sudanese 'Black' raised in Cairo. Arrested in Wadi Halfa on his return from leave in Egypt, he was accused of being the head of the Workmen's League. He was employed by the Public Works Department workshops as head artisan. His son was 'Abd al-Qādir Aḥmad Sayyid, an early member of the White Flag League; he carried the League's flag during the demonstration of June 23; and was subsequently imprisoned for six months. 'Abd al-Qādir had been

[70] *Al-Riwāyāt*, pp. 385–86. Al-'Āzza states that this was before the demonstration by the Cadets, which was held on August 8, but it is likely that she is referring to the large demonstration of August 15.

primary school educated, then worked for a while as a clerk in a mercantile company. Subsequently he ran a shop in the *deims*, the working-class neighbourhood south of Khartoum, which his father had bought him.[71] Thus, not only his father could afford to send him to primary school, but he could also make an investment to 'settle down' his son. The second example is that of Nafīsa Surūr, the girl who sewed the cadets' flag. Her mother was described as a washerwoman at the Khartoum civil hospital; Nafīsa's family was therefore much less advantaged than families such as that of 'Alī 'Abd al-Laṭīf, as it can be evinced from the fact that al-'Āzza, the wife of 'Alī 'Abd al-Laṭīf, never worked until her death, and this despite the fact that her husband spent the rest of his life confined. Yet, Nafīsa's family was able to purchase their own house in the centre of Omdurman.[72]

However, workers lacked visibility and recognition, particularly at a political level. They could negotiate their salaries, change their employers, but they were not entitled to a voice in the various colonial initiatives on labour, trade, or economic reforms, not to mention wider political issues. For instance, Sudanese workers were not consulted on how to steer an institution such as the Central Labour Bureau. 'Sudanese servants' learnt how to make use of it to find work, but had no influence on the way it was shaped. As for wider issues, politics at the time was simply not conceived as an arena in which men of 'little education' might participate. Uneducated, employed in manual jobs, far from government channels, with few contacts with the 'powerful,' they were considered as the lowest social order not only by the British authorities, but also by local notables. They were the diametrical opposite to the class that the British were prepared to admit into the political arena. While economic development brought wealth, this alone was not sufficient to secure any change in their status.

The White Flag League was the first political movement in Sudan to realize the importance of integrating this group. As seen, workers were involved in the activities of the League early on and extensively: they were included in the leadership of the movement, asked to swear the oath of the League, chosen to lead demonstrations and spread anticolonial leaflets. And so they did. It is possible to argue that the alliance of this group with the White Flag League was particularly meaningful for both. On its part, the League was seeking to create a broad social alliance, and, following the example of Egypt, its leaders believed that any political victory had to involve the masses. On the other hand, skilled and unskilled workers found a framework within the League's nationalist message in which to express their own grievances. Here, the League was especially successful,

71 'Notes on person arrested in connection with recent demonstration' in Khartoum, 23.6.1924, FO 141/810/3, NA; DI to More, SA, 3.7.1924, FO 141/806/1, NA.

72 For *osta* Aḥmad and his son: (Telegram, unsigned), Khartoum to High Commissioner of Egypt, Cairo, 13.9.1924, FO 141/805/2, NA; 'Notes on person arrested in connection with recent demonstration,' Khartoum, 23.6.1924. FO 141/810/3, NA; Report from Gov., Khartoum to DI, 16.9.1924, Kordofan 1/13/62, NRO. For Nafīsa Surūr: Confession, Ali Ahmed Saleh, 1.8.1924, p. 14, FO 141/805/3, NA. Nothing is said about her background in her interview in *Al-Riwāyāt*: 467-488.

in that it managed to give a shape, means and purpose to the workers' issues and their desire for recognition. This in turn affected the way in which the workers saw themselves, as actors in a collective struggle, and as a part of what was now imagined as the Sudanese nation.

CONCLUSION TO PART FOUR

These fragments of narrative on the participation of workers in 1924 – more a story of what is not known than the contrary – also calls for reflections on a quite different issue: the historian's gaze. Why this aspect of 1924 is so persistently overlooked in the historical narratives? This in turn leads to the problem of the 'story of the story', and to Trouillot's question about the various moments in which silence affects the processes of historical production.

The contemporary archives reveal not only the way colonial rulers saw Sudanese society, but also how they attempted to shape it. Well before the official inauguration of the doctrine of Indirect Rule, first in its 'mild' form, with the Lee Stack Dual Policy, and then much more decisively after 1924 with Civil Secretary Harold MacMichael, the colonial government ruled by proxy. The authority of the state was asserted through men who had been selected on the basis of their willingness to collaborate with the colonial state and by their community's recognition as leaders. For the British, however, a leader's legitimacy, at least in Northern Sudan, was determined by blood, family prestige and religious and literary reputation. Indeed, the main difference between the native policy before the First World War and Indirect Rule was a matter of intensity: more powers were devolved, and shaykhs were sought more systematically in each community, including urban centres.[73]

The archives are, therefore, much richer with information about urban and rural notables and religious personalities than any other social group. Offices such as the Intelligence Department produced numerous and lengthy files describing histories, family trees, connections and relational networks of religious, rural, and urban notables.[74] This information reveals

[73] A description of Indirect Rule in Daly, *Empire on the Nile*, pp. 360-379; on a specific case, see Willis, 'Tribal Gatherings: Colonial Spectacle, Native Administration and Local Government'; on the question of legal devolution: Sachs, '"Native Courts" and the Limits of the Law in Colonial Sudan: Ambiguity as Strategy.' Finally, the description of Indirect Rule by one of its main defenders: Harold A. MacMichael, *The Anglo-Egyptian Sudan* (London: Faber and Faber, 1934), pp. 233-257.

[74] The file series 'Intelligence' in the National Record Office is particularly rich. But see also, the 'Handbook of the Gezira' (Civsec1 57/37/138, NRO), which is a

an attempt to acquire an intimate knowledge of this group and of their alliances, tensions, and rifts. Furthermore, it was a way of anticipating reactions and acquiring informed opinions on policies to be tested and difficult decisions to be made. This is clear from 1924: when the initial disturbances occurred, the Director of Intelligence immediately sought the advice of *sayyid* 'Abd al-Raḥman al-Mahdī and *sayyid* 'Alī al-Mīrghanī. By controlling the top echelons, the British hoped to keep a hold on society as a whole. The notables were the only political interlocutors that the British were prepared to listen to, besides the tentative attempts of Lee Stack to create a young, educated class of nationalists.

This is the narrative that emerges from the colonial archive, but anything that lies outside the bright light cast by the political interests of the colonial government is more difficult to fathom. However, it is precisely in these shadows that a historian can discover some of the causes that led to the 1924 Revolution.

The pieces of the puzzle finally come together to reveal that the changes that were set in motion by colonialism mined the very system of rule by proxy and co-optation that the British rulers considered to be the key to successful colonization. There were two reasons for this: first, the expansion of Sudan's economy, the construction of the basic infrastructures required for the state to function, and second, the need to administer and defend Sudan, all of which set up a chain reaction that evaded state control. This is most evident in the case of the working class, whose salaries continued to increase, at least during the period under discussion. Those were processes that no state initiative could control.

The second reason is that colonial theory was roundly defeated by praxis, as in the case of colonial education, which was intended to reinforce existing hierarchies, thereby offering a further layer of legitimacy – education – to the notable families through which the British ruled by proxy. In practice, however, the school created an educated elite that had quite different interests, and a quite dissimilar composition, from the elite of descent, the so-called 'notables'.

The final point is that while the colonial archive offers one view of the state of society, it must not be confused with the vision that various social groups had of themselves and their own position and the way in which the state acted towards these hierarchies. There were evident gaps in perception. As discussed, the government selected pupils from the primary school level based in part on their origins. However, the existence of a racial quota in the Education Department's statistics can be only inferred by historians with figures in hand, and was never openly claimed or declared by the authorities. Moreover, the government's racial classifications lacked consistency, so that it is difficult to assess the extent to which people understood that they were being selected by race. In the Egyptian army, officers of slave descent were able to reach the highest administrative positions opened to Sudanese. As seen, Sudanese

(*contd*) Who's Who list of all the heads of the various communities and hamlets, not only in the Gezira Province, but also in Khartoum and Tuti Island, and the Blue Nile Province.

who were rejected at the secondary school level believed the reason was political, and had no inkling that it was due to their origins.

Thus, while British colonial officers were busy writing up the genealogies of the notables, a rich, yet barely recorded array of social unfolding was under way. This lack of visibility must also be seen as a consequence of the discrepancy between what the colonial government wanted for the Sudanese society and therefore was able to record, and what was actually happening. A historian can only track these changes through dedication and effort, by piecing together archival fragments, thrown into a constant state of uncertainty and doubt because the fragments contrast so markedly with the way in which Northern Sudanese Society is perceived today. These fragments describe 'black' Sudanese being educated in colonial schools together with 'Berberine' and Egyptians; descendants of slaves securing the best jobs; unskilled wage-workers getting high salaries, and yet demanding more rights and finally – and most famously – a 'black' being selected as leader of a political movement by friends from well-established Northern Sudanese families.

Nationalist narratives shaped an ideological framework that was partially lost after the revolution; in that version of nationalism, people had to 'be united like brothers', everybody belonged to the Sudanese nation, and this identity encompassed all manner of social, religious and ethnic differences.[75]

[75] 'A Call to the Sudanese Generally and to the Natives of Kordofan, Invocation of God,' signed by the Head of the Society of El Helal, Omdurman/El Obeid, 17.8.1924, FO 141/805/2, NA.

11

The Colonial Gaze, History and the Archive[1]

> Professional historians alone do not set the narrative framework into which their stories fit. Most often, someone else has already entered the scene and set the cycle of silences.[2]

Given its logic of accumulation, the archive would appear to be a location where knowledge of the past is safely stored. The very existence of a state archive, such as the colonial one, gives the historian the impression that continuity of government goes hand in hand with continuity of memory. Yet the memory of states is often extremely short: what is a source for a historian is a piece of intelligence for a state that has been produced for a certain function. Once this has been accomplished, the file can be closed and safely forgotten, with the certainty that it can be retrieved any time. The purpose for which a certain item of information has been collected often goes unrecorded, however. It may or may not be retrieved at a later date, but even if it is, the reason for that recovery usually has very little to do with the context in which it was first recorded. Most often it provides answers to problems that have little to do with the original issues or the circumstances under which it was created.

A process of selection, omission, and reinterpretation is applied to the available information for it to be of use where it is relocated. This process implies assigning a new meaning to a past event. This, for instance, is what Shahid Amin demonstrated in his study of the Chauri-Chaura uprising in 1922: it became a 'metaphor' for the national history of postcolonial India.[3] But the meaning of an event can be altered much earlier than that: a single year may suffice. As early as 1925, John Murray Ewart picked out certain pieces of information from the previous year's intelligence records to bring

1 Some of the material in this chapter has previously appeared in 'Setting the Scene of the Crime: the Colonial Archive, History, and the Racialization of the 1924 Revolution in Anglo-Egyptian Sudan', the *Canadian Journal of African Studies* (2015), vol. 49, n. 1.

2 Trouillot, *Silencing the Past*, p. 26.

3 Shahid Amin, *Event, Metaphor, Memory: Chauri Chaura 1922-1992* (Delhi: Oxford University Press, 1996).

some order to the chaos of 1924, and thus the meaning of the revolution began to change. Ewart not only affected the subsequent course of events by providing powerful justifications for the hardening of Indirect Rule with the clear objective of containing nationalism, but he also wrote perhaps the most influential version of the 1924 Revolution.[4]

KNOWLEDGE PANICS AND THE INTELLIGENCE DEPARTMENT

In the historiography of the 1924 Revolution, it is often claimed that the inefficiency of the Intelligence Department played an important part in the events.[5] The basis for this view lies in the debate on the way responsibilities for the events of 1924 were to be shared. Ewart was seconded to Sudan from his position with the Indian Police in Punjab at the end of 1924 to look into this issue, even before the assassination of the Governor General. In 'Memorandum on the Reorganization of the Intelligence Department',[6] commissioned two weeks before Stack was assassinated on 19 November, Ewart listed a number of flaws in the current intelligence-gathering system. Suffice to note here that the report criticized Charles Armine Willis, the director of the Intelligence Department, for having amassed useless 'inchoate details' on political agitation.[7]

Criticism of Willis had been widespread well before Ewart came on the scene.[8] Willis's withdrawn personality made him unpopular in the colonial government.[9] Furthermore, there was a longstanding grudge between him and Harold MacMichael, Assistant Civil Secretary to the Governor General, whose star was rising. The mistrust felt by the other officers towards Willis was related not only to his character, but also to the grey area the Intelligence Department occupied. The powers of the Director of Intelligence were inherited from the position of Inspector General, an *ad hoc* role that had been created by Wingate for Rudolph von Slatin Pasha, an Austrian national who had had a long and adventurous sojourn in Sudan.[10] Slatin had broad powers in matters of a political and sensitive

[4] Precisely on this point, see: G. N. Sanderson, 'Indirect Rule in the Northern Sudan as an Anti-Nationalist Strategy 1920-1939', in Mahasin Muhammed Ahmed al-Hajj al-Safi, *The Nationalist Movement in the Sudan* (Khartoum: Institute of African and Asian Studies, University of Khartoum, 1989), pp. 63-11.

[5] Daly, *Empire on the Nile*, p. 330.

[6] Memorandum on the Reorganization of the Intel. Dept. by Ewart. Officer on special duty, CID, Khartoum 20.12.25, Civsec1 36/1/1, NRO.

[7] Ibid. See also in Daly, *Empire on the Nile*, pp. 329-332, in which Daly follows Ewart in explaining the flaws of the Intelligence Department.

[8] Charles Armine Willis joined the Sudan Political Service in 1905, was seconded to the Intelligence Dept. in 1915, and became its Director in 1920. From 1905 to 1910 he served in various provinces, such as Kordofan and Red Sea (*Sudan Political Service* 1958, 16).

[9] According to Daly, 'In a private letter to MacMichael [the Deputy Civsec] in 1924, Schuster [the financial secretary]... joked that "CMG" might be our slogan', meaning 'Charles (or "Chunkie", Willis's nickname) must go'. (Daly, *Empire on the Nile*, p. 332).

[10] Richard L. Hill, *Slatin Pasha* (London: Oxford University Press, 1965).

nature, from tribal mapping to border conflicts, slavery, and the treatment of political prisoners. However, he was much disliked by his colleagues, as was Willis, for similar reasons. He was accused of courting the religious notables. There was some truth in this: after his retirement Willis was hired as personal advisor to *sayyid* 'Abd al-Raḥman al-Mahdī.[11]

Ewart began his career in India in 1905, after the reform of the Indian Intelligence Department pursued by Lord Curzon, Viceroy of India from 1899 to 1905. Curzon considered that the Indian revolts of the previous century were not due only to local circumstances but to the inefficiency of the intelligence gathering system, and he put himself to the task of renewing and rationalizing it.[12] In his view, the old system had been good only for amassing information, and not for using it in any sensible manner. Taking the new standards as a yardstick, Ewart considered Willis's work during the revolution to have been flawed.

It is difficult to agree with Ewart's assessment, at least in the light of the enormous amount of work that the Intelligence Department carried out in 1924. Over a period of seven months, from May to December 1924, its employees wrote accounts of every open political agitation, and wrote bulletins on the political situation on an almost daily basis. They registered the names of known participants in demonstrations, and wrote personal files on all those who sent telegrams to the government or wrote articles to Egyptian newspapers. With the help of provincial staff, activists were tracked down and arrested in every province. This activity is all the more extraordinary if one considers how scant the resources of the Intelligence Department actually were.[13] In 1924, besides Willis, the Intelligence establishment consisted of Arthur W. Skrine, its Assistant Director, who was replaced by Reginald Davies in July; Captain Philips, its Deputy Assistant; the Syrian Samuel 'Aṭiya; and finally a superintendent in Cairo. In addition to these men, 'the department employed in Khartoum ... seventeen classified staff, most of whom were clerks.'[14] This chronically understaffed and hopelessly overburdened department produced or passed an imposing number of documents.

The quantity of intelligence produced in 1924 reminds us of what Christopher Bayly, an historian of India, has called 'knowledge panics':

> Far from being rational responses to the needs of the modern state, 'knowledge

[11] Douglas H. Johnson, 'CA Willis and the "Cult of Deng:" A Falsification of the Ethnographic Record', *History in Africa* (1985), vol. 12, pp. 131-150.

[12] C. A. Bayly, 'Knowing the Country: Empire and Information in India', *Modern Asian Studies* (1993), vol. 27, n. 1, pp. 39, 41; C. A. Bayly, *Empire and Information : Intelligence Gathering and Social Communication in India, 1780-1870* (Cambridge; New York: Cambridge University Press, 1996). Richard Popplewell, *Intelligence and Imperial Defence: British Intelligence and the Defence of the Indian Empire, 1904-1924* (London; Portland OR: F. Cass, 1995).

[13] The Sudan Government was chronically lacking in materials and human resources, and so it was quite common for an establishment to be so limited. See in particular: A. H. M. Kirk-Greene, 'The Sudan Political Service: A Profile in the Sociology of Imperialism', *The International Journal of African Historical Studies* (1982), vol. 15, n. 1, pp. 21-48.

[14] Daly, *Empire on the Nile*, p. 33.

> panics' sent official agencies through curious parabolas of growth. New agencies were formed. They built up huge data-bases and armies of informants. They developed their own lore, often in isolation from other departments of government. They then atrophied and became obsolescent.[15]

A similar parabola of growth took place in 1924. All things considered, however, the Intelligence Department was quite successful in making good use of it: within a month after the beginning of the agitations, all the most important members of the White Flag League had been arrested or exiled. An 'agent saboteur' had infiltrated the movement, so the Intelligence Department had a fair idea of what the League's plans were.[16] The Intelligence Department's fears were neither exaggerated nor unfounded; indeed, the demonstrations, riots, and mutinies far exceeded colonial expectations. In August 1924 an Intelligence officer commented: 'Recent events have gone to show that the information obtained has been an understatement rather than an overstatement of the seriousness of the situation.'[17]

Knowledge panics do not happen randomly; they reflect precise moments at which a government's categories of understanding break down. This is what happened in 1924, when British colonial officers realized that people had stopped talking politics in the language of what was disparagingly defined as 'religious fanaticism' or 'fanatical religious movements', referring to the Mahdist insurgencies that had occurred so frequently during the period up to the 1920s.[18] Nor did what was happening resemble 'tribal rebellions', as local insurgencies were labelled and belittled. One telling comparison can be made with the revolt in Southern Darfur in 1921, the so-called 'Nyala Rebellion'. In spite of the breadth of the insurgency in Darfur and the thousands of people involved – as many as, if not more than, in 1924 – it never provoked the same amount of paperwork as the 1924 Revolution did, because it was believed to have been provoked by 'fanatics', and confined to the margins of Sudan. The rebellion was bloodily crushed, a few reports were produced, and the matter closed.[19]

In 1924, new sections of the population of Sudan began to claim that they had the right to decide on their own government. Such rhetoric did not fit a country that was considered by its administrators to be extremely 'backward' compared with other regions of the British Empire such as India or Egypt. Because what was happening was so difficult to explain, it evoked fears that were typical of situations in which the worst-case scenario seemed always about to happen, such as Egypt and the Egyptians taking over Sudan, or Sudanese killing their British rulers. For instance, like many other men, Ewart was convinced that 1924 was but the first step in a long struggle: 'For the moment there is a period of quiescence, but it would be futile to suppose that there will be no "next

[15] Bayly, 'Knowing the Country: Empire and Information in India', p. 38.
[16] Confessions of Ali Ahmed Saleh, FO 141/805/2, NA.
[17] Note from the Acting DI, 13.8.1924, FO 141/805/2, NA.
[18] Cudsi, 'Sudanese Resistance to British Rule, 1900-1920', H. A. Ibrahim, 'Mahdist Risings Against the Condominium Government in the Sudan, 1900-1927', *The International Journal of African Historical Studies* (1979), vol. 12, n. 3, pp. 440-471.
[19] Daly, *Empire on the Nile*, p. 282-84. Intel 9/1/8 and Darfur 1/19A/102, NRO.

time".'[20] Trying to comprehend the incomprehensible was what led the Intelligence Department to its enormous effort of record production.

1924 INSURGENTS IN THE RECORDS OF THE INTELLIGENCE DEPARTMENT

High-level British officers such as Willis understood the causes of the 1924 Revolution by linking them to the political activists who organized it. Insurgents were depicted as a particular 'revolutionary type'. This enabled British officers to support certain conclusions about the causes of the agitations.

In the period between May and December 1924, as mentioned elsewhere, the Intelligence Department gathered information on more than 900 people (see Appendix 2). They were reported for signing telegrams, leading or taking part in demonstrations, making public speeches, or for any kind of act interpreted as seditious. Beside the notes of the Intelligence Department, there were those drafted by other high officials, such as Governors and their Deputies in the provinces, British inspectors, the Civil Secretary, officers in the military establishment. Provincial officers forwarded their notes to Khartoum, either directly to the Intelligence Department or to the Civil Secretary, the Governor General, or other authorities. The content of these reports varies a great deal. Some documents simply include long lists of names of political activists, other are several paragraph long. It is important to emphasize that these people corresponded to those who were *seen* by the Department, and not to those who actually became involved in the insurgency. For that reason, some categories, such as government staff are overrepresented while others, such as workers underrepresented. One category – women – was completely invisible. All the women supporting the movement from behind the scenes, such as the wife of 'Alī 'Abd al-Laṭīf, are excluded from the colonial records.

The most recurrent information was – perhaps understandably – the nature of 'seditious' activities. The second one was the profession of the activist, mentioned in 75% of cases. Information on origins, including nationality, ethnicity, family, and home town, on the other hand, is available in only 393, or 43%, cases. Information such as age or sex is hardly ever provided: ages of only 26 out of 917 people are known.

Specific patterns of representation can be discerned in relation to a certain number of factors, such as profession, family background, and origin:

a) Nationalism as deviance

The first and most visible characteristic is that British officers did not portray insurgents as political opponents but as criminals. Thus, together with brief descriptions on their backgrounds and professions and the nature of their political involvement, the Intelligence Department's notes

[20] Ewart Report, p. 171, but see also the whole section, pp. 169-172.

tended to include what type of unfortunate circumstance in their past or careers had led them to join the nationalist movement. One example is the note written on al-Tuhāmī Muḥammad 'Uthmān, a member of the second committee of the White Flag League, arrested for participating in a demonstration in Khartoum on June 26:

> ...a Jaali of 20 years of age, is a man of little education and by profession a carpenter at Khartoum. He is a person of no standing and position and it is believed he has been led into his present action by his friends[21] ...an ex-convict of the lowest character.[22]

The significance of his political participation is played down by connecting his political choices to a tainted social and moral world: al-Tuhāmī was involved in politics because he was uneducated, of the 'lowest character', and lacking in standing. Similarly, one of the five founders of the White Flag League, Ḥassan Ṣāliḥ, was described in a biographical note on the signatories to a telegram to which he had contributed:

> Hassan Saleh: Clerk, Telegraph Office, Khartoum, son of an Egyptian by name Saleh El Matbaji, who used to be in charge of the Printing Press under the old Government. Hassan is a muwallad, but registers himself as a Sudanese in the Posts and Telegraphs Department – Mother also an Egyptian of bad character. An insignificant individual from all points of view; in his Department he is known to his chiefs as an obstructionist, and of a quarrelsome disposition. [23]

Descriptions of this kind are extremely pervasive, not only in sources written by Willis and his associates in the Intelligence Department, but also in those of British officers outside the capital. One example written by the Deputy Governor of the Kordofan province is that of an activist from El Obeid:

> Abdalla Abu Gaseisa: This man was formerly a Government rate-collector in El Obeid, and was sentenced to a term of imprisonment and a large fine for embezzlement in 1922 ... I regard him as a dangerous man of evil intent & menace, & consider that he is the very type of person from whom political agitators are made.[24]

In other words, political agitators were made from a specific 'type' or category of person – that is, malcontents – based on their personal flaws, 'evil' disposition, 'bad nature', and hereditary defects.

Even in sources of a very factual nature such as chronologies, descriptions of the moral qualities of agitators' occupied almost as much space in the text as events. One such is the 'Chronicle of events during the period of political excitement in Khartoum (June-August 1924)' produced by the Intelligence Department at the beginning of August.[25] The demonstration of 19 June is described as having been started by

[21] Deputy Adjunct DI, Notes on the signatories of the telegram of 3.6.1924, Khartoum, FO 141/806/1, NA.

[22] Telegram from Khartoum to the High Commissioner for Egypt, Cairo, 4.7.1924, FO 141/801/6, NA.

[23] Notes on signatories to a telegram of protest to his Excellency the Governor General, Khartoum, 10.6.1924, FO 141/806/1, NA.

[24] Note from the Deputy Gov. on the accused, undated, Kordofan 1/14/69, NRO.

[25] Chronicle of Events in Khartoum, June-August 1924, FO 141/805/2. NA. All the quotes in this paragraph are taken from the same document.

'Hag el Sheikh Omar... a Jaali merchant of small standing with a fanatical reputation.' The demonstration of 27 June was led by a certain Aḥmad Idrīs 'Abu Ghālib, '...a Muwallad clerk in the Sanitary Department', accused 'of having misappropriated about LE 70 worth of Sanitary Stores'. The other 'ringleaders' of the demonstration were tarred with the same brush: Ḥassan Aḥmad Fāḍil had had problems with the police, and Ismā'īl 'Abd al-Majīd was 'the most fanatical of a fanatical family'.

Some of these descriptions are pure gossip and paint a vivid picture of the moral world of the colonial officers. Some activists were accused of challenging professional hierarchies – for example in their 'impertinence', disrespect towards superiors, ingratitude, truculence, and lack of restraint in their work – or more explicitly of embezzlement, theft, corruption, and idleness at work.[26] Other defects imply an absence of moral and rational order in their world, as 'araki sodden',[27] 'sullen fanatics'[28], 'medically certified catamites',[29] or lunatics.[30] A few references hint at the foreignness of an insurgent, as was the case with one activist from a prestigious family who was dismissed as 'not really a Mahassi' because his mother was a Fellata – that is, of West African origin.[31] Finally, political activism was linked to a grudge that certain members of a family held against the British, as in the Intelligence Note on the activist Ḥusayn Yūsif Ḥusayn: '... father was shaykh of a quarter in Omdurman, discharged for ill practice.'[32]

The common thread in these profiles is that the accused represented challenges to an established order, be it social, professional, or moral. Men's lives and actions were interpreted as testing authority and a set of social norms, as a craving for something that was forbidden, as a desire for the unlawful. It is significant that the chaos was moral before it was political, as if the issue at stake went well beyond forms of government into the very core of society and its values. The British rejected the demands of the nationalists not on the grounds of the lack of soundness in their political ideas, but because they were personally incapable of conducting a truly political discourse.

26 Some examples may be found in: Notes on the signatories to the telegram of 15.5.1924, FO 141/806/1, NA; Deputy Adjunct DI, Notes on the signatories of the telegram of 3.6.1924, Khartoum, FO 141/806/1, NA; Notes on signatories of a telegram of protest to his Excellency the Governor General, Khartoum, 10.6.1924, FO 141/806/1, NA.

27 Note from the Deputy Gov. on the accused, undated, Kordofan 1/14/69, NRO.

28 DI to the Gov. of Khartoum, Khartoum, 8.7.1924, Palace 4/10/49, NRO. Another example, 'semi-insane fanatic', in a telegram from Khartoum to the High Commissioner for Egypt, Cairo, 4.7.1924, FO 141/801/6, NA.

29 Chronicle of events during the period of political excitement in Khartoum, June/ August 1924, FO 141/805/2, NA.

30 The accusation of madness was one of the most frequent. Among many examples, see: Sudan Monthly Intelligence Report no. 362, September 1924, WO 33/999, NA; Disturbances 1924, History Sheets, Northern Prov. 1/21/217, NRO.

31 From the DI to Gov. Khartoum, Khartoum, 8.7.1924, Palace 4/10/49, NRO.

32 Notes on the signatory to a telegram to His Excellency the Governor General, 3.6.1924, FO 141/810/3, NA.

b) On Origins

The Intelligence Department noted, as seen, the profession of activists more frequently than origin, except for people labelled as *Muwalladīn*. Similarly, the Department tended to record the background of a person if he was from Egypt. Thus, of 393 people out of 917 whose origin is known, 51 were identified as *Muwalladīn*, and 126 as Egyptians. Nevertheless, surprisingly, even when it was obvious from the name or from other details that an activist came from Egypt, the sources could fail to mention this explicitly. For instance, during the revolt in Atbara, the origin of the insurgents can be only evinced contextually, because the lists of activists only report their names.[33] Even the origins of the leaders of the Atbara revolt, Jamāl al-Dīn Muḥammad and Ḥilmī Būsa'īd, are nowhere to be found in the colonial records available for this study.

Besides nationality, the ethnic origins of the activists, even of major figures, are also notable for their absence. Even when this information was occasionally and randomly noted, mistakes were quite common. Besides 'Alī 'Abd al-Laṭīf, whose dual Dinka and Nuba origin was a source of endless confusion in colonial sources, there is al-Tuhāmī Muḥammad, who is described in some places as a Ja'ali and elsewhere as Shayqi. Similar confusion continually occurs with the origins of the cadets who mutinied in August.[34] These uncertainties indicate that such information was not only probably difficult to obtain, but also relatively unimportant in the eyes of the Intelligence Department. But more crucially, it is clear from these records that British officials did not systematically connect a specific ethnic background with insurgency. In other words, ethnic background was not considered a cause of political mobilization.

c) On Status and Profession

What impact did the insurgents' family background have on the way they were represented? One of the 'agitators' who opened the season of demonstrations was al-Imām Dūlayb Khalīl, one of the earliest members of White Flag League. Willis observed: 'He and his brother come from a prestigious family and are regarded as a "social asset" to the League',[35] yet an Intelligence Department Note offered this bleak description of him:

> El Imam Doleib, has a third name – El Khalil. He is about 26 years of age and is connected with the Doalib of Kordofan and the family of Sayed Ismail el Azhari.

[33] List of ringleaders in Atbara, according to the fifth witness Sol Awad eff. Attia, Railway Battalion, 19.8.1924, Palace 4/10/52, NRO.

[34] He is described as a Shayqi in SA to First Secretary, Cairo, 13.7.1924, and as a Ja'ali in Deputy Adjunct DI, Notes on the signatories to the telegram of 3.6.1924, Khartoum, FO 141/806/1, NA. For the cadets: compare the list of sentences, White Flag League conspiracy trial, Northern Prov. 1/21/207, NRO, with R.H. Dunn, Chief Justice of the Sudan Govt. to Private Secretary Khartoum 29.3.1925, Intel 2/10/71, NRO, and the list of the Military Cadets who took part in the demonstration in August 1924, who were released under guarantee: unsigned, undated, Kordofan 1/11/45, NRO.

[35] C. A. Willis, 'The League of the White Flag', Khartoum 20.7.1924, FO 141/810/3, NA.

> His cousin Ahmed el Imam Doleib received a religious robe at the beginning of this year. Owing to the lack of education he could not find employment but he was repeatedly recommended by the Intelligence Department owing to his family connections and was given a situation (through District Commissioner Omdurman) as rate collector. He resigned this on the ground of ill health at the beginning of this year and got a temporary job in Khartoum North. He has been out of work for several months and has no means of subsistence. His relations [sic] heard that he has been seen in the company of Ali Abdel Latif but he swore that this was only a chance meeting, but it appears he was lying. He has been a constant source of trouble to his relations.[36]

The description of Mudaththir Aḥmad Ibrāhīm, who was a member of the second committee of the White Flag, and came from a notable family that had been closely connected to the Mahdī, was very similar:

> Ahmed Mudassir Ibrahim is 25 years of age and was educated free in the Omdurman Primary School, where he attained the 3rd year level in 1913. He was then appointed as a telephone operator, but was subsequently discharged for gross impertinence. In view of his family connections, he was reinstated and employed as a telephone operator in the Palace. He has been living away from his family for some months. His father was keeper of the Privy Seal to the Khalifa Abdullahi. He surrendered to General Wingate after the battle of Omdurman and has lived on the bounty of the Government ever since. He has some land in Berber Province and receives £120 a year, and has on several occasions been enabled to go on pilgrimage to Mecca at the expense of the government. He is now in Mecca for the 14th time. He and his family are under great obligation to the Sudan Government.[37]

These examples demonstrate that the Intelligence Department was no kinder to activists from a notable background than it was to common Sudanese. On the contrary, the above description, like many others, follows the same pattern as those reported previously: Mudaththir was discharged on the grounds of 'gross impertinence', and al-Imām Dūlayb Khalīl was 'a constant source of troubles'.

At the same time, these records cast light on the 'debt' these families owed to the government. Leniency towards the irresponsible children of notables was presented as a personal favour that consequently placed their families in a situation of obligation towards the government. Indeed, insurgents from notable families served shorter terms of imprisonment than common Sudanese – if they were imprisoned at all – as in the cadets' demonstration in August: although all the fifty-one cadets from the Military School marched together, sixteen were released 'under guarantee'. This meant in practice that their relatives used their influence to convince the British to let them go and guaranteed their 'good behaviour'.[38] Among the cadets released were sons or relatives of *'umda* or established merchants. As 'Abdallāh Mabrūk put it bluntly: 'The ranked cadets were sentenced five years. And those who were sentenced,

[36] Translation of a telegram addressed to His Excellency the Governor General, Khartoum, 3.6.1924, FO 141/806/1, NA.

[37] He had signed the same telegram for which al-Imām was noted. Translation of a telegram addressed to His Excellency the Governor General, Khartoum, 3.6.1924, FO 141/806/1, NA.

[38] List of Military Cadets who took part in demonstration in August 1924, who were released under guarantee, unsigned, undated, Kordofan 1/11/45, NRO.

their fathers were not influential enough.'[39] Finally, one of the clearest examples is the execution of the officers held responsible for the November mutiny. One, 'Alī al-Bannā, was pardoned at the very last minute. 'Alī was the only one among the four officers not only to be from Northern Sudan but to have powerful connections. On the one hand, his family was related to *sayyid* 'Abd al-Raḥman al-Mahdī, who apparently was the one to whom he owed his life spared; and on the other, his brother, Muḥammad 'Umar al-Bannā, was well known as a representative of the pro-British faction among the graduates, and had composed a number of poems pro-colonization.[40]

How were people from less eminent backgrounds, of southern origins, or from slave-soldiers families represented? Our first example is that of an educated government employee from a Dinka background, 'Abd al-Qādir Aḥmad Sayyid, who led the demonstration of 23 June in Khartoum:[41]

> Abdel Gader Ahmed Said – Dinkawi, age 19 years. Ex-student of Gordon College. Served as clerk to Sudan Mercantile Co. for 6 months and was discharged with a bad character.
>
> Wrote an abusive and somewhat seditious letter to Director of Intelligence on 16.1.1924, in which he said he had decided to wage a peaceful war against the Government so as to be put in gaol, or slain. His father opened a small shop for him in the deims, at the end of January.[42]

Another example is that of Officer Zayn al-'Ābdīn 'Abd al-Tām, whose family background was also in Southern Sudan:[43]

> Mulazim Awal Zein el Abdin Abdel Tain – Sub-mamur, Nuba Mountains Province. 12 years' service in Egyptian Army. Character very good.
>
> Dinkawi. Military School Khartoum. ... Was described in telegram from certain of the League of White Flag in Cairo as forming, with Mohammed el Mahdi, a delegation from the Sudan to express loyalty to King Fuad.[44]

A final example is that of the leader of the White Flag League, whose origin is not even mentioned:

> Ali Abdel Latif: the ex-Sudanese Mulazim Awal, IX Battalion, was tried in June 1922 for attempting to incite dissatisfaction against the government of the Sudan, found guilty, and sentenced to 12 months imprisonment. Released from prison in April, 1923. Since then he has always been the centre of a body of native young men, chiefly malcontents, criticising the Government and spreading adverse political ideas.[45]

In these examples, nationalist participation is still as a flaw related more to character than to origin. This demonstrates that this British 'catalogue of crimes' – the types of defect that colonial officers attributed to the

39 *Al-Riwāyāt*, p. 492.
40 On 'Umar al-Bannā, Najīla, *Malāmiḥ Min al-Mujtama' al-Sūdānī*, p. 62.
41 From the DI to the Gov. of El Obeid 24.6.1924, Kordofan 1/12/54, NRO.
42 Notes on persons arrested in connection with recent demonstration in Khartoum, 23.6.1924, FO 141/810/3, NA.
43 Chronicle of events during the period of political excitement in Khartoum, June/August 1924, FO 141/805/2. NA.
44 Ibid.
45 Notes on persons arrested in connection with recent demonstration in Khartoum, 23.6.1924, FO 141/810/3, NA.

insurgents to explain their activism – did not include being of Southern or slave descent.

Finally, how did the professional background affect the representations of the insurgents? In a significant majority of cases, the records are extremely concise, as in these examples, which are fairly typical: Bashīr Naʿīm, a butcher, 'Tried for having thrown stones in the demonstration in Omdurman';[46] a cook: 'Abdel Khalil Tahmush. He is alleged to have attempted to organize a demonstration in Khartoum, 21.9, with 5 others, crying for Egypt in Mosque Square; found not guilty';[47] or 'Mustafa Yusef, ivory turner, Aswani Egyptian, sentenced 2 months.'[48]

Such brevity is connected to what has been seen in the previous chapter: first, the Intelligence Department had much less information on the working classes than on government employees. Second, it was the sign of the relative lack of government interest in such insurgents, as if there was no point in gathering more information about them because they had no real weight.

Overall, colonial sources written while the events were taking place tended to lump all political activists in one large category of criminals and to dismiss their political participation in terms of low moral fibre. Irrespective of class, origin, and status, activists were all depicted as demented, thieves, drunkards, social parasites, losers, and people whose 'bad character' had led them down the wrong path. Yet in spite of their constant reference to the revolutionaries' personal defects, officials could not help but diligently note the occupations, origins, and statuses of the insurgents, because the records were produced specifically as evidence for intelligence and judicial purposes.

One remarkable feature of the insurgency emerges from these descriptions, altogether unrecognized by the authorities: White Flag League supporters came from extremely diverse backgrounds. The information in these personal records is like a snapshot commented on using a caption that does not fit with the image. Even though government officials used very similar terminology to depict various political activists, they also reveal the enormous diversity of professional and social backgrounds. As Ranajit Guha put it, this diversity was a 'necessary and pervasive element within that body of evidence'[49]: the carpenter Tuhāmī Muḥammad did not have much in common with the *sūdānī* ranked officer Zayn al-ʿĀbdīn ʿAbd al-Tām, and the unemployed religious man Dūlayb Khalīl did not share much with ʿAbd al-Qādir Aḥmad Sayyid, a Dinkawi, who was a clerk in a mercantile company. Yet all of them were members of the White Flag

[46] Baily, Gov. of Khartoum Prov. to the Civsec, Khartoum, 29.6.1924, Palace 4/10/49, NRO.

[47] The Gov. of Khartoum Prov. to Private Secretary 22.9.1924 and 28.9.1924, both in Palace 4/10/48, NRO.

[48] List of convictions in connection with the demonstration of 15.8; and Corbyn to Private Secretary, Khartoum, 19.8.1924, both in Palace 4/10/48, NRO.

[49] Ranajit Guha, 'The Prose of Counter-insurgency', *Selected Subaltern Studies*, Guha, Ranajit, and Gayatri Chakravorty Spivak eds. (New York: Oxford University Press, 1988), p. 13.

League. The records of the Intelligence Department attempted to organize, but did not erase, the histories of the insurgents.

TO EXPLAIN AND INTERPRET: THE EWART REPORT ON POLITICAL AGITATION

John M. Ewart joined the Indian Police in 1905, the same year in which C. A. Willis had been appointed to the Sudan Political Service. Ewart had quickly climbed through the ranks, serving as District Officer and Frontier Constabulary, Punjab and North-West Frontier Province before joining the police.[50] In his capacity as 'expert', he came to Sudan to help with the reorganization of the Intelligence Department. As events unfolded at the end of 1924, confirming the reputation of that department for inefficiency, Ewart was given another task to match his qualifications: the 'Report on Political Agitation in the Sudan', published early on after the crisis in April 1925.

The report was intended to explain a number of issues: the 'real' reasons for the insurgency; whether there was any connection between the events of 1924 and other major perceived threats to the Empire, such as 'Bolshevism' and 'Pan-Islamism'; and how it was related to the Anglo-Egyptian conflict. It is noteworthy that Ewart quietly but systematically erased the name of the former Director of Intelligence, C. A. Willis.[51] He wrote the main report himself, and asked one of Willis's subordinates, Reginald Davies, and the Deputy Governor of Khartoum Province, Robin E. H. Baily, to write the appendices. By erasing almost all traces of the disgraced director, Ewart was more than condemning a man much disliked by the British administration; he was also dismissing Willis's understanding of the insurgency. Ewart rejected both Willis's description and interpretation of the events because he considered them flawed and useless.

The following pages demonstrate that the entire Ewart Report resonated with two fundamental beliefs about why the Sudanese became politically active. The report maintained that only one factor was critical: the role of Egypt: 'the Revolution of 1924 ... is merely and solely a product of Egyptian politics' (Ewart Report, 172). It further argued that only 'perverted' elements of Sudanese society could have been affected by the corrupting Egyptian influences: 'denationalized Sudanese', and chief among them, 'detribalized negroids'.

a) The Egyptian 'Infection'

The idea that the events of 1924 were a product of Egyptian 'machinations' was certainly not new. As early as July 1924, Willis wrote in a report: '... the system is Egyptian, the expenses have no other obvious source and

[50] In 1932 he was promoted to be Inspector-General of the Punjab Police, and in 1936 he became Director of Intelligence in India. He died in 1939, aged 55. *The Glasgow Herald,* December 9, 1939.

[51] He was only mentioned in one section authored by 'the Director of Intelligence', a one-page 'Appreciation of the situation as on July 1, 1924' (Ewart Report, p. 176).

are attributed to Egyptians, and the appeal is invariably to Egypt and the nature of the propaganda is Egyptian.'[52] Willis lacked direct evidence, but he increasingly found informants who were ready to swear that Egyptians were behind everything. Proof of this kind was so eagerly awaited that its consistency was hardly checked.[53] Ewart did not disagree on this point in 1925, but sought to erase any possible doubt on Egyptian responsibility. Testimonies of people who had turned King's evidence were adjusted slightly to fit expectations.[54] Insistence on Egyptian participation in 1924 became far more pervasive, as reflected in a number of narrative strategies.

First, the description of Egyptians and their influence on the nationalist movement was replete with references to racial, criminal, moral, and sexual deviancy. Ewart depicted the Egyptians as 'Orientals', prone to intrigue, seduction, and obscure political manoeuvres: 'There is evidence that this series of riotous outbreaks was deliberately instigated from Egypt and organised by the Egyptian secret members of the league acting through Ali Abdul Latif' (161); 'the Sudanese were, if possible, less amenable than ever to seduction by the anti-British insinuations of Egyptian officials by means of seditious circulars' (154); 'in this they met with considerable success by methods of flattery and the painting of seductive pictures of what the educated Sudanese might hope' (156). Another pervasive theme was the depiction of Egypt as an 'infectious agent' spreading dangerous ideas amongst the Sudanese: 'the seed of unrest was beginning to germinate' (159).

Constant repetition of the words 'Egypt' and 'Egyptians' throughout the report hammered home the theme. For example, on page 154, these words occur 22 times, and on page 155, 18 times. Finally, according to the Report, Egyptians and Egypt were the causative agents of all actions taking place in Sudan in 1924, directly or indirectly. This is exemplified in the content titles of the Report. Section Two is headed 'Propaganda by Egyptians from 1921 onwards' (155), Section Three 'Development of organisation in Egyptian hands' (157), and Section Four 'Hafiz Bey Ramadan's Visit to Khartoum. Organisation of Demonstrations by Sudanese'. (Ḥāfiẓ Bey was one of the leaders of the Watanist party in Egypt). Furthermore, every event was systematically connected to Egypt: thus, the cadets' mutiny of August 9 was 'deliberately organised by Egyptian army officers' (164); in Atbara, the Railways Battalion mutinied because it had been instigated by 'civilian Egyptian and Muwallid railway employees' (164); in Port Sudan, demonstrations were organized by 'Egyptian and Sudanese clerks and by Egyptian soldiers from the Railway Battalion' with 'the connivance of

52 C.A. Willis, 'The League of the White Flag', 20.7.1924, FO 141/810/3, NA, p. 10.
53 The clearest case in point is the confession by 'Alī Aḥmad Ṣāliḥ, who gave information he could not possibly have been privy to, as he had not sworn the oath of the League. Confessions of Ali Ahmed Saleh, FO 141/805/2, NA.
54 '31st Dec. The following evidence must be taken. Ali Ahmed Saleh and others must agree about meeting in May – and about Egyptians present at the meeting, and in particular as to why some say they saw the Egyptian present while others deny.' 'Ali Ahmed Salih is a spy employed by me.' Baily Diary 1924 Oct 7 – 1926 Mar, SAD 422/3/28.

the Egyptian mamur and his assistant' (163). Finally, even in the White Flag League, which as the report made clear officially excluded Egyptians there were nevertheless Egyptian 'secret members' who were covertly directing the League's tactics and decisions (159). Egyptian conspiracy was everywhere.

b) 'Denationalized Sudanese' and 'Detribalized Negroids'

The second major difference between the Ewart Report and the earlier records of the Intelligence Department lies in the role played by 'race' in determining nationalistic allegiances. For Ewart, while 'pure-bred' Sudanese were not attracted to Egyptian machinations, there were certain categories of people who were particularly vulnerable to them: first of all the *Muwalladīn*, and second, those of what he labelled the 'denationalised' class:

> The 'denationalised' class is peculiar to Sudan. It consists of Sudanese of mixed extraction, Egyptians born and domiciled in the Sudan, and negroids of slave and ex-slave extraction and often mixed descent. All these elements are outside the orbit of normal control or of appeal to tribal or national sentiment ... (154).

From these quotes, it can be argued that there was a glaring difference between the way the Ewart Report defined 'abnormality' compared with the records of the Intelligence Department. In the latter, nationalism sprang from forms of deviance which was interpreted as a personal deficiency of a moral or professional nature that was almost never connected with the perceived race of the insurgents. Blood entered the picture only in the case of people with Egyptian forebears. In the Ewart Report, on the other hand, abnormality described another type of Sudanese, one that did not have a clearly identifiable 'tribal belonging' and race.

As a box within a box, among the 'denationalized' people who lacked tribal ties, there was one particularly pernicious group, to which Ewart returned at several points in his report. These were the 'detribalized negroids', 'a most unsuitable class', mostly comprised of officers of the Egyptian Army (170). Support from 'Black' officers for Egypt was perfectly logical for Ewart. First, it was a desire for revenge against 'the Arabs': 'the "blacks" [believe they are] the real Sudanese, and should rule the country' (159). Second, it was a natural consequence of their race. As Baily put it in one of the appendices to the report, 'Blacks are capricious and arrogant, and are easily influenced by plausible statements, spoken or read.'[55] For Ewart too, the 'Blacks' were and would remain 'savages', and as such were suitable for manual labour, not for the subtleties of politics:

> A man who joins the army from his tribal home returns to his old niche there when he returns. The ex-officers class now referred to has no niche anywhere. Its members claim to be Dinkas or the like; their fathers have served creditably as soldiers or even as officers, they come of slave stock, uprooted a generation or more ago from their tribal home, and have no ties, no traditions and no trade to which to turn, once they have left the army. ... Those who have become officers are the less able and willing ... to revert to the only level they can occupy in civil life, that of manual labour. Among such men, with mentality little, if any, above that of a savage, idle hands are especially prone to mischief, and their sons, with a veneer

[55] Baily Report, Appendix 7 to the Ewart's Report, p. 181.

> of college education imposed upon the same mentality, and infected with political ideas, have proved exceptionally unamenable. (171)

While destined by their race to take subordinate positions, this class had been 'fatally prominent throughout the political history of recent years' (163). For Ewart, it was essential to reverse the dangerous situation that had been brought about by previous political ineptitude. He noted how men of such 'unstable slave stock' had been educated in large numbers and given positions of responsibility in the government because of their ties to the army:

> This class has shown itself readier in the past than most others to avail itself of the educational facilities offered since the British occupation, and is, consequently, strongly represented in the lower ranks of officials, military and civilian, and similar capacities in commercial life. (155)

Their principal error was to have aspired to a role in society that was inappropriate to their racial destiny. Naturally, they had embraced and fostered Egyptian intrigue.

Ewart was adding one additional category – race – to the 'catalogue of crime' outlined here. His alacrity in applying a racial factor to the insurgency in a context with which he was unfamiliar reveals that such rhetoric was shared across the Empire. At the same time, it does not imply that the government before 1924 was free of racial policies or attitudes. As discussed throughout this study, racial considerations were at work, and Ewart acknowledged the fact. Indeed, the picture painted by Ewart in his report was that before 1924, the colonial state had had an incoherent racial policy, as reflected in career of people like 'Alī 'Abd al-Laṭīf. Being defined as 'Black' had important implications for a person's life: it determined, for instance, what kind of school he might have access to and the type of career to be pursued. However, this did not coincide with a destiny of economic or professional marginalization, at least during the period covered by this study. The distinction rather indicated a relaxed racial division of labour, which had brought 'Black' officers to the top of the professional ladder within government administration, a situation Ewart regretted. This was soon to change, however: just as there was no place for 'half breeds' and 'detribalized negroids' in society, so there was no place for such people in the development of the kind of national consciousness that Ewart envisaged for the country.

c) Notables, and therefore Allies

In perfect symmetry with Ewart's belief that 'bad blood' was synonymous with 'bad politics', the politically respectable elements of Sudanese society were those that were not 'mixed'. The racially pure were impervious to Egyptian propaganda:

> For a long time [the denationalised class] and the Egyptians in the Sudan were the sole propagandists, and their efforts to disturb <u>the true sons of the soil</u> were effective only to the extent of creating a certain degree of unrest by means of wholesale misrepresentation, but failed to provoke the smallest sign of an Egypto-Sudanese *entente* (155).[56]

[56] The italics are in the original text, but the underlining is mine.

Ewart portrayed the religious and secular leaders of the country and their offspring as the rational and orderly force of Sudanese society; they were 'responsible Sudanese' who made the right choices: they chose Britain over Egypt early and naturally, and enthusiastically petitioned the government for safeguards against Egyptian claims:

> Leading natives in the provinces of the Northern Sudan were ... invited to express their wishes. This signal produced a number of addresses to the Governor General, protesting the desire of the signatories and those they represented to remain under British tutelage until such time as they were able to govern themselves. (159)

This narrative placed racially pure, politically responsible tribal and religious leaders on one side, and racially degenerate insurgents on the other. This oppositional structure further delegitimized the national movement. In Sudan, there was a politically minded group made up of the 'best elements of the country', who had 'acquired definite conceptions as regards rights and national developments' (170). If certain elements from this group had given their support to Egypt, it was a matter of pure strategy (172), as their real objective was to demand more political rights for the Sudanese:

> Formulated by minds less ill-balanced than that of Ali Abdul Latif, these sentiments represent views honestly held and certain to be pressed, within constitutional bounds, with growing persistence by some of the best elements in the country (156).

In Ewart's narrative, this group served as a contrast to the 'denationalised Sudanese' who were supporters of the White Flag League: *Muwalladīn*, blacks, and other 'low-grade clerks ... and the dregs of the town population' (163). This argument was founded on the fiction that a part of the population of Sudan was 'pure-bred' Arab. After 1924, this came to play an increasingly important role in politics and in the image of the Sudanese nation.

The report's vigorous style, the fact that it had been written by a capable 'expert' in police work, and its claim to be based on months of research lent it great authority and gave its assumptions a veneer of evidential truth. The cracks in the narrative are extremely well hidden, only showing up when the report is compared with the 'vast amount of inchoate detail', as Ewart described the records of the Intelligence Department. In practice, they are undetectable without a thorough and deep dive into the sources on 1924, to read them against the grain.

CONCLUSIONS: THE COLONIAL GAZE AND SUDANESE NATIONALISM

Trouillot wrote that the way in which layers of representations of the past are superimposed on each other might be compared to a crime scene where an intruder reshuffles the evidence.[57]

[57] Trouillot, *Silencing the Past*, p. 26.

The first part of this chapter offered an analysis of the records produced by the Intelligence Department during 1924. Day by day, these records bear witness to the government's anxiety that things might get out of hand, and that events might outrun imagination. The Department was, therefore, careful to record any relevant detail, to paint a clear picture of the 'revolutionary type' in order to be able to act fast and arrest all possible suspects to avoid the spread of discontent. During 1924, the British officers noted something over which they had only limited control and even less idea of how it would end. Obviously, not all this information would be used, but it was felt essential to record as much as possible. Despite the overriding colonial tone of these sources, that all insurgents were criminals, this mass of information is the best available source to counter the view of 1924 as a minor event that engaged only an immature intelligentsia and a handful of army officers. The records attest to the heterogeneity of the insurgents in terms of geographical origin, family background, status, education, and profession. They also confirm that groups previously untouched by nationalist ideas as well as those in remote provinces the country were moved by the idea that the Sudanese were one nation, endowed with a certain set of rights, and able to choose their own destiny. To this day participants remember it as a *thawra*, a revolution; as this study has demonstrated, it was a revolutionary departure in Sudanese history.

By 1925, the revolution had been quashed. The Egyptian army had left the country, most of the 1924 activists were in prison, and the government was eliminating Egyptians from the administration. Willis was removed from duty, and in 1926 he was shunted sideways to a post of equivalent seniority as Governor of the Upper Nile, in Southern Sudan, where he was supposed to be less harmful. The Intelligence Department became a 'sub-department' attached to the office of Harold MacMichael, appointed in 1926 as Civil Secretary, who had finally risen to become the most prominent figure in the colonial government.

In this context, there was no need and no space for superfluous and unsettling information. Published in the White Papers, the Ewart Report was to be the final and definitive word on the 1924 Revolution. Inconsistent elements, fragments that did not fit, and incomprehensible details could be set aside because the aim of the report was to give the 'right' meaning to recent events. Names were reshuffled, details removed and others inserted so that the report's two hypotheses could be proved: that the 1924 Revolution was an Egyptian product, and 'detribalized negroids' had a crucial role in it. The 'Black Sudanese' and people of Egyptian origin became the scapegoats for the revolution, while the network of alliances upon which colonialism rested was safeguarded – even strengthened. The British graciously forgave the renegade sons of notable families, and erased their presence from the records of the insurgency. In the historiography of Sudan, the explanation provided by the Ewart Report has had the greatest impact on the way the revolution has been read. It has outweighed the impressive mass of intelligence gathered in 1924, and has defused the subversive force of the event, both in the past and in the present.

The knowledge of 1924 represents potentially a paradigmatic breakdown in the historiography of modern Sudan, which is still riddled with Orientalist assumptions. 1924 was a moment in which mass protests were organized without the intervention of the notables of the country, or the mobilization of ethnic divisions. Even the issue over the Sudanese struggle against British 'Christians' was of minimal importance, as is evident from the telegrams of the White Flag (See Appendix 1). In short, none of the mechanisms which are so often described as 'working' well in Sudan and more widely African politics – tribalism, sectarianism, clientelism – are useful for an understanding of 1924. But as Sudan is seen as 'not yet modern' today, still mired in warfare and tribalism, how could it have been better one hundred years ago? In a linear conception of history as a movement from darkness to civilization, the fact that as early as 1924, the 'masses' may have been politicized not by religion or ethnic links, but by a concept as 'modern' as the White Flag's version of nationalism, that is, a struggle for self-liberation and for the claim of people's rights, seems highly improbable. Similarly, it seems very unlikely that a movement such as the White Flag League may have been politically possible: the explosion of social hierarchies, finely visualized in the first photograph of the five founding members of that league is so unimaginable that it is easier to think that it never happened at all or that it was meaningless. These are some of the reasons that have contributed to the fixing of the image of 1924 as a non-event. Hopefully, this book has contributed some possible ways to rethink 1924, which was about people who were beginning to think of themselves as Sudanese nationals, searching for ways to assert their rights against a colonial government.

Epilogue: Memory and the Racialization of the 1924 Revolution

It is often thought that it is a historian's job to establish taxonomies of credibility among different narratives in order to recover a certain past, but sometimes these same narratives have multiplied to such an extent that this proves downright impossible.[1] This is true not only for the colonial records on 1924 – multiplied, as seen, by the 'knowledge panic' caused by the events – but even more for the memories that were produced later. Finally, each version is corroborated and then contradicted by other accounts, be they colonial or local, in unpredictable ways, and new versions continue to be produced.

In this brief epilogue, I would like to return once again to two questions: the memory of 1924 and the 'racial theme' of the Revolution. The first point concerns the reason for the unending proliferation of accounts on 1924 – in other words, what this wealth of versions tells us about the past. The second wonders about the way in which racial issues may have affected the memory of 1924. What most interests me here is the manner in which the memory of 1924 is structured – the configuration of its recurrences, silences and omissions – and the way in which the various actors remember it, always bearing in mind the oscillations of 1924 within the national discourse. I believe that the multiplicity of local narratives about 1924 is not only a product of the various nationalist interpretations of the past that have followed one after the other – the efforts made to construct the Sudanese nation at the time of independence, the socialist phase of al-Numayī, or the new Islamic past of the present government – but also a consequence of the ways in which different social actors felt about, and reacted to, the trauma of 1924, and dealt with the racial theme that emerged after 1924. To make this point, I will take a brief look at the history of the ones who produced memories about 1924.

The first published accounts of the Revolution of 1924 came out after the Second World War, and were written by educated Sudanese who made

[1] The main argument of this epilogue is fully developed here: Vezzadini, *'Spies, Secrets, and a Story Waiting to Be (re)told'*.

up part of the country's intellectual elite. One of the earliest works on the 1924 Revolution, for instance, published in 1948, was *al-Sirā' al-musallaḥ 'alā al-wahda fī al-Sūdān,* by one of the country's first semi-professional historians, Muḥammad 'Abd al-Rahīm.[2] The work is an apology for the nationalist movement in which the 1924 activists are depicted as national heroes working together to build the Sudanese nation. Special praise was reserved for 'Alī 'Abd al-Latīf, and the author was particularly disturbed by the accusation of 'low birth', which he complained about in these words: '[it] was nonsense and made-up, imaginary tales, and [the offender] missed out the fact that 'Alī Effendi was from the Dinka, which is one of the largest and sternest tribes in Sudan... maybe you think that these people are not human or were only made for slavery... all people are equal and no Arab is better than anybody else, except in his belief'.[3] Similarly, in the influential *Malāmiḥ min al-mujtama' al-sūdānī*, which was first published in 1964, Ḥassan Najīla describes 'Alī 'Abd al-Laṭīf in this way: 'It was the peak of colonization. This young man had a job that was an ambition for many, and he threw it away to wrestle an irresistible power, with no weapons except for his own faith'.[4] Another well-known author of memories is Sulaymān Kisha, who began writing about the insurgency as early as 1932, and who had written two books on the Revolution by 1970.[5] Kisha honoured 'Alī 'Abd al-Laṭīf and his colleagues, and described the links between himself and the 'hero' of 1924, whom he knew personally, and whom he used to visit at his home.[6]

Contrary to the belief of present-day historians, the racial theme is never mentioned as a cause of the failure of 1924. On the other hand, these authors all mention the 'secret work' of spies. For Ḥassan Najīla, betrayals even preceded 1924: 'Duplicity was begun by one person who enjoyed high standing among us [in the Sudan Union]';[7] Muḥammad 'Abd al-Raḥīm talks about various unnamed spies, and dedicates a number of angry passages to the most famous of British informants, 'Alī Aḥmad Ṣāliḥ.[8]

In spite of the positive descriptions of 1924 that were expressed by the first generation of authors, the activists of 1924 and their families viewed these accounts as incomplete and inadequate. However, I believe that this criticism was addressed more at the authors than it was at the content of the memoirs, which, as we have seen, were full of praise for the 'martyrs' of 1924, in line with their nationalist agenda. This can be understood if

2 Muḥammad 'Abd al-Raḥīm, *al-Ṣirā' al-musallaḥ alā al-waḥda fī al-Sūdān, aw, al-Ḥaqīqa 'an ḥawādith 1924* (al-Khurṭūm: Maṭba'at Klūt Bak, 1948). On this author, see 'Alī Ṣāliḥ Karrār, Yaḥyā Muḥammad Ibrāhīm, and Rex S. O'Fahey, 'The Life and Writings of a Sudanese Historian: Muḥammad 'Abd Al-Raḥīm (1878–1966)', *Sudanic Africa* (1995), no. 6, pp. 125–36.

3 'Abd al-Raḥīm, *al-Ṣirā' al-musallaḥ*, pp. 39-46.

4 Ḥassan Najīla, *Malāmiḥ*, p. 31.

5 *Index for Primary and Secondary Sources on the 1924 Revolution in the Sudan*. The books were: *Sūq al-dhikryāt* (1963) and *al-Liwā' al-abyaḍ* (1969). See bibliography.

6 Kisha, *al-Liwā' al-abyaḍ* pp. 6, 14.

7 Hasan Najila, *Malāmiḥ*, p. 171.

8 'Abd al-Raḥīm, *al-Ṣirā' al-musallaḥ*, p. 13.

we view it in the light of broader social issues. These early historians came from the same social group as the politicians who led the country to independence. They were also the very people who were considered to be responsible for 'betraying' the aspirations of the South and allowing the country to fall into a catastrophic civil war. Their political choices went hand in hand with a double standard: the nationalists affirmed that everybody in Sudan was equal, but in actual practice they worked to consolidate their own power. Similarly, some of the first historians' enthusiasm for 1924 was seen as rather dubious. The best case in point is Sulaymān Kisha, who, as seen, is rumoured to have been the person who tarnished the reputation of 'Alī 'Abd al-Laṭīf in *al-Ḥaḍāra* and betrayed the Sudan Union. This suspicion of double standards also involves some of the 1924 activists. One example of this is Mudaththir al-Būshī, the judge who was interviewed in *al-Riwāyāt*. In it, he described 'Alī 'Abd al-Laṭīf as 'an extraordinary officer' and praised the joint actions of officers and civilians like him in Wad Medani; however, he later became one of the champions of the Arabization of education in Southern Sudan, and later still a supporter of the Islamic Charter Front.[9]

As I pointed out in the introduction, a wide-scale project of collecting oral witnesses on 1924 was launched during the time of al-Numayrī, resulting in *al-Riwāyāt al-shafawiyya li-thuwwār 1924*. As the volume included interviews with 1924 activists – women, wage-workers and soldiers, as well as numerous army officers – it cast new light on various fascinating aspects of 1924, such as the connections among the actors, their intellectual backgrounds and the centres of insurgency. In spite of these new elements, however, perhaps surprisingly, in terms of interpretation these accounts do not differ substantially from those we have discussed above, and they share at least three fundamental assumptions: first, they never describe open disagreements among activists, stating, on the contrary, that the various social groups always worked hand in hand; second, they never mention the issue of the 'high' or 'low' background of certain activists as a causative factor of the events; and third, they also consistently view spies and traitors as causes of the failure of the revolution. People from entirely different professions and origins, who did not know each other, shared these general assumptions.

What was present in the accounts of *al-Riwāyāt* to a much larger extent than had been the case in previous memoirs is the topic of 'secrets'. I have discussed the centrality of secrecy to the structure of the League and the different levels of access to information according to the type of membership (see Chapter 4). These secrets continued to bind the activists as late as the 1970s, and I even encountered the problem during my fieldworks in the 2000s. This meant, for instance, that none of the many officers interviewed in *al-Riwāyāt* talked about the Sudan Union of 1924 (meaning the association of officers) or the plan to resort to violent action if there were an Egyptian evacuation, or the agreement with the Egyptian officers. Even civilian members of the League

9 Abdullahi Ali Ibrahim, *Manichaean Delirium: Decolonizing the Judiciary and Islamic Renewal in Sudan, 1898–1985* (Leiden/ and Boston: Brill, 2008), p. 108.

refused to talk about other associations, and often even about their own. Finally, the names of supposed 'spies' are also usually kept secret. In the few occurrences in which the name of a 'spy' was suggested (in most cases unconfirmed by colonial documents, which instead named other informants), they were either civilian members of the League or Sudanese from notable families, as with 'Alī al-Bannā and 'Abdallāh Khalīl. One officer told the following story: 'Abdallāh Khalīl was transferred to Wad Medani. He swore the oath, and was given the responsibility of keeping a list of League members. After some time, he was promoted to *miralai*, and all the other officers were punished by a transfer'.[10] All these stories suggest a theme of betrayal caused by greed. Again, the accounts are consistent: activists became spies – that is, they broke their oaths and revealed secrets – not because of any kind of racial rift, but as a result of personal ambition.

But what lies behind the keeping of these secrets for decades after the end of the Revolution, and continuing to denounce the acts of those who did not? I believe that this says more about the audibility of certain voices in the history of Sudan than about the existence of secrets that are still waiting to be disclosed. What is inaudible – that is, unexpressed and unacknowledged in elite histories of 1924 – is not so much what happened in 1924, *but after it*. It is precisely there that the theme of the racial split is situated, almost invisibly.

We saw in the last chapter that from the end of 1924, the British began to interpret the 1924 Revolution along racial lines. They attributed responsibility for the Revolution almost solely to 'Detribalized Blacks' and to Egyptian elements living in Sudan. As seen, after the expulsion of Egyptians, it was the group of 'Black officers' who had to bear the worst consequences for the crushed revolution. There are two aspects of the strategy of variations in punishment that crucially affect the way in which 1924 is remembered. First, it created divisions within a political movement that was explicitly and persistently concerned with overcoming social divisions relating to origin, ethnicity and occupation. Second, there were also long-term consequences. As we discussed in Chapters 8 and 9, the British became more careful about associating education with origin, admitting fewer Sudanese from a southern or western background into colonial schools and shutting down the Military School. As a result of this, at least until the Second World War, it became more difficult for people from these origins to attain the same position as their fathers, people like Zayn al-'Ābdīn 'Abd al-Tām, and 'Alī 'Abd al-Latīf, who were part of the educational and occupational elite. This is not only clear from the figures about the 'origins' of pupils in the 1930s, discussed in Chapter 8, but it was also recounted by some of their families. As one informant told me:

> When the League was destroyed, things started. After the Revolution, there was a new system that worked in this way: if you were Nuba or Dinka, there was no way for you; you could not go to the army and find a place there. The Dinka especially suffered a great deal: they were not wanted any more – they were too brave. In this

10 *Al-Riwāyāt*, Hassan Ismā'īl al-Muftī, p. 136.

situation, people from the northern tribes took advantage of this to get closer to the British; that is why there was racism later.[11]

This made it very difficult to attribute responsibility and to heal the wounds caused by the involuntary, posthumous betrayal of a section of the 1924 activists who were identified as 'the Arabs'. They were not responsible for the separate forms of punishment that followed the Revolution, for being released from prison or graced. Despite this, people identified as 'Arabs' failed to acknowledge either their own empowerment in the enhanced privileges that they came to enjoy or the fact that these privileges had come at the cost of the marginalization of other groups. This is the part of the story that is missing from the accounts of the first 'Arab' historians, in spite of all their praise for 1924.

The resentment generated by this form of injustice is sometimes explicitly expressed in testimonies. For instance, in 2005, in a conversation with the family of one of the three executed officers, Thābit 'Abd al-Rahīm, I learned that 'Alī al-Bannā and Thābit were close friends and neighbours. The family believed that 'Alī al-Bannā's relatives could have interceded to save Thābit's life as well: 'why did they not do it?' they asked. He died when he was only twenty-one, leaving a wife and an infant child that he would not see grow up; even today, his death is anything but a part of the past. While it is hard to believe that Thābit's life could indeed have been spared, this account reveals a story of shattered solidarities and painful divisions for which there has never been redress. Therefore, spy stories tell us less about disloyalties during 1924 than they do about the irreparable fractures that followed.

The 'Black Officers' and the other activists who paid the highest price for 1924 were caught up in a situation that made it extremely difficult for them to talk. 1924 was both a great political victory and a terrible loss. It was a moment of social unity and the point in time after which this same unity was shattered. Their loyalty to secrets that continue to be meaningful decades after 1924 seems to me to be a sign of their rejection of narratives that have failed to acknowledge the whole story. Even in the cacophony of *al-Riwāyāt*, the activists abridged their narratives, relating their stories while at the same time conveying the idea that they would not tell *all*. The keeping of secrets represents both a strategy of resistance, and – paradoxically – an incentive to continue to remember 1924, because for as long as the master narrative does not change, the past cannot be laid to rest.

[11] Interview by the author, tape recording, Omdurman, December 2004. I prefer to keep this informant anonymous.

Appendix I: Telegrams of the White Flag League and Other Protesters

TELEGRAMS

Table 15 Geographical distribution of texts, including telegrams

Place	Number of Texts
Khartoum/Omdurman	29
Port Sudan	15
Atbara	5
Medani	3
El Obeid	3
Abu Hamed	2
Bara	2
Al-Nuhud	1
Barakat	1
Halfa	1
Hassahissa	1
Merowe	1
Shendi	1
Total of texts the origin of which is known	**65**

Sources: NA: FO 141/810/3, FO 141/806/1, FO 141/805/2; WO 33/999. NRO: Palace 4/9/44, Palace 4/9/46, Palace 4/9/49, Palace 4/10/50, Kordofan 1/12/53, Kordofan 1/14/65, Northern Province 1/21/213, Northern Province 1/20/191. CRO: 0075-049751

A Note on the Language

These texts are poor English translations of originals in Arabic that I could not locate in any archives I visited. The quality of the language must be put in context: the overburdened translators employed by the Intelligence

Department had too much work and very little time to carry it out properly. Also, the main task of these translators was not to produce grammatically correct documents, but to convey the general meaning of these political texts, often as fast as possible. Such translations must be seen as drafts, and as the only fragments we have of voices that were certainly much more eloquent in Arabic, but which are now lost.

1) *Translation of an Arabic telegram, Khartoum, Saleh Abdel Gadir, Ali Abdel Latif, Hassan Sharif, Hassan Saleh, Obeid El Haj El Amin to Governor General, Khartoum, 15.5.1924, FO 141/806/1, NA.*

We beg to conveyance of this our protest to both the Egyptian and British Parliaments. Our dignity will not permit us to be bought and sold like animals who have no voice in their disposal. We protest with all our strength for not giving our people the legal freedom to say their word openly and to send those who will be selected by the nation from her sincere sons to at least to be aware of the true decision on the settlement of their future during the Negotiations. It is not for any other person than they, whatever the state may be, to settle the question of its future because the word is only for the nation and she is the owner of the right. We also protest against the secrecy and compulsory work which are adapted for the separation of the Sudan. All what we can do is to communicate this to you and to send someone to convey our opinion to our Exalted King and to the Consuls of the European Powers in Cairo.

2) *Translation of a Telegram, Mohammed Idris Babikr, El Imam Doleib, Ahmed Mudassir Ibrahim, El Tuhami Mohammed Osman, Hussein Yusif Hussein, to Governor General, Khartoum, 3.6.1924, FO 141/810/3, NA.*

We unceasingly support the telegrams of our friends to Your Excellency and assure you that we do not want any substitute for Egyptian rule and we disengage ourselves from anyone who deceived us in the past and we pay no attention to the falsehoods in the papers.

3) *El Tayeb Babikr, Sheik Omar Dafalla, Izzeidin Rashek, Abu El Amin Abu El Gasem, Mohammed Sirr El Khatim, Ali Abdel Latif to Egyptian Newspapers (The Editors of: El Balagh, El Akhbar, El Ahram) and the President of the Chamber, in DI. to SA Cairo, Khartoum, 19.6.1924, FO 141/806/1, NA.*

In the name of the Sudan nation, we beg to protest and to express out disgust at the policy [of] boycottage [sic] used to prevent the Delegation from departure in order to submit the documents of the loyalty of the majority of the Sudan natives to the King of the Country. We persistently demand the interference of the Government in the matter, with all the bravery and friendliness at her disposal, in order to put a stop to all kinds of persecution. Because the whole Egyptian nation is responsible before History for any calamity that befalls the servants of the Egyptian Crown wherever they are found. We are confident that a ship, at the helm of which is Saad Pasha, will never strike a rock however dark and stormy the times may be.

4) *Ahmed Omar Bakhreiba (Vice-President of the White Flag in the Blue Nile) to the President of the Egyptian parliament and the Honourable members, Cairo, 21.6.1924, FO 141/806/1, NA.*

We congratulate the Egyptian nation in the person of our Great King Fuad on the occasion of the outburst of the volcanoes of loyalty to the throne of the Kingdom which has been legally founded in the Sudan for the last 100 years. Petition of protests are being prepared, during demonstrations held in the name of HM the King and submitted from all sides against the British administration which is stealing signatures from weak natives by means of commission agents and traitors.

We beg further to draw your attention to the necessity of ordering that the new Egyptian flag be used throughout the whole of the Sudan.

Long Live the King.

5) *Translation of Arabic telegram, signed by 38 Army officers to the President of the Parliament, the Minister of War and the Press Syndicate, Cairo, 24.6.1924, FO 141/806/1 (copy in FO 141/810/3 with 36 signatures), NA.*

Whilst the officer Zein el Abdin was taking a picture of the demonstration he was arrested and imprisoned. We protest against this and against the imprisonment of four employees, and the beating of those who were shouting "Long live the King of Egypt and the Sudan" by swords.

6) *Translation of telegram, Saleh Abdel Gader, Ali Mallasi, Bashari Abdel Rahman to Governor General, Port Sudan, 25.6.1924, FO 141/810/3, NA.*

We protest against the arrest of our brother Mulazim Zein el Abdin Abdel Tam, Mohammed eff. Ibrahim Ismail, and their fellows, assuring you that they express the wish of the Sudanese Nation and her feelings towards her famous King Fuad I., the King of the Nile Valley. Your [sic] this treatment contravenes the liberty of expression of ideas; the Nation has the right of choice to declare in lawful ways for deciding their fate and no one else than her sincere sons have the right to demand her designs. Your confiscation of our ideas is an oppression which cannot be allowed by the Law of your high Nation and your candid people, who struggle for reformation.

7) *Translation of telegram, Saleh Abdel Kader, Ali Malasi, Bashri Abdel Rahman to Prime Minister, President of the Two houses, Press Syndicate, Cairo, 25.6.1924, FO 141/810/3, NA.*

We have declared the sayings of the truth but we were persecuted. We have sent our delegates to you to act on our behalf but they were arrested and imprisoned. We have expressed our love to our country and our beloved king Fuad, but we were tried and sentence [sic] to imprisonment. How is that, while we only stand by our great Egyptian throne and we apply for the freedom of the Nile Valley [?] What will be the position of the noble Egyptian nation and the position of their benevolent men with regard to the treatment which we the Sudanese receive[?] – We protest with all our strength against the arrest of our brethren Mulazim Awal Zein El Abdin Eff. Abdel Tam, Mohammed Eff. Ibrahim Ismail and others of the sons of the country which still has the hope to live with you.

8) *Translation of telegram, Mohammed Hediya, Ebeid Idris, Ahmed Ali, El Tayeb Abdin to His Excellency, the Governor General of the Sudan, Port Sudan, 27.6.1924, FO 141/806/1, NA.*

In continuation to the telegram addressed to you by our colleagues in Port Sudan, we beg to protest in the name of the Sudan nation against the severity used in dealing with our brethren the sons of the country who have been thrown into prison –whose only crime is the expression of their feelings of loyalty to their country and to their Great King Fuad I. We beg to repeat our assurance that they have not declared anything but truth, which is the aspiration of every Sudanese and which is the wish of the whole nation namely the non-division of the Nile Valley. The strong ties that bind us with our brethrens [sic] the Egyptians are not dissolvable and this is why we found no reason why we should not express our feelings of loyalty to our King. The persecution of our principles, and imprisonment of our brethren who express our feelings, is an encroachment on our rights which we are claiming by legal and peaceful means – and we did not expect you would obstruct us in this doing.

9) *Translation of telegram, Ahmed Omar Bakhreiba, Vice President of the White Flag League in the Blue Nile Province, Wad Medani, to Prime Minister, Members of the House of Representatives, President of the House of Commons, Cairo, 28.6.1924, FO 141/810/3, NA.*

In the name of the King, the Sudanese nation, the representatives of the two nations, the legal rights and Law, we protest against the British administration of arresting Zein Abdin Abd el Tam and Mohammed Eff. El Khalifa Abdalla El Taishi, Sheik Omar, Sheik Dafalla and their brethren who demonstrated in a peaceful manner. The public opinion of all the natives, the Sudanese officials in the Government departments both military and civil in all the Provinces, are inclined to make peaceful demonstration within the legal limits against the British administration which pretends that they vote in its favour. We also protest against the British administration for using swords against the White Flag League who are sincere to their dear country. These demonstrations are like strong washouts but they are in good order and therefore the responsibility of all the acts that took place should fall on the shoulders of the armed British administration. We beg you to consider this as a notification from us to all the ambassadors of the powers in Egypt especially to that of England, and we ask for its publication in the Egyptian and Sudanese newspapers. Long live the King.

10) *Translation of Telegram, Ali Abdel Latif, to the president of the parliament and the Press syndicate, Cairo, 30.6.1924, FO 141/810/3, NA.*

The peaceable demonstrators have been tried and sentenced to six months for shouting long live the King – It is an insult and it would please us, and we the people of the Sudan shall wait to see how and when the noble Egyptian nation would come forward to wash it.

11) *Translation of telegram, Ali Abdel Latif to the Right Honourable Ramsey MacDonald, The Times, The Daily Herald, 3.7.1924, Khartoum, FO 141/810/3, NA.*

The Association of the White Standards backed by the masses vehemently protests against statements of responsible Britishers concerning alleged British rights in Sudan stop No true Sudanese can ever accept imperialistic tactics and capitalistic schemes intended annex Sudan forcibly into British Empire stop Separation means death both Sudan and Egypt.

12) *Translation of a Telegram, from a Party of Sudanese, to Parliament and press syndicate, Cairo, 4.7.1924, FO 141/810/3, NA.*

The government prohibited the despatch of the national movement news from the Capital (Khartoum) to you. They will arrest Ali Abd al Latif. The British officials are publishing their propaganda in the country and they are spreading the spirit of enmity against Egyptians with all the power they possess and if we are on parliamentary election. We beg for mercy.

13) *Ahmed Omar Bakhreiba, Representative of the White Standards, and members in Medani to Officials, officers, NCO's and men of the Police in all Provinces of the Sudan, 5.7.1924, Medani, FO 141/806/1, NA, excerpts.*

You are no doubt aware of the dispute which is taking place between the Govt. of HM the King of Egypt and the Sudan, and the British administration in the Sudan: ... There is no doubt that you are perfectly aware that you owe loyalty exclusively to the Govt. of HE king Ahmed Fuad, the King of Egypt and the Sudan, by the law and the oath of obedience taken from you, and by the religion which binds you together. ...

We do not ask you to disobey the law by disobeying your Superiors – No. A thousand times no. Or to commit any crime against public security and order; we only ask you to remember what you owe legally to the King and to your brethren, peaceful demonstrators against the British administration, who have contravened the condition laid down in the agreement of partnership made between them, and have done much towards robbing the riches of the country and enslaving its people.

You know that the matter is a peaceful one and does not require the raising of a stick or a whip, but requires management, reminding and calling attention of parliament in Europe and Egypt by legal means and proper arguments, lest intrigue, deceit, disorder, lies etc. prevail.

14) *Obeid El Haj El Amin, Vice president of the League to the Governor General of the Sudan and the Director of Intelligence, Khartoum, 5.7.1924, FO 141/806/1, NA.*

We vehemently protest against the acts of terror towards those who express their loyalty to the Egyptian Crown. This action is not worthy of the honour of the Great Britain who pretends educating the nations. We also protest against your arrest of Ali Eff. Abdel Latif, Arafat Eff. Mohammed, Shaykh Omar Bakhreiba and others for no reason. We also protest against the secret courts recently adopted.

15) *Telegram from El Tayeb Abdin, Mohammed Hadeyah, Ali Mallasi, Ebeid Idris, Bashari Abdel Rahman to Governor General, Port Sudan, 5.7.1924, FO 141/810/3, NA.*

Power has been completed [sic] and the house of Saleh effendi Abdel Gader has been inspected and documents of loyalty of the Sudanese nation to her King Fuad I, have been taken. We protest with all our strength against this obstruction and ask your pity on this nation as to declare with demanding for the security of the future of her country because this is one of her lawful rights.

16) *Telegram from Obeid El Haj El Amin, Khartoum, to Prime Minister President of the Parliament, Press Syndicate, Cairo, 5.7.1924, FO 141/810/3, NA.*

The Tyrannical authority has begun arresting the men of action who have expressed their feelings towards the Great King. All those who have been arrested in the demonstrations have been tried in a Secret Court and have been imprisoned with thieves and murderers. Yesterday Ali Abdel Latif, Arafat Mohammed, Saleh Abdel Gader and Shaykh Omar Bakhreiba have been arrested with no crime except their clinging to the Egyptian throne. This is the honour of the English who pretend having come to the Sudan to educate and civilize its people. They arrest all those who contradict their opinions, persecute them, and treat them in the most abominable manner. Let those English know that we shall die to the last man, rather than accepting humiliation, and we accept no substitute for the Egyptians.

Let the advanced European nations bear witness of their treatment of humanity in the 20th Century.

17) *Saleh Abdel Kader, Aly Mallasi, Bashari Abdel Rahman, Ebeid Idris, El Tayeb Abdin, Mohammed Hadeyah to Governor General, Port Sudan, 8.7.1924, Palace 4/10/49, NRO.*

The using of power in searching the house of officer Ali Eff Abdel Latif, in his absence, taking his papers and his confinement, – we deny it – and protest against it by the name of the whole Sudanese nation. Every action wished with it to kill our national motion and our peaceful demands will strong [sic] our steadiness, union our lines and increase us in believe, steadily and bravery young and old men without caring to the dark of prisons and heaviness of fetters, and every hardness that you met us with it will increase our hate on you and our despair from you and double our love to our country and our King Fuad I, the king of the Nile Valley.

18) *Party of officers and natives to Acting Governor General of the Sudan, 8.7.1924, Palace 4/10/49, NRO.*

For keeping his life, it should be in your notice that has anything happened to him touching his life, you would be held responsible before the European Governments.

19) *Unsigned, to Anisa El Rashidi, President of the Women's Society, Alexandria, undated, but between 8.7.1924 and 24.7.1924, FO 141/810/3, NA.*

The flower of young men has been sentenced to three years imprisonment by the tyrannical power. This is a sacrifice to the country. Protests were sent to the Prime Minister. Long live the country and may complete independence come for Egypt and the Sudan.

20) *Obeid El Haj El Amin, Vice president of the White Flag League, Omdurman, to Parliament and Press Syndicate, Cairo, 8.7.1924, FO 141/810/3, NA.*

The imprisoned liberals are being beaten and threatened with cruelty with makes humanity tremble, in order to cause them to relinquish their principle and pretend that their acts were due to the abetment of the Egyptians. We have protested against this to the British Parliament.

21) *Unknown sender, Port Sudan, to Hakimam, Khartoum, 5.8.1924, Palace 4/10/50, NRO, excerpt.*

The repetition of the confinement accident (imprisonment) and (the) punishing of our innocent brothers who are loyal to their country and their King Fuad I, is an act which will increase the Sudanese in steadiness and their immovable belief and in continuing with demand by the non division of the Nile Valley....

22) *Mahmoud Mohammed Farghali, "For White Standards Society", Abu Hamed, to High Commissioner for Egypt, 7.8.1924, FO 141/810/3, NA, excerpt.*

Innocents who are loyal to the Egyptian throne here [are] imprisoned and treated as ordinary criminals, Lately native engineer Sirelkhatm was sentenced to three months' imprisonment for crying out verses of Koran and cheers to King Fuad in mosque. Alas, where is liberty of religious [sic] and justice of British Government [?] Is it just, in century of liberty and independence, to treat a nation in such cruelty which is unused for animals [?] There are animal reservations societies but none that ask about Sudanese who are seriously suffering of depression from British Government agents who announce to all that they are alleys to justice, but in fact this is contrary. ...

23) *'Translation of a seditious letter copied in a hectograph, addressed in English to the Director of Intelligence, Khartoum, and posted in Khartoum,' 10.8.1924, FO 141/805/2, excerpt.*

... Do not contemplate escaping from the field of national "Jihad" but stand fast and hold on to the last. If you escape you will only be deserting a right which has no defender and a religion complaining to God of a nation which had caused its destruction, and friends who have deserted it. God shall see your doings and remind you of them in the next world.

Your enemies desire to deprive you of your rights and you desire them to send their troops away from your country. They desire to torture you and enslave you, and you desire to die in the way of your independence. They desire to usurp your lands and weaken you, and you desire to obtain a paradise as big as heaven and earth which has been allotted to the inhabitants. ...

24) *Unsigned notice pasted in the civil hospital, signed "Forward patriots", and addressed "To my respected countrymen", Khartoum, 11.8.1924, Palace 4/10/50, NRO, excerpt.*

... Boycott the British completely and hate them as religion, nationality, character, the Nile country, God and his Prophet order you to hate them. Long live the Nile, long live the king of the Nile Fuad the first, long live Saad Zaghlul pasha, long live Ali Abdel Latif, long live the progressive young men, long live the sacrifice and down with the tyrannical and oppressive British.

25) *A call to the Sudanese Generally and to the natives of Kordofan, signed Head of the Society of el-Helal, Omdurman, 17.8.1924, FO 141/805/2, NA, excerpts.*

... What is the reason of your laziness? Are you pleased with your tyrants or are you depressed? Are you mere bodies to be guided like a flock of sheep, or are you slaves to be trodden on, or are you articles of merchandize to be sold in the open markets? Are you pleased with the present state of affairs and content to remain silent, which strengthens the hand of the British, or are you cowards? ... Do not be deluded by this mirage, this blind policy of colonization, the policy of those who will bury you under taxes, rob you of your money, your land and your livelihood, while you are inattentive, you know the treatment and torments, but are afraid. We also be of you by God, His Prophets and by the love of your dear native country to avoid your brothers the merchants. Pay no attention to your races or religions, do not be traitors, do not be spies, but be united like brothers. God Help you and Farewell.

26) *Translation of a seditious circular found in the streets of El Obeid on Friday 31st of August, entitled 'A call to the Sudanese Generally and to the natives of Kordofan', signed by President Crescent society, 27.8.1924, FO 141/805/2, NA, excerpts.*

In the name of God the merciful the compassionate. O Ye free patriots, men and women of the future, etc (God is your refuge and strength and help in trouble nor shall we fear through the earthquake and mountains be overturned into the sea – Holy Bible). We speak to you with heart filled with freedom, undismayed by bombs and guns etc. Where are you? Are you willing to put up with this tyranny or are you slaves to be trampled underfoot and be bought and sold in the market etc?

Khartoum, Omdurman, Atbara, Wad Medani, Port Sudan and every town in the Sudan is working for freedom for Egypt and the Sudan. ... So just as the crescent and the cross have followers so Egypt and the Sudan shall not be separated. So get together and organize peaceful demonstrations and show your feelings toward your country and its happiness and do not suffer this policy of colonisation, this policy of those who plunder your goods and lands, while you stood by from excess of fear. We call upon you in the name of God and by the life of our dear native country. We hope you will not cause or receive any harm. Call on your friends the merchants to help you, and do not play the part of traitors. God give you victory. Peace on you.

27) *Othman Mohammed Hashim, member of the White Flag League, Published in Muqattam, 31.8.1924, FO 141/805/2, NA, excerpt.*

... The Society [of the Sudan Union] was founded by the best and most enlightened of the natives of the country and of the most famous families and by leaders of opinion in it. Previous to its organization individual members were seeking to oppose the colonization by various methods and they were assisted in this by reason of their position in administrative posts in touch with the masses of the people. This Society has done good work in preparing the nation and rendering it inflammable and ready to respond to the first spark of true patriotism (nationalism). There were also circumstances that assisted this work.

Now when the White Flag League began to work openly the United Sudan Society was working unseen and no difficulty was experienced in leading the nation to its patriotic campaign. When member of the White Flag League were arrested the United Sudan Society broke into revolt and by its circulars gave an open lead and call to the nation to be as one mass in its support.

28) *Tayeb Babiker, 'What is there in the Sudan!', Published in al-Akhbar, 3.9.1924, FO 141/805/2, NA, excerpt.*

... They have filled the prisons with the innocent who are only charged with having cheered and expressed their loyalty to the King of the Nile Valley who is lawfully and naturally the king of the country. ... They were not content with prohibiting demonstrations but went so far as to prevent meetings and gathering ... on the occasion of banquets, lamentations, burials and 'Zikrs' such as has been our custom.... They have oppressed us to an extent such as is forbidden by the laws of nature. They have also filled the walls, mosques and streets of every city with notices of threat, promising severe punishment to whoever contravenes them. They have on the whole used all kind of oppression and menace, demonstrations are proceeding everywhere, and the inhabitants who consider that the separation of the Nile is like death to them have been made to experience all kinds of oppression.

We look on these acts of cruelty as vaccinations against our unity. Let them increase the wounds and let them also double the power of the vaccins [sic] lymph for that would not affect us. They depend in their policy on their fading power whereas we depend on the strength of our rights and on the power of our belief. Let them deprive us of our rights, let them exercise their cruelty and let them also do whatever they like to human beings for these are only lessons which we require much in our practical life.

We would, however, ask our Government [Egypt] to change her policy in regard to such actions. She has already been silent for a long time and it is time she said her last word to the English and defend us, at least in their capacity as a partner, although we believe that no partnership exists, as all that is on the Nile is Egypt's ....

29) *'A call', addressed to 'my dear Countrymen', signed Society for the national defence, 13.9.1924, FO 141/805/3, NA, and Kordofan 1/4/65, NRO, excerpt.*

... Your country is what is going to remain for you and your offspring. It is therefore the biggest shame that a nation should come from overseas to strip you of your property and enslave you, your children, and your women and that you should be unaware of this.

You should be aware that the time for you to rise up has arrived. You should not be lazy; the hour when you should be awake has arrived, don't be sleepy but fight the cause of your country so that the colonizer might understand that whenever a party is suppressed another would appear to claim our right in a more emphatic way than the first. Let the British officials understand that whatever oppression they undertake others are to reap the outcome of their work and they would remain guilty before God ...

30) *Unsigned letter sent to the Nazir El Obeid School, 28.11.1924, Kordofan 1/14/65, NRO, excerpts.*

I beg you to salute on behalf of the honoured heroes of our rising [,] [e]specially ALI ABDUL LATIF and his civil and military companions; those people who offered their dear souls and future for the sake of rendering services to their sacred native land – Wadi El Nil ; those innocents who were imprisoned by the cruelty of colonization and the policy of dispersion. They are waiting [for] you with their hearts full of confidence and of faith, to advance with the affair of your native land or carrying through the lawful means such as peaceful demonstrations and open protests in order that you may declare your indignation against the oppressors, their cruelty and their deviation from the right course. You must perform these things without fearing their bullets, guns, aeroplanes, testudos [sic], police and spies.

You have already done this but have to tell you, with the deepest sorrow which overflows my hearts and companionship, that your absolute silence caused the opponent to say that the Sudanese agitation was fictitious and that it was excited, secretly, by money.

You have never been an instrument which is set to motion by means of a foreign hand. The opponents forgot that they have treated you unjustly by their martial and exception laws. Moreover, they have deprived you from knowledge, imposed [illegible] and driven you away from the hand of your fathers and grandfathers.

Appendix 2: Sources on Members of Political Associations in 1924

BACKGROUND OF PROTESTERS AND PARTICIPATION IN DEMONSTRATIONS

The lists of White Flag members and other activists

The historiography of 1924 has unanimously considered that the White Flag League included 120 members, whose names are all known, thanks to a list found by the Intelligence Department in the home of one of them.[1] This list offers us an unequivocal picture of the socio-professional background of the members, which in turn is often quoted to justify the apparent failure of the League to reach outside the 'Effendi' group that made it up. We know the professions of half of these 120 members, and 90% of this half were educated Sudanese. Most of them worked in departments such as the Railways and the Post and Telegraph, followed by discharged Egyptian Army officers and a handful of artisans and traders, but no serving officers.

It is extremely problematic, however, to attempt to base membership of the White Flag League on this list, for several reasons. First of all, the list has a number of peculiar features that might lead to its authenticity being questioned. Besides the fact that it was found at the home of Ḥassan Midḥat, who was one of the main witness for the prosecution (*The White Flag Trials*, pp. 58-68), there are some strange features regarding the individuals included in it. For example, it contains *en bloc* the names of a group of discharged officers who had signed two petition-telegrams a few weeks earlier (their names spelled exactly in the same way, which is unusual in colonial documents), but who otherwise never came to the

[1] The list I refer to is the 'List of 120 Members of the White Flag League and the suggested leaders in the future', undated and unsigned; however, it could be from just after or around 3 July, since it includes the name of 'Alī 'Abd al-Laṭīf, accompanied by the word 'arrested' in pencil. The list was found at the home of Ḥassan Midḥat, Northern Province 1/21/207, NRO. The account of the discovery appears in Chronicle of events during the period of political excitement in Khartoum, FO 141/805/2, NA.

attention of the Intelligence Department for having taken part in any other protest.[2] But even if we do not go so far as to believe that the list might be a forgery, the fact that it does not include some of the League's most famous members, such as Zayn al-'Ābdīn 'Abd al-Tām, or Ṭayyib Bābikr – both of them were instead included the list of about twenty early activists kept in the house of 'Alī 'Abd al-Laṭīf – or again 'Alī Malāsī, one of the leaders of the League in Port Sudan, leads to the question of its value. Second, this is by no means the only existing list of White Flag members. On the contrary, the colonial archives are particularly rich in lists. These include a number of members that varies from 118 to 20, and the names do not coincide with those on the first list. Furthermore, none of all the lists available includes the cadets of the Military School, the Atbara rioters, and the officers who took part in the November mutiny. The following is a comprehensive 'list of lists' of political activists present in different archives.

Colonial archives

- 'Members of the White Flag League and the suggested leaders in the future' (list found in the house of Ḥassan Midḥat), undated, unsigned, Kordofan 1/13/5, and Northern Province, 1/21/207 NRO, 120 members.
- 'List of political agitators', undated, unsigned, Kordofan 1/13/61, NRO, with 118 named individuals (only 26 people appear in both). The profession is known for 50% of them, and it includes quite equally officers, cadets, civilian employees, and merchants.
- 'List of members of the League', undated, unsigned. In pencil: 'Usual distribution asking to inform us which of these men are govt. employees and to which dept. they belong', Palace 4/10/50, NRO, 43 members. The profession is known only for 16 of them, all of them government or private employees, except for two officers.
- 'List of members of the WFL in Obeid', in Information regarding the activities of the League of the White Flag in El Obeid, Director of Intelligence, Khartoum, 10.8.24, FO 141/805, NA. 39 people. The profession is known for 37, equal distribution of officers, government employees and traders.
- 'List of Members of the WF Society as given by sheikh Omer Tenai', 21.8.1924, Kordofan 1/16/68, NRO. 19 members, most of them merchants and government employees.

These two last lists, which were both found in Kordofan, together include 58 people; only one name among the 58 is to be found also in the 120-name list of Ḥassan Midḥat, although these two lists include protesters active in all Sudan and not only in Kordofan.

- 'List of members of the 'Sudan Union' who are said to have recently taken the oath', Intelligence, 21.9.24, Telegram from Hakiman, Khartoum, to Stack, London, and More, Cairo, 22.9.1924, Palace 4/9/45, NRO. 65 members, all of them officers except 4 government employees.

2 Appendix K to the Willis Report: the League of the White Flag: Translation of Arabic telegram addressed to The Press Syndicate and the President of the Council of Ministers, Cairo, (erroneously) dated 24.7.1924, FO 141/810/3, NA.

Private hands

- List kept by the Durriyya Muḥammad Ḥusayn, grand-daughter of 'Alī 'Abd al-Laṭīf (20 members).
- List of about 200 members. It belongs to the family documents of one of the mutinous cadets, 'Abdallāh Mabrūk. This list, in the great majority officers, include only very few people known by the Intelligence Department. This list seems to prove that the overwhelming majority of the military establishment of the time was involved in the 1924 Revolution.

SOURCES FOR THE GEOGRAPHY OF 1924 ACTIVISTS IN THE PROVINCES (EXCLUDING THE CAPITAL, PORT SUDAN, EL OBEID, SHENDI, ATBARA, AND WAD MEDANI)

In alphabetical order

Abu Deleiq: Intelligence note, Khartoum, 18.7.1924 Northern Province 1/20/192, NRO.

Abu Hamed: all the file Northern Province 1/21/207, NRO.

Argo: Intelligence Department Khartoum, 3.8.1924, Phipps for Director of Intelligence, Palace 4/10/50, NRO.

Bahr al-Ghazal, province, general: Extract from a letter from the Sudan Agent, Cairo to the Director of Intelligence, Khartoum 7.10.1924 Kordofan 1/14/68, NRO .

Bara: Leaders as Signalled by Cooke, 21.9.1924 Kordofan 1/12/55, NRO; DC, Northern Kordofan to Gov. Kordofan, Bara 14.11.1924, Kordofan 1/12/57, NRO.

Berber: Information, Director of Intelligence to Gov. Berber, 18.7.24, Khartoum, Northern Province 1/20/192, NRO.

Delgo: Acting Governor of Halfa to Director of Intelligence, Halfa 7.9.1924 FO 141/805/2, NA; Chronology – Appendix no. 13 in Kordofan 1/13/62, NRO.

Dilling: Assistant District Commissioner to Governor Nuba Mountain Province, Dilling, 21.8.1924, Kordofan 1/12/56, NRO.

Dongola: Translation of a letter of information, Intelligence Department, 28.7.1924, Palace 4/10/49, NRO.

El Damer: Director of Intelligence, Information to Governor Berber, Khartoum, 18.7.1924, Northern Province 1/20/192, NRO.

El Dueim: Extract from a letter from the Sudan Agent, Cairo to the Director of Intelligence, Khartoum, 7.10.1924, Kordofan 1/14/68, NRO.

El Fasher: Governor Fasher to Director of Intelligence, 20.8.1924, FO 141/805/3, NA; Telegram from Director of Intelligence to Governor, El Fasher, 18.12.24, Palace 4/9/47, NRO.

El Nuhud: Information, El Obeid, 20.7.1924, and Intelligence Dept., Khartoum 4.8.1924, both in Palace 4/10/50, NRO; Assist. DC to Gov. El Obeid, El Nahud, 7.9.1924, Kordofan 1/14/65, NRO.

Geteina: Extracts form Governor White Nile Province, 3.9.1924, FO

141/805/2, NA.

Halfaya al-Maluk: Information by informer n. 150, El Obeid, 9.9.1924, Kordofan 1/12/55, NRO.

Hassahissa: Intelligence Notes, 22.9.1924, Palace 4/9/45, NRO.

Hillet Shiqayla (Shigeila): Summary of Agent's Report received from the Gezira, Intelligence Notes 25.8.1924, Northern Province 1/21/215, NRO.

Kabushiya: Director of Intelligence, Information to Governor Berber, Khartoum, 18.7.1924, Northern Province 1/20/192, NRO

Kamlin: Summary of Agent's Report received from the Gezira, Intelligence Notes, 25.8.1924, Northern Province 1/21/215, NRO.

Khashem el Girba : Acting Sirdar to Acting Governor General, 9.10.24, Palace 4/9/46, NRO.

Kodok : List of members of the 'Sudan Union' who are said to have recently taken the oath, Intelligence, 21.9.1924, Palace 4/9/45, NRO.

Kosti: ADC Northern Kordofan to Governor Kordofan, 3.12.1924, Bara, Kordofan 1/13/60, NRO.

Makwar: Mukhabarat to Governor, 16.7.1924, Kordofan 1/12/56, NRO.

Malakal: Miscellaneous files in Palace 4/9/45, Palace 4/9/46, NRO, and FO 141/669/8, NA.

Nurayet (Berber): Gov. Berber Prov. to DC Berber, El Damer, 27.9.24, Northern Province, 1/21/215, NRO.

Renk: List of members of the 'Sudan Union' who are said to have recently taken the oath, Intelligence, 21.9.1924, Palace 4/9/45, NRO.

Sharkayla: miscellaneous files in Kordofan 1/12/55, NRO.

Shembe : List of members of the 'Sudan Union' who are said to have recently taken the oath, Intelligence, 21.9.1924, Palace 4/9/45, NRO.

Singa: Bence-Pembroke, Governor, Singa, to Director of Intelligence, Khartoum, 11.9.1924, Palace 4/9/45, NRO; Intelligence Notes 21.10.1924, Palace 4/9/47, NRO.

Talodi: miscellaneous files Palace 4/9/45, NRO.

Taqali: Notes on the activity of the White Flag Society at El Obeid, Gov. Kordofan Prov. to Director of Intelligence, El Obeid, 8.8.1924, Kordofan 1/14/68, NRO.

Umm Ruwaba: whole files, Kordofan 1/12/55, Kordofan 1/12/56, Kordofan 1/12/57, NRO

Wadi Halfa: miscellaneous files in FO 141/805/2; from Arkan Harb, Halfa, to HE Sirdar, Khartoum, 14.7.1924, Palace 4/10/49, NRO. Extract from a letter from the Sudan Agent Cairo, to the Director of Intelligence, Khartoum 7.10.1924, Kordofan 1/14/68, NRO.

Wau: Miscellaneous files in Palace 4/9/44, Palace 4/9/45, Palace 4/9/46, NRO.

Table 16 Occupation and origin of individuals arrested for participating in the disturbances of June and July in Khartoum.

Key D= Demonstration; S= Speech; L = organized by the League

Date	Type	Name	Occupation	Origin	Role in the WFL
19.6	S+D L	*Shaykh* Wad 'Umar Ḍayfallāh	Religious man	Ja'ali	Member of the League, according to 'Alī's list
20.6	S	*Shaykh* Ḥassan al-Amīn al-Ḍarīr	Religious man	Mahasi Relative of *'umda* of Tuti Island	
23.6	D	Ḥāmid Ḥusayn	Carpenter	Muwallad	Member of the Markazia 2
	L	'Alī Aḥmad Ṣāliḥ	Clerk in private company	Mahasi	Close to the League, main witness for the prosecution
		Ismā'īl Ibrāhīm	Clerk in the Tanzimat office	Muwallad (relative of Ṣāliḥ 'Abd al-Qādir)	Member of the League, according to 'Alī's list
		'Abd al-Sālim Sid Aḥmad	Unemployed	Dinka	
		Muḥammad Makkī Ibrāhīm			Member of the League, brother-in-law of Sāliḥ 'Abd al-Qādir
26.6	D	'Abd al-Karīm al-Sayyid	Carpenter	Muwallad	Member of the White Flag League, who wrote a long memoir on 1924
		Fu'ād 'Alī	Bookmaker	Hashimi	Pleaded innocent.
		Tawfīq Ḥassan	Tailor	Muwallad	
		Tuhāmī Muḥammad 'Uthmān	Carpenter	Shayqi	Member of the Markazia

Table 16 (contd)

27.6	D	Aḥmad Idrīs Abū Ghālib	Clerk at the Medical Office	"Moorish Muwallad"	
		Khalīl Kabsūn	Teacher at the American Missionary School	Dinka	Relative of Ḥassan Faḍl al Mūlā
		Ḥassan Aḥmad Faḍl	Small merchant	Muwallad	
		Ismā'īl 'Abd al-Majīd	Small merchant	Muwallad	
6.7	Attempted		Tailor	Muwallad	
	D		Tailor	Furawi	
12.7	S	Muḥammad Sirr al-Khātim	Clerk in the Irrigation Dept.	Mahasi from Halfa	Member of the League
22.7	D	'Alī Ḥassan Dabba		Ja'ali	
2.8	D	Muḥammad 'Abd al- 'Āl	Carpenter/ stonecutter	Muwallad	This was the second demonstration he was in
15.8	D	Ḥassan Muḥammad Yāsīn	Shoemaker	"Harbabi"	
	17 people arrested, but only 8 names	Muḥammad Sulaymān	Clerk	Ja'ali	Named on a "list of political agitators"*
		"Bedawi" Ḥusayn Badrān	Merchant	"Eligi"	
		Muṣṭafā Yūsif	Ivory turner	Egyptian	
		Muḥammad Khamīl	Merchant	'Abbasi	
		Aḥmad 'Alī	Merchant	Ja'ali	
		'Abd al-'Azīz "Gama"	Merchant	Egyptian	
		Aḥmad al-Māḥī		Maḥasi	
21.9	D	'Abd al-Khalīl "Tahmush"	Cook	"Berberine"	Pleaded innocent, acquitted
	5 people arrested, but only 4 named	'Abd al-Raḥman Ḥassan	Fishmonger	Muwallad	
		Ḥusayn 'Alī	Pedlar, owner of a coffee stall	"Eligi"	
		Mūsā Aḥmad ('Antar)	Coffee shop owner	Ja'ali	Named on "list of political agitators"

* Intelligence, political activities of various persons, Index to files 36-m-5-3, Kordofan 1/13/61, NRO.

Sources: NA : FO 141/805/2, FO 141/806/1, FO 141/810/3. NRO: Kordofan 1/12/54, Kordofan 1/13/58, Kordofan 1/13/59, Kordofan 1/13/61, Palace 4/10/48, Palace 4/10/49, Palace 4/10/50

Bibliography

PRIMARY SOURCES

Archives

National Record Office, Khartoum (NRO)

Civsec 1-58-167 Nationality Analysis 20-30
Civsec 5-6-33 Colonization Schemes
Civsec 5-8-49 Applications to Military School
Civsec 17-1-3 Education Fees
Civsec 37-1-3 Labour, Discharged Soldiers
Civsec 50-14-61 Staff Khartoum Province
Civsec 50-8-38 Trial Obeid Haj al Amin. doc
Civsec 57-35-133 Handbook Khartoum Province
Civsec1 1-58-165 Gordon College Complaints
Civsec1 1-58-168 Prospect of educated Sudanese
Civsec1 1-58-169 Prospect of educated Sudanese
Civsec1 1-58-170 Prospect of educated Sudanese
Civsec1 10-1-1 Unlawful societies ordinance 1919
Civsec1 10-2-5 Revision grading system
Civsec1 17-2-6 Education expansion 1920-30
Civsec1 17-24-2 Education of Nubian boys and Employment in Sudan Government
Civsec1 17-3-14 Education system in the Sudan 1938
Civsec1 17-5-25 Application for free or assisted education
Civsec1 20-2-6 Provinces, Analysis of Staff 1933
Civsec1 20-5-23 Education 1930s
Civsec1 36-1-1 Intelligence Department, Re-organisation 1925-27
Civsec1 36-14-11 Rumour of strike in Atbara 1919
Civsec1 36-4-16 1924
Civsec1 37-1-2 Discussions among Labour Commitee 1930s.
Civsec1 37-1-3 Labour bureau for ex-soldiers and Police
Civsec1 37-2-6 Tramway strike in Khartoum
Civsec1 5-1-3 General Ruling Re. Pagan serving in Northern Province
Civsec1 5-5-24 Recruitment 1928
Civsec1 5-5-31 SDF boy technical school
Civsec1 5-6-35 Radif
Civsec1 5-6-40 Army at dardanelli
Civsec1 5-7-44 Pension Army
Civsec1 5-8-52 Recruitment SDF 1935
Civsec1 9-13-53 Rents for officers
Civsec2 24-13-204 Shinnawi

Civsec2 24-38-471 Mamurs sub-mamurs Whos who
Civsec2 4-2-10 Army
Civsec2 4-2-11 Sudan Defence Force and mutiny
Darfur 1-2-7 Unrest
Darfur 1-2-11 Army Reservist
Darfur 1-19-98 Haradat
Darfur 1-19-100 Mahdi Influence in Darfur
Darfur 1-19A-102 Nyala
Darfur 1-23-128 Nebi Isa Cult
Darfur 3-2-16 Seditious Circulars
Darfur 4-1-6 Slavery
Department Reports 7-43-163 The New Cost of Living Indices
Department Reports 20-1-1 Gordon Memorial College, reports and accounts to 31st December 1927
Intel 1-2-105 Memorandum Intelligence Deptartment
Intel 1-11-50 Miscellaneous Intelligence 1924
Intel 1-20-106 Censorship 1914-1919
Intel 1-21-111 Bhar al Ghazal, anonymous letters
Intel 2-10-71 Muzamil Ali Dinar
Intel 2-14-121 HM King's visit, return of Shaykhs and Dinkas
Intel 2-31-253 Administration by Native Notables 1922-23
Intel 2-41-341 Settlement for Mahdi and Khalifa's families
Intel 2-44-370 Census of the Sudan 1909-1913
Intel 2-48-407 Organization of Secret Service and Intelligence in the Provinces, 1914-1915
Intel 2-48-409 Seditious literature 1915
Intel 4-1-1 Labour in Deims around Khartoum
Intel 4-1-3 Samples of contracts
Intel 4-1-6 Registration of Labour
Intel 4-1-7 Labour Supply 1921
Intel 4-2-8 Labour Miscellaneous files
Intel 4-2-9 Restriction of Recruiting of Labourers
Intel 4-2-10 Miscellaneous file labour, 1921-23.doc
Intel 4-2-11 Labour miscellaneous files
Intel 4-3-15 Labour Reports 1909-12
Intel 4-3-16 Labour Report 1912-13
Intel 4-3-17 Labour Report 1910
Intel 4-4-29 Memo on the agricultural labour in the Sudan
Intel 4-5-38 Black List of Sudanese Servants
Intel 4-5-42 Report Riverain estate labour supply
Intel 4-5-44 Scarcity of Labour
Intel 4-7-54 Wages of labour at Port Sudan
Intel 4-7-56 Gum porters El Obeid
Intel 4-7-58 Army recruits
Intel 9-1-8 Nyala 1921
Intel 9-2-20 Who's Who Madhist Khartoum
Khartoum Province 1-7-176 Personnel Rulings and General Correspondence
Khartoum Province 1-5-78 25 Birthday of King Fuad, procedures
Khartoum Province 1-6-98 Complaint against merisa brewing
Kordofan 1-11-45 Mutiny at Talodi and Khartoum
Kordofan 1-11-51 3 Future status of the Sudan, expression of Public Opinion
Kordofan 1-12-53 Anonymous Letters
Kordofan 1-12-54 Demonstration
Kordofan 1-12-55 Intelligence, Future Status – WF Society
Kordofan 1-12-56 Intelligence, future status of the Sudan, Political agitation in the Sudan, Activities of various persons
Kordofan 1-12-57 Future status of the Sudan Political agitation in the Sudan, actiyities of various persons
Kordofan 1-12-58 Intelligence, Future Status, Activities
Kordofan 1-13-59 Intelligence, Future status of the Sudan, Political agitators and various persons
Kordofan 1-13-60 Intelligence, Future status of the Sudan, Political agitators and various persons
Kordofan 1-13-61 Intelligence, political activities of various persons
Index to files 36-m-5-3
Kordofan 1-13-62 Intelligence, future Status of the Sudan, Activities of organizations
Kordofan 1-13-63 Memorandum, Archer
Kordofan 1-13-64 White Flag League
Kordofan 1-14-66 Action to be taken against seditionists
Kordofan 1-14-70 Bolshevism Intelligence
Northern Province 1-19-117, History

Sheet, Henry Hanalla (Hamdalla)
Northern Province 1-19-119 Bimbashi Hamid Saleh el Mek
Northern Province 1-19-122 El Tayeb Babikr of Shendi
Northern Province 1-19-128 Bayoumi Sayah Shendi
Northern Province 1-20-191 Atbara telegrams
Northern Province 1-20-192 Atbara, disturbances of August 1924
Northern Province 1-20-195 Trial of Hilmi Bisaida, Gamal el Din Mohammed, Seddik el Mekki el Shafie, Aba Yazid Ahmed
Northern Province 1-20-198, Disturbances in Shendi 1926
Northern Province 1-20-199 Gordon College Strike
Northern Province 1-21-207 White Flag League Conspiracy Trial, 1924
Northern Province 1-21-211 Mutiny in Khartoum 1924
Northern Province 1-21-212 Military School mutiny 1925
Northern Province 1-21-213 Seditious Telegram 1925
Northern Province 1-21-214 Sedition Pamphlets 1924
Northern Province 1-21-215 Pro-Egyptian Propaganda: General, 1924
Northern Province 1-21-217 Mahmoud Mohammed Farghali, Disturbances 1924
Northern Province 1-21-221 Omar Dafalla
Palace 4-1-3 Gordon College Office, statistics
Palace 4-1-4 Gordon College Office
Palace 4-8-41 Petition by old soldiers
Palace 4-9-44 1924
Palace 4-9-45 1924
Palace 4-9-46 1924
Palace 4-9-47 1924
Palace 4-10-48 1924
Palace 4-10-49 1924
Palace 4-10-50 1924
Palace 4-10-51 Prison Mutiny
Palace 4-10-52 Atbara Mutiny
Palace 4-11-54 Talodi Mutiny
Palace 4-11-55 Khartoum Mutiny
UNP 1-19-160 Reorganisation of the Intelligence Department
UNP 1-25-191 Irrigation Dep. employees
UNP 1-25-192 Suspects Mohammed Mabrouk El Zani
UNP 1-26-194 White Flag League
UNP 1-26-195 Bolshevism, communist activities, Wafd

The National Archives, Kew, London (NA)

FO 141/42/1 Sudan: The Education (Non-Government Schools) Ordinance, 1927.
FO 141/494/8 Murder of Major General Sir Lee Stack
FO 141/494/9 Sudan Mutiny of 1924
FO 141/504/4 Press situation following the murder of the Sirdar
FO 141/532/4 Education in the Sudan, 1935
FO 141/582/3 Sudanese independence from Egypt
FO 141/586/1 1921 Public Order Ordinance, 1925 Public Order (Amendment) Ordinance
FO 141/607/1: War services of the Sudan administration and Egyptian Army
FO 141/640/2 Slave trade and slavery in the Sudan, Egypt and Abyssinia
FO 141/669/8 Egyptian Political Situation 1924-27
FO 141/692/13 Exemption of Sudanese nationals from conscription in the Egyptian Army, 1931
FO 141/705/4 Reports on educational policy in Northern and Southern Sudan, 1933
FO 141/709/22 Report of a strike by pupils at Gordon Memorial College
FO 141/713/8 Information provided to the League of Nations about slavery in the Sudan
FO 141/719/1 Gordon Memorial College, Khartoum
FO 141/739/1 Questions relating to the political and financial status of the Anglo-Egyptian Sudan
FO 141/751/2 Egyptian Propaganda in the Sudan 1924
FO 141/777/1 Negotiations between British and Egyptian Governments on

the future status of the Sudan
FO 141/787/9 Sudan local government 1924-29
FO 141/790/11 Intelligence Bureau memorandum on 'The Formula of the Self-Determination of Peoples and the Moslem World'1918
FO 141/790/16 Sudan: movement for independence from Egypt 1922-1925
FO 141/805/2 Sudan Disturbance 1924
FO 141/806/1 Sudan Disturbance, 1918-1924
FO 141/806/8100 Re Sudan Disturbances
FO 141/807/1 Miscellaneous Egyptian political intelligence
FO 141/807/2 Saad Pasha Zaghloul and Party
FO 141/810/2 Egyptian self-government propaganda
FO 141/810/3 Reports on disturbances and demonstrations by political groups in Egypt and the Sudan and British reactions 1924
FO 141/812/27 Egyptian army labour for Sudan railways
FO 141/819/16 The invocation of King Hussein at Friday prayers in mosques in the Sudan 1925
FO 141/825/1 The administration of Gordon Memorial College, 1929.
FO 371/1361 Egypt. Code 16 Files 25 – 4781 includes Report on GMC 1910
FO 407 Series: Foreign Office: Confidential Print Egypt and the Sudan: Further Correspondence, Parts from LXIII (1905) to XCVIII (1925)

FO 407/201 Ewart Report on Political Agitation in the Sudan, Khartoum, 21.4.1925
WO 32/6383 Omdurman Mutiny: Insubordination by officers of Egyptian Army 1900
WO 32/5588 Question of control and organization of Egyptian Forces in Sudan, 1923-24

Cairo Record Office (in Arabic and French)

0069-002076 Report on Sudan, 1924
0075-049751 Sudan 1924 (Soudan, Protestation a la suite des évènements et troubles – archives confidentielles)
0075-049751 Soudan, Protestation a la suite des évènements et troubles – archives confidentielles
0075-049752 Évènements et troubles, August 1924, 1ère partie
0075-049753 Évènements et troubles Novembre et décembre 1924
0075-049754 Évènements et troubles August 1924, 2ème partie
0075-049755 Évènements and troubles, 1924

Sudan Archive Durham (SAD)

110/11/1-89 IX Sudanese Regimental Historical Record
188/3/203-4 Legal secretary to the Gov. Gen, 28.12.1913
212/8/5-8 CA Willis, notes on his part in the disturbances of 1924, typescript.
270/1/99 Slatin to Wingate, 27.1.1900
271/2/4 Wingate to Cromer, 21.02.01
294/6/1-43 AC Parker, Atbara 1924
301/3/29-30 J. J. Asser, 'Report on tour of Bahr el-Ghazal, Tewfikia and Malakal, 08.09.1911
430/6/5-6 Appeal to the Sudan Government by the Sudanese Notables against the liberation of slaves, 2.10.1898 to HE the Sirdar
438/653 Slatin Papers
479/7/53 Scheme E (Evacuation of the Egyptian army), Intelligence notes on the mutiny of 27-28 November. 1924
533/2/1-17 REH Baily, 1924 Mutiny, comments

549/6 Sudan Government, Annual Report of the Education Department, 1928
550/11/1-63 Gordon Memorial College Trust 1929, Report of a commission of inspection on the GMC, February 1929
552/4/1-38 Annual Report 1930: 1930 Report on GMC
553/6/1-25 Annual Report 1931
553/8/24 Gordon Memorial College Trust for 1932
555/6/1-29 Annual Report of the education department for the year ended the 31st December 1933.
558/7/1-84 Gordon Memorial College Trust, 1939
710/11/23 Draft on "The status of slavery in Islam", addressed to all governors (except upper Nile and Equatoria) 6.5.1925
741/3/1-64 JHR Orlebar "Account of events at the time of the mutiny in 1924 by ex-miralai Adair bey"
780/1/4 CG Dupuis to Lady Jane, 21/12/24

Mahmoud Saleh Collection (Special collection on Sudan), Centre for Middle Eastern and Islamic Studies [SMI], University of Bergen

[[Great Britain]. Foreign Office (Historical Section)] *Anglo-Egyptian Sudan* (1919)
[Anglo-Egyptian Sudan] *A Handbook of the Anglo-Egyptian Sudan* (1922)
Army Orders and Special Army Orders, 1910 to 1924 included
Sarsfield-Hall (E.G., Compiler), *Handbook of Khartoum Province* (Khartoum, 1930, unpublished government report)
The Sudan Penal Code, 1899, Cairo: National Print Office

Government and institutional publications

Handbook of the Egyptian Army (Department Reports 5/5/26, NRO)
Handbook of the Gezira (Civsec1 57-37-138, NRO)
Memorandum on Education Policy 1923 (Civsec1 17-6-34, NRO)
Province Education Officers Handbook (Khartoum Province 1/4/46, NRO)
Sudan Railways, *Port Sudan Harbour* (Quays: Port Manager's office, 1966)
The Sub-Māmūr's Handbook. Lectures on the Penal, Criminal Procedure and Civil Codes, and Notes on Accounts, Agriculture, Forestry, Sanitation, &c. (Printed by M. Corquodale & CO. LTD, 1926) (SMI)

Government reports

Reports on the Finance, Administration and Condition of the Sudan, 1908 to 1913 (accessible http://www.dur.ac.uk/library/asc/sudan/gov-genl_reports/)
Governor General Annual Reports, 1900 to 1925, (idem)
Sudan Monthly Intelligence Reports Nos 294-341 (May 1919-March 1923) and Intelligence Department annual reports 1921 & 1922, WO 33/997, NA
Sudan Monthly Intelligence Reports 1923-1925 (April 1923-August 1925) with indexes for 1922-1924 and Intelligence Department annual reports 1923 and 1924, WO 33/999, NA

Interviews conducted by the author

'Abd al-Majīd al-Hājj al-Amīn, interview taken in his house in Omdurman, 28.01.2005.
'Abd al-Nūr Khalīl Faraḥ, grandson of Khalīl Faraḥ, interview in his house of Khartoum with Nāzik Nūr al-Hudā.
'Abd al-Raḥman al-Ṭayyib, relative of Muḥammad al-Mahdī. Interview taken in his house in Omdurman, 11.12.2004; 2.01.2005; 10.01.2005, with Aḥmad 'Abd al-Wāḥid.
Amīna Bilāl Riziq, wife of Zayn al 'Ābdīn 'Abd al-Tām. Interview taken in her house in Khartoum with Prof. Mu'taṣim.

Fāṭima Sayyid Faraḥ, daughter of officer Sayyid Faraḥ, interview taken at the main Khartoum hospital, 05.04.2008 with Prof. Mu'taṣim.
Durriyya 'Alī 'Abd al-Laṭīf: Interviews taken in her house, 8.12.2004; with her husband and her son Mu'āwyyia Aḥmad Badrī, 30.12.2004; several informal conversations via email and Skype with Mu'āwyyia, 2005 to 2014.
Ibrāhīm Muḥammad, relative of Muḥammad Faḍlallāh al-Shinnāwī, interview taken in his house in Omdurman together with Yoshiko Kurita and Aḥmad 'Abd al-Wāḥid, 24.05.2005.
Idrīs al-Bannā, nephew of 'Alī al-Bannā, interview taken in his house of Omdurman, 13.2.2005 and 26.2.2005.
Khadīja, granddaughter of 'Abd al-Faḍīl al-Māẓ, Omdurman, 1.05.2006, with Mu'āwyyia al-Badrī.
Lamiyā Ibrāhīm Badrī, daughter of Ibrāhīm Badrī, interview taken in her house of Khartoum, 25.4.2008.
Munā 'Alī Al-Bannā, daughter of 'Alī Al-Bannā, interview taken in her house in Omdurman, 18 and 24.02.2005.
Sa'd Ṣāliḥ 'Abd al-Qādir: one of the sons of Ṣāliḥ 'Abd al-Qādir, 26.01.2005; 30.01.2005; and April 2008 in his house in Khartoum North, with Aḥmad 'Abd al-Wāḥid.
Thābit 'Abd al-Raḥīm, interview taken in his house of Omdurman, 30.12.2004 with Aḥmad 'Abd al-Wāḥid and Naṣr al-Dīn Kafī.
Zayn al-'Ābdīn Ḥusayn Sharīf, nephew of Ḥusayn Sharīf, interview taken in his house of Omdurman, 29.4.2006 with Mu'āwyyia al-Badrī.

Interviews conducted by others

Al-Riwāyāt al-Shafawiyya li-Thuwwār 1924. Al-Khurṭūm: Ma'had al-Dirāsāt Ifrīqīya al-Āsīwīya, 1974.
'Alī Mūsā, 28.5.1974, Institute of Afro-Asian Studies, tape n. 1163.
'Izz al-Dīn Ḥusayn Rāsiq, Institute of Afro-Asian Studies, tape n. 1575.
Aḥmad Ibrāhīm Diyāb, Tape-recorded interview that he made with al-'Āzza, wife of 'Alī 'Abd al-Laṭīf, undated.

Manuscripts, pictures, songs, tape-recorded interviews and handwritten notes

Amīna Bilāl Riziq: picture series on 1924.
Family of 'Alī 'Abd al-Laṭīf: Treasury of the White Flag League; list of members.
Ibrāhīm Muḥammad: handwritten notes of Muḥammad Faḍlallāh al-Shinnāwī: The laws of the 1924 cadets' rights defence society; autobiographical note; "what has the Military School done in Khartoum and Why"?; list of cadets of the military school; a song, "to the martyr students of the Sudanese military school"; pictures.
Idrīs al-Bannā: short essay on Sudanese nationalism, including song.
'Abd al-Nūr Khalīl Faraḥ: offprint of various publications copied on Khalīl Faraḥ.
Munā 'Alī al-Bannā: letters by 'Alī al-Bannā to Numayrī and Sādāt.
Zayn al-'Ābdīn Ḥusayn Sharīf: offprint of *Bākūra al-wa'ī bil-thāt. Silsilat maqālat katabahā al-marḥūm. Al-sayyid Ḥusayn Sharīf fī al-sanatayn 1919-1920.*

Primary printed sources in Arabic and works on 1924 and on the insurgents

'Abd al-Karīm al-Sayyid, *Al-Liwā' Al-Abyaḍ, Thawrat 1924: Mudhakkirāt Wa-mushāhadāt Sajīn* (Khartoum: Jāmi'at al-Khurṭūm, Kulliyat al-Ādāb, Shu'bat Abḥāth al-Sūdān, 1970)
'Abd al-Wahhāb Aḥmad al-Raḥīm, 'Naḥwa ta'rīf jadīd "lithawra" 1924', in *Al-Ḥaraka Al-Waṭaniyya fī al-Sūdān: Thawra 1924,* Maḥāsin 'Abd al-Qādir Ḥājj

al-Ṣāfī ed., pp. 11-84.
'Awāṭif 'Umar 'Abdallāh, *Ṣāliḥ 'Abd Al-Qādir: Ḥayātuhu Wa Shi'ruhu* (Bayirūt: Dār al-Jīl, 1991).
Aḥmad Ibrāhīm Diyāb, *Thawrat 1924: dirāsa wa-waqā'i'* (Khartoum, 1977).
Aḥmad Ibrāhīm Diyāb, *al-'Alāqāt al-miṣrīya al-sūdāniyya: 1919-1924* (al-Qāhira: al-Hai'a al-Miṣrīya al-'Āmma lil-Kitāb, 1985).
Bākūra al-wa'ī bil-thāt. Silsilat maqālat katabahā al-marḥūm. Al-sayyid Ḥusayn Sharīf fī al-sanatayn 1919-1920; offprint, undated; publisher unspecified
Ḥassan Najīla, *Malāmiḥ Min al-Mujtama' al-Sūdānī* (Bayrut: Dār Maktabat al-ḥayāh, 1964).
Maḥāsin 'Abd al-Qādir Ḥājj al-Ṣāfī, *Al-Ḥaraka Al-Waṭaniyya Fī al-Sūdān: Thawra 1924* (Al-Khurṭūm: Ma'had al-Dirāsāt al-Ifrīqīya al-Āsīwīya, Jāmi'a al-Khurṭūm, 1992).
Maḥjūb 'Umar Bāshirī, *Ma'ālim Al-Ḥaraka Al-Waṭaniyya Fī al-Sūdān* (al-Khurṭūm: al-Maktaba al-Thaqāfiyya, 1996).
Maḥjūb Muḥammad Bāshirī, *Rūwād Al-fikr Al-Sūdānī* (Bayrūt: Dār al-Jīl, 1991).
Muḥammad 'Abd al-Raḥīm, *Al-Ṣira' Al-musallaḥ 'alā Al-waḥda Fī al-Sūdan, Aw, Al-Ḥaqīqa 'an Ḥawādith 1924* (al-Khurṭūm: Maṭba'at Klūt Bak, 1948).
Muḥammad 'Uthmān Yāsīn, *Al-Shā'ir Tawfīq Ṣalīḥ Jibrīl: Dhikrayāt Wa-aḥādīth* (Bayrūt: Dār al-Thaqāfa, 1971).
Muḥammad al-Makkī Ibrāhīm, *Al-Fikr Al-Sūdānī: usulubuhu wa taṭawwuruhu* (al-Khurṭūm, 1989).
Sulaymān Kisha, *Sūq Al-dhikryāt* (al-Khurṭūm: sharika al-ṭaba'a wal-nasha, 1963).
Sulaymān Kisha, *Al-Liwā' Al-Abyaḍ* (al-Khurṭūm, 1969).
Tawfīq Ṣāliḥ Jibrīl, Muḥammad Ibrāhīm Abū Salīm, and Muḥammad Ṣāliḥ Ḥasan, *Diwān Ufuq Wa-shafaq* (al-Khurṭūm: Jāmi'at al-Khartūm, Dār al-Ta'līf wa-al-Tarjama wa-al-Nashr, 1972).
Saeed Mohd. Ahmed El Mahdi ed., *The White Flag Trials* (Khartoum: Institute of African and Asian Studies, The Department of Private Law, University of Khartoum, 1974).

Journals

Muḥammad Ibrāhīm Ḥatīkābī: "'Ubayd min qabīla al-maḥas wa 'Alī 'Abd al-Laṭīf khandaqāwī wa laysa min al-dīnkā" ['Ubayd from al-mahasi tribe and 'Alī 'Abd al-Laṭīf from Khadaq and not from Dinka,] *Al-Rāy al-'ām*, 17.5.2002.
'Manzil al-za'ym 'Alī 'Abd al-Laṭīf maṭ'am baladī!!', *Ajrās al-ḥurriyya*, 3.11.2009, issue 540, p. 1.

SECONDARY SOURCES

Books and articles

Abdel-Rahim, Muddathir, *Imperialism and Nationalism in the Sudan: A Study in Constitutional and Political Development, 1899-1956* (Oxford: Clarendon Press, 1969).
Abdelkarim, Abbas, 'Wage Labourers in the Fragmented Labour Market of the Gezira, Sudan', *Africa: Journal of the International African Institute* (1986), vol. 56, n. 1, pp. 54-70.
Abdin, Hasan, *Early Sudanese Nationalism, 1919-1925* (Khartoum: Institute of African & Asian Studies, University of Khartoum, 1985).
Ahmed, Jamal Mohammed, *The Intellectual Origins of Egyptian Nationalism* (London; New York: Oxford University Press, 1960).
Amin, Shahid, *Event, Metaphor, Memory: Chauri Chaura 1922-1992* (Delhi: Oxford University Press, 1996).

Anderson, Benedict, *Imagined Communities : Reflections on the Origin and Spread of Nationalism* (London; New York: Verso, 1991).
Arai, Masami, *Turkish Nationalism in the Young Turk Era* (Leiden; New York: E.J. Brill, 1992).
Aya, Rod, 'The Third Man; Or, Agency in History; Or, Rationality in Revolution', *History and Theory* (2001) vol. 40, n. 4, pp. 143–52.
Aya, Rod, 'Theories of Revolution Reconsidered', *Theory and Society* (1979), vol. 8, n. 1, pp. 39–99.
Ayalon, Ami, *The Press in the Arab Middle East: A History* (New York: Oxford University Press, 1995).
Babiker, Mahjoub Abd Al-Malik, *Press and Politics in the Sudan* (Khartoum: Univ. of Khartoum, 1985).
Badrawi, Malak, *Political Violence in Egypt, 1910-1924: Secret Societies, Plots and Assassinations* (Richmond: Curzon, 2000).
Bakheit, Jaafar Muhammad Ali, *Communist Activities in the Middle East Between 1919-1927, with Special Reference to Egypt and the Sudan* (Khartoum: University of Khartoum, 1975).
Bakheit, Jafaar, 'British Administration and Sudanese Nationalism 1919-1939' (PhD Thesis, University of Cambridge, 1965).
Baldwin, James E., 'Petitioning the Sultan in Ottoman Egypt', *Bulletin of the School of Oriental and African Studies* (2012), vol. 75 n. 3, pp. 499-524.
Banerjee, Sikata, *Muscular Nationalism. Gender, Violence, and Empire in India and Ireland, 1914-2004* (New York: New York University Press, 2012).
Baron, Beth, *Egypt As a Woman. Nationalism, Gender, and Politics* (Berkeley: University of California Press, 2005)
Barua, P., 'Inventing Race: The British and India's Martial Races', *Historian* (1995), vol. 58, n. 1, pp. 107-116
Bashkin, Orit, *The Other Iraq: Pluralism and Culture in Hashemite Iraq* (Stanford, Calif.: Stanford University Press, 2009).
Batatu, Hanna, *The Old Social Classes and the Revolutionary Movements of Iraq* (Princeton NJ: Princeton Univ. Press, 1978)
Bayly, C. A., 'Knowing the Country: Empire and Information in India', *Modern Asian Studies* (1993), vol. 27, n. 1, pp. 3-43.
Bayly, C. A., *Empire and Information : Intelligence Gathering and Social Communication in India, 1780-1870* (Cambridge; New York: Cambridge University Press, 1996).
Bayly, C. A., and Eugenio Biagini eds. *Giuseppe Mazzini and the Globalization of Democratic Nationalism, 1830-1920* (Oxford: Oxford University Press, 2008).
Badri, Babikr, *The Memoirs of Babikr Bedri* (London; New York: Oxford U.P., 1969)
Beeley, Brian W., 'The Turkish Village Coffeehouse As a Social Institution', *Geographical Review* (1970), vol. 60, n. 4, pp. 475-493.
Beinin, Joel and Zachary Lockman, *Workers on the Nile: Nationalism, Communism, Islam, and the Egyptian Working Class, 1882-1954* (Cairo: American University in Cairo Press, 1998).
Bernal, Victoria, *Cultivating Workers : Peasants and Capitalism in a Sudanese Village* (New York: Columbia University Press, 1991).
Beshir, Mohamed Omar, *Revolution and Nationalism in the Sudan* (New York: Barnes & Noble Books, 1974).
Bjørkelo, Anders, *Prelude to the Mahdiyya: Peasants and Traders in the Shendi Region, 1821-1885* (Cambridge: Cambridge University Press, 2003).
Blaustein, Albert P., Jay A. Sigler, and Benjamin R. Beede eds., *Independence Documents of the World* (Dobbs Ferry, N.Y.: Oceana Publications, 1977).
Blondheim, Menahem, *News Over the Wires : The Telegraph and the Flow of Public Information in America, 1844-1897* (Cambridge, Mass.: Harvard University Press, 1994).
Boltanski, Luc, *Les Cadres: La Formation d'un Groupe Social* (Paris: Éditions de

Minuit, 1982).
Boltanski, Luc, *L'amour et la Justice comme Compétences : Trois Essais de Sociologie de L'action* (Paris: Métailié, 1990).
Bredin, G. R. F., 'The Life Story of Yuzbashi 'Abdullah Adlan', *Sudan Notes and Records* (1961) vol. 42, pp. 37–52.
Bush, Barbara, *Imperialism, Race and Resistance: Africa and Britain, 1919-1945* (London, New York: Routledge, 2002).
Callahan, Michael D., *Mandates and Empire. The League of Nations and Africa* (Brighton: Sussex Academic Press, 1999).
Callahan, Michael D., *A Sacred Trust : The League of Nations and Africa, 1929-1946* (Brighton; Portland, Or.: Sussex Academic Press, 2004).
Casciarri, Barbara, and Abdel Ghaffar Mohammed Ahmed, 'Pastoralists under Pressure in Present-Day Sudan: An Introduction', *Nomadic Peoples* (2009), vol. 13, n. 1, pp. 10–22.
Casciarri, Barbara, 'De l'altérité et de l'invisibilité des groupes pastoraux au Soudan. Repenser les études soudanaises en partant de leurs marges mobiles', *Canadian Journal of African Studies,* (2015), vol. 49, n. 1.
Cerutti, Simona, 'Histoire Pragmatique, ou de la Rencontre entre Histoire Sociale et Histoire Culturelle', *Tracés. Revue de Sciences Humaines* (2008) vol. 15, pp. 147–68.
Chakrabarty, Dipesh, 'Minority histories, subaltern pasts', *Economic and Political Weekly* (1998), vol. 33, n. 9, pp. 475-479.
Chalcraft, J., 'Engaging the State: Peasants and Petitions in Egypt on the Eve of Colonial Rule', *International Journal of Middle East Studies* (2005), vol. 37, n. 3, pp. 303-325.
Chatterjee, Partha, *Nationalist Thought and the Colonial World: A Derivative Discourse* (Minneapolis: University of Minnesota Press, 1993).
Chatterjee, Partha, *The Nation and Its Fragments: Colonial and Postcolonial Histories* (Princeton, NJ: Princeton University Press, 1993).
Clayton, Anthony, and David Killingray eds., *Khaki and Blue : Military and Police in British Colonial Africa* (Athens, Ohio: Ohio University Centre for International Studies, 1989).
Cole, Juan R., *Colonialism and Revolution in the Middle East. Social and Cultural Origins of Egypt's 'Urabi Movement* (Princeton, N.J.: Princeton University Press, 1993).
Collins, Robert O., *Land Beyond the Rivers; The Southern Sudan, 1898-1918* (New Haven: Yale University Press, 1971).
Collins, Robert O., *Shadows in the Grass : Britain in the Southern Sudan, 1918-1956* (New Haven: Yale University Press, 1983).
Condie, R. H. B., 'Egypt's Trade with the Sudan', *Sudan Notes and Records* (1955), vol. 36, n. 1, pp. 57-63.
Connor, Walker, 'When Is a Nation?', *Ethnic and Racial Studies* (1990), vol. 13, n. 1, pp. 92-103.
Connor, Walker, 'The Timelessness of Nations', *Nations and Nationalism* (2004), vol. 10, n. 1-2, pp. 35-47.
Constable, P., 'The Marginalization of a Dalit Martial Race in Late Nineteenth-and Early Twentieth-Century Western India', *Journal of Asian Studies* (2001), vol. 60, n. 2, pp. 439-478.
Cooper, Frederick, *Decolonization and African Society : The Labor Question in French and British Africa* (Cambridge U.K.; New York: Cambridge University Press, 1996).
Cooper, Frederick, 'Rethinking Colonial African History', *Reading Subaltern Studies: Critical History, Contested Meaning and the Globalization of South Asia*, David Ludden ed. (London: Anthem Press, 2002), pp. 256-303.
Cooper, Frederick, *Africa Since 1940: The Past of the Present. New Approaches to African History* (Cambridge, U.K.; New York: Cambridge University Press, 2002)

Cope, Nicholas, 'The Zulu Petit Bourgeoisie and Zulu Nationalism in the 1920s: Origins of Inkatha', *Journal of Southern African Studies* (2007), vol. 16, n. 3, pp. 431-451.

Cross, Peter, 'British Attitudes to Sudanese Labour: The Foreign Office Records As Sources for Social History', *British Journal of Middle Eastern Studies* (1997), vol. 24, n. 2, pp. 217-260.

Cudsi, Alexander S., 'Sudanese Resistance to British Rule, 1900-1920' (PhD Thesis, University of Khartoum, 1969).

Currie, James, 'The Educational Experiment in the Anglo-Egyptian Sudan, 1900-33. Part I', *African Affairs, Journal of the Royal African Society* (1934), vol. 33, n. 133, pp. 361-371.

Currie, James, 'The Educational Experiment in the Anglo-Egyptian Sudan, 1900-33. Part II', *African Affairs, Journal of the Royal African Society* (1935), vol. 34, n. 134, pp. 41-59.

Daly, Martin W., *British Administration and the Northern Sudan, 1917–1924: The Governor-Generalship of Sir Lee Stack in the Sudan* (Leiden: Nederlands Historisch-Archaeologisch Instituut te Istanbul, 1980).

Daly, Martin W., 'The Egyptian Army Mutiny at Omdurman January-February 1900', *British Journal of Middle Eastern Studies* (1981), vol. 8, no. 1, pp. 3-12.

Daly, Martin W., *Empire on the Nile: The Anglo-Egyptian Sudan, 1898-1934* (Cambridge [Cambridgeshire]; New York: Cambridge University Press, 2000).

Dedering, Tilman, 'Petitioning Geneva: Transnational Aspects of Protest and Resistance in South West Africa/Namibia After the First World War', *Journal of Southern African Studies* (2009), vol. 35, n. 4, pp. 785-801.

Deeb, Marius, *Party Politics in Egypt : The Wafd and Its Rivals, 1919-1939* (London: Ithaca Press, 1979).

Della Porta, Donatella and Mario Diani, *Social Movements : An Introduction* (Malden, MA: Blackwell Pub, 2006).

Della Porta, Donatella, and Sidney G. Tarrow, *Transnational Protest and Global Activism* (Lanham, MD: Rowman & Littlefield, 2005).

Deng, Francis M., *War of Visions: Conflict of Identities in the Sudan* (Brookings Institution Press, 1995).

Deng, Francis M., *Green Is the Color of the Master. The Legacy of Slavery and the Crisis of National Identity in Modern Sudan*, Paper presented at 'From Chattel Bondage to State Servitude: Slavery in the 20th Century', 6th International Conference of Gilder Lehrman Center for the Study of Slavery, Resistance, and Abolition, 2004.

Derrick, Jonathan, *Africa's 'Agitators': Militant Anti-colonialism in Africa and the West, 1918-1939* (New York: Columbia University Press, 2008).

Derrida, Jacques, *Archive Fever: A Freudian Impression* (Translated by Eric Prenowitz. Chicago: University of Chicago Press, 1996).

De Waal, Alexander, *Famine Crimes: Politics & the Disaster Relief Industry in Africa* (African Rights & the International African Institute, 1997).

Duffield, Mark R., *Maiurno : Capitalism & Rural Life in Sudan* (London: Ithaca Press, 1981).

Dunn, John P., *Khedive Ismail's Army* (London; New York: Routledge, 2005).

Durkheim, Emile, *The Elementary Forms of Religious Life* (Translated by Karen E. Fields. New York: Free Press, 1995 1st ed. 1912).

El-Amin, Mohammed Nuri, 'A Leftist Labour Movement in the Sudan in the Early 1920s: Fact or Fiction?', *Middle Eastern Studies* (1984), vol. 20, n. 3, pp. 370-378.

El-Amin, Mohammed Nuri, 'Britain, the 1924 Sudanese Uprising, and the Impact of Egypt on the Sudan', *The International Journal of African Historical Studies* (1986), vol. 19, n. 2, pp. 235-260.

El-Dawi, Taj-el-Anbia Ali, 'Social Characteristics of Big Merchants and Businessmen in El Obeid', *Essays in Sudan Ethnography,* Ian Cunnison and Wendy James eds.

(London: C. Hurst, 1972), pp. 201-216.
El-Dawi, Taj-el-Anbia Ali, 'The Residential Ecology of El Obeid', in *Urbanization and Urban Life in the Sudan,* Valdo Pons ed. (Hull: Dept. of Sociology and Social Anthropology of the University of Hull, 1980), pp. 322-351.
Ellis, Stephen and Ineke I. V. Kessel eds. *Movers and Shakers: Social Movements in Africa* (Leiden; Boston: Brill, 2009).
Emirbayer, Mustafa, and Jeff Goodwin, 'Symbols, Positions, Objects: Toward a New Theory of Revolutions and Collective Action', *History and Theory* (1996), vol. 35, n. 3, pp. 358–74.
Eppel, Michael, 'The Elite, the Effendiyya, and the Growth of Nationalism and Pan-Arabism in Hashemite Iraq, 1921-1958', *International Journal of Middle East Studies* (1998), vol. 30, n. 2, pp. 227-250.
Erickson, Bonnie H., 'Secret Societies and Social Structure', *Social Forces* (1981), vol. 60, n. 1, pp. 188-210.
Ewald, Jane, *Soldiers, Traders, and Slaves: State Formation and Economic Transformation in the Greater Nile Valley, 1700-1885* (Madison: University of Wisconsin Press, 1990).
Fahmy, Khalid, *All the Pasha's Men: Mehmed Ali, His Army and the Making of Modern Egypt* (Cambridge University Press, 1998).
Fahmy, Ziad, *Ordinary Egyptians: Creating the Modern Nation Through Popular Culture* (Stanford, California: Stanford University Press, 2011).
Fawzi, Saad Ed Din, *The Labour Movement in the Sudan, 1946-1955* (London, New York: Oxford University Press, 1957).
Foran, John, and Jeff Goodwin, 'Revolutionary Outcomes in Iran and Nicaragua: Coalition Fragmentation, War, and the Limits of Social Transformation', *Theory and Society* (1993), vol. 22, n. 2, pp. 209–47.
Foran, John, *Theorizing Revolutions* (London; New York: Routledge, 1997).
Foster, Susan Leigh, 'Choreographies of Protest', *Theatre Journal* (2003), vol. 55, n. 3, pp. 395-412.
Foucault, Michel, *Les Mots Et Les Choses: Une Archéologie Des Sciences Humaines* (Paris: Gallimard, 1966).
Gellner, Ernest, *Postmodernism, Reason and Religion* (London; New York: Routledge, 1992).
Gellner, Ernest, *Nations and Nationalism* (Malden, MA: Blackwell, 2006, first ed. 1983).
Gelvin, James L., 'Demonstrating Communities in Post-Ottoman Syria', *The Journal of Interdisciplinary History* (1994), vol. 25, n. 1, pp. 23-44.
Gelvin, James L., 'The Social Origins of Popular Nationalism in Syria: Evidence for a New Framework', *International Journal of Middle East Studies* (1994), vol. 26, n. 4, pp. 645-661.
Gelvin, James L., *Divided Loyalties Nationalism and Mass Politics in Syria at the Close of Empire* (Berkeley: University of California Press, 1998).
Gelvin, James L., 'Arab Nationalism Meets Social Theory', VV.AA. 'Questions and Pensées: "Arab Nationalism": Has a New Framework Emerged?', *International Journal of Middle East Studies* (2009), vol. 41, n. 1, pp. 10-21.
Gershoni I. and J. Jankowski, *Egypt, Islam, and the Arabs the Search for Egyptian Nationhood, 1900-1930* (New York: Oxford University Press, 1986).
Gershoni, I., 'From Pharaonism to Islam and Arabism : The Use of History by Egyptian Nationalist Writers', *Conference Proceedings of the Middle East Studies Association of North America* (1992).
Glassman, Jonathon, *Feasts and Riot: Revelry, Rebellion, and Popular Conciousness on the Swahili Coast, 1856-1888* (Portsmouth: N.H.: Heinemann, 1995).
Goldberg, Ellis, 'Peasants in Revolt-Egypt 1919', *International Journal of Middle East Studies* (1992), vol. 24, n. 2, pp. 261-280.
Goldschmidt, Arthur, Amy J. Johnson, and Barak A. Salmoni, *Re-envisioning Egypt 1919-1952* (Cairo; New York: American University in Cairo Press, 2005).

Goldstein, Daniel, *Libération ou Annexion: aux Chemins Croisés de l'Histoire Tunisienne, 1914-1922* (Tunis: Maison tunisienne de l'édition, 1978).
Goldstone, Jack A., 'Toward a Fourth Generation of Revolutionary Theory', *Annual Review of Political Science* (2001), vol. 4, pp. 139–87.
Goldstone, Jack A. ed., *Revolutions: Theoretical, Comparative, and Historical Studies* (San Diego: Harcourt Brace Jovanovich, 1986).
Gong, Gerrit W., *The Standard of "Civilization" in International Society* (Oxford: Clarendon Press, 1984).
Goodwin, Jeff, and Adam Isaiah Green, 'Revolutions', *Encyclopedia of Violence, Peace, and Conflict*, Lester K. Kurtz ed. (Academic Press, 2008), pp. 1870-1880.
Goodwin, Jeff, James M. Jasper, and Francesca Polletta, *Passionate Politics: Emotions and Social Movements* (Chicago: University of Chicago Press, 2001).
Guha, Ranajit, and Gayatri Chakravorty Spivak, *Selected Subaltern Studies* (New York: Oxford University Press, 1988).
Guha, Ranajit, *Dominance without Hegemony: History and Power in Colonial India* (Cambridge, MA: Harvard University Press, 1997).
Gwynn, Charles G., *Imperial Policing* (London: MacMillan and Co. 1934).
Hanes, Wiliam T., *Imperial Diplomacy in the Era of Decolonization: The Sudan and Anglo-Egyptian Relations, 1945-1956* (Westport, Conn.: Greenwood Press, 1995).
Hargey, Taj, 'The Suppression of Slavery in the Sudan, 1898-1939' (PhD Thesis, University of Oxford, 1981).
Hargey, Taj, 'Festina Lente: Slavery Policy and Practice in the Anglo-Egyptian Sudan', *Slavery & Abolition* (1998), vol. 19, n. 2, pp. 250–72.
Harvey, David, *The Condition of Postmodernity: An Enquiry Into the Origins of Cultural Change* (Oxford U.K.; Cambridge, Mass.: Blackwell, 1990)
Hazelrigg, Lawrence E., 'A Reexamination of Simmel's "The Secret and the Secret Society": Nine Propositions', *Social Forces* (1969), vol. 47, n. 3, pp. 323-330.
Headrick, Daniel R., *The Tools of Empire : Technology and European Imperialism in the Nineteenth Century* (New York: Oxford University Press, 1981).
Headrick, Daniel R., *The Tentacles of Progress : Technology Transfer in the Age of Imperialism, 1850-1940* (New York: Oxford University Press, 1988).
Hebbert, G. K. C., 'The Bandala of the Bahr El Ghazal', *Sudan Notes and Records* (1925), vol. 8, pp. 187–94.
Hibbeln, Paul, 'Supervising Imperialism: Petitions to the League of Nations Permanent Mandates Commission, 1920-1939', *Proceedings of the Ohio Academy of History* (2001).
Hill, Richard L., *Egypt in the Sudan, 1820-1881* (London: Oxford University Press, 1959).
Hill, Richard L., *Slatin Pasha* (London: Oxford University Press, 1965).
Hill, Richard L., *Sudan Transport. A History of Railways, Marine and River Services in the Republic of the Sudan* (London: Oxford University, 1965).
Hill, Richard L., *A Biographical Dictionary of the Sudan* (London: Frank Cass, 1967).
Hill, Richard L. and Peter C. Hogg, *A Black Corps D'Élite. An Egyptian Sudanese Conscript Battalion with the French Army in Mexico, 1863-1867, and Its Survivors in Subsequent African History* (East Lansing: Michigan State University Press, 1995).
Hodgkin, Katharine, and Susannah Radstone, *Regimes of Memory* (London ; New York: Routledge, 2003).
Hodgkin, Katharine, and Susannah Radstone, *Memory, History, Nation: Contested Pasts* (Transaction Publishers, 2005).
Holt, P. M, and M. W Daly, *A History of the Sudan: From the Coming of Islam to the Present Day* (Harlow, England; New York: Longman, 2000).
Huntington, Samuel P., *Political Order in Changing Societies* (New Haven: Yale University Press, 1968).
Ibrahim, Ahmed Uthman Muhammad, *The Dilemma of British Rule in the Nuba Mountains, 1898-1947* (Khartoum; London: Graduate College, University of

Khartoum, 1985).

Ibrahim, Hassan A., 'Mahdist Risings Against the Condominium Government in the Sudan, 1900-1927', *The International Journal of African Historical Studies* (1979), vol. 12, n. 3, pp. 440-471.

Ibrahim, Hassan A., *Sayyid 'Abd Al-Rahman Al-Mahdi: A Study of Neo-Mahdism in the Sudan, 1899-1956* (Boston: Brill, 2004).

Idris, Amir H., *Identity, Citizenship, and Violence in Two Sudans: Reimagining a Common Future* (Basingstoke: Palgrave Macmillan, 2013).

Isaacman, Allen, and Derek Peterson, 'Making the Chikunda: Military Slavery and Ethnicity in Southern Africa, 1750-1900', *International Journal of African Historical Studies* (2003), vol. 36, n. 2, pp. 257-281.

Jābir, Jum'a, *Al-Musiqā Al-Sūdāniyya : Tārīkh, Turāth, Hawiyya, Naqd* (al-Khurṭūm: Sharikat al-Fārābī, 1986).

Jaffrelot, Christophe, *The Hindu Nationalist Movement in India* (New York: Columbia University Press, 1996).

Jankowski, James P., *Egypt, Islam, and the Arabs: The Search for Egyptian Nationhood, 1900-1930* (New York: Oxford University Press, 1986).

Jankowski, James P. and I. Gershoni, *Rethinking Nationalism in the Arab Middle East* (New York: Columbia University Press, 1997).

Jasper, James M., 'The Emotions of Protest: Affective and Reactive Emotions in and Around Social Movements', *Sociological Forum* (1998), vol. 13, n. 3, pp. 397-424.

Jasper, James M., *The Art of Moral Protest Culture, Biography, and Creativity in Social Movements* (Chicago, Ill.: University of Chicago Press, 1999).

Jenkins, J. 'Resource Mobilization Theory and the Study of Social Movements', *Annual Review of Sociology* (1983), vol. 9, pp. 527–53.

Johnson, Douglas H., 'CA Willis and the "Cult of Deng:" A Falsification of the Ethnographic Record', *History in Africa* (1985), vol. 12, pp. 131-150.

Johnson, Douglas H., 'Sudanese Military Slavery From the Eighteenth to the Twentieth Century', in *Slavery and Other Forms of Unfree Labour,* L. Archer ed. (London: Routledge, 1988), pp. 142-156.

Johnson, Douglas H., 'The Structure of a Legacy: Military Slavery in Northeast Africa', *Ethnohistory* (1989), vol. 36, n. 1, pp. 72-88.

Johnson, Douglas H., 'Tribe or Nationality? The Sudanese Diaspora and the Kenyan Nubis', *Journal of Eastern African Studies* (2009), vol. 3, no. 1, pp. 112-131.

Kaddache, Mahfoud, *Histoire Du Nationalisme Algérien* (Paris: Paris-Méditerranée, 2003).

Kamrava, Mehran, 'Revolution Revisited: The Structuralist-Voluntarist Debate', *Canadian Journal of Political Science/Revue Canadienne de Science Politique* (1999), vol. 32, n. 2, pp. 317–45.

Kelidar, Abbas, 'The Political Press in Egypt, 1882-1914', in *Contemporary Egypt Through Egyptian Eyes: Essays in Honour of Professor P.J. Vatikiotis,* Charles Tripp ed. (London; New York: Routledge, 1993).

Kenyon, Susan M., 'Zainab's Story: Slavery, Women and Community in Colonial Sudan', *Urban Anthropology and Studies of Cultural Systems and World Economic Development* (2009), vol. 38, n. 1, pp. 33-77.

Kenyon, Susan M., *Spirits and Slaves in Central Sudan: The Red Wind of Sennar* (New York: Palgrave Macmillan, 2012).

Khalidi Omar, 'Ethnic Group Recruitment in the Indian Army: The Contrasting Cases of Sikhs, Muslims, Gurkhas and Others', *Pacific Affairs* (2001), vol. 74, n. 4, pp. 529-552.

Khalidi, Rashid ed., *The Origins of Arab Nationalism* (New York: Columbia University Press, 1991).

Khan, Noor-Aiman I., *Egyptian-Indian Nationalist Collaboration and the British Empire* (New York: Palgrave Macmillan, 2011).

Khogali, Mustafa M., 'The Migration of the Danagla to Port Sudan: A Case Study on the Impact of Migration on the Change of Identity', *GeoJournal* (1991), vol. 25, n. 1, pp. 63-71.

Killingray, David, 'Repercussions of World War I in the Gold Coast', *The Journal of African History* (1978), vol. 19, n. 1, pp. 39-59.

Killingray, David, 'The Maintenance of Law and Order in British Colonial Africa', *African Affairs* (1986), vol. 85, n. 340, pp. 411-437.

Kirk-Greene, A. H. M., 'Damnosa Hereditas: Ethnic Ranking and the Martial Races Imperative in Africa', *Ethnic and Racial Studies* (1980), vol. 3, n. 4, pp. 393-414.

Kirk-Greene, A. H. M. 'The Sudan Political Service: A Profile in the Sociology of Imperialism', *The International Journal of African Historical Studies* (1982), vol. 15, n.1, pp. 21-48.

Kramer, Robert S., *Holy City on the Nile : Omdurman During the Mahdiyya, 1885-1898* (Princeton: Markus Wiener Publishers, 2010).

Kramer, Robert S., 'The Death of Bassiouni: A Case of Complex Identity in the Sudan', *The Canadian Journal of African Studies,* forthcoming (2015).

Kurita, Yoshiko, 'The Concept of Nationalism in the White Flag League Movement', in *The Nationalist Movement in the Sudan,* Mahasin Abdel Gadir Hag Al-Safi ed. (Khartoum: Institute of African and Asian Studies, University of Khartoum, 1989), pp. 14-63.

Kurita, Yoshiko, *'Alī 'Abd Al-Laṭīf Wa-Thawrat 1924: Baḥth Fī Maṣādir Al-Thawra Al-Sūdāniyya* (Cairo: Markaz al-Dirasāt al-Sūdāniyya, 1997).

Kurita, Yoshiko, 'The Role of 'Negroid but Detribalized' People in Modern Sudanese History', *Nilo-Ethiopian studies* (2003), vol. 8-9, pp. 1-11.

Kurita, Yoshiko, 'The Daughters of Omdurman: The Role of Women in the Sudanese Mahdist Movement and Its Significance for the Subsequent Historical Process', *JCAS Symposium Series* (2004)

Kyle, Keith, 'Gandhi, Harry Thuku and Early Kenya Nationalism', *Transition* (1966), vol. 27, pp. 16-22.

Lamothe, Ronald M., *Slaves of Fortune : Sudanese Soldiers and the River War, 1896-1898* (Woodbridge, Suffolk; Rochester, NY: James Currey, 2011).

Lampen, G. D., 'The Baggara Tribes of Darfur', *Sudan Notes and Records* (1933), vol. 16, n. 2, pp. 97–118.

Landau, Jacob M., 'Prolegomena to a Study of Secret Societies in Modern Egypt', *Middle Eastern Studies* (1965), vol. 1, n. 2, pp. 135-186.

Lawrance, Benjamin N., Emily E. L. Osborn, and Richard R. L. Roberts eds. *Intermediaries, Interpreters, and Clerks: African Employees in the Making of Colonial Africa* (Madison, Wis.: University of Wisconsin Press, 2006).

Leith, J., 'Revolutions, History of', *International Encyclopedia of the Social & Behavioral Sciences*, Neil J. Smelser and Paul B. Baltes eds. (Oxford: Pergamon, 2001), pp. 13302-13306.

Leopold, Mark, 'Legacies of Slavery in North-West Uganda: The Story of the "one-Elevens"', *Africa* (2006), vol. 76, n. 2, pp. 180-199.

Lev, Yaacov, 'David Ayalon (1914–1998) and the History of Black Military Slavery in Medieval Islam', *Der Islam* (2013), vol. 90, n. 1, pp. 21–43.

Lewis, B.A, 'Deim El Arab and the Beja Stevedores of Port Sudan', *Sudan Notes and Records Sudan Notes and Records* (1962), vol. 43, pp. 16–49.

Lewis I.M. ed., *Nationalism & Self Determination in the Horn of Africa* (London: Ithaca Press 1983)

Lockman, Z., 'Imagining the working class: Culture, nationalism, and class formation in Egypt, 1899-1914', *Poetics Today* (1994), vol. 15, p. 2, pp. 157-190.

Lonsdale, J. M., 'Some Origins of Nationalism in East Africa', *Journal of African History* (1968), vol. 9, n. 1, pp. 119-146.

Lunn, Joe, '"Les Races Guerrieres": Racial Preconceptions in the French Military About West African Soldiers During the First World War', *Journal of Contemporary History* (1999), vol. 34, n. 4, pp. 517-536.

Lyman, Stanford M., 'Chinese Secret Societies in the Occident: Notes and Suggestions for Research in the Sociology of Secrecy', *Canadian Review of Sociology/Revue Canadienne de Sociologie* (1964), vol. 1, n. 2, pp. 79–102.

MacMichael, Harold A., *A History of the Arabs in the Sudan* (London: F. Cass., 1967, 1st ed. 1922)

Mahjoubi, Ali, *Les Origines du Mouvement National en Tunisie (1904-1934)* (Tunis: Université de Tunis, 1982).

Makris, G. P., *Changing Masters: Spirit Possession and Identity Construction Among Slave Descendants and Other Subordinates in the Sudan* (Evanston, Ill.: Northwestern University Press, 2000).

Manchuelle, François, 'Assimilés ou patriotes africains? Naissance du Nationalisme Culturel en Afrique Française (1853-1931)', *Cahiers d'Études Africaines* (1995), vol. 35, n. 138/139, pp. 333-368.

Manela, Erez, *The Wilsonian Moment: Self-determination and the International Origins of Anticolonial Nationalism* (Oxford; New York: Oxford University Press, 2007).

Manger, Leif O. ed., *Trade and Traders in the Sudan* (Dept. of Social Anthropology, University of Bergen, 1984).

Manger, Leif O., 'Pastoralist-State Relationships among the Hadendowa Beja of Eastern Sudan', *Nomadic Peoples* (2001), vol. 5, n. 2, pp. 21–48.

Marjomaa, Risto, 'The Martial Spirit: Yao Soldiers in British Service in Nyasaland (Malawi), 1895-1939', *The Journal of African History* (2003), vol. 44, n. 3, pp. 413-432.

Masselos, Jim, *Indian Nationalism: A History* (New Delhi: Sterling Publishers, 1985).

McCarthy, John D., and Mayer N. Zald, 'Resource Mobilization and Social Movements: A Partial Theory', *American Journal of Sociology* (1977), vol. 82, n. 6, pp. 1212–41.

McDougall, James, *History and the Culture of Nationalism in Algeria* (Cambridge: Cambridge University Press, 2006).

McLoughlin, Peter F. M., 'Economic Development and the Heritage of Slavery in the Sudan Republic', *Africa* (1962), vol. 32, n. 4, pp. 355-391.

Meyers, R., 'Slave Soldiers and State Politics in Early 'Alawi Morocco, 1668-1727', *International Journal of African Historical Studies* (1983), vol. 16, n. 1, pp. 39-48.

Mills, David E., 'A Failed Nationalist Endeavor: Egyptian-Sudanese Textile Trade', *British Journal of Middle Eastern Studies* (2004), vol. 31, n. 2, pp. 175-194.

Mills, David E, *Dividing the Nile: Egypt's Economic Nationalists in the Sudan, 1918-56* (Cairo, New York: The American University in Cairo Press, 2014).

Milne, Janet C. M., 'The Impact of Labour Migration on the Amarar in Port Sudan', *Sudan Notes and Records* (1974), vol. 55, pp. 70–87.

Miura, Toru, and John J. E. Philips, *Slave Elites in the Middle East and Africa : A Comparative Study* (London; New York: Kegan Paul International, 2000).

Mohammed Salih, Mahgoub, 'The Sudanese Press', *Sudan Notes and Records* (1965), vol. 46, pp. 1-7.

Moore-Harell, Alice, 'The Turco-Egyptian Army in Sudan on the Eve of the Mahdiyya, 1877-80', *International Journal of Middle East Studies* (1999), vol. 31, n. 1, pp. 19-37.

Moyd, Michelle, 'Making the Household, Making the State: Colonial Military Communities and Labor in German East Africa', *International Labor and Working-Class History* (2011), vol. 80, n. 1, pp. 53–76.

Natarajan, Swaminath, *A History of the Press in India* (Bombay; New York: Asia Pub. House, 1962).

Negib, Mohammed, *Memorie di Mohammed Negib (1919-1973)* (Firenze: La Nuova Italia, 1976).

Neguib, Mohammad, *Egypt's Destiny* (London: Gollancz, 1955).

Nickles, David P., *Under the Wire: How the Telegraph Changed Diplomacy* (Cambridge,

Mass.: Harvard University Press, 2003).
O'Brien, Jay, 'Agricultural Labour Force and Development in the Sudan' (PhD Thesis, University of Connecticut, 1980).
O'Brien, Jay, 'The Formation of the Agricultural Labour Force in Sudan', *Review of African Political Economy* (1983), vol. 26, pp. 15-34.
O'Fahey, Rex S. and Jay L. Spaulding, 'Hāshim and the Musabba'āt', *Bulletin of the School of Oriental and African Studies, University of London* (1972), vol. 35, n. 2, pp. 316-333.
O'Fahey, Rex Seán, *Arabic Literature of Africa. Vol. III: The Writings of the Muslim Peoples of Northeastern Africa* (Leiden: Brill, 2003).
Oliver, J., 'Port Sudan: Its Growth and Function', in *Urbanization and Urban Life in the Sudan*, Valdo Pons ed. (Hull: Dept. of Sociology and Social Anthropology of the University of Hull, 1980), pp. 297-321.
Omer, El-Haj Bilal, *The Danagla Traders of Northern Sudan: Rural Capitalism and Agricultural Development* (London: Ithaca Press, 1995).
Öztürk, Serdar, 'The Struggle Over Turkish Village Coffeehouses (1923–45)', *Middle Eastern Studies* (2008), vol. 44, n. 3, pp. 435-454.
Parsons, Timothy H. '"Wakamba Warriors Are Soldiers of the Queen": The Evolution of the Kamba As a Martial Race, 1890-1970', *Ethnohistory* (1999), vol. 46, n. 4, pp. 671-701.
Parsons, Timothy H., *The African Rank-and-File: Social Implications of Colonial Military Service in the King's African Rifles, 1902-1964* (Portsmouth, NH: Heinemann, 1999).
Passerini, Luisa, 'Memories Between Silence and Oblivion', in *Contested Pasts: The Politics of Memory*, Katharine Hodgkin and Susannah Radstone eds. (London and New York: Routledge, 2003), pp. 238-54.
Paul, Andrew, *A History of the Beja Tribes of the Sudan* (Cambridge: Cambridge University Press, 1954).
Perkins, Kenneth J. '"The Best Laid Out Town on the Red Sea": The Creation of Port Sudan, 1904-09', *Middle Eastern Studies* (1991), vol. 27, n. 2, pp. 283-302.
Perkins, Kenneth J., *Port Sudan: The Evolution of a Colonial City State, Culture, and Society in Arab North Africa* (Boulder: Westview Press, 1993).
Perkins, Kenneth J., *A History of Modern Tunisia* (New York: Cambridge University Press, 2004).
Polletta, Francesca and James Jasper, 'Collective Identity and Social Movements', *Annual Review of Sociology* (2001), vol. 27, pp. 283-305.
Popplewell, Richard, *Intelligence and Imperial Defence: British Intelligence and the Defence of the Indian Empire, 1904-1924* (London; Portland, Or.: F. Cass, 1995).
Pott, Alexander J., *People of the Book* (Edinburgh and London: W. Blackwood & Sons, 1932).
Potter, S., 'Communication and Integration: The British and Dominions Press and the British World, C. 1876--1914', *The Journal of Imperial and Commonwealth History* (2003), vol. 31, n. 2, pp. 190-206.
Pouchepadass, J., 'A proposito della critica postcoloniale sul "discorso" dell'archivio', *Quaderni Storici* (2008), vol. 43, n. 3, pp. 675-690.
Provence, Michael, *The Great Syrian Revolt and the Rise of Arab Nationalism* (Austin: University of Texas Press, 2005).
Prunier, Gerard, 'Military Slavery in the Sudan During the Turkiyya, 1820-1885', *Slavery & Abolition* (1992), vol. 13, n. 1, pp. 129-139.
al-Qaddāl, Muḥammad Sayyid, *Tārīkh Al-Sūdān Al-Ḥadīth: 1820-1955* (al-Khurṭūm: Markaz 'Abd-al-Karīm Mīrghanī, 2002).
Qāsim, 'Awn a-Sharīf, *Mawsū'at Al-qabā'il Wa-al-ansāb Fī Al-Sūdān Wa-ashhar Asmā' al-'Ālam Wa-al-amākin*, 6 vols. (Khartoum: Maktabat Āfiruqrāf, 1996).
al-Rafi'ī, 'Abd al-Raḥman, *Thawra 1919: Tārīkh Miṣr al-qawmī min sana 1914 ilā 1921* (Cairo: Maktaba al-Nahḍa al-Miṣriyya, 1968, 3rd ed.)

al-Rafiʿī, ʿAbd al-Raḥman, *Fi āʿqāb al-thawra al-miṣriyya : Thawrat sanat 1919* (al-Qāhira: Dār al-Maʿārif, 1987).
Ranger, Terence, 'The "New Historiography" in Dar Es Salaam: An Answer', *African Affairs* (1971), vol. 70, n. 278, pp. 50-61.
Ranger, Terence, 'Nationalist Historiography, Patriotic History and the History of the Nation: The Struggle Over the Past in Zimbabwe', *Journal of Southern African Studies* (2004), vol. 30, n. 2, pp. 215-234.
Read, Donald, *The Power of News: The History of the Reuters* (Oxford, New York: Oxford University Press, 1999).
Reid, Donald M., *Whose Pharaohs: Archaeology, Museums, and Egyptian National Identity From Napoleon to World War I* (Berkeley: University of California Press, 2002).
Rejwan, Nissim, *Arabs Face the Modern World: Religious, Cultural, and Political Responses to the West* (Gainesville: University Press of Florida, 1998).
Revel, Jacques, 'L'Institution et le Social', in *Les Formes de l'Expérience. Une Autre Histoire Sociale,* Bernard Lepetit ed. (Paris, Albin Michel, 1995), pp. 63–84.
Revel, Jacques, *Jeux D'échelles: La Micro-Analyse à l'Expérience* (Paris: Seuil, 1996).
Salih, Kamal O. 'British Colonial Military Recruitment Policy in the Southern Kordofan Region of Sudan, 1900--1945', *Middle Eastern Studies* (2005), vol. 41, n. 2, pp. 169-192.
Salih, M. A. M., 'Agro-Pastoralists Response to Agricultural Policies: The Predicament of the Baggara, Western Sudan', in *Adaptive Strategies in African Arid Lands,* Proceedings from a seminar at the Scandinavian Institute of African Studies, Uppsala, Sweden, April 1989, pp. 59–75.
Sandars, G.E.R, 'The Amarar', *Sudan Notes and Records* (1935), vol. 18, n. 2, pp. 195-220.
Sanderson, G. N., 'Indirect Rule in the Northern Sudan as an Anti-Nationalist Strategy 1920-1939', in *The Nationalist Movement in the Sudan,* Mahasin Muhammed Ahmed al-Hajj al-Safi ed. (Khartoum: Institute of African and Asian Studies, University of Khartoum, 1989), pp. 63-111.
Sanderson, Lilian, 'Education and Administrative Control in Colonial Sudan and Northern Nigeria', *African Affairs* (1975), vol. 74, n. 297, pp. 427-441.
Selbin, Eric, *Revolution in the Real World: Bringing Agency Back in* (New York: Routledge, 1997).
Seri-Hersch, Iris, 'Histoire Scolaire, Impérialisme(s) et Décolonisation(s): Le Cas du Soudan Anglo-égyptien (1945-1958)' (PhD, Aix-Marseille Université, 2012).
Shahvar, Soli, 'Tribes and Telegraphs in Lower Iraq: The Muntafiq and the Baghdad-Basrah Telegraph Line of 1863-65', *Middle Eastern Studies* (2003), vol. 39, n. 1, pp. 89-116.
Shanafelt, Robert, 'The Nature of Flag Power: How Flags Entail Dominance, Subordination, and Social Solidarity', *Politics and the Life Sciences* (2008), vol. 27, n. 2, pp. 13-27.
Sharkey, Heather J., 'Arabic Literature and the Nationalist Imagination in Kordofan', in *Kordofan Invaded: Peripheral Incorporation and Social Transformation in Islamic Africa*, Endre Stiansen and M. Kevane eds. (Leiden, Boston: Brill, 1998), pp. 165-179.
Sharkey, Heather J., 'Colonialism, Character-building and the Culture of Nationalism in the Sudan, 1898-1956.' *International Journal of the History of Sport* (1998), vol. 15, n. 1, pp. 1-26.
Sharkey, Heather J., 'A Century in Print: Arabic Journalism and Nationalism in Sudan, 1899-1999', *International Journal of Middle East Studies* (1999), vol. 31, n. 4, pp. 531-549.
Sharkey, Heather J., 'Christians Among Muslims: The Church Missionary Society in the Northern Sudan', *The Journal of African History* (2002), vol. 43, n. 1, pp. 51-75.

Sharkey, Heather J., *Living with Colonialism: Nationalism and Culture in the Anglo-Egyptian Sudan* (Berkley and Los Angeles: University of California Press, 2003)
Sharkey, Heather J., 'Arab Identity and Ideology in Sudan: The Politics of Language, Ethnicity, and Race', *African Affairs* (2007), vol. 107, n. 426, pp. 21-43.
Shepperson, George, 'The Place of John Chilembwe in Malawi Historiography', in *The Early History of Malawi*, B. Pachai ed. (London: Longman, 1972), pp. 405–28.
Sibeud, Emmanuelle, 'A Useless Colonial Science? : Practicing Anthropology in the French Colonial Empire, Circa 1880-1960', *Current Anthropology* (2012), vol. 53, n. 5, pp. 83-94.
Sikainga, Ahmad A., *Slaves Into Workers: Emancipation and Labor in Colonial Sudan* (Austin: University of Texas Press, 1996).
Sikainga, Ahmad A., 'Military Slavery and the Emergence of a Southern Sudanese Diaspora in the Northern Sudan, 1884-1956', in *White Nile, Black Blood: War, Leadership, and Ethnicity From Khartoum to Kampala,* Stephanie Beswick and Jay Spaulding eds. (Lawrenceville, NJ: Red Sea Press, 2000), pp. 23-37.
Sikainga, Ahmad A., *City of Steel and Fire : A Social History of Atbara, Sudan's Railway Town, 1906-1984* (Portsmouth, N.H.: Heinemann, 2002).
Sikainga, Ahmad A., 'A Short History of Sudanese Popular Music', in *The Sudan Handbook.* John Ryle, Justin Willis, Suliman Baldo, and Jok Maudt Jok eds. (Oxford: James Currey), pp. 145-152.
Silvestri, Michael, '"The Sinn Fein of India": Irish Nationalism and the Policing of Revolutionary Terrorism in Bengal', *Journal of British Studies* (2000), vol. 39, n. 4, pp. 454-486.
Simmel, Georg, 'The Sociology of Secrecy and of Secret Societies', *American Journal of Sociology* (1906), vol. 11, n. 4, pp. 441-498.
Simon, Reeva S., 'The Education of An Iraqi Ottoman Army Officer.' *The Origins of Arab Nationalism* Rashid Khalidi ed. (New York: Columbia University Press, 1991), pp. 151-166.
Skocpol, Theda, *States and Social Revolutions: A Comparative Analysis of France, Russia, and China* (Cambridge; New York: Cambridge University Press, 1979).
Smith, Anthony D., *Nationalism and Ethnosymbolism History, Culture and Ethnicity in the Formation of Nations* (Edinburgh: Edinburgh University Press, 2007).
Soghayroon, Thorraya, 'Sudanese Literature in English Translation: An Analytical Study of the Translation with a Historical Introduction to the Literature' (PhD, University of Westmister, 2010).
Spaulding, Jay and L. Kapteijns, 'The Orientalist Paradigm in the Historiography of the Late Precolonial Sudan', in *Golden Ages, Dark Ages: Imagining the Past in Anthropology and History,* Jay O'Brien and William Roseberry eds. (Berkeley: University of California Press, 1991), pp. 139-151.
Stiansen, Endre, 'The Gum Arabic Trade in Kordofan in the Mid-nineteenth Century', *Kordofan Invaded: Peripherial Incorporation and Social Transformation in Islamic Africa,* Endre Stiansen and Michael Kevane eds. (Leiden: Brill, 1998), pp. 60-85.
Stoler, Ann Laura, 'Colonial Archives and the Arts of Governance', *Archival Science* (2002), vol. 2, n. 1, pp. 87-109.
Stoler, Ann Laura, *Along the Archival Grain: Epistemic Anxieties and Colonial Common Sense* (Princeton: Princeton University Press, 2009).
Streets, H., *Martial Races: The Military, Race and Masculinity in British Imperial Culture, 1857-1914* (Manchester Univ Press, 2004).
Subrahmanyam, Sanjay, 'Connected Histories: Notes Towards a Reconfiguration of Early Modern Eurasia', *Modern Asian Studies* (1997), vol. 31, n. 3, pp. 735-762.
Switzer, Les, 'The Ambiguities of Protest in South Africa: Rural Politics and the Press During the 1920s', *The International Journal of African Historical Studies* (1990), vol. 23, n. 1, pp. 87-109.
Tarrow, Sidney, *Power in Movement. Social Movements and Contentious Politics*

(Cambridge, U.K.; New York: Cambridge University Press, 1988).
Tauber, Eliezer, *The Formation of Modern Syria and Iraq* (Ilford, Essex, U.K.; Portland, Or.: Frank Cass, 1995).
Tauber, Eliezer, 'Secrecy in Early Arab Nationalist Organizations', *Middle Eastern Studies* (1997), vol. 33, n. 1, pp. 119-127.
Tauber, Eliezer, 'Egyptian Secret Societies, 1911', *Middle Eastern Studies* (2006), vol. 42, n. 4, pp. 603-623.
Thomas, Martin, *Empires of Intelligence: Security Services and Colonial Disorder After 1914* (Berkeley: University of California Press, 2008).
Thompson, E. P., 'Patrician Society, Plebeian Culture', *Journal of Social History* (1974), vol. 7, n. 4, pp. 382–405.
Tilly, C., L. Tilly, and R. Tilly, *The Rebellious Century: 1830-1930* (Cambridge: Harvard University Press, 1975).
Traugott, Mark, *Repertoires and Cycles of Collective Action* (Durham: Duke University Press, 1995).
Trouillot, Michel-Rolph, *Silencing the Past: Power and the Production of History* (Boston, Mass.: Beacon Press, 1995).
Vezzadini, Elena, and Pierre Guidi, 'Contested Memories, Subalternity, and the State in Colonial and Postcolonial Histories of Northeast Africa', *Northeast African Studies* (2010), vol. 13, no. 2, pp. v–xviii.
Vezzadini, Elena, 'Making the Sudanese: Slavery Policies and Hegemony Construction in Early Colonial Sudan', in *Sudan's Wars and Peace Agreements*, Jay Spaulding, Stephanie Beswick, Caroline Fluher Lobban, and Richard Lobban eds. (Newcastle: Cambridge Scholar Publishing, 2010), pp. 71-101.
Vezzadini, Elena, 'Une "élite exclue". Les militaires soudanais entre ordre et révolte au Soudan colonial britannique (1900-1924)', in *Maintenir l'Ordre Colonial. Afrique et Madagascar, XIXe-XXe Siècles*, Jean-Pierre Bat and Nicolas Curtin eds. (Rennes: Presse Universitaire de Rennes, 2012), pp. 85-110.
Vezzadini, Elena, 'Spies, Secrets, and a Story Waiting to Be (re)told: Memories of the 1924 Revolution and the Racialization of Sudanese History', *Northeast African Studies* (2013), vol. 13, n. 2, pp. 53–92.
Vezzadini, Elena, 'Nationalism by Telegrams: Political Writings and Anti-Colonial Resistance in Sudan, 1920–1924', *The International Journal of African Historical Studies* (2013), vol., 46, n. 1, pp. 27–59.
Warburg, Gabriel R. *Islam, Nationalism and Communism in a Traditional Society: the Case of Sudan* (London: F. Cass, 1978).
Warburg, Gabriel, 'From Mahdism to Neo-Mahdism in the Sudan: The Role of the Sudanese Graduates in Paving the Way to Independence, 1881-1956', *Middle Eastern Studies* (2005), vol. 41, n. 6, pp. 975-99.
Warf, B. A. S., *The Spatial Turn : Interdisciplinary Perspectives* (London; New York: Routledge, 2009).
Watenpaugh, Keith D., *Being Modern in the Middle East : Revolution, Nationalism, Colonialism, and the Arab Middle Class* (Princeton, N.J.: Princeton University Press, 2006).
Willis, Justin, 'Violence, Authority, and the State in the Nuba Mountains of Condominium Sudan', *The Historical Journal* (2003), vol. 46, n. 1, pp. 89-114.
Willis, Justin, 'Tribal Gatherings: Colonial Spectacle, Native Administration and Local Government in Condominium Sudan', *Past & Present* (2011), vol. 211, n. 1, pp. 243-268.
Windel, Aaron, 'British Colonial Education in Africa: Policy and Practice in the Era of Trusteeship', *History Compass* (2009), vol. 7, n. 1, pp. 1-21.
Wipper, Audrey, 'Kikuyu Women and the Harry Thuku Disturbances: Some Uniformities of Female Militancy', *Africa* (2011), vol. 59, n. 3, pp. 300-337.
Zhou, Yongming, *Historicizing Online Politics: Telegraphy, the Internet, and Political Participation in China* (Stanford: Stanford University Press, 2006).

Index

Abadba 112, 224, 246
al-Abbasiyya 31, 88
Abdallah, Arafat Muhammad/ Mohammed, Arafat, Eff. 28, 74, 283
Abdallah, al-Azza Muhammad 59, 81-2, 95, 98, 150, 168, 169, 172, 226, 250, 251, 259
Abdallah, Muhammad 207, 208
Abdallahi, Khalifa 3, 70-1, 162, 178
Abdin, Hasan 9, 58
Abdin, al-Tayyib 113, 123, 281, 283
Abduh, Muhammad 47
Abdun, Husayn 240
Abu Deleiq 84, 290
Abu Hamed 84, 153, 274, 290
Abu Sinn, Yuzbashi Ahmad Hilmi 223
Abu Sinn family 195
accountability 96, 108, 153, 163
Adham, Adam 139, 207
al-Afghani, Jamal al-Din 47
Africa 21-3 passim, 234; East – Association 11, 20; North 19; South-West 20, 46; sub-Saharan 21; West 213, conference 19, 20
'Africans'/Africanness 8, 28-30 passim, 36, 37, 67, 180
agents 112-14, 134, 139, 156, 258, 278
agreement, Condominium 2
agriculture 140-1, 243-4, 246, 249
Ahmad, Gharib 207, 208
Ahmad, mahdi Muhammad 2, 70
Ahmad, Mahmud Khamis 184, 197, 210
Ahmad, 'Osta' 239
al-Ahram 51, 53, 69
Ajabna, Sultan 219
Ajras al-Hurriyya 5
Algeria 19, 20, 47
Ali, Ahmad 102, 281, 293
Ali, Khedive Muhammad 160, 210
Allenby, Viscount 4, 42, 79-81 passim, 88, 90-1, 151
Amin, Qasim 44
Amin, Shahid 255
al-Amin, Nuri 238
al-Amin, Muhammad 100
al-Amin, Ubayd al-Hajj 2, 16, 62, 67, 68, 73-5 passim, 98, 99, 102, 109, 149, 179, 180, 182-6 passim, 199, 203, 279, 282-4 passim
ancestry 158, 160, 179-80, 268 see also origins
Anderson, Benedict 21, 22
Anglo-Egyptian Bank 240
Anja, Hamadan Abu 212
Antar, Musa Ahmad 171-2, 236-41 passim, 293
Arabs/Arabness 8, 25-30, 33-7 passim, 43, 49, 74, 78, 126, 127, 158, 180, 182, 196-9 passim, 224, 229, 245-8 passim, 268
archives 15, 16, 215, 253-66 passim, 286
Argo 85, 183, 290
Arifi, Adham Pasha 212, 214
army, British 77-8, 82-4 passim, 87, 91, 92, 94, 127, 137, 216-17; Arab Corps 220, 221; Egyptian 4, 59, 87, 90-5 passim, 116, 127, 137, 156, 172, 174, 182, 195, 209-31 passim, 271, Handbook of 219, 223, pay 228, recruiting 218-21, 223; Sudanese Battalion 4, 36, 87, 93, 101, 106, 172, 206-33 passim, Sudan Defence Force 218, 221; Turco-Egyptian

Jihadiyya 209-14 passim, 218; see also officers
arrests 2-4 passim, 28, 40, 72-6, 83-7 passim, 91, 101-5 passim, 124-5, 128, 136-7, 153, 155, 157, 170-2 passim, 240, 245, 257, 278
articles 39-42 passim, 51-2
artisans 3, 38, 73, 78, 86, 101, 110, 114, 138, 139, 182, 235-7 passim, 245, 247, 250, 253
assassinations 4, 54, 61-2, 89, 90, 116, 256
Atbara 3, 39, 76-9 passim, 120, 124, 126, 134, 153, 168, 235, 239, 247, 267, 278
Atiya, Samuel 257
Austria-Hungary 44
Aysa, Sulayman 103
al-Azhari, Isma'il 88, 195, 223, 262

Babikr, Tayyib 84, 100, 102, 104, 105, 108, 162, 164, 166, 279, 286-7
Badri, Babikr 187
Bahr al-Ghazal 85, 208, 211, 219, 290
Baily, Robin E. 59, 75, 95, 239, 266, 268
Bakheit, Jafaar 9, 29, 41, 175, 237-8
al-Bakhit, Muhammad Abd 75, 208
Bakhriba, Ahmad Umar 102, 112, 115, 159, 160, 280-83 passim
Bakri, Tafiq Ahmad 184
al-Banna, Ali 4, 93-5 passim, 224, 229, 264
al-Banna, Muhammad Umar 264
Baqqara 36, 74, 134, 140, 141, 214, 246, 247
Bara 59, 133, 134, 143, 153, 196, 197, 206, 226, 278, 290
Barakat 72, 75, 153, 278
Bayley, C.A. 55, 257-8
Beinin, Joel 234-5, 238
Beja 125-32 passim, 145, 249
Berber 70, 144, 196, 246, 290
Berberine 33, 130, 143, 196-8 passim, 237, 247, 254
Beshir, Mohamed Omer 11, 190, 195
Bihari, Abd al-Wahhab 206, 207, 209
Black/Sudani 33-7 passim, 76, 139, 180, 182, 195-8 passim, 212-13, 218, 224, 228, 229, 245-7 passim, 254, 268-71 passim
Britain/British 20, 36-8 passim, 89. 103, 129-30, 132, 151, 187, 216-18 passim, 253, 256-9; and Egypt 1, 2, 4, 10, 22, 34, 60, 88-91, 112, 117, 209-13 passim, 215, 216, 266-8 see also Condiminium; and Sudan 1-3 passim, 7, 20, 31, 40-4 passim, 51, 69-76, 87-9, 93-5 passim, 115, 116, 124, 127-8, 133, 139-42, 155- 7 passim, 159, 160, 164-6 passim, 169, 171, 186-99, 200-3, 209, 213-18 passim, 220, 222-5 passim, 248, 251-2, 256-66 passim, anti-Britain 32, 39, 42- 8, 69, 71, 162, 163, pro 28-9, 31-2, 38, 41, 43, 47; see also Ewart Report; Indirect Rule; Intelligence Department
al-Bushi, Mudaththir 30, 45, 53, 54, 59, 62, 105, 185, 199, 232, 241

cadets 3, 79-83, 81, 92, 110, 168-9, 172-4 passim, 206-7, 207, 222-5 passim, 233, 263, 267; origins 224-5, 262
Camel Corps 36, 58, 119, 133, 135, 140, 207, 221, 226, 230, 249
Cameroun 46
casualties 3, 78, 94, 126, 167
Chilemba, John 11
China 63
Christianity 43, 272
circulars 39-43 passim, 60, 64, 85, 109, 136, 150, 153-4, 157-8, 163, 184, 267
civil servants 16, 29, 71, 110-11, 114, 137-8, 181, 182, 200-5 passim, 217, 240, 249; pay grades 200-3; SPG 200, 242
civilization 41, 44, 47-9, 152, 156
class factors 14, 30, 235-6
Cole, Juan 24
coffee houses 172, 237, 239-42, 253; Qahwat al-Halwani 240-1
colonialism 16, 19-64, 129-30, 154-7 passim, 235, 246, 249, 252-4, 270-2 passim; anti- 20, 22, 24, 28, 30, 39, 41, 43-6, 53-6 passim, 60, 72, 84-5, 98, 105, 106, 108-14 passim, 132, 158, 233, 234, 241
colonization 1, 24, 39, 43, 47, 63, 157, 161-3, 166, 171-5 passim, 179, 186, 216-17, 253
Condominium, Anglo-Egyptian 1, 2, 4, 9, 40, 50, 90, 117, 143, 145, 195, 212, 215, 221, 243, 245, 249; invasion 209-13 passim, 216
Cowan Pasha 93
culture 13, 16, 33, 44, 160, 176, 183, 243
Currie, James 187, 188, 199
Curzon, Lord 257

Dabba, Ali Hassan 75, 293
al-Dahab, sayyid Ahmad Suwar 88
Daly, M.W. 10, 40, 91
dams 141, 244
al-Dar, Muhammad Jabr 113, 133-5 passim
Darfur 8, 60, 122, 180, 211, 213, 217, 226; 'Black Block' 207; Nyala Rebellion 258
al-Darir, Hassan al-Amin 72, 292
Davies, Reginald 257, 266
Dayfallah, Muhammad 100
Dayfallah, Shaykh Umar (aka Dafalla, Sheikh Omar / Omar, Hag el Sheikh/ Shaykh, Umar al-Haj/al-Hajj al-Shaykh Wad Umar) 71, 72, 167, 261, 279, 281, 292
declarations 31, 88
delegations 1, 3, 42, 46-7, 49, 70-1, 151, 178, 264
demonstrations 1-4 passim, 10, 15, 19, 39, 71-87 passim, 96, 97, 101, 103, 113, 114, 124-9, 134-7, 166-73 passim, 183, 234-9 passim, 242, 250, 257, 258, 267; ban on 3, 72, 85, 120
'denationalized Sudanese' 266, 268-70 passim
'detribalized negroids' 8, 225, 266, 268-70 passim
devolution 187, 252
al-Dhakir, Ahmad Isma'il 134
Dhingra, Madan Lal 54
Dinar, Muzammil Ali 92, 162, 171, 173, 184, 202, 222
Dinka/'Denka' 7, 33, 98, 111, 178, 179, 210, 224, 225
Diyab, Ahmad Ibrahim 9
Dongola 34, 40, 85, 112, 290
droughts 130-1, 140, 145
Dulayb, Shaykh Ahmad al-Imam 29, 32, 99, 263, 279
Dunn, John P. 211-12
Durkheim, Emile 165

economy 140-6 passim, 243-4, 253
education 41, 178, 182-99 passim, 236, 253-4, 269; admission 188-90, 198-9, 204; attrition 191, 203; Dual Policy 187, 252; girls' 187; selection 187, 194-9 passim, 204; sociology of education 185-205 passim
Effendi class 35, 71, 97, 101, 117, 119, 120, 234, 242, 250, 288
Egypt/Egyptians 1-4 passim, 20, 24, 26-7, 39-47 passim, 49, 51, 54, 60-4 passim, 69, 77-9, 89-92 passim, 128, 144-5, 150-1, 168, 195, 197-8, 212, 228, 234, 254, 262, 271 see also army; Condominium; press; and Britain 1-4 passim, 10, 22, 26, 53, 69, 88-91 passim, 116, 119, 152, 162, 209-13, 216, 266-8, 53, 69, 119, 267, anti-Britain 53, 69, 119, 267; Protectorate 1; Revolution (1919) 1, 13, 19, 20, 39, 52-3, 119, 120, 164, 173, 238, Urabi 24; and Sudan 1-3 passim, 28, 34-5, 40, 43, 47, 52-4 passim, 60-1, 69-70, 86, 92-5, 116-21 passim, 124, 144-5, 152, 160-3, 172-4, 178,95, 197-8, 200-2, 205, 209-19 passim, 239, 258, 266-9, anti-Egypt 31, 46, 69, 90, 92, 266-9; pro- 2, 3, 29-32 passim, 35, 39, 43, 47, 69, 86, 129, 160-2 passim, 173-4; Turco- 7, 29, 34-5, 117, 129, 143, 146, 209-14, 218; Umma Party 26, 27; Wafd 2, 27, 46, 116, 120, 238; Watanist Party 26, 27, 51,69, 116, 267
El Fasher 85, 86, 134, 290
elites 7, 20, 21, 30, 38, 97, 180, 205, 221-31, 253
El Nuhud 53, 57, 134, 143, 153, 226, 278, 290
El Obeid 3, 4, 16, 58, 84, 110, 122, 132-46, 153, 196, 197, 215, 235, 241-2, 260, 278; White Flag League in 137-42
employment 130, 140-1, 182, 191-4, 199-205 passim, 248, see also labour
emotions 158, 164-76 passim, 233
Erickson, Bonnie 56, 62, 182
ethnic factors 7-8, 21, 33, 37, 139, 178, 259, 262, 272
Europe/Europeans 13, 19, 22, 23, 48, 54, 130, 132, 152, 159
Ewald, Janet 209-10
Ewart, John Murray 255-7, 266; Report 33, 62, 69, 77, 83, 266-71 passim
executions 4, 40, 94-5, 233, 264
exports 117, 140, 143, 145, 243

Fadil, Hassan Ahmad 261, 293
Fahmi, Abd al-Rahman Bey 238-9
Al-Fajr 28
family background 7, 98-9, 134, 195-9 passim, 204-5, 223, 225, 262-5
Farah, Khalil 27, 175-6
Farah, Sayyid 4, 93, 94, 197, 215
Farghali, Mahmoud Mohammed 284
al-Farraj, Ahmad 106

Fatuh, Yuzbashi Mohammad Effendi 59
Fawz 175, 176, 241
Fawzi, Ahmad 86
al-Fawzi, Muhammad Abd 75
fees, school 188, 191, 195
Fellata 130, 139, 246
el-Fiki, Abu El Gasim 112
Five Brothers, Society of 58
flags 67, 73, 80-1, 86, 125, 129, 156, 165, 167, 168; 'incident' 86, 174
Foster, Susan L. 166
France 27, 45
Frost, Thomas 63
Fuad, King 74, 75, 77, 81, 87, 118, 125, 129, 134, 158, 161, 164, 167
Fur 224

Gaelic American, The 55
Gandhi, Mahatma 19, 55, 159
Garang, John 7
Gaseisa, Abdulla Abu 260
Gellatly & Hankey 102, 143, 186, 200, 240
Gelvin, James 25, 165, 166
Gezira and Jebel Awlia Irrigation Scheme 43, 53, 88, 91, 117, 145, 243, 244
Ghali, Butrus 61
Ghallab, Ahmad Idris 73, 293
Gharib, Shaykh Abd El Magid 144
Gillan, Sir Angus 219
Gold Coast 19
Gong, Gerrit W. 48
Gordon College 29, 30, 123, 183-6, 188-95 passim, 198-9, 222-4 passim, 232; Primary School 184-5, 222-3, 231
Gorst, Eldon 51-2
Grand Mufti 74, 88, 109, 205
Guha, Ranajit 265
Guma, Mahmud 239
Gwynn, Sir Charles 216

Habbaniyya 134; Shaykh of 112
Hadarat al-Sudan 2, 7, 31, 32, 38, 40-2 passim, 45, 47, 52, 69
Hadendowa 125, 126, 224, 225, 246
El-Hadi, Abd El Majid 172
al-Hadi, Ibrahim Abd 185
Hadiya, Ali 172, 240-1
Hadiya, Muhammad (Mansur) 113, 123, 172, 240-1, 281, 283
Halfa 34, 278
Hamid, Ali 204
Hanes, William 20
Hashim, Uthman Muhammad 113, 286
Hashimab 195
el-Hashimi, Khalid Bin 19
Hassahissa 75, 153, 278, 291
Hassan, Yuzbashi Abd al-Khaliq 71
Hassan, Abd al-Rahman 237, 293
Hassan, Tawfiq 292
al-Hay, Abd al-Aziz Abd 59, 80, 116, 184, 208, 215-16, 223, 225, 226
al-Hay, Idris Abd 80, 81, 171, 172, 210, 223, 225
Haykal, Muhammad Husayn 45
al-Hindi, sayyid Yusuf 2, 28
al-Hindiyya 2
history/historiography 5-12, 14-16, 20-30 passim, 33, 97, 116, 119, 160-1, 167, 234, 242, 252-6 passim, 271-2
Hizb al-Umma 62
Holt, P.M. 10
Hudayb, Muhammad Amin 39
Huddleston, Hubert 4, 80, 89, 93, 94, 200
Huntington, Samuel P. 12-13
Husayn, Durriyya Muhammad 299
Husayn, Husayn Yusif 100, 261, 279

Ibrahim, Ahmad Mudaththir 29, 99, 103, 106, 108, 263, 279
Ibrahim, Bayyid 139
Ibrahim, Isma'il Muhammad eff/ Ibrahim Israil 32, 161, 292
Ibrahim, Muhammad al-Makki 32, 100, 292
Ibrahim, Wahba 123
Id, Habiballa and Hussein 144
ideology 13, 15, 16, 21-4 passim, 26, 27, 39, 41, 97, 147-76 passim, 180, 254
Idris, Abdel Hai 213, 223
Idris, Ahmad 135
Idris, Muhammad/Babikr, Mohammed Idris 99, 279
Idris, Ubayd 113, 123, 281, 283
imperialism 21-3 passim, 38, 183; anti- 43, 162
imprisonment 2, 3, 54, 72-7 passim, 85-6, 92, 95, 103, 137, 170-2 passim, 237, 249- 51 passim, 263
independence, 20, 26, 40, 45, 47, 48, 162; Egypt 1-2, 26, 40, 45, 136, 162, 'Reserved Points' 2; Sudan 2, 3, 11, 20, 26-8 passim, 40, 43, 45-7 passim, 136, 162
India/Indians 44, 51, 54, 55, 63, 130, 159, 213, 257; Ahimsaa 19; Chauri-Chaura uprising 255

indirect rule 10, 132, 142, 187, 188, 221, 252-3, 256
infrastructure 117, 132, 141, 145, 244, 253
injustice 155, 159, 163, 170-3 passim
intelligence, political 49-55
Intelligence Department 32, 60, 69, 88, 96, 106, 110, 111, 114, 115, 119, 120, 124, 133-4, 140, 165, 176, 215-16, 236-7, 247, 256-66, 268, 270, 271, 288
intermarriage 34, 35
international community 159-60, 163
international relations 44-9 passim, 152
Iraq 35, 63, 64; revolt (1920) 13, 19
Irish Free State/Ireland 19, 54
Isma'il, Khedive 24
Isma'il, Muhammad Eff. Ibrahim/Israil Ibrahim 32 161, 275, 276
Italy 13, 45

Ja'aliyyin 34, 99, 100, 111, 139, 143, 224, 237, 247, 260-2 passim
al-Jak, Yuzbashi Kabsun 208
Jama (Ajma) Fumi 219-20, 232
Jamiyyat al-Liwa al-Abyad see White Flag League
Jamiyyat al-Tadamun al-Akhawi 61-2
Jankowski, James 26
Japan 48
al-Jarida 51
Jasper, James M. 97, 170
Jibril Yazb. Muhammad Eff. Salih/ Gibril, Yazbashi Mohammed Eff. Saleh 59, 112, 119, 135-6, 215
Jibril, Tawfiq Salih 2, 29, 85, 135
Jihadiyya 211-14
justice 156-7, 159, 163
Justice! 48, 55

Kabsun, Khalil 208, 293
Kamil, Mustafa 26, 27
Kassala 214, 247
Keays, G. A. V. 230
Kenya 11, 20, 213
Khalil, Abdallah 27-8, 31, 223, 229
Khalil, al-Imam Dulayb 32, 262-3, 265
Khalil, Khalfallah 28
Khartoum 3-5 passim, 43, 60, 76, 81-3 passim, 86, 110-11, 113, 124, 142, 235, 239, 240, 244, 247-8, 260, 278; North 4, 43, 55, 71, 82, 93, 110, 168, 172, 178
al-Khatim, Muhammad Sirr 74, 104, 109, 118, 237, 240, 293
Khatmiyya 2
Khan, Noor-Aiman 55, 56
Killingray, David 20, 217
Kisha, Sulayman 2, 29, 31, 37, 57, 180
Kitchener, Lord 195
'knowledge panics' 257-8
Kober prison 4, 55, 72, 82, 85, 92, 104, 168, 172, 182, 183
Kordofan 36, 57, 60, 62, 67, 70, 84, 99, 112, 133-5 passim, 140-3 passim, 186, 197, 210, 221, 224
Korea 19
Kurita, Yoshiko 9-10, 37, 167, 173, 179-80, 225

labour 130-2, 140-1, 234-54 passim; Central – Bureau 245, 247-9 passim, 251; costs 243-5; market 188-94, 203, 204; registration 245, 246; shortage 243-4, 247; Syndicate 238
Lamothe, Ronald M. 211, 213, 218
al-Latif, Ali Abd 2, 5-10 passim, 27, 30-2 passim, 37, 53, 63, 67, 68, 80-2 passim, 98, 101-2, 105, 106, 118, 157, 207, 226, 231, 263-4, 267, 269, 270, 279, 282-3 passim, 287; arrest/ imprisonment 2, 3, 73, 74, 80, 100, 109, 159, 169, 170; origins 7, 8, 28, 67, 179-80, 225, 262
law 106, 159, 232; international 48; martial 88; Sudan Penal Code 239
Laz, Ali Musa 74, 75, 100
League of Nations 45, 46, 48-9, 159; Covenant 48
legality 71, 156, 159, 161, 253
letters 3, 39, 41, 85, 150, 153
liberation 154, 155, 157, 166, 173
literature 174-6
Al-Liwa 51, 54-5
Lockman, Zachary 234-5, 238

Mabruk, Abdallah 210, 263-4, 290
MacDonald, Ramsay 90, 120, 151, 282
MacMichael, Harold A. 188, 252, 256, 271
Maghreb 214
Mahas 111
al-Mahdi, sayyid Abd al-Rahman 2, 28, 31, 60, 74. 88, 109, 153, 178, 179, 253, 257, 264
al-Mahdi, Muhammad/el-Taishi Muhammed, Eff. El Khalifa 3, 70-1, 73, 109, 155, 162, 178-80 passim, 228, 264, 281

Mahdiyya/Mahdists 11, 36, 195, 212, 213, 216-17, 258
Mahmud, Husayn Mukhtar 203
al-Majid, Isma'il Abd 261, 293
al-Mak, Muhammad Salih 105, 133, 135, 136, 139
Malakal 4, 87, 229, 291
Malasi, Ali 51, 53, 56-8 passim, 60, 62, 113, 123, 125-9 passim, 170, 173, 179, 186, 199, 205, 280, 283, 289
Malawi 11
mamur 3, 59, 70, 117, 126, 136, 204, 208, 230-1
mandates 48
Manela, Erez 44-5, 47, 49, 50
al-Mardi, Ali 32
markets 145, 240-2 passim, 250, 253
al-Maz, Abd al-Fadil 4, 5, 93-5 passim, 215
McDougall, James 20
merchants 28, 29, 38, 49, 52, 87, 101, 109-11 passim, 117, 138, 139, 142-6 passim, 194, 195, 250, 263
Merowe 72, 75, 153, 278
Mesopotamia 25
Metemma 35, 98
Mexico 210, 211, 214
Middle East 19, 23, 25, 234
Midhat, Hassan 75, 288
migration 34, 130, 246-8 passim, 250
Military School 3, 79-83, 101, 166, 172, 194, 195, 206, 207, 214, 221-3 passim, 225, 228, 230
Milner, Lord 2; commission 2
al-Mirghani, sayyid Ali, 1, 28, 88, 253
al-Mirghani, Tayyib 185
Mirsal, Musa 239
missionaries 186, 187
mobility 204, 226, 231, 232; social 248, 250
Morocco 27
al-Muayyad 51
al-Mufti, Hassan Isma'il 58, 59, 104, 105, 208, 223, 226, 232
Muhammad, Farajallah 86
Muhammad, Jamal al-Din 262
Muhammad, Sulayman 4, 93, 94, 206, 207
al-Mula, Hassan Fadl 4, 59, 87, 93, 94, 208, 226
Mulazmin 214
al-Muqattam 51-3 passim, 115, 238
Musa, Ali 58, 60
Mushli, Fatima Ibrahim 35
mutiny 4, 55, 79-83, 91-5 passim, 115-16, 214, 224, 258, 267; 27 November 4, 5, 55, 93-5, 115, 120, 156, 159, 167, 172, 206, 209, 215, 219, 233, 264, 289
Muwallad/Muwalladin 33-5 passim, 76, 111, 128, 139, 143, 196, 224, 247, 262, 268, 270

Nada, Fathallah 207, 208
Na'im, Bashir 237, 265
Najib, Muhammad (or Neguib) – former president of Egypt 34, 60-1
Najila, Hassan 29, 33, 37, 43, 53, 174-5, 241
narratives 14-15, 27-31, 69
Nasir, Sami 112
al-Nasr, Hamdi Bey 69
al-Nasir, Jamal Abd 26, 235
nationalism 1-16, 19-64, 142-6, 157-63, 239-42, 250-2, 259-72 passim; see also Sudan Union; White Flag League
nationality 33-7, 196, 198, 259
news 50, 51, 54, 55; agencies 50, 51, 258
Nickles, David P. 152
Nile Valley 143, 160; Unity of 2, 3, 37, 58, 161-3 passim, 173, 174, 239
notables 1, 28, 30-2 passim, 41, 42, 46, 69, 74, 88, 118, 169, 180, 223-4, 251-4 passim, 262-3, 269-72 passim
Nuba/Nubians 35, 67, 98, 99, 109, 111, 139, 198, 224, 237; Mountains 7, 36, 70, 91, 112, 134, 150, 180, 209, 233
Numayri, Ja'far 5
al-Nur, Abdallah 109, 208
al-Nur, Ubayd Abd 175-6
Nurayet 84, 112, 291

occupations/professions 86, 100, 102-4 passim, 111, 128, 138-40 passim, 178, 198-9, 236-7, 240, 241, 259, 262, 265-6
officers, British 60, 78, 187, 209, 213-18 passim, 271; Egyptian 4, 39, 59, 78, 86, 90, 91, 94, 114, 115, 117, 119, 121,182, 195, Club 75, 83, 176; Sudanese 3, 4, 8, 10, 29, 36, 49, 58-60 passim, 69, 86, 87, 90, 91, 93-5 passim, 106, 109-16 passim, 133, 135, 138, 159, 174, 182, 206, 207, 209-13, 221-33, 268-9, 271, Club 119, 135, 137, dismissed 109, 208, 216; privileges 226, 228-9
officials, Sudanese 3, 8, 41, 49, 73, 138,

145, 195 see also civil servants
Omdurman 31, 38, 39, 43, 57, 82, 88, 99, 109, 110, 196, 198, 199, 212, 247, 251, 253, 265, 278
origins 7-8, 25-7, 33-6, 98-100 passim, 111, 128, 139, 158, 178-80, 196-8 passim, 224, 225, 247, 253-4, 262
Ottoman Empire 26, 27, 34, 40, 44, 47, 63, 198, 214 see also Egypt, Turco-
Ozturk, Serdar 240

pamphlets 39, 41-3 passim, 49, 127
pastoralists 36, 131, 140-1, 246
patrols 217-20 passim, 232
patron-client relations 141, 234
pay 130, 140, 226, 228, 236, 242, 244, 248, 249, 253
Peace Conferences 44, 49; Paris 46, 47
peacefulness 79, 159, 165
Perkins, Kenneth 127, 130, 249
petitions 3, 39, 46, 47, 69-70, 86, 101-4 passim, 106, 109, 149-63 passim, 171, 208, 237
Philips, Captain 257
police 76-7, 81-3 passim, 100, 124-6 passim, 136, 168, 235; secret 61, 85-6, 172
Political Service, Sudan 216-17
politics 2, 3, 14-16, 19-64, 87-90 passim, 106, 110-46 passim, 171-2, 175, 185, 231-6, 240-2, 250-72 passim
Polletta, Francesca 97
Port Sudan 3, 16, 62, 69, 76-7, 113, 122-32, 143, 153, 168, 173, 186, 196, 197, 235, 237, 244, 249, 267, 278; White Flag League in 127-9
Portugal/Portuguese 45, 55
Post and Telegraph Department 2, 51, 60, 62, 72, 76, 98, 102, 103, 105, 123, 150, 175, 185, 186, 288
Pott, Alexander 213, 223
power 14-16
press 20, 39-44, 49-55 passim; British 32, 52, 53, 55, 90, 151; Egyptian 1, 39, 51-4 passim, 88, 145, 152, 238, Syndicate 150; Sudanese 2, 5, 52; see also under individual titles
protests/protesters 1, 3, 13, 16, 19-21 passim, 39, 46, 47, 55, 70, 73-84 passim, 89, 96, 98, 108, 113, 127, 147-63, 164-272 passim

al-Qadir, Salih Abd/Gadir, Saleh Eff. Abdel/Kader, Sahel Abdel 2, 3, 30, 32, 58, 59, 62, 67, 68, 72, 76-8 passim, 98, 102, 105, 112, 113, 123-5 passim, 137, 149, 184, 185, 190, 203, 205, 279, 280, 283; arrest 3, 72, 124-5
Qalilat, Mustafa 52
al-Qardawi, Hamid 119, 139
al-Qasim, shaykh Abu 88
al-Qasim, Mohammad al-Amin Abu/ Gasem, Mohammad al-Amin Abu 279

racism 8, 36, 181, 196-9 passim, 204, 213-14, 218, 253, 268-70 passim
al-Radi, Abd al-Rahman 206, 207
Ra'fat, Mahmud 86
Rahma, Salih 135
al-Rahman, Bashiri Abd 113, 123, 280, 283
al-Rahman, Ibrahim Abd 59, 216
al-Rahim, Thabit Abd 4, 93-5 passim, 206, 210, 229
al-Rahim, Abd al-Wahhab Ahmad Abd 12
al-Ra'id al-Sudan 52
Railways Battallion 3, 39, 77-9 passim, 117, 120, 125-7 passim, 129, 267
Railways Department 60, 78, 123, 185, 186, 235, 240, 288
Ramadan, Muhammad Hafiz Bey 69, 267
Rashayda 246
Rasiq, Izz al-Din Husayn/Rashek, Izzeidin 103, 105, 106, 170-1, 279
Ratib, Mohd 172
religion 21, 28, 38, 43, 44, 87, 160, 167, 186, 258, 270, 272
revolts 12-14 passim, 19, 43, 55, 257, 258, 262; Iraq 13, 19; Syrian 13, 19
Reuters 50-1
Revolution (1924) 1-16 passim, 24, 27, 55, 64-146 passim, 164, 166, 180, 206, 233- 54 passim; definition 12-14; Egyptian 1, 2, 13, 19, 24, 39, 52, 119, 120, 164, 173, 238; French 164; Russian 43, 44; Urabi 24
Rif'at Bey 94
rights 19, 43, 44, 48, 272
Rihan, Abdallah (tailor) 239
Rihan, Abdallah 208, 225
Rihan, Husayn 207, 208
riots 77-9, 92-3, 96, 120, 183, 184, 239, 258
risk 56, 167, 170
al-Riwayat al-Shafawiyya li-Thuwwar

1924 5, 52, 80, 97, 133, 183-5 passim, 209, 216, 219, 232, 236
Riziq, Amina Bilal 70, 72, 167, 207
Riziq, Yuzbashi Bilal 207
Rowlatt Committee Report 63
Rufa'a 112, 187, 199
Rustum, Muhammad Surur 59, 207

sacrifice 157-8, 163, 167, 171, 173
Sa'd, Hassan 172
Sa'd, Iskander 203
al-Safi, Mahasin Abd al-Qadir Hajj 11
Salih, Ali Ahmad 52, 63-4, 105, 112, 200, 203, 237-8, 241, 292
Salih, Hassan (Al-Matbaji) 2, 67, 72-3, 75, 98, 149, 260, 273
Salih, Taha 31-2
Salih, Zayn al-Abdin 207
Sawakin 125, 129, 186, 199
Sayah, Bayumi 204
Sayf, Muhyi al-Din Abu 184
al-Sayyid, Abd al-Karim 31, 73, 102, 179, 236, 292
Sayyid, Abd al-Qadir Ahmad 72, 167, 250-2, 264, 265
Sayyid, osta Ahmad 250-1
schools, Elementary Vernacular 187, 189, 190, 196; girls elementary 187; Quranic (khalwa) 187, (kuttab) 184, 190, 197, 198; military 187; primary 184, 187, 189-94 passim,197-8; secondary 187, 189-90; Vocational Workshop 187, 194
Scotland 55
secrecy 32-3, 96, 104-5, 156; secret societies 2, 33, 39, 55-64, 69, 96, 120, 182, 208, 231
self-determination 20, 44-8 passim, 70, 159, 161, 258
al-Shafi, shaykh Babikr al-Hajj 32
Shahata, Sayyid 184, 206, 207, 209, 216, 226, 229
al-Shahid, al-Amin Labib 118
al-Shallali, Abayzid Ahmad Husayn 55, 184
Shaigi/Shayqi 33, 36, 100, 139, 262
Sharaf, Hassan 207, 208
Sharif, Hassan 2, 67-9 passim, 68, 72, 75, 98, 102, 149, 203, 279
Sharif, Husayn 31, 32, 38, 40, 45, 52
Sharif, Muhammad 40, 136
Sharif, Dr Muhammad Abd al-Fatah 106, 135
Sharif, Yusif 106
Sharkey, Heather J. 42, 230
Shendi 3, 4, 35, 83-4, 100, 104, 108, 113, 134, 153, 170, 196, 229
al-Shinnawi, Muhammad Fadlallah 81, 209-10; origins 224-5
Shinqiti, Muhammad Salih 8, 28
Sikainga, Ahmad A. 242, 248, 249
Silvestri, Michael 54
Skocpol, Theda 12-14 passim
Skrine, Arthur W. 257
slaves 7, 8, 33-6 passim, 141, 178-80, 210-14 passim, 218-19, 242-3, 245, 246, 265, 269; in army 70, 210-13; trade 178, 211
social movements 16, 24, 27, 97, 164
songs 114, 174-6 passim
South Africa 20
Stack, Sir Lee 4, 28, 36, 79, 89, 90, 116, 174, 187, 230-1, 252, 253, 256
Sterry, Sir Wasey 74, 88, 89
strikes 74, 76, 78, 92, 125, 127, 248-9; Cairo tram 238
students 79-83, 92, 109-11 passim, 123, 126, 189-99 passim, 206
Subrahmanyam, Sanjay 22, 44, 47
Sudan Commission 70; Committee 69
Sudan lil-sudaniyyn 2
Sudan, Southern 4, 5, 8, 10, 36, 67, 86, 111, 180, 186, 229, 233
Sudan Union 2, 25, 27, 28, 30-3 passim, 41, 42, 57, 59-63 passim, 86, 110, 111, 114-16 passim, 123, 153, 175, 180, 183, 185, 215, 286, 289
Sulayman, shaykh Abu Zayd 88
Suq al-Arabi 5, 172, 228, 240, 241
Surur, Nafisa 81, 251
symbols 121, 164-6 passim, 171, 173-6, 233
Syria 25-7 passim, 46, 51, 63, 64, 151, 196; Ba'ath Party 26; Revolt 13, 19

Ta'aisha 74, 140, 224, 246-7
Tagore, Rabindranath 44
Tahir, Ali 225
Tahmush, Abdel Khalil 265, 293
Talodi 91, 99, 233, 291
al-Tam, Zayn al-Abdin Abd/el-Abdin, Zein 3, 16, 67, 69-72 passim, 86, 100, 106, 155, 161, 167, 170, 178-9, 206, 207, 228, 231, 264, 265, 280, 281, 289
Taqali 134, 209, 212, 291
taxation 88,145; education tax 188, 212
Tayallah, Hassan 112-13
telegrams 3, 16, 41, 67, 74, 75, 79, 85, 86, 100-4, 106, 109, 113, 114, 120,

123-7, 149-63 passim, 169, 170, 257, 259, 278-87
telegraph 39, 49-50, 51, 152
Tenai, Shaykh Omer 289
Thaalbi, Abd al-Aziz 19
Three Towns 111, 112, 122, 153, 250
Thuku, Harry 11, 20
Togo 46
Tokar 197, 247
totemism 165
trade/traders 8, 71, 88, 97, 110, 111, 114, 117, 122, 129-30, 140-6 passim, 182, 194, 236, 253
trade unions 238-9
trials 5-6, 32, 53, 62-4 passim, 74, 85, 118, 127
tribes 33, 37, 139-42 passim, 213, 225, 258, 268, 272; United – Society 58-9
Trouillot, Michel-Rolf 14-15, 252, 270
Tunisia 19, 23, 47
Turkey 19 see also Ottoman Empire; -Egyptian rule 7, 29, 35, 117, 129, 143, 145, 173, 209-13 passim, 219; Turkiyya 195

Uganda 213
Umar, al-Hajj al-Shaykh Wad 71, 72, 167
Umm Ruwaba 84, 106, 134, 206, 291
unemployment 111, 191
United States 13, 44-5, 48, 55
Uthman, Ibrahim Sayyid 80, 173, 184, 210, 222
Uthman, Muhammad Sayyid 229
Uthman, al-Tuhami Muhammad/ Muhammad, al-Tuhami/Osman, El-Tuhami Mohammed 73, 99-101 passim, 260, 262, 265, 279, 292

Von Slatin, Pasha Rudolf 216, 256-7

Wad Medani 3, 45, 58-62 passim, 75, 85, 104, 105, 110, 113, 153, 229, 232
Wadi Halfa 71, 84, 153, 178, 198, 212, 250, 291
wage-workers 3, 8, 13, 16, 73, 86, 97, 101, 110, 111, 114, 117, 120, 121, 128-31 passim, 138, 139, 169, 180, 182, 234-54
war, civil 8, 10; Crimea 211; Irish liberation 19; World War I 1, 16, 19-21 passim, 50, 56, 58, 59, 133, 216, 217, 243, post- 16, 19-24, 44-9, 178-272 passim; World War II 23, 166, 176
al-Wardani, Ibrahim Nassif 61-2
Warburg, Gabriel 10
Watenpaugh, Keith 151
Wau 4, 86, 174, 214, 226, 233, 291
Weymouth, HMS 77, 127
White Flag League 2-5 passim, 10, 15, 16, 25, 31, 32, 35-7 passim, 49, 51, 53-4, 61-3, 67-70, 72-6, 85-7, 96-123, 126-9, 133-42, 161-72, 182-5, 234-9, 250-2 passim, 258, 265, 268, 272, 282, 284, 286, 288-9 passim; organization 97-108, markazia 98-100, 108-10 passim, 113, membership 97-109 passim, 283; oath 96, 104, 105, 113, 251; trials of 5, 32, 53, 55, 62-4 passim, 74, 85, 112, 118
Willis, Charles Armine 73, 76, 185, 256-7, 259, 260, 262-3, 266-7, 271
Willis, Justin 218
Wilson, Woodrow 19, 44-5, 50; 14 Points 44, 50
Wingate, General Reginald 1, 187, 213, 216, 217, 223, 243, 256
women 41, 44, 157, 168, 200, 246, 250, 259; Society of Alexandria 150, 284
Workmen's League 85, 86, 237-9 passim, 250
Wyllie, Curzon 54

Yemenis 127, 130-1, 249
Yusif, Mustafa 237, 265, 293

Zaghlul, Sa'd 1, 2, 4, 26, 27, 46, 49, 53, 69, 81, 88-91 passim, 112, 150, 161, 167, 172, 180
Zayd, Ahmad Sabri 52-3, 55, 123, 125, 173, 183-6 passim, 199, 200, 204, 222
Zayd, Muhammad Abd al-Mun'im 69, 123, 125, 183-6 passim, 199, 204, 222
al-Zayn, Hassan 207-8, 231
Zhou, Yongming 152
al-Zubayr Pasha, Ahmad al-Trifi 85, 184, 204
Zubeir Pasha 113

EASTERN AFRICAN STUDIES

These titles published in the United States and Canada by Ohio University Press

Revealing Prophets
Edited by DAVID M. ANDERSON & DOUGLAS H. JOHNSON

East African Expressions of Christianity
Edited by THOMAS SPEAR & ISARIA N. KIMAMBO

The Poor Are Not Us
Edited by DAVID M. ANDERSON & VIGDIS BROCH-DUE

Potent Brews
JUSTIN WILLIS

Swahili Origins
JAMES DE VERE ALLEN

Being Maasai
Edited by THOMAS SPEAR & RICHARD WALLER

Jua Kali Kenya
KENNETH KING

Control & Crisis in Colonial Kenya
BRUCE BERMAN

Unhappy Valley
Book One: State & Class
Book Two: Violence & Ethnicity
BRUCE BERMAN & JOHN LONSDALE

Mau Mau from Below
GREET KERSHAW

The Mau Mau War in Perspective
FRANK FUREDI

Squatters & the Roots of Mau Mau 1905-63
TABITHA KANOGO

Economic & Social Origins of Mau Mau 1945-53
DAVID W. THROUP

Multi-Party Politics in Kenya
DAVID W. THROUP & CHARLES HORNSBY

Empire State-Building
JOANNA LEWIS

Decolonization & Independence in Kenya 1940-93
Edited by B.A. OGOT & WILLIAM R. OCHIENG'

Eroding the Commons
DAVID ANDERSON

Penetration & Protest in Tanzania
ISARIA N. KIMAMBO

Custodians of the Land
Edited by GREGORY MADDOX, JAMES L. GIBLIN & ISARIA N. KIMAMBO

Education in the Development of Tanzania 1919-1990
LENE BUCHERT

The Second Economy in Tanzania
T.L. MALIYAMKONO & M.S.D. BAGACHWA

Ecology Control & Economic Development in East African History
HELGE KJEKSHUS

Siaya
DAVID WILLIAM COHEN & E.S. ATIENO ODHIAMBO

Uganda Now • Changing Uganda Developing Uganda • From Chaos to Order • Religion & Politics in East Africa
Edited by HOLGER BERNT HANSEN & MICHAEL TWADDLE

Kakungulu & the Creation of Uganda 1868-1928
MICHAEL TWADDLE

Controlling Anger
SUZETTE HEALD

Kampala Women Getting By
SANDRA WALLMAN

Political Power in Pre-Colonial Buganda
RICHARD J. REID

Alice Lakwena & the Holy Spirits
HEIKE BEHREND

Slaves, Spices & Ivory in Zanzibar
ABDUL SHERIFF

Zanzibar Under Colonial Rule
Edited by ABDUL SHERIFF & ED FERGUSON

The History & Conservation of Zanzibar Stone Town
Edited by ABDUL SHERIFF

Pastimes & Politics
LAURA FAIR

Ethnicity & Conflict in the Horn of Africa
Edited by KATSUYOSHI FUKUI & JOHN MARKAKIS

Conflict, Age & Power in North East Africa
Edited by EISEI KURIMOTO & SIMON SIMONSE

Property Rights & Political Development in Ethiopia & Eritrea
SANDRA FULLERTON JOIREMAN

Revolution & Religion in Ethiopia
ØYVIND M. EIDE

Brothers at War
TEKESTE NEGASH & KJETIL TRONVOLL

From Guerrillas to Government
DAVID POOL

Mau Mau & Nationhood
Edited by E.S. ATIENO ODHIAMBO & JOHN LONSDALE

A History of Modern Ethiopia, 1855-1991(2nd edn)
BAHRU ZEWDE

Pioneers of Change in Ethiopia
BAHRU ZEWDE

Remapping Ethiopia
Edited by W. JAMES, D. DONHAM, E. KURIMOTO & A. TRIULZI

Southern Marches of Imperial Ethiopia
Edited by DONALD L. DONHAM & WENDY JAMES

A Modern History of the Somali (4th edn)
I.M. LEWIS

Islands of Intensive Agriculture in East Africa
Edited by MATS WIDGREN & JOHN E.G. SUTTON

Leaf of Allah
EZEKIEL GEBISSA

Dhows & the Colonial Economy of Zanzibar 1860-1970
ERIK GILBERT

African Womanhood in Colonial Kenya
TABITHA KANOGO

African Underclass
ANDREW BURTON

In Search of a Nation
Edited by GREGORY H. MADDOX & JAMES L. GIBLIN

A History of the Excluded
JAMES L. GIBLIN

Black Poachers, White Hunters
EDWARD I. STEINHART

Ethnic Federalism
DAVID TURTON

Crisis & Decline in Bunyoro
SHANE DOYLE

Emancipation without Abolition in German East Africa
JAN-GEORG DEUTSCH

Women, Work & Domestic Virtue in Uganda 1900-2003
GRACE BANTEBYA KYOMUHENDO & MARJORIE KENISTON McINTOSH

Cultivating Success in Uganda
GRACE CARSWELL

War in Pre-Colonial Eastern Africa
RICHARD REID

Slavery in the Great Lakes Region of East Africa
Edited by HENRI MÉDARD & SHANE DOYLE

The Benefits of Famine
DAVID KEEN

www.ingramcontent.com/pod-product-compliance
Lightning Source LLC
Chambersburg PA
CBHW051558230426
43668CB00013B/1899
* 9 7 8 1 8 4 7 0 1 2 0 9 8 *